THE DRAGOMAN RENAISSANCE

The Dragoman Renaissance

*Diplomatic Interpreters
and the Routes of Orientalism*

E. Natalie Rothman

CORNELL UNIVERSITY PRESS

ITHACA AND LONDON

First published 2021 by Cornell University Press

Library of Congress Cataloging-in-Publication Data
Names: Rothman, E. Natalie (Ella Natalie), 1976– author.
Title: The dragoman renaissance: diplomatic interpreters and the routes of orientalism / E. Natalie Rothman.
Description: Ithaca [New York]: Cornell University Press, 2021. | Includes bibliographical references and index. |
Identifiers: LCCN 2020042673 (print) | LCCN 2020042674 (ebook) | ISBN 9781501758492 (paperback) | ISBN 9781501758485 (pdf) | ISBN 9781501758508 (epub)
Subjects: LCSH: Dragomen—Turkey—History—16th century. | Dragomen—Turkey—History—17th century. | Orientalism—Europe—History—16th century. | Orientalism—Europe—History—17th century. | Turkey—Relations—Europe—History. | Europe—Relations—Turkey—History. | Turkey—History—Ottoman Empire, 1288–1918.
Classification: LCC DR479.E85 R67 2021 (print) | LCC DR479.E85 (ebook) | DDC 327.560409/032—dc23
LC record available at https://lccn.loc.gov/2020042673
LC ebook record available at https://lccn.loc.gov/2020042674

Cover illustration: *Dragoman Marcantonio Mamuca della Torre* (Istanbul, 1636 – Vienna, 1712). Oil on canvas, 222 x 150 cm. Poreč (Croatia), Museum of the Poreč Territory, ZMP 1680.

S|H The Sustainable History Monograph Pilot
M|P Opening up the Past, Publishing for the Future

This book is published as part of the Sustainable History
Monograph Pilot. With the generous support of the
Andrew W. Mellon Foundation, the Pilot uses cutting-edge
publishing technology to produce open access digital editions
of high-quality, peer-reviewed monographs from leading
university presses. Free digital editions can be downloaded
from: Books at JSTOR, EBSCO, Hathi Trust, Internet
Archive, OAPEN, Project MUSE, and many other open
repositories.

When you cite the book, please include the following
URL for its Digital Object Identifier (DOI):
https://doi.org/10.7298/fxrs-fn65

We are eager to learn more about how you discovered this
title and how you are using it. We hope you will spend a few
minutes answering a couple of questions at this url:
https://www.longleafservices.org/shmp-survey/

More information about the Sustainable History Monograph
Pilot can be found at https://www.longleafservices.org.

For Tamouz and Nour

CONTENTS

FIGURES

All figures referred to in the book are available here: https://dragomans
.digital.utsc.utoronto.ca/islandora/object/dragomans:TableofFigures

0.1. Vanmour, *Audience*
https://ark.digital.utsc.utoronto.ca/ark:/61220/utsc5880

0.2. "Dragoman" in *Figurae 294 colorite*
https://ark.digital.utsc.utoronto.ca/ark:/61220/utsc5881

1.1. The Venetian bailate ca. 1660
https://ark.digital.utsc.utoronto.ca/ark:/61220/utsc5882

1.2. Families Represented in the Venetian Dragomanate, ca. 1570–1720
https://ark.digital.utsc.utoronto.ca/ark:/61220/utsc5883

1.3. Intermarriage across Istanbul's dragomanate, ca. 1570–1720
https://ark.digital.utsc.utoronto.ca/ark:/61220/utsc5884

2.1. The Borisi-Scoccardi-Mascellini Family
https://ark.digital.utsc.utoronto.ca/ark:/61220/utsc5885

2.2. The Brutti-Borisi-Tarsia Dragoman Dynasty
https://ark.digital.utsc.utoronto.ca/ark:/61220/utsc5886

3.1. Altarpiece of San Felice, Venice
https://ark.digital.utsc.utoronto.ca/ark:/61220/utsc5887

4.1. Gian Rinaldo Carli
https://ark.digital.utsc.utoronto.ca/ark:/61220/utsc5930

4.2. Gian Rinaldo Carli
https://ark.digital.utsc.utoronto.ca/ark:/61220/utsc5888

4.3. Sultan Mehmed III
https://ark.digital.utsc.utoronto.ca/ark:/61220/utsc5889

TABLES

ACKNOWLEDGMENTS

This book began nearly two decades ago as a couple of dense dissertation chapters that needed more room to grow. Over the years, these chapters developed rhizomatically, taking me in unanticipated methodological and spatiotemporal directions. As the project matured, what I originally conceived as a straightforward social history of an understudied group was enriched by scholarship in fields as diverse as philology, linguistic anthropology, and art history, to say nothing of book history, Turkology, and Translation Studies. My decidedly undisciplined poaching would not have been possible without the immense generosity of colleagues, friends, and students.

First and foremost, I would like to thank the many students and research assistants with whom I have worked over the years. Ted Adamo, Selin Eksioğlu, Nick Field, Erdem İdil, Dr. Mehmet Kuru, Giovanna Licata, Sanja Ljaskevic, Dr. Sarah Loose, Dr. Vanessa McCarthy, Dr. Kathryn Taylor, Dylan Wilkerson, Dr. Murat Yaşar, and Dr. Gülay Yılmaz have all contributed to this project, and their questions and insights have deeply informed my own.

Research for this book has taken me to archives and libraries in Italy, Turkey, Croatia, Slovenia, France, Germany, Russia, and the United States, and has benefited from access to digitized collections in all these countries, as well as in the UK, the Netherlands, and Austria. My special thanks to Dr. Daria Vasilyeva, head of the Byzantium and the Middle East Section of the Oriental Department of the State Hermitage Museum in St. Petersburg, for her kind invitation and exceptional hospitality during my research visit, and to Dr. Lupold von Lehsten, deputy director at the Institut für Personengeschichte in Bensheim, Germany, for warmly welcoming me there. I am grateful to Dr. Vltava Muk, curator at the Museum of the Poreč territory (Croatia), for facilitating access to digital reproductions of portraits in the museum holdings, and to Dr. Luka Juri, director of the Koper Regional Museum (Slovenia), for kind permission to reproduce portraits from that collection as well. Additional thanks are due to Frank Tong in Interlibrary

Loan services at the University of Toronto Scarborough Library, and to the excellent staff at the UTSC Office of the Vice-Principal, Research. Their support has been vital in securing grants that were key to the project's completion, including a Standard Research Grant and an Insight Grant from the Social Sciences and Humanities Research Council of Canada, a Mellon Residential Fellowship at the Newberry Library, an Early Researcher Award from the Government of Ontario, and several University of Toronto grants.

Beyond institutional support, the University of Toronto community in general, and the Department of Historical and Cultural Studies at the University of Toronto Scarborough in particular, have been a most wonderful space in which to gestate this book. I am immensely grateful for the friendship and insight of Frank Cody, Paul Cohen, Lucia Dacome, Natalie Zemon Davis, Anver Emon, Drew Gilbert, Alex Gillespie, Atiqa Hachimi, Jens Hanssen, Monica Heller, Katie Larson, Jeannie Miller, Nada Moumtaz, Andrea Muehlebach, Melanie Newton, Yigal Nizri, Bhavani Raman, Walid Saleh, Nick Terpstra, Nhung Tuyet Tran, Tamara Walker, Yvon Wang, and many other colleagues. Beyond U of T, this book has benefited immeasurably from comments and advice from Danna Agmon, Virginia Aksan, Gadi Algazi, Benny Arbel, Megan Armstrong, Marc Aymes, Karen Barzman, Günhan Börekci, Marie Bossaert, Palmira Brummett, Guy Burak, Guillaume Calafat, Clare Carroll, Georg Christ, John Christopoulos, Libby Cohen, Tom Cohen, Jocelyne Dakhlia, David Do Paço, Eric Dursteler, Tolga Esmer, Heather Ferguson, Emine Fetvacı, Paula Findlen, Maartje van Gelder, John-Paul Ghobrial, Claire Gilbert, Dena Goodman, Toby Graf, Aslı Gürbüzel, Gottfried Hagen, Randy Head, Daniel Hershenzon, Diane Owen Hughes, Mariusz Kaczka, Gábor Kármán, Rajeev Kinra, Tijana Krstić, Cristian Luca, Ron Makleff, Nabil Matar, Ed Muir, Serap Mumcu, Carla Nappi, Laurie Nussdorfer, Nil Palabiyik, the late Maria-Pia Pedani, Leslie Peirce, James Pickett, Helmut Puff, Valentina Pugliano, Cesare Santus, Ana Sekulić, Nir Shafir, Housni Shehada, Henning Sievert, Amy Singer, Dan Smail, Elżbieta Święcicka, Emmanuel Szurek, Baki Tezcan, Toni Veneri, Polona Vidmar, Filippo de Vivo, Margarita Voulgaropoulou, Veruschka Wagner, Josh White, Tom Willette, Ali Yaycioğlu, and Selma Zecevic.

In the process of writing I have been fortunate to present different iterations of various parts of this book at dozens of universities, including Brigham Young, Brown, Central European University, Chicago, CUNY,

Duke, École des Hautes Études en Sciences Sociales, Harvard, Lund, Michigan, NYU, Pennsylvania, Pittsburgh, Rochester, Stanford, Syracuse, UC Berkeley, UCLA, and Zadar, as well as the Folger Shakespeare Library, Grinnell College, the Institute for Advanced Study, the Newberry Library, annual meetings of the American Historical Association, International Congress of Medieval Studies, Middle East Studies Association, Renaissance Society of America, Sixteenth-Century Studies Conference, Turkologentag, and, on numerous occasions, at the University of Toronto. I thank my hosts and audiences at all these venues for their engagement and hospitality.

I have previously published parts of this book, often in a significantly different form. Sections of Chapters 1, 2, and 6 appeared in "Interpreting Dragomans: Boundaries and Crossings in the Early Modern Mediterranean," *Comparative Studies in Society and History* 51, 4 (October 2009). Some passages in Chapter 1 have appeared in "Dragomans" and "Jeunes de Langues," in *Routledge Encyclopedia of Interpreting Studies*, ed. Franz Pöchhacker (London: Routledge, 2015). A section of Chapter 2 appeared in "Accounting for Gifts: The Poetics and Pragmatics of Material Circulations in Venetian-Ottoman Diplomacy," in *Cultures of Empire: Rethinking Venetian Rule, 1400–1700. Essays in Honour of Benjamin Arbel,* eds. Georg Christ and Franz-Julius Morche (Leiden: Brill, 2020). Earlier versions of parts of Chapter 3 appeared in "Self-Fashioning in the Mediterranean Contact Zone: Giovanni Battista Salvago and his *Africa overo Barbaria* (1625)," in *Renaissance Medievalisms*, ed. Konrad Eisenbichler (Toronto: Centre for Reformation and Renaissance Studies, 2009) and in "Afterword," *Things Not Easily Believed: Introducing the Early Modern Relation*, eds. Thomas Cohen and Germaine Warkentin. Special issue of *Renaissance and Reformation/Renaissance et Réforme* 34, 1-2 (2011). An earlier version of a section of Chapter 4 appeared in "Visualizing a Space of Encounter: Intimacy, Alterity, and Trans-Imperial Perspective in an Ottoman-Venetian Miniature Album," *Osmanlı Araştırmaları / Journal of Ottoman Studies* 40 (2012). Earlier versions of parts of Chapter 7 appeared in "Dragomans and 'Turkish Literature': The Making of a Field of Inquiry," *Oriente Moderno* 93, 2 (2013) and in "Afterword: Intermediaries, Mediation, and Cross-Confessional Diplomacy in the Early Modern Mediterranean," *Journal of Early Modern History* 19, 2–3 (2015).

Close, ongoing collaboration with Kirsta Stapelfeldt and her fabulous team in the Digital Scholarship Unit at the UTSC Library has not only made possible this monograph's companion digital repository, but has enriched the work conceptually and methodologically at every step along the way. More recently, I have been fortunate to work with Emily Andrew, Alexis Siemon, Allegra Martschenko, and Ange Romeo-Hall at Cornell University Press, and Ihsan Taylor at Longleaf Services. Emily's sharp eye and the detailed comments from Alex Bevilacqua and another manuscript reviewer have greatly enriched the book's argument. Elsa Dixler's copyedits greatly improved its presentation.

As this manuscript is going to press amid a global pandemic and a terrifying resurgence of state-sanctioned violence, I am heartened by scholars and students across the globe calling for a reckoning with institutional racism, brutal academic labor precarity, and their attendant, unsustainable modalities of knowledge production. I hope this study of a key moment in the genealogy of the modern knowledge/power nexus and its imperial entanglements contributes to an urgently needed collective transformation.

Finally, I owe this book to my fiercest critic and most generous, imaginative, and brilliant interlocutor, Alejandro Paz. I dedicate it to Tamouz and Nour, our own shared work-in-progress.

ABBREVIATIONS

ASVe   Archivio di Stato di Venezia
BaC   Bailo a Costantinopoli
Bapt   Santa Maria Draperis, Liber Baptizatorum
BnF   Bibliothèque nationale de France, Paris
BNM   Biblioteca Nationale Marciana, Venice
BOA   Başbakanlık Osmanlı Arşivleri, Istanbul
BUB   Biblioteca Universitaria, Bologna
CCD   Capi del Consiglio dei Dieci
Conj   Santa Maria Draperis, Liber Conjugatorum
DT   Documenti Turchi
ED   Ecnebi Defteri
FHL   Family History Library, Salt Lake City
FM   Fondo Marsigli
IS   Inquisitori di Stato
LAC   Lettere di Ambasciatori, Costantinopoli
MCC   Museo Civico Correr, Venice
Mort   Santa Maria Draperis, Liber Mortuorum
ÖNB   Österreichische Nationalbibliothek, Vienna
SDelC   Senato, Deliberazioni Costantinopoli
SDispC Senato, Dispacci Costantinopoli

NOTE ON NAMES, TERMS, AND TRANSLITERATION

As Claire Gilbert shows, the processes by which historians of non-English speaking societies come to translate their sources are neither self-evident nor value neutral.[1] Indeed, it is a particular challenge of a book about translation that its source material is rendered in English translation throughout, thereby risking eliding the very textual transformations it studies. In an effort to allow readers to assess the arguments for themselves, I provide transcriptions or transliterations of the relevant passages of all source materials in the notes. Unless otherwise noted, all translations are mine.

Early modern orthography was notoriously lax. Italianate (and other Latinate) authors habitually mangled Ottoman names beyond recognition. As much as possible, I have opted for modern Turkish conventionalized renderings of Ottoman terms (e.g., *paşa*, *çavuş*) and normalized proper names, except for names that might already be familiar to readers in an Anglicized orthography (e.g., Mehmed, Bayezid). I have mostly kept Italian proper names as their bearers spelled them (hence Christoforo Tarsia but Cristoforo Mamuca della Torre). The inconsistent orthography of sources for several family names in this study (e.g., Peron/Perone/Pirone/Pironi/Piron; Naon/Navon/Navone/Navoni) necessitated some arbitrary choices in the interest of cross-reference.

Introduction

> How did philology, lexicography, history, biology, political and
> economic theory, novel-writing, and lyric poetry come to the
> service of Orientalism's broadly imperialist view of the world?
> What changes, modulations, refinements, even revolutions take
> place within Orientalism? What is the meaning of originality,
> of continuity, of individuality, in this context? How does Orien-
> talism transmit or reproduce itself from one epoch to another?
> In fine, how can we treat the cultural, historical phenomenon
> of Orientalism as a kind of willed human work—not of mere
> unconditioned ratiocination—in all its historical complexity,
> detail, and worth without at the same time losing sight of the
> alliance between cultural work, political tendencies, the state,
> and the specific realities of domination?
>
> —Edward W. Said[1]

A LARGE OIL-ON-CANVAS PAINTING (figure 0.1) offers a variation on a theme repeated by the artist dozens of times: the Ottoman sultan receiving a European ambassador for a formal audience. It comes from the studio of a Flemish-born, Istanbul-based artist, Jean Baptiste Van-mour (1671–1737), whom the French king Louis XV appointed "Ordinary Royal Painter in the Levant." Perfect symmetry and order characterize Vanmour's audience scenes, with the Sultan seated on his throne on the left, and the ambassador, his retinue, and Ottoman dignitaries standing on the right. Adjacent to the ambassador stoop, almost invariably, one or two figures, distinguished unmistakably by their regalia and grooming style from both foreign diplomats and local ministers. The ambiguous figures in-between, and the subject of this book, are dragomans, diplomatic trans-lator-interpreters who accompanied ambassadors on their audiences and acted, ritually, as their mouth and ears, mediating the unfolding ceremony. Who were the dragomans? Where did they hail from, and what, exactly, did they do? How were they understood by contemporary political and diplomatic circles in Istanbul and beyond, and what role did they play in systematizing and circulating knowledge of the Ottoman Empire, its histories, languages, and societies?

At almost the exact same time that Vanmour was executing his oil canvases, a substantially different perspective on dragomans' work was proffered in an illustrated album presented to a Habsburg prince:

> Dragoman: any interpreter who frequents the Divan, [depicted here] as he is dressed; there is the Divan of the Grand Vizier, which is frequented almost daily by the interpreters of the Holy Roman Emperor, the interpreters of the Porte, of England, France, Venice, Poland, Holland, Ragusa etc. who stay there to solicit the interests of their Prince, or of merchants and consuls. And it is rare to see them at the Divan unless for some necessity, which allows them to appear in the Grand Divan, where the Grand Vizier is assisted by the two Kazaskers, that is, the two Grand Chancellors, for any important matter of justice.[2]

This definition serves as a gloss for a miniature (figure 0.2) depicting a dragoman, one of 294 visual-cum-textual representations of officeholders of the Ottoman Empire. The miniatures are bound in a three-volume manuscript album presented in 1723 to Prince-Elector Charles Albert of Bavaria (the future Holy Roman Emperor Charles VII) and, at an unknown date, to Prince Eugene of Savoy (1663–1736), a Habsburg military commander and courtier, renowned for his field victories against the Ottomans. Other exemplars may have been presented to other courtly patrons in Vienna and Hanover.[3]

The definition highlights three aspects of the dragomans' craft: first, that they engage in independent negotiation—as opposed to ventriloquizing an ambassador's words as in Vanmour's portrayal; second, that dragomans form a cohesive professional "type," whether employed by a foreign embassy, an Ottoman vassal state, the sultan's court, or merchants and consuls; and third, that they are a distinctly Istanbulite formation, fully integrated into the workflow of the Ottoman divan (chancery). The highly conventionalized, typological visual presentation of the dragoman's figure in the albums, following contemporary Ottoman style, strips him of most contextual backdrop and props, with the exception of his distinct livery and the scroll he clutches in his right hand (presumably a *berat*, or sultanic letter patent), both common iconographic features attesting to a dragoman's professional identity. Yet the verbal gloss makes it apparent that—even absent Vanmour's lavish visual cues—dragomans are entirely of the courtly Istanbulite world they inhabit.

The series of albums in which this miniature and its gloss appear is remarkable on several counts, not least its author-compiler, Cristoforo Mamuca della Torre (1681–1760). Cristoforo was the scion of a long and distinguished dragoman dynasty. His father, paternal great-uncles and great-grandfather, as well as maternal cousins, uncles, grandfather, and great-uncles—at least a dozen relatives in all—had lived and worked as (mostly Venetian) dragomans in Istanbul from the 1590s onward. Cristoforo himself was born in the Ottoman capital and apprenticed as a Habsburg dragoman there before moving to the newly established Habsburg Free Port of Trieste, where in 1749 he became Empress Maria Theresa's official representative for Ottoman merchants and, in 1751, their Consul.[4]

Mamuca della Torre's perspective on who dragomans are and what they do fully reflects his professional trajectory and his pedigree in what it says and, especially, in how it says it. It is lodged in a specific material form—the album—that carefully melded multiple distinctively Ottoman and Italianate visual and textual genres of representation to form a miniature album-cum-political-manual, a consummate diplomatic gift.[5] Bespoke, and yet reproducible, this series of codices—and Mamuca della Torre's quest for courtly patronage through them—leveraged Italian prose and the rhetoric of Ottoman "barbarity" to flaunt deep intimacy with Ottoman society, politics, and language in an effort to secure social mobility in the heart of Europe.[6]

This book tells the story of Cristoforo Mamuca della Torre's forebears. It shows how, by obviating the need for foreign diplomats to master the Ottoman language prior to assuming a position at the Porte, dragomans contributed to the sense of Ottoman alterity among European elites—an alterity that ensured their continued relevance. Dragomans, however, were neither great conspirators bent on keeping their diplomatic masters ignorant and misinformed, nor faceless pawns and mindless tools in the transposition of official speech from one linguistic code to another. Rather, they served as key nodes in the production and circulation of current knowledge about the Ottomans to European-wide publics.[7] More than simple "information," what dragomans mediated to early modern European publics were elite Ottoman perspectives on politics, language, and society. These perspectives—as refracted by dragomans—lay at the heart of an emergent early modern field of Ottomanist knowledge.

What Are Dragomans?

The institution of the dragoman (Italian *dragomanno*; Greek *dragouma-nos*; French *drogman/truchement*; Spanish *trujamán/dragomán*), an official state or diplomatic interpreter, developed in the context of premodern Mediterranean statecraft from antiquity onward. A staple of diplomatic practice, dragomans were crucial actors in many of the political and commercial arenas of the region, where their role far exceeded rendering a speaker's message in another language. Dragomans' social background, as well as the institutional parameters of their work, evolved over the centuries thanks to their sustained interactions across linguistic and juridical boundaries.

The etymology of "dragoman," a foreignizing loanword, betrays its Mediterranean roots, and can be traced to the cognates *targemān, turgeman, dragoumanos, tarjumān, tarjomân,* and *tercüman* in Aramaic, Hebrew, Greek, Arabic, Persian, and Ottoman Turkish, respectively.[8] References to *dragomanni* can be found in Italian sources as early as the thirteenth century, mostly in the context of negotiations with the Fatimids and Mamluks in Egypt and with Turkic principalities in the Black Sea region. Similar etymologies can be traced for the word's several European cognates. In the medieval Mediterranean basin dragomans served various political, commercial, and diplomatic functions as essential intermediaries between the rulers and the ruled. In the following centuries, and especially outside that region, dragomans—often attached to chanceries and boards of trade—came to be associated almost exclusively with interpreting and translation to and from "Oriental languages" such as Arabic, Turkish, and Persian. This close, if belated and narrow association between dragomans and Islamicate-European diplomacy alerts us already to their special place in the genealogy of Orientalism, as the "shifty" figure of the dragoman came to mark multiple and mutually reinforcing uncertainties about ethnolinguistic, religious, and political boundaries.

The scholarship on dragomans has mostly followed the sharp divide between studies of dragomans of the Ottoman Imperial Council (*Divân-ı Hümâyûn tercümanı*) on the one hand, and studies of dragomans employed by European powers in their own capitals as well as in Istanbul, on the other. However, dragomans of the two types not only were heirs to a largely shared, circum-Mediterranean body of diplomatic and chancery practices but often sustained strong and enduring ties with one another.[9] Sometimes they were actually one and the same person, whose career trajectory led to work for multiple employers and across several empires.[10] This book accordingly emphasizes the circulation of dragomans' recruitment and employment patterns and kinship alliances, as well as interpretive practices (and, indeed, their very concepts of interpreting and translation) across linguistic, juridical, and confessional boundaries, while helping to articulate these very boundaries.

Several ancient precedents exist for the use of official diplomatic and state interpreters. Especially noteworthy are the empires of Pharaonic Egypt and Rome, where dragomans already featured many of the characteristics that appeared later, such as their role in mediating relationships between a sovereign and various subject populations, construed along lines of linguistic difference; the merging of diplomatic, commercial, proto-ethnographic, and juridical roles; the blending of written and oral communicative techniques; the effort to train cadres at the imperial center drawn from youth recruited in the provinces; and, more broadly, the discursive emphasis on polyglotism as the hallmark of imperial governmentality.[11] These features came into full bloom in the premodern Mediterranean and Indian Ocean. Dragomans' translingual disposition and multi-perspectival habitus, extended social ties, and flexible patronage relations proved highly desirable, whether in the context of flourishing courtly societies interested in facilitating literary and theological translations,[12] or in pilgrimage sites, port cities, and other commercial hubs that attracted large numbers of foreign sojourners. Thus, we find Mamluk, Ottoman, Safavid, and Mughal dragomans serving as diplomatic emissaries as well as commercial brokers, pilgrim guides, and even spies.[13] Ottoman dragomans especially were ubiquitous in a variety of state institutions, ranging from provincial and ministerial chanceries to customs houses and courts.[14] Indeed, in their role as intermediaries between the sultan and his polyglot subjects as well as (inevitably lesser) foreign rulers and vassals, Ottoman dragomans performed as ritual figurations of sovereignty itself, of which mediated—rather than direct—communication increasingly became an essential aspect.[15] Similarly, in the sprawling colonial administration of late medieval and early modern Venice, interpreters, while not always bearing the title of "dragoman," performed equally diverse functions, both in Venice's Dalmatian and Aegean colonial territories and in the city proper.[16]

The ubiquity of dragomans across diverse sociopolitical spaces speaks to the importance of linguistic plurality to premodern conceptions of imperial power.[17] In the Ottoman Empire, dragomans' value continued to grow with the massive territorial expansion of the fifteenth and sixteenth centuries, which brought into the imperial orbit large numbers of Greek, Slavic, and Arabic speakers. Throughout Ottoman lands, dragomans served as vital, though by no means exclusive, intermediaries between the sultan's representatives and non-Turkish-speaking subjects well into the nineteenth century.[18] At the same time, Mehmed II's conquest of Constantinople in 1453 transformed that city, already richly multilingual, into a veritable polyglot metropolis, with sizable populations of enslaved persons from sub-Saharan Africa and the Black Sea regions; Slavic-and Greek-speaking elite soldiery and government bureaucrats drawn largely from rural communities in Southeastern Europe; Arabic and Persianate scholars from the Arab provinces and from Central Asia; and, of course, Greek-, Judeo-Spanish-and Armenian-speaking merchant communities.[19]

A corollary to Istanbul's military and political ascent was its growing significance in diplomatic circles.[20] By the late sixteenth century, the city's suburb of Galata-Pera boasted a large number of foreign consulates and resident embassies. With Ottoman Turkish now the dominant language of court ceremonial, but the sultan himself largely inaccessible to all but his innermost circle, dragomans came to embody Ottoman alterity, at least to their foreign employers. For unlike other capitals, where command of the local courtly language(s) would grant a resident ambassador direct access to the sovereign, lack of direct communication with the sultan made dragomans de rigueur in Ottoman diplomatic practice. Ironically, dragomans' ubiquity may have provided a further disincentive for diplomats sent to the Porte to acquire fluency in Ottoman Turkish themselves. This, in turn, exacerbated perceptions of the language as inaccessible, and of the Ottoman political system as arcane and impenetrable.[21]

Istanbul, a Trans-Imperial Nexus

As numerous studies have shown, the early modern period witnessed an intensifying European awareness of and fascination with things "Turkish." Ottoman practices of dress, imperial governance, and military discipline informed English and French elite fashion, Italian political theory, Dutch military reform, and Habsburg court music, to mention just a few examples.[22] At the same time, many other aspects of Ottoman social life were objectified as signs of alterity supposedly incommensurable with "European" practices. In the context of ongoing warfare, both the structural similarities between the Ottomans' and their neighbors' political and religious institutions, on the one hand, and the growing appetite for exoticizing *Turcica* on the other, were fueled by a fledgling European print culture, in which the Ottomans were a favorite (though not always favored) topic. At least 6,000 distinct publications on *Turcica* were printed in Europe before 1700.[23] Knowledge of Ottoman society and culture relied on the unprecedented textual and visual output of sojourners in the Ottoman capital—travelers, missionaries, merchants, and, especially, diplomats. These long-term visitors became authorities on things Ottoman, and their extensive sojourns in the Ottoman Empire—shaped by the increasingly codified protocols of contemporary diplomacy—a requisite practice for producing legitimate knowledge.[24] Such foreign visitors, in turn, relied crucially on a network of local (or localized) intermediaries for gaining familiarity with and developing their own perspective on Ottoman society. This mediation is rarely acknowledged, let alone studied in detail, in much of the scholarship on Ottoman-European diplomacy.[25]

The largest and most vital cadre of diplomatic intermediaries was the corps of dragomans employed by foreign embassies at the Porte. Whether born and raised in the Ottoman capital or merely long-term sojourners, dragomans were ubiquitous in the city's Christian suburbs, chiefly in Galata-Pera, the site of most foreign embassies. They appeared as regular guests both at court and in Ottoman officials' homes. Unlike modern diplomatic interpreters who engage in simultaneous oral interpretation between two parties, dragomans often acted independently as emissaries and negotiators, only later producing oral and written reports to their employers about their interactions with Ottoman officials. They served as principal actors in their own right in the production and circulation of news in and of Istanbul.[26] Dragomans' interpretive work crucially informed foreign diplomats and their numerous guests about Ottoman politics and society. They did not simply make "information" available, but shaped many discourses about the Ottomans that were then inscribed in official diplomatic dispatches and reports. Such reports themselves circulated widely. Some, although secret by definition, were copied and sent off to Rome, while others were translated and anthologized into "manuals of political theory" for European-wide consumption.[27]

Early modern European knowledge of the Ottoman Empire, it should be emphasized, was far from a unified enterprise. It emerged in diverse genres intended for an array of publics. Missionaries, scholars, pilgrims, travelers, artists, and former captives all contributed in fundamental ways to European knowledge about the Ottomans. In focusing on the contributions of dragomans to an emergent field of knowledge, this book does not simply privilege one (admittedly central) group of cultural brokers. Rather, it makes the case that the articulation of a "dragomans' perspective" and its impact can be traced even in knowledge produced in non-diplomatic milieus, as dragomans' networks extended far and wide, and, especially, as dragomans' positionality, epistemologies, and methods became enmeshed in a much broader Ottomanist discourse.

Consider, for example, the following short letter, which Giacomo Tarsia, an Istanbul-born-and-based dragoman in Venetian service, sent to William Lord Paget, the English ambassador-extraordinary to the Ottoman court in June 1695:

> Most Illustrious and Excellent Signor, My Most Honorable Patron and Master,
>
> With all [my] submission I have received the wonderful letters written by Your Excellence between the 12–22 [of the previous month], and was much consoled to learn of your revered satisfaction with my work on the Turkish history.
>
> The book purchased by Your Excellency and sent to me is indeed of great purpose to you; it begins at the time of the coronation of Sultan Mehmed, and ends with the Porte's decision to march its armies to invade Hungary, and then proceeds with the siege of Vienna, in the year of Muhammad 1093, toward the end of the Christian year 1682.
>
> In following the supreme orders of Your Excellency, I will continue in this thread of the history, and will not omit [anything] in this matter or in any other, as I see myself honored by your precious prescriptions to always recognize Your Excellency as long as I live.
>
> Pera, 20–30 June, 1695
> Your most Humble, Devoted, and Obsequious Servant
> Giacomo Tarsia[28]

The letter, written in Italian, discusses a translation of an Ottoman chronicle that Paget commissioned from Tarsia. The chronicle spanned the years 1642 to 1682, a fateful period in Ottoman history and historiography which coincided with the War of Crete (1645–1669)—the longest Venetian-Ottoman military conflict on record.[29] Tarsia's letter speaks to the great intellectual ferment of late-seventeenth-century Istanbul's diplomatic milieu, where bibliophile diplomats vied with one another to procure Ottoman manuscripts for several growing "Oriental libraries," whether royal, university, or privately owned.[30]

The letter also highlights dragomans' unique role as mediating this process of mobilizing Ottoman knowledge. While the overall significance of Istanbul's diplomatic scene for the genealogies of Orientalism is increasingly acknowledged, the epistemological implications of its diplomatic nexus, personnel, structures, and procedures are still not well understood. For keen as they may have been to gain meaningful knowledge of their surroundings, in their quest for such knowledge foreign representatives vitally depended on the mediation of localized underlings, secretaries and, especially, dragomans, many Venetian-trained. With a few notable exceptions, even the most bookish among the Porte's early modern resident diplomats lacked formal training in Ottoman Turkish, let alone in Ottoman history and literature.[31] With limited contacts in local scholarly milieus, diplomat-bibliophiles often relied on dragomans to identify worthwhile manuscripts to procure, to negotiate their acquisition, to translate them once acquired, and to provide digests, glosses, inventories, and other appropriate "contexts" for their reading.

Giacomo Tarsia was one such well-connected intermediary, equally at home at the Ottoman court and in Venetian patrician palaces, fluent in multiple languages, and adept at serving multiple masters, at times concurrently. It was likely on his advice, if not that of his brother Tommaso (the Venetian grand dragoman) or some other dragoman colleague, that Paget purchased the unidentified Ottoman chronicle that is the subject of the letter quoted above. Beyond the platitudes of patronage, what we have in Tarsia's letter to Paget is a trace of the condensation of multiple levels of mediation, historiographical frameworks, and linguistic codes at work in the production of Ottomanist knowledge in early modern Istanbul's diplomatic milieu. The dragoman's polyglot habitus and implicit claim to local know-how thus served as the linchpin of a broad system of material circulation and semiosis that entangled Istanbul with other centers of knowledge production.

Contemporary diplomatic correspondence from Istanbul bears out the important role of dragomans in framing the Ottoman world for their employers through daily material and textual practices. European scholars who sojourned in the Ottoman Empire in search of ancient manuscripts, artifacts, and inscriptions similarly betray in their accounts a heavy reliance on local intermediaries, especially embassy dragomans, in their scientific endeavors. Sojourners' accounts tended to focus on the practical nature of such mediation, for example in acting as guides and in obtaining permits for archeological excavations from Ottoman officials. They were more taciturn about other, highly skilled labor performed by dragomans, yet the evidence suggests that the latter's contributions went far beyond "local arrangements." As part of the quest for manuscripts, artifacts, and inscriptions on behalf of sojourning patrons, dragomans often engaged in extensive negotiations—both face-to-face and through written correspondence—with the owners and custodians of libraries and ancient sites, whether urban courtiers and booksellers in Istanbul, clergy on Mount Athos and Mount Lebanon, or provincial governors in Athens and the Peloponnese. These negotiations relied both on dragomans' diplomatic skills and on their sometimes vast and region-wide professional and kinship networks. As important, they also depended on dragomans' ability to read and identify the manuscripts once procured, to ascertain their authenticity and significance, and to copy and translate manuscripts from Greek, Arabic, and Ottoman Turkish.[32] It is unsurprising that dragomans' interventions profoundly shaped the resultant knowledge.

By focusing on dragomans' roles in articulating Ottomanist knowledge, this book contributes to a broader effort to decenter and "declass" a once dominant Eurocentric and scholastic vision of the Republic of Letters in general, and of early modern Orientalism in particular.[33] It also critiques a still pervasive tendency to treat "center" and "periphery" as stable and binary categories that can be mapped onto distinct institutional spaces. Dragomans were not, at least prima facie, "typical" Ottoman subjects. They rarely embraced Islam and often enjoyed the juridical status of non-Ottoman subjects, whether by virtue of their birth outside the empire, or through the conferral of their diplomatic employer's subjecthood and exemption from local taxes. At the same time, dragomans spent much of their lives in Istanbul or other Mediterranean commercial/political hubs, cultivating a metropolitan sensibility. Their writings often betray a deeply metropolitan disdain for the provinces and suspicion of non-elites, whether Ottoman or other. Their perception as "exceptional" may thus stem more from modernist, nationalist commitments than from their actual divergence from classical Ottoman and Venetian patterns of subordinate elite subject-making, as discussed in Chapter 1.

Dragomans and "Orientalism's Genesis Amnesia"

In his seminal book *Orientalism*, Edward Said famously charted some of the entwined epistemological principles and methodological procedures that underlie the scholarly-cum-political production of the Orient as a geopolitical category and a textual topos: the conception of Islam as a unified civilization, the collapsing of spatiotemporal distinctions among Islamicate societies,[34] and the treatment of variegated Arabic, Persian, and Turkish texts as forming a single tradition, regardless of their particular modes of transmission and sites of enunciation. Said saw these epistemological and methodological procedures as inextricably linked to modern European imperial power. Other scholars, while taking issue with one or more aspects of Said's work, have largely shared this assumption.

This book challenges both the spatial and temporal boundaries of Orientalism. It suggests, first, that the genealogies of Orientalist epistemologies and methodologies, while profoundly shaped by Enlightenment scientific preoccupations and by myriad colonial endeavors thereafter, have longer routes that meander, inter alia, through the inter-imperial contest of the sixteenth-century Mediterranean and its reworkings over a long seventeenth century. As a corollary, the spaces in which Orientalism as a set of epistemologies and methodologies initially formed were not only (or even primarily) those of metropolitan European scholarship. Rather, the diplomatic milieu of early modern Istanbul, and its close engagement with Ottoman courtly and learned elites, played a decisive role in shaping some of Orientalism's most distinctive features. Among those were its philological and prescriptive bent and its keen interest in political narrative history, coupled with a tendency to elide important temporal, spatial, and sociocultural differences to produce "the Orient" as a coherent and cohesive object.

Rather than designate Orientalism simply as a myopic yet all pervasive representation by and for Europeans, therefore, this book considers it to be the culmination of specific communicative circuits and institutionalized genres of knowledge production that entangled Ottoman courtiers and scholars with diplomatic sojourners through complex, multidirectional processes of commensuration. William Hanks helpfully defines commensuration as textual procedures that bring "two languages into alignment, so that meaning can move from one to the other."[35] This book extends this definition to include numerous semiotic practices (translation in the strict sense, glossing and calquing, commentary, analogy-making, and so forth) that explicitly or implicitly call attention to the presumed commensurability of two systems, be they linguistic or otherwise. Following Hanks's own analysis, it points to the emergent nature of the boundary between any two sociocultural systems, forged precisely through processes of commensuration.[36] Under Orientalism, understood here and throughout the book as a capacious field of knowledge transcending modern disciplinary boundaries, the resultant systems were "Europe" and "the Orient." Both were—and continue to be—deeply unstable in their valences.

Such a reframing of Orientalism is not entirely new. In the four decades since the publication of *Orientalism*, we have come to appreciate how early modern efforts to produce knowledge about regions that ultimately became objectified as "the Orient" involved people, sites of enunciation, and genres of writing far beyond European metropoles. As Talal Asad noted already in 1980, Orientalism's modes of authority cannot be reduced to its geographical provenance in an amorphous "West." An inquiry into the power of Orientalist discourse, he suggested, must attend to "the particular conditions within which this authoritative discourse was historically produced."[37] This book explores one such nexus of knowledge production, focusing on how seventeenth-century dragomans mediated epistemological and methodological procedures for understanding the Ottoman world between Istanbul and Venice, Paris and Vienna. This does not deny the significance of other genealogies of Orientalism, particularly in the courtly encounters of various South, East, and Central Asian learned elites with missionaries, travelers, and European colonial administrator-scholars.[38] Nor does it negate the transformative role that the Enlightenment eventually played in "the secular, institutionalized study of the Orient by specialists capable of understanding oriental languages and handling primary source material."[39] It does, however, underscore the centrality of Istanbul, its diplomatic milieu, and, especially, its dragoman cadres, to the European articulation of specific ideas about the Islamicate world, its histories, languages, and the special place of the Ottoman Empire therein.

Recent scholarship has emphasized how remarkably similar procedures to those of Orientalism—viz., the warping of space and time and the homogenizing of distinct political and textual traditions in an effort to distill a canonical conception of Universal (Islamic) Empire—evolved at the heart of the Ottoman Empire itself in the course of the sixteenth century. As Ottomanists have shown, during the age of Süleyman the Lawgiver (r. 1520–1566) Ottoman scholars undertook a massive project of synthesizing and re-appropriating the intellectual fruits of earlier imperial formations, whether Greco-Roman, Arabic, Turco-Mongol, or Persian, in an effort to forge an Ottoman imperial tradition, as part of a self-conscious project of *translatio imperii et studii.*[40] Others have traced the genealogies of this imperial formation even further, to Mehmed the Conqueror (r. 1444–1446 and 1451–1481).[41] As Karen Barkey argues, Ottoman imperialism reworked not only the forms of previous empires, but their conceptual apparatus. The Ottoman concept of empire, she writes, "was not just Ottoman, Turkish, or Islamic. It was all these combined with Roman and Byzantine, Balkan, and Turco-Mongol institutions and practices."[42] This Ottoman project resulted, according to Marc Aymes, in "a historical phenomenon so literally matching a concept of *empire* that it did not need to boast the title at all times."[43]

The Ottoman project of *translatio imperii* was premised on deep familiarity with prior imperial formations, as well as on the cultivation of communicative circuits that kept Ottoman scholarly and political elites enmeshed in broader Eurasian networks of exchange.[44] The Ottomans, after all, fashioned themselves not only as heirs to numerous previous empires, but as universal monarchs, a claim that brought them into direct competition with their Habsburg, Safavid, and Mughal contemporaneous imperial rivals.[45]

In this vein, Ottomanists have noted how early modern Ottomans engaged not only with European political theology but with diverse practices of knowledge production, whether geographic, cartographic, theological, or legal.[46] Very much in conversation with this growing historiography, this book charts out how a significant body of knowledge about the Ottomans that circulated among the empire's early modern European observers might have operated not as an outsiders' misreading but rather as a refraction of elite Ottoman perspectives themselves on the land and its histories, politics, and languages.

More specifically, this book considers how decidedly entangled (and often shared) Ottoman/European epistemologies of translation, commensuration, and re-appropriation and their attendant hermeneutical practices became the foundations for the field of knowledge eventually known as Orientalism. It explores some of the institutions, agents, and communicative circuits through which modes of inquiry were mediated from Istanbul to other sites of knowledge production, and the impact of these channels of mediation on the shape of the knowledge thus produced. It foregrounds, moreover, how these processes of mediation between the Ottomans and

nascent European reading publics crucially involved dragomans as paradigmatic trans-imperial subjects, social actors who straddled and helped
broker political, religious, and linguistic boundaries across various imperial
centers.[47] In thematizing specific trans-imperial practices and practitioners
of mediation, this study joins a growing body of scholarship that has sought
to go beyond the enumeration of typological similarities between "Europe"
and its "Others" to address particular institutional domains in which contemporaries observed, categorized, and compared social phenomena across
boundaries, and to consider how these processes of commensuration lay
at the heart of intense communicative circuits that undermine any facile
civilizational divides.[48]

If Said and his postcolonial heirs have often situated Orientalism in the
context of nineteenth-century and later imperialisms, scholars of early
modernity have emphasized the much longer genealogies of the relationship between new knowledge practices and the rise of global consciousness.[49] Within the sizable body of work that has attended to "Old World"
encounters, one strand has focused largely on "representations" of Muslim alterity in myriad European literary genres, underscoring the inherent
blind spots of metropolitan knowledge makers.[50] More recently, scholars
have significantly broadened their scope and methodological toolkit, to
consider the diverse genealogies of Orientalism in humanist philology, Renaissance antiquarianism, confessionalized sacred history, travel-writing,
and missionary proto-ethnography.[51] This shift from literary "representations" to the social history of scholarship has alerted us to the substantial,
if insufficiently acknowledged, role of individuals of Ottoman or North
African descent in Orientalist scholarly production in places like Rome,
Paris, Leiden, and Oxford, whether as translators, language instructors,
secretaries, or informal collaborators.[52] Such belated recognition of Muslim, Eastern Christian, and Jewish presences at the heart of metropolitan
sites of scholarly production further unsettles the notion that philology, sacred history, and antiquarianism were a distinctively European pursuit.[53] It
further challenges a once prevailing understanding of Islamicate societies
as an inert backdrop against which enterprising Europeans "discovered" a
mute and immutable object.

Such a "bootstrapping" understanding of Orientalism's genesis in European minds, if not always in the European metropole, has been decisively
challenged in relation to Indo-Persian worlds of knowledge. In that context,
as multiple scholars have now shown, "the Orient" emerged out of intense

interactions between European scholars and writers and elite members of powerful contemporary Islamicate states. Islamicate elites brought to these engagements different interpretive methods, epistemologies, religiopolitical institutions, and modalities of knowledge production.[54] Less well studied is the significance to Orientalist projects of Europeans' interactions with Ottoman peers and with Ottoman textualities and visualities, of the mediated nature of the knowledge thus produced, and of its institutional embedding in Istanbul's imperial and diplomatic chanceries.[55]

The glaring absence of the Ottomans as subjects rather than mere objects of early modern Orientalism is especially consequential given the centrality of the Ottoman Empire to an early modern European system of states, as Daniel Goffman argues.[56] This absence is also analytically myopic, given that contemporary Ottoman elites cultivated myriad philological and historiographical practices to support their claims to imperial continuity and classical heritage. Indeed, the entwined diplomatic and conceptual engagements between the Ottomans and their neighbors are essential to address for a less linear and teleological understanding of Orientalism's genealogies. As Mohamad Tavakoli-Targhi memorably puts it:

> The formation of Orientalism as an area of European academic inquiry was grounded on a "genesis amnesia" that systematically obliterated the dialogic conditions of its emergence and the production of its linguistic and textual tools. [. . .] As a hegemonic and totalizing discourse, Orientalism celebrates its own perspectival account as scientific and objective while forgetting the histories and perspectives informing its origins.[57]

In this vein, the book centers on the diplomatic milieu of the early modern Ottoman capital as a particular site of such engagements. Combining the prosopographical study of dragomans' kinship and social networking strategies with an in-depth exploration of the texts and images they produced, it situates the articulation of a field of Ottomanist knowledge in relation to contemporary Mediterranean diplomacy and scribal and print cultures. Through this combined methodology it offers a more fine-grained periodization of changes in European understandings of Ottoman society, politics, history, and religion. It shows, furthermore, how the writings that emerged from Istanbul's diplomatic milieu participated in the project of constituting Europe, a project informed from its inception by competing ideas about the relationship between civilization, language, religion, and political subjecthood.[58] Thus, the book underscores how the diplomatic and scholarly networks through which Ottomanist knowledge circulated crucially involved members of the Ottoman elite themselves in intimate and ongoing conversations with long-term sojourners in the Ottoman Empire.[59] Premised on the notion that the genealogies of Orientalism must take into account Istanbul itself as a key site of cultural production, the book explores early modern Istanbul's forms of scholarly sociability, while recognizing that such sociability inevitably entangled the city with other spaces and their inhabitants, metropolitan and provincial alike.[60]

The "Dragoman Renaissance," in this sense, is an exploration of the deep entanglement of philological knowledge-production practices at the heart of the Renaissance's humanist project with the Ottomancentric lifeworlds of a cadre of trans-imperial dragomans who called the Ottoman capital home. It is neither a nostalgic celebration of putative "rebirth," nor simply an exercise in periodization, a revalorization of seventeenth-century Mediterranean sociocultural developments long overshadowed by the better-studied fifteenth and sixteenth centuries. Rather, it refers to an era of dragomans' mutually articulating professional formation, social consolidation, and substantial intellectual-cum-political impact.

Lifeworlds and Semiotic Practices

Over the years, the history of Istanbul's dragomans has attracted some scholarly attention through studies of individual dragomans,[61] reconstructions of dragoman lineages,[62] surveys of policies related to the dragomans of specific embassies,[63] or appraisals of the functions of dragomans in a particular sphere of administrative activity.[64] Whereas the extant scholarship has documented, if sometimes anecdotally, the social and institutional dimensions of dragomans' lifeworlds, it has devoted much less attention to their semiotic practices.[65] This book brings these perspectives together, in an effort to overcome the fragmentation that has limited comparative insight. It combines a sustained study of dragomans' social and professional trajectories with granular analysis of their semiotic practices and engagement with the broader sphere of diplomatic knowledge production. While focusing on the Venetian dragomanate as the largest, most enduring, and self-conscious cadre of dragomans in early modern Istanbul, the book never loses sight of this cadre's extensive mobility. Especially in later chapters, emphasis on the trans-imperial nature of dragomans' modalities of knowledge production and circulation necessitates a close look at Paris and Vienna (among other locales) as much as at Istanbul and Venice.

To illustrate the importance of dragomans' positionality for emergent trans-imperial practices of diplomatic knowledge production, the first two chapters explore the dialectical relationship between several processes that gave shape to the Venetian dragomanate. We begin with the centripetal forces at work in dragomans' recruitment, training, and socialization in the *bailate*, the household of the *bailo*, or Venetian permanent representative to the Porte. We consider how a localized caste of dragomans was forged out of youth recruited throughout Venetian and Ottoman territories. From their at times mercurial remaking via both marriage and officeholding in Istanbul's Catholic community, dragomans became a deeply endogamous group, whose functioning relied precisely on the network effect created by their various connections beyond embassy compounds and the sultan's court. Dragomans' socio-professional mobilities across disparate spaces and increasingly formalized diplomatic and colonial-bureaucratic institutional coordinates worked in tandem with the trans-imperial circulations of objects (through gift-giving) and of persons (through kinship) as interlinked dimensions of successful diplomacy. In particular, kinshipping—the rhizomic expansion of dragomans' social resources through far-reaching patronage, strategic marriage alliances, and localized property ownership and legal know-how—illuminates the formative roles of dragomans' womenfolk in their kin's performance *qua* dragomans.

Whereas the first two chapters emphasize the thoroughly relational practices through which dragoman cadres were forged, the next two attend to dragomans' textual and visual self-inscription, respectively. Chapter 3 considers how four Venetian dragomans' reports from official diplomatic missions, or *relazioni*, articulated the relationship between their object of observation and their authorized public. It explores the hermeneutic strategies that dragoman authors developed for representing Islamicate—Ottoman as well as Safavid, and metropolitan as well as provincial—sociocultural practices within a Venetocentric, humanistically inflected political vocabulary. The chapter addresses the varieties of subject-positions that dragomans' *relazioni* foreground for their trans-imperial authors vis-à-vis their intended readership in Venice's political class, and the rapport they cultivate with a nascent public keenly interested in eyewitness accounts of foreign lands. Rather than simply identify commonalities in a genre known for its highly conventionalized rhetorical strategies, the focus is on authors' evolving understanding of their relationship to the Venetian and Ottoman states and to various spaces and social groupings within their orbit in light of their differentiated personal and professional trajectories.

Following suit, Chapter 4 considers Venetian dragomans' practices of visual (self-) representation by comparing two sets of artifacts. The first is a miniature album of ca. 1660, whose visual program and narrative gloss reveal dragomans' trans-imperial perspective on Istanbul and on Venetian-Ottoman history. The second is a cluster of more than a dozen large oil portraits of dragomans of the Tarsia-Carli-Mamuca della Torre families and their spouses, produced at the turn of the eighteenth century and hung in their ancestral palaces in Koper and Poreč (today in Slovenia and Croatia, respectively). Despite their contrasting media and intended audience, both miniatures and portraits use the visual conventions of their respective genres to offer a congruent sense of dragomans' self-presentation and positionality as proper Ottoman Catholic urbane elite.

The last three chapters return to the question of how dragomans mediated Ottoman epistemologies of translation and their attendant hermeneutical practices to a nascent European discipline of Orientalism. Chapter 5 takes up dragomans' role in the institutionalization of Ottoman language studies in Europe, tracing their substantial output of Ottoman-language grammars, dictionaries, lexicons, and vocabularies. It contrasts dragomans' works with those of other professional groups, particularly seminary-trained missionaries and university-trained philologists, and teases out their unique contributions to the study of the Ottoman language and its ideological framing.

Chapter 6 surveys dragomans' translational oeuvre to underscore its embedding in a rich intertextual web. Moving beyond cataloging what dragomans translated, the chapter asks how they did so. By contrasting two dragomans' divergent translations of the same sultanic decree, and by tracing the evolution over time in dragomans' translations of Ottoman historical works, it considers how specific translation practices such as glossing, commensurating, and voicing related to individual dragomans' intimate ties to multiple bureaucratic elites and imperial institutions. These ideas are further foregrounded in Chapter 7, which explores the unique features of dragomans' participation in a sprawling Republic of Letters. It analyzes how dragomans' positionality in specific circulatory regimes not only allowed them to mediate between Ottoman authors and European reading publics but impacted the ultimate shape of knowledge thus produced. The Epilogue then considers the legacies of Istanbul's Venetian dragomanate, from kinshipping to language acquisition, and suggests how their unique mode of immersive apprenticeship—firmly rooted in diplomacy—eventually became an important aspect of foreign language pedagogy more broadly.

Studies of the dragomanate to date have aimed mostly to reconstruct individual biographies and familial genealogies, with the underlying premise that dragomans were heroic, if marginal, Europeans who operated in a culturally foreign East. With the renewed interest in the early modern Mediterranean as a space of entangled histories, however, it has become more and more evident that the very categories of "Europe" and "the East" must be understood relationally. In developing a historical account of such relationalities and entanglements, this book explores the roles that dragomans' semiotic practices played in articulating the multilayered, evolving relationship between the Ottomans and their neighbors. Throughout, it emphasizes the collaborative nature of dragomans' modalities of knowledge production, belying any facile distinction between "local" and "foreign," "eastern" and "western," "Islamic" and "Christian." Exploring dragomans' variegated strategies of representing the Ottomans as a set of mediation practices, it shows how such practices relate to dragomans' divergent backgrounds, training, kinship patterns, professional ties, and intended publics. By situating dragomans' mediation practices alongside and in relation to other networking activities that repeatedly crossed juridical and ethnolinguistic boundaries, particularly kinshipping and gift-giving, the book questions prevailing ideas about the nature of linguistic mediation in this diplomatic milieu, and the role that Ottoman elite perspectives played in shaping enduring understandings of the Ottomans in early modern Europe. The book thus offers both a fine-grained portrait of an impactful but understudied group of intermediaries, and a sustained methodological and conceptual reflection on the long genealogies of Orientalism as the mutual imbrication of geopolitics and cultural knowledge production in a vital world region whose reverberations are felt to this day.

CHAPTER I

Localizing Foreignness

Forging Istanbul's Dragomanate

A MINIATURE PAINTING OF THE *bailate*, the Venetian consulate in the Ottoman capital ca. 1660, offers us a rare contemporary visual representation of the institutional space in which dragomans were, quite literally, made (figure 1.1). It depicts a two-story building, fenced off from its surroundings, and encircled by a tree-lined garden. Seated on a wooden platform in the garden with their backs to the house are three men in Venetian breeches, cassocks, and ruffs, sporting rounded orange-striped caps on their heads. At the corner, a laborer, wearing a distinctly plainer shirt, breeches, and fez, draws water from a well. Through a window on the ground floor another man, dressed similarly to the ones gathered outside, is seen holding an open book. On the second-floor veranda three figures—a bearded man and a beardless youth in simple kaftans and fur-trimmed caps and another youth in Venetian clothing—lean against the railing. The bearded man and the Venetian youth seem to be conversing, while the other youth is standing aloof.

Through minute sartorial difference, this image codifies several intersecting socio-legal, ethno-religious, professional, and age hierarchies within the bailate. It underscores the volatile identity of dragomans and apprentice dragomans, who inhabited the bailate in growing numbers in the seventeenth century, and who at once formed its institutional core and its most contentious links to the surrounding Ottoman world beyond its walls. It is hardly an accident, therefore, that the two beardless apprentice dragomans in the image are clad in prototypical high-status Venetian and Ottoman Christian garb, respectively. These two sartorial prototypes are here metonymic of two important sources of recruitment into the dragomanate. They also index the transformative capacity of long apprenticeship in the bailate to turn local Catholic youth into loyal Venetian subjects while refashioning Venetian-born citizens into effectively localized members of Istanbul's courtly and diplomatic milieu. A text accompanying the image reads:

> Image of the house, where the Excellent Baili reside, enclosed by part of the orchard, and the hallway above, through which one walks. Below it are the rooms where usually the apprentice dragomans reside.[1]

The spatial and social reconfiguration of dragomans through long residency in the bailate is at the heart of this chapter, which centers on the myriad mechanisms through which apprentice dragomans were recruited, trained, employed, and imbued with a particular trans-imperial habitus. In order to appreciate the pivotal role of the bailate as a space of transformative socialization for future dragomans, the chapter first situates the evolution of the institution of the dragomanate itself at the intersection of Venetocentric, circum-Mediterranean, and Ottomancentric practices for mediating language and power. It then considers why and how dragomans became central to Venetian-Ottoman diplomacy, that is: how dragomans' sources of recruitment and modes of socialization gave shape to particular modalities of diplomatic knowledge production.

Patrimonial Households and Trans-Imperial Spaces of Encounter

Historians of the early modern Ottoman state have long noted the important role played by large elite households in entwining domestic hierarchies with imperial politics. Through their far-reaching recruitment and training programs, it has been suggested, such households institutionalized and perpetuated ethnic heterogeneity at the empire's core.[2] These patrimonial households—starting with the imperial palace in Istanbul and extending to the households of military-bureaucratic elites in the provinces—served as training grounds for a large body of young cadets, who functioned simultaneously as both domestic and civil servants. Initially, candidates for the Ottoman imperial household were captured primarily through raids beyond the frontier and from among captives and prisoners of war. From the early fifteenth century, additional recruits were obtained through the formalization of the practice of *devşirme*, or child levy. This institution ensured the steady supply of enslaved boys for the imperial household from among the non-Muslim rural population of the provinces, especially the Balkans, where a changing percentage of boys and youth were removed from their parental homes and sent to the imperial center. By the late six-teenth century, however, raids, war booty, and the *devşirme* ceased to be the exclusive source of recruits into the imperial household. To supple-ment them, specialized personnel with specific skills or technical know-how were sometimes enlisted from among converts, "foreigners" beyond the frontier, and groups in Ottoman society previously deemed "unfit" for service.[3]

Regardless of provenance and method of mobilization, patrimonial households had the capacity to profoundly transform their inductees. Upon recruitment, cadets underwent a lengthy and rigorous regimen of what Cornell Fleischer has termed "deracination, education, and Ottomaniza-tion," which molded them into loyal subjects suited for lifelong service to the dynast in key military and administrative roles.[4] This protracted train-ing could easily last over a decade. Recruits were first assigned to rural Anatolian (Turkish Muslim) families to learn the language and become accustomed to hard labor. Only then, after being schooled or apprenticed within the imperial household for several years, did they enter a variety of positions in the state's expanding military-bureaucratic apparatus.[5] Whereas cadets' marriage was at first strictly limited, by the late sixteenth century the rules relaxed to the point that true service dynasties began to emerge, particularly among members of the imperial cavalry and other elite officeholders. Here, for the first time, membership in the Ottoman imperial household became a potentially heritable status, with sons of re-cruits gaining a sense of privilege by descent. These swelled the ranks and ultimately made the *devşirme* superfluous, leading to its de facto disap-pearance in the late seventeenth century.[6]

The transformation in household recruitment patterns at the turn of the seventeenth century and its implications for conceptions of subjecthood, loyalty, and bureaucratic professionalization have been well-documented not only in the Ottoman capital, but also in the military-bureaucratic elite households of the Ottoman Balkans, Egypt, North Africa, and the Arab provinces.[7] Far less understood are the roles of recruitment into and train-ing within expansive elite households in contemporary Venetian society. To be sure, Venetian historiography has emphasized rather the exclusivity and endogamy of the metropolitan patrician and citizen classes.[8] Yet even in hyper-endogamous Venice, studies of elite households have outlined how extended, bilateral kinship orientation was instrumental in consoli-dating a patrician grip on political institutions, allowing families to weave dense networks of patronage through both the paternal and the maternal lines.[9]

Significantly, thus far the shared patrimonial principles and purposes—though not always actual practices—of Ottoman and Venetian elite households have gone unnoticed for the most part. This understudied confluence is especially intriguing in light of the prescribed, long sojourns at the Porte of many prominent members of Venice's elites in their youth, precisely as a political and commercial apprenticeship. It is well worth asking, therefore, how assumptions about loyalty and subjecthood were engendered by Venetian and Ottoman elite kinship and household structures, and how associated roles were inhabited and manipulated by people who were familiar with—indeed, familiars of—both.

Such familiarity was cultivated most clearly in the Venetian bailate in Istanbul, an institution that served as a model for numerous other diplomatic residences in the Ottoman capital in its functioning as a central node in the production and circulation of dragoman-mediated knowledge. In fact, the Venetian dragomanate in Istanbul and its offshoots throughout the Venetian maritime colonies and in Venice proper are a prime example of how the Venetian state adapted prototypically Ottoman mechanisms of subject-making and integration through a large elite household. The emergence and transformation of the Venetian dragomanate underscores how Venetian and Ottoman household patterns and affective ties interacted and sometimes converged in the making of trans-imperial professional cadres.

Recruitment

By its heyday in the late seventeenth century, the Venetian dragomanate came to consist of no more than a dozen families, who supplied the bailate with most of its new apprentice dragomans generation after generation. Throughout the early modern period these families intensely and repeatedly intermarried, securing their tight control over apprentice dragoman positions, which became de facto heritable. Sojourning in the bailate in the 1770s, the physiologist Lazzaro Spallanzani observed that as soon as dragomans' families have sons, "they dress them *alla dragomana* and lead them in their father's footsteps."[10] The intergenerational transfer of skill and status embodied in dragoman positions was facilitated by the institutionalization of a specific official, subaltern dragoman rank, that of *giovani di lingua* (literally language youth, a calque of the Turkish *dil oğlan*), glossed here as "apprentice dragomans."[11] This neologism underscores both the strong element of apprenticeship and subordination implied by apprentices' junior position, as they honed their linguistic and diplomatic skills and shadowed more seasoned dragomans, and the reality of their service as de facto dragomans, from regularly translating official Ottoman records into Italian to their more occasional and haphazard participation in court protocol, during public ceremonies, and when substituting for their seniors on their day-to-day rounds to the divan and to Ottoman officials' home.

Initially, apprentice dragomans were to be recruited across Venetian territories with the explicit purpose of equipping them with the high skill and decorum required for diplomatic work in the Ottoman court. "There is no doubt," observed the bailo Paolo Contarini in 1583,

> that the service of one's own [subjects] is more advantageous and has more public dignity than that of Turkish [i.e. Ottoman] subjects, because the [former], who are not preoccupied with showing respect, speak with daring, whereas the Turks are afraid to do so.[12]

Paul Rycaut, then secretary in the English embassy in Istanbul, was to make a very similar observation in *The Present State of the Ottoman Empire* almost a century later, pinpointing the problem of dragomans' meek speech to their compromised juridical position as Ottoman subjects:

> The reason of which Tyranny and presumption in these prime Officers over the Interpreters, is because they are most commonly born subjects of the Grand Signior, and therefore ill support the least word misplaced, or savouring of contest from them, not distinguishing between the sense of the Embassadour, and the explication of the Interpreter; and therefore it were very useful to breed up a Seminary of young Englishmen, of sprightly and ingenious parts, to be qualified for that Office; who may with less danger to themselves, honour to their Master, and advantage to the publick, express boldly without the usual mincing and submission of other Interpreters, whatsoever is commanded and declared by their Master.[13]

Rycaut's fantasy of "a seminary of young Englishmen," however, like similar projects hatched in other contemporary embassies, was never to materialize. Even the Venetians, who made mighty efforts to send Venetian youth to the bailate, had to concede that the attempt was only partially successful, and certainly not without its perils. The bailo Sebastian Venier, for example, placed little hope in Venetian youth sent to the bailate to be apprenticed as dragomans on his watch:

> Those [Venetians] who are of tender age, either their parents do not permit them to come here, or if they do little can be done to prevent them from falling prey to a thousand strange accidents; if they are of mature age, beyond their inability to learn languages, they have been brought up not in what I would call liberty, but rather in such license, that it is impossible to make them accommodate the customs here, and not disturb the house of the poor baili . . .[14]

The apprentices' official title already suggests the significance attributed to young age as a precondition for the transformation presumed to result from long apprenticeship. And while most apprentices, particularly those sent from Venice, began their tenure in the bailate around the age of fifteen or eighteen, apprentices as young as ten, or even younger, were not uncommon. It was that youthfulness, however, that proved, as Venier observed, a source of many challenges, especially for sojourning apprentices hailing from faraway Venice. In fact, over the course of the seventeenth century fewer Venetians were sent to Istanbul, and fewer still successfully completed their apprenticeship in the bailate. The majority of dragoman apprenticeships became the purview of local dragomans' sons and nephews, whose sisters in the meantime married other dragomans and apprentices, forging a truly endogamous Istanbulite dragoman caste.

Such intense endogamy emerged haphazardly, since the 1550s, from three very different bases of recruitment: the Venetian citizen class, the urban elites of Venice's Adriatic and eastern Mediterranean colonies, and the Ottoman (mainly Istanbulite) Catholic community. Understanding the differing ties that eventually bound these three groups to one another and to Venetian diplomacy is essential for any inquiry into their role in mediating Venetian-Ottoman relations.

In Venice, *cittadini originarii* (citizens by birth) formed a de facto second tier of the metropolitan elite. Men belonging to this clearly self-conscious estate were barred from officeholding and voting, but constituted the government's bureaucratic core, largely sharing patrician understandings of the state. As service in Istanbul was generally considered a stepping-stone to more prestigious government employment in Venice, numerous citizen families, with a long tradition of supplying secretaries to the ducal chancellery, were willing to send their sons into apprenticeship in the bailate.[15]

A second group of recruits to the dragomanate came from the Venetian colonial elite in the Adriatic and eastern Mediterranean, increasingly undermined by the Ottoman conquest of Venice's Dalmatian hinterland in the early sixteenth century and of Cyprus in 1571. In the aftermath of these conquests, many feudal families sought refuge in Venetian territories or in Venice itself. Placing a son in diplomatic service in Istanbul reinforced these threatened elites' claims to enduring colonial loyalty. It also offered concrete prospects for social and economic mobility by linking young apprentices with powerful patrons, and by opening up distinct future commercial opportunities in both Venice and Istanbul.[16]

Finally, the third and largest group of recruits to Venice's dragomanate came from the Ottoman capital's Latin-rite (Roman Catholic) community, known as the *Magnifica comunità*. Members of this community traced their roots to Genoese, Pisan, and Venetian settlement in Byzantium even prior to the Fourth Crusade. Permanent Genoese settlement in the bustling port district of Galata dates from the 1260s.[17] Local descendants of these early settlers retained their close ties to the city's political and commercial nerve centers after the Ottoman conquest of 1453.[18] It was in the second half of the sixteenth century, however, as several foreign embassies relocated to Pera (today Beyoğlu), a leafy hilltop quarter just behind Galata, across the Golden Horn from the sultan's Topkapı palace, that the bailo began recruiting his dragomans from among members of several prominent local Catholic families.

In joining his large household, permanently based in Pera after 1571, local dragomans gave the bailo direct access to the area's centers of power, while increasing their own status. The local prestige of the dragoman's position is evident from the tight correspondence between its holders and the highest officers—priors and sub-priors—of the *Magnifica comunità*—who oversaw the community's significant real estate holdings and were entrusted with negotiating with Ottoman authorities periodic maintenance and repairs for the area's numerous Catholic churches and convents. Between 1570 and 1670, Venetian dragomans or their immediate kin served as priors or sub-priors of the *Magnifica comunità* thirty-two times, for a cumulative total of eighty-eight years. Between 1670, when elections became more sporadic, and 1705 (the latest date for which information is available), ten of thirteen Community officials were dragomans, though not necessarily Venetian. Dragomans also served in other capacities in local Catholic churches. In 1626, Giovanni Antonio Grillo, the Venetian grand dragoman, was appointed Procurator of St. Francis. That same year, two members of another dragomans' family, Matteo and Bartolomeo Piron, became Procurators of St. Peter and St. George, respectively.[19]

From local recruits' perspective, Venetian employment spelled not only a steady income, but a source of authority within the shrinking, conflict-riddled Catholic community. Venetian employment served, furthermore, as legal protection, granting dragomans immunities and exemptions from Ottoman law, at least in principle.[20] Most important, dragoman posts offered several distinct familial advantages. A dragoman was well positioned to keep relatives abreast of political, economic, and military developments both at home and abroad. Access to such timely news was essential to long-distance traders. Beyond trading in information, dragomans' intense and varied contacts among the political-cum-commercial elites of Istanbul and Venice (or, London, Marseille, and Amsterdam) greatly benefited merchant relatives by offering concrete business opportunities. For such merchants, the ability to extract profit depended on accessing often highly monopolistic markets as well as on securing preferential tax levels therein. Both depended on contracting deals (and, ideally, forging partnerships) with foreign merchants.[21] The connection between English, French, or Dutch merchants and their respective embassies was more or less explicit, as the former practically ran the latter, or at least retained a high degree of financial leverage over it.[22] If in the Venetian case the power dynamic was not as simple (certainly by the seventeenth century), the bailo still had to cultivate the good will of his advisory council, which consisted of locally based Venetian merchants.

From the perspective of Venetian officialdom, the recruitment of dragomans from among Pera's most powerful Catholic families could curb, at least partially and temporarily, French and Papal inroads into the community. The strategic and iconic significance of the *Magnifica comunità* was well recognized by the various Catholic powers of the period, all of whom vied to claim their protection of specific Christian Ottoman holy sites and institutions.[23] More important, it gave Venice access to diffuse social networks that facilitated the elusive task of information gathering across Ottoman territories, particularly given Pera families' frequent marital ties to the Catholic and Orthodox elites of the Aegean and Ionian, the Dalmatian coast, and the Danubian principalities, as well as the Ottoman capital itself.

In recruiting apprentice dragomans, the Venetians gave clear preference to the sons, sons-in-law, and nephews of acting and former dragomans, making them de facto hereditary posts.[24] Local families were keenly aware of this practice and the inroads into dragoman apprenticeships in the bailate that kinship ties provided. When a local dragoman or apprentice passed away or retired from service, his relatives would immediately petition the bailo to take another kinsman in. For example, when Ippolito Parada died of the plague only a few months after starting an apprenticeship in 1637, his family promptly asked that he be replaced by his fifteen-year-old younger brother, Michele. The bailo Alvise Contarini, who approvingly forwarded the request to the Senate, suggested that "Your Serenity could do no greater work of charity than this."[25] On another occasion, the dragoman Giovanni Battista Navon, whose father, Pasquale, and brother Tommaso had already served in that office, petitioned to have his son Alessandro admitted into the bailo's service as an apprentice dragoman. Navon did not fail to mention his father-in-law, Marcantonio Borisi, who had been executed by the Ottomans while in Venetian service, and the stipends disbursed to his now-deceased wife and her sisters in recognition of Borisi's merits. Citing both families' long service, the bailo recommended admitting Alessandro so that "excited by this stimulus of public kindness he will diligently apply himself to his studies as faithfully and devotedly as is typical of his family [casa]."[26]

This mechanism of recruitment proved very effective, and within a couple of generations the Venetian dragomanate was populated overwhelmingly by members of the Catholic community of Pera. Throughout the late-sixteenth and seventeenth centuries several of the most distinguished local Catholic families had at least one son employed as a Venetian apprentice dragoman at almost any given moment. This system of virtually guaranteed employment to certain local families reproduced on a smaller scale the Venetian strategy of granting citizens by birth a monopoly over specific positions in the state bureaucracy, forging alliances and securing goodwill and collaboration.[27]

Table 1.1 and figure 1.2 show the different juridical composition and kin resources of the bailate's apprentices and dragomans from the late-sixteenth to the early-eighteenth centuries. Of a total of thirteen Venetian citizen families represented in the dragomanate, six produced only apprentices who failed to achieve dragoman rank.[28] In contrast, all seventeen Ottoman families represented in the pool secured at least one dragoman appointment.[29] If we consider that, unlike Venetian citizens, many Ottoman and Venetian colonial families represented in the dragomanate had multiple members in service throughout the period—some up to half a

TABLE I.I Juridical composition of the Venetian dragomanate in Istanbul, 1570–1720

Rank	Venetian citizens	Venetian colonial subjects	Ottoman subjects	Unknown	Total families
Apprentice-only families[a]	7[b]	2[c]	—	1[d]	11
Dragoman families	6[e]	4[f]	17[g]	2[h]	28
Total families	13	6	17	3	39

a. Excluding families with both apprentice dragomans and dragomans.
b. Garzoni, Scaramelli, Torre, Tosi, Velutello, Vico, and Zon.
c. Agapito and Ausonio.
d. Cornaro, likely Venetian citizens or subjects.
e. Alberti, Bon, Darduin, Imberti, Marucini, and Vecchia.
f. Borisi, Brutti, Carli, and Tarsia.
g. Balsarini, Coressi, Fortis, Gioveni, Girachi, Grillo, Gulianò, Mascellini, Navon, Negroni, Nicolini, Olivieri, Parada, Piron, Ralli, Salvago, and Sanguinazzo.
h. Calavrò-Imberti (possibly of Istrian/Venetian colonial or Venetian citizen provenance) and Scassi.

dozen or more—their relative share of the dragomanate becomes significantly greater: in the 150-year period analyzed here, only seven bailate dragomans hailed from Venetian citizen families, and, with the exception of the Marucinis early in the period, every Venetian citizen dragoman was an "isolate," with no blood relatives employed as either apprentices or dragomans.[30] In contrast, the four Venetian colonial families in the dragomanate had a total of twenty-four individuals in service, and the seventeen Ottoman families at least fifty-five.[31] Venetian citizens, then, accounted for only 16 percent of the dragomanate in this period (fifteen out of a total of ninety-four individual apprentices and dragomans), compared with 25 percent Venetian colonial subjects and nearly 59 percent Ottoman subjects, respectively. That dragomans tended to be lifelong bailate employees, whereas apprentices typically worked in the bailate for a decade or less, means that Ottoman majority at any given time was even more pronounced than can be gleaned from simple percentages or head counts.

Of course, representing dragomans through their membership in decidedly patriarchal and patrilineal families hardly gives a complete picture of their multiple, at times trans-imperial kin relations. But it does provide a reasonable shorthand for individuals' juridical status (acquired largely through patrilines), and the growing dominance of Istanbul's Catholic elite in the Venetian dragomanate. It is also noteworthy that all four families of Venetian colonial subjecthood represented in the dragomanate—Borisi, Brutti, Carli, and Tarsia—were intermarried among themselves as well as among Catholic Istanbul's elite families, including several other dragoman dynasties, as figures 1.2 and 1.3 further demonstrate. Figure 1.2 reveals the significantly greater propensity of Ottoman families represented in the Venetian dragomanate to contract marriages with other such families, as well as with Venetian colonial dragoman families, compared to Venetian citizen ones. Figure 1.3 broadens this picture to underscore Catholic Pera's intense endogamy across dragomanates, as well as the integration of foreign dragoman families (Venetian colonial and other) into that milieu through marriage. Here, too, Venetian citizen families are the outlier.

This dynamic suggests that by the late sixteenth century the institution of the bailate, albeit of much longer, Byzantine roots, came to weld classical Venetian patterns of endogamy and social reproduction with Ottoman practices of exogamous recruitment and training. On the one hand, admission into Venetian service in Istanbul—not unlike other positions in Venice's expansive state apparatus—relied heavily on kinship and descent. On the other, it entailed the restructuring of these same familial ties. For upon entry into service, young apprentice dragomans were removed from their (predominantly Istanbulite) homes and from the domestic care of their (predominantly Greek-speaking) mothers, and placed into the all-male, Italianate space of the bailate. There, for the next seven years or more, they were entrusted into the paternal care of their dragoman fathers, uncles, older brothers, and, of course, the bailo himself. The latter, although customarily ignorant of Turkish, personally supervised his apprentice dragomans' linguistic progress and reported on it in his periodic dispatches to the Venetian Senate and in his comprehensive *relazione* upon return from office.[32]

The discussion so far has suggested a simple, tripartite division of the dragomanate into denizens of Venetian, colonial, and Istanbulite Catholic families. This division is in line with the logic of the early modern Venetian state itself, which carefully distinguished between citizens, subjects, and non-subjects, each possessing a supposedly inherent and fixed degree of affinity to the Venetian state, and a set measure of willingness to put the state's interests before one's own. Suspicion of the supposed disloyalty and dishonesty of Pera-born dragomans, which would characterize Venetian debates about the dragomanate throughout the seventeenth and eighteenth centuries (and permeates some modern scholarship too), resulted in repeated, if largely failed, attempts to secure quotas for Venetian secretaries' sons among apprentice dragomans, and to facilitate training programs in Venice prior to dispatching youth to Istanbul.[33] Indeed, the recruitment of Venetian citizens and colonial subjects as apprentice dragomans was intended precisely to counteract the proverbial disloyalty of Pera-born dragomans who were, after all, Ottoman subjects.

Yet the very division of the dragomanate into Venetian citizens, colonial subjects, and Istanbulite non-subjects was much eroded by the forms of sociability engendered by the bailate and the wider Ottoman city. So much so that by the seventeenth century the boundaries between the three groups became increasingly difficult to maintain. Venetian subjects and citizens sent to be trained in Istanbul could "go native" in ways unforeseen and unappreciated by their employers. Some embraced Islam, quit the service, and sought employment elsewhere in the Ottoman capital. For example, in the span of just three years, from 1627 to 1629, Venice lost three of its Venetian-born apprentice dragomans. Camillo Garzoni was convicted of an unnamed crime (possibly leaving Istanbul without the bailo's permission), exiled to Zara (Zadar, today in Croatia) for three years, and barred from public office for life. Another apprentice, Fontana, converted to Islam. A third, Antonio Torre, also became Muslim, leaving behind a long list of creditors.[34] Some apprentice dragomans took local concubines or lovers in clear transgression of expected affective boundaries,[35] while others still were absorbed into the Latin community of Pera through marriage, acquiring in the process in-laws from among more senior dragomans or other wealthy and well-connected denizens. Out of dozens of Venetian citizens who apprenticed in the bailate over the century, only a handful became dragomans.

For those who did, marriage into local families facilitated quick integration into the Latin community. In fact, by the mid-seventeenth century, the high degree of intermarriage among the three groups of Venetian dragomans in Istanbul led to the establishment of veritable dragoman dynasties, more or less permanently settled in Istanbul despite their diverse roots across Ottoman and Venetian territories. Dragomans' intergenerational and trans-imperial bonds were both capitalized upon by dragomans themselves and seen by their Venetian patrons as vital to the success of their enterprise in the Ottoman capital.

The high degree of endogamy and integration across juridical lines is further indicated by the numerous cases of colonial émigré dragomans who came to assume prominent positions in the Latin community. Cases in point are those of the Venetian dragoman of Albanian and Istrian origins Christoforo Brutti, who was appointed sub-prior of the *Magnifica comunità* in 1623, and Brutti's nephew, Christoforo Tarsia, born in Venetian Capodistria (Koper, now in Slovenia), who in 1652 became the community's prior.[36] Whereas the granting of the prestigious title of prior or sub-prior was a clear sign of these parvenus' ultimate recognition as elite members of the local community, it also marked their reciprocal adoption of a local, deeply endogamous practice that wedded elite status, service to the Venetian bailate, and communal title-holding.

From the Ottoman state's point of view, too, dragomans were both "foreign" by virtue of serving foreign embassies, and "local" by virtue of their numerous relations in the Ottoman capital and provinces, and their wives' and sisters' at times significant real-estate ownership in the city.[37] Dragomans themselves often complicated this juridical situation further by placing different sons with different embassies, thus making claim to various forms of foreign protection, if not outright subjecthood. For example, in the late-sixteenth and early-seventeenth centuries, members of the Olivieri family worked in both the French and Venetian embassies. Nicorosio Grillo, a cousin of the Venetian grand dragoman Giovanni Antonio, was employed by the Dutch ambassador Cornelis Haga in 1616. Other local families, including the Navon, Piron, and Parada, similarly had some sons working for the Venetians and others for the French, the English, the Dutch, and the Habsburgs.[38]

Officially, the Venetians disapproved of their dragomans' immediate relatives working for other powers for fear of espionage. However, extended kin and friendship networks offered dragomans vital access to local and inter-imperial information, often proving beneficial to their Venetian employers too. Panaiotis Nicousios (1613–1673), for example, who served the Habsburg legation in Istanbul and later became Ottoman grand dragoman, maintained a decades-long friendship with Ambrosio Grillo, as well as other Venetian dragomans and baili, providing vital information on political maneuvers in other embassies and the chambers of the grand vizier himself.[39]

Over time, even the long-standing chasm between Istanbul's Catholic and Orthodox (Phanariot) elites—though ideologically still powerful—was sufficiently eroded through intermarriage that some Venetian dragomans became directly related to the Porte's Phanariot grand dragomans of the Mavrocordato and Ghika families.[40] The two sons of the Ottoman grand dragoman Alexander Mavrocordato (in office from 1673), Nicholas (grand dragoman from 1689) and Yanaki (grand dragoman from 1709), married Cassandra Cantacuzeno and Zamfira Gulianò, Ambrosio Grillo's grand-daughter and niece, respectively. Nicholas and Cassandra's son married Maria Gulianò, likely Zamfira's niece. By the eighteenth century, the Mavrocordatos became related through marriage to the Ralli family, several of whose sons served as Venetian dragomans.[41] The advantages of such unions for Venetian diplomacy were hardly lost on the baili. Upon Cassandra Cantacuzeno's marriage to Nicholas Mavrocordato in August 1700, the bailo Lorenzo Soranzo reported to the Senate that he had taken the opportunity to cultivate both families' good will by sending Cassandra a gift of four robes "with other gallantries."[42]

The Phanariot connection's significance goes beyond purely genealogical reasons. It was dragomans' Phanariot kin—especially mothers—who facilitated early acquisition of Greek at home and who greased the wheels of the highest echelons of the Ottoman government, where Phanariots played a decisive role. Venetian dragomans' Phanariot connections—their mothers' membership in the post-Byzantine Orthodox aristocracy—also bolstered their elite status. The prestige and power enjoyed by such Orthodox Istanbulite elites, modeled on Ottoman forms of the grandee household, were recognized by courtly society even more than that of their Catholic counterparts.[43]

The long-term employment of several entry-level apprentice dragomans who displayed only minimal linguistic skills but who were well connected in Istanbul attests to the political usefulness of maintaining members of various local elites on the bailate payroll. In an extensive report on dragomans' performance in 1641, two outgoing baili, Pietro Foscarini and Alvise Contarini, cautioned against discharging any from service, regardless of poor performance, since they would immediately be recruited by the French and English.[44] A dispatch by the Venetian Resident (de facto bailo) Giovanni Battista Ballarino in 1655 confirmed that the aging Giovanni Piron, who had been employed as an apprentice dragoman for twenty years, had finally mastered some languages, and endorsed his petition for promotion to the level of dragoman. Yet in 1664 Piron, aged seventy-five, was still listed on the payroll as an apprentice. According to Ballarino, for the previous six years Piron had visited the bailate only at Easter and Christmas. Given his brother Antonio's position as an English dragoman, and Giovanni's fast friendship with Giorgio Draperis, the English grand dragoman, Ballarino considered his absence from duty an advantage, since it kept the disgruntled apprentice from disclosing sensitive information to Venice's commercial rivals.[45]

Training

The Venetian dragomanate's tight endogamy, which sometimes pulled Venetian recruits into Ottomancentric milieus, could also operate in the reverse, imbuing local recruits with cultural frameworks, bodily repertoires, and social contacts that signaled their incorporation into a Venetocentric trans-imperial project. A former dragoman turned abbot, Antonio Olivieri, provides intriguing vignettes into the world of the bailate in the later seventeenth century and its transformative capacity for local recruits. Born in 1655, Olivieri joined the bailate as an apprentice dragoman ca. 1670. The scion of a local Catholic dragoman dynasty, Olivieri was the son of Giovanni, a long-time Venetian dragoman, and the grandson and great-grandson of Carlo Olivier and Domenico, senior French dragomans at the turn of the seventeenth century. His mother, Cassandra Cantacuzeno, on the other hand, was the daughter of a distinguished Orthodox Phanariot family.[46] In his memoir, Olivieri describes how the foreign embassies of Galata and Pera jointly sponsored a large masquerade ball of 150 persons for the 1676 carnival season, and then, in an explicit effort by the French and Venetian representatives to outdo one another, commissioned lavish, public theatrical productions the following year, in which some dragomans also performed. Olivieri himself was asked by the bailo Morosini to participate in a production of Don Giovanni.[47] Despite Olivieri's protestations that his Italian was poor and that he would become the laughingstock of the community, he was left with no choice but to recite the prologue and to play the sheriff who attempted to prevent Don Giovanni from visiting a bordello.

Beyond the reaffirmation of hypersexual heteronormativity, a prerequisite of the bailate's strictly homosocial space (despite periodic breaches), this theatrical production partook in a process of turning local youth into

distinctly "cosmopolitan" courtiers. Of course, the use of public spectacle to convey courtly power was not unfamiliar to denizens of the Ottoman capital—the Porte sponsored such spectacles on various occasions,
and even commissioned their immortalization in lavish albums.[48] But the
specific genres chosen by the bailo—masquerade and comedy—were distinctly foreign.[49] "Don Giovanni" itself was a work whose diverse iterations
across Spanish, French, and Italian stages (and, eventually, in Habsburg
Central Europe) made it a particularly potent sign of cosmopolitan cultural connoisseurship. In the immediate context of the performances orchestrated by Istanbul's embassies in 1676 we should note the trappings of
lavish costumes and masquerade. These departed sharply from the clear
demarcation of hierarchy, position, and communal belonging through sartorial regimentation that characterized early modern Ottoman urban society in general, and dragomans' livery in particular. As significant were the
temporary redrawing of communal boundaries as to include all embassy
staff, and the designation of the public space of the embassy district as
culturally foreign by importing fashionable theatrical genres and mounting
stages, backdrop scenery, and other visual props.

Beyond the topsy-turvy spacetime of carnival season, the process of so-
cializing future dragomans continued to unfold more mundanely through
protracted apprenticeship and residence in the bailate. As their name suggests, most *giovani di lingua* started their apprenticeship in their teens.
Initial legislation in 1551 set apprentices' minimum age at twenty, but over
the years, children as young as eight or ten were regularly admitted.[50]
Teenage diplomatic employment was hardly unusual at the time. French
apprentice dragomans' average age upon arrival in Istanbul was seventeen to nineteen, and the initial decree signed by Louis XIV's minister
Jean-Baptiste Colbert had envisioned an even earlier start, at nine or ten.[51]
Youth employment was customary in other settings too. Starting in the
1630s, the colonial administration of seventeenth-century New Spain preferred very young employees, as Mark Burkholder observes. Despite their
lack of maturity and inexperience, he contends, young bureaucrats held
the prospect of long years of future service.[52] This was vitally important
for dragomans, whose protracted linguistic training and upkeep were particularly costly.

Apprentice dragomans' youthfulness nevertheless posed challenges.
During their initial sojourn in the bailate they had to undergo not only
language training, but comprehensive general education as well.[53] Various

baili sought different solutions to this problem. In 1577, the bailo Giovanni Correr endorsed a proposal by the Turkish language instructor in his house to go to Venice to train young children there before they are sent to Istanbul.[54] In a dispatch to the Heads of the Council of Ten a few years earlier, the bailo Antonio Tiepolo went so far as to suggest that the two apprentice dragomans in his house at the time, Matteo Marucini and Marchiò Spinelli, be sent to live outside the bailate, "in the house of one of the Turkish dragomans," to give them better opportunities to practice the language. Tiepolo did not elaborate on the identity of the proposed foster family, but the very idea of sending Venetian youth to live outside the bailate was novel (although "Turkish" here is curious, it could be understood as meaning local Ottoman Christians rather than Muslims, let alone ethnic Turks). Tiepolo suggested that in this way the two youth might gain command of the language in a year or two.[55] This estimate is interesting, since by that point Marucini and Spinelli had lived in Istanbul for over six years. Yet the proposal, endorsed by the two apprentices themselves, was apparently rejected by the Venetian authorities. And although in 1623 the Senate favored proposals to send apprentices to be schooled in an Armenian college, suggesting that "staying in a place where one only speaks, reads and writes in Turkish, it is to be believed that the fruit hoped for will be produced faster," the plans remained unrealized.[56]

Upon appointing two apprentice dragomans, Bernardin Zon and Camillo Garzoni, in 1625, the Senate repeated verbatim the decision to have them attend an Armenian college in Istanbul.[57] Yet no indication survives of any Venetian apprentices ever actually attending the Armenian colleges in either Istanbul or Izmir. In fact, after Venetian dragoman apprenticeship in Istanbul was instituted by law in 1551, all incumbents were strictly confined to the bailate for the duration of their apprenticeship, normally lasting seven years or longer. This held true even for local apprentices who, in order to become dragomans, needed to be re-socialized as Venetian subjects first.

Formally, then, an apprentice dragoman's training began upon entry into the bailate. In reality, however, many had started their preparation long before. Venetian citizens often trained as secretaries in the ducal chancellery in St. Mark's Square for several years prior to traveling to Istanbul. Pera-born youth, especially the sons and nephews of active dragomans, received home instruction in several languages before they were formally admitted to the ranks of apprentices. In a 1700 petition, the dragoman Giacomo

Tarsia, the son and younger brother of several dragomans in Venetian service, described how his two sons, eighteen-year-old Christoforo and thirteen-year-old Giovanni Battista, had already learned several languages at home. Christoforo, argued the proud father with perhaps a tinge of hyperbole, had already mastered Italian, Latin, French, Greek, Turkish, Persian, and Arabic.[58] Giacomo himself had been taught languages at home by his father, Christoforo, in the 1660s.[59] These were hardly exceptional cases. In 1672 the Venetian traveler Cornelio Magni observed the early linguistic training of Pera's future dragomans:

> [I]t is certainly quite remarkable seeing that not only adults, and older men, but also young children as soon as they learn to babble loosen their tongue in three of four very different languages, and these in perfection.
>
> The Greek language is their original, being the common spoken idiom of the country, and in it they are educated by their mothers, who cultivate that language.[60]

Early modern Istanbul's plurilingualism was pervasive. Yet it is important to point out that dragoman households often used Greek alongside (or instead of) Italian for everyday interaction, whether due to marriage into local Orthodox Phanariot or Catholic émigré families from Greek-speaking islands, or to Greek's enduring cultural prestige among post-Byzantine elites. In 1614 the Roman traveler Pietro della Valle, while sojourning in Istanbul, noted that "there remain in Pera few families of ancient times, who are all Greek in their clothes and customs, and preserve the Latin rite and Italian language, concurrently with the Greek idiom."[61] In 1680, an Irish vicar apostolic, John Baptist Burke, listed Pera's dragoman households in general, and the Tarsias in particular, as "Greeks of the Latin Rite."[62] Eighteenth-century parish records from Galata's largest Catholic church, SS Peter and Paul, show that "Greeks" formed the lion's share of this French-sponsored church's parishioners (e.g., 68 percent and 61 percent of brides and grooms, respectively; 63 percent and 55 percent of mothers and fathers of baptized children; and 55 percent and 34 percent of female and male deceased). The term "Greek" here clearly referred to language rather than confession, as the parishioners of SS Peter and Paul were Catholic, mostly members of the local Latin-rite community (the former *Magnifica comunità*, dissolved in 1680), or émigrés from the islands of Chios, Tinos, and Syros. As Edhem Eldem shows, this interpretation is further borne out by the strong endogamy within this Greek element of the community, with some exogamy vis-à-vis French residents in Istanbul.[63] The term "Greek," however, like the term "Turk," derived some of its potency precisely from its bivalency as both an ethnolinguistic and a religious marker. This bivalency was the source of much anxiety among early modern sojourning diplomats, while proving invaluable to dragomans' access to Greek-speaking Ottoman elites.

As significant as Greek was as a marker of local cultural fluency, it was Ottoman Turkish that was understood as the sine qua non of dragomans' training. The 1551 decree regulating apprentice dragomans' training entrusted their instruction to a local Catholic resident of Pera, Pietro Maruffo.[64] But very soon the bailo hired a Muslim Turk to serve as *cozza* (from Turkish *hoca*, schoolmaster) for several hours a day. Periodic accounts found in baili's dispatches concerning apprentices' education suggested only limited progress, in part due to the lack of a shared language between the teacher and his students, in part due to the former's personality and pedagogical shortcomings (drinking problems and a reluctance to force unwilling students to attend classes were among the recurring problems cited). In 1577 the bailo Giovanni Correr reported that the *hoca*, one Mehmed Çelebi, had good command of Italian and a pleasing manner.[65] He also seems to have been perennially in debt. A power of attorney granted by the dragoman Matteo Marucini to Girolamo Alberti in 1581 authorized the recovery from Mehmed of a debt of 2,100 aspers.[66] The dragoman Stefano di Gioveni's 1599 will similarly mentions that the *hoca* owed him 6,000 aspers.[67] In later decades things seem to have gone from bad to worse. A 1641 report on the performance of dragomans by the bailo Girolamo Trevisan praised the Turkish teacher for his erudition, knowledge of Ottoman law, and refined Arabic, Persian, and Turkish. But it acknowledged that the *hoca*

> Does not understand any Italian or Greek. Thus he would not be fit to teach the beginners, because they will not understand each other, but for those who have some foundations he is very useful in perfecting them when they apply themselves to it. He visits the house, but does not have a designated room in which to hold classes; no such room is available, [therefore] he teaches whoever comes to him, but will neither reproach, nor seek those who do not; he is not without his great faults; he is so dedicated to wine that he is often overcome by it, and

with age, which advances, this vice always grows. He dresses like a Dervish, which is like a religious habit, but he is not scrupulous at all about [religious] law, and it is widely agreed, that he doesn't care much about either [law or religion], which is why, in the many years he has served the House he has never said a word to any of his students regarding matters of religion, or any Muslim persuasion, as anyone very zealous could easily have done.[68]

Two months later, the baili Pietro Foscarini and Alvise Contarini stressed even further the shortcomings of apprentices' current training:

Because the apprentice dragomans, especially those of the land, have a great need to learn to speak good Italian, with which they could then more easily improve their Turkish, since the hoca, otherwise valorous in the Turkish, Persian, and Arabic languages, does not understand Frankish [i.e. Italian], and so neither one nor the other knows the validity of words, and their true signification, the young apprentices lose their first two or three years of studies, or spend them with very little profit: We remind you with all reverence, how necessary overall it is, to provide these youth with a person, who will instruct them in the Italian language, and will also teach them to write, with good phrases and characters, which is very important for the translation of letters and other writings which are sent from Venice, and the ones that the baili write: This person could be either the Chaplain of the current Excellent Bailo, with some increase in salary, or one of the Franciscan or Dominican Fathers that are sent to Istanbul, who as [Venetian] subjects also receive some annual monies, which the *Cottimo* fund of Your Serenity pays them; and it could in that case be asked of their superiors to send for that effect someone experienced in belles lettres, and in the most appropriate conditions of such a position.[69]

A dispatch in 1643 similarly reported that due to space shortage the *hoca* had no place to hold classes, and had therefore taken to arriving in the house only around lunchtime and leaving shortly thereafter.[70] A room was evidently found, finally, to accommodate the *hoca* Omer Effendi and his students, for in 1655 Secretary Ballarino's account books list expenses for fitting the room, as well as for the apprentice dragomans Brutti and Leonardo Tarsia's purchases of Turkish books.[71]

Yet the problems with apprentices' training did not consist only of space and teaching materials. As the baili's dispatches suggest, mastery of Ottoman Turkish was but one component of apprentices' required training. The youngest, barely literate in any language, needed basic schooling. Local-born youth required instruction in Italian and Latin as much as in Ottoman, as their home language was often demotic Greek (and, far less frequently, Slavic or Armenian). Early language instruction proved advantageous given the limited pedagogical resources available for formal training programs in the bailate. Most critically, unless arriving from the Venetian chancery, apprentices had to master the basics of diplomacy, letter-writing, and secretarial work as well, for which abundant pedagogical literature existed in Italian.

Part of the solution to the shortcomings of the *hoca*'s formal instruction was found in the apprenticeship system itself: classroom learning was often supplemented by substantial on-the-job training (shadowing senior dragomans on their daily runs, observing, and imitating) and by lengthy appointments to less prestigious posts in Venice's Mediterranean and Adriatic colonies prior to assuming the rank of bailate dragoman. Anecdotal evidence for the regularity of this de facto *cursus honorum* abounds in apprentice dragomans' petitions for promotion. In his 1652 petition to be appointed dragoman, Ruggiero Tarsia detailed his lengthy career as an apprentice for a whopping twenty-four years. According to Tarsia, after taking up Ottoman Turkish, he was posted in Crete, Corfu, and in the navy. He participated in eleven trips to Istanbul to accompany the Venetian baili Girolamo Trevisan, Pietro Foscarini, and Alvise Contarini on their journeys to and from the Ottoman capital, substituted for Grand Dragoman Grillo when the plague struck the latter's house, accompanied the road dragoman Giovanni Battista Salvago on his trips to Venice to assist Nicolò Dolfin on his (never to materialize) trip to Istanbul, and also served as a public interpreter both in Venice and under Captain General Foscolo in Sebenico (Šibenik, now in Croatia) and Zara.[72]

The Venetian method of apprentice training in situ was by far the most systematic among Istanbul's contemporary embassies. Anecdotal evidence suggests that others often attempted (sometimes successfully) to poach dragomans who had undergone the Venetian training system. As late as the 1670s some aspiring dragomans of large legations such as the French still resorted to improvisation, supplementing whatever limited linguistic and diplomatic training they had acquired prior to arriving at the Porte with ad hoc private Arabic, Persian, and Ottoman tutors.[73] It was only from the 1670s onward that other powers began to develop in earnest their own dragoman schools, with varying degrees of success.

Given the many complications associated with training apprentices in Istanbul, it is remarkable that a school for Ottoman language was never established in Venice. Early on, the Senate's appeal to the bailo Antonio Erizzo (1555–1557) to ship Ottoman-language instructional books to Venice was declined on the grounds of their cost.[74] Two decades later, in 1577, it was actually the bailo, Giovanni Correr, who enthusiastically relayed to the Senate the *hoca's* proposal to relocate to Venice and establish a school there. Correr endorsed the proposal, arguing that since children were quicker language learners, instruction in Venice would allow them to "learn Turkish as their maternal language." Correr added that the teacher had good manners and was fluent in Italian. Furthermore, the costs of his upkeep in Venice surely would not exceed those of accommodating apprentices in the bailate.[75] But the Senate never approved the move. Fifty years later, in 1627, it decreed a search for a Turkish instructor for young apprentices in Venice, specifying, however, that he must be Christian, perhaps Greek or Armenian.[76] Such a person was never found. Instead, throughout the period, in order to become dragomans Venetian-born apprentices had to spend much of their youth in Istanbul.

Several other legations sought to adopt and adapt the Venetian practice of sending young apprentices for long sojourns in the Ottoman capital. Starting in 1626, French apprentice dragomans were lodged and trained in the Capuchin convent adjacent to the French embassy in Pera. Initially, the program meant to enroll between eight and twelve students annually, but these numbers clearly were not met. In 1669, a royal decree established that six *Jeunes de langues* would be sent to Istanbul annually, to be schooled by the Capuchins.[77] Other embassies, too, attempted, mostly unsuccessfully, to establish training programs of their own. Starting in the late sixteenth century, the Polish crown periodically sent young nobles to Istanbul on a bursary in order to learn Ottoman and diplomacy at court—on more than one occasion under the Polish converts turned imperial dragomans, Ibrahim Bey and Ali Ufki Bey.[78] A mid-seventeenth-century proposal by a dragoman in Polish service to establish a school in Warsaw to train future diplomats, missionaries, and merchants (to be recruited, respectively, from among Polish nobles, clergy, and commoners) never materialized.[79] It may well have inspired, however, future efforts undertaken by the Habsburgs

in Vienna and the Bourbons in Madrid to systematize dragoman training programs, which, like the Polish school, emphasized fencing and good
manners, as much as Ottoman grammar.

Most of these attempts faltered, as efforts to send youth to Istanbul met
with very mixed pedagogical results, while proposals to recruit a suitable
faculty and instructional materials for use outside the Ottoman Empire
proved financially or politically inexpedient. In the French case, this led the
government to embark on a radically different program of training. In 1700
twelve scholarships were established for "Oriental children" to study at the
Jesuit Collège Louis-le-Grand in Paris. By 1721, all boys destined for dragoman apprenticeships, whether hailing from French or Ottoman-Christian
families, were to be trained at the Parisian Jesuit college first, and only
then, after about eight years, travel to Istanbul. Although this program
underwent various modifications over the years (and eventually admitted
an equal number of "Levantine" and French students), it kept intact the
basic model of extensive formal linguistic training in Latin, Ottoman, and
Arabic in the French metropole prior to going to Istanbul.[80] This method
of training officers in the metropole bears close similarity to later colonial
policies, both French and other.[81] Even earlier, this model further inspired
similar programs elsewhere in Europe. A late-seventeenth-century attempt
by the English Levant Company to send several Greek Ottoman subjects
to Gloucester College, Oxford, to learn English, with a view to employ-
ing them as dragomans on their return, was not repeated. Conversely,
more successful and long-lasting was the parallel transformation of the
Habsburgs' dragoman training method from a Sprachknaben-Institut (Institute for Language Boys) attached to the Imperial Residence in Istanbul
to a Kaiserlich-königliche Akademie für Orientalischer Sprachen (Imperial-Royal Academy for Oriental Languages), which opened in Vienna in
1754, though earlier efforts to train dragomans in Vienna date back to 1674.
Like its Parisian counterpart, the Viennese institution—similarly reliant
on Jesuit involvement and pedagogies—proved long-lasting, training some
of the greatest dragomans of the late-eighteenth and nineteenth centuries,
including Joseph von Hammer-Purgstall, perhaps the most prolific and influential Orientalist of his time.[82] The French-Habsburg model was also
the explicit template for an (ultimately failed) Spanish program to create a
School of Oriental Languages in Madrid in 1781.[83]

For the duration of the seventeenth century, however, and lacking systematic apprenticeship programs either on their own soil or in Istanbul,

most other embassies continued to recruit Greek Orthodox, Armenian, and Jewish dragomans regularly, as well as Catholic graduates of the Venetian and French apprenticeship programs.[84] Their dragoman cadres, as a result, lacked the strong endogamy and confessional cohesion that characterized the Venetian dragomanate, but perhaps offered ties to wider Ottoman commercial and political networks, particularly given the more dispersed geography of non-Catholic dragomans' places of provenance.[85]

The enduring reliance on local Istanbulite recruits had important implications for the nature of Venetian dragoman apprenticeship. Formally, an apprentice dragoman's training began upon entry into the bailate. But as we saw, many apprentices had started their training long before. As the sons, younger brothers, or nephews of acting dragomans, boys destined for the dragomanate often received language instruction at home in preparation for and in anticipation of their formal admission to the rank of apprentices. At the same time, protracted residency in the bailate proved essential to Venetian dragoman apprenticeships not simply for its role in developing linguistic competence (in both Ottoman Turkish, the employers' written language, and less frequently in Arabic, Persian, or Slavic). It also—perhaps primarily—served to socialize young men of widely diverse backgrounds into homosocial masculinity and to carefully instill a command of diplomatic protocol premised on a more or less shared, circum-Mediterranean elite courtly culture.

The imperative to cultivate forms of literacy directly tied to elite genres of sociability is well borne out in the memoirs of a consummate French dragoman, François Pétis de la Croix, who wrote ca. 1684 that

As for my studies in the Turkish language, I have done in Istanbul the same things I had done in Persia. I have had teachers for language, writing, and music; I have frequented the learned; I have read several good books in prose and in verse. I have endeavored to understand all sorts of legal, financial, and disputational [*chicane*] records, and even arithmetic, philosophy, and other sciences, and I have studied in the last place the book of a learned man, entitled the Perfect Secretary, which contains letters of all Styles and all characters for kings, princes, viziers, friends, enemies, and all other kinds of conditions. Finally, I tried to learn everything that could be learned from this language and its different characters in Qrmalı, Sulsy and Dyvany, and to make a full exercise of what I had learned, I translated for Mr

Ambassador Nointel a quantity of Curious pieces, of which he has
charged me, among which were all the letters written beforehand from
France to the Ottoman Porte, and from the Porte to the French Court,
which comprised a large volume, and several Other books in the languages which I knew, of which this lord has reported to the court.[86]

Pétis de la Croix makes evident that the dragoman's essential work tools
went far beyond the (laborious) acquisition of oral fluency in Turkish.
Rather, they entailed a deep command of a variety of Ottoman literary
genres and a thoroughgoing understanding of official chancery practice,
including those inscriptional technologies that contemporary Ottoman bureaucratic elites acquired from similar letter-writing books and exercises.
The process of becoming a dragoman, in other words, prepared apprentices
to engage with Ottoman officialdom by emulating the very bodily practices (inscription, copying, and translation) and aesthetics of prose literary
writing (*inşa*) that marked a growing cadre of scribes in the contemporary Ottoman divan (chancery).[87] This was hardly a coincidence, as the
functions of embassy dragomans and the imperial divan closely mirrored
each other.[88]

In this context, the Venetian apprenticeship program proved relatively
effective and enduring not simply thanks to its endogamous elements, but
likely because—precisely like the Ottoman training program for scribes—
it facilitated a community of practice. Membership in this community,
cultivated inter alia through prolonged cohabitation in the bailate, underscored the practical and performative aspects of dragomans' habitus. It
also fostered greater awareness of the intricacies of elite domestic social
hierarchies (which in several fundamental ways were comparable across
Ottoman and Venetian elite households) that helped young apprentices
navigate the maze of political intrigue and competing interests at the Porte.
Here again, apprentices hailing from long-established local dragoman dynasties had a clear advantage over recruits from elsewhere, allowing them
to acquire the performative dimensions of the craft from a very young
age from their dragoman fathers, uncles, and older siblings. Being part
of familial information networks that crossed juridical boundaries and
provided access to family archives of translations and copies of essential diplomatic records were also important, if rarely discussed, training
resources. Unattached apprentices from faraway Venice and Istria had
to rely on the good will of senior dragomans who were understandably

reticent to share the secrets of their trade, especially if they felt threatened by parvenu younger competitors, or if they sought to secure apprenticeships for their own kin.

More than anything, then, a successful dragoman's apprenticeship was characterized by the acquisition of versatile written and oral genres of communication, by integrating into a community of practice in order to master different aspects of courtly habitus, by learning through emulation how to perform measured deference to a carefully scalar range of local officials and diplomatic representatives, by showing to advantage one's familiarity with Istanbulite elite culture, and by moving across institutional spaces, linguistic registers, and social contexts with "effortless" ease and confidence, embodying Castiglione's much-celebrated ideal of *sprezzatura*. Beyond linguistic fluency in this or that language, dragomans' extensive apprenticeship, on-the-job training, and long sojourn in Istanbul and in Venetian colonies rather than in Venice proper thus fundamentally shaped their practices of translation and mediation, and proved key to their ability to successfully insert themselves in dense trans-imperial networks of patronage, to become trans-imperial courtiers themselves.

Employment

If dragomans' trans-imperial provenances and trajectories were ultimately advantageous to the bailate, so were their trans-imperial employment patterns. Perhaps the most distinctive feature of the dragomans' profession was their spatial mobility, often spanning multiple jurisdictions. Embassy dragomans' daily activities were far from limited to interpreting during the bailo's rare formal audiences with the grand vizier and other Ottoman ministers. Rather, they entailed diverse diplomatic, consular, and commercial duties across offices and locales. Dragomans regularly translated written documents to and from Ottoman. Even more frequently, they engaged in independent visits to the imperial divan and to Ottoman officials' residences, where they acted as de facto Venetian representatives in their own right. To perform such duties, they cultivated a dense network of alignments and loyalties in Istanbul, in Venice, and, as important, in other Ottoman commercial hubs and in the Venetian-Ottoman Dalmatian borderlands.[89] Beyond regular sojourns to the border and short-term assignments to conflict areas, several dragomans were tasked with delicate diplomatic missions further afield—to Persia, North Africa, and the gates of Vienna. They recorded these missions in extensive reports, or *Relazioni*, presented to the Venetian Senate upon their return, much like patrician ambassadors.

Beyond these "exceptional" (and exceptionally well-documented) missions, dragomans also traveled far and wide on more mundane assignments. In fact, assistance in border negotiations and periodic postings throughout Venice's Mediterranean and Adriatic colonies were customary phases in many apprentices' and junior dragomans' training before assuming more prestigious positions in either Venice or Istanbul. The Pera-born Stefano di Gioveni, a dragoman's son who had served the Venetian consul in Alexandria since 1581, was recalled to Istanbul five years later to replace the deceased dragoman Ambrosio Grillo.[90] The Istanbul-born Giuliano Salvago was sent to Aleppo to serve the Venetian nation there in 1605, and continued to shuttle back and forth between Aleppo and Istanbul until his premature death in 1619.[91] Throughout the seventeenth century, at least half a dozen Istanbul-based dragomans were sent to Venice's maritime headquarters in Zara to work for periods ranging from several months to several years in the service of the Venetian governor-general in Dalmatia, before returning to the Ottoman capital.[92]

While mobility characterized dragomans' trajectories across all ranks, over time, a fairly rigid division of labor emerged to create a hierarchy among specific kinds of dragomans, each associated with different forms of mobility. At the bottom of the pyramid were the *giovani di lingua* or apprentice dragomans, who were largely confined to the bailate, where their training sometimes morphed into work as they honed their skills by translating incoming Ottoman records and by shadowing more senior members of the corps on their errands. Next was the *protogero*, a low-level dragoman-clerk in charge of naval and commercial affairs, who spent much of his time at the customs office at the port in Tophane. Higher in status was the *dragomanno di strada* (road dragoman), entrusted with accompanying Venetian representatives to and from Istanbul, followed by several appointed dragomans (sometimes distinguished by seniority, if not by salary, and referred to, variously, as *dragomanno ordinario*, *dragomanno publico*, or simply *dragomanno*), charged with translation to and from Ottoman and with visiting Ottoman officials and other embassies. The grand dragoman, the most senior of the corps, appeared in audiences in front of the grand vizier and served as the mission's "eyes and ears"—an oft-repeated trope in senior diplomats' reports from their missions.

In addition, a dragoman—occasionally referred to in the eighteenth century as *dragomanno generalizio*—was regularly assigned to the Venetian governor-general in Zara, the Venetian colonial headquarters. At least one *dragomanno consolare* (consular dragoman) was attached to each of the Venetian consulates in Alexandria, Aleppo, and later Izmir. Finally, a *dragomanno publico* (public dragoman) was also attached to the *Cinque Savii alla Mercanzia*, Venice's Board of Trade, to help translate incoming correspondence, assist sojourning Ottoman merchants and dignitaries while on Venetian soil, and produce intelligence reports and memoranda concerning Ottoman and Safavid affairs. With few exceptions, all dragomans appointed to this prestigious and lucrative post were Venetian subjects (though not necessarily citizens) with significant prior history of consular service in the Ottoman capital.[93] Others still, though rarely enjoying the title of dragomans, served in colonial chanceries and courtrooms throughout the Venetian maritime empire, especially in locales with large Greek- and Slavic-speaking populations, such as Corfu, Cyprus, Crete, Dalmatia, and the Istrian peninsula.[94]

Venice's dragomanate was probably the largest in early modern Istanbul, but it was not the only one. Various Ottoman subjects—including Jews, Orthodox Christians, and converts to Islam, served as Porte dragomans, often without formal title, as early as the fifteenth century.[95] By the late-sixteenth and seventeenth century, Ottoman ad hoc court interpreters were sometimes supplemented with government-appointed chancery dragomans, especially in urban centers throughout the empire's Arabic-, Greek-, and Slavic-speaking provinces.[96] Like their Venetian counterparts, some Ottoman chancery dragomans stationed in the Ottoman-Habsburg borderlands were involved in border negotiations and other delicate diplomatic missions.[97] More formalized dragoman positions emerged within the Ottoman administration by the early 1670s, including, in addition to the dragoman of the Imperial Council (*Divan-ı Hümâyûn tercümanı*), the dragoman of the fleet (*donanma tercümanı*), who was second in command to the grand admiral, and the dragoman of the Imperial Army (*tercüman-ı ordu-yu Hümâyûn*). Unlike provincial dragomans who were evidently recruited largely from among the local populace, and who often supplemented their income with tax collecting, the more senior dragoman ranks to emerge in the following century were reserved for Phanariots, were centrally appointed by the Imperial Council, and frequently served as a stepping-stone to even more senior and lucrative positions as *voyvodas* (viceroys) of Moldavia and Wallachia.[98]

Besides the bailate and the Porte, other foreign consulates, too, sought to keep at least one, and often several, dragomans exclusively on their payroll. While generally following the Venetian division of labor, the seniority and power of individual consulate dragomans could not always be gleaned fully from their titles, as there was no necessary correlation between qualifications and career trajectories, let alone age. In fact, as noted earlier, some dragomans were even kept on the payroll for years while essentially not performing any work, simply due to their family connections to other consulates, and therefore out of fear that, if dismissed, they might reveal state secrets to a rival power.

Dragomans' uncertain loyalty was only compounded by their at times mercurial juridical status, which has been the subject of some scholarly debate. Under Ottoman law, local dragomans who served foreign powers enjoyed a special status as *beratlı*, namely the holders of a *berat*, or patent, which offered distinct tax exemptions, commercial privileges, and freedoms. The *ahidname*, or imperial charters granted by the sultan to friendly foreign powers, often included several clauses concerning dragomans, enumerating their numbers, privileges, and responsibilities. And whereas the majority of *beratlı* were bona fide dragomans, by the nineteenth century a certain number enjoyed this status without performing any actual diplomatic duties, contributing in no small measure to the reputation of the system as corrupt and unsustainable. Ottoman authorities themselves sought to limit the number of dragomans allotted to each embassy for precisely this reason. Dragomans' legal immunities as "subjects" of their employers (even as the vast majority were born Ottoman subjects) exacerbated an already complex situation.[99]

The ambiguity of dragomans' legal status was nowhere more apparent than in their fraught relationship to the bailate as an institution that provided them with coveted legal privileges and which bolstered their standing in the community, but whose own modes of authority vitally depended on the cultivation of myriad patronage bonds with dragomans' own independent households throughout the capital. It is to these households, and their profound role in shaping the dragomanate's lifeworlds, that we now turn.

Kinshipping

Casting Nets and Spawning Dynasties

> Having dragomans get married here must be considered of no
> small prejudice and impediment to public concerns: as they are
> relieved of the requirement to reside in the bailate so are they
> also relieved of its interests, all their efforts and application
> are turned to their families, who, being established in the land
> of the Turks, thus oblige them to circumspection and reserve
> [toward the Ottomans].
>
> —Bailo Alvise Mocenigo, Dispatch to the Senate,
> May 21, 1713[1]

O N JULY 25, 1587, the Venetian Senate enthusiastically resolved to deliver a gift of 400 sequins (gold ducats) to the Ottoman Porte dragoman Hürrem Bey on the occasion of his only daughter's wedding.[2] The gift was justified

> [a]s a sign of our Republic's satisfaction with the service he has pro-
> vided on different important occasions, and the readiness with which
> he has proven his wish to continue doing so in the future. . . . it be-
> hooves public service to satisfy him so that, as is well known to every-
> one, this being a person of high status at the Porte, he could perform
> many important services, as he has done in the past, as is understood
> from the letters of our bailo and his predecessors.[3]

This act of gift-giving in itself was not particularly remarkable. Gifts to foreign dignitaries and officeholders were part and parcel of early modern diplomacy's transactional costs, an expected—indeed required—aspect of doing business in Istanbul and elsewhere. Hürrem Bey, in fact, would have been a "natural" recipient of such gifts. A convert to Islam from

Lucca, he had been on the bailate payroll (and a frequent guest for dinner) for at least several years prior. What is more, his was a high office—as Porte dragoman he was directly answerable to the powerful Grand Vizier Sokollu Mehmed Paşa. He was also a key political protagonist in his own right, embroiled in ongoing double-dealings for the Florentine, French, and Habsburg legations, for which he was regularly—and lavishly—paid.[4]

Nor was the occasion of this act of gift-giving—the wedding of Hürrem Bey's daughter—exceptional. Absent a clear-cut distinction between public and private, between the office and the officeholder, kin often played a pivotal role in the professional lives of early modern diplomats. Weddings—where women helped embed their kinsmen into new networks of patronage—were particularly auspicious and common occasions for such gift-giving. Two years after the gift to Hürrem Bey, a bailate dragoman, Pasqual Navon, petitioned for, and was granted, a gift of 150 sequins on the occasion of his daughter's marriage. His petition referred to a similar gift he had been given a few years earlier.[5] Other Venetian dragomans were likewise rewarded upon their—or their womenfolk's—marriages in the following decades.[6] While ubiquitous, the bailate's gifting practices vis-à-vis dragomans laid bare a key paradox of dragomans' operation as both high-level diplomatic employees and full members of Ottoman society.

The gift to Hürrem Bey, the need for Senate approval to effect it, and its textual elaboration therefore go to the heart of the "dragoman problem" that the Venetians—like virtually all other diplomatic legations in Istanbul—faced, namely: how to secure the affective attachment of a notoriously mercurial specialist cadre, much in demand, and far too grounded in multiple social webs to ensure its exclusive dependency on the bailate? To a large extent, the Venetian state cultivated extensive patronage ties between baili and their dragomans' kin precisely to mitigate dragomans' proverbial disloyalty and dishonesty. As much as dragomans sought to secure apprenticeships and stipends for their children in order to foster long-term bonds of mutuality with the bailate, Venetian representatives, on their part, recognized the importance of such bonds beyond the individual merit or skill of any particular dragoman.

And here lay the problem. For dragomans as prototypical intermediaries networking was everything. In a world of supposedly global and instant connectivity, it is easy to overlook the labor of network-making, its non-metaphorical qualities, as well as its shifting textures and uneven distributions, which ultimately produce and sustain distinct regimes of

circulation. Early modernists have rightly cautioned against the facile, cel-
ebratory tone of much public discourse about late modern globalization,
and have challenged the supposed newness of circulation, networking, and
connectivity per se. And yet, studying earlier forms of trans-imperial consciousness and connectivity reveals not so much that the world was already
networked in the seventeenth century but that "network," then and now,
is better thought of as a verb than as a noun. In dragomans' networking,
secrecy, subterfuge, omission, and circumspection were essential tools of
the trade, resulting in different parts of their elusive "networks" decidedly
kept "in the dark" about their other contacts.

Moreover, dragomans' deep embedding in Ottoman society, which to their
Venetian metropolitan observers often seemed problematic, was, in reality,
an essential aspect of dragomans' lifeworlds. Taking its cue from a recent
definition of kinshipping as the "moving through time and space by means of
relationship and exchange,"[7] this chapter explores how by forging kinship ties
dragomans challenge our (and many of their contemporaries') assumptions
about what separated Venice from Istanbul, provincial settings from metropolitan ones, and the temporalities of past, present, and future that these
spaces helped reconfigure. It emphasizes how kinshipping operates not as
moving through (ostensibly inert) time and space, but rather as the production
of spatiotemporal categories inherent in all acts of relating and exchanging.

Kinshipping: Networked Households

Dragomans' intense and recurring kinshipping strategies were shaped by
multiple imperatives. For if dragomans' households served as crucial nodes
in the acquisition of local prestige and power, they did so in part through
the cultivation of trans-imperial kinship networks that furthered the circulation of timely political, diplomatic, and linguistic expertise. While
bailate dragomans celebrated their loyalty to Venice in one petition after
another, their immediate kin and affines—brothers, sons, brothers-in-law,
and nephews—were otherwise employed in Istanbul. Some became dragomans for neighboring foreign embassies, others married French, Dutch, or
Danish merchants and physicians active in the Ottoman capital (and often
in the sultan's court itself),[8] and yet others married into the nobility of the
southern and central European Ottoman-Habsburg borderlands.

The mutual benefits of multigenerational marriage alliances between
local and localized dragoman families, on the one hand, and newly arrived

dragomans (as well as other professional and merchant émigrés) on the other, can be illustrated through the case of the Borisi-Scoccardi-Mascellini family (figure 2.1).[9] In the first generation represented we see the Venetian grand dragoman Marcantonio Borisi marrying Alessandra Piron and then, upon Alessandra's death, Caterina Olivieri. Both women were descendants of established Pera dragoman families, and marrying them helped localize the Borisi dynasty. In the second generation, one of Marcantonio and Alessandra's daughters, Francesca, married Pelegrino Testa, the scion of a local Catholic family. That short-lived union (annulled a few years later) produced a daughter, Asanina, who married another local Catholic, Bartolomeo Dane. Francesca Borisi's second marriage to the Danish physician Hans Andersen Skovgaard ("Scoccardi") also produced an only daughter, Gioia, who married the Pesaro-born physician Giovanni Mascellini.[10] Of that couple's three children, one, Francesco, became a Venetian apprentice dragoman; another, Laura, married the Venetian dragoman Giacomo Tarsia; while Lucia, their third, married another locally based physician, Charles LeDuc, a Frenchman. Of the three LeDuc daughters one, Teresa Maria, married Luca Chirico, a Ragusan consul turned British dragoman. The Chiricos' descendants remained in Istanbul, where at least one later served as a dragoman for the Russian legation and consular representative for the kingdom of Sardinia.[11] Similar patterns—combining marriage into foreign-born, Istanbul-based dragoman and other professional families, on the one hand, and into the established local Catholic elite on the other—typify the marriage strategies of most siblings in these and following generational cohorts as well.

This dual movement of simultaneously "going local" and forging extended trans-imperial kinship networks becomes even more significant when we zoom out of the specific case of Francesca Borisi's descendants and look at the entwined strategies of the Borisi, Brutti, and Tarsia clans as a whole (figure 2.2). These three closely intermarried dragoman dynasties traced their roots to then current or former Venetian colonial territories in Albania, Montenegro, and Istria. Despite their diverse origins, by the seventeenth century certain branches of all three families were firmly settled in Istanbul. In the course of the century between 1570 and 1670, they produced five generations of dragomans in Venetian service, totaling at least thirteen men. At the same time, these dragomans' immediate relatives were placed all across the Venetian and Ottoman Empires, and their daughters and sisters married into at least five other dragoman families in the Ottoman capital, as well as into Venetian, Habsburg, Danish, Polish, and Moldavian aristocracies and merchant elites. By the mid-seventeenth century the Borisi-Brutti-Tarsia extended family had spanned three empires and over a half dozen locales.

These complex genealogies underscore the importance of marriage alliances for transforming Istanbul's dragomans into a unified and socially mobile group, regardless of their diverse origins. Indeed, the forging of kinship networks that crisscrossed political, spatial, ethnolinguistic, and estate divisions not only furthered dragomans' internal cohesion and self-consciousness as a professional cadre. It also aligned them with a truly trans-imperial—rather than specifically Venetian—milieu. The group's resultant uncertain political loyalties were, not surprisingly, at the heart of Venetian concerns over the services rendered by dragomans, who were all too localized but possibly not sufficiently "Venetianized."

These concerns were not uniquely Venetian. As the French consul on Chios Louis de Riantz wrote to his ambassador in Istanbul, Pierre-Antoine de Castagnères Châteauneuf (in office 1689–1692), to complain about the "Greek" dragoman of the French Embassy [Domenico] Fornetti:

> Conditions being good, Your Excellency sent Fornetti, Your dragoman of the Greek nation [*Grec de nation*], to a port [*Eschelle*] where the French Consul has no relationship with the Greeks and has operated here easily for 30 years until Fornetti, hiding in his hood, said he was an Arab and gave me two parcels [*pacquets*] of your Excellency, in which there is no mention of Fornetti's commission for Chios nor of my consular house.[12]

Châteauneuf rejected the allegations in an angry marginal note:

> What does he mean when he says that Mr. Fornetti is of the Greek Nation? Is he saying that [Fornetti] is of the Greek rite? That is not true, he professes the Roman and Apostolic Catholic Religion, in which all his ancestors were raised, lived, and died. Is he saying that he was born in Greece? It seems clear that he was born in Turkey, but from that it should not be concluded that he was either a Greek or a Turk. He is from an ancient family originally from Genoa, his ancestors had the honor of serving the King and having worked for His Majesty's Ambassador at the Porte in the capacity of First Dragoman without interruption from father to son for the past 150 years. His great

grandfather had a patent for that office from King Henry III [r. 1574–1589]. It is in order to continue in this assignment that they have stayed on and established themselves in this country and that Mr. Fornetti was born here. Far from something that he should be reproached for, on the contrary, it is honorable for him and for the grandsons of French dragomans who are at the Porte today, who will be in the same situation as he is if they are destined for the same employment.[13]

Other evidence corroborates the sense that Greek was not only the dominant language of communal and domestic interactions among Catholics in Galata but that women in particular were often literate in Greek more than in Italian. Some Catholic women's signatures in Greek on Italian notarial records in the bailate chancery archives confirm this. Such are the signatures of Battistina and Cassandra Grillo, the late dragoman Ambrosio Grillo's sister and daughter, respectively, who in 1682 authorized—in Greek—the transfer to a local Catholic church of a debt owed them by the bailo, in compliance with Grillo's last testament.[14] The 1652 testament of Caterina Salvago, widow of Stefano Fortis and niece, granddaughter, and great-granddaughter of five Salvago dragomans, was similarly written in Greek.[15]

As these examples show, being Grecophone and being Catholic were not perceived as inherently contradictory as far as the local Latin-rite community was concerned. Yet the bivalence of "Greekness" as both an ethnolinguistic and a confessional marker, combined with dragomans' occasional marriage across confessional lines into Istanbul's Phanariot (Orthodox) elite, did lead to some baili's suspicion vis-à-vis certain members of the dragomanate, including the Grillos. Thus, a copy of a letter of June 1677 by the bailo Morosini to his uncle, Monsignor Gianfrancesco Morosini, the Patriarch of Venice, confirms that among the six Venetian dragomans at the Porte at the time "none are schismatic." Moreover, the bailo continues, in order to avoid any suspicion,

> I have not availed myself of our First Dragoman Grillo, who is experienced, well-versed, and of the highest credentials, and have employed instead Tarsia, who is second in order, only because Grillo has schismatic relatives, even though he himself is of pure faith [*fede incontaminata*].[16]

Morosini had a point: Ambrosio Grillo, the dragoman in question, was married to the Greek Orthodox Cassandra Catargi, and their daughter

Cassandra was married to Demetrio Cantacuzeno, a scion of a noble Byzantine family. Grillo's sister, Battistina, had married a Phanariot man as well, Constantino Gulianò. At the same time, Morosini may have made a virtue out of necessity here, as the dragoman Ambrosio Grillo was by that point quite elderly, and his rivalry with the Tarsia dragomans truly legendary and toxic for the bailate as a whole.

Grillo's extensive ties in Istanbul's elite Orthodox circles highlight the role of marriage as a form of dragoman localization neither anticipated nor encouraged by Venetian authorities. Despite efforts by both foreign employers and Catholic nuncios to police the boundary between Catholicism and Orthodoxy, the Ottoman capital offered ample opportunities for its Christian denizens to forge kinship alliances that disrupted confessional logics. Confessionally mixed households seem to have been rather common in early modern Istanbul, even if to Venetian (and other foreign Catholic) eyes they appeared inherently suspicious.

The dangers—and advantages—of local marriage were not lost on newly arrived dragomans either. In 1644 the Venetian citizen and dragoman Paolo Vecchia married the daughter of the Latin, Pera-born grand dragoman Giovanni Antonio Grillo (Ambrosio's father). In his florid petition to the Venetian government on the occasion of his wedding, Vecchia suggested that the sole purpose of the union was to let him "stay in the country and devote myself until the last breath to the service of Your Serenity," alluding to the Ottoman view of a foreign resident's marriage to an Ottoman subject as a clear indication of intent to naturalize.[17] Five years later, following Grillo's execution by Ottoman authorities, Vecchia, now living in his late father-in-law's house, claimed that Grillo "with all tenderness sought to love me with affection exceeding that of a father."[18] In addressing the Venetian authorities, Vecchia therefore downplayed his affective ties to Grillo's daughter, who is not even mentioned by name, as such ties could be seen as conflicting with his undivided loyalty to his Venetian employer and sovereign. Rather, he professed deep and reciprocated affection for his father-in-law. In invoking the all-male bond among dragomans themselves, he conveniently bracketed the important role played by wives, daughters, and sisters in cementing these bonds in the first place.

Over the centuries, bailo after bailo bemoaned the danger of local marriage. In 1719 the Venetian Senate even passed a decree prohibiting dragomans from contracting marriages in Ottoman lands without the express permission of the bailo. The decree followed similar regulations issued by the French crown only three years prior, prohibiting all their subjects from marrying in Ottoman territories. French merchants who married Ottoman-born women, the decree stipulated, risked being, along with their descendants, "excluded from all offices and public administrations of the body of the Nation, even the faculty of admission to its assemblies."[19] Like its French precursor, the Venetian decree was reiterated for decades, alongside lamentations of dragomans' extensive kinship ties in Istanbul, confirming its limited effects in practice.[20] As "compromising" as they may have appeared to their employers, local kinship alliances secured dragomans' important economic and political interests, allowing them to diversify their professional trajectories beyond the dragomanate.

The confessional mix of dragomans' households was coupled with, indeed premised on, fierce class endogamy—a shared commitment to the perpetuation of metropolitan elite status. Such status was articulated through the display of wealth and taste in acts of public consumption on the occasion of weddings and baptisms, recursively cementing class-endogamous kinship alliances. A particularly vivid description of one key moment in this unfolding process is captured in the diary of the young Antoine Galland, who in 1673 was apprenticing as a dragoman in the French embassy in Istanbul. Between April 20 and 23, Galland spent over 1,500 words in four breathless, consecutive diary entries describing the trousseau and festive arrangements for the forthcoming nuptials of what can only be described as the dragoman power couple of the decade, Giustiniana Tarsia and Marcantonio Mamuca della Torre.[21] Galland was clearly impressed by what he saw, and while trying to mask his voyeuristic giddiness as a carefully calculated ploy to pay a visit to two powerful diplomatic households, his sense of ethnographic estrangement and awe is palpable throughout. He repeatedly describes the bride's trousseau as produced in the style of the country or "à la turque," replete with kaftans and turban-like headgear. He notes the separate seating arrangements for the wedding feast for the "Franks" (on benches) and the "Greeks" (on sofas). The wedding procession, he writes, was headed by janissary guards and a troupe of Jewish dancers and musicians, while the invitation list numbered a hundred ninety households, transcending the city's confessional divides.

Galland's description not only belies Christoforo Tarsia's (the bride's father) chronic complaints about poverty, a staple in his petitions for salary increases and promotions over the years. It also confirms our understanding of Istanbul's elite society as rather well-integrated across confessions, sharing a ceremonial aesthetic that melded janissary bands with Jewish dancers and musicians. More directly, Galland hints at the Tarsias' and Mamuca della Torres' own extensive ties within the Greek Orthodox community. The couple's wedding godfather, we learn, was none other than Prince Grigor Ghika, the Ottoman-appointed hospodar of Moldavia. Ghika was represented at the wedding by a Greek trader, who presented the bride a gift of 100 gold ducats.[22]

Galland's account speaks to Marcantonio and Giustiniana's embedding in an elite Istanbulite milieu that was deeply local precisely in its consistent traversing of confessional boundaries. Such elite interconfessional kinship was forged not only at the altar but also at the baptismal font, Tridentine prohibitions on baptismal sponsorship by non-Catholics notwithstanding. Thus, for example, the June 14, 1685, baptismal record for eighteen-month-old Pantaleone, son of Giorgio Lomaca, the Polish grand dragoman, registers the godparents as Cassandra Grillo (daughter of late Venetian dragoman Ambrosio, mentioned above) and Ghighorasco Cantacuzeno, a scion of a leading Phanariot family (and possibly Cassandra's own brother-in-law or son).[23]

While bailate records regularly reported invitations for the bailo to serve as a godfather for a dragoman's newborn child, or as a guest of honor at a daughter's wedding, they remain practically silent on the vast patronage network that bound dragomans to other denizens of the Ottoman capital. The bailate archives prove particularly limited on the structure and wealth of dragomans' households, even though dragomans often expressed their elite status by maintaining large households with significant numbers of domestic servants and enslaved people. If anything, bailate records paint a misleading picture of dragomans' chronic poverty, often used as a trope in petitions for salary raises, bonuses, and promotions.

Much more ample evidence on the patterning of dragomans' sociality and domestic arrangements comes from the parish records of Santa Maria Draperis, a Pera church patronized in the seventeenth century by many Venetian dragoman families (and virtually all other Catholic embassy dragomans).[24] The church's baptism, marriage, and burial registers, which survive from ca. 1662 onward, paint a picture of intensive, recurring baptismal sponsorship among Pera's leading Catholic families, including dragomans and their womenfolk. A record of May 10, 1671, registers the baptism of Ludovico, son of Henning [Vold] and Girolama Mamuca [della Torre], with the Venetian bailo Alvise Molin as the godfather. The officiating priest was the bailate chaplain, Fra Francesco.[25] Henning Vold was a

Dutch merchant and physician. His wife, Girolama, was the granddaughter of the martyred Venetian dragoman Marcantonio Borisi and the sister of the Habsburg dragoman Marcantonio Mamuca della Torre. Baby Ludovico's godmother, Battistina Zanetti, was the wife of the Venetian dragoman Christoforo Tarsia and the mother of three dragomans herself. Another record, from April 11, 1678, registers the baptism of Antonio, son of the French dragoman Francesco Testa and Maria Fortis (a descendant of two Venetian dragoman lineages). Here, the godfather was the child's paternal grandfather, while the godmother was his paternal aunt Susanna, wife of the Venetian dragoman Tommaso Navon.[26]

Dragomans and Domestics

Parish records also reveal another vital—and far less explored—dimension of dragomans' domesticity: slavery. The practice of domestic slavery in virtually all dragoman households in Pera contradicts dragomans' habitual complaints about abject poverty. It underscores how these households served to counterbalance the bailate as patrimonial households in their own right. That the enslaved did not simply provide domestic labor but also contributed in significant ways to the weaving of dragomans' patronage networks is fully borne out by the distinctive patterns of their marriage and baptism, discussed below, and by dragomans' varied roles as sponsors and witnesses in enslaved persons' sacraments.[27]

As with Ottoman *kadı* records, which historians have mined to great effect to study domestic slavery in early modern Galata (and elsewhere), parish records provide an inherently partial perspective on the enslaved parishioners they record.[28] Even when discounting for the patchy chronological coverage of these records (which begin in 1662), and the survival of records from only some of the churches patronized by dragomans' households, parish records, by their nature, mention only those enslaved persons who had undergone Catholic sacraments (baptism, marriage, last rites). Non-Catholics, those whose rituals had been administered by other clergy, and those who may not have been recorded as enslaved by the parish priests, are inevitably not accounted for.[29] More fundamentally, the information is necessarily filtered through the genre conventions of Tridentine parish records and the perspectives of the clergy producing them. While some differences between the records produced by different priests are noticeable, and call for further investigation, entries generally consist of a bare-bones formulary that includes dates, names, and, on occasion, certain identification such as approximate age, provenance, and residential neighborhood (for those enslaved parishioners owned by denizens of the Ottoman capital other than dragomans). The names of baptismal sponsors, especially when they were the owners or their immediate kin, are often noted in shorthand, e.g., "Her Excellency Catherina," presumably because they were easily identifiable in the small community of Pera. Given these significant limitations, surviving parish records hardly lend themselves to systematic analysis, let alone to an in-depth exploration of enslaved persons' own perspectives on their living and working conditions in dragomans' household (or any other aspect of their lives, for that matter). It is conceivable, for example, that dragomans and other local Catholics might have understood the purchasing of enslaved Christians as an act of charity, protecting the enslaved from the eventuality (unlikely as it may have been) of conversion to Islam at the hands of Muslim masters. It is also possible that the sentiment was shared by some of the enslaved. In that case, baptism of enslaved persons of evidently Christian background—strictly prohibited for Catholics in principle—could have been understood as religious reaffirmation. But these are purely conjectural possibilities absent other documentation to corroborate either enslaved persons' or their masters' understandings of their actions. With these caveats, what follows is necessarily a tentative account of the patterns of dragomans' ownership and baptismal sponsorship of enslaved domestics.

The proportion of Christians among enslaved persons in dragomans' households is impossible to compute given parish records' obvious selection bias. Yet the number of dragoman-owned enslaved persons listed in parish records is both significant (several dozens in the three decades examined here, 1662–1694), and accords with those for baptisms of enslaved persons in non-dragoman Catholic households in Pera and adjacent neighborhoods (notably Kasımpaşa and Beşiktaş). This indicates that the practices of Christian slaveholding, and marriage, reproduction, and baptism of enslaved persons were all quite pervasive among Catholic households in the Ottoman capital.

Marriages and baptisms of enslaved persons—typically conducted under the aegis of their masters or masters' immediate relatives—helped further cement ties within the small community of Pera. A baptismal record of February 22, 1665, for Nicolò, the son out of wedlock of Elisabetta of Bohemia, an enslaved person in the household of the Dutch merchant and physician Henning Vold, lists as the godmother Gioia Mascellini. This was, in all likelihood, Gioia Scoccardi (née Mascellini), the cousin of Henning Vold's wife, Girolama Mamuca della Torre. Both were granddaughters of the Venetian dragoman Marcantonio Borisi, and directly related to several other dragomans of the Piron and Tarsia families.[30] The baptisms of two enslaved women owned by the Venetian dragoman Gian Rinaldo Carli on August 2, 1685, were similarly held in the house of his first cousin Giustiniana Tarsia (daughter of the late Venetian dragoman Christoforo Tarsia and wife of the Habsburg dragoman Marcantonio Mamuca della Torre). The two enslaved women, Elena, an Albanian ("Zuria"), and Anna, a Mingrelian, were sponsored by Giustiniana's children, Cristoforo and Maria, ages four and seven, respectively. Numerous baptisms of enslaved persons in the Tarsia-Mamuca della Torre household over the next decade followed a similar pattern. An entry on July 23, 1692, lists Cristoforo Mamuca della Torre and his aunt, Laura Mascellini, as the godparents of baby Maria Maddalena, daughter of a Russian enslaved couple, Elena and Andronico. On May 5, 1693, a baptismal record for Stefano, son of the enslaved Russian Foti and his enslaved wife, Anna, lists Cristoforo Mamuca della Torre again as the godfather, this time with "Orena his slave" as the godmother. A third baptismal record listing Cristoforo as the godfather comes a year later, on July 7, 1694.[31] The enslaved baptizee, Giorgio, belonged to Cristoforo's mother, Giustiniana Tarsia Mamuca della Torre.

The godfather in all these cases, Cristoforo Mamuca della Torre, was the descendant of dragoman dynasties on both sides. That he himself was a child at the time of these baptisms (he was born in 1681) suggests either the impromptu nature of enslaved persons' baptismal sponsorships, or, more likely, their function in cementing preexisting ties of kinship and patronage. In this sense, Cristoforo stood in for his respective lineages. His father Marcantonio's residency in Vienna away from the family, since 1683, may have given special poignancy to his young son's elevated role as a token of dynastic continuity in a social milieu particularly attuned to lineal succession. A similar case could be made for Cristoforo's elder brother, Leopoldo (b. ca. 1674), an apprentice dragoman in the Habsburg legation since 1684, who on April 26, 1687, served as the godfather for Gregorio, the son of Giuseppe and Sofia, enslaved persons in his mother's household. Not coincidentally, the godmother on this occasion was Leopoldo's octogenarian paternal grandmother, Cecilia Borisi, reinforcing the importance of lineage to the household's status.[32] The Mamuca della Torre family evidently had a particular penchant for keeping baptisms of enslaved persons "in the family," but they were hardly the only ones to appoint their children as enslaved persons' godparents. In 1690, the English dragoman Antonio Piron held a baptism ceremony at home for Margarita, the daughter of an enslaved couple, Zibunner and Zachari. The godfather was Piron's son, Giovanni, who could not have been more than eight or nine at the time, and possibly much younger.[33]

Not all enslaved baptizees were newborns. Quite a few were older children and adults. A few were baptized on their deathbed, as was the case for Gregorio, an enslaved man in the house of Marcantonio Mamuca della Torre, who received conditional baptism a day before his death on November 29, 1682.[34] On most occasions, however, adult baptism of enslaved persons was registered without further comment, suggesting its ubiquity. Of special interest is a cluster of baptisms of mostly young enslaved women, sometimes with their infants or children, in 1682–1683. These women hailed from the households of at least a half dozen Venetian, Habsburg, French, Dutch, and Ragusan dragomans. They included Anastasia, a twenty-year-old enslaved woman in Tommaso Tarsia's household, twenty-year-old Caterina of Georgia, similarly enslaved by Tarsia, who was baptized alongside her nine-month-old baby, Pietro, with Francesco Mascellini, an apprentice dragoman and Tommaso's brother-in-law, designated as godfather of both mother and child. Also baptized that same year were Soffia, an enslaved woman in the household of Marcantonio Mamuca della Torre; Caterina and Maria, enslaved women in the household of the Ragusan dragoman Luca Barca; Anna and Anastasia, enslaved by Francesco Testa; Zaffirra, a ten-year-old enslaved Circassian girl in the household of the French dragoman Bartolomeo Dane; Anna and her son, Basilio, both enslaved by the Dutch grand dragoman Willem Theijls; an unnamed enslaved boy alongside two enslaved women, Apollonia and Anastasia, in the household of Marcantonio Mamuca della Torre; and Basilio and Simone, enslaved Georgians in the household of Tommaso Tarsia.[35] The identification of these enslaved baptizees as Mingrelian, Circassian, and Georgian raises the possibility that they had all been purchased in close succession. Similar references to (evidently Catholic) enslaved persons in dragomans' households can be found in the parish burial registry, as in the 1682 death notice for Cosmo, enslaved by the Venetian grand dragoman Tommaso Tarsia.[36] This calls for further comparison with broader Istanbulite slaveholding patterns.

The extent and occasions of manumission in dragomans' households are unknown, despite evidence for enduring bonds between the formerly enslaved and their owners. A wedding record for Maria of Russia and Renato ("Marsan") of France in 1690 describes the bride as the "liberated slave of Mr. Tarsia," though there is no indication that Tarsia or any other household member witnessed the wedding.[37] Manumitted persons' marriages also underscore the strong ties between various dragoman households: only a week after Maria's wedding, another one took place between Martino Ziurgi (i.e., Georgian), formerly enslaved by "Sultaniza Navon," and Caterina of Mingrelia, formerly enslaved by the Venetian dragoman Antonio Olivieri.[38] Sultaniza was in fact Susanna Testa, wife of the Venetian dragoman Tommaso Navon, and sister of the French dragoman Francesco (Draco) Testa. The Olivieri and Navon families were also related by marriage.

Not all matrimonies of enslaved and manumitted persons hailing from dragomans' households were with others freed persons of the same Pera milieu. A Russian woman enslaved by Tommaso Tarsia married Nicoletto, enslaved by Süleyman, an Ottoman naval officer. Annusa, formerly enslaved by Tommaso Tarsia, married the Calabrian Biaso Conti, enslaved in the Ottoman *bagno*. Mariora, daughter of an (unnamed) person formerly enslaved by Demetrio Timoni, the second dragoman in the English embassy, married Giovanni Paradissi of Chios (with two of Timoni's sons as witnesses). Repanzo, formerly enslaved by the Dutch dragoman Willem Theijls, married a certain Leopoldo Vidali.[39]

Slavery—including the ownership of enslaved Christians by Christian masters—was hardly unusual among early modern urban elites in both Ottoman and Venetian territories.[40] The specific pattern of slavery in dragomans' households, however, suggests some important variations from the typical patterns of Ottoman urban slavery in general, and in Galata and Pera in particular. As Charles Wilkins and others show, elite Muslim households in this period included significant numbers of enslaved persons of sub-Saharan and Italian provenance, and generally kept many more men than women.[41] This makes the preponderance of enslaved women from the Black Sea region in dragomans' households particularly notable, as is the virtual absence from these households of enslaved persons of Western European provenance, who do appear regularly in other baptismal, marriage, and burial records in the same register.[42] These divergent patterns may suggest Catholic dragomans' particular distaste for keeping enslaved persons deemed ethnically related to themselves. The absence from the records of enslaved persons of sub-Saharan provenance, on the other hand, may attest either to their underrepresentation in dragomans' households, or to the reluctance to baptize potentially Muslim enslaved persons, given political sensitivity. Here, as in many other cases, the evidence is inconclusive.

In seeking further to understand the phenomenon of slavery in dragomans' households, one important question is the degree to which baptism may have signified a particular bond between the enslaved and their masters. Who initiated the baptism? Were the sacraments negotiated with the understanding that they might prompt manumission and sustain future patronage? Were the enslaved baptizees involved at all in the selection of baptismal sponsors for themselves or their children? If so, was the selection of elite sponsors a simple emulation of sponsorship patterns for elite children's baptisms? Was it staking a particular claim of belonging in the household? How should we interpret the repeated appearance of certain dragomans' young children as baptismal sponsors of enslaved persons in their parents' households, given that Tridentine rules considered children to be "defective" sponsors? And, as the vast majority of enslaved persons in dragomans' households hailed from ostensibly Christian territories and were purchased as adults, why were so many (re)baptized when the Catholic Church strictly prohibited repeated baptism?

The ubiquity of enslaved Christians in dragomans' households indicates the degree to which these households maintained a key hallmark of elite status in this period, namely a sizable number of domestics.[43] These numbers further raise the still unexplored role of intimacies in forging horizontal and vertical ties that facilitated the circulation of knowledge within and across households. While the full extent of sexual relationships between masters and enslaved persons in this context is impossible to determine from the extant documentation, the preponderance of young women among baptized enslaved adults in dragomans' households (i.e., those likely to have been enslaved and purchased recently, in adulthood), as well as several cases of baptized newborns of unknown paternity recorded as the sons of dragomans' enslaved women (and often with the master, mistress, or their immediate relatives serving as godparents), raise the distinct possibility of sexual slavery.[44] In 1676 the French dragoman Michel Dantan (about twenty-five-years old at the time, and unmarried) served as godfather in the at-home baptism of Marziale, son of an enslaved woman in his household, registered without an indication of paternity. Two consecutive baptismal records the following year note the in-house baptisms of eight-year-old Elisabetta and year-old Anna, both "Russians," and daughters of an enslaved woman in the household of the Habsburg dragoman Marcantonio Mamuca della Torre. The paternity of neither one is disclosed. To avoid imputation of paternity, at least one baptismal record of an enslaved woman's child mentions explicitly that the mother was purchased "when she was pregnant."[45] The vast majority of enslaved persons in dragoman households hailed from the Black Sea region, and were identified in parish records as "Russian," "Mingrelian," or, less frequently, "Georgian" or "Circassian." Both Ottoman and Italian slaveholders prized women from the Black Sea region for their fair features, though their prevalence in Muslim households in Istanbul was evidently more limited than in the sample of dragomans' households examined here, calling for further research into the relationship between Catholic slaveholding patterns and those of broader elite Istanbulite society.

The Dragomanate of Women

Alongside confessional exogamy, most dragoman families practiced clear class, and eventually caste, endogamy, as we saw. By recursively marrying within the dragomanate over multiple generations families not only cemented their hold on the profession but, willy-nilly, accelerated the blurring of ethnic and juridical lines between dragomans' different provenances across the Venetian-Ottoman ecumene. When viewed as a long-term marriage strategy, the dragomanate's intense endogamy highlights the vital role of women in integrating the bailate into larger economic, legal, and affective spheres. Although their activities are poorly documented, dragomans' womenfolk were busy and well-informed participants in an economy based on the circulation of objects (through gifts) and persons (through kinship). An exploration of women's centrality to the dragomanate thus brings into sharper relief the gendered nature of ostensibly homosocial diplomatic practice. This gendered aspect of courtly homosociality is particularly noteworthy given that the same period that saw the dragomanate institutionalized through elaborate recruitment, training, and resocialization practices was also the height of what Ottomanists once called "the Sultanate of Women," a period when women of the imperial household—queen mothers and sultans' consorts in particular—wielded significant political power.[46]

If the lives of Ottoman courtly women are still relatively obscure, we know even less about those of Pera's Catholic elite women, including dragomans' wives, sisters, and daughters. Mothers' special role in the early linguistic preparation of sons destined for the dragomanate was noted above.

Women's other important, if rarely acknowledged, roles in Venetian-Otto-man diplomacy stemmed from their involvement in managing real estate in Galata, the hub of foreign diplomacy and commerce at the Porte. This can be gleaned from their sporadic appearance in Ottoman and Venetian records (and particularly the intersection of the two).

Two records from summer 1608 preserved in the Ottoman archives con-cern a legal dispute between Alessandra Borisi née Piron and a trustee of a local pious endowment (*vakf*).[47] The dispute revolved around ownership of a house in Galata, which Alessandra claimed had been in her family's possession for hundreds of years. Fortunately for Alessandra, the district's previous *kadı* and the imperial archives keeper both testified that the prop-erty was hers. They even issued her husband a document of ownership to that effect. These records confirming her ownership (dutifully summarized in the "Register of Foreigners") were provided at the behest of the bailo Simone Contarini, whose interest in the case likely had to do with the iden-tity of Alessandra's husband, Grand Dragoman Marcantonio Borisi (ca. 1570–1622), a power broker not only within the bailate but more broadly in the city's political and diplomatic circles.

Alessandra emerged victorious in this case thanks not only to the bailo's patronage but to her own ability to navigate the jurisdictional maze of the Ottoman capital. A descendant of an extremely wealthy and distinguished local Catholic family, Alessandra was hardly unique in providing her émi-gré dragoman husband with powerful financial backing firmly rooted in Galata's real estate market and long-distance trade.[48] Independent family capital, frequently managed by women, was de facto a prerequisite for many dragomans' ability to perform their duties in the bailate, especially given salaries sometimes years in arrears. Unlike their frequently peripa-tetic dragoman kinsmen, women stayed put, generating wealth and connec-tions that proved essential for the professional success of their menfolk—dragomans, merchants, and professionals alike.

It is thus noteworthy that several dragomans' wives and daughters seem to have wielded both significant real estate properties in the city and the juridical know-how to maintain family wealth.[49] Besides Alessandra Piron there was Francesca, daughter of the dragoman Pasquale Navon and wife of the dragoman Nicolò Coressi, who sold a house she owned to the Catholic Church in 1585;[50] Despina, daughter of the dragoman Francesco Brutti, who in 1639 rented rooms to various Venetian merchants in Pera;[51] Gioia, daugh-ter of the dragoman Giovanni Antonio Grillo and granddaughter and niece of several dragomans of the Olivieri family, who in her will of 1658 left to the churches of the Madonna and San Giorgio "my part of the shop or tavern in Bahic Bazaar";[52] Franceschina, daughter of the late Marcantonio Borisi, who in 1660 appointed her son-in-law, the bailate physician Giovanni Mascellini, to get hold of property in Capodistria left to her by her paternal uncle, Francesco, and currently in the hands of her brother Pietro;[53] and, finally, Franceschina's daughter, Gioia Scoccardi, herself mother of the apprentice dragoman Francesco Mascellini, who in 1675 was involved in a legal dispute over ownership of a "herbalist's shop on Bahce street."[54] In his will and last testament of 1712, Grand Dragoman Tommaso Tarsia bequeathed a mill he owned near the English embassy in Istanbul, as well as the family's house, to his unmarried sister, Angela, who for decades had already served as the *Madonna e Patrona* of her brother's household and possessions.[55] Angela was soon to marry dragoman Stefano Testa, a maternal great-great-grandson of Gianesin Salvago the Elder and a nephew of the Fortis dragomans, helping to cement further dragoman endogamy and property accumulation.

Beyond anecdotal evidence, the most sustained documentation of dragomans' womenfolk as real estate owners and operators comes from the history of the bailate itself. The protracted, at times acrimonious negotiations between Venetian representatives and the house's landlady, Gioia Salvago—granddaughter, niece, wife, and aunt of several dragomans—are documented in painstaking detail in the bailate archives and reconstructed in modern scholarship.[56]

It is precisely in their capacity as landowners of extensive properties across Istanbul and its environs that dragomans' womenfolk appear in the bailate's notarial and chancery records as engaged in ownership litigation with relatives, tenants, Ottoman pious endowments, and Ottoman state institutions. Their firsthand knowledge of the complex legal landscape of early modern Istanbul positioned women as important intermediaries between the bailate and surrounding metropolitan society. In 1587, Caterina Gagliano, the wife of the road dragoman Mateca Salvago and mother of three other dragomans, sued her two brothers over their father and uncle's substantial inheritance. Both the capital and the further business opportunities generated by Caterina proved immensely important for her son Gianesin Salvago's future career.[57] In 1610, Caterina Piron filed suit with the bailo against Gianesin, requesting to receive her dowry in return for divorcing his younger brother, Benetto. The bailo accepted Gianesin's argument that, since both Caterina and her spouse were Ottoman subjects, the case should be argued in front of an Ottoman magistrate rather than the bailo. Yet the very fact that Caterina took her case to the bailo in the first place suggests familiarity with the complex inter-imperial juridical system and "jurisdictional plurality" of Istanbul and a readiness to exploit it.[58] A few decades later, Gianesin's cousin, Caterina Salvago, was to give the bailo much grief as the embassy's landlady, threatening to evict the consulate and to bring Muslim tenants in, forcing the bailo to pay out of pocket for the building's much needed repairs.[59]

Another important dimension of the lives of dragomans' womenfolk was their involvement in a dense web of patronage that bound together the bailate, the economic elite of Pera's Latin community, and the political class of the Ottoman metropole. An anecdote in the memoir of Venetian drago-man turned abbot Antonio Olivieri illustrates this point. When his paternal aunt Caterina discovered that her second husband, the dragoman Giovanni Antonio Grillo, had been executed by the Ottoman authorities due to his involvement in a Venetian spying scheme in 1649, she quickly paid a visit to the sultan's mother (*valide sultan*) Kösem Sultan, carrying gifts of "silk, cloth, and embroidery," pleading for her husband's grave to be opened and for the body to be exhumed. When her wish was granted, she took the corpse to Pera, where the Dominican friars held a Catholic burial in the Church of St. Anna, replete with a public procession attended by candle bearers from two local confraternities, as well as the French embassy's staff and janis-saries.[60] The context of the ongoing Venetian-Ottoman War of Crete makes particularly noteworthy Caterina Olivieri's access to Kösem, the empire's regent and arguably most powerful political personage at that point, and the two women's role in negotiating such a delicate diplomatic matter. Similarly, when Caterina and Giovanni Antonio's daughter, Gioia Grillo, passed away in 1658, the Venetian Resident Ballarino instructed that, in order to demon-strate the great esteem with which her family was held, she should receive a public funeral, accompanied by bailate staff and janissaries "as is customary for dragomans and others who are awarded public recognition."[61]

Through traces in the bailate chancery records—and especially in the remaining bailate cash ledgers—we learn further details about the role of dragoman's womenfolk in the Venetian-Ottoman gift economy. At the sim-plest level, they appear as beneficiaries of allowances and pensions for their deceased menfolk, especially dragomans. The ledgers of the late 1650s list Sobrana, Ornota, Battistina, and Vittoria, daughters of Grand Drag-oman Grillo, as stipendiaries on numerous occasions a decade after their father's execution. *Assegnamenti* (allowances) for Franceschetta, Gioieta, and Cecilia, daughters of Grand Dragoman Marcantonio Borisi, are similarly listed, decades after their father's death in 1620. Their sister, Salvagia Borisi, appears in the ledgers even more regularly over several years. Entries in 1681 still mention payments to Angela and Giustiniana Tarsia, Gioia Scoccardi Mascellini, Cecilia Borisi, and Battistina Grillo, daughters and granddaughters of deceased dragomans, some octogenarian.[62] The linchpin connecting all these women was their twice-widowed mother/stepmother Caterina, though beyond her contacts with Kösem Valide Sultan noted above, little is known about this evidently powerful matriarch.

The entries in the bailate cash ledgers fill important gaps in our knowledge of specific women, whose very names are rarely mentioned in other records. (A good example of this are the repeated reference to "the wife of Giovanni Battista Salvago," discussed below—virtually the only indication that Salvago had a wife, even though the bailate archives document in great detail practically every other aspect of this distinguished dragoman's long life.) These entries do not, however, radically change our understanding of a common pattern of Venetian benevolent paternalism vis-à-vis the descendants of deceased public servants both in Venice and overseas.

Of greater interest is the appearance of dragomans' wives in the bailate cash ledgers as the recipients of specific gifts in kind. To be sure, these women formed only a tiny fraction among the bailo's giftees, the overwhelming majority of whom were Ottoman courtiers and state officials.[63] Upon closer look, however, there emerges an intriguing pattern. Several entries refer to three women in particular as the recipients of a set of items that includes dusters,[64] velvet, soap, flowers, gloves, perfumes, scallops, civet pelts, velvet-encased mirrors, refined sugar, and baskets.[65] Significantly, almost the same combination of household and luxury goods was gifted on earlier occasions to a few prominent Ottoman courtiers, including the above-mentioned queen mother, Kösem Valide Sultan, the grand vizier, the sultan's chief equestrian, and a certain Halil Paşa (likely Damat Halil Paşa, the former and future grand vizier).[66] The repeated appearance of a cluster of three Catholic women giftees alongside these four exceptionally powerful Ottoman courtiers is especially striking since, in general, very few other non-bailate employees or Ottoman courtiers and state functionaries appear in these gift lists at all.

Who, then, are these three women giftees? One is the wife of Giambattista Orlandi, a long-term local resident who hailed from Bergamo and who played a certain role in the small community of Venetian merchants that centered on the bailate.[67] His wife first appears in the account books as the recipient of a shirt on April 18, 1625, with a note stating that the gift was occasioned by an invitation for the ambassador to serve as a godfather for Orlandi's child.[68] This is one of very few explanations for gifts throughout the account book—a similar annotation appears several times more alongside Orlandi's name in entries for various other gifts.[69] These annotations suggest that Orlandi's status may not have warranted such lavish gifts otherwise. They therefore underscore the importance of the bonds forged through baptismal godparenthood (and hence co-parenthood with birth parents) in this trans-imperial milieu, incorporating the resident bailo (or, in this case, a visiting ambassador) into local elite Catholic circles, whose members ranged greatly in their juridical and affective ties to Venice.[70]

If Orlandi's identity remains somewhat obscure, that of the other two women who consistently appear alongside her as gift recipients is clearer: these are the wives of Giovanni Battista Navon and of Giovanni Battista Salvago, both long-time road dragomans in Venetian service and the scions of prominent Istanbulite Catholic dragoman dynasties. While the ledger does not identify either woman by her own name, we can infer from other sources that Navon's wife was Bartolomea Coressi, whose likely father, Bartolomeo Coressi, was an Ottoman court physician sent as an envoy to Venice in 1601.[71] Bartolomea was not only Navon's wife but also the niece of another dragoman, Nicolò Coressi, who had served as Venetian public interpreter on Crete and who married Navon's sister, Francesca.[72]

These examples illustrate women's centrality to the weaving of dense, highly endogamous dragoman dynasties that cemented Venetian diplomatic power in Istanbul long after the Venetian state lost some of its political clout elsewhere. But the nature of the gifts given to these particular women and the occasions on which they were presented may hold further significance. At the time the gifts were made in April 1625, the dragoman Giovanni Battista Navon was en route to Venice with the returning bailo Giorgio Giustinian, while his colleague, Giovanni Battista Salvago, was in North Africa on the Serenissima's behalf, negotiating the ransom of enslaved Venetians. That both Navon and Salvago were road dragomans may have carried particular significance in this context. It was during extended trips, while much of the bailate was on the road that a special rapport could develop between the bailo and his dragomans. This is because, unlike other employees, dragomans did not usually reside in the bailate but rather maintained their own households nearby. As we have seen, these households often wielded their own power and authority through multilateral kinship ties and complex real estate investments in which dragomans' wives played vital roles. Road dragomans' extended absence from home was thus rife with meaning for their wives and local affines. Gifts from the faraway Serenissima—and luxury items explicitly marked as feminine at that—may have served therefore to signal the bond that connected dragomans' womenfolk with a Venetian world of goods, and also, more subtly, that positioned these women as the linchpin in a system of circulation and signification where the lines between Venetian and Ottoman elite consumption patterns could be contested.

These three women are virtually the only gift recipients listed in the surviving cash ledgers other than Ottoman officials and—very occasionally—dragomans and a few other members of the bailate's *famiglia alta*, like his accountant and physician. This makes particularly noteworthy the nature of these gifts as highly gendered luxury items for personal and domestic consumption (such as mirrors, soaps, and refined comestibles), as opposed to the livery gifted to bailate staff, including dragomans.[73] In a context where baili sought—unsuccessfully—to direct their dragomans' affective ties away from local relatives and, as much as possible, limit their marriage, the patronage and power conveyed by these lavish gifts to dragomans' wives, all hailing from prominent local families, served as an unmistakable acknowledgment of the importance of such ties for dragomans' successful service, and, perhaps, of the evolution of taste in these rarefied households to resemble at least partially those of the Venetian patriciate and Ottoman imperial household themselves.

Comportment

Beyond emulation, the bailate cash ledgers allow us to envision the bailo's evolving gifting practices as fractal recursivity within an Ottomancentric system.[74] A petition in 1598 by the bailate's aging physician, David Valentino, asked to be given the same *regalie* (livery) that was customary for apprentice dragomans, suggesting these objects' functioning as a quasi-contractual obligation, part of apprentices' regular compensation.[75] Bailate chancery records and Senate deliberations on new apprentice and dragoman appointments all meticulously registered the allocation of one to four annual sets of livery as part of their "benefits package," understood as perhaps the most crucial element in the making of dragomans' professional identity.[76] A Senate decree of 1630 authorized the bailo to provide two sets of livery to an Armenian dragoman, Giovanni Molino, in recognition of his service.[77] The bailate ledgers systematically record the disbursement of formal robes (kaftans) to dragomans and apprentices. Such entries—in a variety of financial records for both internal and external consumption—never fail to detail the precise occasion, date, type, color, and number of items allotted to each recipient.[78] Similarly, the phrases *un paro di vesti per regalia* (a pair of garments for livery) and *regalie di vesti e di denari* (livery of garments and money) appear in many deliberations for dragomans' salary increase, as well as in baili's lamentations about the costs of keeping apprentices and dragomans in their service.[79]

Significantly, this periodic distribution of livery to bailate staff mirrored the sultan's own presentation of robes of honor to Ottoman officials (and to foreign emissaries) on festive occasions, part and parcel of a broader system of gifting luxury textiles throughout the empire.[80] When the bailo Nicolò Barbarigo described his secretary's and dragoman's visit to the residence of a paşa in 1579 to deliver a gift of gyrfalcons,[81] he specifically emphasized that his two delegates were "dressed honorably," here understood clearly as a defining feature of their successful performance.[82] In his relazione of 1622, the returning bailo Almorò Nani emphasized that

> In appearing in the Divan, and at the doors of the Magnates of Istanbul, [dragomans] must dress with much expense conforming to the customs of the land, for public reputation, and they must make themselves welcome according to the occasion in order to facilitate the negotiation of public matters.[83]

Dragomans' petitions for salary raises similarly emphasized the requirement to "dress with dignity," to acquire "the customary clothes for appearing in front of Turkish ministers" and to "survive in Istanbul with a prominent profession especially subject to the wasteful manner of the court." The costliness of garments was often mentioned as grounds for raises.[84] One dragoman in 1643 insisted that his four sets of clothes "barely suffice to meet what is proper for the appointment I hold of public servant and minister."[85] It is probably not accidental that the same supplicant, the Venetian citizen Paolo Vecchia, also lamented in his petition his twenty-one years of "service rendered in the lands of barbarians." The "extravagant" dress code of Ottoman officialdom thus becomes emblematic of the empire's overall perceived excess.

Fanciful as Ottoman formal robes may have been, they clearly were the yardstick by which dragomans' garments were measured. Typical dragoman outfits were frequently made of bright, expensive satin. An expenditure list on the occasion of Giovanni Capello's special embassy to Istanbul in 1654 detailed the colors of each dragoman's satin dress (crimson, aquamarine, silver, white, yellow-brown Isabella color and marble-white *pavonazzo*), as well as their twill outer robes in olive green, amber and gold, "florid wine-color," and rose-pink.[86]

Given the meticulous sartorial regimentation of officeholders in both the Venetian and Ottoman empires, it is small wonder that dragomans' dress was the subject of extensive codification throughout the period. A key element of an Ottoman safe-conduct issued for Giovanni Battista Salvago in 1642 was a permission to don a turban like a Muslim.[87] This is quite remarkable, as in contemporary legal opinions (*fetva*) the donning of the turban by a non-Muslim effectively meant conversion to Islam.[88] Far from limited to distinguishing between Muslim and non-Muslim dress, the Ottoman system of sartorial codification also marked specific ethnoreligious and professional groups, and helped differentiate urban from rural folk. Outside the Ottoman Empire these sartorial taxonomies were much celebrated as they were popularized in costume albums. Ottoman sartorial hyper-distinction and lavishness thus became themselves indexical signs of Ottoman imperial grandeur (or, from another perspective, excess and decadence). The careful registration of gradations of cloth allocated to different dragomans therefore accentuated their partaking in an Ottoman—rather than a Venetian—semiotic system. After all, Venetian ideologies of male dress insisted on simple, unified black garb across the patrician and citizen elite, and, as a corollary to the meticulous regimentation of social and moral boundaries through sartorial codes, gendered most fanciful dress as feminine.[89] Dragomans, on the other hand, were expected—not least by their Venetian patrician employers—to wear outlandish livery in order to respectfully and respectably interact with Ottoman officials.

If the accouterments of the dragoman's office figured prominently on their minds, as on those of their employers, it is because they constituted a locus of anxiety over the dragoman's status. Charles Fonton, an eighteenth-century dragoman employed by the French ambassador to the Porte (and a direct descendant of the Navon family of Venetian dragomans), summarized the problem thus:

No doubt oriental clothing confuses [dragomans] with tax-paying Ottoman subjects [*reaya*], and makes them seem what they are not. The authorities always misapprehend this outward appearance, and very few of them know, very few even want to believe, that our Dragomans are truly French.

[. . .]

One has often seen Dragomans detained for the tribute [*haraç*], and when the tribute collector [*haraçlı*] was assured that they were French and exempt from the tribute, he was satisfied to claim that it was a mistake, and that after all one cannot read on the face of a Frenchman dressed *à la turque* either his name or his country.[90]

Fonton cast the uncertain identification of the clothed dragoman as "French" as opposed to "Turkish" as a problem of imperial governance, of mistaken claims by a foreign sovereign's agents. But for many of Fonton's colleagues, the challenge was just as much to "act" or perform Frenchness (or Venetianness), to have one's alliances and affect directed appropriately. In theory, bailate dragomans who were recognized by the Porte through a *berat* could claim the status of Venetian juridical subjects, and hence exemption from Ottoman law and taxes.[91] However, in practice, such Venetianness was often in tension with other claims and identifications—not only by the Ottoman state, but by kin and church, for example. These claims were not always compatible; their friction was exacerbated by dragomans' pervasive endogamy, which constituted families of multiple, sometimes antagonistic jurisdictions. As Alexander de Groot observes, locally born dragomans "were only seemingly binational because of the status they had acquired of protégé of a foreign capitulatory power. But this status had, after all, to be granted by the Ottoman Porte upon the request of the foreign ambassador concerned."[92] Since dragomans' extraterritorial juridical status was neither fixed, nor securely premised on the usual markers of communal membership in that period—lineage, place of provenance, or name—it required special cultivation, in part through sartorial regimentation, which the donning of Ottoman-style robes clearly disrupted.

The challenge of misidentification, however, runs deeper than the mistaken interpellation of individual dragomans, and lies at the heart of Istanbul's diplomatic enterprise, where the question of Venetian representatives' sovereignty vis-à-vis the sultan was far from settled. For one, as noted above, livery served not only to mark its wearer's station, but also as a diplomatic gift, a true "sign of recognition" with its real potential for failure, as Webb Keane argues.[93] In 1660, at the height of the War of Crete, Secretary Ballarino sent one of his dragomans to deliver a gift of four sets of clothes to the Ottoman minister Ibrahim Paşa, notorious for his anti-Venetian sentiments, in the hope of appeasing him. Ibrahim not only refused to accept the garments, but exclaimed: "The slaves of our Emperor have no need to be dressed by those who make war with him."[94] As Ballarino himself later admitted in his report of the fiasco to the Senate, he had meant the garments as tokens of friendship, substitutes for more lavish gifts, which he was unable to send given his long house arrest and empty coffers. The garments, he reported, had been handed "with expressions of appreciation for [Ibrahim Paşa's] merit, and in hope of allowing him in due course to test with livelier effects the sincere disposition of the Serene Republic toward him."[95] Ibrahim, too, clearly understood that the garments stood not only for other future gifts, but more important, for the Republic's good intentions and affirmation of an Ottomancentric political order. In declining the gift he thus refused to recognize the sincerity of intention behind it, rejecting Venetian patronage along the way.

The risky business of attire was therefore integral to the trans-imperial economies of gift and affect that underwrote dragomans' performance of mediation in early modern Istanbul. Yet other semiotic practices were not without their hazards too. "He has proven himself as full of affect and of loyalty, as of value." Thus the Venetian Senate urged the bailo Pietro Foscarini to promote the Pera-born Giovanni Antonio Grillo to the position of grand dragoman in 1636.[96] As we saw, "affect" and "loyalty," when properly invested in the Venetian Republic, were deemed key to the performance and advancement of dragomans. Generous toward dragomans who had proven themselves properly affectionate toward the Republic, the Venetian authorities acted harshly toward those whose affect was "misplaced," i.e., invested in the wrong objects, and who thereby transgressed the boundaries of a moral community centered on the bailate.

Familiarity

Even in peacetime baili frequently lamented their profound dependency on dragoman-generated knowledge, a dependency redoubled by the former's short term in office of typically only two years and almost uniform ignorance of Ottoman Turkish. In his relazione to the Senate of 1576, the bailo

Antonio Tiepolo complained at some length about dragomans' mediation and his inability to establish direct lines of communication with Ottoman ministers,

> From which follows that because of the great difficulty of interpretation . . . the bailo can never do anything by himself, since he cannot express his own reasons as effectively as necessary. Therefore, absent this efficacy of words, and absent also the virtue of the bailo's skill in reasoning, from which the Paşa would understand proper respect rather than cowardice or fear, the dragoman, who is often impeded by the difficulty of interpreting, and even more by failing to apprehend not only the issues, but also the bailo's mode of impressing these issues, weakens the arguments and exhibits that timidity which is never the bailo's share; for which reason if [the dragoman] is not aided by the bailo in what to say, and by a face full of confidence, and by a steady voice, the Paşa might dare to refuse or make difficult that which would have been most simple in itself. This disadvantage of the bailo, or rather of Your Serenity, is augmented when negotiating in the divan, where it is not customary for the bailo to go; because the dragoman, while Christian, because he is nonetheless a Turkish [i.e., Ottoman] subject, is fearful by his nature, and even more so for having neither the talent nor the experience to negotiate as would be needed in matters of any import.[97]

Early modern diplomacy was deeply rooted in humanist notions of eloquence.[98] Unsurprisingly, forced reliance on the linguistic mediation of dragomans in the bailo's communications with Ottoman officialdom came to be seen as an insurmountable problem. The challenge was compounded by the perceived gap between the prototypical speech styles of the bailo and the dragoman, which are here mapped very clearly onto their distinct "nature"—their status, personhood, and capacity for confident self-presentation.

Yet if Tiepolo contrasted the bailo's "proper respect" with the dragoman's "cowardice" and "fear," dragomans' tenacity as intermediaries was undoubtedly due in no small measure to their ability to inhabit a deferential role vis-à-vis both Ottoman and Venetian elite interlocutors. This ability was cultivated through their lifelong service in Istanbul and extensive contacts in the city. Such "localization" also made dragomans much more familiar with Ottoman diplomatic protocol and court affairs than their Venetian employers could ever be.

Ultimately, it was precisely dragomans' sense of appropriate self-presentation—not just their linguistic skills or juridical status—that lent authority to their pronouncements on local "custom." The bailo Andrea Badoer's report of an encounter between the dragoman Mateca Salvago and an Ottoman provincial governor in 1573 illuminates dragomans' power to speak authoritatively in the name of tradition. Upon arrival at the governor's residence, Salvago was asked whether he had brought the governor his gift. Salvago responded in the positive, and added that, as usual, the gift consisted of silken cloth and other fine textiles. The governor exclaimed: "But where are my one thousand sequins?" Salvago, according to Badoer's report, asserted that monetary gifts were not customary. Moreover, when the governor protested that textiles were not customary gifts either, and demanded to see the bailo himself, Salvago retorted that this would be "superfluous," since even the bailo could not offer him a monetary gift, adding that the governor "could not say what was not true."[99] If some baili complained that Ottoman subjects made timid and complacent dragomans, Salvago's dealing with the governor implies quite the opposite.

Evidently, their deep familiarity with customary diplomatic practice allowed some dragomans to effectively represent Venice to Ottoman officials, and to continue to monopolize this position against possible alternative channels of communication. Several Venetian diplomats recognized this. In 1553, the bailo Bernardin Navagero praised Gianesin Salvago for his long, loyal service, and the respect he had earned in the divan. Not only did Salvago "understand very well the humors of that nation [i.e., the Ottomans]," but "he is most obliged to the paşas, and especially to Rüstem, with whom he has become very close, and [shows] such familiarity that he speaks without respectful address, and laughs with him."[100]

Whereas Navagero finds Salvago's familiarity with Rüstem Paşa remarkable, dragomans' cultivated ability to flex the otherwise rigid registers of deferential address that define stranger sociality was a critical aspect of their successful diplomatic performance. It was precisely the prerogative of dragomans *qua* dragomans, an indexical sign of their positionality "in between," as those who deliberately cross the carefully enforced boundaries of ostensibly distinct linguistic codes and sociojuridical groupings. This policing of the linguistic boundary was itself a well-orchestrated performance, as suggested by numerous anecdotes about Ottoman officials of European background listening to their compatriots in their first language, but responding only in Turkish, via a dragoman.[101]

Yet dragomans' authority derived not only from their familiarity with Ottoman officials and diplomatic protocol. It was also grounded in their embedding in a deeply endogamous community of practice and ability to mediate understandings of the "local" to their sojourning diplomatic interlocutors (and, often through them, to circulate these understandings to a wider Republic of Letters). The following anecdote illustrates this point.

On November 12, 1671, the Venetian dragoman Christoforo Tarsia signed an affidavit of a rather peculiar kind. In it, he explained the circumstances that led to the burial of his son Leonardo in 1663 in the Orthodox ("Greek") church of St. Demetrios in Edirne. Leonardo, the father explained, had traveled to Edirne as a dragoman in the entourage of Venetian Resident Giovanni Battista Ballarino, following the Ottoman court. While there, he contracted the plague, to which he succumbed seven days later. Accompanied by Venetian representatives and all of the city's "principal Greeks," his body was carried to the church, where it was interred near the great altar. The Greek religious, after performing the funeral rites and reciting prayers for his soul, placed a silver lamp over Leonardo's tomb, which was lit in perpetuity to commemorate his soul. His gravestone included "Latin and Greek letters in honor of his virtue, birth, and status." In the absence of the bailate chaplain, Christoforo added, his son had been confessed by a Greek priest, who administered absolution and Holy Communion. This was followed by a visit by a Ragusan (Catholic) chaplain, who, having arrived too late and hearing that the last rites had been performed already by a Greek priest, performed the final absolution. Before his death, however, Leonardo had given written testimony to Ballarino that "in front of God and the world he confessed dying a true Catholic and Roman Apostolic, recommending for his protection his old father and his dearest mother."[102]

This account was included in a series of testimonials as to the union between the Orthodox and Roman Catholic Churches collected by the French ambassador to the Porte, Marquis de Nointel, from various members of Istanbul's Catholic community, among others. Starting in 1674, these testimonials, alongside numerous professions of faith, appeared in several editions of *La perpetuité de la foy de l'Eglise catholique touchant l'Eucharistie*, an anti-Calvinist polemical book authored by the Jansenist theologians Antoine Arnauld and Pierre Nicole. In gathering these materials, Ambassador de Nointel was assisted by his secretary (and former apprentice dragoman) Antoine Galland, who translated many of the testimonials from Arabic, Greek, and Latin into French.

These testimonials, and Arnauld and Nicole's publication project as a whole, were part of the broader Eucharistic controversy between Calvinists and Jansenists. They were meant to bolster the latter's position about the Christian universality of belief in true transubstantiation by refuting the Huguenot minister Jean Claude's assertion that Eastern Christians denied transubstantiation, as well as the true presence of Jesus Christ in the host and the veneration of saints.[103] The Eucharistic controversy, however, also had a more immediate Ottoman context, namely the ongoing negotiations between several Ottoman Christian Orthodox Hierarchs and European representatives (diplomatic and missionary both) over protection and confessional identity in this period.

Arnauld and Nicole's book was reprinted dozens of times throughout the late-seventeenth and eighteenth centuries. The circumstances that led to the inclusion of Tarsia's testimony in it underscore European diplomats' heavy reliance on their dragomans for authenticating "local knowledge." In this case, Tarsia's statement is meant to corroborate the fine points of theological difference (or lack thereof) among various Christian denominations in an age of confessionalization. The inscriptional labor of the French dragoman Galland also reminds us of the significant, and often overlooked, role of dragomans in commissioning, transcribing, editing, and translating the speech of local informants, turning it into entextualized voices.

But what does this episode tell us about dragomans' relationship with their sojourning diplomatic patrons? About their embedding in local institutions and communities of practice? What does it say more specifically about Tarsia's own positionality vis-à-vis these various matrices of belonging? First, it suggests that Catholic good standing and strong familial attachments formed the two primary axes of self-identification for members of Pera's Latin-rite community. Both for Leonardo on his deathbed and for his father, Christoforo, recalling these painful events eight years later, of paramount importance was that "he confessed dying a true Catholic and Roman Apostolic, recommending for his protection his old father and his dearest mother." Neither juridical status (as an Ottoman subject), nor place of provenance (Christoforo hailed from Venetian Istria, where the family continued to hold land and noble title), let alone partaking in a geopolitical or civilizational block (as "European") seem to have held much sway in this context.

Given Christoforo Tarsia's trajectory as an émigré from faraway Istria, and his occupation as Venetian dragoman, more significant still is the very fact that he was asked to provide this attestation in the first place, in the context of a French Eucharistic controversy. Why was he deemed, at least in the French ambassador's eyes, to possess an authoritative perspective on Orthodox theology or on Orthodox-Catholic relations? The key to this question is found a few pages earlier in Arnauld and Nicole's tome, in the list of signatories of a collective statement by "the Community of Perots," namely representatives of Pera's Latin-rite community.[104] Of the nineteen signatories, at least ten were dragomans employed by the French, English, and Venetian embassies, Christoforo Tarsia among them. Many of these dragomans, and virtually all other signatories, had also been elected community officials (councilors, priors, and sub-priors) and closely related to other dragomans by birth or marriage. Tarsia's status as an elderly and respected Venetian dragoman was metonymic of his standing in the local Latin-rite community of Pera, and vice versa.

This case illustrates the authority that dragomans, as quintessential trans-imperial intermediaries, derived vis-à-vis European publics from their elite membership in Pera's Latin-rite communal organizations and from their extensive local kinship ties. It also demonstrates how their access to diplomatic channels of communication and, especially, to the enormous circulatory potential of print enhanced and projected this authority.

The double-edged sword of dragomans' familiarity with juridical and confessional others goes to the heart of the tensions between centrifugal and centripetal forces in the forging of the dragomanate. Similar to Arabic translators' successful performance of "fiduciary translation" in early modern Spain, as Claire Gilbert productively shows, dragomans' professional bona fides could never rely on linguistic competence alone, but necessitated a "variety of discursive and social strategies."[105] In the long run, deep familiarity with Ottoman society, indeed embedding therein, was not an aberration, but rather a constitutive and enduring prerequisite of dragomans' successful diplomacy at the Porte. Sojourning representatives' perennial concerns about dragomans' loyalty and trustworthiness pivoted on the latter's demonstrably deep embedding in Ottoman society. Yet it was precisely this embedding that enabled dragomans to fulfil their mission. Rather than contradictory, dragomans' professional and familial strategies reinforced one another, generating productive tensions and ambiguities, opportunities and constraints that were to typify dragomans' trans-imperial itineraries for centuries to come.

CHAPTER 3

Inscribing the Self

Dragomans' Relazioni

In Istanbul, Anatolian Turks are not admitted to the Porte, nor to the military or the ministries, because they are considered uncouth and rustic, as opposed to Europeans, who are deemed to be valorous, while they [Anatolian Turks] are deemed to be cowardly. Yet in Barbary, they are the most numerous and most eminent. It can be believed that from this difference is born the gut hatred that the Barbary Turks harbor for the Ottoman Porte, their repudiator. And therefore, abandoning their native huts and the plough, they rush to ennoble themselves in Barbary, where they can marry Moorish women. Their sons, called Culogli, that is, sons of soldiers,[1] succeed their father but, due to their ties to their Moorish mother, [since they are] spurious in a certain way and degenerate, are not esteemed as much as the renegades and the original Turks. This mixing of renegades and Turks creates a third species of Turks who speak Italian and Castilian. The renegades do not understand Ottoman grandeur, which they have never seen, and the Turks expect from [the Porte] neither honors nor offices, and therefore it is little wonder if they lack in effective obedience, which is professed by mouth only.[2]

THIS PASSAGE, PENNED IN 1625 by Giovanni Battista Salvago, a native of Istanbul and a life-long Venetian dragoman, captures some of the complexities of the author's effort to establish himself as a cultural intermediary between Ottoman and Venetian political elites. As a descendant of an elite Istanbulite Catholic family that traced its roots to Genoese settlers in Constantinople in the wake of the Fourth Crusade, and as the scion of a dynasty of dragomans who had all served the Venetian bailo at the Porte, Salvago was ideally positioned to claim expert knowledge of Ottoman society, history, and culture. He couched many of his observations of things Ottoman in the classicizing language of humanist learning, prompted perhaps by his broad education and extensive sojourns in Venice. This text fashions its author as an educated metropolitan Venetian by simultaneously claiming insider knowledge of the Ottoman world and yet distancing himself from it, by developing spatiotemporal categories of Ottoman difference. It suggests in particular how Salvago both appropriated medieval discourses of Turkish ethnogenesis and sought to commensurate Ottoman notions of ethnicity and status with Venetian ones.

In order to situate Salvago's performance within the early modern Mediterranean space of encounter, this chapter compares his report on North Africa to three other Venetian dragomans' *relazioni*—the only extant exemplars of this genre before 1700: the Cypriot-born Michele Membrè's 1542 account of his mission to the court of the Safavid Shah Tahmāsp (r. 1524–1576) two years prior, Venetian secretary Vincenzo degli Alessandri's 1574 narrative about his (ultimately failed) mission to the same court the previous year, and the dragoman Tommaso Tarsia's 1683 report from the second Ottoman siege of Vienna. These relazioni differentially articulate dragomans' trans-imperial perspective on the Ottoman and Venetian worlds they claimed to mediate.

Despite their divergent places of provenance and professional trajectories, the four authors examined here shared several important characteristics, namely their birth or extended sojourns in Ottoman lands and their prior service to the Venetian government, whether in Istanbul or in Venice. How did these trajectories shape dragomans' relazioni? How can we read this corpus as (heterogeneous) trans-imperial self-fashioning? And to what extent might we observe an arc of transformation from Membrè's mid-sixteenth-century relazione to Tarsia's late-seventeenth? Taken as a whole, these relazioni underscore how tropes of Ottoman alterity were often employed precisely by those who, like Salvago, could make a strong claim to intimate knowledge of things Ottoman by dint of their Ottoman juridical subjecthood, birth, or extended sojourn and service in the empire. They allow us to consider the distinctly metropolitan Istanbulite perspective on the Ottoman Empire these authors evince, a perspective largely commensurable with that of contemporary Venetian (and other Italianate) readers.

What is a Relazione?

Before turning our attention to specific relazioni, however, a few words
are in order about the genre itself. Relazioni, as masterfully analyzed by
Filippo de Vivo, hold pride of place in Venetian historiography and in European diplomatic and political history more broadly.[3] From the Latinate
root "to relate," relazioni aimed to provide a highly conventionalized report
about a foreign court as seen through the eyes of an official Venetian representative. As Andreas Motsch elaborates, their poetics were vitally shaped
by their performative and institutional matrix as reports about matters of
great political import to be read out loud, enacted in front of an audience—
in the Venetian case, the assembly of the Senate. Even more significantly,

> While referential in nature and in intent, the value of this discourse
> depends on the competence of the speaker, who bears witness out of
> personal experience and thus personal knowledge, so that the moral
> and epistemological value of what is said is indeed based on the wit-
> ness' experience, prestige, and ethics.[4]

Unsurprisingly, then, the vast majority of Venetian relazioni were penned
by members of the highest echelons of the patrician political elite. Highly
structured and formal, these ambassadorial reports did not shy away from
offering firsthand accounts and astute, explicit political commentary,
whether about faraway courts or Venetian policies. Yet they often positioned the author as an all-knowing observer, somehow detached from his
object of observation. The relazioni analyzed in this chapter are markedly
different. Neither patrician nor all-knowing, their authors had to struggle
to establish the very legitimacy of their authorship in a deeply hierarchical
diplomatic order which admitted few non-patricians as bona fide representatives of the Serenissima. Rather than accept them as disinterested
eyewitness accounts that add to our positive knowledge of developments
in Ottoman and Safavid lands, as these relazioni have been treated by most
scholars who have cited them, this chapter focuses on how dragomans'
relazioni perform and position their authors vis-à-vis their intended patrician Venetian readership.

Indeed, it is not purely the biographical anomaly of these relazioni's authors that warrants closer scrutiny. Rather, what makes these texts remarkable is the epistemological work they aim to achieve. These texts and their
authors represent a crucial, if neglected, phase in the process of articulating

the relationship between Europe and neighboring Islamicate polities, particularly those that eventually came to be known as the Levant.

Relazioni were conceivably dragomans' most impactful writings, and certainly the most circulated. Yet they were not the only type of first-person narratives dragomans produced. Chapters 5 through 7 will discuss dragomans' different forms of self-inscription in the paratexts of their dictionaries, grammars, translations from Ottoman, and historical discourses, while Chapter 4 considers their strategies of visual self-presentation. These are just some of the textual and visual genres through which dragomans' subjectivities were inscribed. No seventeenth-century Venetian dragoman is known to have left extensive "diaries," "memoirs," or "autobiographies" akin to those penned by the Frenchman Antoine Galland, the Transylvanian Dávid Rozsnyai, the Ottoman of Polish/Ruthenian birth Ali Ufki Bey, or, in the following century, the Ottoman Osman Ağa, the Ragusan Miho Zarini, the Hungarian François Tott, and, most famous and influential, the Austrian Joseph von Hammer-Purgstall.[5] But at least one seventeenth-century Venetian apprentice dragoman, Antonio Benetti, wrote a travelogue describing his journey to and sojourn in Istanbul in the entourage of the bailo Giovanni Battista Donà in the early 1680s.[6] This was followed in 1725 by the unauthorized publication of the memoirs of a Venetian dragoman turned priest, Antonio Olivieri, which covered the same tumultuous period, as well as several earlier episodes involving the bailate and its dragomans from the late 1640s onward.[7] At least one eighteenth-century travelogue remains unpublished, describing the journey from Istanbul to Tenedos of the Venetian dragoman siblings Cosmo and Giambattista Calavrò-Imberti.[8]

Beyond this corpus, we can glean dragomans' self-presentational strategies from a host of other practices. Even dragomans' most minute inscriptional and translational activities can be read in relation to their professional and personal trajectories, not as neutral "sources" but as curated reflections and refractions of divergent genres, institutional frameworks, and, indeed, understandings of self. The discussion of Venetian dragomans' relazioni here is therefore inevitably partial, focusing on one important but hardly exhaustive set of texts and their institutional contexts of performativity.

As scholars have shown, both the relazione's etymological roots in the verb *riferire* and its actual performance in front of the Senate upon an ambassador's return from his mission evoke the act of "bringing back"—a spatiotemporal relation of circulation.[9] In this circulation, the narrator is

typically cast as the go-between, a privileged, heroic figure who singularly
ventured out and is now in a position to relate that which is distant (in time,
space, or both) to the listeners or readers. Inherent in this enactment of
circulation is the tension between localizing the subject matter, on the one
hand, and reinforcing its spatiotemporal distance on the other. This "dual
vision," the effort to "demonstrate both . . . otherness and . . . sameness"
in a single oratorical performance, allows for the "other" and the "self"
to emerge as distinct and clearly delineated. Thus, in making an object
accessible, the relazione's narrative mode foregrounds its *unfamiliarity, its
inaccessibility except through the narrator's mediation.*

As De Vivo fruitfully argues, the performance, consumption, and circulation of early modern Venetian diplomatic relazioni were all complex
processes. These moments and actions, however, were preceded by several
necessary steps, including the collation, distillation, and purification of
disparate previous texts, both oral and written ("information"), and their
transformation into a "new" text, what linguistic anthropologists call the
process of entextualization.[10] This process constitutes not only an identifiable text, but an unambiguously namable author. The heterogeneity of any
relazione's "sources" and their complex mechanisms of composition thus
call attention to the institutional sites where relazioni were crafted and
"sources" were constituted as such (e.g., by observing, overhearing, elic-
iting, quoting, summarizing, copying down, paraphrasing, or transcribing
portions of oral speech or written texts). It also makes evident the need for
a detailed analysis of the semiotic devices that helped inscribe the spatiotemporal distance between object and readership, including deictics, the
conscious "borrowing" of lexical items from other linguistic codes, glossing, explication, and commensuration of "foreign terms," and myriad other
strategies of translation in its broadest sense, as discussed in Chapter 5.

To a large extent, the very act of textual "composition" is never singular.
Authorial practice always involves assembling and reordering previous text
fragments, as well as distributing responsibility for the textual utterance
across different persons presumed to have taken part in its composition.
Indeed, as De Vivo notes, many Venetian diplomatic relazioni were not
penned by the ambassadors who read them in front of the Senate, but were
"ghost-written by secretaries and others."[11] In order to produce their reports—indeed, in order to engage in any diplomatic activity—relazioni
authors relied heavily on collaborators, including spies, informants, and
other variously positioned members of the host society. The words of these

knowledge producers were themselves mediated, often by dragomans. Thus, while some Venetian diplomats acknowledged it more openly than others, it is hard to overstate the degree to which their ability to produce and circulate timely news from Istanbul relied on dragomans' local embedding and interpretive work.

It was, for example, with some pride that the bailo Almorò Nani informed the Senate in 1616 of his secret contacts with a Hungarian dragoman who debriefed him about events in the Habsburg court and in Dalmatia, a region of key importance to the Venetians. In another dispatch a few months later, Nani reported on the missions of his two dragomans, Giuliano Salvago and Barnabà Brutti, to the Ottoman governor of Bosnia and to Ibrahim Ağa, the military governor of Buda, respectively. The dragomans' letters, which Nani summarized, included detailed diplomatic, military, commercial, and ethnographic information concerning various Ottoman provinces.[12] Similarly, during the protracted War of Crete (1645–1669), and especially during its later phases, it was largely thanks to his dragomans that the Venetian Resident Giovanni Battista Ballarino—variably imprisoned, exiled to Edirne, or placed under house arrest—was able to continue to send frequent and lengthy dispatches to Venice. These dispatches—in sharp contrast with more polished and rhetorical relazioni—often read as a minimally edited concatenation of reported speech, summarizing in written form what Ballarino's dragomans had relayed to him orally of their wheeling and dealing with Ottoman officials and other diplomats in the capital.

Even a preliminary consideration of the Venetian diplomatic relazione's "discursive footprint" must therefore address the actors and perspectives that forged it, often embedded in the narrative as vital compositional techniques. These multiple collaborators brought to the process their own ideas about what was new and noteworthy and, as important, about proper ways of reporting and relating, indeed, of engaging in discourse. Such diverse points of view and (thoroughly mediated) perceptions of the relazione's presumed audience are inextricably entwined with those of the nominal author.

In recognizing this process of laminating a variety of perspectives inherent in the forging of cohesive relazioni, the goal is not to "recover" submerged voices, to "let the subaltern speak" in any simple way, or to assume Ottoman interlocutors' a priori subalternity. For the very attempt to "translate" or "relate" interlocutors' words would have already engaged to some extent their conceptual frameworks, including their understanding of text and circulation. The resultant multifocality of the relazione as a genre is therefore not a background noise to be reduced (let alone filtered out completely), but an essential aspect of its narrative mode. It is, moreover, an aspect that merits careful attention if we are to trace the genre's genealogies and truth claims. For example, we are only beginning to understand the legacies of medieval Islamicate travel literature in its variegated forms—including the pilgrimage narrative and the *rihla* (personal account of travel)—for early modern Ottoman practices of narrating that which is new and foreign.[13] Given Venetian ambassadors' ongoing interactions with Ottoman narrative conventions and with oral interlocutors fully schooled in Ottoman diplomatic protocol, these practices surely played a role in shaping Venetian relazioni from the Porte as well, a role not yet fully fleshed out.[14]

All these considerations alert us to the pervasive polyphony of diplomatic discourse, which grafted to one another multiple potentially competing perspectives.[15] For truth-effect, early modern relations very much relied on extensive direct citation, whether explicitly framed as such or not. Such strategies call for further inquiry into the relazione's voicing structure, and into the discursive mechanisms that at times purged the final text of the vestiges of competing voices, while at others built precisely on their presence as authenticating and legitimizing the author's own truth claims.[16] It may well be worth asking, therefore, how a singular authorial voice was produced out of the variety of voices that served as sources, and how the tension between competing perspectives was suppressed in the forging of a coherent relational narrative. Indeed, to what extent was that a conscious goal, and how well was it achieved?[17]

Venetian diplomats themselves often acknowledged—if grudgingly—their reliance on other intermediaries and therefore on not-quite-patrician perspectives. Giovanni Battista Ballarino, serving as the de facto Venetian Resident in Istanbul from the mid-1650s to the mid-1660s, struggled to keep producing meaningful political knowledge for his masters in Venice while under house arrest, and thus often resorted to reporting almost verbatim his dragomans' oral communications with Ottoman officials. Conversely, and as noted in previous chapters, baili's dispatches and missives to the Senate repeat ad nauseam their fears of betrayal by local dragomans, suggesting that reliance on local intermediaries necessarily compromised Venetian interests. This anxiety concerned not just local intermediaries' "loyalty" and competence, but the very processes of producing and articulating knowledge in diplomatic discourse. Significantly, acknowledgement of reliance on other intermediaries is less explicit in ambassadorial relazioni, the final, carefully crafted and highly redacted ex post facto product of embassies, than it is in periodic dispatches. This was not because, once home, returning ambassadors somehow "forgot" their indebtedness to other diplomatic practitioners and intermediaries but rather because the genre demanded that well-groomed patrician envoys fashion themselves as eloquent orators and sole authors of their own narrative.

Of course, for envoys to acknowledge the multiple layers of mediation and diverse perspectives underwriting their relazioni would have undermined their narrative's autoptic authority and clear anchoring in a singular timespace on which the authorial voice rested. Furthermore, such an acknowledgement might have cast doubt on the uniqueness (and hence value) of the confidential information that the author purported to divulge. To position oneself as an "information broker" is to undermine the claims of others to provide this vital service, and to imply that the information one offers is not only unique but coherent and fungible.

The stakes of such positioning are particularly acute in the context of early modern "spilling around the planet" of European politics and commerce. Beyond doubt, early modern European relation-writers sought to account on an unprecedented scale for what we might call, in retrospect, cultural difference. At the same time, as scholars have shown, early modern relation writers reporting from virtually all corners of the earth struggled to fit new engagements into familiar narrative frames. These frames were shaped, first and foremost, not by paradigmatic "first encounters" in New Worlds but rather by centuries of sustained interaction, indeed by metaphorical rubbing shoulders, with proximate societies, including the Byzantines, the Mamluks, and their eventual Ottoman successors. It was precisely these societies' uncanny closeness and (incomplete) familiarity that required significant discursive elaboration to articulate their foreignness and the political sensibilities that go along with it.

This elaboration leaves us with more questions than answers: were there prototypical early modern discursive strategies for foregrounding spatio-temporal distance across relations' widely disparate sites of production, performance, and circulation? More generally, what does the consolidation of the relation as a paradigmatic and immensely popular genre tell us about early modernity? What role might it have played in constituting Venetian (and other) self-consciousness through multiple encounters abroad?

Clearly, the relational mode has now largely been subsumed by other modalities of claiming truth.[18] But this should not obscure its foundational role in various disciplinary epistemological procedures, from ethnography to philology. By focusing on dragomans' relazioni, we can begin to observe some of this subgenre's entanglements and triangulations, further moving away from a bootstrapping, Eurocentric account of the emergence of ethnographic reportage.

Dragomans' Relazioni: Some Typologies and General Observations

Above and beyond linguistic prowess, dragomans' social and cultural capital derived from (and in turn reinforced) their positionality as "information specialists" who gathered and rearticulated useful knowledge for their patrons. They performed this specialized craft through a mixture of genres, some written, some oral, which depended simultaneously on their ability to distinguish themselves both as individual bearers of unique knowledge and expertise and—especially with respect to the Venetian dragomanate—as members of a community of practice shaped by apprenticeship, commensality, and endogamy. Their successful performance thus required a careful self-fashioning as denizens of a "space of encounter," masters of an intercultural habitus and of specific genres of proto-ethnographic reportage.

At the same time, in writing relazioni, dragomans by necessity departed from the more familiar territory of oral negotiations. Orality defined much of dragomans' daily interactions, whether with Ottoman dignitaries or embassy staffers, reporting to the bailo, or petitioning the Senate or the Porte, always intended as an oral performance by the supplicant or a representative thereof. In inhabiting the writerly persona of a relazione author, dragomans assumed the mantle of "professional interlopers": for non-patricians (and, in some cases, non-Venetian subjects) who penned relazioni to be presented to the Venetian government, the stakes involved were higher than for patrician ambassadors and baili. If Ottaviano Bon, who was accused of turning his relazione into a polemical pamphlet "with a demonstrative and apologetic aim" was an outlier among his patrician peers, such apologetics were rather a prerequisite for non-patrician dragoman relazione authors.[19] After all, they had to demonstrate their very authority to write in this genre—and, by implication, to be legitimate diplomats. To do so, they had to comply with the genre's rigid expectations. Composing a well-formed relazione that demonstrated all the stylistic trappings of the genre

established, first, their authority to write it (and, by extension, the legitimacy of their claims to have served as high-level representatives of the
state). It also, on a secondary level, underscored authors' membership in
an exclusive Venetian elite milieu by virtue of their command of a rarefied
literary culture.

Beyond the challenge of their non-patrician status, three of the four
relazioni-writing dragomans examined in this chapter—Alessandri being
a notable exception—were further hampered by their non-Venetian lineage
and/or place of birth far from the Lagoon city. Membrè and Tarsia were
nominally Venetian subjects: Membrè was born on Cyprus at a time when
the island was still a Venetian colony; Tarsia was born in Istanbul, but
to parents who hailed from Venetian Capodistria. Salvago was an Istanbul-born Ottoman subject, a scion of a local dragoman dynasty of Genoese
descent. For these three authors, writing about the Ottoman and Safavid
empires posed a double challenge: how to describe foreign polities (which,
in some cases, were one's birthplace) in a way that conveyed authority
without betraying excessive intimacy? Put another way, if successfully
claiming to be an enculturated Venetian was a pre-condition for these authors' performances, how did they frame their expert knowledge of the Ottoman and Safavid worlds so as to simultaneously substantiate their claim
to full membership in a Venetian cultural sphere?

Here, it becomes especially important to recognize the relazione as a
paradigmatic "contact genre," whose explicit aim is to present one society,
political system, or cultural complex to a readership external by definition
to the object being described. As Alejandro Paz defines it, a contact genre
is an "interactional (Bakhtinian) genre where the participants are positioned as across some socio-cultural boundary, and where the participants
perceive themselves as exchanging information about the other or engaging
otherwise in issues of their own alterity."[20] This raises the question of how
the relazione text itself marks its production in an epistemological, juridical, as well as physical space of encounter. What makes a relazione "Venetian"? What makes it "about" contact? Clearly, a relazione about, say, Man-
tua, articulated its object's alterity rather differently than a relazione about
Persia. Moreover, as a contact genre, the relazione relied on an extended
network of mediation to derive its authority and verisimilitude. Intermediaries themselves had different expectations about and understandings of
the nature of political communication. In order to understand dragomans'
relazioni, it is therefore not enough to know something about Venetian

readership and textual conventions. One must consider how authors' (at times invisible) Safavid and Ottoman interlocutors—who supplied much of dragomans' knowledge of those societies—thought about diplomacy, testimony, and knowledge itself.[21]

We can disaggregate this trans-imperial perspective further, by considering how a Venetian colonial subject like Membrè was informed by his embeddedness in distinctive patronage networks across the eastern Mediterranean, as well as by his extensive contacts among Ottoman merchants. His perspective surely differed from that of Salvago or Tarsia, who grew up in established dragoman families in Istanbul, apprenticed in the bailate from a very young age, were well integrated into the Catholic Latin community of Pera, and had close friends and patrons among other ambassadorial households and courtly elites. Their perspective also contrasted with that of Alessandri, a Venetian-born citizen and a distinguished secretary to the Senate. Alessandri had lived in Istanbul for seven years prior to his assignment but acquired only limited knowledge of the Islamicate world beyond the Ottoman metropole. Further, whereas Salvago descended from an established Genoese family who had resided in Constantinople since Byzantine times, Tarsia's father had emigrated from Venetian Capodistria to become a dragoman only a few decades prior. While the Tarsias carefully contracting marriage alliances among Istanbul's Catholic elite, they also maintained kinship ties and property in Venetian Istria.

Beyond biographical differences, other pertinent questions concern the potential difference between relazioni from Ottoman territories (Salvago, Tarsia) and from Safavid lands (Membrè, Alessandri), between wartime relazioni (Alessandri, Tarsia) and those written during periods of prolonged Venetian-Ottoman peace (Membrè, Salvago). In an effort to explore these questions more systematically, let us consider each of the four relazioni in turn.

Alessandri: Refracting Persia through Ottoman Lenses

Despite its basis in diplomatic failure and egregious misrepresentations of the Safavid court (at which the author was in fact never received), Vincenzo degli Alessandri's relazione from Persia, read to the Senate on September 24, 1572, circulated widely among contemporaries.[22] Well over three dozen distinct manuscript copies, summaries, and adaptations of the report survive in libraries and archives from Venice, Verona, and the Friuli to

Florence, Rome, Rimini, Paris, Vienna, Madrid, and London. It was also anthologized alongside Venetian reports from the Ottoman Empire and other foreign lands.[23] This large number of manuscript copies attests to its significant contemporary circulation and potential impact. Moreover, thanks to his sojourn in Safavid lands Alessandri became a Safavid "expert" in Venetian officials' eyes. When a Safavid envoy, Xwāje Mohammad, appeared in Venice a year after Alessandri's return from mission, seeking military alliance against the Ottomans, Alessandri hosted him and facilitated meetings with other government representatives.[24]

How did that come to be? Alessandri, a secretary in the ducal chancery, served in the bailate in the early-to-mid 1560s. In 1566 he petitioned successfully to be admitted to the first cohort of apprentice dragomans. He returned to Venice in 1570, only to be tasked immediately with traveling to Persia, in an effort to convince the Safavid shah Tahmāsp to join a league against the Ottoman sultan Selim II. Alessandri's letter of commission ordered him to present the shah with a letter, appraise him of the war in Hungary and of the Ottoman attack on Cyprus and Dalmatia, and urge him to join forces with Venice and a Christian anti-Ottoman league. The letter of commission listed Alessandri's qualifications laconically as "your experience of Turkish matters."[25] This assessment proved quite apt, when we consider how much Alessandri's report of Persia is shaped by a decidedly Ottoman metropolitan perspective.

Alessandri's *relazione* is a relatively short text of approximately 7,000 words.[26] Like other *relazioni*, it opens with an assurance to his Senate audience that "I will not say anything that I have not seen, or have been told with certainty by various men worthy of faith."[27] Alessandri occasionally inserts himself into the narrative by using first-person verbs and pronouns ("I saw," "my letter"), proclaiming that he has seen things with his own eyes, gleaned information directly from knowledgeable individuals, and visited the court daily.[28] Yet the rate of first-person verbs and pronouns declines precipitously after the opening paragraph, spiking again only in the closing one. The remainder of the narrative includes about a dozen such usages in total.

Although Alessandri never concedes that he was unable to meet with the shah, by all accounts his diplomatic mission was a complete and utter failure.[29] The value of his narrative, it seems, lay largely in its reasonably systematic description, which followed the organizational structure of ambassadorial *relazioni*. Although this is never made explicit, Alessandri's depiction of Shah Tahmāsp, his court, and his realm serves as a (largely distorted) mirror image of his near contemporary, the Ottoman sultan Sü-leyman the Lawgiver (r. 1520–1566), with whom Alessandri was more familiar. This mostly implicit comparison would have likely been evident to well-informed contemporary readers, as Süleyman's reign was idolized not only by contemporaneous Ottoman commentators (and certainly upon his death a few years before Alessandri's mission) but also by European observers, among whom the sultan's political success and military prowess were legendary. Süleyman, as his Ottoman moniker kanuni (the lawgiver) attests, was fabled for his effort to systematize imperial rule, centralize institutions, and promulgate more accessible legal codes and practice (epitomized by the ability to directly petition the divan). By contrast, Alessandri presents Tahmāsp as decidedly uninterested in the people's plight. His account of the masses ("hundreds and even thousands at a time") hurling their complaints at the palace walls unacknowledged while avaricious judges overrun the country, stands in implicit contrast with Süleyman's subjects, who regularly accessed the court through a highly streamlined petitioning process.[30] Alessandri's charge that Tahmāsp had shirked his obligation to hear petitions was particularly grave given the centrality of promulgating justice to the performance of Muslim kingship, and contrasts with the assessment of other near contemporary observers of Safavid court life.[31]

Whereas Süleyman was frequently seen in public, whether through well-orchestrated festivals or when leading his armies on (fabulously successful) military campaigns, Tahmāsp is described as decidedly uninterested in military affairs, staunchly secluded (not having left the palace in twelve years), and infatuated with women and money rather than ruling his realm. That Alessandri systematically refers to Tahmāsp as *re* (king) rather than emperor is telling in this regard. As Elton L. Daniel notes, while shah was routinely translated as king, this fails to convey the institution's historical associations with great antiquity, legitimacy, power, and authority, and specifically with the Persian ideal of sacred kingship. The Safavids in particular adopted the term shah as "the particular and distinctive title of the dynastic rulers of the Iranian plateau."[32] In so doing, they cultivated the long Persianate tradition of divine kingship that understood the ruler as "the Shadow of God"—a divine incarnation to some extent. This tradition found fertile ground in the Twelver Shi'i notion of the Hidden Imam, articulated powerfully in the figure of Shah Ismail, who proclaimed himself a reincarnation of 'Alī. This doctrinal particularity, continued under

Ismail's son Tahmāsp, seems to have been entirely lost on Alessandri, who was likely more familiar with the Christian notion of the king as a temporal power—a sovereign, to be sure, but subordinate to both pope and emperor,[33] especially at a time when kings increasingly struggled to parlay the "social power of religious commitment . . . into political ascendancy."[34]

Yet importantly, Alessandri's main frame of reference for Tahmāsp was hardly European kingship. Rather, he was evidently informed, like most Venetians, by official Ottoman intelligence on the Safavid realm.[35] In fact, he seems to have measured the Safavid ruler against a decidedly Ottoman yardstick, though he barely mentions the Ottomans explicitly. Thus, if Süleyman was renowned for military prowess and for personally leading troops in battle, Alessandri's Tahmāsp is timid and avoids military campaign. If Süleyman's magnificence was legendary, Tahmāsp "frequently sells jewels and other merchandise, buying and selling with the subtlety of a mediocre merchant."[36] If Süleyman's three consorts stayed in his harem, countless women are described as habitually exiting Tahmāsp's court on horseback, meddling in politics, and keeping the shah away from more important engagements. If Süleyman surrounded himself with wise and capable administrators (epitomized by his beloved Ibrahim Paşa, and later by a host of highly competent chancellors and secretaries), Tahmāsp, according to Alessandri, was at the mercy of Kurdish guards and buffoons, resulting in murder and injustice throughout his realm.[37]

Alessandri does not limit the Safavid/Ottoman contrastive relationship to the figure of the ruler, but extends it to other dimensions, particularly material culture. Safavid women, Alessandri writes, "are mostly ugly, though of beautiful features and noble appearance, because their clothes are not as refined as those of Turkish women."[38] Even when Alessandri finds something praiseworthy—the unsurpassed quality and beauty of Persian horses—it turns out to be the result of breeding Karaman and Arab horses, left behind by the Ottoman sultan Bayezid's retreating armies.[39]

Alessandri reserves his greatest contempt for Safavid cities, which he claims are unsightly and dusty, the site of lawlessness and vigilante justice. He describes Tabriz in particularly disparaging tones: "the buildings are most ugly, and there are no mosques or other [monuments] to lend charm to these cities . . . the roads are ugly due to all the dust, making them hard to walk, and as a result in the winters there are extreme mudslides."[40] Plenty of evidence—architectural and narrative alike—suggests that at the very same period that Alessandri was writing this, the shahs initiated massive building projects, including mosques, public squares, and grand avenues throughout Safavid lands.[41] It is true that when Alessandri visited Tabriz it was no longer the capital of the Safavid realm (which had moved to Qazvin ca. 1550, only to be relocated again to Isfahan half a century later, in 1598). However, Tabriz was not entirely abandoned. In fact, it was in Tabriz that the Safavids had inherited from Uzun Hasan an entire new quarter, Nasriyya, which included, in addition to the ruler's private garden complex, "a market, madrasa, mosque, and hospital."[42] The aesthetic qualities of these public projects were the focus of several contemporary European observers, who represented them both textually and visually, and whose works were accessible to the same elite public that Alessandri addressed.[43] Circa 1510, a Venetian merchant marveled at Tabriz's "immense palaces" and "splendid houses."[44] In 1540, Membrè, whose relazione I discuss below, described the entrance to Tabriz as "all gardens and mosques with blue vaults," and noted the presence of multiple squares, baths, bazaars, and caravanserai. He devoted special admiring attention to the Blue Mosque complex, built in the fifteenth century "with well colored marbles," and a "very pretty stream." "The mosque is so well built," Membrè concluded, "that neither in the land of the Turk, nor in all the lands I have seen, have I found another such building."[45] More generally, as Rudi Matthee notes, Venetian writings of the period tended to present Iranians as "refined" and as "heirs to an ancient civilization, in contradistinction to the barbaric and belligerent Turks, who were thought to be the descendants of uncultured tribesmen."[46] Alessandri's reversal of this trope is thus especially noteworthy.

As Ottomanists have convincingly argued, the image of Süleyman the Lawgiver as a paragon of imperial rulership had been carefully crafted during his lifetime by the likes of his grand vizier, Ibrahim Paşa, and the secretary litterateurs Mustafa Ali and Celālzāde Mustafā, only to be further elaborated by later observers.[47] That Tahmāsp and his realm made such a poor impression on Alessandri speaks less to his subject's shortcomings than to the observer's thoroughly Ottomanized outlook.

If the Ottomans are largely an implicit presence in Alessandri's account, most references to them follow the emergent distinction (enforced precisely by diplomatic usage of the time) between Ottoman and Turk. Alessandri applies the former term to the state and its institutions.[48] The latter he uses as an ethnonym for individuals or social groups.[49] Significantly, Alessandri makes no parallel distinction between Safavid and Persian, using the term

Persiani throughout for both, in keeping with Ottoman usage. The term Uzbek is mentioned once (in reference to the ethnicity of an individual, 173). The Qizilbash are not named as such at all, even though the term was regularly mentioned (and translated as "red hats") in other contemporary relazioni.[50]

These nomenclatural choices gain particular significance in light of the enormous political and military importance of the Qizilbash. Their absence from Alessandri's narrative underscores not only the limited empirical basis of his observations but, especially, his reliance on an Ottoman perspective. This is further confirmed by the almost complete absence of Persian nomenclature from the text. To an extent, one would expect the use of Turkish nomenclature, given the functioning of Turkish as the lingua franca of Ottoman and Safavid elites alike. However, Alessandri uses only three unglossed Turkish terms throughout, *çavuş* (ciaussi), *paşa* (bascia) and *voivode* (vayvoda), all exclusively to refer to Ottoman offices. Safavid offices, on the other hand, are almost entirely rendered through silent glosses to Italian.[51] The few glossed terms are similarly of Turkish provenance, including *sultani*—which Alessandri variably glosses as "meaning simply the main leaders of the military," princes, noblemen, or provincial governors, a polysemy in keeping with contemporary Safavid usage, even if its nuances were lost on Alessandri.[52] His overall general avoidance of either Persian or Turkish nomenclature for Safavid offices in favor of silent glossing suggests that his main interest lay less in Safavid cultural alterity and more in the shah's supposed political-cum-ethical failures.

Salvago: Humanism, Medievalism, and Alterity

If the perspective on the Safavid world proffered by Alessandri, a Venetian citizen and secretary, was indelibly shaped by the author's seven-year sojourn in Istanbul, we can observe a mirror process of "Venetianization" in the relazione from North Africa of Giovanni Battista Salvago, an Istanbulite who spent significant time in Venice. Born to an established Catholic dragoman dynasty in Pera in the 1590s, Giovanni Battista was admitted to the bailate as an apprentice dragoman around 1610, following in the footsteps of his paternal grandfather, father, and two older brothers.[53] Nine years later, already fluent in Greek (likely his first language), Italian, Turkish, and Latin, he was appointed road dragoman in place of his brother Giuliano, who had died of the plague a few months earlier.

Giovanni Battista continued to work as road dragoman until 1645, when war broke out between Venice and the Ottomans over the island of Crete. He died shortly thereafter.

In his capacity as road dragoman, Salvago traversed the Ottoman-Venetian border dozens of times to accompany Venetian baili and ambassadors on their way to Istanbul and back. He thus served as a crucial link between two metropoles, often carrying news and material objects from one city to the other. His repeated trips helped Salvago forge ties not only in both capitals but in various provincial settings along the way. In 1642, as the route between Istanbul and Venice became more dangerous, he acquired a safe-conduct from Sultan Ibrahim (r. 1640–1648), which permitted him to dress as a Muslim, don a turban while on the road, and even carry arms—a true testament to his diplomatic stature.[54]

Little is known about Salvago's education beyond his initial language training in the bailate, but a few data points allow us to reconstruct his early trajectory. From 1622 to 1624, he was delayed in Venice, waiting for the newly elected bailo Michele Foscarini to recover from illness. It is quite possible that during these two years he advanced his education, either in Venice itself or in the nearby University of Padua.[55] It was during those two years that Salvago drafted several substantial texts: in 1624 he composed an "epigraph" and a "sonnet" in praise of Doge Francesco Contarini.[56] More revealing are several translations and adaptations of Turkish religious, legal, and historical texts he produced in 1622, conceivably at Foscarini's behest, which underscore Salvago's great interest in recent Ottoman history and in Muslim ritual practice. In particular, Salvago's narrative concerning the deposition of Sultan Osman II in 1622—the first Ottoman regicide and a foundational moment in what Baki Tezcan has dubbed the Second Ottoman Empire—and his portrayal of Muslim ritual practice suggest a conscious attempt to act as an intermediary, introducing Ottoman religious and historical thought to an Italian readership.[57] These texts showcase Salvago's deep familiarity with classical Ottoman genres and his embeddedness in Ottoman intellectual milieus. His report from North Africa, to which I now turn, while evincing a similarly insider understanding of Ottoman imperial governance, also suggests Salvago's effort to distance himself from things Ottoman and to establish his unambiguous position as a loyal, useful, and humanistically inclined Venetian.

In October 1624, rather than accompany the new bailo from Venice to Istanbul, the Senate instructed Salvago to travel as its official representative to the North African Regencies. There he was to negotiate the release of twenty Venetian subjects captured by corsairs the previous June off the shores of Venetian Dalmatia.[58] The relazione he submitted to the Senate upon his return from mission consisted of forty-eight folios ten by ten inches in size, as well as pen drawings of "the famous cities" of Algiers, Tunis, and Bizerte.[59]

Salvago's report is kept in the Venetian State Archives as part of the series of *Relazioni degli Ambasciatori veneti* (B3). Its classification as an ambassadorial report is significant, giving insight into the author's ambiguous position as both an Ottoman subject and a Venetian ambassador.[60] At least two autographed copies of part 2 of the relazione survived outside the Ducal Chancery.[61] Such "leaked" copies of ostensibly secret reports were, of course, fairly common at the time. According to Lucette Valensi, Venetian relazioni enjoyed great popularity among European political elites thanks to their ability to "observe and read the political realities of their day" through an "admirable grid" that followed "a codified order" and articulated "what advantage Venice could gain from the existing situation."[62]

Salvago's relazione from North Africa certainly adheres to many of the rules of the genre regarding the ordering of information and in its analytical rather than descriptive intent. It consists of three unequal parts, corresponding to the three sets of questions that Salvago had been instructed to address in writing in his letter of appointment.[63] The first part describes his negotiations with officials in North Africa regarding the ransoming of enslaved Venetian subjects (pages 20–52), including a section on the corsairs' objections to the Venetian position (34–36); the provisional agreement reached (36–38); and a translation of a response to the doge's letter by Hüsrev Paşa, the regent of Algiers (50–52). The second part of the relazione describes the North African Regencies (53–90). It includes, in addition to an historical overview of the region since Roman times (53–55) and a discussion of the evolution of the corsairs' naval technologies (56–65, 78–79), appraisals of the Regencies' political institutions (65–72), material culture (69, 73, 76, 81–83), and ethnic composition (75, 77–78). It concludes with physical descriptions of the cities of Algiers (83–85), Tunis (85–86), and Bizerte (86–87) as well as cursory mentions of other North African urban centers, including Cairo, Tripoli, and Fez. Finally, the third and shortest part of the relazione (91–98) provides details on the enslaved Venetians held in Algiers and Tunis, including their numbers, places of provenance, previous professions, and current employment.[64]

While mostly disparaging in tone, Salvago's interpretation of Ottoman
North Africa tacitly acknowledges the complexities of Ottoman social and
ethnic distinctions and signals their continuities with Roman and medieval political structures. His report sometimes reinforces a binary view of
"Europeans" versus "Ottomans" but at others undermines it. This chapter's epigraph suggests Salvago's acute historical and proto-psychological
analytical skills. In that passage, Salvago seems to capture some of the
main contradictions of colonial societies in general, and of Ottoman North
Africa in particular, addressing processes of social mobility and reproduction, the intersection of ethnicity and gender, perceptions of "mixing," and
the historical transformation of both metropolitan and colonial elites over
time.[65] By recognizing the social distance between Ottoman metropolitan
and provincial elites, and the growing autonomy of North Africa from
Istanbul, Salvago professed a distinctly metropolitan Ottoman perspective.[66] At the same time, he harnessed historical analysis and his humanist
learning to the service of Venetian rather than Ottoman imperial aims.
He regularly distances himself from the people he observes along the way
and, by extension, from their allies, the Ottomans, using several strategies.

First, Salvago assumes a specifically Venetian perspective, one that envisions the North African corsairs; the Ottomans; and their Western allies,
chiefly the Dutch, French, and English, as equally distant. He repeatedly
reminds his readers that if it were not for the Atlantic seaboard powers,
the corsairs would be long gone.[67] These Atlantic powers also happened
to be Venice's fiercest commercial rivals in the early seventeenth century.
Salvago suggests that it is not only through cunning and violence but also
through friendship and alliance that the North African corsairs have obtained from "the Ponentine nation" vital artisans and much needed skilled
professionals.[68]

Second, Salvago portrays North Africa societies as "mixed," using a
hodgepodge of religious, social, historical, and climactic explanations
to account for their composition. He distinguishes between many ethnic
groups: *Africani, Barbareschi, Turchi, Turchi primitivi, Turchi nativi, Turchi asiatici, Mori, Mori terazzani, Mori bianchi, Arabi,* and finally, *Culogli*
(from the Turkish *kuloğlan,* literally sons of the sultan's slaves). The latter,
according to Salvago, are the offspring of Turks and local *cittadine bian-
chissime,* or "very white female town-dwellers."[69] This consciousness of
Ottoman North Africa's great ethnic and racial diversity and of "Turk" as
an ethnic rather than a juridical descriptor is particularly noteworthy.

Contemporaneous inhabitants of the region often referred to the Ottoman military-administrative elite as "Turks," a term that those elites themselves sometimes accepted.[70] Yet according to Maria-Pia Pedani, the first recorded use of *turco* in Venetian documents to describe ethnic belonging rather than membership in the Ottoman dynastic ruling family dates to a 1637 relazione by Secretary Angelo Alessandri that distinguishes between *turchi* and *turchi nativi*, as well as between *impero ottomano* and *ottomani*, recognizing that the state was Ottoman, not Turkish.[71] Salvago, whose relazione predates Angelo Alessandri's by over a decade, was one of Alessandri's chief dragomans during the latter's term of office in the bailate in the late 1630s. This suggests the potential role that Salvago and fellow dragomans may have played in introducing Venetian diplomatic and bureaucratic elites to the Ottoman Empire's ethnic complexity and in elaborating a terminology for discussing it.[72] At the same time, like many of his Venetian predecessors, Salvago occasionally conflates Turkish with Ottoman. Ultimately, he presents the Turkish element as what unifies North Africa's ethnic heterogeneity, imputing to the Turks nothing less than the creation of Barbary as a political unit:

> The corsairs of the province are called Barbaresques, but in reality they are a mass and a gang of ruffians of many races and progeny. The founders were Turks and they instituted a new militia of Janissaries in Barbary, ordaining that, except for Moors, Romani, and Jews, all the Nations should be admitted.[73]

If Salvago credits the Turks with being the *originarii* (founders) of the North African regencies while recognizing that others—Moors, Romani, and Jews—were there first, chronologically speaking, it is because for him it is Ottoman law that reigns in the region and defines its political structures.[74] In that sense, Salvago's perception of North African society and politics was distinctly Ottomancentric, bracketing the region's other genealogies and pre-Ottoman continuities.[75] His perception is a telling product of its time in accepting as a given the corsairs' predominance in Algerian and Tunisian military-political structures as a whole.[76]

Notwithstanding the Ottomans' foundational role in Salvago's account of North African state formation, the legal and political relationship between the region and its Ottoman overlords in his narrative is far from settled. In fact, the passage above continues to characterize the Turks who arrive in the Regencies as "evil-doers, transgressors, murderers, assassins, swindlers, dropouts, forgers, vagabonds and wanderers"; that is, marginal people and outlaws, hardly representative of the Ottoman Empire's political core. Moreover, according to Salvago, these marginal social types are assisted by renegades and adventurers from Christian Europe.

In some sense, Salvago's attention to North Africa's ethnic heterogeneity serves to authorize his implicit claim to profound knowledge of the local society despite the brevity of his sojourn there. It also serves to erase the region's Roman past, a legacy it could otherwise share with other parts of the Ottoman-Venetian ecumene, thus unsettling any easy civility-barbarity dichotomy.[77] According to Salvago, Algiers and Tunis may have been Roman cities, but their current inhabitants are all parvenus: Turkish criminals, Granadan Muslims exiled from Iberia, merchants from the East (the Levant) and the West (the Netherlands, England and France), and renegades from Italy. These non-autochthonous elements also account, in Salvago's eyes, for what little industry exists in North Africa. Salvago credits no inventions to locals, strictly speaking.[78] Manufacturing gunpowder and building harquebuses are the only technologies he assigns to the Moors, but even these inventions, he is quick to note, came from Fez, where the Moors had learned them from their brethren expelled from Granada.[79] It is these newcomers who had introduced metal foundries to North Africa, but "with little success, and it is believed they will not make much profit."[80]

Salvago denies North Africa not only industry and innovation but indeed any civility. It is on this issue in particular that his divergence from Leo Africanus, by far the best read early modern Italianate authority on the region, becomes most clear.[81] In Leo's narrative, binary oppositions operate to define *his* Africa—white, urban, socially stratified and culturally Arabized—in stark contrast to both the nomadic tribal Berbers lurking outside city walls and the unknown societies of sub-Saharan Africa. Port cities, for Leo, are sites of civility and civilization; they are nodes that connect the Mediterranean's North African shores with larger networks of exchange encompassing both Europe and Arabia. To his contemporary European readers, everything in Leo's description of Algiers and Tunis would have evoked a sense of familiarity and orderliness, a link between Arab and European high learning.[82]

Past or present Arabic letters, or indeed any sense of a larger cultural sphere in which the societies of North Africa partake, are largely absent from Salvago's account. For him, Africa "in ancient and modern times, whether due to celestial influence or to natural antipathy, has always been in various guises inimical and troublesome on the opposite side of Europe."[83] Salvago contrasts Africa with Europe, rather than the Mediterranean with sub-Saharan Africa, as did Leo and, we may add, the many classical authors on whom Leo built, including Pliny.[84] For Salvago, the networks that connect North Africa with the outside world are only those of corsairs who raid the opposite shores of the Mediterranean in search of captives.

For Leo, clothing could operate as a sign not only of civility but of cosmopolitan refinement. In his elaborate, fifty-six-page-long description of the city of Fez, Leo mentions that "the inhabitants of the city, that is, the nobles, are really civilized people, and in winter they wear clothes made of foreign wool."[85] For Salvago, the same wool is the mark of simplicity: "The corsairs, both great and small, wear absolutely nothing but woolen cloth and never silk, very different from the superb dress of Constantinople."[86]

Salvago's contrast between corsairs' woolen cloth and the lavish silk of Istanbul underscores his vision of the Regencies as a colonial backwater. Throughout his report he shows little interest in fitting the Regencies into any larger contemporary Ottoman framework. He pays much greater attention to the corsairs' ships, military might, and trafficking in captives than to the Regencies' social hierarchies or political structures. Rather than contextualize these structures within the broader Ottoman polity of which they clearly formed a part, Salvago employs a classicizing and archaizing vocabulary to describe them as a "popular republic" and a "military democracy" or a "republic" now turned into a "despotic regime" through the "tyranny" of the dey.[87]

These archaizing and classicizing gestures are central to Salvago's self-fashioning as a learned man of letters. They underscore both the spatiotemporal distance of his object—the North African Regencies—from the Ottoman imperial metropole and the author's own classical erudition. They are, indeed, in line with at least some late humanists' archaizing strategies in translating Ottoman historical narratives into Latin and European vernaculars.[88] As a final example, here is how he introduces the "Turks" in his narrative, collapsing widely disparate temporal and spatial units into a supposedly coherent and cohesive account of origins:

New Thracians, native Tatars, people of Gog and Magog as the Divine Historian St. John calls them in the Apocalypse and so characterizes them with occult mystery; having renounced the pastoral life in the Caspian Mountains, wishing to rule they had long ago left Scythia, commonly called Tartary, and had come to occupy Thrace, today called Romania, a place where for the duration of centuries, not of decades or years, they had contact with all sorts of civil people, but still they have not acquired any kind of urbanity, that is they have not departed from their harsh Scythian and ferocious Thracian [origins], and in every way maintain the original rustic harshness and the inborn savagery, which they have never relinquished nor forgotten.[89]

Combining biblical, Greek, Roman, and medieval tropes of Otherness, such as Gog and Magog, the Scythians and the Tatars, Salvago presents seventeenth-century Turks as the epitome of barbarity.[90] Despite centuries of contact with the civilized world of Christendom, Salvago suggests, "Turks" are impermeable to change, as barbarity runs in their blood. As noted above, Salvago was born and raised in Istanbul, and had many friends among Ottoman elites.[91] His framing the account of Barbary within a schema of Turkish barbarity tells us little about his own understanding of either the Ottomans or of North Africa; it reveals, instead, how much he trusted his Venetian readers' predisposition to accept such a biblically and classically inflected account of Turkish ethnogenesis, and his willingness to tell them just what they expected to hear.

Other Venetian dragomans in Istanbul invoked the trope of "barbarity" too, often for the same purpose of implicitly reaffirming their own affinity with Venice and distance from the Ottomans. In 1649, Christoforo Tarsia sought Venetian backing in a civil litigation in which he was involved, claiming that without it he would surely turn into "food for the voracity of these barbarians."[92] A decade later Tarsia again deployed "Turkish barbarity" in an effort to mobilize more junior colleagues into collective bargaining.[93] While that attempt was crushed shortly after its inception, it left an indelible impression, forcing Venetian authorities more fully to take dragomans' interests into consideration and to acknowledge their collective power. These and other similar cases highlight the extent to which dragomans sought to play on Venetian fears of alleged Ottoman "barbarity" to achieve their own ends. They thus underscore the role in articulating emerging discourses about Ottoman otherness of precisely those, like Venetian dragomans, who could claim insider knowledge of Ottoman society.

The analysis of Salvago's North African relazione has underlined the importance of his claims to insider knowledge in authorizing his role as diplomat and intermediary, but also these claims' unstable and paradoxical nature. Intimacy with things Ottoman (and a partially Ottoman-metropolitan perspective on the Ottomans' North African colonial periphery) was a precondition for Salvago's claims to knowledge. Yet his authority also depended, or at least so he thought, on ultimately distancing himself from his Ottoman object of description. By presenting Turks as barbarians and Scythians, Tatars, and people of Gog and Magog, Salvago drew on a humanist trope of some political urgency, as well as on long-standing medieval topoi.[94] However, more than signaling the Turks' barbarity, in his *relazione* Salvago was indexing his own worthiness as an "acculturated" Venetian subject, fully grounded in classicizing humanist thought and the medieval tradition that formed its basis.

Membrè: Bivalence at Court

Having considered two metropolitan dragomans who had spent substantial time "on the other side," let us now examine a *relazione* by a colonial subject who hailed from a socially and spatially marginalized location, but who climbed up the ranks to become one of the most successful dragomans of the era.

Very little is known of Michele Membrè's early life, and opinions vary as to his provenance. Born on Cyprus ca. 1510 (he reported his age as thirty years old at the time of his mission to Persia in 1539), he claimed Greek as his native tongue, and shared ancestry with the Catholic-Greek nobleman Bernardo Benedetti, in whose household in Nicosia he grew up. Yet he also spoke Arabic and Turkish (perhaps thanks to his work as a commercial agent in Syria and Anatolia in his youth), and asserted Circassian roots and command of Persian as well.[95] It is possible that he had some Arab Christian ancestry, given his interest in Arabic Christian liturgy later on in life, and evident command of literary Arabic and Syriac.[96] As Arbel notes, it was undoubtedly his linguistic acumen (and, we might add, evident entrepreneurial spirit) that catapulted Membrè from Cyprus to Isfahan, and from Istanbul and Cairo to Venice, where he eventually became the longest-serving public dragoman on record, and amassed significant influence. This was in no small part thanks to his powerful position with the Board of Trade, which he monopolized from 1550 until his death in 1594.[97] One indication of Membrè's unusual wealth is his patronage of a massive altarpiece for the parish church of San Felice (figure 3.1). The work, by the renowned Florentine artist Domenico Passignano (Cresti), was commissioned during Passignano's Venetian sojourn in the 1580s. The inscription unmistakably identifies Membrè as the patron: CHRISTO RE-DEMP. ALTARE AVGVSTISS. MICHAEL MAMBRE REIP[UBLIC]AE FIDELIS INTERPRES RELIGIONIS GRATIA FACIĒ[N]DVM CVRAVI ("The faithful interpreter of the Republic, Michele Membrè, took care to restore the altar of Christ the Redeemer for the love of religion"). The painting depicts the elderly Membrè on the lower left, praying to Jesus and San Felice, a saint with strong connections to Mediterranean commerce whose father hailed from Syria.[98]

Membrè's artistic entrepreneurship did not begin with his patronage of Passignano, however. As early as 1550 he collaborated with the Venetian cartographer Giacomo Gastaldi to produce a map of "all the cities and realms in the parts of Asia, from the Mediterranean sea eastward, including the whole of Anatolia, Syria and Persia with the land of the Sophi, and then toward the northeast, to the land of Cathay and southward to India and the Spice Islands."[99] Three years later, in 1553, he assisted the fabled cosmographer Giovanni Battista Ramusio in preparing a world map (or possibly maps). In 1568 a Senate resolution linked him to the printing of a heart-shaped world map designed ca. 1559/60 for the Ottoman market. Membrè, as Arbel suggests, may well have played a significant role in producing this enigmatic and ambitious object, a role masked by the pseudonym of "Hajji Ahmet," a purported North African princely author.[100]

When Membrè presented his report from Persia to the Senate in 1542, however, he was still a colonial upstart, an unknown quantity to his patrician audience, and, to boot, a man of rather tenuous claim to any formal status in Venice. This subaltern position strongly shapes his narrative. As Morton notes, Membrè's style, structure, and thematic foci differ markedly from those of more elite and better-educated Venetian relazioni writers of the time. He largely avoids analytical "synoptic statements" about the Safavid army or geography, for example, makes no reference to Christian Safavid subjects beyond the borderlands, and in general keeps his observations chronological and anecdotal.[101]

Not only does Membrè's narrative style diverge from a standard relazione but it bears strong affinity with a different genre altogether, the picaresque novel. Membrè presents himself throughout as a social outsider both to the Ottoman and Safavid realms he traverses and the rarefied circles of the Venetian metropolitan patriciate he addresses. In a series of hair-raising adventures, his cunning allows him first to reach the Safavid court against all odds, then to "escape," cross the Strait of Hormuz to Goa, and sail to Portugal. By presenting his departure from the Safavid court as an escape, even when extant documentation clearly points to the shah having granted him permission to depart, Membrè once again turns readers' attention to his own ingenuity. And like the *picaro*, Membrè does not achieve personal growth from his spatial and social mobility. Rather, mobility serves to repeatedly affirm his unwavering loyalty to—and orientation toward—Venice as both the object of his political quest and his ultimate destination. (This does not prevent him from presenting himself to the shah at his first audience as "a Venetian gentleman.")[102]

Both Membrè's marginal social and spatial provenance and his limited encounters with the Safavids' Persian-speaking populations are crucial to keep in mind, as Membrè's relazione can be read as an extended apologia, an effort to demonstrate his affective attachment to Venice as a loyal and worthy subject. The following anecdote, in which he positions himself not only as a diplomatic emissary, but as a cultural and theological translator too, illustrates both aspects of his writing:

> As I was talking to the Sayyids [of Osku], they said that I should tell them why the Venetians had a lion for their coat of arms; for they marvelled much at that, saying that the lion belonged to the Shah, for 'Alī is an invisible lion. To men it appeared that he was a man, but he was a lion, sent by God to destroy the idolaters. So, in their histories, the arms of 'Alī are represented as a lion. That was why they wished to know. To which I replied that from this they could see by trial whether the Signoria was a friend of the Shah or not; for they have such love for 'Alī that they carry his arms and adore him, and are more devoted to him than others. They said to me that I must tell how that had come to pass. I said to them,
>
> "At the time when 'Alī was alive, although in these parts he was in the form of a man, in the parts where Venice is he used to go in the form of a lion and appeared so visibly; and he spoke in the ears of holy men of the word of God, of God's miracles, and of heavenly things. So they wrote it all down, which has made a book, which they now call Gospel, and in Turkish İncil."
>
> And he said to me that they admitted that the said Gospel was true, and they too believed in the said İncil. And with that they were left well-informed by me; and they said that I should be called *muvālī*, that

is a person beloved of 'Alī; and that it would be a greater sin to kill one Venetian than a thousand Ottomans.[103]

This passage allows us to move beyond the question of representations of Otherness, so palpable in Salvago's writings. Instead, it suggests how dragomans—inherently instrumental in commensurating Venetian socio-conceptual vocabularies with those of Islamicate societies in which they became embedded—also sought to capture that process of commensuration in their own texts. In this specific example, Membrè underscores not simply his nimbleness at addressing fraught spiritual questions and harnessing them to specific political agendas (i.e., furthering the cause of a Safavid-Venetian anti-Ottoman alliance). Rather, he intimates his capacity to engage in the theological disputation beloved by the Safavid court, "accommodating" Shi'a cosmology to some extent, while never relinquishing a staunchly Catholic Venetian perspective.[104]

Through the use of the dialogue form and its simulacrum of verbatim reporting of face-to-face interaction, Membrè recounts a conversation he purportedly had with a group of sayyids (i.e., descendants of the Prophet Muhammad through his grandson) in the town of Osku (now in Iran's East Azerbaijan province). In his narrative, it is the dignitaries who beseech him to interpret the Venetian iconography of the Lion of St. Mark and thus act as a cultural intermediary. By framing the conversation thus, Membrè turns the narrative on its head and glosses for his readers the intricacies of Safavid Shi'a theology instead. In the carefully wrought explanation he provides, ostensibly for his Safavid listeners (but, in effect, for his audience in the Venetian Senate), Membrè turns a potentially controversial theological disputation into a political parable about the natural affinity between Safavids and Venetians (and their shared hatred of Ottomans). Along the way, he morphs 'Alī the Messenger into Mark the Apostle—not as two figures bearing some affinity, but as one and the same, collapsing significant spatiotemporal divides between Islamic and Christian cosmologies. In the story's coda, Membrè's keen listeners confer on him the epithet *muvālī*, "one beloved by 'Alī," while at the same time making him a token of the type "Venetian." Earlier in the narrative, he presents himself to the sayyids as "Venetian" and even a "Venetian nobleman." Their proclamation thus secures rhetorically his Venetian identity.

A final confirmation of his Venetian identity was provided months later in Hormuz, when Membrè found himself in an audience in front of a Portuguese captain who suspected his motives and believed him to be an Ottoman spy. To the rescue—at least according to Membrè—came a Safavid ambassador en route to the Mughal court, who recognized Membrè from Tabriz and vouched for his identity as a true Venetian ambassador. As a colonial subject of only tenuous affinity to the metropole he had yet to set foot in, Membrè made a dual move, first to arrogate to himself Venetian title, and then to reinforce it through the reported speech of others. His strategy illustrates the work of self-positioning that non-Venetian, non-patrician dragomans' relazioni were meant to achieve. It underscores the primary address of relazioni to a Venetian patrician audience which, by accepting the relazione's truth claims, was also to accept its author as, aspirationally if not juridically, a member of its exclusive club.

Ultimately, and like other dragoman authors, Membrè's effort to position himself not simply as a Venetian but as a consummate representative of Venetian interests is also worked out through his enactment of linguistic and political mediation. Even as the narrative arc takes Membrè away from the Venetian-Ottoman maritime borderlands to the heart of the Safavid realm and beyond, to the Indian Ocean and to Portuguese Goa, he continues to filter his interactions through the lens of Venetian-Ottoman relations. Linguistically, Turkish elements permeate his narrative throughout. In the example above, Membrè uses the term *seitler* (Turkish plural of *seit*, from the Arabic *sayyid*, an honorific for descendants of the Prophet) to describe his courtly Safavid interlocutors.[105] He also provides glosses for Turkish terms, in some cases repeatedly, throughout the narrative. He glosses *caravassarà* (caravanserai) using the Venetian construction *zoè fontego* (that is, a fondaco) five out of the ten times he mentions the term, all in close succession.[106] He explains that minarets (*minara*, using the Turkish term again) are *come campanelli alti* (like tall bell-towers).[107] While he occasionally glosses entire phrases, the vast majority of his glosses are of (Turkish) nomenclature for officeholders, in line with dragomans' translation practices more broadly. As Morton points out, Membrè's deep embedding among the Qizilbash is at least partly to blame for his Turkophone-inflected account of Safavid society, and his relative neglect of the empire's settled, Persophone rural and property-owning urban populations, including the educated elites who dominated the administration.[108] As in Alessandri's case, Membrè's Turkophone bent may have reflected his own linguistic limitations. Certainly his overwhelming focus on the court, not unlike that of other dragoman relazione authors, was also informed by the strictures of the genre and, especially, by an aspirational identification with courtly society more generally.

Tarsia: The Picaresque

Such self-positioning as a cultural intermediary and commensurator extraordinaire became less available a century and a half later, when Tommaso Tarsia penned his relazione in 1683. Instead of cultural commensuration, Tarsia's relazione stands out in cultivating the authorial voice. If Membrè's narrative sees little character development, Tarsia's operates as a drama centered on the author's actions, thoughts, and feelings. In a remarkable divergence from the genre's usual thematics and poetics, Tarsia says less about his ostensible topic, the second Ottoman siege of Vienna, than about his own household's trials and tribulations. A bold parallelism between domestic and political affairs informs the entire concluding section of his relazione, in which Tarsia demonstrates how his diplomatic acumen allowed him to put an end to the travails of both family and Venetian representatives, persecuted by a local Ottoman deputy in the author's absence. While under arrest and fully expecting an impending death sentence, Tarsia is interrogated by the grand vizier and the mufti. He recounts his attempt to clear the name of his brother Giacomo, who had assisted the Venetian secretary Capello to escape. In defending his brother Tarsia also strives to represent the Venetian perspective on said escape, which precipitated a sharp deterioration in Venetian-Ottoman diplomatic relations. Overcoming political, financial, and physical adversity, Tarsia makes his way from Vienna via Belgrade to Edirne, where the sultan had relocated his court. There, he charms his contacts at court, secures a sultanic edict and safe passage, and promptly presents these to the local deputy in Istanbul, thus bringing to an end the woes of both his *famiglia* (family) and the *fameglia* (bailate). The Tarsias take possession of their house, the bailate dragomans all come out of hiding, and Tommaso himself retires to a nearby village to recover and await new orders from Venice. Tarsia's ability to serve simultaneously as a Venetian emissary (vis-à-vis the Ottomans) and as a dragoman (relating the exchange back to his Venetian masters) is premised on collapsing the distinction between the two. His relazione, at this point, reads like a dispatch from a head of mission. In the closing sentence Tarsia marks his retreat from public view so he could put his life and family affairs in order, while assuming the voice of a mature civil servant awaiting further order from his Venetian masters.[109]

The telos of Tarsia's lengthy narrative of over 24,000 words is thus the dual celebration of both Venetian public interest and the author himself as its undisputed champion. His feat gains special poignancy when we recall that Tarsia's father, Christoforo, had narrowly escaped Ottoman imprisonment in Edirne *and* lost the family house to fire only a few decades earlier. The son's triumph here is not only in restoring patriarchal order but in superseding his father. Fittingly, his narrative includes over 150 first-person verbs and pronouns, distributed throughout, but particularly prominent toward the end, as Tarsia aims to fuse the political-diplomatic and the personal.

The self-involved nature of Tarsia's *relazione* is well illustrated in the following report of Tarsia's conversations with Ottoman officials, wherein they plead with him to assume the position of Ottoman grand dragoman in the wake of the demise of the former incumbent, Alexandros Mavrocordato:

Since the Christmas holiday was on the same day that immediately followed the execution of the late Grand Vizier, out of reverence for that venerable day I, with others, did not attend court, but the next day, letters from Thököly arrived and I was promptly called to translate them. I went immediately, and found out that the Grand Chancellor had taken the aforementioned letters to the ağa of the Janissaries, himself formerly a top general, and therefore the *kapıcılar kahyasi* [head chamberlain] with the *çavuş başı* [head messenger], who were there, told me to wait with them for a while, as it could not be long before the same Grand Chancellor would appear with the letters to be translated. To that effect, as I stayed over with them, they began to talk to me of various things, and in conclusion, under seal of full confidentiality, communicated to me that it was certain that Mavrocordato would be deposed from the dragomanate of the Porte, and that if I were in the least so inclined, they have a feeling that in that case that office would be leaning toward me ["my weakness"]. To which they urged me as good friends not to resist, but rather to embrace with good will the opportunity, which should not preclude my serving another prince, given that at other times dragomans of the Porte had been subjects who had also served the Caesarean Emperor [i.e., the Holy Roman Emperor], and to hasten my trip toward Edirne to that effect. Surprised by this extravagant proposal, I did not know what to add in order to avoid this appointment other than my inadequacy for the position, and with that, given the late hour and with the letters not having arrived I excused myself, to come back to translate them the next day. Mavrocordato having heard of my being visited by the two above-mentioned ministers, unsuspectedly passed his note to the Grand Chancellor (with whom he held the closest trust), supplicating that he had already intended to publicly translate the above-mentioned letters.[110]

Tarsia continues to narrate the suspenseful episode in some detail. Its successful conclusion underscores his tactful ability to extricate himself from an undesirable appointment. The not-so-subtle point of the story is both to suggest to his Venetian patrons his excellent reputation and hence his lucrative career prospects at the Ottoman court and his consummate diplomatic skill. Along the way, he makes sure to remind his audience of his fast friendships with top Ottoman courtiers—the head chamberlain, head messenger, and grand chancellor—and the calculating nature of those friendships, all intended, in the final account, to serve Venetian interests, to which Tarsia once again hyperbolically declares his allegiance. It is Venice, he proclaims, for whom he would "rather live and die with that incorrupt faith, suckled with milk under the propitious auspices of my natural and invincible Prince." [111]

In keeping with his focus on diplomatic mediation, Tarsia establishes a sense of Ottoman alterity less by engaging in ethnographic description, and more by repeatedly denouncing Ottoman political forms. His relazione reads at times as a laundry list of anti-Ottoman slogans, where variations on the qualifiers "tyrannical," "barbarous," and "despotic" figure prominently.[112] Such denunciations allow Tarsia to retain his ideological distance from the Ottomans even while flaunting his great social familiarity with several courtiers. In contrast, and unsurprisingly, the League's forces are described as valorous, courageous, and heroic.[113]

Tarsia conveys his familiarity with the Ottomans through linguistic mastery too. As a seasoned dragoman fully trained in Venetian diplomatic protocol, Tarsia uses glossing to underscore his superb command of both Ottoman and Latin. He offers a handful of glosses of Ottoman nomenclature, particularly official titles, such as *talhiszi, o refferendario, caimacam, cioè suo luogotenente appresso il sultano*, but he also introduces a substantial number of unglossed Ottoman terms.[114] This strategy of non-translation may signal his trust in his intended audience's familiarity with the intricacies of Ottoman government and military structures; more likely, it enables Tarsia to display his own command thereof.[115] The same can be said for his use of Latin.[116]

As a lifelong dragoman, and by far the latest of the four dragoman relazioni writers discussed here, Tarsia may well have possessed the most standardized translation practices, informed by an implicit style sheet that defined which terms required glossing and which ones did not. He was also, notably, reporting about unfolding political and military developments in the culturally familiar Ottoman-Habsburg borderlands, rather than offering an ethnographic account of a geographically and epistemologically distant court, such as Isfahan or Tunis. These differences in objects of observation, however, are hardly the only or even primary determining factors shaping Tarsia's linguistic choices. Of greater impact was the growing conventionalization of Ottoman nomenclature in Venetian diplomatic writings in the course of the seventeenth century. Thus, throughout his relazione, Tarsia maintains a relatively consistent distinction between *Ottomano, ottomano/i, Turco/chi, turco/chi,* and *Mussulmani.* The upper-case form *Ottomano* appears primarily to designate the state and military.[117] The lowercase forms *ottomano,* and, especially, *ottomani,* refer to collectivities of Ottoman subjects. *Turchi* is used for roughly the same purpose, whereas *turchi* is applied mostly as the ethnic mark of individuals and, especially, of social groups, such as enslaved persons and merchants.[118] The term *Mussulmani* is used to refer exclusively to the collectivity of Muslims, often in explicit or implicit contrast to *Christiani.* Awareness of difference between ethnolinguistic, confessional, and juridical categories of belonging once again serves, inter alia, to underscore Tarsia's cultural fluency and thoroughly Venetianized outlook.

On a more granular level, Tarsia notes ministers' place of provenance mostly as an occasion to disparage them.[119] For example, the executed former grand vizier and military commander Kara Mustafa Paşa was "of the vilest birth," having originated from Merzifon (in north-central Anatolia).[120] Elsewhere, Tarsia also imputes moral character based on ethnicity when describing a near-rape case and stating that the assailant, "in order to get greater revenge, turned to fraud, the usual style of this nation."[121] Perhaps Tarsia was aiming in these statements to approximate for his Venetian readers the Ottoman awareness of *cins* (ethnoregional identity), which, as Metin Kunt has argued, often informed contemporary Ottoman elites' solidarities.[122] In doing so he also reflected long-standing Istanbulite courtly disdain for the rural backwaters of Anatolia.

READING THE FOUR relazioni by Alessandri, Salvago, Membrè, and Tarsia contrastively has highlighted how their positionality, sense of audience, and biographical trajectories profoundly shaped their narratives, from the events, places, and people they report on to the minute linguistic strategies they deployed. The highly conventionalized patrician Venetian relazione, well established as a genre by the middle of the sixteenth century, was undoubtedly an important yardstick by which decidedly non-patrician (and sometimes non-Venetian) dragomans measured their own diplomatic-cum-literary performance. At the same time, as seen throughout the chapter, if dragomans' relazioni repeatedly aimed to make visible the work of mediation and to sustain their authors' claim to trans-imperial cultural fluency, these claims ultimately reaffirm dragomans' deep embedding in Ottoman courtly society.

The relazione is just one genre where dragomans' enduring contributions to knowledge of Ottoman and Safavid worlds in early modern Europe are evident. As part of a broader field of textual and visual production, these relazioni underscore why their dragoman authors cannot be viewed merely as an "appendix" to the grand narrative of Mediterranean history, working in the shadow of powerful ambassadors and consuls. If the "new diplomatic history" has highlighted the role of relatively subaltern social actors in the development of diplomatic practice and protocol, the point is not simply to "set the record straight," but to consider how such actors contributed substantively to the "methodization of observation," the articulation of enduring epistemologies and methodologies in the study of society and culture.[123] The remainder of this book explores how dragomans' diverse contributions—inscribed materially in their hands, implicit in their reported speech throughout diplomatic correspondence, and epistemologically vital for the synthesis of metropolitan Ottoman and Venetian sovereignty regimes—in fact *generated* the diplomatic archive and shaped some of its key modalities of knowledge production.

CHAPTER 4

Visualizing a Space of Encounter

A THREE-QUARTER PORTRAIT (FIGURE 4.1) shows a young man in semi-profile, exhibiting several of the hallmarks of early modern elite masculinity: a paunchy figure, a protruding elbow, and a carefully trimmed mustache. The dagger under his belt, whose hilt he holds in his right hand, and his clothing—a cream-colored brocaded kaftan and matching pink fur-lined coat and *kalpak* cap—proclaim his profession as a dragoman and his setting as Ottoman, as do the tassels that hang from the dark drapes that frame his figure.[1] The man's left hand casually rests on his cap, positioned strategically on a side table next to a letter bearing a large seal (his *berat*, or letter patent) and a pile of books. The spines read *Galice, Grece, Turcice, Persice,* and *Arabice,* alluding—with some degree of hyperbole, no doubt—to the owner's multilingual prowess. A family's coat of arms hangs to his left, while an inscription to the right identifies the subject as Gian Rinaldo Carli, the son of Girolamo of the nobility of Capodistria, and as "the Most Serene Venetian Republic's interpreter at the Ottoman Porte," aged twenty-two in the year 1679.

A second portrait of Carli (figure 4.2) bears the inscription "Serenissimae Repvblicae Venetiarum Interpres Magnvs"—Grand Dragoman of the Most Serene Republic of Venice, a title he obtained in 1716, at age seventy. This full-length portrait both recalls and updates the earlier representation.[2] Here Carli is wearing a similar brocaded kaftan (now with an Ottoman slipper clearly visible underneath), but the fur-trimmed coat has been replaced by a more regal, salmon-pink silken mantle with a shimmering blue lining and golden clasps, and the brocaded sash is replaced by a gilded belt, calling attention to Carli's more rotund figure. Gone are the youthful dagger, the sealed *berat* and the multilingual dictionaries, the family coat-of-arms, and much of Carli's hair. The older Carli stands in semi-profile on a checkered marble floor in front of a dark curtain that accentuates and focuses attention on his obligatory outward-pointing elbow, while his receding hairline unmistakably signals his more advanced age.[3] Rather than resting on a table to call attention to the subject's professional legitimacy (metonymically captured in the earlier portrait by the dictionaries and *berat* as signs of linguistic and juridical authorization), the now oversized cap is held by a young black page, partially camouflaged by the dark curtain but lavishly dressed to match his master's livery.[4] The page's diminutive figure and obsequious posture clearly mark him as an enslaved person, in keeping with a long iconographic tradition.[5] His physiognomy is fittingly stereotypical, with a bright white eye in the middle of a face in profile and wide red lips. His livery—a striped, gilded, and silken white kaftan with pearl buttons and a pendant pearl earring—reflects his master's wealth. The page nearly mimics Carli's posture, standing in the same angle with his right elbow bent, while keeping his arm close to the body, to avoid the implication of aggressive mastery. His right hand holds his master's grotesquely oversize cap, while his left, outstretched arm is partially hidden behind the curtain. If Carli's face is turned to contemplate the viewer with an expression of impenetrable confidence, the page attentively tilts his face toward his master.

The presence of the page distinguishes Carli's portrait from a series of dragoman portraits discussed below, and adds a potential twist: in contemporary European iconography young black pages—particularly those wearing livery and pearl earrings—were closely associated with "Turkishness." The representation here might therefore imply that, regardless of his distinctly Ottoman garb, Carli is a master over Turks.[6] This may explain why the page is represented as phenotypically black at a time when, as we saw in Chapter 2, most persons enslaved in Istanbulite dragomans' households hailed from the Black Sea and Mediterranean regions.

In addition to the Black page, both Carli's by then well-established Istanbulite identity and his elite status are further bolstered by the pendant portrait of his wife, Caterina de Negri (figure 4.39), in whose direction Carli's finger points. I return to these and other portraits in the series at the end of the chapter in order to consider what visions of dragomans' Istanbulite lifeworlds they mediated to audiences far away. But first, in order to understand what professional and genealogical claims such visual representations were understood to stake, and what relationships they established between subjects and their publics, I situate them within a broader field of production that constituted a Mediterranean space of encounter.

It is now "common knowledge" among Ottomanists (though not necessarily among early modern Europeanists) that the *translatio studii* that undergirded the great synthesis of the Süleymanic era melded humanist ideals and epistemological procedures with those of earlier imperial formations—be they Greco-Latin, Arabic, or Persianate.[7] If the self-consciously synthetic nature of Ottoman imperial culture of the era is relatively well studied, we know far less about how contemporaneous emergent European human sciences reappropriated and rearticulated Ottoman metropolitan perspectives on the empire's history and culture.[8] The growing presentism of much historical scholarship, and the power of teleological narratives to color our understanding of pre-Enlightenment spaces of encounter between newly emergent "Europeans" and their myriad neighbors make it even more imperative that we look at the multidirectional modalities of knowledge production in the early modern Mediterranean.

To this end, the chapter considers two sets of artifacts that both "represent" dragomans and in whose production dragomans were involved. These articulations of a space of encounter raise broad methodological and epistemological questions about the history of Ottoman-European interactions, and underscore the need to attend to the particular circulatory regimes of diplomacy that defined dragomans' mobility, and through which they forged representational strategies. Comparing and contrasting the media, producers, purposes, and audiences of these two sets of artifacts suggests how the visual archives of Venetian-Ottoman diplomacy functioned as a vital site where trans-imperial perspectives on Ottoman courtly culture were formed.

Diplomacy and Trans-Imperial Perspective in a Split Album

Our first example is an illustrated album about Ottoman politics, diplomacy, and everyday life, which both represents dragomans, visually and textually, and in whose production dragomans were crucially involved. The album, which dates to the early 1660s, is now split between two codices, one in Venice (henceforth the Cicogna Codex) and one in St. Petersburg (henceforth the Taeschner Codex).[9] This ur-codex, referred to henceforth as "the Ballarino album" for reasons to become clear shortly, articulates a trans-imperial perspective on Ottoman (and more specifically, Istanbulite) history, society, and culture that defies easy classification as either "Ottoman" or "Venetian." The Ballarino album contained at least 113 folios (fifty-nine now in Cicogna, fifty-four in Taeschner), all but three featuring an illustration in gouache mounted on the recto (four as double-size bifolds). All inserts have red, gray, or gilded pen borders. An extensive Italian gloss precedes and follows the insert, and sometimes "spills over" onto the verso. Thematically, the visual program of the album can be divided roughly into three broad sections: (1) Sultans' portraits (fols. 1–16 in Cicogna and fols. 5 and 9 in Taeschner);[10] (2) genre scenes, monuments, and vessels (fols. 17–34 and 50–54 in Cicogna and fols. 1–4, 6-8, 10–13, 15–50, 54–55 in Taeschner); and (3) diplomatic and military battle scenes from the Venetian-Ottoman War of Crete (1645–1669) (fols. 35–49 and 55–59 in Cicogna and fols. 14 and 51–53 in Taeschner).[11]

The original integrity of Taeschner's and Cicogna's codices is supported by several facts. First, the only two sultanic portraits included in the Taeschner Codex—Osman II on folio 5 and Ahmed I on folio 9—are precisely two of the three missing from the otherwise mostly chronological sultanic sequence in the Cicogna Codex (the third one being Murad IV, 1623–1640, now lost).[12] Second, both codices feature identical hand, ink, color scheme, and style, but without visual duplication (cf. figures 4.3 and 4.4). Furthermore, textual references in the narratives in one codex to illustrations found in the other make it clear that the author intended leaves from both to form an integral work, and that the order of the leaves, at least in the Taeschner Codex, is not original (cf. figures 4.5 and 4.6). The circumstances in which the Ballarino album was split are unknown, and the division is at least partially haphazard (e.g., the exclusion of three sultans from the largely chronological sequence in Cicogna), though it has lent the two resulting codices distinct flavors, discussed below.

At first blush, the Ballarino album fits squarely in the genre of costume albums, which enjoyed great popularity among late-sixteenth and seventeenth-century Ottoman and foreign readers alike.[13] It even shares a few stock images with other contemporary Istanbulite albums, indicating a likely provenance in the same atelier.[14] For example, its barbershop scene (figure 4.7) is identical in composition and style (if not entirely in color scheme and detail) to an illustration in an album commissioned by the Swedish ambassador Claes Rålamb in 1657 (figure 4.8).[15] Several of its sultans' portraits also bear strong stylistic resemblances to those in other contemporary albums. Conversely, illustrations depicting the misfortunes of the Venetian diplomatic corps during the Venetian-Ottoman War of Crete seem unique, as their value for patrons beyond the bailate would have been rather limited.[16]

Earlier scholars have often characterized costume albums as mnemonic devices. As vicarious travel, they "captured" and recalled imperial difference by offering manifold visual typologies of gender roles, status, and professional, regional, and ethnic varieties, either in a particular imperial setting or as a simulacrum of the globe-trotting merchant, now sublimated in the armchair traveler perusing the album from the comfort of home. More recent scholarship has questioned the catchall usefulness of "costume album" as a genre designation, pointing out the diplomatic patronage of many of these artifacts, as well as their collaborative—and diverse—nature as assemblages of both local and foreign expertise, perspectives, and intended readers/viewers.[17]

The Ballarino album, for one, is no hapless souvenir, mass produced by careless bazaar artists and procured in a market stall by clueless sojourners. Rather, it reflects a specific narrative program and fuses entrepreneurial artistic technologies, Ottoman and Italianate genres of visual representation, injected with a clear Venetian diplomatic agenda. That it is more appropriately situated in the context of Mediterranean diplomacy than of armchair travel is made evident by both images and text. The narrative gloss marks its intended audience throughout as members of the Venetian political elite and erases any gap between the narrator's voice and such authorized readers. It does so by using the first person plural to refer to Venetian collective action, by heavily emphasizing Venetian-Ottoman relations, and by implicitly presupposing readers' prior knowledge of the history of these relations. Rather than a memento for armchair travelers, I suggest it was intended as a diplomatic handbook for Istanbul-bound Venetian diplomats on Ottoman society and politics, and, more specifically, as a cautionary tale about the vital importance of dragomans for Venetian diplomacy at the Porte. Assembled in the bailate in the early 1660s, it was the culmination of careful collaboration among its author, the long-time Venetian secretary and de facto Resident at the Porte Giovanni Battista Ballarino, his dragomans, and several Ottoman and Italianate artists.

The extent to which the Ballarino album embodies its multiple provenances, technologies, perspectives, and purposes becomes clearer once we consider the various genres from which it derived its representational techniques, such as illustrated *şehname* (book of kings), *kiyafetname* (physiognomy study), *silsilename* (genealogical sultanic portraiture), *muraqaa'* (anthology), and *album amicorum* (scrapbook). Similar to the latter, the Ballarino album was a potentially open-ended artifact, in which stock and more bespoke images were combined. Its technique of mounting a gilded illustration on a page with an accompanying, recontextualizing gloss closely resembles *muraqqa'* and *album amicorum* production techniques.

In important ways, all of the genres with which the Ballarino album corresponds articulated a space of encounter in at least two senses. First, they were engaged in ongoing cross-fertilization that traversed political and linguistic borders, as humanist learning proliferated in the Ottoman court and as Ottoman manuscripts circulated beyond the empire. Second, they highlighted and celebrated Ottoman ethnic diversity and objectified Ottoman difference vis-à-vis European polities and societies while also suggesting their potential commensurability. These genres then point to the deep embedding of European sojourners in Ottoman elite milieus, and to their compilers and patrons' capacity to engage both. Even if some of the images in the Ballarino album were intended to tantalize their viewers, categorizing them as "bazaar art" is therefore unhelpful analytically and problematic empirically. Instead, their production, whether by local artists associated with the court or by European artists attached to diplomatic missions, is better understood in the context of sustained interaction rather than as merely an exoticizing gesture toward an anonymous, uninformed marketplace.[18]

The album opens with a series of conventionalized representations of Ottoman sultans, accompanied by a narrative detailing their military accomplishments and relations with Venice. Such a political and military chronology was considered part of the necessary education of any foreign diplomat arriving at the Porte,[19] and the Ballarino album was not unique in using sultans' portraits as its hinge. Indeed, the use of serial sultanic portraiture as a structuring device was common to several Ottoman genres, such as the *silsilename*, *şehname*, *kıyafetname*, and their immensely popular humanist cognates, such as the "Lives of the Sultans" produced by the likes of Paolo Giovio, Francesco Sansovino, and Pietro Bertelli.[20] Unlike either its Ottoman or humanist models, however, the chronology in this album is abbreviated enough to suggest it was intended as a mnemonic device for someone already familiar with that history (as, indeed, any Venetian diplomat sent to Istanbul would have been), rather than as an introduction for a layperson.

Beyond overall similarity in organizing principles to specific Ottoman genres, the Ballarino album shows affinity with more diffuse contemporary Ottoman painting conventions. In addition to sultanic portraiture it closely resembles the shape and color scheme used to depict certain vessels (cf. the sultan's kayık in figures 4.9 and 4.10) and Ottoman representational

techniques for naval battle scenes overall (cf. the setup, elevation, and juxtaposition of camps in figures 4.11 and 4.12).

Descriptions of architectural monuments in the Ballarino album also
bear strong affinities to Ottoman visual and narrative conventions of representing architectural space. As Walter Denny suggests:

> In such works [. . .] of city-description, either in travelers' accounts
> or in compilations of architectural monuments [. . .] the concern is in
> enumerating long lists of buildings, in some arbitrary order, whether
> alphabetical, chronological, or by size, location, or degree of holiness;
> each building on the list is often given a brief note as well. The pro-
> vided information rarely, if ever, deals with an architectural descrip-
> tion of the building's form except in poetic metaphor or hyperbole;
> rather, in the same enumerative tradition, the treatise will discuss the
> number of minarets, the number and type of dependencies, or will
> provide anecdotes about the designer of the stained glass or the in-
> scriptions, together with information on the founder and the burials
> at the mosque.[21]

Similarly, the Ballarino album often dwells on the social functions and
(Venetocentric) historical significance of specific buildings. For example, it
distinguishes between *hans* and *caravanserais* based not on their architectural features but on their social uses. Thus, the gloss for the caravanserai
on folio 1 (Taeschner Codex) reads:

> Shape of a Caravanserai, which is constructed in spacious fields for the
> convenience of travelers, with a large covered courtyard inside, where
> the horses are kept [. . .] but the people stay in the building itself with
> their arms and their tools, as there are many hearths neatly [positioned]
> to serve everyone. The Turk comes with the keys to open the door, and
> on the next page one sees the true shape of the open Caravanserai.[22]

That promised "next page" now constitutes folio 32 of the Cicogna Codex
(figure 4.13), where the gloss repeats many of the same themes:

> This is the open caravanserai, with the door, guarded by chains, with
> the hearths and fire for the convenience of travelers, whose weap-
> ons are seen hanging on the wall, with the horses downstairs, in the
> same place, where all sorts of Turks stay, in the same manner that in
> Christendom taverns are used.[23]

Significantly, the gloss not only explains the building's function, but suggests a calque, "tavern," as a familiar, "Christian" equivalent institution. Such calques and ethnographic details are a clear departure from Ottoman genres of description, and serve to make their objects more familiar. The generic visual representation and textual explication offered for *hans* (fol. 19r Cicogna) are almost identical to those given for caravanserais, but with an important additional reference to their urban character, underscoring the narrative's metropolitan-mercantile orientation, as befits a representation of the Ottoman capital for a Venetian readership:[24]

> Image of a han in Istanbul, where men and horses take a break from their travels; the door is crossed by chains, guarded by custodians; outside, adjacent to the same han, are shops of different kinds of merchandise, for the convenience of the same passengers and travelers.[25]

Yet hans feature in the album not only as generic architectural types but also as concrete monuments, the site of specific historical events, e.g., on folio 15v (Cicogna), as the place of Venetian ambassador Giovanni Capello's detention, and on folio 44r (Cicogna), where it is identified as "the first Han of Edirne." Two other hans are visually and textually represented in the Codex: the Büyük Valide Han on folio 22r (Cicogna), and another, unspecified han of Edirne on folio 49r (Cicogna). In describing the Büyük Valide Han, the narrative not only identifies the structure's patron, the *valide* (queen mother) Kösem Sultan (ca. 1589–1651, mother of sultans Murad IV and Ibrahim I), but adds that "it is built of marble with great skill and expenditure; inside are many rooms, to keep the belongings of merchants; in the center, a mosque for prayer, and a fountain for washing and drinking."[26] By recalling the mosque in the courtyard of the Büyük Valide Han and detailing its various ritual and public functions, the author is pointing to hans' social significance as nodal points in urban life, rather than as mere tourist attractions.[27]

The album's interpretive approach, which seeks to familiarize and commensurate Ottoman urban life with Venetian customs, is equally palpable in several glosses of Islamic ritual practices and spaces, including the "Bell tower of a mosque," "Mosque of Sultan Mehmed," "Bayram," "Bayram at court," "Sheikh," "Prayer in a Mosque," "Circumcision," "Calls for Prayer," and "Tekke."[28] In conformity with the remainder of the text, the glosses for these images seek to render Islamic practice and nomenclature commensurable with Christian Italianate terminology. For example, the gloss for the image of a minaret (figure 4.14) refers to its object as "Bell tower [campanile] of a mosque" and calls the muezzin simply a "cleric." While the holiday of Ramadan is mentioned by name, it is immediately followed by a gloss as *Quadragesima* (Lent), lending it a decidedly Catholic, familiar feel.

Another significant feature of the album's selection of architectural views is the absence of any monuments from the "classical period" of Süleyman the Lawgiver (1520–1566), setting it apart from contemporary Ottoman albums that list monuments of the city. While some of the monuments featured in the album recall Istanbul's deep past, either Roman and Byzantine (the aqueducts, the hippodrome), or early Ottoman (Rumeli Fortress, the Castle of the Seven Towers, and the Fatih Mosque), others were very recent, mid-seventeenth-century constructions: the Büyük Valide Han in Istanbul and the Valide Han in Edirne (built in 1650 and 1651, respectively) and the Grand Pavilion (whose construction began in the 1620s but continued throughout the seventeenth century). No reference is made to the multiple impressive building projects carried out under Süleyman the Lawgiver, such as the vast Süleymaniye complex (completed in 1557).[29] Instead, the main criterion for inclusion in the album seems to have been military or commercial interest, as indeed befits a diplomatic manual as opposed to a souvenir.

Perhaps the most critical departure of the Ballarino album from the costume album tradition is its insistence on the key interpretive role of its author(s) in making sense of the visual material presented to the reader. Whereas most early modern Ottoman costume albums compiled pictorial anthologies with only brief descriptive captions, the Ballarino album conjoins Ottoman illustrations with extensive accompanying Italian glosses. Indeed, its lengthy narratives are sometimes illustrated by the images, rather than the other way around. By superimposing a narrative gloss on images predicated on multiple genres, the album simultaneously proclaims the images' limited intelligibility on their own, as the products of a foreign world, and assumes the voice of their most qualified "interpreter." The act of cultural mediation thus becomes metonymic of the very role of Venetian diplomats and dragomans at the Porte.

The departure from the costume album tradition is especially evident in the use of genre scenes as a prompt for discussing contemporary Ottoman urban life.[30] In contemporary costume albums, attire typically functioned as iconic signs of ethnic, gender, and professional diversity.[31] Although the costumes throughout the Ballarino album do stand for different social types (e.g., Muslims, Franks and Latins, court officials, street vendors), the figures wearing them are mostly situated in genre scenes rather than appearing as stand-alone abstractions. They are not prototypes but inter-actionally defined persons.

The relatively little elaboration of dress codes as metonymic of social types also sets apart the Cicogna and the Taeschner codices. While the former is split almost evenly between a sultanic chronicle, a panorama of city views, and an account of recent Venetian-Ottoman hostilities, the latter devotes its lion's share to ethnographic genre scenes at the expense of historical, diplomatic, and military analysis. In addition to two illustra-tions of ethnic types ("a Muslim Indian" and "a Turkish lady on her way to the bath," fols. 43 and 17, respectively), it shares several stock images with other contemporary albums, and offers several other stereotypical illus-trations of, e.g., mendicant dervishes, a barber, the ağa of the janissaries, a sheikh, whirling dervishes, dwarfs, the chief equestrian, and a pair of Cairene spahis. The difference between the two codices in the treatment of costume as a marker of personhood is not only visual but textual as well. The only explicit textual reference to dress in the entire Cicogna Codex concerns some hastily drawn "varied sorts of slippers, that is, shoes, boots, and ankle-boots, used by Turkish men and women."[32] In contrast, the gloss for turbans in the Taeschner Codex reads: "various grades of turbans, some of which are used by Turks according to their estate and their profession, such as spahi, jurists, authors, artists, nobles, plebs, and similar."[33] If the shoes are presented as belonging to no particular order of society, the tur-bans become metonymic of their wearers, and serve as a visual "hinge" for a condensed survey of Ottoman urban society that underscores its internal stratification and diversity.

These different thematic foci of the two codices are matched by another important divergence between them, namely in the scope allotted to his-torical-political narrative. Not only does the Cicogna Codex incorporate most of the sultan's portraits (and the dynastic chronicle that glosses them), it also dedicates eighteen illustrations to Venetian-Ottoman negotiations and military campaigns throughout the 1650s. The Taeschner Codex barely mentions either, and offers a decidedly more positive "spin" when it does: all three of its diplomatic scenes describe benign (and more generic) Vene-tian-Ottoman interactions, such as "the bailo accompanied to audience," "the bailo at audience with the Grand Vizier," and "the bailo perfumed by the Grand Vizier during audience." In contrast, the acrimonious narrative of the Cicogna Codex spans eleven illustrations of humiliation, incarceration, and assorted executions of Venetian diplomats and their aides.

The obscure circumstances of the album's eventual splitting preclude any conclusions about the intentionality behind the differences noted above. Yet much can be inferred about the provenance of the original artifact within Venetian diplomatic circles in Istanbul, and about its intended use as a practical handbook in that milieu. Appended at the end of the Cicogna Codex are two oversized and highly detailed plans of Ottoman fortresses, the *Yedikule* (Castle of the Seven Towers) and the *Rumelihisarı* (Rumeli Fortress), drawn in sepia and black pen following geometrical perspective (figures 4.15 and 4.16). The artist(s) entrusted with executing these plans commanded not only the Italian language (as evinced by the detailed legend accompanying the plan on fol. 59r), but also up-to-date Venetian conventions of visual representation of architectural space.[34] The plan on folio 59r (figure 4.16), in black ink, measures forty-three by sixty centimeters, and is signed by "Antonio Prinsaji," who remains unidentified. Its striking similarity to a plan of the same fortress drawn by the Vicentine artist Francesco Scarella ca. 1685 has been noted by Franz Babinger.[35]

That both plans were included in the album from its inception is clearly indicated on an earlier folio, where the author tells us that "a description of the two other fortresses, renovated, is on another page, done by a very careful hand, and will be in the back of this book."[36] This underscores the album's original integrity, and suggests its intended use as a practical handbook.[37] Indeed, it is not so much the provenance of the illustrations per se, but rather their relationship to the narrative that provides important clues as to the album's author and approximate date. The last sultan featured in the album is Mehmed IV (ruled 1648–1687). Mehmed acceded to the throne at age seven, and his early portraits frequently presented him as a beardless youth, as does his portrait here (Cicogna, 15r). The narrative accompanying Mehmed IV's portrait ends in 1660, even though he ruled until 1687. Similarly, the latest firmly dated events mentioned in the album as a whole are the Ottoman conquest of Varadino, now Oradea in Romania (Cicogna, 15v) and the great fire of Istanbul (Cicogna, 34r), both dating to 1660. No reference is made to the conclusion of the Ottoman conquest of Crete in 1669, a momentous event in the history of Venetian-Ottoman relations that surely would have warranted mention had it taken place before the album was produced.

Another important event not reported in the album—which therefore helps date it—is the change of the guard in the bailate in the mid-1660s. In 1660 Secretary Ballarino, still in Edirne (where he and his staff had relocated intermittently from 1652 to 1664), was elected Venetian grand chancellor—the highest position open to members of the non-patrician citizen class.[38] By then Ballarino had spent over eleven years in the Ottoman Empire.[39] His dispatches to the Senate and private correspondence convey an anxious desire to return to Venice to assume his new and prestigious post. This he never accomplished. The war delayed his departure from Ottoman territory, and he died in Macedonia on his return trip to Venice in 1666. Yet it is likely that upon receiving news of his election as grand chancellor in late 1660, he expected to leave for Venice soon. He may have initiated production of this album at that time as a handbook for his successor.

An emendation on Cicogna folio 35v further confirms Ballarino's authorship. It concerns the rumor of an impending death order, issued for Ballarino by the Ottoman grand vizier. Whispered to Ambassador Giovanni Capello by his French counterpart, it was overheard by the apprentice dragoman Tarsia. The pronoun *mia* (my) that precedes the word *morte* (death) is crossed out and "di Ballarino" is added after (figure 4.17). This is the only place in the entire narrative where Ballarino discloses his identity, for a brief moment, only immediately to resume the first person plural of a generalized Venetian collective. Ballarino was not so much hiding his identity (the word *mia* is crossed out but remains easily legible). Rather, he may have considered the third person to be a more appropriate register, which would strengthen the sense that he intended the work not as a personalized souvenir to take back to Venice, but rather as a professional diplomatic guide for his successor.

Ballarino was a career bureaucrat who dedicated his life to Venetian civil service. In that respect, his social position mirrored in interesting ways that of some *şehnameci*s, official Ottoman court historians of the late sixteenth century, whose works the album parallels. Like the *şehnameci*s, Ballarino was embedded in a dense network of patronage, which made him acutely aware of the collaborative nature of statecraft (in his case: running the bailate and negotiating during wartime), and the need to please both his patrons in Venice to whom he owed his appointment, and his bailate staff, particularly his dragomans. In other words, his perspective was multifocal by default. Also similarly to the *şehnameci*s, Ballarino was not groomed to be a member of the top echelons of his society, yet found himself entrusted with considerable authority and tasked to delicately communicate in writing to his employers the challenges of his daily work. This inclined him to be less invested in the self-aggrandizing textual strategies of patrician diplomats.

Ballarino's multifocal perspective and keen sense for the collaborative dimensions of diplomacy were shared by the dozen or so bailate dragomans he employed. As seen in previous chapters, these dragomans could be—much like Ballarino himself—highly educated individuals with some humanist training and extensive ties within the Venetian elite, but not patricians themselves. Unlike Ballarino, however, dragomans were also for the most part native or long-term residents of Istanbul, well embedded in local networks of patronage, fluent Ottoman speakers, with access to the city's courtiers, artists, and scholars, and potentially some familiarity with those diverse elite Ottoman genres of representing genealogy, history, and society that the album recalls.

We can deduce dragomans' involvement in the album's production from its formal correspondence with Ottoman representational strategies, and, on a more basic level, from the very practicalities of commissioning paintings from local artists under conditions of war, and while Ballarino was under house arrest and periodic exile in Edirne. Dragomans' intervention is further evinced by the prominent place they are assigned throughout the album, both visually and textually. Dragomans or their apprentices are mentioned by name in five of the thirteen folios devoted to Venetian diplomacy and are depicted visually on five others, in ways that subvert the official Venetian order of precedence. For example, on folio 43r Cicogna (figure 4.18), a dragoman (identifiable by his dress) is riding a horse flanked by two Ottoman officials *ahead of* Secretary Ballarino, his assistants, and apprentice dragomans. The dragoman's visual alignment with—and enclosure between—Ottoman officials, apart from the rest of the Venetian contingent behind, suggest his hinge status, as simultaneously Ottoman and Venetian. His visual positioning may also represent his imagined or actual elevated status in the bailate, against the official order of precedence that subordinated him to Ballarino.[40] A similar assertion of the dragoman's high status is made in the gloss to folio 53r Taeschner, which specifies that the grand dragoman, like the bailo and the secretary, mounted on horseback during formal processions to the divan, even though the image clearly shows him on foot among other members of the bailate.

The dragomans' perspective is further reflected in the sequencing of visual representations of alleged Ottoman executions of Venetian representatives, starting with the strangling of Grand Dragoman Giovanni Antonio Grillo in 1649 (fol. 38r Cicogna, figure 4.19), and moving through the hanging of Grand Dragoman Marcantonio Borisi (fol. 39r Cicogna, figure 4.20) to the undated hooking and impalement of two letter carriers (fols. 40r–41r Cicogna).[41] Archival evidence strongly suggests that Borisi's killing in 1620 stemmed not simply from Ottoman caprice but rather from a secret plot by the Venetian state inquisitors, who suspected that he had spied for the Spaniards.[42] Placing Borisi's hanging among several Ottoman executions of Venetian diplomatic employees (rather than in the equally long list of Venetian officials secretly killed by the government for suspected treason) could thus be read as an effort to fix his memory as a loyal, martyred Venetian subject, and as an ominous precedent for Grand Dragoman Giovanni Antonio Grillo's execution twenty-nine years later.

Even more significant for our understanding of how the dragomans' perspective shapes this album is the role both image and text ascribe to a specific apprentice dragoman in preventing his Venetian employers, the bailo Giovanni Soranzo and Secretary Ballarino, from exacerbating an already precarious situation during their interrogation by the Ottoman grand vizier in 1649.[43] On folio 35r (figure 4.21) the apprentice visually figures as the person situated *in between* the Ottoman interrogators, who are standing to the right, and the Venetian diplomats Soranzo and Ballarino, who are seated to the left. His in-between-ness is conveyed by his placement, which is higher and more central than that of his employers. His bright orange cloak and distinct, fur-lined headgear single him out as neither a Muslim nor a "Frank," but rather a "Latin." The gloss refers to him obliquely as *giovane della lingua Tarsia* (apprentice dragoman Tarsia) and therefore does not allow us to determine his exact identity. The future Grand Dragoman Christoforo Tarsia, a noble from the Venetian colony of Capodistria, lived and worked in the bailo's house from 1620. His two younger brothers and three sons were all either born or raised there. In the late 1640s, when the events described took place, several Tarsia family members were employed as apprentice dragomans in the bailo's house.[44] Whoever the specific person in the picture, the very positioning of a young member of the Tarsia family at the center of this politically charged narrative and image, and his crowning as the savior of Venetian diplomats, strongly suggest Tarsia family involvement in the album's production, particularly given dragomans' failed unionization attempt led by Christoforo Tarsia very shortly before the album was created.[45]

In other ways too, the album reflects dragomans' perspective as consistently Venetian, and therefore external to its Ottoman objects while claiming intimate knowledge of them. Several mechanisms are at work in producing this trans-imperial perspective. First, the narrative repeatedly oscillates between admiration for and critique of the sultans by interspersing the chronicle of their accomplishments with anecdotes invoking their cruelty.[46] In addition to their dramatic effect, such anecdotes reinforce distance from the Ottomans, who are otherwise depicted in a rather admiring tone. One could argue that emphasis on cruelty might serve to enhance the narrative's affective force rather than to cast the Ottomans in a particularly negative light. In addition to generic cruelty, both text and images pay special attention to personal atrocities that the Ottoman rulers committed against their political rivals. In particular, the album rarely fails to specify—both verbally and visually—the exact form of capital punishment meted out to such rivals, impalement most prominently.[47]

The onset of the War of Crete saw trans-imperial subjects in general, and dragomans in particular, increasingly emphasizing Ottoman barbarity in their petitions to Venetian officialdom.[48] Dragomans were not unique in this respect: as Lucette Valensi has shown, Ottoman capricious cruelty, and especially the sultan's despotism, became key tropes of an emerging early modern Venetian anti-Ottoman discourse.[49] And certainly the graphic representation of lurid Ottoman violence also served as a building block of wider contemporary European visual culture, fueled by popular voyeuristic prints.[50] Yet, parallel to its emphasis on Ottoman cruelty, the album also makes noticeable and repeated gestures to Ottoman-Venetian parity, not only military, but political, economic, and artistic as well. These seemingly paradoxical refractions of Ottoman worlds are perhaps another indication that the album was intended as a multifocal handbook for a seasoned diplomat.

As discussed above, the Ballarino album achieves a sense of intimacy with the Ottoman world in part through the particular juxtaposition and merging of several visual and textual genres. The skilled manipulation of multiple genres reinforces the sense that a successful diplomat must be able to assume a very particular perspective, integrating knowledge that emerged from distinct though not a priori unrelated cultural centers. It is exactly in such acts of mediation by those in-between, both overtly and tacitly, that the interdependence as well as the boundaries between Venetian and Ottoman cultural centers were established. The dragomans' perspective places the intermediary in the center of the text, and by so doing, subordinates Ottoman narratives to Venetian ones. Here, then, we see the production of a trans-imperial perspective on the Ottoman world. The ability to manipulate multiple genres, both Ottoman and European, and merge them into a unique, individualized whole, gains ironic additional meanings here. Like the sultan's *muraqqa'*, the Ballarino album was meant as a "diplomatic gift" that celebrates the Ottomans, yet also showcases its author's power of discernment and ability to outwit them, which he does, to be sure, with the help of his dragomans, such as when the apprentice dragoman Tarsia is described as advising Ballarino to remain silent in order to avoid incurring the grand vizier's wrath.

To conclude, as the album's author-compiler, Ballarino exercises his chief right of selecting and reorganizing the visual material.[51] By adding a detailed gloss, rather than mere captions, he makes explicit his own remarkable knowledge of things Ottoman. His occasional deletions, corrections, and interlineal additions serve the same overall purpose by amplifying his connoisseurship and position as ultimate arbiter of the text's authority, accuracy, and completeness.[52] At the same time, by granting such extensive narrative and visual space to dragomans' accomplishments, Ballarino acknowledges their specialized knowledge and unique perspective, without which his own authority would be greatly diminished.

The Ballarino album evinces a particular double perspective thanks not only—or even primarily—to its author's position but to dragomans' heavy involvement in its production. As key "invisible technicians," they served as behind-the-scenes intermediaries who procured the expertise of Ottoman artists and who literally translated Ballarino's narrative program to them, and their visual program back to Ballarino. In the process, this program itself came partially to reflect dragomans' own multifocal and trans-imperial perspective. It is this perspective that explicitly thematizes dragomans as visual and textual objects of representation in many of the album's folios, as the hinge of Venetian diplomacy at the Porte, recording their knowledge and sacrifices in great detail.

Genealogy and Place-Making in Serial Portraiture

A useful counterpoint to the Ballarino album is a different set of visual representations of dragomans' trans-imperial perspective in over a dozen large-canvas oil portraits. Despite the very different medium, a comparison of these two representations is warranted by their partially overlapping cast of characters, drawn from among the Tarsia-Carli-Mamuca della Torre dragoman dynasty (figure 4.22). As in the Ballarino album, so too in their portraits dragomans form both objects of representation and subjects actively involved in crafting the representation itself. In commissioning their portraits, however, dragomans collaborated not with Istanbul-based miniaturists and drafters but with portrait artists in the Venetian-Otto-man-Habsburg borderlands in Istria, the Tarsias' and Carlis' ancestral home.

At first blush, the very seriality of the portraits warrants an explana-tion, as they fall into two distinct clusters. Five Tarsia dragoman portraits now in the Koper Regional Museum (and formerly displayed in the Tarsia family palace in Koper) are attributed to a single Koper-based artist, Nata-lis Bertolini. The five portraits—featuring Christoforo, Ruggiero, Marco, Tommaso, and Giacomo Tarsia (figures 4.23, 4.24, 4.25, 4.26 and 4.27), all dragomans in Venetian service in the seventeenth century—share a three-quarter view and similar dimensions (approximately 150 by 95 cen-timeters). All provide a Latin inscription that identifies the sitters, their profession, and their Venetian subjecthood.

At least eight additional portraits of dragomans, apprentice dragomans, and their womenfolk now in the Museum of the Poreč territory (and for-merly in the Carli palace in Koper), are more diverse in format and style. Seven full-length portraits (approximately 220 by 150 centimeters) fea-ture early-eighteenth-century sartorial styles and have been tentatively at-tributed to Sebastiano Bombelli or his atelier.[53] Among these are pendant portraits of Grand Dragoman Gian Rinaldo Carli (figure 4.2) and his wife, Caterina Negri (figure 4.39), both with identifying inscriptions. Additional portraits of the same provenance lack an inscription (or have been dam-aged, rendering the inscription partially or entirely illegible) but similarly depict Istanbulite regalia-clad dragomans sporting professional and em-blematically Ottoman accoutrements. Three of the previously anonymous sitters can be tentatively identified as the dragoman Marcantonio Mamuca della Torre (figure 4.28), his wife, Giustiniana Tarsia (figure 4.29), and one of their sons, possibly Leopoldo, who died prematurely while serving as Habsburg dragoman in his native Istanbul (figure 4.30). Two additional full-length portraits of the same provenance feature dignitaries, possibly Marcantonio Mamuca della Torre in his old age (when he served as a coun-cilor in Vienna) and his son Cristoforo, who served as imperial agent in Trieste (figures 4.31 and 4.32). Also of the same provenance are several portraits in three-quarters, including a youthful depiction of Gian Rinaldo Carli (figure 4.1), featuring his family's coat of arms.[54]

Both the Koper and the Poreč clusters include other, non-dragoman relatives of the Tarsia and Carli dragomans, respectively. The Koper set includes at least four late-fifteenth-and early-sixteenth-century Tarsia ancestors, namely Domenico, Jacopo (b. 1467, figure 4.33), and his sons Nicolò and Damiano (b. 1525, figure 4.34). Strong stylistic similarities and shared format and inscription patterns suggest that these portraits, like those of their dragoman descendants, were created sometime in the second half of the seventeenth century. The Poreč set includes several Carli ancestors as well, all in three-quarter format and similar dimensions (approximately 120 by 95 centimeters). In addition to two recent ancestors, Giovanni Stefano Carli (now lost, bearing the date 1644) and Bradamante Tarsia (figure 4.38), i.e., the dragoman Gian Rinaldo Carli's paternal uncle and mother, respectively, the Carli set includes two more distant forebears, the fourteenth-century Leonardo Carli and his son Cesare (figure 4.36). It also came to include three descendants: a pendant of Stefano Carli (Gian Rinaldo Carli's great-nephew) and his wife, Cecilia Manzini Carli, both bearing the date of their union, 1772 (figures 4.37 and 4.35),[55] and a young, beardless count Carli in formal Ottoman Christian garb, including a silk fur-trimmed overcoat and brocaded gown. The subject of this latter (now presumed lost) portrait is unidentified, but could well have been Stefano Carli in his youth as an apprentice dragoman in Istanbul. At least according to one art historian who examined the "well preserved" original in the interwar period, this portrait was created by the same artist as that of Giovanni Stefano Carli, confirming that the ancestor's portrait—indeed like Bradamante Tarsia's—was a retroactive addition to the series, in this case likely dating to the mid-to-late-eighteenth century.[56]

Thus, within the Poreč cluster, the portraits of turn-of-the-eighteenth-century dragomans and their spouses, all but one full-length, are markedly different in format from those of ancestors and progeny, which are all in three-quarters, and, with the exception of Bradamante Tarsia, significantly less ornate. Of especially low quality and lacking in detail is the portrait of the fourteenth-century Cesare f. Leonardo Carli (figure 4.35). The inclusion of this distant ancestor (in oddly eighteenth-century stern garb) signals the aristocratic-genealogical purpose for which the portrait was presumably commissioned, but also the limited financial resources at the disposal of the portrait's patrons.

This brief overview highlights an important difference between the purely agnatic and patrilineal series of Tarsia dragoman portraits, with their largely Venetocentric orientation, and the decidedly cognatic series of Carli and Mamuca della Torre portraits, featuring both men and women, sometime in pendants, and oriented largely toward the Holy Roman Empire. Indeed, the only evident linchpin connecting the Carlis to the Mamuca della Torres was Giustiniana Tarsia, the dragoman Christoforo Tarsia's daughter, who was both Gian Rinaldo Carli's maternal first cousin and Marcantonio Mamuca della Torre's wife. At the same time, if their selection criteria seem to diverge on which contemporary and near-contemporary relatives to feature, the Tarsia and the Carli clusters cohere in their selection of ancestors. In both cases the individuals commemorated are not necessarily the family's most illustrious forebears.[57] Rather they are, without fail, either military men in Venetian service (e.g., Domenico Tarsia, who led Venetian armies against the Ottomans in 1516), or those who secured the family's noble title (e.g., Cesare Carli, knighted by the Holy Roman Empire in 1348, or Giacomo Tarsia, who in 1478 became an imperial count palatine).[58] Inscriptions on these ancestors' portraits provide only a name and a date, the latter not necessarily that of birth but rather of achieving a familial milestone, further underscoring these portraits' role in buttressing "serialized" genealogical claims.

Much about the portraits' circumstances of production and intended purposes remains uncertain. We do, however, have evidence that all the portraits hung in the Carli and Tarsia family palaces in Capodistria/Koper.[59] The strong ties between the Tarsias and the Carlis and their palaces' physical proximity further warrant a consideration of these portraits in relation to one another. Beyond the particular motivations for their commission and the distinctive stories they were meant to convey, these portraits' shared provenance allows us to draw some tentative conclusions about their intended purposes. Together, these portraits also bring into sharper relief the gap between the emergent genealogical understandings of Istanbul-based dragoman families and their Istria-based kin. Indeed, they palpably articulate the unresolved tension between two models in dragomans' practices of self-representation: the Istanbulite metropolitan grandee (expressed, above all, in both men's and women's careful sartorial codes) and the Italianate provincial aristocrat, reinforced by the very choice of genre (the large-canvas oil painting), posture, and, in most portraits, Latin inscription.

Another salient characteristic of most dragoman portraits in both clusters is the elaborate attention to dress, reflecting the latest Istanbulite fashion. The only exception, significantly, is the portrait of the first Tarsia dragoman, Christoforo (figure 4.23), whose more somber attire, though replete with Ottoman fur trimmings, is coupled with large golden *peroli* buttons *alla veneziana*.[60] Christoforo's biography embodied the transition from Capodistria to Istanbul, from a provincial Venetian to a metropolitan Ottoman setting.

Besides Christoforo, all other dragoman portraits across both clusters are already dressed in the lavish garb of well-to-do Istanbulite Catholic grandees.[61] Their luxurious outfits and confident posture suggest the compatibility, even commensurability, of Ottoman and Italianate elite material cultures, but also their distinctiveness, much like other forms of *Turquerie*.[62] Adherence to Ottoman sartorial style, coupled with specific emblematic props, such as a letter patent, tassels, an interior/exterior view, classicizing balustrades, and abundant drapery, typified baroque portraiture of Ottomancentric diplomats from Holland to Poland.[63] Some of these stock iconographic elements were understood to conventionally represent "Eastern" emissaries, as several contemporary portraits of Ottoman and Safavid ambassadors confirm, while others were more generic markers of diplomatic high status.[64] That the Tarsia dragomans and their cousins chose this particular representational convention for their formal portraiture is significant: Though the portraits were to be hung in the families' ancestral palaces in Capodistria, quite possibly commissioned as mementos of the successful relatives in faraway Istanbul, they make no effort to blend the two milieus.

Further evidence that these portraits were intended as a statement about the commensurability-in-distinctiveness of the two milieus comes from the intricate interrelationship between the three female portraits in this series. One, in three-quarters, features Bradamante Tarsia Carli—Christoforo Tarsia's sister and Gian Rinaldo Carli's mother (figure 4.38). The other two, in full length, feature Caterina Negri (figure 4.39) and, presumably, Giustiniana Tarsia (figure 4.29)—Bradamante's daughter-in-law and niece, respectively.[65]

Although divergent in representational conventions, the three portraits are near-contemporaneous, datable to the very late seventeenth or early eighteenth century. Bradamante's portrait presents her as a young belle with the inscription "Anno 1615." That date, however, marks her year of birth, rather than the painting's completion, as both her posture and her garments clearly date the painting to the turn of the eighteenth century, and exhibit remarkable similarity with another female portrait from the region (figure 4.40), dated to 1700–1710, now on display in Trieste but acquired from Poreč in 1933.

Other portraits in the series also bear dates marking milestone events in sitters' lives rather than when they were painted. Gian Rinaldo Carli's first portrait (figure 4.1) proclaims its subject as "aged 22" in 1679, when Carli was in fact thirty-three. The date on his second portrait (figure 4.2), 1716, reflects his promotion to the post of Grand Dragoman, even though the portrait presents him as a middle-aged man rather than as a seventy-year old. Tommaso Tarsia's portrait bears the date 1681, presumably when he was promoted to the office of grand dragoman. If these dates are approximate at best, Bradamante could hardly have been a young woman in 1615, given that she married in 1635 and gave birth to Gian Rinaldo Carli in 1646. The inscription of her date of birth may draw further attention to her genealogical positionality and hence to her role in connecting the Tarsia and Carli families and in ensuring dynastic continuity. It also—like the dates on other portraits in the series—indicates the posthumous commissioning of several of the paintings decades (sometimes centuries) after their subjects' death, when their precise dates of birth may have been long forgotten.

The genealogical function of young Bradamante Tarsia's portrait is brought into sharper relief when viewed in conversation with the other female portraits in the series. Bradamante, as befits her patrician upbringing in Capodistria, is portrayed as an Italianate, corseted aristocrat sporting typically Istrian three-pearl earrings. In contrast, her Istanbul-born daughter-in-law and niece are dressed as unmistakably Ottoman metropolitan Christian ladies in flowing kaftans and *entaris*. All three don an impressive headdress: Bradamante's is a distinctively European fontange, the latest Parisian fashion in the 1680s,[66] contrasting with the turban and feather arrangements of her two Ottoman relatives. The latter's extravagantly bejeweled headgear, the height of contemporary Istanbulite female fashion, underscores their participation in an Islamicate courtly aesthetics that was distinct yet fully commensurable with that of contemporary European nobilities.[67]

The commensurability of status between the three female portraits is not left to viewers to infer from visual cues alone. In case of any doubt about her noble bona fides, the Latin inscription on Caterina's portrait proclaims her as *Cattarina Carli ex Familia Nigrorvm Nobilivm Genvensis Reipublicae* (Cattarina Carli from the Negri family of the Nobility of the Genoese

Republic). Such reassurance seems aimed to preempt concerns about the sitter's elite status, particularly among a less informed viewership faraway. Unlike her husband, Gian Rinaldo, an Istrian transplant to the Ottoman capital, Caterina was an Ottoman subject, born and raised in Pera to a distinguished local Catholic family. Her ancestors' claim to Genoese nobility was in keeping with many in that community who traced their descent to Genoese settlers in Byzantium in the wake of the Fourth Crusade.[68] While her high status and Italianate credentials would have been evident to any Istanbulite, they may have needed glossing in faraway Istria. Beyond the Latin inscription, several other props in Caterina's portrait serve both to underscore her connection to and compatibility with the Carli noble line and her distinctiveness as an exogamous spouse. The black drapes in the left half of her portrait offer visual continuity with her husband's, and further serve to transition the viewer from the solemn indoor scene of Gian Rinaldo's portrait to the controlled outdoor background of Caterina's. A tassel hanging from the drapes' top edge mirrors the black egret feather in Caterina's headgear (both recalling Ottoman sultanic aigrettes and *sorguç*, or ceremonial plumes), and draws further attention to the massive, extravagant turban—the height of contemporary Istanbul's elite female fashion—that encircles her suitably youthful, pale face, drawing an additional contrast with the diminutive black page behind Gian Rinaldo. Like her husband, Caterina sports multilayered flowing garments of expensive silks topped by an *entari* and a kaftan, and a wide, bejeweled belt, on which she lays delicate fingers. A flower arrangement (including several tulips and daffodils, prototypically Ottoman flowers), a silhouette of cypresses, and a classicizing balustrade complement the view of her outside loggia, referencing the city's Roman past. A ray of light highlights a miniature female nude Greek statuette, visible through an opening in the balustrade. The statuette offers a secondary focal point to the right of the protagonist and further underscores her Renaissance (curvaceous) bodily shape, despite her concealing garments. The "controlled nature" and classicizing gesture of the open loggia as a background for Caterina is worth dwelling on. It appears similarly as an engraving in an Ottoman costume album by George de la Chappelle, printed in Paris in 1648 (figure 4.41), where "the sovereign of Athens" is shown against a background of Grecized columns and cypresses. This background, significantly, distinguishes the Athenian's portrait from about a dozen other female portraits preceding it—of Greek, Jewish, Armenian, Turkish, Persian, and Tatar women of various walks of life—all of whom are set against backdrops bustling with details of commercial life, whether urban, rural, or maritime.

Whether Caterina's portrait was explicitly referencing La Chappelle's engraving is hard to ascertain, though copies of the latter work did circulate in the region, as attested by some two dozen large-canvas oil paintings imitating La Chappelle's engravings (including the one above) held by the Herberstein family in Vurberk Castle, near Ptuj, 250 kilometers northeast of Koper.[69] Significantly, several of the portraits in that series have replaced La Chappelle's cityscapes with drapes and loggias. The "Athenian sovereign," in both La Chappelle and the Styrian painter's imitation is presented as a lady of the sultan's harem.[70] Like her fabulous headgear, the loggia bolstered Caterina's claim to belong in Istanbul's highest echelons and to partake in a distinctly courtly material culture.

The third female portrait in the series (figure 4.29) has yet to be identified definitively. It bears striking similarity to Caterina's, leading several art historians to attribute it to another artist in the same atelier. It too seems to be a pendant of a dragoman's portrait (figure 4.28), which can be identified more firmly: based on the subject's large medallion of the Order of the Holy Sepulcher of Jerusalem, and the inscription, which describes the subject as dragoman for the Holy Roman Emperor, we can safely name the sitter as Marcantonio Mamuca della Torre. It follows that its pendant female portrait likely depicts Giustiniana Tarsia, Marcantonio's wife, who, like Caterina Negri, was born in Istanbul, and who maintained her household there even after her husband relocated to Vienna in 1683.

The presence in the Carli family palace of several portraits tentatively identifiable as members of the Mamuca della Torre family, and their unmistakable stylistic unity with the Carli portraits, disrupt any simple agnatic or patrilineal account of the series' purpose and performance of genealogy. It is only by envisioning dragomans as a caste, whose members are imbued with a bilateral, strongly cognatic consciousness, that the seriality and cross-referentiality of these portraits cohere. This cognatic consciousness is further corroborated by numerous archival traces of enduring ties between the Tarsias and their Carli and Mamuca della Torre matrilineal affines in Istanbul and in Vienna.[71] In Istanbul, parish records attest to members of the three families regularly serving as baptismal godparents and marriage witnesses for one another's children. In 1688 Leopoldo Mamuca della Torre (Marcantonio and Giustiniana's eldest) served as baptismal godfather for his first cousin Anna Maria (Giacomo Tarsia's daughter). Angela Tarsia

(Giacomo's, Tommaso's, and Giustiniana's sister, who remained celibate for many years) served as godmother for at least ten of her Tarsia and Mamuca della Torre nephews and nieces between 1680 and 1697.[72] Extensive correspondence between Marcantonio Mamuca della Torre in Vienna, his wife, Giustiniana Tarsia, and her brothers Giacomo and Tommaso in Istanbul confirms that the siblings remained in close contact through adulthood.[73]

The cognatic outlook conveyed by the portrait series contrasts starkly with other representations of Tarsia and Carli genealogy. These include a Tarsia manuscript narrative genealogy penned ca. 1730 and kept in the family archives,[74] and at least two late-eighteenth-century family trees, one in oil (Carli), and one in print (Tarsia).[75] The Carli family tree (figure 4.42) conforms to similar measurements as the three-quarter portraits of family members, and was similarly hung in the family palace. We can thus reasonably read it as intended to complement the portraiture series. As Bralić and Burić note, the tree is patrilineal and primogenital, with its trunk consisting exclusively of twenty continuous generations of first-born sons (along with their year of birth), reflecting contemporary Istrian (as well as Venetian and Austrian) succession patterns.[76] Branches represent male siblings (but not female siblings or spouses). This particular genealogical understanding—which renders all but male heirs literally invisible—contrasts sharply with the centrality of wives and mothers in the Carli and Mamuca della Torre dragoman portrait clusters, which emphasize these women's high status and wealth.

Of further note is the portraits' origin at the turn of the eighteenth century—the height of the Tarsias', Carlis', and Mamuca della Torres' dragoman careers and bids for noble titles. Many of the sitters and their children spent significant time in Venice, Capodistria, Dalmatia, and Vienna, where they most certainly did not wear kaftan, fez, and ermine-trimmed cloaks. The very existence of these portraits, which harness such a prototypically elite European genre and technology, is premised on the sitters' patronage of Istrian Italianate artists rather than Istanbulite ones. Why, then, this particular fashion statement?

Regalia, as discussed in Chapter 2, was essential for performing the role of an Istanbulite dragoman, conforming to the careful sartorial regimentation of Ottoman courtly society. It was also a primary vehicle of ethnic, estate-based, gendered, and professional classifications in several visual genres, and applied with especial enthusiasm in typologies of foreigners across Eurasia.[77] As late as the 1760s, young Parisian apprentice dragomans were required by law to dress "as Orientals . . . to indicate their status and function."[78] The donning of regalia was similarly de rigueur for European official portraiture at the turn of the eighteenth century; "Oriental" garb and *Turquerie* were particularly in vogue among sitters returning from missions to Ottoman lands and further east—less as masquerade than as a recollection of a personal connection, particularly given the importance of formal portraiture to the contemporary Eurasian diplomatic gift economy.[79] We can thus see the dragomans' distinctly Ottoman regalia as carefully orchestrated professional self-fashioning—not at the individual level necessarily, but at that of the dragoman segment of the dynasty as a multigenerational whole, asserting its importance and sense of place.[80]

These portraits were embedded in a broader genealogical context that included other, non-Istanbulite members of sitters' extended families. This begs the question how these portraits engaged an audience in dragomans' ancestral "home," Capodistria.[81] It is precisely in relation to this audience in a spatiotemporal "elsewhere," far from their primary residence in Istanbul, that these portraits used the idiom of kinship to celebrate dragomans' skill at mediating and commensurating Ottoman and Latinate worlds, but also the Istanbulite women who formed the dynasty's linchpin and that helped localize it in situ. The repeated use of similar iconographic conventions across the series—the distinctly Ottoman regalia, the heavy drapery, the tassels, and, for the male sitters, the *berat* and dictionary pile—help achieve this localization, Ottomanization, and congruity. Although the works are painted by multiple hands, the effort to forge a coherent series is unmistakable, both iconographically and in the repeated references to the sitters' parentage. In its selective genealogical claims, however, the series leaves out other aspects of dragomans' lifeworlds, other filiations and affiliations, other parts of their ostensible networks. And it crucially depends on the medium of a particular genre—Italianate portraiture—and its representational conventions to tell its story.

This portrait series is but one example of how the knowledge that dragomans helped mediate was embedded in specific institutions and genres, which both produced a particularly metropolitan view of the Ottoman Empire and positioned the intermediaries as the masters of drawing a conveniently shifting boundary between Ottoman and European space. Dragomans, including the Tarsias, Carlis, and Mamuca della Torres, were deeply involved in the production of other representations of themselves and of their Ottoman world as well. In 1723, Count Cristoforo Mamuca della Torre, Marcantonio's son, presented Prince Charles Albert of Bavaria (future Holy Roman Emperor Charles VII) a three-volume album of hand-colored figures with accompanying Italian gloss describing in minute detail the various functions of the sultan's court, professions of Istanbul, and "various strange and barbaric nations." Other exemplars of this work, dedicated to other patrons from Vienna to Hanover, underscore Cristoforo's extensive ambition.[82] Cristoforo was also the compiler, ca. 1738, of ten autographed volumes containing a trilingual assortment of genealogical materials—including seventeen paternal and maternal ancestral coats of arms, several family trees (for example, figure 4.43), and detailed pedigrees as far back as the twelfth century, notarized testimonials about his father's career as dragoman in Istanbul, and a narrative about the dragoman's craft.[83] As with the Ballarino album, these materials, which await a detailed study, tell rather different stories. Their medium and stylistic conventions suggest decidedly different subject positions, grounded in trans-imperial aesthetics and genres.

To conclude, this chapter explored the substantial, as well as profoundly multifocal nature of early modern dragomans' visual footprint. Dragomans' diverse visual archives attest to shifting cultural orientations, affective attachments, and religious and ethnolinguistic identities on the Venetian-Ottoman-Habsburg Triplex Confinium. These archival sightings are "good to think with" precisely because of their multiplicity of perspectives, reflecting the different lifeworlds they both mediated and helped occlude. These sightings, furthermore, raise productive questions about the place of individual biographies in our conceptions of borders, mobilities, and the trans-imperial. Each of these sightings sheds light on specific dimensions of its protagonists' inexorably trans-local lives. But beyond individual itineraries, these sightings underscore the particular social and cultural space that dragomans inhabited in seventeenth-century Istanbul—not as "Europeans" sojourning in an alien, "non-European" Ottoman world (as some of the Tarsias', Carlis', and Mamuca della Torres' descendants would later come to think of them) but as deeply grounded in a milieu that itself both defied and helped forge Enlightenment notions of East and West.[84]

Christine Philliou has warned us that "those [Ottomans] who became 'cosmopolitans' did so not out of a desire for contact with people different from themselves, but to gain access to greater status, power, and wealth by connecting several—insular—groups in the empire."[85] Her point raises several questions: First, were the groups that dragomans connected indeed insular? The answer seems to depend at least in part on the eyes of the beholder. In official contexts, Ottoman and foreign representatives certainly tended to rely on dragomans to mediate their interactions and not to engage one another directly. This formal mediation is well captured by numerous illustrations in the Ballarino album featuring dragomans "in between" Ottoman and Venetian parties. Such forced mediation may have had to do with diplomatic protocol more than with the lack of a shared linguistic code or occasions for less structured sociability per se.[86] Second, dragomans, while self-consciously enacting cultural mediation, did so in their professional capacity, not out of any ethical valorization of "diversity" or a commitment to fostering understanding between "different" peoples. We should be weary of ascribing to them retroactively (proto)nationalist sensibilities. If anything, as their portraits attest, dragomans' emphasis on Ottoman alterity was meant, at least in part, to underscore their own utility as those who were adept at commensurating political and ethnolinguistic difference. Thus, in thinking about the production of knowledge in early modern Istanbul, "difference" is better conceptualized not as a pre-existing fact but rather as co-emergent with the settings, institutions, genres, and practices through which notions of Ottoman-ness were articulated. We might think about dragomans' networking as process rather than about networks as channels, stable or otherwise, through which "knowledge" freely flowed.

Like the *şehnameci*, the Ottoman court historian, and Ballarino, the Venetian secretary, the dragomans who commissioned the artifacts discussed in this chapter might be thought of as "subordinate elites," embedded in complex networks of patronage. The resultant multifocal perspective evinced by their textual-cum-visual artifacts reminds us once again of the entwined histories of Venetians and Ottomans in the early modern Mediterranean, and the need to study practices of cultural mediation, commensuration, and boundary-marking in this space of encounter as inherently relational, saturated with layers upon layers of accumulated imperial and trans-imperial sensibilities.

CHAPTER 5

Disciplining Language

Dragomans and Oriental Philology

What is the use of the Turkish language? Reply: Very little indeed in Theology and Sacred Philology. Unremarkable in Politics. [But] frequent in our dealings with the Ottoman Porte; there the Turkish language matters.

—August Pfeiffer[1]

It is a striking phenomenon that at a time of manifold state connections with the Ottoman Empire, as established already in the fifteenth century by various Western powers, above all by the Venetians, especially in the numerous negotiations of the lagoon city [Venice], France and Austria with the Porte on the affairs of the Venetian War, peace, and commerce, no greater engagement with the Turkish language could be effected beyond these purely practical purposes.

—Franz Babinger[2]

FRANZ BABINGER, arguably the most influential historian of the Ottoman Empire of his generation, was quite perceptive in contrasting early modern Europeans' widespread ignorance of the Ottoman language with their intense diplomatic engagements with the Ottomans. What is especially telling about Babinger's formulation, however, might be its passive construction: while "states" are busy "connecting," "negotiating," and "establishing" diplomatic relations, no one in particular is responsible for "engagement with the Turkish language" (or lack thereof, as the case may be). This agentless absence highlights widespread and enduring European ignorance of Ottoman literature and high culture more generally. It also points to invisible technicians—chiefly dragomans—whose philological, linguistic, and translation efforts have received far less recognition than those of university-based Oriental philologists and their modern hagiographers and disciplinary heirs, the Orientalists. This and the next two chapters consider how dragomans' linguistic and translational works served as key sites for the articulation of Ottomanist knowledge in a broader early modern emergent Republic of Letters.

AS HE WAS preparing to embark on his mission to Istanbul in 1680, the incoming bailo Giovanni Battista Donà decided to learn Turkish. Tellingly, no other bailo since 1544 had taken the trouble to do so.[3] To this end, Donà recruited the services of an Armenian Dominican missionary, Giovanni Agop (Yovhannes Konstandnupōlsec'i), who at the time was assisting Donà's brother, Andrea, in catechizing Turkish-speaking neophytes at the Pia Casa dei Catecumeni.[4] Agop, who was born in Istanbul in 1635, had spent time at the college of the Propaganda Fide in Rome and at the Jesuit college in Lyon, then in Livorno (where he helped establish the Armenian press and served as its censor) and in Marseille. In 1685, he published an Italian-language Ottoman grammar and phrase book, judged by a modern scholar to be among the best of its time, and a testament to its author's deep knowledge of the language.[5] Three years later, when Donà sought to publish a compilation of Ottoman proverbs with Italian and Latin translations and an annotated bibliography of Ottoman science—the fruits of his apprentice dragomans' labor—he turned to Agop for help in copy editing the manuscripts and in securing a suitable typeface. The resulting two publications, *Raccolta curiosissima d'adaggi turcheschi* and *Della letteratura de' Turchi*, made a major impression throughout Europe. They immediately spawned several other publications by members of the same circle of Armenian Catholic scholars in Padua, where Agop had relocated in the meantime to take up a position in a seminary, whose superintendent for Oriental languages was another prelate of Ottoman provenance, the Diyarbakır-born Syriac turned Catholic Timoteo Agnellini (Humaylī Ibn Da'fī Karnūsh).[6]

This vignette takes us back to the question posed at the book's outset: how did Istanbul-based dragomans, through their extensive trans-imperial networking practices, mediate decidedly Ottoman epistemologies of translation and re-appropriation to an emergent field of knowledge eventually known as Orientalism? Previous chapters underscored the centrality of dragomans to the diplomatic institutions through which knowledge about the Ottomans circulated from Istanbul to other sites of intellectual production, and the impact that these diplomatic channels of mediation themselves had on the ultimate shape of the knowledge thus generated. It is now time to explore the role of the dragomanate in the very introduction of the Ottoman Turkish language into an emergent Orientalist curriculum, and its canonization as one of the three "learned languages of Islam" (*elsene i-selase*).[7]

Dragomans and the Routes of Ottoman Studies

Viewed as scriptural languages or auxiliary tools for biblical, philological, or scientific study, Hebrew, Aramaic, and Arabic received significant attention from scholiasts at least from the twelfth century onward.[8] These languages were joined, by the seventeenth century, by the languages of South and East Asia, which were studied as the vehicle of intense Catholic missionizing efforts, and thus of interest to the Propaganda Fide and its printing press.[9] Unlike all these languages, Turkish was little known and rarely studied in early modern Europe. One scholar has recently estimated that "around 1700 there were more Protestant academics with some knowledge of Ge'ez . . . than Persian or Turkish."[10] European ignorance of Turkish at the turn of the eighteenth century was still so profound that even a scholar who was soon to compose a grammar for its study could argue in 1692 that "Turkish related to Arabic as French did to Latin." The author of this puzzling pronouncement, Johann David Schieferdecker, was not alone.[11] Widespread European obliviousness to Turkish was symptomatic of the broader neglect of Ottoman studies in institutionalized programs of instruction, teachers, and pedagogical materials. As Noel Malcolm notes, "for most Oriental scholars in Western Europe [. . .] Turkish was a workaday tongue which they might pick up if they spent some time in Istanbul or Anatolia, but it would hardly feature—excepting the occasional attention paid to some of the Ottoman chronicles—in their scholarly activities."[12] This neglect is crucial to the story of how and why Ottoman Turkish—and the world of Ottoman letters, history, and politics embedded in it—did, belatedly, enter the Orientalist canon. One reason for dragomans' centrality to the constitution of Ottoman studies is precisely the neglect of the Ottoman Turkish language by more established scholars in European universities. A prevailing—and enduring—understanding of the Ottomans as the destroyers rather than the cultivators of classical tradition (with the demise of Byzantium in 1453 as a watershed moment) further disincentivized humanistically inclined scholars to take up the Ottoman language as a serious pursuit.

The glaring absence of Ottoman language and letters from early modern university curricula is significant precisely because the historiography of Orientalism has traced its genealogy primarily (and sometimes exclusively) within the metropolitan academy and among metropolitan scholars. Yet the epistemologies, methodologies, and circuits of knowledge that eventually constituted "Ottoman" as a proper object of study beyond the Ottoman Empire—indeed as a central facet of Orientalism—often circumvented those very institutionalized domains in a kind of early modern alt-academy: contract based, short-term, precarious, and poorly recognized.[13] And paramount in Ottoman's alt-academy circuits of knowledge were dragomans. Attending to dragomans' efforts as students of the Ottoman language reveals a longer and spatially more diffuse genealogy of Orientalism, one that extends back to the sixteenth century and involves Istanbul (and the Ottoman eastern Mediterranean more broadly) as a vital node.

As Daniel Stolzenberg recently argued, being an Orientalist in early modern Europe implied, first and foremost, knowledge of "Oriental languages" as the foundation for any claim of expertise. This held true for both Catholics and Protestants. Based on a representative sample of Latin works on "Oriental languages" published between 1450 and 1750 as cataloged in WorldCat, Stolzenberg suggests a modest beginning in the 1590s and an unmistakable rise in the printing of books on the subject in the 1620s, with a sustained interest throughout the seventeenth and early eighteenth centuries.[14] Even though this is precisely the heyday of the dragoman renaissance, as defined in this book, the relative neglect of Ottoman Turkish in the corpus of academic Orientalism is unmistakable. For example, among twenty-eight Latin titles that enumerate as their subject several "Oriental languages," only six list Turkish, as compared to twenty-three that mention Arabic, and twenty-two each that mention Hebrew, Chaldean,[15] and Syriac.

This disparity in printed matter is paralleled by the relative prevalence of university chairs for different languages: chairs for Arabic had been established in Paris, Leiden, Cambridge, and Oxford as early as 1538, 1613, 1633, and 1636, respectively.[16] Dozens of more generic chairs for "Oriental languages" were established all across Protestant Europe in the seventeenth century, almost always meaning Hebrew and Syriac.[17] In contrast, notwithstanding precocious efforts to establish chairs for Turkish in France (at the Collège Royal in Paris in 1750 and again in 1773) and in Russia (at the University of Kazan in 1828), most major universities did not endow such chairs until the late nineteenth century.

To be sure, instruction in Ottoman Turkish did take place in other institutional settings, particularly in the context of training dragomans and other cadres for diplomatic service. Yet Ottoman Turkish instructors were rarely employed by universities (let alone as "professors of Oriental languages" with endowed chairs).[18] This sociological fact is significant because the scholarship on the discipline of Orientalism has traced its genealogy primarily (and sometimes exclusively) within the academy. Here, in contrast, I consider different epistemologies, methodologies, and circuits of knowledge for Ottoman studies, which often circumvented those institutionalized domains that contemporaries would have recognized as constituting "Oriental languages." Situating what counted as "Orient" and "Oriental" in that period is an important undertaking. If nothing else, the Ottoman language became an "Oriental language" in part precisely through its embedding in an academic, institutionalized curriculum (expressed, inter alia, through the formation of university chairs). At the same time, we should not lose sight of the fuzziness of categories such as "Oriental languages," and of the capacity of objects of inquiry to move across categories.[19]

Who, then, pursued "Ottoman studies" in general, and the study of the Ottoman language specifically, in the seventeenth century? Here, a comparison with the European itineraries of Hebrew and Arabic are instructive, and underscore how the long-standing presence of Hebrew-and Arabic-language communities in Europe may have shaped these itineraries. The expulsions and forced conversions of Jews and Muslims on the Iberian Peninsula from the turn of the sixteenth century onward, and the growing phenomenon of Europe-bound Eastern Christians (propelled, in part, by the establishment of the Maronite College in Rome in 1584) contributed significantly to the European mobility of Hebrew-and Arabic-speakers. These myriad mobilities ensured a steady stream of scholars—some more qualified than others—who eked out a living as language instructors, private tutors, amanuenses, catalogers of Oriental manuscripts, and occasional dragomans for Arabic-speaking North African envoys.[20] It enabled someone like the Dutch Thomas Erpenius (1584–1624), "the greatest Arabist of his generation," to secure a chair of Arabic at the University of Leiden and to publish an authoritative Arabic grammar without ever leaving Europe, simply by taking private lessons in Paris, first with the Cairene Copt Yusuf ibn Abu Dhaqn (known as Josephus Abudacnus or Barbatus), then with the Moroccan of Andalusian descent Aḥmad ibn Qāsim Al-Ḥajarī, and by scouring the Arabic-language collections of libraries in Paris, Milan, Basel, Geneva, and Heidelberg.[21] Similarly, Erpenius's patron and friend, the great philologist Isaac Casaubon (1559–1614), was able to achieve a certain fluency in Hebrew by supplementing his juvenile studies with private tutoring with the Genevan Hebraist Pierre Chevalier and by making extensive use of *Tsemah David / Dittionario Hebraico Novo*, the trilingual Hebrew-Latin-Italian dictionary that the Italian Jewish scholar David de' Pomi published in 1587. Casaubon's Arabic, too, was acquired from his copy of Spey's 1583 *Compendium grammatices arabicae* and through his Parisian private tutors, first Etienne Hubert, then Adriaen Willemsz.[22]

No parallel access to tutors and authoritative printed dictionaries and grammars was available to assist Ottoman language learners in contemporary Western Europe, where very few Ottoman scholars sojourned.[23] Even scholars who ardently sought to acquire the language faced significant challenges in finding tutors.[24] At least until the late seventeenth century, one had to travel to Ottoman lands to learn Ottoman. Once there, one was faced with a complex linguistic situation. Here is how the Ottoman courtier, poet, historian, and administrator Mustafa Ali described the nature of contemporary Ottoman Turkish in 1592:

> The astonishing language current in the state of Rum, composed of four languages [West Turkish, Chagatai, Arabic, and Persian], is a pure gilded tongue which, in the speech of the literati, seems more difficult than any of these. If one were to equate speaking Arabic with a religious obligation, and the use of Persian with a sanctioned tradition, then the speaking of a Turkish made up of these sweetnesses becomes a meritorious act, and, in the view of those eloquent in Turkish, the use of simple Turkish should be forbidden.[25]

What Mustafa Ali astutely described was the convergence of two processes well attested in contemporary Istanbul. On the one hand, courtly circles operated as functionally triglossic environments, where Arabic and Persian were used alongside Turkish for distinct spheres of courtly interaction and cultural production. In the words of Cornell Fleischer, "While Arabic was the language of [early modern Ottoman] science and scholarship, Persian was the language of courtly society and the vehicle of the works of poetry and prose most important to cultivated Ottomans."[26] On the other hand, in the course of the fifteenth and sixteenth centuries, courtly speakers of Turkish incorporated Arabisms and Persianisms throughout grammatical aspects (from lexicon to syntax), as well as literary models, whose quotients in one's speech became a measure of one's cultivation. Ottoman, in this sense, was no one's first language, but rather a highly cultivated register acquired through literacy and a lengthy process of resocialization at a court that was inherently multilingual (in its ethnolinguistic composition), and plurilingual (actively cultivating its members' fluency in multiple idioms and registers).[27] The result—a self-consciously "synthetic" Ottoman language—itself came to be used extensively for administrative and ceremonial functions, not least as a statement of power vis-à-vis foreign ambassadors. This was the case even when other languages (e.g., Greek, Slavic, German, or Italian) were available as a shared idiom for all parties present.[28] Maneuvering through this linguistic complexity thus served as a proxy of courtly refinement, so much so that the affirmation of social hierarchy and boundaries precluded courtiers from speaking "simple Turkish."[29]

Heightened awareness of Turkish-Ottoman diglossia among contemporary courtly speakers may well have derived, at least in part, from familiarity with the well-established Arabic grammatical and philological tradition. Arabic, after all, has maintained a distinction between "high" and "low" varieties (albeit in widely different forms and under different nomenclature) from the time it acquired new speakers beyond the Arabian Peninsula with the conquests of the seventh century CE. At least by the late Middle Ages varieties developed that speakers recognized as "mixed," and which they adapted for specific oral and written functions.[30]

The question of how and why these ideological understandings of diglossia, as developed across Arabophone milieus, were adapted to the Ottoman imperial context remains open, and exceeds the parameters of this study. Clearly, the perceived "difficulty" of Ottoman as a high-register synthesis of Turkish, Arabic, and Persian, coupled with the language's relative lack of scriptural, missionizing, and literary aura, made the proposition of mastering it difficult even for avid language learners. Foreign diplomats bound for Istanbul, with few notable exceptions, opted to rely on dragomans to translate Ottoman words and worlds for them, essentially ceding a niche market to them. The undeniably central role of dragomans in endeavors to institutionalize the study of Ottoman in Europe in the eighteenth century will be revisited in this chapter's conclusion.

But first, let us consider the precautious interventions of dragomans in the study of Oriental philology in general, and Ottoman Turkish in particular, in the period before 1730. To this end, we begin this chapter by tracing dragomans' substantial role in the production of grammars, dictionaries, lexicons, vocabularies, glossaries, and phrase books—what we will call "metalinguistic texts." After comparing dragomans' production of such texts to that of other groups, particularly missionaries, scholars, and lay travelers, the chapter identifies some of dragomans' unique contributions to enduring Ottoman language ideologies (as defined below) and relates them to their professional and familial trajectories. It concludes by considering the significance of dragomans' apprenticeship practices for an evolving pedagogy of immersive language study.

Assembling the Ottoman Language: Grammars and Dictionaries

Ottoman language-learning resources were in short supply in early modern Europe. As noted above, whereas chairs for Oriental languages began to proliferate from the sixteenth century onward, they focused almost exclusively on scriptural languages: Hebrew, Greek, Syriac, and, eventually, Arabic. The first chair for Turkish was established only in 1750 (by some accounts, 1773), and held by the Istanbul-trained French dragoman turned royal secretary interpreter Denis Dominique Cardonne until his death in 1783. Evidence suggests that very little actual teaching took place during much of Cardonne's tenure. To be sure, even before the establishment of chairs for Turkish, some professors of Arabic and Persian (and, more rarely, "Oriental languages" in general) dabbled in the study of the Ottoman language, and on occasion even attempted to produce and circulate pedagogical material for that purpose. Their efforts were often criticized by subsequent generations of scholars as deeply flawed.[31]

Without university offerings in Ottoman, throughout the seventeenth century few resources were devoted to it beyond Ottoman borders. Whatever language-learning materials were available in Europe often circulated in manuscript, through highly unstable patronage and tutelage networks, as even the typeface for printing Ottoman-language materials in Arabic script was difficult to obtain. The Arabic and Persian typeface acquired by François Savary de Brèves at great cost in the early 1600s was lost for the better part of a century. Franciscus Meninski's Ottoman publications—for which he served as his own "compositor, pressman, and proofreader," and which he printed himself with Arabic typeface acquired from the Nürem-berg printer Johann Lobinger—were delayed, and in a few cases lost, due to a fire in his print shop during the Ottoman siege of Vienna in 1683.[32]

This context of limited institutionalization and only haphazard efforts to introduce the Ottoman language to non-Ottoman publics forms the back-drop to the following discussion of "metalinguistic texts," namely linguis-tic treatises, grammars, dictionaries, vocabularies, glossaries, and phrase books. Linguistic anthropologists have proposed the term "techniques of linguistic regimentation" to highlight the role of early modern dictionaries and grammars in broader disciplinary projects that treated language as a "natural scientific object" and intended to reduce and control linguistic (and thereby social) variation by subjecting linguistic phenomena to the dual processes of commensuration and boundary-making.[33] Historically minded linguistic anthropologists have done much to uncover the intimate connection between the production of dictionaries and grammars of lan-guages of colonized peoples and imperial and colonial projects. Their work has called into question the assumption that such linguistic undertakings were merely descriptive vis-à-vis "languages" as a priori self-contained objects of study. Indeed, this body of work has conclusively shown the tight bonds of the mediation of linguistic knowledge not only with lin-guistic codification but with the objectification of religious categories, and with processes of socioeconomic reordering and simplification overall.[34] These insights are fundamental to the approach in this chapter. However, as elaborated below, the production and circulation of Ottoman dictionar-ies and grammars for (primarily) non-Ottoman language learners took shape in a decidedly trans-imperial context. As such, we cannot start by assuming that these lexicographic and grammatical works disciplined their trans-imperial readers in any straightforward way. Something much more complicated was at work. We can observe a dynamic tension between the language ideologies that often informed dragomans' metalinguistic production and their embedding in extra-Ottoman patronage networks, whose own disciplinary capacity vis-à-vis Ottoman speakers was decid-edly limited. Additionally, dragomans' linguistic choices, and, especially, their metapragmatic discourse about the nature of the Ottoman language, aimed to underscore their own linguistic and social cultivation—perhaps more than did the equivalent discourse of contemporary professional gram-marians and lexicographers. This dimension of their work and its height-ened reflexivity, self-referentiality, and metapragmatic awareness, are our overarching concerns here; hence the collective designation of these genres as "metalinguistic texts."[35]

In other ways too, the belated and halting emergence of Ottoman-Latin dictionaries and other metalinguistic texts intended for non-Ottoman publics may be fruitfully contrasted with the sixteenth-century uptick in production (if not always publication) of bilingual dictionaries in other imperial contexts. Such texts—for example, for indigenous languages of the Spanish Empire—were produced mostly by Franciscan and Dominican missionaries and/or by speakers of these languages in the wake of conquest. Authors were aided, in all likelihood, by some kind of "elicitation list," and relied to varying degrees on Antonio de Nebrija's Latin-Spanish metalinguistic works.[36] In other words, these dictionaries were the products either of highly self-conscious efforts at linguistic documentation or of fluent bilinguals who wrote primarily for proselytizing purposes.

In contrast, dragomans were neither sojourning missionaries nor "native speakers" of Ottoman, but rather specialists in the use of Ottoman as a courtly linguistic register. In this sense, while their fluency did not always match that of bona fide Ottoman courtiers, it ideally approximated both the latter's methods of language acquisition (though immersive apprenticeship) and contexts of use (through refined courtly and diplomatic—primarily written—genres). These contexts of acquisition and use had direct implications for the language ideologies that dragomans professed and, ultimately, for their linguistic production more broadly.[37]

Some eighty-four bi-and multilingual grammars, vocabularies, dictionaries, and phrase books of Ottoman Turkish in Latin and Romance languages are known to have been written before 1730 (table 5.1; appendix 5.1).[38] Of those, thirty-four were printed at the time, some going into multiple editions and translations, occasionally copied or excerpted by hand. More than half of the works, however—fifty unique titles—survive only in manuscript, some of limited circulation, but others copied, consulted, and annotated more or less extensively by contemporaries. Combined, these works served as the veritable foundation for the strong philological and comparativist orientation of an emergent field of Ottoman studies. These works varied greatly not only in medium but in length, format, intended audience and purposes, and, especially, authorship, which ranged from scholars to diplomats, missionaries, merchants, pilgrims, and captives.

Of the eighty-four works in this corpus of early modern Ottoman metalinguistic texts, five bilingual dictionaries are of unknown provenance

TABLE 5.1 Ottoman metalinguistic texts in Latin and Romance languages up to 1730, by authorship type

Author type	Manuscript	Print	Total
Dragomans	25	14	39 (46%)
Scholars	7	9	16 (19%)
Missionaries	9	5	14 (17%)
Lay sojourners	4	6	10 (12%)
Unidentified	5	0	5 (6%)
Total	50	34	84

and authorship, though at least three of those seem to have originated in the diplomatic circles of Istanbul.[39] Of the remaining seventy-nine, just over a half are divided roughly evenly between three categories of authors: scholars (sixteen); missionaries (fourteen);[40] and lay sojourners, including travelers, pilgrims, captives, and merchants (ten). The other half—thirty-nine unique titles—were penned by dragomans, apprentice dragomans, and other embassy or consular personnel during or after lengthy sojourns in the Ottoman Empire. For the purposes of the analysis here, diplomatic personnel are treated as part of the dragoman category, as they largely shared methodologies, epistemologies, and readership. This sizable contribution—indeed, plurality of works—by dragomans and other diplomatic personnel lends itself to comparative analysis vis-à-vis those by other author categories to highlight some of the unique and enduring features of dragomans' Ottoman metalinguistic work, and the centrality of this work to trans-imperial statecraft itself.

To be sure, a certain degree of arbitrariness is inevitable in assigning authors to one or another professional category, given complex biographical itineraries, highly collaborative contexts of production, and multiple or uncertain intended readership. For example, what are we to make of William Seaman, the author of the *Grammatica linguae Turcicae* (1670)? Seaman traveled to Istanbul in the late 1620s to learn Ottoman while living and working in the household of the English ambassador to the Porte, Sir Peter Wyche, thus sharing an important educational trajectory with dragomans. He remained in close contact with Wyche's widow and son thereafter. At the same time, he was also an erudite Oxonian who corresponded with the French scholar Louis Picques, among others. His (deeply flawed) translation of the Bible into Turkish was sponsored, among others, by Samuel Hartlib and Robert Boyle, of Royal Society fame. Yet ultimately, sponsorship and clientele for his Turkish publications came mostly from members of the English Levant Company, with decidedly more mundane, commercial interests than the millenarian proselytizing fervor that informed Hartlib, or the comparative philological theories that increasingly animated the Republic of Letters.

Seaman's "mixed" classification is hardly an outlier in the small world of early modern Ottoman metalinguistic text producers. Istanbul-based Capuchins such as Bernard de Paris ("Bernardo de Parigi"), author of the *Vocabolario italiano-turchesco*, were entrusted with educating many of Pera's youth, including, importantly, most French apprentice dragomans. De Paris and his fellow Istanbulite missionaries seemed particularly attuned to the needs of diplomats and thus to the Ottoman linguistic registers spoken and written by courtly elites. De Paris lived in the Capuchin convent in the precinct of the French embassy in Pera for over four decades, and wrote in his introduction that he undertook much of his lexicographic research in the embassy. He was a close friend of the French ambassador, Harlay de Césy, serving as his son's Latin tutor.[41] This anticipated diplomatic—as much as missionary—context of use may explain, at least in part, why the *Vocabolario*, which De Paris had composed in French in 1649, was translated into Italian at the behest of the Propaganda Fide by another Capuchin missionary, Pierre d'Abbeville, and printed in Rome in 1665. Italian, after all, was the common tongue of Istanbulite diplomacy at the time, serving as the primary language of communication between dragomans and the city's diplomatic corps. Conversely, Istanbulite missionaries regularly used grammars produced by dragomans and diplomats, such as André Du Ryer's *Rudimenta Grammatices* (1630, 1633) and Franciscus Meninski's *Thesaurus* (1680, 1687, 1756, 1780).[42] The 1685 printing of the Armenian Apostolic missionary Giovanni Agop's Ottoman grammar at the behest of the Venetian bailo Giovanni Battista Donà was discussed at the chapter's outset.[43] The French dragoman François Pétis de la Croix collaborated with the Roman-trained Maronite scholar Pierre Dipy (Butros Diyab, 1620–1709) on an early catalog of Ottoman manuscripts in the Royal Library, later abridged and copied by the Aleppo-born royal interpreter François Barout in 1718.[44] Conversely, the translational activities of the Maronite scholars Gabriel Sionita (Jibrā'īl aṣ-Ṣahyūnī), John Hesronita (Yūḥannā al-Ḥaṣrūnī), and Victor Scialac (Naṣrallāh Shalaq al-ʿĀqūrī) were clearly shaped, at least in part, not only by their Roman Jesuit education but by the interests of the former French ambassador to the Porte turned typographer and printer, François Savary de Brèves.[45]

If the boundary between diplomatic and missionary imperatives in the development of Ottoman metalinguistic texts seems highly porous, even more challenging is to account for the role of dragomans in mediating other authors' encounter with Ottoman language and language ideologies. What, for example, are we to make of the profound impact—sometimes acknowledged but often unstated—of dragomans' work on other metalinguistic texts?[46] And of the immense impact of the institutions they helped establish for Ottoman language instruction on later generations of Orientalists, diplomats, and missionaries throughout Europe and the Ottoman Empire?[47] The methodological limits of a rigidly comparative framework are evident, particularly as early modern lexicographic and grammatical works habitually plagiarized one another, and as the behind-the-scenes work of dragomans as amanuenses and assistants to various European sojourners in Ottoman lands, while evident anecdotally, remained, for the most part, unacknowledged or understated.[48] In a similar vein, we should retain the analytical distinction between the professional identity of authors and their intended readership, as dragomans sometimes addressed their works to a decidedly scholarly and humanistically inclined audience. A case in point is Filippo Argenti, who was a secretary to the Florentine consul in Istanbul, but dedicated his work to the latter's son, Rodolfo Lotti, and other learned friends.[49] A similar scholarly orientation is evident in the works of Viennese dragoman scholars a century and a half later, including Meninski, Podestà, and, to a lesser extent, Bratutti, as discussed below.

Finally, the question of readership raises the problem of ascertaining circulation. Given the dearth of available pedagogical materials, we cannot assume that manuscript dictionaries and grammars enjoyed only circumscribed circulation, to say nothing of long-term scholarly impact. Plenty of evidence suggests, for example, that manuscripts played an important role in entrenching analytical frameworks and structural conventions within this corpus, often bolstering the reputation of printed texts. For example, the Theatine missionary Francesco Maria Maggio (b. 1612 in Palermo) reports that, prior to departing on his mission to the Caucasus in 1636, he received from his Turkish instructor, none other than the intrepid Roman traveler Pietro Della Valle, a summary of the latter's Turkish grammar (written years earlier during his sojourn in Isfahan in 1621).[50] While in the field, Maggio also acquired a manuscript copy of a Turkish grammar by another missionary, Jacobus Stephanus, likely composed in Istanbul ca. 1640. These, along with Du Ryer's grammar (published 1630), proved foundational for Maggio's own work, which itself appeared in print in 1643 and again in 1670.[51] Maggio's grammar, faulty as it was, is cited numerous times by Meninski in his quadrilingual grammar, which was first published in Vienna in 1680 and which quickly became the gold standard for Ottoman grammars, used far and wide (including in the Venetian and French consulates in Istanbul).[52] In this Latinate Republic of Letters, Isfahan and Istanbul, Rome, Paris, and Vienna, all played a part, and missionary linguistics could not be separated out easily from diplomacy and philology.

Similarly, even an older work such as the anonymous quadrilingual *Vocabulario Nuovo* (1574) is known to have gone through numerous editions and to have existed in the French Royal Library, where it would have been accessible to future dragomans, students of the Collège Louis-le-Grand.[53] Argenti's manuscript *Regola del parlar turco* (1533) likewise is known to have been copied, edited, and redacted multiple times, both by its author in Istanbul and by his readers in Florence. Giovanni Molino's *Dittionario della lingua italiana-turchesca* (1641) not only "inspired" the grammar section of Antonio Mascis's *Vocabolario Toscano e Turchesco* (1677), as well as Arcangelo Carradori's unpublished Italian-Turkish dictionary (completed ca. 1650), but spawned manuscript copies now in the British Library and in the Bibliothèque nationale.[54] William Seaman's 1670 treatise on Turkish grammar was copied in 1717 by Johann Eberhard Rau (Ravius, 1695–1770), professor at Herborn.[55] Multiple manuscript translations and copies of Du Ryer's and of Holdermann's grammars were still undertaken by students at the École des langues orientales in Paris as late as 1829 and 1831, respectively, as well as in Leiden. A plagiarized, quasi-verbatim Spanish translation of Holdermann, completed in 1799 by Juan Antonio Romero, an *Interprete por Lenguas Orientales*, also survives.[56]

As this overview suggests, a taxonomy of authors' professional trajectories is largely heuristic. At the same time, it underscores the outsize contribution of dragomans to the corpus, and their decisive role in the (uneasy) introduction of Turkish, particularly Ottoman Turkish, to a budding early modern scholarly field of Oriental philology. The following sections introduce this corpus, consider its most salient features, and outline how it helped shape the epistemological framework through which Ottoman Turkish became legible to a European public. In particular, I show how these works gave "Turkish" as it was studied in Europe a decidedly elite Istanbulite flavor. I suggest that dragomans did not simply refract Ottoman elites' linguistic register but their language ideologies as well, namely "the ideas with which participants and observers frame their understanding of linguistic varieties and map those understandings onto people, events, and activities that are significant to them."[57] I then bring into sharper relief some of the salient features of dragomans' understanding of Ottoman Turkish in relation to other "Oriental languages" by considering the citational practices of Meninski, arguably the most influential early modern dragoman turned Ottoman lexicographer and grammarian.

A Dragomans' Ottoman Metalinguistic Corpus

The earliest dragoman contribution to the Ottoman metalinguistic corpus is Filippo Argenti's *Regola del parlare turcho* (1533), the first grammar of Ottoman ever to appear in Europe. Linguists considered it to be "the richest and most important work on Ottoman by a European throughout the sixteenth century."[58] Argenti, a secretary to the Florentine legation in Istanbul from 1524 to ca. 1533, intended his work as a gift to his friends and patrons among humanist circles in Florence. Although the *Regola* was never printed, it is known to have circulated in multiple manuscript copies, and to have served as the basis for several later bilingual vocabularies and dictionaries.[59]

Other works by dragomans had an even greater impact on the history of Ottoman language learning in Europe, particularly in the seventeenth century. First to be printed was the Alexandria-based French dragoman and consul André du Ryer's *Rudimenta grammatices linguae turcicae* (1630, 1633), which is known to have circulated widely and to have been plagiarized, at least in part, by a few other authors.[60] Less than a decade later, in 1641, the first printed Turkish-Italian dictionary, *Dittionario della lingua italiana-turchesca* was published in Rome. The work was authored by the Armenian Yovhannes Ankiwrac'i ("John of Ankara"), known in Italianate circles (and self-identified on the colophon of his dictionary) as Giovanni Molino. Before moving to Rome, Molino, who was born in Ankara ca. 1592, had served as a French and later Venetian dragoman in Istanbul.[61] The survival of dozens of copies of his dictionary in university libraries not only throughout Italy but in France, Germany, the Netherlands, Switzerland, Denmark, Poland, Sweden, the UK and the US attests to the work's enduring relevance well into the eighteenth century.[62] Other metalinguistic works by dragomans soon followed, including the Transylvanian dragoman and diplomat Jakab Harsányi Nagy's *Colloquia familiaria Turcico-Latina* (Cologne, 1672), the Tuscan dragoman Antonio Mascis's *Vocabolario Toscano e Turchesco* (1677), the Venetian bailo Giovanni Donà and his apprentice dragomans' *Raccolta curiosissima d'adaggi turcheschi* (1688), three late-seventeenth-century manuscript French-Ottoman dictionaries by the royal secretary-interpreters Jean-Baptiste de Fiennes, François Pétis de la Croix, and Antoine Galland, and, finally, the Venetian apprentice dragoman Pietr'Antonio Rizzi's "Memoria locale di precetti grammaticali turchi" (1711) and his French counterpart Jean-Baptiste Couët's book of "phrases turques et françoises" (1712), both in manuscript and evidently intended primarily for personal use.[63]

While significant for many reasons discussed below, no dragoman's metalinguistic works were as impactful as those that resulted from the epic rivalry between two Vienna-based dragomans, Giovanni Battista Podestà (1624–1703) and Franciscus Meninski (1620–1698), whose publications contributed significantly to Vienna's preeminence in a nascent field of Orientalism. These include Podestà's *Assertiones de principiis substantialibus, accidentalibus proximis et remotis, diversisque differentiis linguarum* (1669), *Dissertatio academica continens specimen triennalis profectûs in linguis orientalibus* (1677), *Elementa calligraphiæ Arabico-Persico-Turcicæ* (1678), and *Cursus grammaticalis linguarum orientalium* (1690–1703), and Meninski's three-volume *Thesaurus linguarum orientalium* (1680a, 1680b) and *Complementum thesauri linguarum orientalium* (1687).[64]

Meninski was a first on many fronts. His *Thesaurus* included a highly influential and multiply reprinted trilingual Arabic-Persian-Turkish lexicon and a Turkish-Latin dictionary that remained virtually unsurpassed until the nineteenth century.[65] The French ambassador to the Porte Marquis de Bonnac's memorandum of 1719 lamented the difficulty of using Meninski for the instruction of apprentice dragomans, given the book's prohibitive cost and students' limited familiarity with Latin, but these complaints make it clear that few viable alternatives were available at the time.[66] Despite these limitations and the publication's large format (four folio volumes of about 1,000 pages each), the expanded edition of Meninski's work, issued under Empress Maria Theresia's auspices in 1780, still served as the main, and possibly only, dictionary for use by apprentice dragomans in the

French embassy in Istanbul at the turn of the nineteenth century.[67] Among other innovations, Meninski based his dictionary on the literary register of Ottoman, and invented "the first 'academic' transliteration system with fairly consistent rules."[68] He showed exceptional sensitivity to pronunciation and to vowel harmony—a hallmark of Turkish phonology—which many previous authors had missed or misrepresented.[69] As several recent linguistic studies have noted, Meninski adapted the use of the letter "y" to represent the Ottoman Turkish sound nowadays represented by ı (dotless i) in a manner clearly inflected by contemporary German and Polish orthography.[70] This suggests an effort to accommodate his intended readership among patrons in Warsaw and Vienna, where he had served consecutively.

Meninski's peripatetic personal and professional trajectories typified many a dragoman's career, taking him across several imperial capitals, languages, and institutions. Before settling permanently in Vienna and embarking on a program of scholarship, pedagogy, and publication, the Lorraine-born dragoman had traveled first to Rome, where he studied philology with the Jesuit Father Gattini at the Gregorian University; then to Gdansk, where he served as French and Italian language tutor and penned three grammar textbooks for these languages as well as for Polish; and then, in 1654, to Istanbul, where he stayed on and off for several years and served on three different missions as a Polish envoy. In 1660, he proposed to establish a Polish school for apprentice dragomans in Warsaw.[71] Unsuccessful in this pursuit, he relocated to Vienna in 1662, where he was to remain (except for missions to the Ottoman border in 1664 and a trip to Jerusalem and Lebanon in 1669), serving as court interpreter from 1666 and, eventually, as councilor on the Aulic War Council.[72]

While not all dragomans shared Meninski's remarkable spatial and professional mobility, nearly all—whether Ottoman or European-born—had spent extensive periods acquiring Ottoman in situ in an immersive environment, mainly in the courtly and diplomatic circles of Istanbul or, to a lesser extent, in other Ottoman urban settings. What dragomans acquired during such extensive sojourns was not simply linguistic fluency, but a comprehensive sociology of the Ottoman language—how different linguistic registers were to be used effectively in various situations. Such a sociology refracted Ottoman courtly language ideologies.

With few notable exceptions, most authors of Ottoman dictionaries and grammars for European readership—dragomans and others—used Latinate script (and the orthography of one or another non-Ottoman language)

to render Ottoman Turkish words.[73] As a consequence, this substantial corpus of what is often called "transcription texts" has served linguists over
the years to study Ottoman phonetics. Many historical linguists consider
Latin transcription more useful for the reconstruction of early modern pronunciation than materials written in the Ottoman (Arabo-Persian) script,
whose conventionalized rendering of different contemporary vowel systems is virtually impossible to reconstruct. Beyond phonetics, linguists
have used this corpus to explore Ottoman lexicon, morphology, syntax, and
other aspects of grammar. By and large, modern historical linguists studying these "transcription texts," while keenly interested in their differences,
have taken them to be "documenting the spoken codes," i.e., to merely represent—more or less skillfully—an external reality of diachronic language
shifts and the spatial-social distribution of supposedly discrete linguistic
codes.[74] This is true even of a recent volume that, while helpfully calling
such works "mediator texts," still accepts language variation as an independently observable fact and says little about the complex processes of
mediation in which these texts and their authors partake.[75]

The notions that "transcription texts"/"mediator texts" were themselves
implicated in the ongoing drawing of linguistic-cum-social boundaries, and
that they attest to authors' more or less conscious effort to establish their
own linguistic and professional authority, remain largely unexplored in
the extant literature. The following section, in contrast, proceeds from the
premise that authors' positionality, language ideologies, and metalinguistic
awareness—not simply an abstract notion of linguistic competence—must
be taken into account in the analysis of any linguistic fact they purport to
document. It therefore asks not simply what language varieties were "encountered," but how specific authors observed, categorized, and valorized
linguistic differences, and how these processes of observing, categorizing,
and valorizing may have been inflected by authors' backgrounds, professional trajectories, and intended readership. Such a framework challenges
the entrenched assumption that the representation of language variation sits
outside language itself, calling attention rather to early modern sojourners'
participation in the ongoing processes of Ottoman sociolinguistic differentiation. It also points to how Ottoman interlocutors and institutions shaped
non-Ottoman authors' language ideologies and linguistic perceptions.
Thus, beyond mere competence, I ask how the settings in which authors
had acquired Ottoman language competency and their purposes in doing
so combined to produce certain "routinized dispositions" toward the nature

of the Ottoman language, certain expectations about what constitutes "correct," or "refined" Ottoman.[76]

Missionaries' encounter with the Ottoman language, like their encounter with Arabic, often started in Rome, where they made their first attempts to learn the language from other missionaries (and their books), before heading to the Balkans, Asia Minor, or the Caucasus. Once there, in their effort to proselytize, they welcomed interactions with (largely Christian) speakers of a variety of languages in different locales and social settings. Missionaries bound for the Arab provinces similarly acquired Arabic—often from other missionaries or from Arabophone Christians—already in Europe. Yet their goals in learning the two languages were markedly different. Missionaries' foremost goal in cultivating Arabic was proselytizing to Levantine Christians, the majority of whom (with the exception of Maronites) followed liturgies in other languages, e.g., Syriac, Greek, Coptic, and Armenian). This both heightened missionaries' awareness of Arabic written/oral diglossia and inclined them strongly toward local, spoken vernaculars. Conversely, to the extent that missionaries sought to learn Ottoman at all, it was mostly to translate texts into the language, and, rather secondarily, to interact orally with its speakers.[77] Missionaries had few opportunities to interact with Ottoman Muslims, let alone with educated *ulema*, and were rarely interested in reading texts produced in Ottoman, which in any case were only infrequently at their disposal. The overwhelming majority of "Oriental" texts in seventeenth-century Roman collegiate libraries, after all, were Hebrew, Arabic, Syriac, and Greek liturgical works. The Ottoman language was thus at best missionaries' secondary receptacle of proselytizing textuality, not a fount of knowledge in and of itself.

Unlike missionaries in their encounter with Ottoman primarily as a written, bookish language, merchants, captives, and other itinerant people acquired their Ottoman language skills mostly from their Ottoman peers, often in an eclectic and unsystematic fashion, whether during their sojourns in Ottoman territories or through interaction with Ottoman merchants sojourning in commercial entrepots on the Italian peninsula and elsewhere. Unsurprisingly, their metalinguistic works tended to privilege lexical items pertaining to domestic and street life, commodities, and trade. At the morphological level, they focused on the Western Turkish spoken varieties of the Balkans, often employed by bilingual Slavic-, Greek-, Judeo-Spanish, or Armenian speakers.[78]

Dragomans shared merchants' clear preference for urban varieties, having learned their Ottoman overwhelmingly in metropolitan centers—Aleppo, Alexandria, Izmir, and, especially, Istanbul. But their linguistic training differed markedly from both the haphazard language acquisition typical of merchants and the far more systematic (and Latin-centric) training of missionaries. As seen in Chapter 1, dragomans often began learning Ottoman as youths under a *hoca* (tutor), generally a member of the empire's *ulema* scholarly elite, and then honed their skills over decades in courtly-diplomatic settings, where speech sought to emulate the prestige register of written form.

Finally, scholars often combined the language-learning strategies of dragomans (immersive acquisition in situ, frequently as guests of ambassadorial households in Istanbul) and of missionaries (bookish learning combined with private tutoring in European metropoles). The latter strategy became especially prevalent in the later seventeenth century, as the foundations of Ottoman could be acquired from other European scholars, as well as from Ottoman Christian sojourners in places like Leiden, Vienna, Oxford, or Paris.

What impact might these different settings of language acquisition have had on the language (and metalanguage) thus acquired? How might these contexts have shaped authors' divergent claims to proficiency? What, indeed, constitutes linguistic authority in this period for different authors and readers? In order to explore these questions, I begin with an outline of some of the key features of the dragomans' metalinguistic corpus.

The semantic focal point of dragomans' lexicographic work is, without doubt, statecraft. An example of this is a twenty-two-page printed pamphlet, *Opera Nova la quale dechiara tutto il governo del gran turcho* (New Work describing the entire government of the Grand Turk), penned by the Ottoman grand dragoman Yunus Bey and his patron Alvise Gritti, and published in Venice in 1537. True to its title, the pamphlet provided readers with a detailed exposé of the structure of the Ottoman government and proved to be a powerful template for future works on the subject.[79] The pamphlet is organized as a list of officeholders, their function and current salary, followed by numbered lists of the districts of each province. It concludes with the numbers of military personnel of each rank available for war.

While modest in size and appearance, Yunus Bey and Alvise Gritti's treatise was to have a long afterlife. It was incorporated, with small changes, as Book II of Benedetto Ramberti's treatise on the Ottoman government, which itself went through multiple editions and even a German translation. As Snezhana Rakova shows, other printed and manuscript versions of the treatise circulated throughout the 1530s and 1540s—in Istanbul, Venice, Milan, and likely elsewhere on the Italian peninsula.[80]

Yunus Bey was a familiar face in Venice. It may not be accidental that this Latin-speaking convert to Islam turned Porte dragoman was thoroughly familiar with Venetian government, having visited the Lagoon six times as official Ottoman envoy, and having served concurrently both the sultan and Alvise Gritti (1480–1534). The latter, the Istanbul-born natural son of the Venetian bailo and future doge Andrea Gritti and his Greek concubine, was likewise deeply embedded in Ottoman courtly circles and instrumental in the divan's political and diplomatic efforts to build an anti-Habsburg alliance. Given his death two years before the treatise's publication, however, his authorship remains uncertain.[81]

Following the example of *Opera Nova*, dragomans' dictionaries similarly enumerated ad nauseam every office of the sprawling Ottoman state's administrative and military organs, and then sought to identify the Latinate cognates of each. These ongoing processes of elaboration and commensuration helped constitute the boundary between Ottoman statecraft and its European counterparts by positing the former as the focal point of an ostensibly distinct if translatable linguistic system. Even dictionaries that did not focus primarily on statecraft derived some of their lexicon from the semantic domain most familiar to their authors. Du Ryer, for example, drew lexicographic material for his dictionary in part from diplomatic documents, and included in an appendix an entire address delivered by the French ambassador Marcheville in front of the sultan in 1632—first the French original, then Du Ryer's own translation into Ottoman Turkish (a self-referential example if there ever was one!).[82] The same practice was repeated in the 1726 first edition of Holdermann's Ottoman grammar, which included the capitulations of Edirne of 1673 as a reading exercise.[83]

The elaboration of Ottoman nomenclature for government and military offices, and its commensuration with more familiar Latinate titles was pervasive even in dragomans' works of ostensibly entirely different focus. For example, *Le Secrétaire turc*, first published in Paris in 1688 and then running to over a dozen editions in both French and English, purported to offer the key to a Turkish "language of flowers," i.e., the use of words for various flowers and fruits as amorous metaphors and innuendos, as purportedly employed by Ottomans to secretly communicate with their lovers. But even in such a salacious publication the author, Edouard Lacroix—a long-time secretary and dragoman to the French ambassador in Istanbul using the pseudonym Sieur des Joannots Du Vignau—could not resist the temptation to offer a seven-page digression on the various positions of the Ottoman government, thinly masked as a cautionary note on the perils of Ottoman orthography, mispronunciation, and lack of understanding of the difference between *pacha*, *bassa*, and *bassi* (i.e., the bivalence of *paşa* as both the official title of a governor and as a low-level honorific, and *baş*, i.e., "head" as in *yeniçeri başı*, or head of the janissaries' corps).[84] Similarly, Antonio Mascis, interpreter to the grand duke of Tuscany, while pitching his grammar and dictionary for general use among travelers and the curious, appended to his work several thematic vocabularies. If the first ones were generic enough (e.g., body parts, numbers, and "languages spoken throughout the Ottoman Empire"), they were followed by the far more specialized and diplomacy-oriented "Imperij, Regni, Signorie, & Tributarie, che la Casa Ottoman tiene sotto di se" (Empires, Reigns, Seigneuries, and Tributaries that the House of Osman holds), a list of Ottoman sultans (non-chronological, and including several non-reigning princes and multiple redundant entries), and finally, the sultan's honorific titles.[85]

The privileging of the semantic domain of statecraft often lead to the de facto relative neglect of other aspects of Ottoman lifeworlds. When the French consul in Alexandria, André Du Ryer, attempted to offer "a summary of the religion of the Turks" with his Qur'an translation, his method of "us[ing] a Christian vocabulary to describe Muslim practices" resulted in a work that was "prejudiced, as well as containing certain errors."[86] Unsurprisingly, dragomans' works diverged in this respect from those of missionaries, who placed greater emphasis on the intricacies of Ottoman religious life, and from those of travelers and merchants, who paid more attention to Ottoman material culture and sociability. The brief *Opera Nova de M. Pietro Lupis Valentiano. La qual insegna a parlare Turchesco* (1527), for example, is organized thematically, starting with kin terms, professions, animals, and garments, and concluding with foodstuffs, weather, and numbers.[87] Giuseppe Miselli's multilingual vocabulary for travelers, which he included with his highly popular *Burattino veridico*, similarly proceeded thematically ("on the road," "in the tavern" and so forth) and provided mostly basic vocabulary for foodstuffs, numbers, and directions.[88] The French pilgrim Jean Palerne's "Petit Dictionnaire," a multilingual

vocabulary and simple phrase book enclosed with his posthumously published *Peregrinations,* likewise started with place names and "particular
names of various things," continued, predictably, with numbers, foods,
and weather, and ended with swear words—those that Muslims direct at
Christians and those appropriate for hurling at "Moors."[89] It glossed *Gentil
femme* as *Sultanna* and *Seigneur* as *Beig* but left other French honorifics such as *Monsieur, Madame, Maistre,* and *Maistresse* without Turkish
gloss.[90] Like Lupis and Miselli, it did not introduce any nomenclature related to statecraft.

On the other hand, non-dragomans tended to neglect the semantic
field of statecraft in their dictionaries. That this neglect was considered a
problem for contemporary political elites reveals a major focus for using
written works on the Ottomans. Abbé Eusèbe Renaudot's Memoir to the
French conseil de la marine in 1719 articulates this clearly in discussing the
shortcomings of missionaries' linguistic works, based on translations from
the writings of Islamicate scholars that ignored Christian theology and
its vocabulary altogether.[91] And yet, heavy emphasis on Ottoman political
and military nomenclature was not unique to dragomans. For example,
the first nominal declension in Hieronymus Megiser's 1612 grammar is
for *Beg* (*beğ/bey*, glossed as "Dominus"). It is followed by a few kinship
terms and everyday objects like "wood" and "cloud," as well as the likes
of sultan (glossed as imperator), tschelebi (*çelebi*, an honorific glossed as
Nobilis), and elchi (*elci*, ambassador, glossed as "Legatus").[92] Similarly,
of 124 "Turkish and other" words in a vocabulary that the Capuchin friar
(and decades-long Aleppo resident) Justinien de Neuvy/Michel Febure appended to his highly popular *Teatro della Turchia* in 1681, over a third
concerned government offices and fiscal matters.[93]

Beyond statecraft, what Ottoman's prototypical semantic range came to
be in early modern European metalinguistic texts can be observed nega-
tively, by way of what it excluded. Take, for example, Timoteo Agnellini's
Proverbii utili, e virtuosi in lingua Araba, Persiana, e Turca (Useful and
Virtuous Proverbs in the Arabic, Persian, and Turkish Language), published in Padua in 1688 and explicitly designed to appeal to the young
seminarians and missionaries-to-be whom Agnellini served as instructor
of Oriental languages. The work is divided into three sections, each listing
proverbs in one of the three languages with facing Latin-script transliteration and Italian and Latin translations. The fifty-eight Arabic proverbs that
open the book are mostly edifying and moralizing, with a large majority

explicitly invoking the name of God ("Wisdom begins with the Fear of God" and so forth). A few are of decidedly Christian provenance, e.g., "He who is a slave of the Holy Virgin can never be endangered."[94] The Ottoman-language ones, by contrast, while addressing the ethical life to some extent, are largely free of references to God, for example, "The son of a wolf will always remain a wolf, even when elevated among the people," "One foreigner dislikes another; the landlord dislikes both," "Those who bathe do not fear the rain," or "Everyone considers their customs to be good." Of Agnellini's thirty-three Ottoman proverbs, only a half dozen or so allude to religion, either by mentioning God (e.g., "Guide me, Oh God, in the ways of your love, and instruct me how to serve you"), or more obliquely, by reference to prayer.[95] Similarly, of twenty-eight Persian proverbs, one mentions the resurrection, and three others have religious referents, while the rest do not.

The stark contrast between Agnellini's presentation of Arabic as a language of religion, and of Ottoman and Persian as largely inadequate for conveying religious subject matter, is understandable given the author's status as an Arabophone Ottoman Christian operating in a Catholic missionary context. It also conforms to a broader contemporary emergent understanding of these languages' interrelationship in an Ottoman triglossic context, and their prototypical, distinct semantic domains.[96] An understanding of the three languages as complementary registers within the same speaker community makes especial sense in an Ottomancentric milieu, where all three were available (albeit to varying degrees depending on location and education) and used prototypically for different semantic domains. Agnellini, then, seems to have reproduced here an educated Ottoman lens on these languages, helping mediate it to an Italianate Catholic public.[97]

Beyond biographical details, this example suggests how Latinate metalinguistic texts were instrumental in mediating Ottoman courtly language ideologies. The very insistence on the intimate relationship among Arabic, Persian, and Ottoman as "Islamic languages"—while assigning them to distinct semantic domains—was shared by dragomans and Ottoman courtiers (and other Ottoman educated elites, to varying degrees). These dual moves underscore that Ottoman metalinguistic practices, and not only Latinate paradigms and prejudices, shaped the relationship among Ottoman, Arabic, and Persian in contemporary metalinguistic texts. But before addressing the question of how dragomans became acquainted with

Ottoman metalinguistic practices, let us consider a few other characteristics of dragomans' metalinguistic works.

A first key characteristic is a strong preference for Istanbulite elite language varieties, both phonetically, syntactically, and lexicographically, e.g., in the relative absence of borrowed lexemes from other regional languages. The relative absence of Italianisms, Grecisms, and Slavicisms from dragomans' dictionaries contrasts with Bernard de Paris's monumental three-volume *Vocabolario Italiano-Turchesco*. As Luciano Rocchi has recently observed, the *Vocabolario* features quite a few words of old Italian, Venetian, Slavic, and Greek provenance.[98] Greek linguistic mediation, observable throughout de Paris's *Vocabolario*, is particularly intriguing given the author's missionary activities, which would have brought him into daily contact with Istanbul's Greek-speaking inhabitants.

Borrowings from Greek, Slavic, and other languages were especially marked in provincial Rumeli (western) and Karamanlı (Asia Minor) Turkish varieties. We find traces of these varieties, unsurprisingly, in lexicographic works that emerged from mercantile and missionary circles, from Lupis's *Opera Nova* of ca. 1527 to the textbooks of Bosnian Franciscans in the late eighteenth century, through the 1668 manuscript of *Dictionarium turcico-latinum* attributed to Miklós Illésházy but informed by the input of a professional Italophone (likely Venetian) and Germanophone secretaries.[99] Words of Greek, Italian, Slavic, Hungarian, and Romanian provenance abound in the 1630 Latin-Turkish manuscript glossary and grammatical sketch of the Neapolitan adventurer Giovan Battista Montalbano (1606–1646) too.[100]

Despite their paratexts' programmatic declarations to the contrary, Molino's and Meninski's works both largely lack Grecisms, Slavicisms, and Italianisms, as indeed is the case in most other dragomans' metalinguistic production. This is not because dragomans lacked exposure to them. Not only was Istanbul a magnet for migrants from across the Empire, but many of its administrative, military, and educational elite were de facto trilingual, or even quadrilingual. Many top administrators and army officers were recruited as youth through the *devşirme* system from among rural Christian populations, mainly Greek-and Slavic-speakers in Rumeli. Similarly, scholar-teachers in Istanbul's top *medreses* often hailed from Arabophone and Persophone centers of learning such as Cairo, Baghdad, Damascus, Herat, Samarkand, and Tabriz. In the seventeenth century, Istanbul's expat scholarly community expanded further, absorbing Kurds and Azeris (who fled the Ottoman-Safavid wars) as well as Moroccans (in the wake of the collapse of the Saadi dynasty in 1603), who brought with them new philological sensibilities and textual practices.[101] In Istanbul this diverse group came into contact—still surprisingly understudied—with scholars of other ethnolinguistic backgrounds, e.g., Greek-, Arabic-, and Slavic-speaking Christian Orthodox; Armenians; Judeo-Spanish-and Greek-speaking Jews; German, Hungarian, Transylvanian religious refugees of virtually all Christian confessions; and so forth.[102] This mobility and the various regimes of circulation it spawned further reinforced Ottoman elite culture's self-conscious multilingualism.[103]

Istanbul's polyglot environment inevitably proliferated multidirectional and multiscale linguistic borrowings. Dragomans' elision of these intense borrowings in their accounts of Ottoman was not, however, a linguistic purism *tout court*. As discussed below, dragomans were keenly aware of how the Ottoman language incorporated—indeed was more or less explicitly based on—a heavy dose of Arabisms and Persianisms. It is possible that dragomans—who often spoke Greek at home and systematically trained in Italian—became more aware of the boundaries between these languages and the courtly Ottoman variety than French missionaries for whom these boundaries may have been more opaque, particularly in their permutations in distinct speech varieties. An understanding of Ottoman as directly beholden to Arabophone and Persophone linguistic production but somehow unimpacted by other commonly spoken (and often written) regional languages represents a certain understanding of the Ottoman project as decidedly elite and Islamic. It erases not simply the role of other languages, but of their speakers, in Ottoman society and culture.[104]

Dragomans' metalinguistic works are further distinguished by their pervasive conflation of oral and written registers and privileging of the latter over the former. While to some extent such conflation was true of much contemporary lexicography, dragomans' metalinguistic production is particularly marked by it, in contrast with other early Ottoman lexicographers' efforts—at least ideologically—to capture speech.[105] As historical linguists show, seventeenth-and eighteenth-century missionary metalinguistic texts generally paid close attention to local, spoken varieties, even if the literary register shaped their representations of the vernacular to some extent.[106] Scholars and merchant authors, likewise, generally aimed to capture everyday speech, and thus tended to privilege the morphosyntax and, especially, lexicon of spoken varieties.

In contrast, dragomans favored the courtly register, which, in its deliberate effort to approximate written language in oral performance, naturalized
the conflation of different varieties, and indeed treated the written as a
template for the oral. The privileging of written—especially literary—linguistic varieties became the hallmark of virtually all Ottoman and Turkish
grammars through the nineteenth century, even if they did not always explicitly distinguish these varieties from spoken ones.[107] The indiscriminate
use of generic terms such as (*lisan-ı*) *türkî/osmanî* or *türkçe* to refer to both
oral and written varieties of Ottoman Turkish characterized elite Ottoman
language ideology in general, as explained below.[108] Even as this process
unfolded over time, dragomans seem to have embraced it earlier, and more
consistently, than other authors of Ottoman metalinguistic texts.[109]

Third, of the different types of authors of metalinguistic texts, dragomans were the most likely to produce grammars as opposed to lexicographical works (dictionaries, vocabularies, glossaries, and phrase books).
The ratio of grammars to lexicographical materials among dragomans
(12:21 + 6 combined works and treatises) was substantially higher than
among scholars (2:12 + 2 combined work); missionaries (2:8 + 4) and merchants (2:7 + 1).[110] This underscores dragomans' heightened awareness
of the structural aspects governing language. Like scholars, dragomans
tended to model their grammatical paradigms of Ottoman on Latin, even
when the equivalencies could not be found.[111] This contrasts with the more
vernacular production favored by merchants and travelers, five of whose
seven "dictionaries" are fairly modest vocabularies, glossaries, or phrase
books. At the same time, perhaps due to the growth of comparative linguistics, some dragomans' grammatical works also partially followed Arabic
and Ottoman, as well as Latinate, models of grammar.[112]

Dragomans' professional habitus deeply informed both their definition
of Ottoman's key features and their publication program, from lexicography to orthography and from political patronage to intended readership.
Several dragomans addressed these elements in their paratextual appara-
tuses. Molino's brief letter to the reader envisions his ideal public as "the
curious," and accordingly offers a historical overview of the Seljuk and
Ottoman dynasties, explaining that, thanks to their imperial conquests,
the Turkish language had spread far and wide. After noting the extent of
the Ottoman Empire at the time, its divisions in "55 kingdoms and seigneuries" and "33 nations and languages"—invoking a common trope of
Mediterranean hyperdiversity—Molino explains that the Turkish language

is therefore "a composite" of the many languages with which it has come into contact through conquest, including "Arabic, Persian, Greek, and Tatar." Yet after noting the many *modi di parlare* (modes of speech) of the language, he proceeds to state that his work focuses on that of Istanbul,

> which is currently the best, being the residence of the sovereign, and my way of talking ["modo di dire"] is to be considered the most po-lite Turkish language, which is spoken throughout Turkey [i.e., the Ottoman Empire], since I have acquired it from the court itself, having served for many years as interpreter to His Most Christian Majesty, and for the Most Serene Republic of Venice, finding the true inter-pretation, and the proper meanings of Italian words into the Turkish language."[113]

Molino, in other words, posits his ability to distill for readers the most valu-able language variety as directly premised on his professional trajectory as a dragoman.

Significantly, Molino pegs on his professional identity not only his ca-pacity to discern the true signification of words in Italian (which, after all, was his third or fourth language) and to commensurate them with Turkish ones but also, especially, his cultivated familiarity with Ottoman courtly speech. His emphasis on professional qualifications is noteworthy for two reasons. First, as an Armenian hailing from Anatolia, his first language, in all likelihood, would have been vernacular Anatolian Turkish, not the elite Ottoman register.[114] Second, he doubtlessly honed his Italian linguistic skills during his studies at the Roman College of Neophytes, well before embarking on a diplomatic career in Istanbul. By the time he published his dictionary in 1641, Molino had been back in Rome for at least four years, during which time he served as the Armenian Patriarch's representative to the Holy See.[115] That said, Molino had good reason to emphasize his dip-lomatic career in Istanbul rather than his previous and subsequent Roman sojourns. When he had applied to join the Venetian dragomanate some fifteen years earlier, the bailo noted that Molino "knows and speaks well the Turkish language, even if not a very cultivated one, like those who grew up here" and that he had yet to learn how to write the language.[116] The bailo's concern was likely due, at least partly, to Molino's provenance in Ankara and exposure to provincial, rather than metropolitan (let alone courtly) spoken varieties. Like many other non-Muslim Ottomans, Molino probably learned to write the language in non-Arabic script, which would have seemed like illiteracy to the bailo. Linguistic competence here again is clearly tied to a typology of social personhood and status: concerns about Molino's qualifications had to do as much with his atypical trajectories, namely his roots outside the Catholic milieu of Pera and lack of formal apprenticeship in the bailate. The convergence of an endogamous Istanbulite dragomanate and an understanding of Ottoman Turkish primarily through the lens of diplomacy was to inform European formalized study of the language for centuries to come.

Refracting Courtly Language Ideologies

In his appeal to the reader Molino promises to focus on an Istanbulite, courtly language variety. His dictionary carefully notes lexemes of Persian and Arabic provenance (i.e., of the courtly register) while suppressing other borrowings (especially Grecisms). These attest to Molino's self-conscious sensibilities about dialectal and register differences as they were inflected by spatial and social mobility.[117] By his own account, then, his mediation of the Ottoman language was a far cry from having merely "recorded the spoken language of Istanbul from the first half of the 17th century."[118] Like other dragomans, Molino exemplifies the deep effects of language ideology on the nature of the "data" that metalinguistic texts purport simply to transmit.

What, then, were the language ideologies that informed dragomans' highly selective representation of Ottoman? The linguistic anthropological concept of language ideologies is helpful in observing how Ottoman literati and bureaucrats (and their dragoman interlocutors) came to understand "Ottoman" as a self-consciously "synthetic" language of imperial governmentality, heavily reliant on Persian and Arabic lexicon and syntactic forms, yet distinct from other registers and relatively immune to borrowings from other regional languages. Of course, contemporary Ottoman literati themselves may not have distinguished between these different substrata quite in the same self-conscious way as later language reformers, who sought to purify Turkish of its "foreign" elements. Thus, in a highly ironic twist, the poet Nabî's (c. 1630–1712) couplet "O you who sell outlandish words wrapped in poetry! / A book of odes is not a copy of the dictionary!" decries the proliferation of foreignisms while using three "Turkish words" and eleven "Persian" ones, according to one modern scholar.[119]

A similar consciousness of "synthesis" is found in Meninski, who insisted that students of Ottoman must first learn Arabic, and who included in his Ottoman dictionary words from all three languages.[120] In the opening paragraph of the first chapter of his Ottoman grammar Meninski went so far as to say that "those who do not know these two [Arabic and Persian] can never rightfully be said to have knowledge of Turkish."[121] Many other dragoman authors mention the centrality of Arabic and Persian to Ottoman in their paratextual materials, especially in letters to the readers. In the manuscript draft of his 1630 Ottoman grammar, the first to be published in French (or any European vernacular, for that matter), Du Ryer claimed that Ottoman cannot be mastered without knowledge of Arabic and Persian. In the preface to a grammar written in Istanbul in 1689, another French dragoman, Jean Baptiste de Fiennes *père*, likened the three languages to flour, water, and salt, all essential ingredients for the baking of a good bread.[122]

Such a perspective was not limited to dragomans but informed broader early modern perceptions of Ottoman, thanks at least in part to dragomans' mediation and Meninski's outsize influence.[123] Scholars who were familiar primarily with non-courtly registers, however, sometimes dissented. Megiser, for example, opened his Ottoman grammar, *Institutionum linguae Turcicae libri quatuor* (Four Books on the Institutions of the Turkish Language, 1612) with the unequivocal statement that "The Turkish language shares much with Persian and Tatar; but it is entirely different from Arabic."[124] Megiser did concede that Arabic was the preferred scriptural language among Ottomans, who also used the Arabic script for writing down their own language. Significantly, in this formulation Ottoman and Persian are cognate languages, rather than the latter (along with Arabic) as substrata of the former, as most dragomans would have it. For Megiser, then, "Turkish" operated in a triglossic environment, rather than having incorporated and thereby suppressed the differences among the three.

Perhaps the most articulate exposition of dragomans' language ideology is to be found in Giambattista Donà's introduction to his *Della Letteratura*, where he frames the Ottoman language's relationship to Persian and Arabic as commensurable with Italian regional dialects' relationship to Tuscan and Latin:

The Turkish language is like the provincial [idiom] in Italy, in which everyone speaks with the forms, the pronunciation, and the accents of the land. But it is adorned with Persian, like we do with the Tuscan

[. . .] In the same way one also finds the Arabic among the Turks, as the Latin is among us; as the Qur'an is written in that language, the Arabic is necessary to them, as to us is the language in which Sacred Scripture is to be found. Arabic styles [*maniere*], words, and terms [*periodi*] are used entirely for ornamentation, for elocution, and for decorum, especially in the affairs, the commandments, and other orders of major business and negotiations; in letters of the Prince, Ministers, Paşas, and in orders of the Imperial will. In short among them great erudition is elaborated and used by men of the law, who are those who are employed in the courts of law, by their parish priests and other clerics, as they say; and also by the most distinguished men in the notarial, secretarial, and chancery courts, all of whom by professional necessity understand, speak, and write Arabic [. . .][125]

To be sure, Donà's affirmation of the importance of Tuscan and Latin to the speech of educated Venetians was shaped by his own patrician upbringing. But his analysis of the relationship between different registers of Ottoman, and the elite status of Arabisms and Persianisms in courtly varieties in particular, is also deeply informed by his familiarity with members of specific Ottoman professional and status groups, such as legal scholars (mentioned in an earlier passage) and courtiers. To properly use the highest registers of Ottoman, Donà implies, one not only has to belong to an elite group but to operate in the particular socio-professional context that is the purview of statecraft: the imperial divan, the court of law, the notarial or secretarial office.[126]

Other contemporary metalinguistic works similarly evince a strong preference for Istanbulite and courtly registers of Ottoman over other varieties of Turkish, the former understood as dependent on a high quotient of Arabic and Persian lexicon. Bernard de Paris, for example, wrote in his dictionary's "Epistle to the Reader" that the Turks

appear backward, and of uncivil customs to those who cannot deal with them because they do not know their language; but those who do know it find them familiar [*domestici*] and affable, and much more when you speak to them with greater eloquence: that is why, wishing to serve public utility, especially to those who operate in the Ottoman Empire, and to facilitate the acquisition of the Turkish language, we have labored to acquire said language, having associated with the most learned, read their books, considered the royal decrees,

examined the instruments and writings of the law with the most in-
telligent masters to be found in Constantinople, who were paid by the
Most Excellent and Most Noble Sir Count de Cesy of happy memory,
then Ambassador for His Most Christian Majesty, having taught his
always lauded son Monsu di Conti, now for his most rare virtue the
most worthy Bishop of Lodève, whom I also taught the Latin language, who possesses so purely Turkish, Italian, and Greek, as French
is his natural language, to whom we might say this vocabulary is
owed; with his help we have compiled and collected it as the bee
makes its liqueur from diverse flowers, not only the common [*volgari*]
words, but also those that the Turks use in their eloquent speech, in
composing their books, in manifesting the royal decrees, in making
the instruments of law, and in writing their epistles; for this it was
necessary to gather [*raccogliere*] many Arabic and Persian words, for
which those who know the Arabic or Persian language but unfamiliar
with Ottoman writing might be surprised that in this vocabulary so
many are to be found from one language or the other, not knowing the
mixture [*mescolanza*] that the Turks make of these languages, but, on
the other hand, we believe that those familiar with Turkish books will
be astonished, that with so much effort in a single book are gathered
most of the words, which the Turks use in the writings of the law, and
in their literature, for in the former they use the Arabic, and in the
latter the Persian; in the books, however, they use more Arabic than
Persian, and other corrupted [words] according to the region of the
author . . . [127]

De Paris explicitly pitches his dictionary as an aid for those who wish to
converse with Ottoman scholarly and political elites and to read Ottoman
texts. Accordingly, he expresses a clear preference for written varieties,
especially those gleaned from the writings of officialdom. As far as spoken
language is concerned, he prefers the Istanbulite (courtly) register, showing consciousness that use of Arabic and Persian accords with a speaker's
elite status. Indeed, he reveals a real disdain for folk speech. Later in the
epistle, he even explains that his vocabulary often lists synonyms, the first
one being Turkish, followed by (2) Arabic and (3) Persian, "which are noted
with the letters T., A., and P. and distinguished with asterisks, or little stars
to avoid confusion. And the two or three that are not marked are understood by all."[128] In doing so, de Paris incorporates into his vocabulary a

highly self-reflexive sociology of language stratification, recognizing the strong correlation between the frequency of using Arabic and Persian lexemes and the speaker's status. De Paris is, in other words, refracting a core element of Ottoman elite language ideology.

Meninski elaborated the function of Persian and Arabic lexemes in Ottoman even further. In the opening paragraph of the chapter on orthography in his Turkish grammar, he presents the integration of Arabic and Persian lexemes into Ottoman ("Turkish") speech and writing not simply as a matter of necessity due to the "defects" of the latter as originating in a "barbaric language." Rather, it is the intrinsic qualities of the former, viz. the "majesty," "abundance," and "antiquity" of Arabic, and the "sweetness and elegance" of Persian:

> [I]t should be known that the Turks often employ words, phrases, and sentences—as much in spoken language as in writing—from Arabic, a language most noble and ancient in origin, custom, majesty, and abundance of words, as well as Persian (second to none in sweetness and elegance), not only for the sake of supplanting the defects arising from the origin and custom of their own barbaric language, but also for the sake of elegant expression, which may even be called "most cultivated." Thus, he who is ignorant of those two languages [Arabic and Persian], may never rightly be called an expert in Turkish . . . [129]

His civilizational arc notwithstanding, Meninski rehearses here a common trope in contemporary Ottoman courtly writings about the authority and gravitas of Arabic and the aesthetic qualities of Persian as essential elements of elite Ottoman speech and writing. Yet Meninski's articulation of Ottoman's relationship to Arabic and Persian does more than simply rehash contemporary courtly language ideologies. Elsewhere, he observes that:

> Beyond Greek, Italian, Slavonic, (and) Hungarian, from which the Turks took many words for things not previously known to them, they mix in frequently Arabic and Persian, as much in the spoken form as in the written, not only simple words but also conjoined and composite (words), and often verses and whole sayings with which they adorn and amplify their own written works marvelously, and you can hardly attain and understanding of these (texts) without perfect understanding of both (Arabic and Persian).[130]

According to Meninski, the incorporation into Ottoman of lexemes from Greek, Italian, Slavic, and Hungarian was a matter of pure necessity, a process long concluded, and one, moreover, which did not necessarily result in Ottoman speakers' self-consciousness about the provenance of said lexemes. He presents Arabic and Persian, on the other hand, as languages whose presence as such is always on the minds of elite Ottoman language speakers, and especially writers. Indeed, the passage quoted above is followed by two paradigmatic examples of the use of Arabic and Persian in Ottoman courtly letters: that of instructing diplomatic interpreters and "Turks" in reading and that of composing imperial decrees and missives intended for circulation within the empire and beyond its borders. In all these contexts of use, Meninski insists, a text would be considered unacceptable "without the ornament received from Persian and Arabic words and phrases, interwoven tastefully." Thus, for Meninski, the difference in Ottoman public life between the role of Arabic and Persian, on the one hand, and that of other "regional languages" such as Italian and Greek on the other, seems to pivot both on prototypical users' status (elite versus common), users' self-consciousness about foreign provenance (effaced versus heightened), and, especially, registers (primarily oral versus primarily written—or oral that emulates the written). Meninski's perception of the place of Arabic and Persian in the Ottoman language thus vitally depends on his conflation of oral and written varieties, and on his taking courtly contexts of language use as "unmarked"—it was in written Ottoman, and particularly in the writings of officialdom, that Arabic and Persian made their most frequent and orthographically explicit appearance. From the written formal genres, Arabic and Persian borrowings were then extended into the speech genres of those in sustained contact with them, such as courtiers and dragomans. Unsurprisingly, then, the ability to approximate the elite written register in speech (by consciously weaving Arabic and Persian into one's spoken language) is what defines for Meninski the desired Ottoman competency of "interpreters of the language":

[A] Spaniard, for example, is not expected to know exactly which expressions from his own language originate from Arabic, and which ones [originate from] Latin. Indeed, [there are] many who speak Latin excellently who never have heard or learnt [Greek], although it [Latin] has and makes use of innumerable Greek words. And therefore the same ought to be estimated about the other languages. But, for instance, no man would be called an expert in Latin unless he be thoroughly acquainted with the Greek language, and on that account, in most books of learned men sprinklings of pure Greek words and phrases are frequently seen written out in Greek letters. Thus, scarcely would an interpreter of the Turkish language be an expert who does not understand Arabic and Persian, who does not intermingle the words of both [Arabic and Persian] in speaking as much as in writing.[131]

The analogies with the cases of Spanish (vis-à-vis Arabic and Latin) and of Latin (vis-à-vis Greek) are noteworthy. Contemporary Spaniards, after all, had few reasons to flaunt Arabic's presence in their speech, while Latin was celebrated as the undisputed substratum of all Romance languages, not a stylistic element clearly detachable from other linguistic strata. Conversely, those "learned men" who were "expert in Latin" surely sprinkled their Latin texts with Greek "words and phrases . . . written out in Greek letters" to underscore not Latin's dependence on Greek but rather their own command of both. By the late seventeenth century, it is worth recalling, both classical Latin and classical Greek were largely written varieties commanded by the erudite denizens of the Republic of Letters, among whom Meninski clearly counted himself.[132] In referring to himself as a consummate "interpreter of the Turkish language," Meninski emphasized his scholarly credentials by alluding to the analogous aspect of interspersing his manual with Arabic and Persian. In so doing, he was enacting an erudite linguistic persona, rather than "proving" the essence of Ottoman per se to be grounded in its relationship to either Arabic of Persian. If anything, the self-consciousness implied by the use of verbs such as "intersperse" underscored the distinct ontological standing of the three languages (in contrast, for example, with Arabic elements in Spanish, whose etymology had been either forgotten or targeted by linguistic purists).[133]

In the above example, Meninski was evidently mediating Ottoman elites' own self-consciousness about Arabic and Persian as not fully sublimated elements of Ottoman Turkish but rather as stylistic flourishes inserted by highly literate speakers striving to emulate a written register. This raises the question of how he and other dragoman authors became familiar with Ottoman metalinguistic practices (and their attendant language ideologies) in the first place. Du Ryer, like others before him, is known to have owned and consulted several of the most popular Arabic-Turkish and Arabic-Persian dictionaries in circulation in the Ottoman Empire at the time.[134] He was also quite explicit, as we saw, in relying on Ottoman diplomatic documents as a vital lexicographic source.

Unlike Du Ryer's open acknowledgment of his Ottoman metalinguistic materials and largely diplomatic textual corpus, Meninski, while citing several dozen works in Persian, Ottoman, and Arabic as sources, includes very few dictionaries and grammars among them.[135] He organizes his bibliography by language (again, showcasing a consciousness of each linguistic system as distinct), starting with Arabic, then Persian, and finally Ottoman, following the general trajectory of a by then axiomatic Ottoman elite notion of *translatio studii*.

Meninski is remarkably vague on the "various [Arabic] dictionaries and grammars" he consulted, even though several were in extensive use among contemporary Ottoman literati. In general, even while sharing much of the ideological underpinnings of the Ottoman linguistic tradition, his references to specific metalinguistic works are sparse. His citations of Arabic-language sources are likewise few, numbering only five titles other than the Qur'an: three books on Islamic jurisprudence (*fiqh*) and two Arabic translations (by European-based scholars) of David's Psalms and the *Doctrina Christiana*, respectively.[136] Meninski's parsimony strikes an odd balance between three highly popular works of Islamic jurisprudence written in Arabic but framed by Ottoman commentaries, on the one hand, and two Christian missionary texts on the other. More than Arab authors, Meninski relied on available works by European students of Arabic. His Arabic corpus, in other words, is heavily and doubly mediated by contemporary Ottoman *and* European scholarly milieus.

Meninski's Persian corpus is likewise heavily mediated by an Ottoman perspective. Virtually all the Persian works he cites share a strong Sufi flavor and undisputed stature as classics of Persianate poetry. Unsurprisingly, none represented recent Safavid literary production, but rather the antiquarian taste of contemporary Ottoman elites. As important, all of Meninski's acknowledged Persian sources had previously served as templates for significant Ottoman literary production, whether in translations and adaptations or commentaries. As Selim Kuru and Murat Umut Inan show, by the turn of the seventeenth century Ottoman courtly canon-building tastes came to direct exegetical activity toward a rather narrowly defined corpus of Persian poetry.[137] This restrictive tendency is evident in Meninski's citations of Ottoman commentaries on Persian works. It is also evident in the seventh and final chapter of his Turkish grammar, "De Prosodia et arte metrica," where he offers as a reading exercise an excerpt from a Persian *hikayet* (story) with parallel Ottoman and followed by a Spanish translation.[138] Intriguingly, the Persian story is Husayn Va'iz Kashifi's (d. 1505) *Anwar-i Suhaili*, a reworking of a Pahlavi rendition of the Sanskrit Panchatantra, a fourth-century Sanskrit Kashmiri text (itself doubtlessly based on older oral traditions of storytelling), made famous through its Arabic translation by a Zoroastrian convert to Islam, who gave it the title *Kalilah wa Dimnah*. The title that Meninski gave the work, *Hümâyûnnâme*, is taken from Ali Çelebi's (d. 1543) Ottoman translation of Kashifi, dedicated to Sultan Süleyman the Lawgiver, and lavishly illustrated by Istanbulite court miniaturists in the mid-sixteenth century.[139] Meninski's Spanish version is taken from the Habsburg dragoman Vicenzo Bratutti's translation of the *Hümâyûnnâme*, which appeared in Madrid in 1654.[140] Here, too, Meninski's Persian, while certainly inflected by the Persophone cosmopolis, is a decidedly Ottoman (and dragoman-mediated) Persian.

Compared to his Arabic and Persian citations, Meninski's Ottoman citations range more widely in genre and theme (from dream interpretation to chronicles and almanacs, and from medical treatises to love poems and literary formularies). Yet they, too, showcase a distinctly elite taste, privileging works directly sponsored by the court (including several Ottoman sultanic chronicles), or otherwise in vogue in contemporary Ottoman courtly circles. Indeed, Meninski's "bibliography" strongly reflects courtly canon-building tastes. Such an emergent canon was indebted—and in turn contributed—to "centralized educational institutions and bureaucratic offices of the empire, [which] formed a 'republic of letters' that reshaped the Islamicate literary tradition in a Turkish garb."[141]

At the same time, as noted, oddly absent from Meninski's acknowledged sources are any bilingual Arabic-Ottoman dictionaries. The final entry in his section of Persian books consulted is Kemalpaşazade's (d. 1536) *Dekāyıku'l-Hakāyık*, a Persian-Ottoman thesaurus, which the Ottoman polymath composed in Istanbul under Grand Vizier Ibrahim Paşa's patronage.[142] But Meninski does not mention any other contemporary Ottoman-Persian or Ottoman-Arabic lexicographic works, even though several were used extensively in language instruction in Ottoman palace schools, as well as by previous European authors of Ottoman metalinguistic materials, including Du Ryer's almost equally influential *Rudimenta grammatices linguae Turcicae* of 1630.

Meninski's Ottoman sources speak to a classicizing courtly taste that harkened back to the literary production of the fifteenth and, especially, sixteenth centuries. His strong preference for love poetry and historical nonfiction was shared widely among early modern translators of Ottoman works and profoundly shaped European understandings of the Ottoman literary canon. His classicizing tendencies fit well within the contemporary Zeitgeist of academic Orientalism, which often neglected recent works in favor of "the classical period of the language or society they were interested in." According to Monica Heller and Bonnie McElhinny, by the nineteenth century "this was accompanied by an ideology of civilizational decline, with the argument that the highest achievements of the society studied were in the past, and the implication that the European colonial powers were now superior, or justified in their rule, because of this decline."[143] However, it is noteworthy that in our case, dragomans largely shared such ideologies with contemporary Ottoman courtly elites themselves, raising important questions about the operation of civilizational discourses in a trans-imperial framework and in relation to an Ottomancentric ideological framework whose proponents in the Ottoman court may have invoked "the classics" primarily to buttress their own cultural and political program, and not necessarily as part of a declinist perspective.

Ottoman Synthesis and the *Elsene-i selase*

Meninski's differential (if consistently Ottomancentric) access to Arabic, Persian, and Turkish letters raises the question of how dragomans' metalinguistic texts articulated the close interrelationship between these three languages as *elsene-i selase*, or the three learned languages of Islam, a distinctly Ottoman concept. Crucially, the very notion of these three languages as the vectors of specifically Islamicate knowledge came to be foundational for the study of the Islamicate world in a post-Hebraica European discipline of Orientalism. Yet this notion itself was premised on an Ottoman "fabrication." Not because these languages did not matter for Islamicate scholarship, but because their intimate relationship as understood by European philologists derived precisely from their privileged position as high registers and their multiple entanglements in the Ottoman (and, to a lesser extent, Safavid) court. As recounted by the French traveler Jean Thévenot (1633–1667):

> If the Turks in Constantinople wish to be entertained, they bring before them Arabs, whom they make speak in that language; however, it is their holy language, because their Qur'an and all their prayers are in Arabic, and they commonly say that the Turkish language is used in this world and that in Paradise people will speak the Arabic language, and in Hell the Persian, which however is beautiful, and makes the greater part of Turkish poems and songs, but as they hate the Persians extremely, they speak ill of all that concerns them.[144]

That Thévenot, who traveled extensively throughout the Ottoman, Safavid, and Mughal empires, limited these comments to the "Turks of Constantinople" suggests the particularity of this seventeenth-century Istanbulite elite's understanding of Turkish, Arabic, and Persian as simultaneously distinct registers in a triglossic environment and as elements within a unified field of Ottoman literary production. What Thévenot was reporting ethnographically, dragoman authors of metalinguistic texts transformed into generalizable linguistic orthodoxy.[145] By adopting a courtly Ottoman perspective dragomans' metalinguistic analyses shifted the prototypical meaning of "Oriental languages" from "Hebrew and Aramaic" (and Arabic as an auxiliary language) to "Arabic, Persian, and Turkish" as evinced, for example, in Meninski's student and archrival Podestà's three-volume magnum opus, *Cursus grammaticalis linguarum orientalium, Arabicae scilicet, Persicae et Turcicae* (1690–1703), which dedicated a separate volume to each, all with an eye to properly training Istanbul-bound dragomans.

Thus far, I have alluded to this "special relationship" among the three languages under the term "synthesis." But even if we put aside serious methodological challenges in the study of metalinguistic texts, the term "synthesis" is exceedingly vague. At the very least, two understandings of synthesis should be distinguished. One posits the Ottoman language itself as synthetic, having absorbed Arabic and Persian substrata, similar to how Christianity claimed to supersede Judaism, and Islam claimed to supersede Judaism and Christianity both. The other locates synthesis at the level of Ottoman courtly speech, with "Ottoman" as the de facto functional register of statecraft in a triglossic environment where it is concurrently supplemented by an Arabic register for higher learning and theology, and Persian for belles lettres—a more ecumenical approach (to continue with the doctrinal analogy). Both logics are present, explicitly or implicitly, in the corpus of dragomans' metalinguistic texts, sometimes in the same work. Du Ryer described the Ottoman language as "uncultivated and barbaric," an act of "massive theft" from "nearly all other Oriental languages."[146] De Paris, as noted, justified including in his dictionary the plural form of many Ottoman nouns of Arabic provenance on the basis of their divergence from Arabic usage. Molino stated that "Turkish speech is accompanied by Arabic, Persian, Greek, and Tatar, and to better satisfy the curious, I have declared in many places Arabic, Persian, Greek, and Tatar words."[147] The title page of the third volume of Podestà's *Cursus grammaticalis* defined its subject matter as "Vulgar and Literary Turkish, that is: mixed grammatically and syntactically with Arabic and Persian."[148] This cluster of arguments was nicely elaborated by Antonio Mascis, who served as an interpreter to Cosimo III, grand duke of Tuscany (but who seems to have derived his knowledge of Turkish largely from Molino). In the "Letter to the Reader" that prefaced his *Vocabolario toscano, e turchesco* (Tuscan and Turkish vocabulary) of 1677, Mascis stated that

> The Turks claim, with reason, that their speech [*favella*] is the daughter of Arabic, but is also enriched through aid from three other languages, which are Greek, Persian, and Tatar, which one can well believe, given that it [Turkish] has many words in common with them, from which it follows that whichever one of those one speaks, including Turkish, the other languages can easily be understood; that it [Turkish] is mixed with them, that they make it richer and more copious with words, [and] it is not hard to prove that in those parts of the Greek Empire in Asia where Greek used to be spoken, today only Turkish is spoken, which not only the Greeks, but the Armenians, Chaldeans, Tatars, and many other nations do, who have, to their total disgrace, imbibed the milk of the false Mohammedan doctrine.[149]

Mascis draws a direct line between imperial expansion, religious conversion, and linguistic transformation. His hyperbolic claims are nonetheless interesting for our purposes in perpetuating an Ottoman claim to *translatio imperii*, which presented the sultans as heirs to both Hellenic and Persian imperial formations. Particularly striking is Mascis's voicing of an understanding of Turkish as the "daughter" of Arabic—again, to be understood here as an imperial claim to supersession, rather than to lexicographic (let alone grammatical) genetic links.

While related, the claims of these various dragoman authors imply distinct sociological and epistemological relationships among the three languages and their prototypical speakers. This—and especially Mascis's reference to Ottoman Turkish as the daughter of Arabic—takes us back full circle to Schieferdecker's assertion, referred to at the outset, that Turkish relates to Arabic as French does to Latin. Perhaps Schieferdecker was not so wrong after all. The phylogenetic classification of languages that would take hold in the nineteenth century—and that itself was deeply implicated in European imperialism—would relegate Turkish and Arabic to two very different families (the Turkic branch of Altaic and the Semitic branch of Afro-Asiatic, respectively). But Schieferdecker was writing in the 1690s, almost a full century before Sir William Jones postulated what would become known as Proto-Indo-European, the shared ancestor of Sanskrit, Persian, Greek, and Latin, a theory that paved the way for comparative linguistics.[150] Of particular interest here is not the veracity of Schieferdecker's (or Jones's) theories, but rather how both partook in metalinguistic knowledge production that refracted and mediated to European scholars the language ideologies of Islamicate courtly elites. Schieferdecker, in some sense, was merely summarizing what Meninski (whom he surely read) had to say on the subject only a few years earlier:

> [A]nyone in this Imperial Court or the court of any other prince who wishes to be called a complete interpreter of the Turkish language unavoidably ought to be imbued with Arabic and Persian letters, for even the Turks themselves, as soon as they begin to read, zealously perform the important work of studying each language, nor do they in turn write letters either to their own kind or to foreigners without ornament derived from Persian and Arabic words and phrases interwoven fittingly: although many of their less learned [men] do not distinguish Arabic from Persian and Turkish, nevertheless, they understand the meaning of a word and adapt it to their speech from use alone.[151]

What is mixed, according to Meninski, is not "Turkish" in general, but its elite Ottoman register, and what distinguishes courtiers from their social inferiors is the ability not simply to incorporate Persianisms and Arabisms in their speech but to discern the etymological foreignness of such lexemes. Later comparative linguists would posit language as a system independent from any particular social setting or site of enunciation, and thus knowable through algorithmic computations. Meninski, in contrast, was always a dragoman, keenly aware that the Turkish he had mastered from his courtly teachers in Istanbul, and that he sought to impart to his own students in the courtly milieu of Vienna, was the particular Ottoman Turkish of the divan, a language of imperial administration and high diplomacy, whose spoken register was always striving to emulate a written text.[152] In that setting, Ottoman was, indeed, related to Arabic as French was to Latin, and for the exact same reason: even by the seventeenth century, to be a member of the Republic of Letters one still had to be fluent in Latin, just as one had to use Arabic to partake in a decidedly Ottoman elite discourse. Knowledge of Arabic and Persian, Meninski suggests, is essential for its metapragmatic function, namely the enactment of an elite habitus, rather than merely for its referential function. Or, as Sir William Jones himself put it in 1771 in his "Prefatory discourse to an Essay on the History of the Turks":

> [I]t is impossible to understand the classical writings of the Turks without more than a moderate knowledge of Persian and Arabic, to which none can pretend, who have not made those languages their particular study for many years; and this is no doubt the reason, why there are fewer men of letters among the Turks than among us; for though an intimate acquaintance with the Greek and Roman authors is necessary to support the character of a scholar, yet a very slight tincture of the ancient languages is sufficient for a popular writer, and scarcely any is requisite for a superficial reader.[153]

Both Jones and Meninski were social climbers, forever striving to curry favor with their aristocratic patrons by disparaging their social inferiors. That both considered the proper command of Ottoman as inextricable from the performance of elite habitus, and saw the two as predicated on the ability to pepper one's Turkish speech with Arabic and Persian lexicon, ultimately speaks to the commensurability of early modern courtly cultures. It also underscores the ability—and willingness—of a class of intermediaries to buy into Ottoman courtly language ideologies, to accept that the linguistic variety of the Ottoman court was, indeed, both the purest and synthetic to the core.[154]

As the study of Ottoman became more integrated into a rearticulated notion of "Oriental languages" among eighteenth-century European philologists, it carried with it distinctively Istanbulite courtly language ideologies about Ottoman's prototypical varieties (and the social types presumed to be their authentic and authorized speakers). These language ideologies filtered the Ottoman synthesis through the elite lens of the *elsene i-selase*, underscoring the imperative of studying Ottoman through formal, written varieties, and always alongside and in close relationship to Arabic and Persian. Such language ideologies had direct epistemological and pedagogical implications. They privileged the study of certain kinds of texts that exhibited most fully Ottoman's lexicographical and syntactical relationship to Arabic and Persian, required formal, simultaneous or nearly simultaneous instruction in all three languages, and downplayed Ottoman's relationship to other regional languages (viz. Italian, Greek, Slavic) increasingly understood as "European" and hence "not Islamic." In playing a leading role in introducing these language ideologies to a European readership, and in effacing their ideological nature to boot, dragomans helped constitute the Ottoman language as an object of European knowledge, but also bequeathed to this object its unmistakably foreign guise.

CHAPTER 6

Translating the Ottomans

T WO FACING LEAVES FEATURING an Ottoman and an Italian text are among a few thousand such pairs inscribed into thirty-six registers in the fonds of *Carte Turche* (Turkish Charters) in the bailate archives, spanning the two centuries between 1590 and 1790. The textual pair reproduced in figure 6.1 features, on the right, an ostensible copy of an Ottoman sultanic rescript (official summary) of a petition submitted to the Porte by the Venetian bailo Giacomo Querini ca. 1674. On the left is a purported translation of the Ottoman text, signed by the dragoman Giacomo Tarsia.[1] Whereas the Italian text is unmistakably the dragoman's autograph, the Ottoman was presumably rendered by a bailate scribe, probably from an authorized copy forwarded by the Porte to confirm that action had been taken on the bailo's original petition. I use these qualifiers—ostensible, purported, presumable, probable—to signal that much about the actual production of this translational archive is still unknown.[2] The probative value of the *Carte Turche*'s thousands of copies of Ottoman charters in case of a dispute over the substance of the originals would have been rather limited, as they were anything but "authentic copies," lacking the *tuğra* (seal-like monogram) and most *elkab* (obligatory respectful forms of address) that marked an Ottoman sultanic decree's authenticity, and that were the sine qua non of the Ottoman divan's textual production of "original" versions of "official" records in these genres. What, then, is the knowledge that the bailate's copies-and-translation pairs convey? What was their value and for whom?

A systematic analysis of this corpus, which would take into consideration its material-codicological and linguistic features—from *mise-en-page* and binding techniques to paleography and translation practices—awaits future study. But the textual pair in figure 6.1 can serve to illustrate the relationship between translation, chancery procedures, long-term archival instrumentality, and emergent understandings of dragomans' positionality in the power nexus of Venetian and Ottoman statecraft. According to the

Ottoman rescript copied on the right, a petition from the bailo had sought permission to bury a deceased merchant in the church of St. Francis in Galata.³ Above the rescript appear two annotations, whose diagonal lines attempt to replicate the effect of scribal marginal notes. According to the annotations, the *voivode* (district governor) of Galata, Osman Ağa, had been instructed to ascertain whether such burials had been customary and in line with the existing Imperial Charter.

The spatial relationship between supplication (metonymically represented by the rescript) and bureaucratic processing (metonymically represented by the annotations) is reversed in the Italian translation provided by the dragoman Giacomo Tarsia on the left, where the petition's rescript appears first, followed by the two annotations (table 6.1).

These annotations—presented in reverse order—are identified as instructions issued by a *kaymakam* (deputy), but this authorship is nowhere to be found in the purported "source text" on the facing page. It is possible that both Tarsia and the scribe who produced the Ottoman copy in the register were working from yet another version. Alternatively, perhaps Tarsia sought here to flesh out for his readers the procedural hierarchy of Ottoman government—this would also explain why he reversed the order of the two bureaucratic notes, i.e., as an implicit metapragmatic signal about Ottoman chancery procedures.

Beyond these significant divergences in spatial organization, two other differences between the Ottoman and Italian sides belie a simple notion of "source" and "target." The Ottoman text refers to *sultanım* (my sultan) and *sultanımız* (our sultan) in the rescript of the bailo's petition; the Italian addresses him in the salutation as *Illustrissimo, et Eccelletissimo Signore* (Illustrious and Excellent Signor), and then in the body of the petition as *V[ostra] E[ccellenza]*, Your Excellency, an honorific generally used to address a resident ambassador rather than a sovereign. Not only is the latter a significantly more modest and generic address, but it also conveniently avoids the deictic marking of the addressee's sovereignty over the supplicant conveyed by "my sultan." Other differences between the versions abound. The names of certain Ottoman official genres are translated and thus implicitly commensurated with Italian ones: *ferman,* a sultanic edict, becomes *comando*; *kaydın,* or record, becomes *registro;* *'ahdnâme-i hümâyûn,* or imperial charter, becomes *capitolationi.* Others are rendered as foreignizing loanwords (e.g., *buyuruldu*, official order, becomes *Buiurdi*), as are the offices of *vayvoda* (*voivode,* here in the generic

TABLE 6.1 Transcription and transliteration of ASVe, BaC, b. 252, fasc. 340, 87

(rescript) Ill[ustrissi]mo, et Ecc[ellentissi]mo Sig[no]re	(first annotation) Galata voyvodası Osman ağa haliya bu makule mürdlerin elçisi zikr olunan kilisede kadimden defin ola geldiği gibi mürdü mezkurun defnine mani olmayasın.
Per volontà Divina è morto un Mercante Franco, quale per sepelirlo nella Chiesa n[ost]ra di San Francesco in Galatà prego V[ostra] E[ccellenza] d'un Buiurdi diretto al Vaivoda di Galatà; Nel resto il Comando, è di V[ostra] E[ccellenza]	
Il Bailo di Venetia	
Giacomo Quirini Cav[alie]r	
Trad[ott]a dà Giacomo Tarsia	
Drag[oma]no	
(second annotation) Primo Ordine del d[et]to Caimecam	(second annotation) Ahdname-i hümayun kaydından derkenar oluna
Vi debba veder nel Registro delle Capitolationij	
(first annotation) Secondo Ordine del d[et]to Caimecam.	(rescript) Saadetlu ve muruvvetli sultanım hazretlerimiz sağolsun
Al Vaivoda di Galatà Osman Agà, si comanda.	Nasru'l-allahu teala efrenç bezirganlarından biri mürd olup galatada olan san françesko nam kilise mizde defn olunmak babında galata voyvodasına hitaben buyuruldu-i serif rica olunur. Baki ferman sultanımızındır.
Se s'e praticato ab' antico, che li Corpi di simil morti sono stati sepolti nella Chiesa sud.ta, non impedirete, nel sepelire il sopradetto morto.	
	Venedik baylosu Yakumu Karin kavalları.

sense of a district administrator) and *kaimakam* (*kaymakam*, here a grand vizier's Istanbulite deputy). Even the designation of the deceased merchant as *efrenç*, the Ottoman term for a non-Ottoman European Christian subject, is rendered in the Italian version as *franco*, Frankish, preserving an Ottoman juridical category unlikely to have appeared in the bailo's original petition.[4] These choices have several effects: they signal the translator's keen familiarity with the Ottoman bureaucracy's structures and official genres of documentation, and trust in that awareness being shared by

readers among Venetian political elites. By keeping the general categories
and subject pronouns of the Ottoman text intact but turning "My Sultan"
into "Your Excellency" it also quietly commensurates potentially explosive
differences in perspective, subtly reinforcing the role of the dragoman in
reframing the voices he channels.

Tarsia was clearly not operating in a vacuum, but rather building on
well-established conventions and textual procedures. At the same time,
other examples in the bailate's *Carte Turche* corpus suggest considerable
variation in translation practices over time and among individual dragomans. Dragomans—keenly aware of their addressees—employed different
strategies based on readership and purposes of specific genres. This raises
important questions about routinized practices inherent in the bailate's
translational activities in relation to dragomans' uneven access to archives
of textual models.

As Filippo de Vivo notes, Venetian patricians embarking on diplomatic
missions often had access not only to the Senate's secret archives in the
ducal chancery but to personal and even multigenerational family archives
as well.[5] We know very little about dragomans' access to the ducal chancery,
but have every reason to assume that they could and did consult the bailate
archives, and participated in its periodic reorganization. Additionally, it
is likely that some bailate records found their way to dragomans' family
archives, especially among long-established dragoman dynasties like the
Salvagos and Tarsias. As grandsons, sons, nephews, sons-in-law and siblings of multiple current or former dragomans, members of these and other
dragoman dynasties also accessed an extensive store of orally transmitted
knowledge, frequently invoked as authoritative and binding "custom."

In this context, we may well consider the *Carte Turche* as an archive not
only of diplomatic knowledge and legal precedents but of shifting linguistic and metalinguistic practices as well. The survival of structurally similar registers to the Venetian *Carte Turche* in numerous other diplomatic
chanceries in Istanbul supports this perspective. Such registers, with facing
copies of Ottoman sultanic decrees or other official charters on one side and
a contemporaneous dragoman's Italian or French translation on the other,
were kept across Istanbul's English, French, Dutch, and Polish-Lithuanian
embassies.[6] Some, like the Venetian registers, were letterbooks and copybooks compiled as part of the daily textual circulations of both Ottoman
and European chanceries.[7] Others were the product of didactic efforts by
embassy personnel (including dragomans) to train future staff in Ottoman

diplomatics, or to curate document collections for their own varied purposes.[8] These multiple purposes and contexts of production should not obscure the underlying phenomenon of converging diplomatic practices across Mediterranean chanceries. Indeed, this convergence underscores the multidirectional circulation not only of textual artifacts but, more important, of specialized personnel—dragomans—with their embodied expertise, genre understandings, conceptual vocabularies, inscriptional technologies, and language ideologies.

Thus, before considering the broad corpus of dragomans' translations in Chapter 7, it is worth dwelling on dragomans' translation practices. This is especially true given the deeply ideological context of contemporary translation from Ottoman into Italian, as the example above underscores. To understand this ideological terrain, it helps conceive of translation as enmeshed in a host of "translingual practices," which encompass, as Lydia Liu states, "the process by which new words, meanings, discourses, and modes of representation arise, circulate, and acquire legitimacy within the host language due to, or in spite of, the latter's contact/collision with the guest language."[9] In other words, in order properly to understand dragomans' translation practices—those textual transformations that Translation Studies scholars have variously labeled as translation procedures, techniques, shifts, strategies, and solutions[10]—we must situate them in relation not only to dragomans' professional and familial trajectories but also to the translingual regimes of circulation, institutional matrixes, genres, and manuscript and print inscriptional technologies in which translation was effected. The analysis here proceeds from the premise that even dragomans' most minute textual practices—for example, whether to gloss Ottoman nomenclature or not, and how to go about it—were never "innocent" or value-free, that they were "motivated" not necessarily by the strategic, purposive action of individuals but rather by complex articulations of genres and contexts of production and circulation, as well as by conventionalized expectations about intended readers' familiarity with Ottoman statecraft, politics, and history. Attending to these practices and sites of enunciation underscores the role of positionality in mediation work, and translation's inherent function as an act of boundary marking rather than of bridging across a priori distinct systems of meaning-making.[11]

In pursuing this line of inquiry, several methodological limitations should be noted at the outset. First, working drafts of most dragomans' translations are lost, making it impossible to assess any emendations en route to printed or fair autographed manuscript copies. In one case analyzed below, we cannot even establish definitively a single "source text." Absent other comparable studies of dragomans' translations, it is hard to establish whether dragomans shared expectations about which Ottoman nomenclature constituted "common knowledge" (and hence could be left intact) and which required explication. It is also too early to determine whether dragomans followed any overt "style sheet" in glossing, calquing, or commensurating specific Ottoman terms with Italian ones, or even deployed specific routinized "strategies" consciously and intentionally at all.[12] The epistemological challenge is compounded by the virtual absence of metalinguistic discourse by Venetian dragomans, i.e., explicit reflections on their work process, or about the pedagogy used in their training.

By considering translation practices in terms of what they reveal about pervasive language ideologies (see Chapter 5) we can overcome some of these limitations, as well as the conceptually narrow assumption of translator intentionality that still permeates Translation Studies, and which largely defaults to methodological individualism. The approach here also helps address the "problem" posed by an underdetermined "source text." Unlike the prevailing expectation in much Descriptive Translation Studies of "smooth" translation that effaces traces of the translational activity as a default, dragomans varied in their effort to cover their traces, let alone in their desire to render the text "smooth" and accessible. Given this variation, I have opted for "translation practices" rather than "translation strategies" or "translation procedures," in an effort to avoid overdetermining intentionality or consistency. That said, the analysis that follows does suggest, as a preliminary hypothesis, that dragomans were fairly systematic, and likely self-conscious to a degree, in following certain protocols for translating specific nomenclature, as well as in preserving or shifting a text's overall perspective through the manipulation of specific deictics. Whereas the differences between the cases do not confirm unequivocally a single arc of development, they make manifest an evolving logic and a set of assumptions about the relationship between Ottomans and Italianate (mainly Venetian) reading publics.

Marking Voices, Foregrounding Positions

Our first example consists of two translations of a firman issued by Sultan Murad III to Doge Pasquale Cicogna and received on June 8, 1594. The firman concerned a raid on a Venetian galley by North African corsairs in

Ottoman territorial waters in the Adriatic a month prior (14 Şaban 1002AH/
May 5, 1594); it was issued in response to formal Venetian protests.[13] Of
the two translations compared here, one was prepared in Istanbul by the
Venetian-born dragoman Girolamo Alberti shortly after the firman was
received. The second translation was produced by Giacomo de Nores in
Venice in early July, based on the firman, which was enclosed, sans translation, with a dispatch sent to Venice by Bailo Marco Venier. De Nores was
apparently unaware of Alberti's version.[14] In formulating their translations,
Alberti and de Nores were informed by divergent notions of loyalty and
status. These divergences and the translation practices they authorize continued to shape later translations as well.

The two dragomans differed markedly in their life trajectories and in
their connections to Venetian elite milieus. Girolamo Alberti, a scion of a
well-established family of Venetian citizens by birth, was born circa 1561.
He entered the School of St. Mark as a boy, following in the footsteps of
his grandfather, uncle, father, and brother, who had all served as secretaries
in the Venetian chancery.[15] In 1582, his father, Secretary Gasparo Alberti,
requested to have his firstborn, then twenty-one, sent to Istanbul as an apprentice dragoman.[16] The Senate approved, and Girolamo was to stay in the
Ottoman capital for seventeen years, in the course of which he sometimes
served as the bailate's sole translator of Ottoman texts.[17] Already in 1589
Bailo Giovanni Moro sang Alberti's praise, noting,

> Not only does he understand well that which is said in Turkish, and
> translate into Italian the great number of writings which I continually
> send to Your Serenity, and which I require daily, but being the only
> one in this position, he works at almost all hours, and his ready efforts
> give me full satisfaction.[18]

Alberti's command of Venetian chancery practice and fluency in reading
and translating official Ottoman documents were further recognized in
1600, when his request to return to Venice to attend to family matters was
approved.[19] Alberti, then, was a poster child of dutiful civil service by a
Venetian citizen. By 1594, moreover, he had lived and worked in the bailate
for twelve years, and had had ample opportunity to master the intricacies of
Venetian-Ottoman diplomatic translation as practiced in Istanbul.

Alberti's trajectory contrasts sharply with that of Giacomo de Nores.
Born around 1569 in Nicosia, the capital of then-Venetian Cyprus, Giacomo
was the descendant of two of the island's oldest and most distinguished

noble families, the de Nores and the Podocataro, whose Cypriot roots extended back to the Crusades.[20] During the Ottoman conquest of the island in
1571 several dozen members of both the de Nores and the Podocataro families, including the toddler Giacomo himself, were taken captive and sent to
different parts of the empire. Most were eventually ransomed and departed
for Venice, Spain, Rome, or other Christian territories. But a few, including
one of Giacomo's aunts, converted to Islam and stayed in Ottoman territory.
Reputedly, her two daughters later became sultanas to Mehmed III.[21]

Giacomo himself spent his childhood and youth as a slave in the household of an Ottoman officer in an Istanbul suburb. In 1581 he traveled with
his master to the Safavid frontier, where apparently he learned some Persian. He was ransomed six years later.[22] At the time of his manumission and
arrival in Venice in 1587 de Nores was a youth of seventeen or eighteen,
with no experience in Venetian service, and with limited, if any, command
of Italian.[23] Yet starting in 1589, he was employed as a public dragoman—
an official interpreter for the Venetian Board of Trade. This position entailed close interactions with, and oral interpretation for sojourning Ottoman merchants and their Venetian brokers. His written translations in that
period would have consisted primarily of notarial and commercial rather
than diplomatic records. Indeed, what little fluency he was to achieve in
the conventions of diplomatic translation, or, for that matter, in any official
register of Venetian or Italian written language, was apparently acquired
on the job, in Venice.

The two dragomans' translations of Sultan Murad's firman reflect their
divergent trajectories.[24] While the overall structure and content of the two
texts are similar, significant variations in lexicon and person-marking suggest the two dragomans' differing understandings of what constitutes faithful translation and what typifies and thus defines the difference between
Ottoman and Venetian authority, agency, and voice. Furthermore, as the
analysis below shows, Alberti's translation follows what were probably Venetian diplomatic conventions for rendering Ottoman official terminology
in Italian, conventions that had been developed in the bailate over decades.
Systematic training as an apprentice dragoman would have provided Alberti with a clear set of procedures for translating Ottoman diplomatic
vocabulary. He evidently attempted to voice the source as transparently as
possible, fully assimilating the sultan's perspective to his own.

On the other hand, de Nores's more piecemeal training "on the job" in Venice would have exposed him far less to the intricacies of Venetian-Ottoman

diplomacy. His bread-and-butter professional activity was not translating diplomatic correspondence but rather negotiating commercial disputes among merchants and brokers. Not surprisingly, de Nores used what were probably less conventional solutions than Alberti. More important, he was not as consistent at maintaining the sultan's perspective, and used several devices to signal his role as mediator of knowledge. He thereby ended up distinguishing his own perspective from that of the sultan.

In general, throughout his translation de Nores conveys his familiarity with Ottoman political structures, while also showing great sensitivity to the Venetian position. Given his many years in Ottoman service and his familial connections there (and in other territories beyond Venice), he no doubt was keen to defuse any concerns about his loyalty. Certainly this was his aim when he petitioned the Venetian government for a promotion only a few months after producing this translation. The petition dwelled at length on his aristocratic forebears and the blood they had spilled in defense of the lost colony of Cyprus. By emphasizing his noble status and distinguished ancestry, he reaffirmed his ties to Venice, and also reminded his patrician interlocutors of their commitment to his well-being as a dispossessed colonial subject.

At the same time, de Nores's petition did not shy away from capitalizing on his Ottoman sojourn. References to his long Ottoman captivity might have not only induced sympathy for his plight but also lent credibility to his claim to deep knowledge of Ottoman language and society. After discussing his personal merit, the petition reverts to the first person plural to juxtapose "our" customs with "theirs," thus emphasizing the petitioner's role as an intermediary,

> since it is no less useful for that task [of interpreter] to have experience of the habits of the Turks, their inclinations and their manners of negotiation, *which are very different from ours*, Your Serenity can easily be convinced, that being, I might say, born among these people, and to my bad fortune raised and educated [there], having been involved in their affairs for many years, and traveled in many and diverse provinces and lands here and there . . . [25]

By using the inclusive first-person "our" while narrating his tale of a youth spent in enemy lands, de Nores emphasizes his own distance from the Ottomans, who are treated in the third person. By positioning himself squarely within a Venetian moral community, his long sojourn in Ottoman territory becomes an asset rather than a liability; it foregrounds rather than undermines Ottoman alterity. His disenfranchisement by the Ottomans comes in this way to strengthen his claim to special sensibilities and helps underscore his antipathy to his former captors.

A similar perspective on the Ottomans—one that suggests deep familiarity while at the same time projecting a distant, metropolitan Venetian point of view—is evinced in de Nores's translation of the sultan's letter, setting it apart from Alberti's translation. In fact, de Nores's version more explicitly positions the translator as a "cultural broker," whose mediation is required to make the source legible to a Venetian audience. Several devices help to achieve such an effect: calquing and glossing Ottoman terms and concepts, using colloquial Venetian dialect as opposed to the Tuscan standard common in Venetian chancery writings, and switching person-marking at crucial points to separate the sultan's perspective from that of the translator. Part of the difference between the two translations is no doubt due to Alberti's more systematic schooling in institutions that integrated prevailing humanist ideas about rhetoric and translation, such as the emphasis on literalism and on the translator's "invisibility," including the imperative to avoid interpretive intervention as much as possible.[26] On a secondary level, the very fact that de Nores provides glosses and repeatedly interjects himself as a "cultural broker" into the text marks him as an outsider to the norms and expectations of contemporary diplomatic translation, as practiced in the bailate and the Venetian chancery. Whether this is by accident or design is hard to establish, but the differences would have been clear to any Venetian administrator adept at reading diplomatic dispatches.

Several elements contribute to the difference in perspective of the two translations. First, de Nores includes framing devices in the first two sections of the firman, while Alberti does not. These explicitly introduce the source text: *per una supplica presentata hora all'alta mia sedia* (through a petition just presented to my elevated seat); *suggiungendo appresso in essa supplica, che* (it is further added in that petition that). Such frames accentuate that the text came from "elsewhere," further distance de Nores from the sultan's perspective, and constitute him as a channel rather than a source.

Second, on several occasions de Nores uses terminology that simply calques the phrasing of the original Ottoman text, while Alberti uses what must be taken as idiomatic, and more conventional, phraseology. De Nores translates the Ottoman appellation of the sultan's abode as *la felice Porta* (the felicitous Porte), and *la felice mia ressidenza* (my felicitous residence), following almost word for word the original terms used in the sultan's letter to the doge, *asitane-i sa'adete* (threshold of felicity or felicitous threshold) and *destgahımız* (our chief seat). Alberti prefers more classicizing honorifics, and perhaps a more formal Italian register, such as *l'Ecc[els]a Porta*, (the Sublime Porte), and *la mia Imperial et Cesarea Maestà* (my Imperial and Caesarean Majesty).[27]

Similarly patterned differences between calquing and idiomatic translation are visible in the two dragomans' renderings of Ottoman officials' titles, where the translated forms must commensurate administrative hierarchies. In translating Sinan Paşa's title of *kapudanpaşa*, the Ottoman lord admiral, both de Nores and Alberti use a term current in the Venetian navy: *Cap[itan]o del Mare* (Alberti, using a standard Tuscan form) or *Capitano da Mare* (de Nores, using a Venetian dialect form). Both point to the commensurability of Sinan Paşa's title with the Venetian office of lord admiral. But whereas Alberti later glosses Sinan's title simply as *consigliero* (councilor), de Nores includes Sinan's Ottoman title of *vizir* (vizier, minister), and his specific jurisdiction in the matter of corsairing as *custode d'Alger*, the custodian of Algiers (again, following the original firman's *Cezâyir emînleri ile kapudânımız olan . . . vezîrimiz Sinân paşa*). De Nores thus signals both his awareness of Sinan's elevated position, as second in the Ottoman hierarchy only to the grand vizier, as well as his understanding of Ottoman provincial government structure more generally. To describe the lesser Ottoman officials addressed by the sultan, Alberti uses the form *Sig[no]ri del Mare* (lords of the sea), following the Venetian construction of official titles with the Tuscan preposition "del." De Nores adheres to a similar structure, *sanzachi dà mare*. His version, however, uses *sanzachi*, a Venetianized plural form of the Ottoman *sancak* (province, often used in Venetian sources also to refer to the person of the provincial governor, or *sancakbeği*), plus the Venetian dialect form of the preposition *da*. These various examples all foreground de Nores's understanding that the act of translation requires significant cultural mediation.

Indeed, de Nores is more likely than Alberti to provide his readers with glosses for certain aspects of Ottoman "custom," styling himself as an authority on things Ottoman addressing what he took as an uninitiated metropolitan Venetian reader. For instance, he supplements the original letter's lunar Hijri date with its Gregorian equivalent (*14 della luna di saban, ciò è alli 4 di Maggio*), whereas Alberti leaves the date unglossed.[28] Alberti similarly uses the original Ottoman term *'arz*—a recognizable genre of Ottoman diplomatics—to refer to the official report about the corsairs' attack sent by the district governor, Piri Beğ; de Nores transforms it into *notitia et aviso* (notice), a calque of the original *'arz u takrîr*.

On other occasions, de Nores betrayed his imperfect understanding of Ottoman diplomatic and political concepts. He calls the *'ahdnâme* (privileges) granted by the Ottoman sultan to the Venetians, which were ostensibly violated by the corsairs' attack, *conventione della pace, et promessa, che è fra ambi le parti* (a covenant of peace, and agreement between the two parties). Such a notion of bilateralism was quite foreign to contemporary Ottoman diplomacy. Indeed, the original firman refers to the corsairs' attack as a violation of an *'ahdnâme-i hümâyûn*, an imperial letter of oath, and as *sulh u salâh* (contrary to the peace and amity). This much more unilateral Ottoman understanding of the *'ahdnâme* is well rendered by Alberti, who calls the document *giurati Imp[eria]li Capitoli* (sworn Imperial Articles). Similarly, the sultan's domains, which the original firman calls *memâlik-i mahrûse*, are rendered by de Nores as *custoditi nostri paesi* (our well-protected lands), and by Alberti as *mio Custodito dominio* (my well-protected domain). Although de Nores is both grammatically and lexically closer to the original, it is Alberti's use of *dominio* as opposed to *paesi* that suggests greater familiarity with specifically juridical conceptions of sovereignty and rulership underwriting Venetian-Ottoman diplomatic relations.[29]

De Nores's lexical choices also reveal, whether he realized it or not, traces of an Ottoman perspective. For instance, he calls the three corsair vessels that attacked the Venetian ship *Galere Mussulmane* (Muslim galleys), following the original designation as *müslümân kadırgası*, as opposed to Alberti's *Galee turchesche*. To be sure, late-sixteenth-century Venetian readers would have taken *turchesche* to mean "Muslim" as much as "Turkish," making Alberti's translation technically correct, if complicit in a Venetian (and more broadly European) perspective which conflated Turkish ethnicity, Muslim religion, and Ottoman juridical status.[30] By using the less conventional *Musulmane* rather than the much more common but ambiguous *turchesche*, de Nores avoids this conflation, and instead reproduces the original letter's implicit assumption that North African corsairs were not necessarily ethnically Turkish, and that the Porte exerted only limited control over them.

On the whole, though, de Nores's translation suggests an effort to extricate the translator from any complicity in the sultan's perspective and to position himself in a supposedly more "neutral" intermediary space. In translating *beğ*—the title that the sultan's letter uses for the Venetian administrator assaulted by the corsairs—Alberti renders it as *Bei*, thus upholding his supposed "invisibility" as a translator by sticking to probable convention. De Nores, on the other hand, "re-translates" it back to its presumed Venetian form, *Rettore*. He thus avoids using a Turkism as a title for a Venetian official, even though, as noted above, he does not mind using Turkisms when translating the titles of Ottoman officials. De Nores thus marks the boundary between Venetian and Ottoman domains with his lexical choices.

A similar unease about voicing the sultan's perspective is betrayed by several shifts in person-marking toward the end of de Nores's translation. As mentioned, the first two sections of the sultan's letter provide an account, first of the capture of the Venetian galley, and second of the actions already taken by the Porte to identify and punish the attackers and to reprimand the Ottoman provincial officials. Throughout these first two sections both translators use the first person to refer to the sultan, and the second person for the Venetians. The third and last section of the firman marks a subtle but significant shift, as it moves to address the Venetian doge directly, urging him to ensure that in the future, rather than taking matters into their own hands (and risk destabilizing the peace), the Venetians should appeal to the Ottoman court. In this section of the text, where the sultan makes explicit requests of the Venetians, de Nores seems to get "nervous" about using person-marking that treats his Venetian patrician superiors as "you." Both Alberti and de Nores convey the shift in footing by resorting to the second person plural imperative mode to refer to the Venetian addressees (de Nores: *siate certi, levandovi dalla mente*; Alberti: *non habiate à dubitar*). Yet at crucial moments de Nores switches to a Venetian (or, at least, a less overtly Ottoman) perspective. First, on two separate occasions he seems to avoid the use of pronouns that would clearly mark the speaker as Ottoman. What Alberti translates, respectively, as *la buona pace, che è frà di noi* (the good peace that obtains between us)—here, using the only inclusive first person in the firman—and as *amici di nostri amici* (friends of our friends), de Nores translates as *amicitia, et pace che è fra ambi le parti* (friendship, and peace that obtains between the two parties), and as *amici de gl'amici di questa eccelsa Porta* (friends of the friends of this Sublime Porte). Second, what Alberti renders as *non prestarete aiuto à nostri nemici* (do not lend help to our enemies) becomes, in de Nores's translation, *non darete alli suoi nemici alcuna sorte d'agiuto* (do not give *their* enemies any sort of help; my emphasis). By suddenly referring to the Ottomans in the third, rather than the first person, de Nores significantly changes perspective, and interrupts the conflation of the sultan's voice with that of the translator, as instead is implicit in Alberti's "transparency."

Such a dramatic shift suggests the insecurities of a bureaucratic mediator whose foreignness was signaled not only by his Ottoman upbringing but by his lack of ties to an established metropolitan family. As a late learner of Italian, and non-initiate into the conventions of diplomatic translation, de Nores used a register closer to spoken Venetian, which he would have employed daily in his oral interpreting in front of his patrician employers. All of this probably reinforced his sense of alterity. Alberti, on the other hand, from a recognized Venetian citizen family, and trained in the highest registers of chancery Tuscan from youth, had no similar cause for concern. As bailate resident, he was adept at written translation, used a formal style, and inserted few cultural explanations into the translated text. De Nores's glosses for Ottoman custom, the framings he gave the translation, and the shift in person-marking were attempts to distinguish himself from the Ottomans in the act of translation. In so doing, he showed his awareness of the risks inherent in all mediation.

Glossing and Commensurating

The discussion above, and the comparison of Alberti's and de Nores's translations of Sultan Murad's firman in 1594, have both underscored dragomans' differing emergent understandings of what was prototypically Ottoman or Venetian. In order to gain further insight into the transformation of dragomans' translation practices over time, we turn to three larger translation projects, undertaken at different moments in the seventeenth century: Giovanni Battista Salvago's account of the regicide of Osman II (1622), Giacomo Tarsia's translation of a chronicle by Hasan Vecihi (1675), and Gian Rinaldo Carli's *Cronologia historica* (1697), a translation of Katip Çelebi's *Takvimü't-tevarih* (Almanac of Histories). These three examples roughly follow an arc of development in both translation practices and assumptions about readers' access to the text. The analysis explores how their varied textual practices articulated both the boundary between Ottoman texts and their Italianate readers, and dragomans' own evolving relationship to that shifting boundary.

The first case concerns Giovanni Battista Salvago's (ca. 1590–1644) account of the regicide of Osman II. The narrative describes young Osman's ascent to the throne and his increasingly unpopular reign, marred by a failed campaign against Poland and plans to embark on a hajj to Mecca, which some interpreted to be a ploy to replace his disgruntled janissaries and the *spahi* (imperial cavalry) of the capital with Arab soldiery. Salvago's perspective on the regicide, and its linguistic mediation in his report, are especially interesting. As analyzed below, Salvago gives much attention to the grievances of the janissaries, whose rebellion ultimately led to Osman's incarceration, the re-enthronement of his mentally unstable uncle, Mustafa, and ultimately, Osman's execution. In so doing, he both echoed and amplified an ascendant view among contemporary Ottoman historians themselves.

At least two exemplars of Salvago's account of the regicide survive. A first exemplar, evidently a working draft, bears the title, "Unfortunate life and unhappy death of Sultan Osman, son of Sultan Ahmet, and nephew of sultan Mustafa, the present king of the Turks."[31] A fair copy (figure 6.2) prefaces the original title with "The Ottoman Revolutions precipitated by the Unfortunate Life [etc.]," suggesting a conscious effort to cast the text as political commentary, not a mere chronicle.[32] If little is known about the circulation of the fair copy, the working draft's location in a miscellany of some thirty-six Ottoman-themed texts provides important clues as to its purpose.

We do not know how the miscellany wound its way into the possession of the bibliophile Emmanuele Cicogna (1789–1868) who bequeathed it to the Library of the Correr Museum in Venice, but we can hypothesize about its intended purpose from its contents.[33] Among them are various diplomatic treaties and reports from the late sixteenth and early seventeenth centuries, including Sultan Osman II's missive to the Ragusans, translated by another Venetian dragoman,[34] Count Guido San Giorgio's Discourse on the naval battle of Lepanto in 1571,[35] the *'ahdnâme* granted by Sultan Murad III to Venice in 1575,[36] relazioni by Marcantonio Barbaro (1573) and Ottaviano Bon (1609),[37] a 1574 summary of a report on Ottoman possessions in Europe under Sultan Selim,[38] and, finally, Minuccio Minucci's 1584 treatise on the Crimean Tatars.[39] Additionally, the miscellany includes several texts by Salvago himself, including "On the Death of Muhammad, Prophet of the Muslims [. . .] taken from The lives of saintly fathers and martyrs, including Hassan, Hussein, and others," "The Muslim Institution of Crying

Out on their Towers," "On the Oration of the Muslims," "Translation of a Fetva, that is a legal response, by a Mufti, the Pontiff of the Muslims, against the Persians, in justification of the war that the King of the Turks is legitimately making against the King of Persia," "Translation of a letter of reproach against the Persians, directed at the Teacher of the King of Persia, written by an unknown Turkish author," and "On the Form of the Litanies of the Muslims."[40]

Combined, these works refract the theological-cum-political Sunni-Shi'a debates of the time, what Tijana Krstić has aptly dubbed "the Ottoman Age of Confessionalization."[41] The absence of a clear chronological ordering to the materials, and the combination of theological, political, and military works hints at a deliberate editorial selection process, rather than rote copying of a preexisting collection. As a miscellany, this volume thus operates as the purveyor of current knowledge about Ottoman religious and political affairs to an Italianate non-Muslim, non-Ottoman readership. On a secondary order, it showcases the compiler's deep familiarity with—indeed immersion in—both Ottoman and Venetian metropolitan elites' perspectives on the Ottoman world. Virtually all its materials come from the Venetian diplomatic context of the late sixteenth and early seventeenth centuries. Salvago's own writings and signed translations constitute at least one quarter of the miscellany, whereas no other author is responsible for more than one piece. These details suggest that the materials were assembled—likely by Salvago himself—as a dossier to be handed to a Venetian patron preparing for diplomatic assignment in Istanbul.

Salvago, we should recall, was a road dragoman, who in that capacity shuttled between Istanbul and Venice accompanying Venetian representatives on their way to and from their missions. Upon his death in 1645, a similar compilation of preparatory materials for the incoming bailo Nicolò Dolfin was found in Salvago's *sepetto* (hamper or basket, from the Ottoman *sepet*) in the bailate. It included, among other things, a sixteen-folio *relazione* on the Ottoman navy, and an eleven-folio report entitled "news on the War on Crete."[42] These were only the latest in Salvago's long list of writings, all unpublished, but which clearly enjoyed some circulation among the dragoman's many Venetian patrons and acquaintances. His choice of subject matter reveals a great interest in recent Ottoman history as well as in Muslim ritual practice, and Salvago's largely uncredited sources suggest his access to a more popular register of Ottoman textual production, perhaps partly oral. Taken as a whole, Salvago's portrayal of Muslim ritual practice, his 1625 *relazione* from North Africa (discussed in Chapter 3), and his miscellany, including the narration of the deposition and regicide of Sultan Osman II in 1622, to which we now return, underscore his conscious attempt to mediate Ottoman religious and historical thought to an Italianate readership.[43]

In 1622 Salvago was stranded in Venice, awaiting departure for Istanbul in the company of the newly elected bailo Michele Foscarini (1574–1625), who was suffering from severe illness.[44] It was conceivably at Foscarini's behest that Salvago penned his account of Sultan Osman's regicide—alongside seven other texts in that miscellany that Salvago identified as his own writings or translations. Whether or not Foscarini commissioned the account of the regicide, the events it described were clearly of immense interest to Venice's political class, as to other European elites.[45] The placement of Salvago's narrative about the regicide directly after an anonymous letter from Pera concerning Osman's death and Sultan Mustafa's ascent, also dated 1622, confirms its topicality.

Prima facie, Salvago's chronicle of the regicide is not a translation at all. His use of the verb *riferiva*, reported, to describe his role in the production of the text implicitly distinguishes it from other texts he translated and signed as such. In presenting his role as one of reportage, Salvago associates his narrative with the genre of *relazione* that his employers would have performed in front of the Venetian Senate upon their return from the Porte, and indeed that Salvago himself would present three years later, on his return from his ransoming mission to North Africa (see Chapter 3). As we have seen, in the early modern context, the claim to reporting implied a particular eyewitness quality. But Salvago's report on the regicide at no point suggests he saw the events unfold, or even talked directly to any of the protagonists. Rather, it implies a deep intimacy with the metropolitan elite milieu of the actions (to which we will return momentarily), and, even more significantly, employs a voicing structure that partakes in the perspective of a particular party, the janissaries, empathizes with their rebellion, and ultimately exculpates them from direct responsibility for the regicide. This perspective, as Baki Tezcan notes, became the ascendant ideological stance of Ottoman chroniclers in the aftermath of the regicide, and was likewise articulated by the most influential chronicler of the events, Tuği, himself a janissary. But it was far from the only version of events available to contemporaries.[46]

That Salvago at least adapted if not verbatim translated Tuği, using both the Ottoman chronicler's overall perspective and specific legitimizing strategies, yet without ever acknowledging his sources, is itself quite significant as a case of "unacknowledged translation." Such conceit goes beyond the standard early modern laxity in citation practice, and in fact illuminates the particular modes of authority of proto-Orientalist knowledge production. It was common for Venetian diplomats to incorporate into their written dispatches and relazioni knowledge and perspective gained through oral interactions with Ottoman dignitaries, often mediated by dragomans. The sources of such knowledge and their complex channels of mediation were only partially acknowledged. Here we see how a similar process of unacknowledged mediation likely informs Salvago's own writing.

How did Salvago's erasure of mediation and of the boundary between different perspectives shape his translation practices? Among other things, it produced a text relatively free of Ottomanisms. Salvago systematically used only Gregorian rather than *hijri* dates, and substituted Ottoman offices and other nomenclature with Italian glosses: *ministro* for *vezir*, *re* (king) for *padişah*, *saggi Dottori con ragioni scritturali* (learned scholars of scripture) for *ulema*, *governo* (government, governorate) for *beylik*.[47] He also frequently substituted Hellenic toponyms for Ottoman ones, e.g., Babylonia rather than Baghdad and Asia rather than Anatolia.

Two other translation practices likely unique to Salvago are worth dwelling on: first, not once in the manuscript's thirty-two pages did he use the declaratory conjunction *cioè*, "that is," before an Italian gloss of an Ottoman term. This conjunction was commonplace in contemporary translations from Ottoman, including many other dragomans' writings. For example, its Italian (*cioè*), Venetian (*zoe*), and Latin (*idest*) variants appear over 100 times in Yunus Bey and Alvise Gritti's twenty-two-page printed treatise, *Opera Nova* (1537), which provided Venetian readers with a detailed exposé on the structure of the Ottoman government, becoming a template for future discourses on the subject.[48] The *cioè* conjunction is far less prevalent in Book II of Benedetto Ramberti's *Libri tre delle cose de Turchi* (1539), which was largely plagiarized from Yunus Bey and Gritti's treatise, and which mostly followed the structure of its source, but it still precedes about half of Ramberti's glosses for both offices and place-names. The *cioè* conjunction also appears regularly in printed Italian translations of Ottoman texts, relazioni, travelogues, and writings in cognate contact genres throughout the sixteenth and seventeenth century, including the apprentice dragoman Antonio Benetti's account of his journey from Venice to Istanbul in 1688.[49] Though a systematic study of equivalent conjunctions in other languages is not available, anecdotal evidence suggests that this usage was prevalent cross-linguistically, especially in genres whose intent was to educate readers about the Ottoman government's structure.[50]

Even more than Ramberti, and in contrast to Benetti's and to Yunus Bey and Alvise Gritti's style, Salvago's Italian glosses mostly attach to the Ottoman nomenclature without the *cioè* conjunction, as in *Muftì sommo interprete della legge, Cadileschier Giudice di campo*—the latter example appearing after four unglossed previous mentions of *kadilesker*.[51] If the *cioè* conjunction, while intimating equivalency and translatability, calls attention to the fraught act of commensuration, its absence elides such possible epistemic gaps, as well as the very fact of translation.

Second, and even more unusually, Salvago generally reverses the elements of the equivalency, providing the Italian gloss first, and only then the Ottoman term, after the declaratory conjunction *detti* ("[which are] called," plural), e.g., *pellegrini detti Hagì, responsi, detti in Turco Fetfà, questor et essattor publico, che i Turchi dicono Defterdar*, or *Il Moro Eunuco Chislar Agà*.[52] This subtle shift suggests the primacy of a shared meaning over the distinct and foreign nomenclature. It renders not only the events described but their very cultural framing more familiar and commensurable with the lifeworlds of an Italianate readership, without erasing entirely the translator's interpretive, intermediary role.

Beyond these particular syntactical constructions, Salvago's narrative offers other elements of a "syncretic" perspective, e.g., in psychologically justifying and motivating protagonists' actions, both individual and collective, thus implying shared intimacy with them. He also partakes in a decidedly metropolitan, elite perspective on the Ottoman provinces, for example in repeatedly describing the dangers of the hajj to Mecca due to "Arab robbers and marauders,"[53] and in using the term "Ottoman" in the narrow sense of a member of the house of Osman rather than the much more generalized sense of Ottoman subject, for example when explaining that Osman avoided the hajj because "no Ottoman has ever gone there."[54] Finally, Salvago frequently incorporates in his narrative extensive passages of direct speech, particularly to represent the words of aggrieved janissaries. For example, he quotes verbatim a lengthy dialogue that purportedly took place in front of the Fatih Mosque on May 18 between the *spahi*, janissaries, and other stipendiaries of the court on the one hand, and the *ulema* on the other.[55] Such extended direct speech contributes to the narrative's witnessing effect, and is especially striking given that Salvago often summarized the words of other historical agents, granting them much less textual elaboration.

Salvago's rather idiosyncratic textual practices are brought into sharper relief by comparison with those of Giacomo Tarsia's translation of the *Tarih-i Vecihi*, entitled "Relation on the Events of the Ottoman Empire from the Year of Muhammad 1046 through 1071, and of Christ our Lord 1638 through 1660, composed in the Turkish language by Hasan Vezhi [sic] and translated into the Italian tongue by Giacomo Tarsia Venetian dragoman in Pera of Constantinople on October 20, 1675." An autograph bound octavo manuscript of 360 pages is now in the Marciana Library in Venice.[56] Although never printed, the title page of Tarsia's manuscript (figure 6.3) emulates print in its layout and typography-inspired calligraphy. The choice of *relazione* for the translated title also suggests an affinity with a prestigious genre of diplomatic and political reportage with which Venetian reading publics (and Tarsia himself) would have been keenly familiar. As discussed in Chapter 3, diplomatic reports, while officially meant for circumscribed circulation, were often edited, printed, translated, and read far beyond their original intended audience in government. Tarsia's evocation of the genre of Venetian *relazione*, then, exemplifies his strong humanistic awareness and the impact of earlier printed texts on the framing of new texts about the Ottomans, and perhaps his own aspirations to leverage print technologies.

Ironically, we know more about Tarsia than about the work's author, Hasan Vecihi (ca. 1620–1661). The latter was born around 1620 in Bakhchysarai (Tatar: Bağçasaray) in the Crimea and moved to Istanbul at a young age to become a scribe in the chancery of the imperial *divan* (in striking parallel with the itinerary of many Venetian dragomans, including Giacomo's father, Christoforo). As the *mühürdar* (keeper of the seal) of Grand Admiral and future Grand Vizier Kara Mustafa Paşa, Vecihi witnessed the campaign on Baghdad in 1638. His chronicle survives in at least ten copies in both former Ottoman lands and beyond (including Leiden and Vienna), some dating to the 1670s through 1690s, attesting to its continued circulation after Vecihi's untimely death of tuberculosis ca. 1660.[57]

Tarsia's implicit style sheet in translating Vecihi seems guided by an overriding concern for preserving Vecihi's Ottoman perspective rather than the conventionalized forms of contemporary Italian diplomatic translation. Tarsia is particularly attentive to Ottoman honorifics and epithets (for example, he retains the epithet *han* at the end of sultans' names, an obligatory honorific in Ottoman usage not customarily preserved in Italian diplomatic translations of the time, which tended to do away with most Ottoman honorifics and epithets). He similarly retains pejorative terms for the Safavids through Italianate lexical forms, which help convey the text's Ottoman metropolitan perspective. In upholding references to the Ottoman army as *Militia Mussulmana, Essercito Mussulmano* (the Muslim army) he again sustains an Ottoman perspective on the sultanate as the guardian of (Sunni) orthodoxy, rendering the Safavids not only a political rival but, as Shi'a, a heretical sect and a religious abomination. Tarsia even leaves intact and unglossed references to the Venetians in besieged Crete as *ostinati Infedeli* (obstinate infidels) and *l'infedeli Venetiani* (the Venetian infidels).[58]

At the same time, Tarsia is more systematic than Salvago in distinguishing Ottoman and Italian linguistic matter. Rather than silently render all Ottoman nomenclature in Italian, he frequently employs the conjunction *cioè*, "that is," to make more explicit his glosses of Ottoman terms and Gregorian conversions of *hijri* dates. The boundary between the two linguistic-cum-cultural systems now seems less permeable, though clearly not entirely fixed.

Compared to both Salvago's and Tarsia's works, Gian Rinaldo Carli's *Cronologia Historica,* a translation of Katip Çelebi's *Takvimü't-tevarih* (Almanac of Histories) is perhaps the most ambitious, and certainly the most capacious and erudite. It is also the only Venetian dragoman's translation of a complete Ottoman work to be printed to date.[59] That the printer, Andrea Poletti, was responsible, a decade earlier, for printing Donà's two works on Ottoman letters, as well as the apprentice dragoman Antonio Benetti's travelogue, suggests Carli's contacts in Venetian literary circles that would have facilitated the publication.[60]

If Carli operated on the spatial and sociological periphery of the Venetian literary field, Katip Çelebi was certainly at the heart of its Istanbulite counterpart. A true polymath, Katip Çelebi (also known as Haci Halife, 1609–1657) completed the *Takvimü't-tevarih*, a compilation of chronological tables of world history from the beginning to his own time, in 1648. After his death in 1659, Çelebi's highly popular work was continued by several authors. It circulated both within the Ottoman Empire; in Safavid lands in an anonymous, 1674 posthumous Persian translation; and in Europe in a copy prepared in Istanbul shortly after Çelebi's death, and brought to Leiden by Levinus Warner alongside fragments of Çelebi's massive library.[61] Carli's

Italian translation was preceded by Antoine Galland's manuscript French version (before 1682), and followed by Johann Jacob Reiske's Latin version, also in manuscript.[62] In 1733 the *Takvimü't-tevarih* became the twelfth book to be published by the printing press of the Ottoman courtier Ibrahim Müteferrika.[63] Carli's work, then, partakes in a broader system of early Enlightenment scholarly production and circulation.

Perhaps even more than Tuği and Vecihi, Katip Çelebi was a scholar of a decidedly metropolitan outlook, whose work explicitly sought to legitimize the Ottoman imperial project and situate it in a universal temporal scheme. The son of a bureaucrat, he himself traveled in his youth on several military campaigns, but eventually settled back in Istanbul, his birthplace, where he was employed in the chancery. His massive textual output was based primarily on written sources, some acquired on his travels to Aleppo, but mostly obtained in Istanbul, where he spent much of his inheritance to amass "probably the largest private library in Istanbul in his time."[64]

Katip Çelebi's encyclopedic work famously inspired Barthélemy d'Herbelot's *Bibliothèque orientale*.[65] Yet the former's role in the genealogies of Orientalism is not simply one of ideational influence, but of intense material and epistemological circulations in which dragomans played a decisive role. If Antoine Galland was instrumental in collecting manuscripts for d'Herbelot's magisterial book (and owed his own introduction to Katip Çelebi's work to the latter's student, Ḥüseyin Hezārfenn, with whom Galland collaborated while in Istanbul), so Carli was deeply involved in a Venetian equivalent to d'Herbelot's undertaking, Giovanni Battista Donà's massive compilation and publication project. Donà, to whom Carli dedicated his work, was a former bailo and patron of several previous translation projects undertaken by dragomans and apprentices in his employ. Key among those was Carli, who, like his cousin Giacomo Tarsia, had joined the bailate at a young age to apprentice there, and ultimately rose through the ranks to eventually become Venetian grand dragoman in 1716.

The connections between Carli's *Cronologia* and Donà's earlier publication projects of 1688 did not end there, nor with their shared prestigious printer. In his dedication to Donà—which Carli loudly proclaimed on the title page, describing the dedicatee as "Senator and great sage"—the dragoman frames the *Cronologia* precisely as a response to the call sounded in Donà's *Della Letteratura* to disabuse European readers of the assumption of universal Ottoman ignorance.[66]

This intellectual genealogy informs Carli's translation practices through-out, for example in his rendering of temporal data. Given that the whole book is a chronology, it is all the more remarkable that no *hijri* dates are glossed or converted to the Gregorian calendar. The work, Carli implies, is meant to showcase how its author (and, by extension, educated Ottoman elites) understood history, rather than offer a useful lens on the past, Ottoman or otherwise. Repeated marginal notes that point out textual errors and divergences from classical authorities bear this out.

In fact, Carli's marginal annotations represent the culmination of drag-omans' increasing tendency to make their mediation and translation work visible. The visual conventions of early modern print bring out the distinc-tiveness of the marginal notes more forcefully than a manuscript might. Carli's editorial interventions certainly become quite easy to separate out from the body of the text thanks to his liberal use of asterisks to point to the notes, which are rendered in italicized, smaller type. Of significance here are less the typographical affordances of print, however, than the epistemo-logical assumptions of the translator vis-à-vis his readership.[67] In this re-gard, Carli's notes perform several functions at once. At the semantic level, they explicate or gloss terms that the translator assumes his Italianate read-ership would be unfamiliar with. At the same time, the notes allow Carli to use Ottoman nomenclature in the body of the translation and to clearly demarcate Çelebi's words from his own. Thus, in the first marginal note on page 6 (figure 6.4) we learn that *Haci* means pilgrims to Mecca. The second note performs a more complex act of mediation: rather than Ottoman no-menclature, what the note glosses is an Italian calque of the emergent Otto-man concept of a Christian community, *tayifeti'n-Nasraniyye*,[68] which Ve-netian diplomatic translations of the period usually rendered as *[la] nation nazarena* (the Nazarene nation). Similar locutions—"Nazarene Emperor," "Nazarene religion," and so forth—appear multiple times throughout the book.[69] Remarkably, Carli does not "domesticate" the category by silently rendering it as "Christians" in the body of the text—as Salvago or Tarsia likely would have. Rather, he maintains the calque form and then glosses in a marginal note, doubly reinforcing the foreignness of the text as the product of a particular cultural context distant from the readers' and hence requiring the translator's editorial intervention.

The third marginal note on page 6 identifies a place name, the city of Zur. It reads: "I do not know what this city of Zur is, but I know well that Plutarch, Curtius [Quintus Curtius Rufus], and Arrian, all of whom penned works on the life of Alexander, wrote that he died in Babylonia." This note catapults the translator even more firmly into the level of a philologically and historically minded man of letters. Metadiscursively, it intimates that Çelebi's book is very much in conversation with the same classical traditions to which contemporary European scholars were laying claim, an argument undergirding Carli's translation project as a whole.

Similar notes proliferate throughout Carli's translation. He is particularly fond of pointing out when Çelebi's account diverges from known Greek sources on antiquity, for example when he remarks that Humai and her sister, the two Persian (Sasanian) princesses who vied for the throne upon the death of their father, King Ardashir, in the year 5172 "are not mentioned in Greek history."[70] Later on the same page he observes: "This whole chapter contains many implications and anachronisms which are in fact contrary to what the Greek and Latin historians have written." Notes further buttress his own cultural and linguistic competency, for example, when explaining that *Meut* in the name of the fortress *Hissarul Meut* (Fortress of Death) means death in Arabic. More than adding essential information, Carli here reminds readers of his Arabic proficiency.[71]

Beyond "Foreignization" and "Domestication"

What might Salvago's, Tarsia's, and Carli's translation practices tell us about Venetian dragomans' emergent perspective on Ottoman historicity and textuality? Is there an identifiable temporal arc to the deployment of particular practices and their combinations? At least prima facie, we can identify a progression from silent commensuration (Salvago) to sharper distinction between Ottoman and Italian linguistic matter (Tarsia) to even more conspicuous elaboration of dragomans' own mediation and translation labor (Carli). Were these dragomans' practices determined primarily by individual personal and professional trajectories? By genre? By broader sociohistorical processes and intellectual currents? Such a systematic analysis awaits a future study.

Even the preliminary results presented above, however, offer a powerful rebuttal of the supposedly inherent meaning, purpose, and ethics of "foreignization" and "domestication," as developed by the Translation Studies scholar Lawrence Venuti. Building on the work of the German Romantic philosopher Friedrich Schleiermacher, who coined the terms, Venuti posited "foreignization" and "domestication" as a set of translation strategies intended to foster "cultural resistance" through disruption and "cultural intimacy" through smoothness, respectively. Critiques of this model have now become widespread among Translation Studies scholars. Theorists have rightfully taken Venuti to task for his binary model, for his a priori valorization of "foreignization" strategies, and for his assumption that emphasis on cultural difference is inherently ethical and desirable whereas prioritizing fluency and seamlessness is inherently oppressive.[72] Historians of translation, for their part, have amply demonstrated that neither "smooth" nor "faithful" translation necessarily served as the only (or even primary) guiding principles for early modern translators.[73]

Yet both Venuti and his critics seem to share fundamental assumptions about what constitutes translation, what is its function, and, indeed, how it relates to sociocultural worlds. Both camps tend to hypostatize language, culture, and society, treating them as self-evidently coextensive. They take for granted that translation entails two a priori distinct languages-cum-cultures-cum-societies, and that the distinction is palpable and incontrovertible both to members of said language communities/cultures/ societies and to scholarly observers. By and large, they situate translators inherently and squarely within the target language-cum-culture-cum-society, from whence they supposedly address a selfsame readership.[74]

The monolingual and methodological nationalist fallacies undergirding such arguments are belied by dragomans' lifeworlds. Clearly, in Istanbul and other metropoles, dragomans could hardly be assumed to stand apart from the courtly milieu in which they operated or to address only a readership of cultural others in a spatial elsewhere. Whether it was Carli—who grew up in a bilingual Italophone/Slavophone environment in his ancestral hometown, Capodistria, or Salvago and Tarsia, who were born and raised in bilingual Grecophone/Italophone households in Istanbul, dragomans' lifeworlds were fundamentally plurilingual.

The pervasive plurilingualism of early modern Istanbulite dragomans (and other denizens of the Ottoman capital) is only one aspect of the problem. Equally significant is the question of audience: if all three texts examined here are Italian, what is the Italophone readership they are addressing? Does it comprise only fluent speakers of the language? Are such addressees necessarily based in Italophone spaces? Are they axiomatically not Ottoman? Clearly, we cannot answer these questions in the affirmative without ignoring the centrality of Italian to the circulation of diplomatic (and, more generally, political) knowledge in the early modern Mediterranean and beyond.[75] Analyzing dragomans' specific textual practices thus furthers our understanding of the multiple and entangled forms of mediation involved in the production of knowledge about the Ottoman Empire with Italian as the primary vector of that knowledge across the European continent. These textual practices shed light on dragomans' role in naturalizing a particularly metropolitan elite Ottoman Turkish (as opposed to other regional dialects) as "standard," and in European-wide proliferation of Italian-inflected Turkish; for example, in the frequent appearance of morphologically Italianized lexemes (such as *seraglio, agiamoglani, visiriato*, and *sangiacco/sangiaccato*) in English, French, German, and Greek works on the Ottomans.[76] As Peter Burke notes, seventeenth-century English writings about the Ottomans often resorted to Italianate forms of Ottoman nomenclature. "[T]erms such as bascia, dispotto, giannizari, seraglio, gran signor suggest that the Turkish terms reached English via Italian."[77] Not simply via Italian, we might add, but via the institution of the (predominantly Venetianized) dragomanate.

Indeed, the articulation of "Turkish literature" as a field of knowledge can only be understood as simultaneously intensely local (lodged in the specific diplomatic milieu of Istanbul) and trans-imperial (addressing a readership across multiple jurisdictional and ethnolinguistic boundaries). This field, however, was shaped not only by dragomans' evident preference for specific metalinguistic and historiographical genres and authors previously canonized by Ottoman courtly literati but also by dragomans' own strong taxonomic impulse, articulated through their evolving textual practices. Chancery-trained dragomans were particularly attuned to the need to classify, compare, and commensurate Ottoman bureaucratic practices with those of European chanceries. As professional mediators, dragomans were wont to emphasize difference and, moreover, to conceive of it as a binary opposition between two clearly demarcated sides. After all, they made their livelihood by pointing out equivalences and differences, by essentializing and objectifying cultures, languages, and practices as belonging squarely on one side or another, thus justifying their professional labor or mediation and interpretation. In this sense, their role in the articulation of Occidentalism, as well as Orientalism, warrants further consideration. At the same time, dragomans' everyday activities engaged them repeatedly in high-stakes interactions, which required them to "relate" back to imperial employers the substance of interactions elsewhere, thus undermining any simple sense of radical alterity and incommensurability. These oral practices, still not fully charted out, played a pivotal role in defining dragomans' modalities of knowledge production. Analyzing dragomans' translation practices thus requires attending to their multiple publics and interactional genres, both oral and written. It also calls for considering how such practices corresponded to contemporary Ottoman textualities.[78] These dimensions of the dragoman's craft underscore the dialogic nature of mediation, and the specific ways in which dragomans perceived their "syntheses."

In conclusion, the translation and authorial practices analyzed in this chapter—explanatory prefaces, glossing and elaboration, calquing and "foreignisms," ellipsis, reordering of materials, framing devices such as voicing and footing, and modes of referring to sources or their erasure—call into question basic assumptions of the field of Translation Studies. If both Venuti and his critics take the aesthetics of literary translation as their prototype for what translation "is," this chapter has considered myriad other genres—from sultanic decrees and political commentary to historiography. This has also revealed the limitations of the concepts of "foreignization" and "domestication" in a political context in which—far from Venuti's model of *translatio imperii* from weak to powerful language-cum-culture-cum-society—the power relationship between "source" and "target" is yet to be settled.

These numerous instabilities underscore the enduring analytical value of the notion of a "dialogic emergence of culture" as postulated by the linguistic anthropologists Dennis Tedlock and Bruce Mannheim over two decades ago.[79] It is by attending to dragomans' specific and evolving translation practices that we see most clearly their active participation in constituting the boundaries of "Ottoman" and "Italian," in opening up and foreclosing possibilities of commensuration and articulations of cultural specificity and irreducibility. Such possibilities, and the role that dragomans arrogated to themselves (or sometimes shunned) in realizing them, were inherently embroiled in dense ideological struggles, intensely local and personal but also, simultaneously, trans-imperial and consequential. They cannot be separated from contemporary debates about the Ottomans' place in an emergent European system of states, about civilizational decline, and, ultimately, about periodization.

In his preface to the *Cronologia historica*, Carli expressed the hope that his translation of Katip Çelebi's work would "disabuse" the public "from the reprehensive opinion that not a seed of erudition remains among these barbarians."[80] He was echoing the words of his patron, the former bailo Giambattista Donà, who had expressed a similar hope a decade earlier. Dragomans' translations, in other words, participated not only in the constitution of a corpus of Ottoman literature in Italian, but in defining the ideological contours of the synecdochal relations between "literature" and "culture." Indeed, Donà's efforts to introduce an Italianate reading public to the riches of Ottoman literature and scholarship were certainly part of a broader field of translation activity, in which dragomans—both Venetian and other—played an outsize role.

CHAPTER 7

Circulating "Turkish Literature"

Of a great number of observers [who had traveled to the Ottoman Empire] it must be said that they brought away from their
experience only what they had previously sought to find.

—Myron P. Gilmore[1]

The invisible translator is . . . the purest expression of our
resentment for translators—the one whose services are
begrudged because they are so necessary, because they remind
us of the fact that our understanding is borrowed from others.

—Elliott Colla[2]

IN THE FIRST ARTICLE to be published in the flagship journal of the
Royal Prussian Society of Sciences, the *Miscellanea Berolinensia*,
in 1710, the society's president, Gottfried Wilhelm Leibniz, set out to
show how the ancient origins of peoples could be deduced from their current linguistic habits.[3] A few years earlier, in preparation for his study,
"Brevis designatio meditationum de originibus gentium ductis potissimum
ex indicio linguarum" (Brief account of thoughts on the origins of peoples, based principally on evidence from their languages), the distinguished
philosopher corresponded with the Viennese dragoman Giovanni Battista
Podestà (1625–1703). Through numerous inquiries about several regions,
from the Black Sea to Siberia, Leibniz hoped to shed light on the origins of
various ethnolinguistic groups of antiquity based on present-day linguistic
phenomena. For example, he asks why in Transylvania there survive words
that "without being Hungarian or Slavic" are unknown to "other Germans,"
whether in "Tatary-Crimea" one can still find "Germans" or "Goths who
speak German," which people near or under Muscovite rule speak non-
Slavic languages, and what languages are spoken by the people of Siberia.

Podestà obliged his distinguished correspondent, but his responses mostly dampened the philosopher's enthusiasm for (highly speculative) inferences about antiquity. Time and again, the dragoman's answers suggested that the languages spoken by contemporary people in border regions were mixtures of imperial languages. The Tatars of the Volga, he informed Leibniz, spoke a mixture of Tatar and Russian. The ones further east spoke a mixture of Turkish and Chagatai. In Trebizond, they spoke a mix of Turkish and Georgian.[4]

What is especially intriguing about the exchange, however, is not Podestà's argument but his evidence. He repeatedly referred Leibniz to a single source, the works of the Ottoman historian Mustafa Cenābī (d. 1590), hardly a household name in eighteenth-century Europe. As Vefa Erginbaş recently noted, despite Cenābī's profound impact as the author of "one of the most influential universal histories ever written under the Ottomans," this late-sixteenth-century *medrese* professor remains "one of the least known and least studied Ottoman historians."[5] Cenābī began composing his two volume, 900-folio Arabic-language universal history around 1564 and took well over a decade to complete it. His choice of Arabic (a language not widely used by Ottoman historians) was puzzling enough to prompt the sultan to ask him to translate it into Turkish, which Cenābī did, in an abbreviated form (along with an Arabic abridgement). Highly innovative in its comprehensive coverage and source-critical methods, Cenābī's work evidently circulated among contemporary Ottoman connoisseurs, as attested by the dozen and a half surviving copies in Istanbul alone.[6]

In contrast with its relative popularity among Ottoman scholarly elites, however, the only excerpt from this work available at the turn of the eighteenth century in Latin (or in any language other than Arabic or Turkish, for that matter) was *De Gestis Timurlenkii sive Tamerlanis*, a modest quarto publication of 100 unnumbered pages. It was translated by none other than Podestà himself.[7] The translation was printed in 1680 by the Vienna University Printer, Leopold Voigt, with whom Podestà had previously collaborated on several other works. Some of these used Arabic type that Podestà had especially commissioned after his appointment as professor of Oriental languages in the Habsburg capital.[8] Other works, like the ambitious *Ottoman Annals*, which Podestà published in near-concurrent German, Latin, and Italian editions in 1671–1672, had virtually no Arabic type, except for a single word in the Italian edition (printed by Voigt). More than adding substantively to the text's comprehensibility, the typeface seems to have served primarily to flaunt the translator's bona fides and the printer's technological prowess.[9]

Podestà clearly hoped that his translation of the *Ottoman Annals*—although they essentially reduplicated the efforts of Johannes Gaudier more than a century earlier—would reach European-wide circulation and enjoy substantial market appeal.[10] He explained that his own translation was based on "another Turkish exemplar, which contains more relations, and which differs in some narrations" from Gaudier's. He also insisted that "the substance of the original does not permit extraordinary eloquence," further underscoring his own fidelity to the source text (and hence philological acumen). Podestà's hopes for commercial success are evinced in his undertaking to print near-simultaneous editions in three different languages and in describing the work as "part one"—a second anticipated volume, "A life of Süleyman, written by his secretary," never materialized. They are reflected in Podestà's exhortation to the readers on the book's last page: "Let us apply ourselves with humility, and add greater perfection to our talents, so that with great utility to the Homeland, we will raise these letters, born anew in Europe."[11]

A similar civilizational perspective that calls explicit attention to the translator's act of mediation is evident in the *De Gestis Timurlenkii*. Its title page proclaims it to be a "Turkish-Arabic-Persian opuscule . . . extracted from a Turkish-Arabic-Persian manuscript codex that was unknown to many European historians," and which was found in the Imperial Library of Vienna, now brought into Latin ("Latinè redditum"). The repetition of the original work's mixed linguistic provenance in a decidedly Islamic setting, and its precise material condition (i.e., a short manuscript, excerpted from a longer codex, both extant in the Imperial Library) are significant in announcing the original's multiple alterity. These are juxtaposed with the Latinate print product that Podestà advertised as addressing a decidedly European scholarly public. He was, in other words, self-consciously and explicitly positioning himself as an intermediary not only linguistically, but civilizationally and technologically as well.[12] These three elements, as this chapter will discuss, often went hand in hand in dragomans' mediation of Ottomancentric knowledge to European readerships.

In his Letter to the Reader, Podestà further explains that the codex was brought to the Imperial Library by Sebastian Tengnagel (1573–1636), the late Habsburg court librarian, who was an avid collector of Oriental manuscripts commissioned from dragomans and diplomats in Istanbul.[13]

Indeed, the Viennese manuscript contains not only numerous annotations in Tengnagel's handwriting but other clues as to its provenance. Its appendix contains a copy of a letter that Omar, Sultan Osman II's preceptor, sent to the governor of Hungary concerning Bethlen Gábor, the Transylvanian prince who was an Ottoman ally against the Habsburgs. The letter must have been written sometime during Osman's short and ill-fated reign from 1618 to 1622. Cenābī's manuscript, in other words, was likely procured for Tengnagel shortly after it had been created, and was possibly copied especially for him.[14]

Contrary to Podestà's ambitions, his translation of Cenābī seems to have enjoyed only limited circulation, almost entirely within Habsburg territories, as can be gleaned from the current location of the dozen surviving copies.[15] Yet, as the example of his interactions with Leibniz suggests, Podestà's significance cannot be fully measured by the limited readership his publications garnered. Whereas print played a decisive role in consolidating Podestà's reputation as a scholar, it remained codependent on courtly sociability and on the power of epistolary, manuscript communication. It was overwhelmingly through epistolary circulation that Podestà and other dragoman-scholars partook in the Republic of Letters, mediating its engagement with Ottoman peers. Ultimately, Podestà's own position of authority within an Enlightenment scholarly milieu had to do less with his printing prowess, let alone linguistic competence per se, and more with his ability to channel authoritatively metropolitan Ottoman perspectives on the Ottoman periphery (both temporal and spatial) to a highly networked readership among key denizens of the Republic of Letters.

The resonances of Podestà's oeuvre across a dispersed field of knowledge remind us of the importance of Orientalism's multiple infrastructures. These included not only—or even primarily—print but also established regimes of circulation, the "cultivated habits of animating artifactually mediated texts, enabling the movement of discourse along predictable social trajectories," as the anthropologist Francis Cody defines them.[16] The institutionalization of diplomatic channels of communication and their attendant genres and material qualities, the mechanisms that enabled scholars to sojourn at length in Istanbul's embassy compounds and to interact with Ottoman elites (often via dragomans), as well as dragomans' own mobilities between various metropoles while engaging in secretarial and bibliographic work in princely service, all illustrate the unique, and increasingly codified, regime of circulation of an emergent seventeenth-century

Ottomanist field of knowledge. This chapter attends to dragomans' myriad contributions to that field's articulation. It traces the broad contours of the trans-imperial regime of circulation that bound the early Republic of Letters to Istanbul's courtly milieu. It then outlines the arc of development of a corpus of dragomans' writings about the Ottomans—whether as authors, translators, or "invisible technicians," and considers how dragomans' uniquely itinerant biographies, epistemologies, and translation practices helped shape a distinct field of knowledge with its own methodologies and institutional contexts of production.

The Libraries of "Turkish Literature" and Istanbulite Diplomacy

The preface to the Jesuit abbot and scholar Giambattista Toderini's *Letteratura turchesca* (1787), a three-volume work that radically challenged European ideas about Ottoman scientific and literary stagnation, presents the book as the product of the author's sojourn in the Ottoman capital from 1781 to 1786. Toderini had stayed in the house of the Venetian bailo Agostino Garzoni and his wife, Pisana Quirini Stampalia, serving as theologian and tutor for their son.[17] Istanbul's diplomatic milieu in general, and dragomans' decisive role in mediating Toderini's contacts among the Ottoman intellectual elite in particular, proved essential for the abbot's research.[18] The complex trans-imperial perspective on the world of Ottoman letters engendered by the setting of Toderini's Istanbulite sojourn is borne out throughout his remarkable book. It is evinced already on the frontispiece (figure 7.1). Amid various scientific and musical instruments, sheet music, and nautical charts, which the author claims to have seen in Istanbul, he prominently placed the *tuğra* (seal) of the reigning Sultan Abdülhamid I "as he has restored the Ottoman press."[19] Toderini here reflects not only an Enlightenment perspective on print as a transformative cultural tool but a distinctly metropolitan Ottoman view of Ibrahim Müteferrika's Istanbulite printing press as an imperial undertaking.[20]

Perhaps above all else, Toderini's trans-imperial perspective is evident in his collaboration with the dragoman Giambattista Calavrò-Imberti, whom the author describes as "Venetian dragoman, competent in Turkish, and versed in Latin and Italian belles-lettres." Among other things, Toderini tasked Calavrò-Imberti with translating a lengthy 1784 sultanic decree for the renewal of the Ottoman imperial printing press, which laid out the significance of print for Ottoman society (and which abundantly demonstrated the Ottoman circulation of Enlightenment tropes about knowledge and reason).[21] The translation is reproduced at the end of the book. By concluding his monument to Ottoman literature with a sultanic decree that aims to ensure the further circulation, activation, and elaboration of that very corpus, Toderini positions his work not as an exterior lens on an Ottoman world of learning but rather as its refraction, partaking in a shared "enlightened" moment (his criticism of French Enlightenment ideals notwithstanding).

Toderini's reliance on dragomans, however, was not limited to facilitating collaborations with contemporaries in Istanbul. Among others, he quotes passages from the work of the Venetian dragoman Giovanni Medun (fl. ca. 1726–34), who translated the Anatolian scholar and judge Kınalızade Ali Çelebi's *Akhlak-ı Ala'i* (1565) and gave it the title *Alti costumi o sia sapienza pratica, etica, economica, politica del turco Mehemed Effendi Chinalixadè di Dimasco* (Old customs, or rather practical, ethical, economic, and political wisdom of the Turk Mehmed Efendi Kınalızade of Damascus). By the time of Medun's translation in the 1720s or 1730s Kınalızade's work had become "the classic statement of Ottoman social and political morality," a fact that likely motivated the dragoman to undertake its translation.[22] Even though it was never printed, Toderini mentions having read Medun's translation in the personal library of the Venetian senator Benetto Molino—underscoring the role of elite sociability in the trans-imperial circulation of early modern manuscripts.[23]

As we saw in previous chapters, exactly a century before Toderini's *Letteratura Turchesca*, in 1688 two books were published in Venice under the aegis of Giovanni Battista Donà, a former bailo in Istanbul: *Della letteratura de' Turchi* (On the Literature of the Turks) and *Raccolta curiosissima d'adaggi turcheschi* (A Most Curious Collection of Turkish Adages). *Della letteratura* radically challenged contemporary European understandings of Ottoman culture (or lack thereof). The notion of "literature" in this period encompassed all learning and science, and the book surveyed Ottoman studies in the fields of grammar, poetry, logic, mathematics, geometry, optics, music, medicine, herbal alchemy, chemistry, history, politics, geography, and devotion, interspersed with translations prepared by the Venetian dragoman Gian Rinaldo Carli. The book concluded with an exhortation for additional translations of books from Turkish, Persian, and Arabic. Leibniz, passing through Venice in 1690, remarked that *Della letteratura* was the only "new" title he had discovered there.[24]

Donà's and Toderini's "libraries," published a century apart, bookend a dramatic period of growth for a trans-imperial Ottomanist field of knowledge. Like their better-known and hugely successful double, Barthélemy d'Herbelot's posthumous *Bibliothèque orientale* (1697), they catered to a reading public fascinated by the world of Ottoman letters. They offered a first "space of encounter" with Ottoman letters for Enlightenment scholars and readers largely unable to access Ottoman-language texts directly. Such a florilegium, extracting and anthologizing Ottoman (as well as Arabic and Persian) texts, became a leading Ottoman language training technique in both Paris and Vienna, the two foremost European centers for the study of Ottoman letters in the eighteenth century. And, even more than d'Herbelot, both Venetian author-compilers relied extensively on dragomans in mediating Ottoman texts, canonical tastes, and elite perspectives to their diverse readers far from Istanbul: whereas d'Herbelot translated his own texts, Donà's works were, quite explicitly, premised on a compilation and translation project undertaken by a group of dragomans and apprentice dragomans who had worked under Donà in the Venetian bailate in Istanbul during his short tenure there in 1681–1683.[25] Likewise, the extent to which Toderini's much more commercially successful work depended on dragomans' labor and expertise cannot be overstated. By his own admission, Toderini did not speak Turkish.[26]

Toderini's linguistic deficiency should come as little surprise. Throughout the early modern period, embassy employees, especially dragomans and secretaries, proved to be pivotal "invisible technicians" who vitally assisted more illustrious metropolitan sojourners to produce knowledge about the Ottomans and to circulate it to a wider reading public.[27] Istanbul's embassies regularly hosted scholars and artists in residence for extended periods. Such sojourns—which frequently involved traveling in the entourage of the ambassador to various other parts of the Ottoman Empire—facilitated contacts with Ottoman interlocutors, and enabled visitors—some with only minimal prior familiarity with Ottoman language, society, or history—to lay claim to firsthand knowledge of things Ottoman.

Thus, despite authors' frequent assertions of firsthand witnessing, their knowledge was profoundly mediated by the perspectives of embassy dragomans and other local intermediaries. During his extended sojourn in the Ottoman capital, the Roman traveler extraordinaire Pietro della Valle (1586–1652) engaged a group of dragomans in his quest for local knowledge. Among other works, he acquired a miniature album produced by

Ottoman artists, and a copy of a manuscript work on Ottoman government penned by Domenico Timoni (1590–1648), an Istanbul-born dragoman in English service, which he intended to send to Rome.[28]

Like Della Valle before him and Toderini after, the Bolognese count Luigi Ferdinando Marsigli (1658–1730) spent two years in Istanbul (in 1679–1680) as the guest of the Venetian bailo Pietro Civran. Similar to his Roman precursor and other scholarly minded sojourners, Marsigli arrived in the Ottoman capital with no prior knowledge of Turkish, necessitating the extensive services of local dragomans. Upon his arrival, young Marsigli hired a Jewish interpreter, Abraham Gabai, to teach him the Ottoman language, though his success in this endeavor may have been rather modest.[29] He soon became acquainted with numerous courtly scribes and scholars, and began to collect copies of documents and maps. Here is how Marsigli's modern biographer describes the patrician scholar's time in Istanbul:

> Accompanied by his Jewish interpreters or the dragomans of the Venetian embassy, willing if not apt to learn Turkish himself, infectiously eager, young Marsigli managed to become friendly with a handful of well-informed men who moved fairly close to the ruling circles of the Ottoman court. They were doctors, astronomers, geographers, historians. Some were, or accounted themselves, universal experts. Muneğğim-basi, astrologer and herbalist, gave Marsigli the horoscopes of Sultan Mehmed IV and his son Mustafa, and discussed with him the question of calculating Istanbul's latitude; the two differed in their estimates. Hezarfenn, an encyclopaedic author to whom he pays affectionate tribute, generously showed him his own "compendium" of official texts listing the forces of the Ottoman army and navy, with figures for the revenues supporting them. Marsigli was able to have this copied or at least summarized in Italian translation. Another piece by Hezarfenn, who had traveled to Mecca and the Yemen as a young man, discoursed on the coffee plant, coffee-making and the medical virtues of coffee. This too was transcribed for Marsigli.[30]

These interactions were no doubt impactful on the young gentleman-scholar, but their mediated nature cannot be emphasized enough. Indeed, the imprint of the Venetian bailate is evident throughout Marsigli's copious notes from Istanbul. To give just one, rather banal, example: an Italian translation of a pedigree of a pure-bred horse, authenticated by the *kadı* of Galata, is enclosed with a translation of the horse's bill of sale of August 16, 1680, in one of Marsigli's notebooks. Marsigli had purchased the horse, Mendup, from Ahmet Çelebi, a *kiaya* (lieutenant) of Kaplan Paşa, the Ottoman lord admiral. Both the pedigree and the bill of sale were translated into Italian in Giacomo Tarsia's handwriting. Tarsia, it turns out, was himself Marsigli's agent for the sale, while the witness to the transaction was the bailate janissary, Essuf. Tarsia, however, was not merely an agent—his translation bears multiple signs of his self-conscious role in providing Italian glosses and cognates for Ottoman nomenclature, as evinced in the very title he provides for the translation, "Geneologìa del Cavallo Mendup riconosciuta p[er] autentica dal Giud[ic]e di Galata, che hà formato la Scritt[ur]a di Compra d'esso, come Da Turchi si costuma" (Genealogy of the Horse Mendup, recognized as authentic by the Judge of Galata, who made the bill of sale of the above, as is customary among the Turks).[31]

Marsigli's perspective on the Ottoman world was shaped by dragomans' mediation in more profound ways as well. His copious notebooks include, inter alia, a list of epithets that the Venetians used for addressing Ottoman government officials, the equivalent list used by the French, and the one used by the Ottoman divan for the French king—internal chancery documents par excellence that would not have circulated widely beyond dragomans and secretaries.[32] Also among Marsigli's notebooks is a letter from the Habsburg dragoman Meninski, by then already in Vienna, in response to his query about the role of military judges in the adminstration of the Ottoman Empire's Asian provinces.[33] Marsigli further possessed a dragoman's (presumably Tarsia's) Italian translation of an Ottoman catechism.[34] A second miscellany in Marsigli's estate contains military notices, imperial edicts, detailed descriptions of various offices and officials of the Ottoman court, observations on Ottoman diplomatic protocol, revenue lists, tables of provincial and district governorships with their revenues and households, and assorted documents related to Muslim, Orthodox, and Armenian religious beliefs and practices.[35] The bulk of these materials, in other words, would have originated in diplomatic chanceries, would have been intended for highly restricted circulation, and would have required the active help of dragomans to procure and interpret.

These diverse examples from the archives of just one sojourner nicely capture the key role played by dragomans and other diplomatic personnel in the multidirectional production and circulation of scholarly knowledge in early modern Istanbul. Whether by developing conventions for diplomatic translation or as informants and interlocutors to ambassadors and sojourners alike, dragomans facilitated the work of embassies as centers of cultural production. As amanuenses, guides, and interpreters for European embassy guests, dragomans were central, though rarely acknowledged, nodes in communicative circuits that linked visitors with a manifold Ottoman courtly and intellectual milieu. Orally or in writing, dragomans' mediation thus profoundly shaped how Ottomanist knowledge was produced, and how it circulated.

Forming a Canon: Translating and Printing

In addition to hosting assorted visitors, early modern Istanbul's diplomatic households were often the sites of intense cultural production. If sojourning scholars became an increasingly familiar staple of Istanbul's embassies, the diplomatic corps itself cultivated various scholarly pursuits, at times of the highest level. Ambassadors were not infrequently aspiring scholars themselves. The most famous and influential example is the Habsburg ambassador Ogier Ghislain de Busbecq, whose *Turkish Letters* (1555–1562) had a profound impact on generations of readers.[36] A century later, another scholarly ambassador, the German Levinus Warner (1619–1665), who served as Dutch Resident in Istanbul from 1655, played a crucial role in the two simultaneous initiatives to translate the Bible into Turkish.[37]

In addition to ambassadors, other embassy staff also generated enduring representations of Ottoman lifeworlds for European consumption. A most instructive example of such a diplomat-scholar was Paul Rycaut, who first arrived in the Ottoman capital in January 1661 as English chancellor of the Levant Company's factory, and until 1665 served as the private secretary of Embassy. In these roles he traveled to the North African Regencies, Aleppo, and the Balkans. He was then appointed English consul in Izmir, where he remained from 1667 until 1678. The four publications that resulted from his seventeen-year Ottoman sojourn, *The Present State of the Ottoman Empire* (1666), *The History of the Three Late Famous Impostors* (1669), *The Present State of the Greek and Armenian Churches* (1679), and *The History of the Turkish Empire* (1680) all enjoyed enduring popularity and were among the most influential texts about Ottoman society, religion, and history to be published in the seventeenth century.[38] All four books relied heavily on Rycaut's multilingual prowess and contacts among Ottoman scholars, merchants, and government officials.

Other contemporary European works on Ottoman-Christian religious life often featured the fine points of doctrinal disputation. Rycaut's books, by contrast, have a strong ethnographic flavor. They are, moreover, based on direct observation and extensive conversations with a wide cast of characters. These included several personal friends at the Ottoman court, among them the former governor of Cairo and Diyarbakır Şeytan Ibrahim Paşa, the court physician Giovanni Mascellini (who in the 1650s was concurrently on the bailate payroll, treating various dragomans and employees), the dragoman Ali Ufki Bey, and the Habsburg (and, unofficially, Ottoman) dragoman Marcantonio Mamuca della Torre, Rycaut's correspondent for over twenty years. Rycaut's books also incorporated extensive paraphrases—at times bordering on verbatim quotations—from English diplomatic dispatches and other official embassy records.[39] Perhaps because of these methods, Rycaut's account of Greek and Armenian religiosity was notably more empathetic than most contemporaries'.

The enduring impact of Rycaut's textual elaboration of Ottoman lifeworlds on the Enlightenment is comparable to that of the visual repertoire developed half a century later by Jean-Baptiste Vanmour, whose audience scene in the divan ca. 1710 is analyzed in the Introduction (figure 0.1). Vanmour lived and worked in the French embassy in Istanbul from 1699 to his death in 1737 as *peintre ordinaire du Roi en Levant*, officially tasked to produce painted scenes for festivities at the embassy. Beyond his official title, Vanmour's immense popularity in Ahmed III's court and his "considerable contact with local artists during his thirty-year residence in Istanbul" underscore the diplomatic milieu's significance in articulating an enduring visual repertoire (partly based on "Ottoman pictorial tropes") for representing the Ottomans to European publics.[40]

Vanmour's lengthy sojourn followed in the footsteps of several embassy artists, whose visual representations of Ottoman courtly ceremony and urban life was in great demand in Europe.[41] Among the earliest and most enduring European representations of the Ottomans were the sultanic portraits produced by Gentile Bellini (1429–1507) during his 1479 diplomatic sojourn in Istanbul, which was occasioned by Mehmed II's explicit request to Venice. These portraits, which reflect a deep engagement with Ottoman genres, motifs, and sultanic representational strategies, became part of a visual repertory studied and appropriated by Ottoman artists, whose work itself was the subject of later copying by artists employed by the influential Paolo Giovio. The Istanbul sojourns of Pieter Coecke van Aelst (1533–1534), Nicholas de Nicolay (1551–1552), Melchior Lorck (1555–1559), the three Austrian artists in the entourage of the Habsburg ambassador Hans Ludwig von Kuefstein (1628–1630), George de la Chappelle of Caen (1643), the artist commissioned by the Swedish ambassador Claes Rålamb (1657–1658), and the group of artists in the French ambassador Marquis de Nointel's "picture factory" in the 1670s were all employed as part of official diplomatic missions. De Nicolay's images of Ottoman costumes were repeatedly copied and reprinted in later costume albums (including Francesco Sansovino's hugely popular publications in the 1560s and 1570s), and had a long-lasting impact on early modern taxonomies of Ottoman difference.[42] This repertoire, which emphasized (not to say belabored) Ottoman ritualism, extravagance, and the meticulous sartorial codification of social status, was clearly based on a diplomatic perspective shaped primarily by participation in state-sanctioned ceremonial.

Some dragomans, too, followed a scholarly path in Europe before their Ottoman sojourns. An elite educational background no doubt facilitated their eventually becoming published authors and authorities on things Ottoman. Jacobus Golius (1596–1667) studied with Erpenius at the University of Leiden, before serving as dragoman for the Dutch embassy to Morocco from 1622 to 1624, and from 1625 to 1628 sojourned in Syria and Istanbul before returning to his post as professor of Arabic at Leiden and publishing some of the most influential editions of Arabic texts and Latin-Arabic metalinguistic texts of the era.[43] William Seaman (1606/7–1680) spent several years as an employee of the English embassy in Istanbul in the late 1620s, where he learned Turkish, before returning to London and publishing a partial translation of Hoca Sadeddin Efendi's *Crown of Stories* as *The reign of Sultan Orchan, second king of the Turks* in 1652. In the following century, the Venetian Pietro Busenello (1705–1765) spent four years as an apprentice dragoman in the bailate, resulting in a massive study of Ottoman society and polity, which he dedicated to Doge Pietro Grimani.[44] These examples recall dragomans' marked contributions to the methodical linguistic study of Ottoman Turkish and to conventionalizing key translation and commensuration practices across Ottoman and Italianate reading publics and beyond, as discussed in the previous two chapters. It is now time to consider more systematically dragomans' further contributions to the constitution of "Turkish Literature" through their translations of Ottoman works in other genres.

As Chapter 6 suggested, most Venetian dragomans' translations remained in manuscript. For several reasons, including differential trans-imperial itineraries and greater access to publishing infrastructures, their
Habsburg and French counterparts were significantly more successful in
their publication efforts. The Ragusan dragoman Vicko (Vicenzo, Vicente)
Bratutti, who served in Ferdinand III's court in Vienna and later in King
Philip IV's court in Madrid, was able to publish his Italian translation
of Hoca Sadeddin Efendi's (1536–1599) *Tacü't-tevarih* (Crown of Stories)
under the title *Chronica dell'origine, e progressi della Casa Ottomana.*
Bratutti had the first part of his work printed in Vienna in 1649, the second part in Madrid in 1652.[45] The frontispiece of the first volume, quite
tellingly, featured the translator's own bust portrait (figure 7.2) by the
Augsburg engraver Elias Wideman, who specialized in portraits of the
Habsburg political and literary elite.[46] Bratutti's choice of frontispiece,
with its Latin inscription and clear reference to an enduring humanist
genre, was hardly accidental. He was to reproduce the same self-referential portrait five years later in the first volume of his *Espejo político y
moral*, published in Madrid.[47] This suggests how in his myriad publishing endeavors Bratutti meant, first and foremost, to (re)establish his own
stature in new courtly milieus.[48] That Sadeddin was Prince Murad III's
preceptor and a major figure at court—and eventually a *şehülislam* under
Murad's successor Mehmed III—surely played a role in Bratutti's decision
to translate his oeuvre. As Alessio Bombaci points out, despite its many
deficiencies, Bratutti's translation—along with Podestà's Latin translation
of the *Crown of Stories* in 1671, enshrined Sadeddin's triumphalist account
of dynastic conquests as the canonical version of early Ottoman history to
circulate in Europe for years to come.[49] Beyond Sadeddin, Bratutti also
translated Ottoman and Arabic texts into Castilian, including Celālzāde
Mustafa's chronicle, which was published in Madrid in 1678 as *Anales de
Egipto.*[50] An Ottoman version of *Kalilah wa Dimnah*, or the Fables of Bidpai' (the Panchatantra, itself the product of complex Arabic-Persian-San-
skrit cross-cultural interactions), became in his hands *Espejo político y
moral para príncipes, y ministros, y todo género de personas*, the first two
volumes of which were published in Madrid in 1654 and 1658, and again,
posthumously, in 1694.[51] Bratutti's translations later served as the basis for
other European versions as well.[52]

The publication record of Habsburg dragomans is especially remarkable when we include in this category the extensive list of works by the

two Vienna-based dragomans and archrivals, Meninski and Podestà, discussed above. Habsburg dragomans' publication success was overshadowed in the following century by that of French dragomans, in part no doubt thanks to their close association with several Parisian elite institutions, including the Royal Library, the Collège Royal, and the Collège Louis-le-Grand, and their respective scholarly infrastructures. Before Antoine Galland (1646–1715) became the fabled translator-compiler of the international best-selling *Les mille et une nuits*, he served as secretary to French ambassador to the Porte, Charles-Marie-François Olier, Marquis de Nointel (1635–1685), himself an aspiring Orientalist. Galland's first five-year sojourn in the Ottoman capital, for which he left a detailed journal, began in 1670, and was followed by two other extended visits to the empire, in 1677 and in 1679–1688. During these stays Galland used his growing expertise and contacts in the Ottoman capital to acquire Ottoman, Arabic, and Persian manuscripts, which became an important foundation both for his future publications and for French Orientalism more broadly.

Galland was arguably the most influential dragoman to become a published author, but he was by no means the only one. Shuttling between Istanbul and Paris, François Pétis de la Croix (1653–1713), who served as dragoman under Louis XIV, published several of his dragoman father's translations from Ottoman, including the *Histoire du grand Genghiz Khan* (1710). He also contributed a Turkish poem to preface Jean Thévenot's *Voyages en Orient* (1664) and edited the French translation-adaptation-concoction of *Les mille et un jours* (1710–1712), a sequel of sorts to Galland's popular *Les mille et une nuits*.[53] The sequel "was presented as a translation of a Persian original, but later turned out to be a collection of Turkish tales translated by apprentice dragomans in Istanbul, preserved in the Royal Library and rather haphazardly put together and edited by the compiler of the work."[54] The list of Pétis de la Croix's unpublished manuscript works in French, Turkish, and Persian is even longer.[55]

The celebrity status that both Galland and Pétis de la Croix eventually enjoyed had to do not only with their own work but also with its continuation posthumously by their intellectual and institutional heirs. Galland's French translation of Ali Çelebi was published only after his death and was continued by the dragoman turned royal interpreter turned chair of Turkish at the Collège Royal, Denis Dominique Cardonne (1720–1783).[56] Galland's and de la Croix's translation efforts inspired similar projects in the coming decades, spearheaded by the antiquarian Comte Anne Claude de Caylus (1692–1765) and by Cardonne, whose anthologies of "Oriental tales" similarly drew on translations by French apprentice dragomans kept in the Royal Library.[57] Although many other dragomans' and apprentice dragomans' translations remained in manuscript, they too were sometimes used by later authors of "Oriental tales" as sources for their various adaptations.[58]

Dragomans' lasting contributions to eighteenth-century Orientalism went beyond popularizing the "Oriental tale" (itself a deceptively "popular" genre heavily mediated by contemporary genres and literary tastes—both Ottoman and European—and often translated by apprentice dragomans). I return to this instantiation of what Srinivas Aravamudan helpfully dubs "corporate" Orientalism at the end of the chapter.[59] Additionally, and as influentially, dragomans translated historical and other nonfiction genres. Several dragomans' translations were printed promptly by the first Ottoman Turkish press of the polymath (and former court dragoman) Ibrahim Müteferrika, starting in 1729.[60] Other dragomans' works received even greater circulation in French print. Antoine Galland's nephew, Julien, who himself had apprenticed as a dragoman in Istanbul and later served as French dragoman in Sidon, published an account of the rituals and ceremonies of the pilgrimage to Mecca, which was translated into German in 1757.[61] He also translated the Ottoman ambassador Yirmisekiz Mehmed Çelebi's account of his embassy to Paris in 1721, *Sefaretname*, which was published in both Istanbul and Paris in 1757.[62] The French dragoman Charles Fonton (1725–1793), the son of the French first dragoman Pierre Fonton and Pera-born Lucrezia Navon (the Venetian dragoman Giovanni Battista Navon's daughter), published in 1751 a treatise on Ottoman classical music, which became the foundation for an entire subdiscipline. It was deeply informed by previous studies of Ottoman courtly music by members of the court themselves. These include Ali Ufki Bey (the Pole Wojciech Bobowski, 1610–1675), who composed his *Mecmua-ı saz ü söz* (Collection of Instrumental and Vocal Works) ca. 1650, and the Moldavian prince turned Ottoman courtier and scholar Dimitrie Cantemir (1673–1723), who completed his *Kitab-ı 'ilmü'l-müsiki ala vechi'l hurufat* (Book of the Science of Music According to the Alphabetic Notation) in Istanbul between 1700 and 1703.[63] At the same time, as David Irving points out, while Fonton "identified Plato as a common element between European and Ottoman musics . . . he disputed the extent of the Ottoman claim for a direct musical lineage from the Greek philosopher. Evidently he wished to preserve ancient Greek heritage for Europe, in defiance of Ottoman hegemony over Hellenic regions."[64] In true Enlightenment fashion, then, Fonton placed his organographic evidence into the epistemological straitjacket of absolute civilizational divides. In an interesting departure from earlier dragomans' emphasis on commensurability and a common classical filiation, for Fonton the Ottomans became more decisively a civilizational other.

Venetian, French, and Habsburg dragomans were by no means the only ones to participate in an expanding Republic of Letters. Willem Theijls, grand dragoman in the Dutch embassy in Istanbul (and the son of Janszoon Theijls, the Dutch consul in Egypt and of Clara Piron, the daughter of an Istanbulite dragoman dynasty), published in Leiden in 1721 a massive memoir-chronicle concerning recent Ottoman-Venetian-Habsburg military and political negotiations, based on diplomatic sources, which he dedicated to the king of Sweden, Charles XII.[65] Ignatius Mouradgea d'Ohsson (1740–1807), a long-time dragoman of the Swedish legation to the Porte (and the son of an Armenian dragoman for the Swedish consulate in Izmir and a French diplomat's daughter) became a celebrity in the literary circles of Paris, where, beginning in 1787, he published his taxonomical "natural history" of the Ottoman Empire, *Tableau général de l'empire othoman* in three deluxe folio volumes. The work went through another, more modest edition for bourgeois subscribers and was partially translated into English, German, Russian, Swedish, and Polish as well. Notably, upon his return to Istanbul in 1792, Mouradgea presented a copy of the deluxe edition to Sultan Selim III, who rewarded him handsomely for it.[66] Another dragoman employed by the Swedish legation, Antoine de Murat (1739–1813), penned an important treatise on Ottoman music.[67] Franz von Dombay (1758–1810), a decade-long Austrian dragoman in Bosnia, was the author, inter alia, of a history of Morocco and a study of North African dialectology.[68] Another Austrian, Joseph von Hammer-Purgstall (1774–1856), perhaps the most famous and influential Orientalist of his generation, spent eight years in Istanbul and Cairo as an apprentice dragoman (1799–1807). While derided by several contemporary specialists, his ten-volume *Geschichte des osmanischen Reiches*, published in 1827–1835, provides indispensable source material for scholars in the field to this day, and has been translated into half a dozen languages.[69]

The Dialogic Emergence of "Turkish Literature"

Dragomans' significant contributions to the emergence of European Ottoman studies were, quite evidently, trans-imperial in scope. At the same time, they were only one part, albeit a deeply impactful one, of a broader field of activity, encompassing other actors beyond the diplomatic milieu of early modern Istanbul. Indeed, dragomans' translational and publication activities bring to the fore their multiple and evolving relationships with members of the Ottoman capital's intellectual and political elite as well as with a spatially diffuse set of interlocutors across a sprawling Republic of Letters. We thus cannot talk about "Turkish literature," the product par excellence of a European perspective on the Ottomans, without considering how this field of knowledge emerged through sustained (and often dragoman-mediated) dialogue with uniquely positioned Ottoman and non-Ottoman subjects.

An excellent illustration of the complex circulations and mediations at the heart of an early modern European understanding of Ottoman history and historicity is found in Hans Löwenklau's (1541–1594) *Annales Sultanorum Othmanidarum, a Turcis sua lingua scripti* (Annales of the Ottoman Sultans, written by the Turks in their own language, 1588, 1596) and *Historiae Musulmanae* (1591). Almut Höfert has recently described these mammoth, multivolume works as "ground-breaking," "the first in presenting Turkish history to a European audience in a particularly elaborate synthesis on the basis of Ottoman sources." The *Annales* purported to be based on "all hitherto published Greek, Latin, Italian, French, German, Hungarian and other histories," whereas the *Historiae*, which itself was to become a main source for Richard Knolles's highly influential *Generall historie of the Turkes* (London, 1603), used three different Ottoman sources (some of which had also informed the *Annales*, though not as explicitly acknowledged). The first was the "Annales Beccani," named after the Habsburg ambassador Hieronymus Beck, who had obtained it in Istanbul through a French dragoman and brought it to Vienna, where Johannes Gaudier translated it, then published it in Frankfurt in 1567. Beck's chronicle was itself a translation of a work dated 1550 by the Ottoman historian and theologian Mollā Çelebi, which combined and extended several anonymous Ottoman chronicles down to 1549. A second source for the *Historiae* was the "Codex Verantius," gifted to Löwenklau by the nephew of the Habsburg ambassador Antonius Verantius, and based on an anonymous translation of a chronicle from Ottoman into Italian by a Greek scholar. A third source was the "Codex Hanivaldus," a Latin history of the Ottomans, which the Habsburg embassy secretary Philip Hanivald von Eckersdorf commissioned from the Ottoman court dragoman of Hungarian background, Murad Bey. It was largely based on the early-sixteenth-century work of the Ottoman historian Neşri's *Cihannümâ* (Cosmorama), itself "a compilation of a number of Ottoman historiographical traditions."[70] The making of Löwenklau's *Annales* reflects the improvised and precarious nature of sixteenth-century Habsburg diplomacy in Istanbul, before a resident embassy was able to rely on its own dragomans. The result was a thoroughly "mixed" work whose mediation and further circulation depended not only on Ottoman Porte dragomans' labor and expertise but on extensive patronage networks and segmented, multi-sited scholarly expertise.

Ottoman writings on Europe were similarly shaped by specific trans-imperial regimes of circulation and complex collaborations. Upon graduating from the University of Padua in 1692, Emmanuel Timoni, an Istanbul-born descendant of a dragoman lineage, became the physician of the English embassy to the Porte and, following a trip to London in 1703, was appointed to the prestigious Royal Society. A decade later, he published in the *Philosophical Transactions* a letter concerning smallpox inoculation, a method widely practiced in the Ottoman Empire.[71] Timoni was followed by another Istanbulite, the physician of the Venetian embassy, Giacomo Pilarino.[72] Over the next three decades, Timoni's and Pilarino's publications on the matter were translated and published in Venice, Leiden, and Leipzig.[73] Other examples abound: Ali Ufki Bey, after being educated at the Ottoman court for two decades, joined ca. 1657 the service of several foreign ambassadors, including the English and the Dutch. While still in Ottoman employ, he completed a translation into Turkish of the tract *Ianua linguarum reserata aurea* by the Moravian reformer Comenius (1643). His translation projects expanded in the 1650s and 1660s, when he produced a Turkish translation of the Catechism of the Church of England (1653) and of the Old and New Testament and the Apocrypha (ca. 1658), a tract *Concerning the Liturgy of the Turks* (published posthumously in Latin in 1690 and in English in 1712) and another tract on Turkish grammar, *Grammatica Turcicolatina* (1666), which he dedicated to the chaplain of the English embassy.[74] He authored a detailed treatise on the Topkapı Palace, published in German and in Italian in 1665 and 1679, respectively, and a relation of the violent death of Kösem Sultan, Mehmed IV's influential grandmother, published in England by Isaac Barrow.[75] Ufki Bey's Bible translations may have been assisted by another dragoman in Istanbul, the Jew Yahya bin 'Ishak, or Haki.[76] Beyond such local collaborations and his own writings and translations, Ufki Bey was also a crucial link in the further circulation of Ottomancentric knowledge. He was a key informant not only for Rycaut's *Present State*, but for other early Orientalists, including Nointel, Antoine Galland, and Cornelio Magni, who claimed that Ufki Bey presented his manuscripts to various diplomats in exchange for alcohol.[77]

Many other examples survive of scholarly networks connecting Ottoman courtiers and foreign embassy employees. In 1631, the Ottoman lord admiral, who was interested in astrology and cosmography, asked the Venetian bailo for a cartography expert who could help him with some maps he owned. The bailo offered to send his dragoman, Giovanni Battista Salvago.[78] Antoine Galland maintained extensive contacts with Ottoman grand dragoman Alexander Mavrocordato (1641–1709) and with the Ottoman court treasurer and polymath Hezārfenn Hüseyin Efendi (whose name literally means "versed in a thousand arts"). Hezārfenn (d. 1691) could count among his friends not only Galland but Marsigli, who met him in his seventies, and made extensive use of his library. Hezārfenn's universal history, in turn, was based among other things on Greek and Latin sources, which he is known to have accessed through the help of some dragomans.[79] Mavrocordato, like many members of Istanbul's Orthodox elite, was trained at the University of Padua. Years later, he used his time at the gates of Vienna in 1683 to try to purchase as many books as he could in the Austrian capital. He dedicated his first historical work to a study of the grandeur and decline of the Ottoman Empire. Antoine Galland wrote in his diary in 1672: "yesterday I attended a reading of an Italian discourse written by Mr. Mavrocordato, concerning the strength and the weakness of the Ottoman Empire," and confirmed that the work contained precious information about the state of the empire.[80] Mavrocordato later published a three-volume work, *État de l'Empire ottoman*.[81] Hezārfenn's own work of the same title was translated into French by Galland in 1686.[82]

As Alexander Bevilacqua has noted, Barthélemy d'Herbelot's posthumous, monumental, and hugely influential *Bibliothèque orientale* (1697) had "the unmistakable imprint of the commitments and perspectives of his sources," and was particularly indebted—in both contents and organizing principles—to earlier Ottoman bibliographic-encyclopedic endeavors. His most immediate source was the *Kaşf al-ẓunūn* (Unveiling of Opinions) by the Istanbulite polymath Katip Çelebi.[83] That work itself was indebted to an earlier thematic bibliography by Taşköprüzade Ahmed (d. 1561), whose biography was similarly elite and court-centered, having spent most of his career as a teacher and *kadı* in the capital.[84] D'Herbelot had consulted two manuscripts of Katip Çelebi's work in Paris, one in the Royal Library and one in that of Jean-Baptiste Colbert, and had an additional copy made for himself. His very access to Çelebi's book in Paris owed to the collecting mission of Antoine Galland in the 1670s, sponsored by French ambassadors to the Porte. Galland's contributions to the project did not end with procuring Çelebi's work, however, but included writing a preface, proofreading, and indexing the entire work after d'Herbelot's death.[85] Galland, in turn, was introduced to Katip Çelebi's work by none other than the Ottoman scholar's student, Hezārfenn.[86] A set of revisions and additions that Galland undertook in anticipation of a new edition of the *Bibliothèque* (cut short by his death in 1715) underscores the profoundly Ottomancentric and courtly framework in which he operated.[87]

Ottoman mediation was central to the constitution of European Oriental libraries as a whole, not only to their Ottoman-language sections. The early collections of Persian manuscripts now in the Bibliothèque nationale in Paris bear the unmistakable imprint of Istanbul as their primary site of acquisition, and often reflect Ottoman bibliophiles' tastes. At the end of his term as ambassador in Istanbul in 1604, Savary de Brèves brought with him back to Paris some 110 "Arabic, Turkish, and Persian" manuscripts, which served as the foundation for his future typographical efforts, and which notably did not focus on Eastern Christian titles.[88] The scholar Christian Rau (1613–1677), whose collection came to the French Royal Library after his death, purchased many of his Persian (and Ottoman) manuscripts in Istanbul during his sojourn there in 1639–42. Dozens of other Persian manuscripts now at the Bibliothèque nationale were purchased on the instruction of Cardinal Jules Mazarin by Jean de la Hay, the French ambassador to Istanbul from 1639 to 1665. Colbert sent half a dozen of his own envoys to Istanbul for the same purpose starting in 1671.[89]

Modern scholars have often celebrated Katip Çelebi, Hezārfenn, and their contemporaries as the "first" Ottoman scholars to consciously interact with their European counterparts. But this claim—a corollary to the widespread and pernicious idea that early modern Ottoman elites lacked "curiosity" about and knowledge of Europe—is untenable. Many of the interactions between Ottomans and European sojourners in Istanbul were oral, making their traces difficult to recover, but in recent years more and more of the fermentation that characterized this milieu has come to light. As Matthew Melvin-Koushki recently suggested, a widely shared, "renewed enthusiasm for translation from India to Italy . . . would seem to mark the advent of Western early modernity (or modernities)." In a deliberate anti-Orientalist move, Melvin-Koushki crucially makes the case for defining "the West" as "the half of Afro-Eurasia west of South India, incorporating the Arabic, Persian and Latin cosmopolises, that vast realm where the Hellenic-Abrahamic synthesis reigned supreme."[90]

The centrality of translation to the very constitution of Ottoman letters is evident even, perhaps especially, in the field of most intense textual production in this period, namely historiography. Over the fifteenth and sixteenth centuries, Ottoman historiography gradually came to its own through translations of key works from Arabic and Persian, the importation of poetic and hermeneutic models from the Arabophone and Persophone cultural spheres, and, concurrently, the continued composition of Persian-language universal histories by Ottoman scholars at least until the 1570s, in evident response to ongoing demand from a functionally triglossic elite readership.[91]

The majority of translations undertaken by Ottoman scholars until the seventeenth century were undoubtedly from Arabic and Persian, key languages of scholarship and literature in the Islamicate cosmopolis.[92] Yet significant aspects of Latin learning were incorporated into Ottoman culture as well through various intermediaries and genres, often orally. As outlined by Tijana Krstić, the sixteenth century was the heyday of multilingual, multidirectional translational activity in Istanbul. This was already underway during the reign of Mehmed II, who collected Greek manuscripts (and printed books) for his library.[93] Among other works, he commissioned the translation from Greek of Plutarch's *Lives*, of Ptolemy's geography, and of several theological and philosophical treatises by more recent authors, including the Greek Orthodox patriarchs Gennadios Scholarios and Maximos III, and the philosopher Georgios Gemistos-Pletho's *Book of Laws* and rendition of the Neoplatonist, theurgical *Chaldean Oracles*.[94] Mehmed also sponsored the translation from Italian of the *Breve narratione della vita et fatti del signor Ussuncassano* (Brief narrative of the life and deeds of the Sovereign Uzun Hasan).[95] The early sixteenth century saw anonymous Turkish translations of Aesop's fables (via Maximus Planudes) and of various Italian authors, including Abstemius, Rinuccio d'Arezzo, and

Poggio Bracciolini.[96] The Ottoman admiral Piri Reis (1470–1554) synthe-
sized Iberian, Arab, and Indo-Chinese cartographic traditions, explicitly
building his charts of the Atlantic Ocean (1513) and North Atlantic (1528) on
dozens of earlier maps, including Columbus's.[97] In 1572, Hasan bin Hamza
and Ali bin Sinan compiled from assorted French sources and translated
into Turkish the *Tevarih-i Padişahan-ı Françe* (Chronicles of the Kings of
France), commissioned by the Ottoman grand vizier Feridun Bey.[98]

The pattern set by the dragomans Yunus Bey, Murad Bey, and Mahmud
Bey of scholarly translations to and from Ottoman Turkish was followed
and expanded in the next century by Ali Ufki Bey and his students. In
1654, Katip Çelebi translated from Latin Mercator's *Atlas minor* with the
help of a French convert to Islam, and used European cartographers and
geographers for a revised version of his *Cihannüma*.[99] Starting in 1675,
Ebu Bekr of Damascus (d. 1691), a scholar in the retinue of the grand vizier, was entrusted by Sultan Mehmed IV with the task of translating Joan
Blaeu's *Atlas Major*, published in Amsterdam in eleven volumes and previously gifted to the sultan by the Dutch ambassador in 1668. To achieve
this task, which took a decade to complete, he collaborated with Marsigli,
among others.[100] Other seventeenth-century Ottoman scholars translated
and adapted Latin astronomical tables, as well as French and Spanish Para-
celsian medical and anatomical texts, sometimes in collaboration with European colleagues who practiced in Istanbul.[101]

Imperial patronage of and interest in translations only increased in the
eighteenth century. In 1722 the dragoman Osman Ağa of Temeşvar, who
had spent the decade 1688–1699 in Austrian captivity, translated from the
German an abbreviated history of Austria from 800 to 1662.[102] A few years
later, the Ottoman grand vizier Mehmed Rağib Paşa commissioned two
dragomans, Paolo Eremiani (a graduate of the French apprentice dragomans' program at the Collège Louis-le-Grand) and Santi Lomaca (a Greek
dragoman at court) to translate into Turkish the Jesuit Jean-Baptiste du
Halde's history of China.[103] In the 1730s and 1740s the founder of the Ottoman press, Ibrahim Müteferrika (1674–1745) undertook several extensive
translations and writings on European society, history, and science—and
at least one Jesuit missionary's work on the collapse of the Safavid Empire
in the wake of Afghan invasion in 1722.[104] In 1792, the Swedish dragoman Mouradgea d'Ohsson was involved in Sultan Selim III's reform efforts, which were based on the supposed adoption of European military
reform.[105]

As this brief overview suggests, much of the European Orientalist scholarly perspective on Ottoman culture was shaped by the intensive interactions and textual circulations among a relatively small group of erudite
Istanbulites—courtiers, scholars, and dragomans—many native or long-
time residents of the capital. The formative period for these interactions
spanned roughly a century and a half, from the 1570s to the 1720s. This was
the age of the dragoman renaissance. It is the perspective of this courtly
Ottoman milieu—which encompassed both an admiration for Arabic, Persian, and Turkish learning, and a deep sense of "crisis" and need for reform,
ultimately giving birth to the famous (and now debunked) paradigm of
Ottoman decline—that has colored Orientalist scholarship for three centuries since. This durability is a testament to the power of the dragomans'
synthesis and its particular regime of circulation, as well as to its epistemological limitations.

Toward a History of Ottomanist Translations

What was the impact of the extensive textual and visual output of Istanbulite diplomacy's regime of circulation, and how are we to understand this
corpus in relation to dragomans' personal trans-imperial itineraries, training, and precarious position both in Istanbul and in an emergent Republic
of Letters? What follows is a schematic answer, in the hope of sparking
further research on these admittedly large questions and especially on how
the corpus of translated Ottoman relates to the canon of translated Arabic
and Persian, given the more limited circuits of the former. Whereas dragomans were involved in translations from all three languages, the "dragoman
effect" was particularly strong in the case of Ottoman works.

Istanbulite dragomans, whose bread-and-butter activity involved
bi-directional diplomatic translation and interpreting, were uniquely positioned to appreciate the importance of Ottoman as a language of imperial
power. The advantages of commanding Ottoman became especially evident not necessarily in the context of everyday communication in Istanbul,
where several other languages could be used, but rather in accessing the ad-
ministrative-bureaucratic heart of the empire. After all, As Jan Reychman
and Ananiasz Zajączkowski noted over 50 years ago, the roots of Ottoman
diplomatics—a branch of philology and archival studies preoccupied with
historicizing Ottoman documentary practices—are firmly grounded in the
translational and copying activities at the core of dragoman training.[106]

This highly institutionalized context of acquisition and prototypical use of Ottoman—and the language ideologies that attended it—directly informed dragomans' choices of texts to write or translate. As described in previous chapters, aside from dictionaries and grammars, dragomans' texts focused overwhelmingly on Ottoman politics and statecraft, to the neglect of other spheres of sociocultural production. It is thus hardly surprising that dragomans' translation projects show a clear preference for historical genres, a preference shared by many of their closest interlocutors at court and beyond.[107]

In contrast, other Ottoman genres are significantly underrepresented in the corpus of dragomans' translations. Most conspicuous in their absence are Ottoman poetry, theology, and scientific writings, as well as non-courtly literary production more generally. The neglect of the first two genres, poetry and theology, warrants special attention, given their tremendous popularity in contemporary courtly Ottoman circles. Recent scholarship has underscored the vibrancy and originality of Ottoman theological and philosophical writings.[108] The contribution of divan poetry to the development of the Ottoman language itself is undeniable. By the seventeenth century, it had become *the* Ottoman literary genre par excellence, spawning significant Ottoman-language poetry in various subgenres.[109] Indeed, as Hatice Aynur shows, by that point it had become a prime vehicle for punctuating Ottoman time and space, literally embedded in the built environment and in elites' everyday rituals of social life.[110] But Ottoman poetry's pervasive incorporation of Persian and Arabic lexemes likely made it much harder for dragomans to translate. Conversely, the rare dragomans with the requisite knowledge of Arabic and Persian tended to prioritize Persian poetry, even if their aesthetic sensibilities were themselves unmistakably shaped by contemporary Istanbulite courtly tastes, bibliographic traditions, and interpretive frameworks.[111] Ottoman theology likewise enjoyed a real renaissance in the seventeenth century, given the tremendous religious fermentation that followed the rise of puritan *kadızadelis* and their rivalry with Sufi groups, resulting in significant textual production on both sides.[112]

One explanation for the relative neglect of poetry, theology, and science in dragomans' translations is the perception of these genres—again, by Ottoman elites as much as by their dragoman interlocutors—as prototypically "Arabic" or "Persian" rather than "Ottoman," irrespective of the actual prevalence (indeed, relative popularity) of writings in Ottoman in these different domains. Another explanation may have to do with dragomans' limited access to the social milieus where these genres thrived, e.g., the salons of Istanbul and the literary coteries they were premised on. As Helen Pfeifer shows, "these salons operated largely as by-invitation-only gatherings, attended by well-to-do Muslim men for the purpose of social and intellectual exchange."[113] As historians of early modern literary culture elsewhere (but with clear relevance for our case as well) have noted, coteries were "linked by ties of friendship founded upon, or deepened by, mutual encouragement to original composition; the production and exchange of manuscript materials to celebrate the group and further its members' interests; and the criticism of one another's work and of shared reading materials."[114] These conditions would have made it particularly hard for dragomans to penetrate Istanbul's contemporary poetry scene and its media outputs.

Be that as it may, by neglecting to translate Ottoman poetry, theology, and science, dragomans were perhaps unwittingly advancing a dominant (if declining) Ottoman language ideology that saw the Ottoman language as not particularly suited for these genres, and that mandated diglossia for its courtly elites.[115] This neglect reinforced a still pervasive prejudice against Ottoman literature among contemporary European scholars and readers, and an understanding of Ottoman as a primarily "practical" language of bureaucratic governance, a perception that was to change in Europe, slowly and very partially, only in the nineteenth century.[116]

It is thus largely thanks to dragomans that the early modern European notion of "Turkish literature" was so heavily tilted toward historical and political genres. Through their selection of Ottoman texts to translate, dragomans played a pivotal role in defining for their European publics a sense of Ottoman canonicity. Dragomans' choices, however, were themselves informed by a complex intellectual network, and, in a very real sense, voiced Ottoman elites' own imperial ideologies about the Ottoman synthesis of prior Islamic knowledge. This dimension calls for much further investigation, but several examples help illustrate how dragomans refracted the perspectives of the courtly scholars and authors with whom they conversed, either literally or metaphorically.

The first example illustrates how an Ottoman-metropolitan perspective permeated early Orientalist knowledge even through dragomans' translations of ostensibly non-Ottoman texts. As part of their training, in the 1730s and early 1740s, a team of French apprentice dragomans in the Ottoman capital undertook the translation of at least half a dozen works on Islamic history, ranging from the Caliphate to the Mamluks.[117] Among others, their translations included the magisterial fifteen-volume *Tarih-i Mısır-ı Cedid* (New History of Egypt), which the scholar Celālzāde Salih (d. 1565), the younger brother of the Ottoman courtier Celālzāde Mustafa, completed in 1550. As Giancarlo Casale shows, Celālzāde himself relied quite heavily on Ayyubid and Mamluk-era histories, especially al-Maqrizi (d. 1442), who accounts for well over half of the contents of the *New History*.[118] That even works originally composed in Arabic were initially translated into French not from the original but rather from their Ottoman Turkish adaptations (often produced as part of local scholars' quest for imperial patronage in the immediate aftermath of Ottoman expansion in Arab lands) already suggests how a metropolitan Ottoman reframing may have shaped their future reception.[119] While the selection criteria for works to be translated by apprentice dragomans warrants further study, the perspective on Islamicate and Egyptian history reflected therein was clearly shaped by Ottoman imperial power and sultanic patronage.

The second example concerns the lasting effect of the preponderance of chronicles, annals, and other overtly political and court-centric historical genres in the corpus of dragomans' translations. As noted above, in addition to dragomans' own privileging of historical genres over others, their translations also became foundational for "libraries," or rather *catalogues raisonnés* of Ottomanist knowledge, which served as the basis for further textual production. Donà's, d'Herbelot's, and Toderini's anthologies, which explicitly acknowledged dragomans' curation and translation labor at their core, all belong in this category. But perhaps the clearest example of this relationship between dragomans' mediation of Ottoman letters and further Orientalist production is Vincent Mignot's (ca. 1725–1791) *Histoire de l'Empire ottoman*, published in Paris in four volumes from 1771 to 1773. Despite its many critics and detractors, it was translated into multiple languages (including German in 1774, Polish in 1779, English in 1787, Russian in 1789). Mignot, who was Voltaire's nephew, was an Enlightenment author par excellence, and his influence on Ottoman historiography proved surprisingly enduring.[120] It is thus especially relevant that his authority was premised firmly on access to diplomatic archives, as his English translator, A. Hawkins, relates in his preface:

> The access which the author [i.e., Mignot] had to the king of France's repository of foreign affairs, through favor of the duke of Choiseul,

furnished him with the most authentic and interesting accounts of the Ottomans, and which must necessarily confer on his history a superiority over every other that has yet been published.[121]

Mignot himself explicated his sources of authority more fully, and revealingly. After conceding to have "no knowledge of oriental languages" and listing his main published sources,[122] he wrote:

> I have had the good fortune to find assistances which I had no reason to expect; they have determined me to undertake this work, of which, to speak properly, I am nothing more than the compiler. Mr. Cardonne, secretary interpreter to the king of France for the oriental languages, and professor of the Arabic tongue in the royal college, who has served the court, and the French commerce, in quality of druggerman, in several Turkish ports during twenty years, has taken the pain to translate the most interesting and instructive parts of the three Turkish annalists, Naima Effendi, Rachid Effendi, and Tchelebi Zadé, which commence in the year 1594 of the Christian æra, and finish in 1727. He has been so obliging as to let me see his manuscript before it was deposited in the king's library. Mr. Bejault, keeper of the manuscripts of this library, has likewise been so kind as to intrust me with several translations of Turkish originals, which contain interesting parts of their history.[123]

Mignot mentions two additional manuscript sources: François Baron de Tott's (1733–1793) yet-to-be-published memoirs of his fifteen-year sojourn in Istanbul (as an ambassador's secretary and military consultant) and, most interestingly, French ambassadorial reports kept in the "repository of foreign affairs."[124] That Mignot described himself as *redacteur*, a mere compiler, may be read as a standard performance of self-deprecation so characteristic of early modern authors' prefaces. Yet the elaborate credit he gives to the dragoman turned professor Denis Dominique Cardonne and the (unnamed) apprentice dragomans whose translations he consulted in the Royal Library seems genuine enough. It underscores dragomans' profound role in constituting knowledge of the Ottoman world for a burgeoning Republic of Letters, by establishing a canon of Turkish literature in translation and through specific interpretive practices.[125] It reminds us how much dragomans' perspectives on Ottoman history, as refracted to Mignot, themselves recalibrated contemporary Ottoman courtly tastes.

In fact, the three Ottoman historians Mignot explicitly mentions as his sources in translation, Mustafa Naima (1655–1716), Mehmed Raşid Efendi (d. 1735), and Ismail Asım Küçükçelebizade (1685–1762), were all contemporary or near-contemporary *vakanüvis* (official court historiographers) of a decidedly Istanbulite outlook, who enjoyed wide popularity and circulation among Ottoman elites, in no small measure thanks to their appearance in print through the first Ottoman Turkish printing press in Istanbul.[126]

The almost exclusive reliance on these exact same official court chroniclers as a source for the recent history of the Ottoman Empire was to characterize the work of other eighteenth-and nineteenth-century European historians. In an era of exploding historiographical activity, with hundreds of historians operating across the Ottoman Empire, and with historiographical methods expanding rapidly in Europe as well, it is particularly noteworthy that the canon of Ottoman historiography in translation remained remarkably constricted and metropolitan. Even in the 1740s, over a decade after Naima appeared in print, many dozens of pages from his chronicles pertaining to the 1590s were assigned to two French apprentice dragomans to copy by hand and to translate.[127] In the following century, none other than the doyen of Ottoman historiography, the Austrian dragoman turned orientalist Joseph von Hammer-Purgstall (1774–1856), was to use the same chronicles and give them further circulation through his immensely influential ten-volume *Geschichte des osmanischen Reiches* (1827–1835). Despite its title page's claim to be based "in large part on hitherto unused manuscripts and archives," Hammer-Purgstall's project, like Mignot's half a century earlier, relied heavily on the official Ottoman chronicles of Naima, Raşid, and Asım.[128]

These examples of dragomans' mediation of a decidedly metropolitan and courtly Ottoman historiographical canon clearly do not reflect the entire edifice of early Orientalist scholarship. The "Oriental folk tales" that decisively entered the European canon in the early eighteenth century through the serialized publications of the dragoman-scholars Galland and Pétis de la Croix offer counterexamples pointing to a much more diffuse set of intermediaries. These tales became immediate publishing sensations, appearing in dozens of editions and translations. They were added to by subsequent generations of dragomans well into the nineteenth century.[129] Neither Galland's nor Pétis de la Croix's works constitute simple "translations" of preexisting texts, let alone direct transfers from extant Arabic or Persian originals, respectively. Their impact cannot be overstated, having "changed the world on a scale unrivaled by any other literary text."[130] By the end of the eighteenth century, copies of the English translations of Galland's work had reached North America, Australia, and South Asia. By the early twentieth century, the early French or English texts had been further translated into dozens of other languages, often in multiple versions.[131] It was, in other words, Galland's and his immediate successors' vision of "the Oriental folk tale" that circulated globally across Arabophone, Turkophone, and Persophone (as well as Russophone, Japanophone, etc., etc.) reading publics. Yet, the "folk" that French Enlightenment dragomans proffered was itself heavily mediated not only linguistically but spatiotemporally as well. Its circuits included the anonymous Anatolian authors who adapted largely Persian sources in the fifteenth-century compilation *Ferec ba'd eş-şidde* (Relief after Hardship); urban storytellers, including Galland's own Istanbulite *hoca*, or language teacher; and cosmopolitan, Europe-bound intermediaries like Galland's scribe, the Aleppo-born Joseph Lazare, or the Jesuit-educated Maronite scholar Hanna Diyab. During interviews with Galland in Paris in 1709, Diyab told the savant—in French—some of the *Nights'* most iconic stories, including "Ali Baba and the Forty Thieves." Diyab, as recent scholarship has revealed, may have built in part on genres, tropes, and even entire narratives with long European genealogies.[132]

Like most dragoman authors discussed in this chapter, both Galland and Pétis de la Croix were deeply enmeshed in Ottoman courtly and scholarly circles, even as they were attuned to their European public. They represent the entrepreneurial dragoman who is able to parlay his cultural capital—premised on thorough grounding in Ottoman elite culture and languages—into social capital (including concrete economic resources) in Europe through several commercial-cum-epistemological transactions. This phenomenon attests yet again to dragomans' precarity—like that of other scholars who relied on patronage and short-term employment in a variety of auxiliary professions (from tutors to correctors). While the phenomenon gained much of its momentum at the turn of the eighteenth century, it was rooted in translation practices, spatial arrangements, and, indeed, habitus, that Istanbul's dragomanate had developed for over a century prior.

This chapter has charted the long temporal arc of dragomans' translation and publication activities, positioning them squarely within an emergent Ottomanist field of knowledge. That field's specialized work practices and regimes of circulation, deep embedding in a courtly and diplomatic Istanbulite milieu, and, especially, dragomans' centrality to it, have been largely forgotten—a testament to the multiple erasures at work in the articulation of modern disciplines. Rather than anachronistically think of the profoundly trans-imperial world that dragomans inhabited as exceptional (let alone "hybrid"), we are prompted by their hefty epistemological and methodological legacies to recognize, once again, the enduring power of Orientalist myopia to obfuscate its own nonlinear genealogies.[133] If "modernity—including modern philology—was not *something done to a supine Asia* by colonialist operatives [but] rather . . . was everywhere co-produced and dizzyingly multiple"—this multiplicity was itself vitally mediated, co-creating the boundaries its proponents claimed to transcend.[134] As dragomans set circulation in motion they also, inevitably, reinforced a view of the world as deeply fractured along ethnolinguistic, religious, juridical, and, increasingly, civilizational lines. We are that world's heirs, in ways both evident and less so.

Epilogue

Dragomans and the Routes of Orientalism

AN OBITUARY IN *Il Corriere Ordinario*, Vienna's quasi-official Italian-language gazette, on April 16, 1712, mourned the death of Count Marcantonio Mamuca della Torre (b. 1635) a week earlier: "In the course of 62 years [he] served the House of Austria, with added benefit to the Holy Roman Empire, and to all of Christendom." The notice continued to eulogize the count's "endless efforts and evident dangers, memorable and relevant services," his "great zeal and devotion in protecting the Holy Sepulcher from the irregular taxes [*avanie*] and oppressions of the Turks and in assisting the clergy against the persecution of schismatic Christians . . ." It concluded by describing the interment of the deceased—clad in Franciscan garb—in a Viennese Benedictine church, alongside his wife, Countess Giustiniana Tarsia, as instructed by their sons, Counts Leopoldo and Cristoforo.[1] That brief eulogy completed a process set in motion two decades earlier, with Marcantonio's ennoblement procedures. Those procedures were captured, rather unusually, in a print publication, Vincenzo Giulio Lodi's *L'Immortalità del Cavalier Marcantonio Mamuca della Torre* (The Immortality of the Cavalier Marcantonio Mamuca della Torre), in 1701.[2] What the eulogy did not mention, quite deliberately, were Marcantonio's very deep roots in the Ottoman Empire, his extensive kin and patronage ties far beyond the Habsburg realm and Catholic Christianity, and, especially, his occupation in the course of those sixty-two years of loyal service: Marcantonio was a dragoman, who split his time between Istanbul, his birthplace, and Vienna, his place of residence from 1683 on. In Istanbul he worked at the interface of Ottoman ministers and several diplomatic representatives, often serving multiple parties simultaneously. Later, in Vienna, in the wake of the failed Ottoman siege of 1683, he became attached to the Imperial War Council, but likewise continued to share detailed intelligence with the Venetian and English ambassadors to Vienna, among others, as well as to cultivate extensive correspondence networks with acquaintances in Istanbul.[3] Meanwhile, his wife, Giustiniana Tarsia, maintained the family household in the Ottoman capital and raised five children. The parties she threw at the family's summerhouse in Belgrade Forest, just outside Istanbul, were legendary among the city's elite, who regularly frequented the area's hunting grounds. Giustiniana's ability to continue cultivating this circle of visitors from the highest echelons of Ottoman society depended, in no small part, on her access to a wider world of goods, thanks to her husband Marcantonio in Vienna. Giustiniana corresponded with her husband regularly, and asked him periodically for specific commodities to be sent over, demonstrating an impeccable urbane taste.

If Marcantonio and Giustiniana's professional path was profoundly trans-local (and, indeed, trans-imperial), their familial trajectories were even more multipronged. On the paternal side, Marcantonio descended from the Catholic (Messinese and Genoese) merchant colonial elite of Chios in the eastern Mediterranean.[4] On the maternal side, he was named after his eponymous grandfather Marcantonio Borisi, a fabled Venetian grand dragoman who spawned a veritable dragoman dynasty with Venetian, Habsburg, French, Dutch, and English offshoots. Through marriage, the Mamuca della Torres cultivated strong ties to the Orthodox patriciate of Istanbul as well.[5] Giustiniana's ancestors hailed from Capodistria in the Venetian-ruled Adriatic (nowadays Koper in Slovenia), as well as several other Venetian colonial families who traced their roots to Bar in Albania, among other places. Both bride and groom, then, descended from several deeply intermarried dragoman dynasties whose multiple branches converged in Istanbul.

Within a generation, however, all of this was to change. Marcantonio and Giustiniana's children all married into Habsburg magnate families. Like other members of the dragomanate, Marcantonio and Giustiniana placed both their sons in dragoman apprenticeships early on. Leopoldo (named after the Holy Roman Emperor) served as a Habsburg diplomat until his premature death a few months after his father. His younger brother, Cristoforo (named after his dragoman maternal grandfather), left the dragomanate to enjoy a long career as a courtier, spending much of his time in the newly declared Habsburg Free Port of Trieste, where he actively lobbied the Habsburg authorities to secure freedom of worship for Orthodox Christian and other Ottoman merchants. In 1749, he became Empress Maria Theresa's official representative for "Greek merchants."[6] Several of Cristoforo's sons remained in Trieste, where they pursued political and military careers and were eventually absorbed into the local high bourgeoisie.

Marcantonio and Giustiniana's three daughters did not fare too poorly either. The youngest, Lucia, accompanied her father to the Viennese court, where she became a lady-in-waiting and eventually married the imperial counselor for Tyrol, Count Sbardelatti. Her eldest sister, Maria Francesca, married first the Transylvanian count Ádam Kálnoky, then the Moldavian Boyard Constantin de Neniul, thus consolidating the family's Orthodox ties, already apparent in previous generations. Their middle sister, Vittoria, remained in Istanbul for many years, and eventually married Carl Christof, future Reichsgraf von Watzdorff. Within a few generations, then, the family catapulted itself from the commercial and diplomatic milieu of Pera into the Central European aristocracy.

Their timing was impeccable. By the nineteenth century, the Venetian state was no more. The Ottoman Empire, once a towering political and economic power controlling three-quarters of the Mediterranean basin, with a capital serving as a commercial and diplomatic hub that aspiring global players could ignore only at their own risk, was becoming, at least from the perspective of its westerly neighbors, "the sick man of Europe."[7] While several of Istanbul's dragoman dynasties, like the Testa and Draperis, continued to hold on to their positions practically through the end of the empire, most, like the Carli, Tarsia, and, indeed, Mamuca della Torre, were absorbed into the aristocracy and high bourgeoisie of other regional states, leaving their dragoman days behind. As the Mamuca della Torres' case illustrates so vividly, they often parlayed their dragoman bona fides and specialized expertise for sociopolitical capital beyond the Ottoman Empire, in courtly positions or professional advancement in other metropoles.

Yet this metamorphosis did not spell the end of the dragomanate's impact on the nascent discipline of Orientalism. The afterlives of dragomans' "ways of knowing," their institutional and epistemological imprint, their textual practices and language ideologies are ingrained across the modern humanities.

Institutionalization and Language Immersion Pedagogy

Emmanuel Szurek argues that "the intellectual and political construction of Turkishness is a fundamentally transnational undertaking."[8] As this book has shown, the epistemological and institutional genealogies of the modern projects of Ottoman studies and Turkology can be traced back to the seventeenth century, and to the efforts of Istanbulite dragomans to carve out a space for the study of Ottoman language, literature, and history within an emergent discipline of Orientalism that was otherwise interested primarily in Semitic languages, and, by the eighteenth century, Chinese, Persian, and South Asian languages. Dragomans did so not only by authoring the lion's share of Ottoman metalinguistic texts, indelibly shaping this corpus. Rather, they helped lay the groundwork for a budding scholarly field of Ottoman studies by procuring Ottoman manuscripts in Istanbul, by serving as royal/imperial interpreters in European capitals where they were often entrusted with cataloging and commissioning further manuscripts and cultivating a readership for Ottoman texts in translation, and, finally, by setting up and staffing academies for Oriental languages. In so doing, they articulated fundamental methodologies and epistemologies for the study of Ottoman worlds, cementing the field's embedding in the institutional matrix of Mediterranean diplomacy.

At the height of the dragoman renaissance of the seventeenth century, dragoman training and language acquisition were premised on socialization in core imperial institutions. Porte dragomans were trained in the Ottoman Palace School as young *devşirme* recruits and war captives. Embassy dragomans received their training largely as apprentices in consular chanceries. In the former case, their education reflected a metropolitan view of Ottoman elite culture, one that was self-consciously "synthetic," based on the integration and re-appropriation of a heavy dose of Arabic and Persian literary models.[9] In the latter case, embassy dragomans' perceptions of Ottoman language use were shaped not only by their daily lessons with *medrese*-trained *hocas* (a staple of dragoman apprenticeship in the Venetian bailate and beyond), but by humanist ideals of eloquence and possibly Eurasian-wide ideologies that linked vernacular languages with political power.[10]

The immersive, relatively direct access to Ottoman linguistic-cum-pedagogical practices that became the cornerstone of seventeenth-century dragoman apprenticeships was to be eroded in the following century. The demise of Istanbul's consulates as sites of Ottoman language learning, however, opened up new incentives and opportunities for publishing metalinguistic texts. As discussed in Chapter I, in both Paris and Vienna (and elsewhere) new educational institutions aimed to systematize the teaching of the Ottoman language outside the Ottoman Empire and to formalize the training of diplomatic interpreters as two intimately related activities. Part of the unstated but essential pedagogical logic behind such institutions was the notion that core linguistic competencies could be acquired in a class-room setting and not just in a fully immersive environment. The embod-ied practices of written and especially oral diplomatic mediation—drago-mans' bread-and-butter activities—could be cultivated later, through the shadowing of more seasoned dragomans in situ. This abstraction of lan-guage-learning from specific sites of social interaction—attesting to strong Jesuit influence on pedagogical currents in both Paris and Vienna—came hand in hand with a renewed emphasis on mastering grammatical para-digms and on written translation. These emphases outlived the suppression of the Jesuit order and its banishment from France in 1764 and from Austria a decade later.[11]

It is to this shift in pedagogy that we owe much of the early corpus of French and Latin translations from Ottoman Turkish. Throughout the eigh-teenth century, young apprentice dragomans attending the Parisian school were routinely required to translate texts from Ottoman (as well as Arabic and Persian) as part of their training. Their translations—numbering in the hundreds—were deposited in the Royal Library, forming the nucleus of a larger collection of bilingual "classics" and supplemented by those "Ori-ental manuscripts" that French diplomats in Istanbul were instructed to purchase for the king, even at exorbitant prices. Aiding these translational and transactional activities were scores of manuscript Ottoman-language dictionaries, grammars, and phrase books kept in the school library. It was dragomans and apprentices who then annotated, excerpted, and copied these materials, which bear signs of extensive use by generations of stu-dents. Following numerous permutations, the school library's collections, as well as those of the Royal Library, found their way to the Bibliothèque nationale.[12]

Students and faculty in Vienna's Orientalische Akademie, with their strong links to Habsburg diplomatic circles in Istanbul, played a similarly vital role in systematizing and disseminating Ottoman linguistic knowl-edge. Here, too, the impact of apprentice dragomans' translational activ-ities, modeled explicitly on Venetian and French precedents, cannot be overstated.[13] Tight connections between dragomans or other embassy staff and the development of "diasporic" Ottoman-language libraries have been traced in the eighteenth-century Polish case as well, albeit on a more mod-est scale.[14]

Dragomans' role in institutionalizing Ottoman studies was not limited to circulating and translating manuscripts, of course. As important, dragoman careers (or, at a minimum, a dragoman apprenticeship followed by a few years of diplomatic or consular service in the Ottoman Empire) became the classic route into professorships of Oriental languages at the Collège Royal and into appointments as bibliographers or other key positions in the Royal Library in Paris. The first catalog of Ottoman and Persian Manuscripts at the Royal Library, printed in 1739, took Pierre Armain, a graduate of the dragoman program, five years to prepare. Armain later became an instructor of Oriental languages at the Collège Louis-le-Grand.[15] Similar professional trajectories typified other French proto-Orientalists, from the ambassador turned printer François Savary de Brèves (1560–1628) and the bibliophile ambassador turned priest Achille Harlay de Sancy (1581–1646), whose private collection eventually became a cornerstone of the Bibliothèque nationale's Oriental manuscript holdings,[16] to the dragomans turned authors, François Pétis de la Croix father (1622–1695) and son (1653–1713) and Antoine Galland (1646–1715), to dragoman –and comparative musicologist *avant la lettre* Charles Fonton (1725–1793).[17]

An equally long list could be produced of Vienna-based Orientalists who had acquired their Ottomanist bona fides through sojourns as dragomans in the Ottoman Empire, including Michel D'Asquier, Meninski, Podestà, and, more than a century later, Franz von Dombay (1758–1810), Thomas von Chabert-Ostland (1766-1841),[18] and, most influentially, their schoolmate and collaborator, the renowned historian of the Ottoman Empire Joseph von Hammer-Purgstall (1774–1856). Notably, Dombay, Chabert and Hammer-Purgstall founded "one of the earliest learned international orientalist journals, *Fundgruben des Orients*, which appeared in Vienna from 1809 to 1818."[19] Its French equivalent, the *Journal Asiatique* (established 1822) was similarly the fruit of dragomans' labor.

Significant eighteenth-century Parisian and Viennese efforts to institutionalize the study of Ottoman Turkish bring to a sharper relief the relative absence of Venetian dragomans from this area of activity. Despite—or perhaps precisely because of—their outsize importance in shaping the dragomanate as a professional group, a community of practice, and a kin-based caste, Venetian dragomans played only a secondary role in the production of Ottoman metalinguistic texts. The two exceptions to this generalization, discussed in Chapter 5, are Giovanni Molino's dictionary (published, tellingly, under the aegis of the Roman papacy rather than of the Venetian state) and Giambattista Donà's publications (to which apprentice dragomans were pivotal, though perhaps unwitting, contributors). Molino, of course, was hardly a typical Venetian dragoman, hailing from an Armenian family in Ankara rather than the Catholic milieu of Pera. Rather than marry into other dragoman families, he left the Ottoman Empire permanently to establish himself as a scholar in Italy. In Donà's case, the apprentice dragomans who collected and translated his two books' Ottoman sources did so under direct instructions from their employer rather than on their own initiative.

The explanation of why, throughout the period, Venetian dragomans largely left the production of metalinguistic texts to others seems to lie in a combination of factors. In part, it was the economic and political woes of eighteenth-century Venice in general, and the relative stagnation of its publishing industries in particular, especially compared to the Dutch and French. Other perhaps more immediate reasons have to do with Venetian dragomans' lifeworlds. The Venetian dragomanate's centuries-old endogamy fostered a community of practice whose training was overwhelmingly apprenticeship-based and familial. Such training relied heavily on dragomans' access to chancery archives and manuscript collections, including the bailate's *Carte Turche* registers, a large, meticulously preserved and indexed corpus of transcribed Ottoman charters and their translations. These modes of knowledge transfer possibly obviated, or at the very least lessened, the need for formal textbooks, certainly in print.[20] Finally, as a resolutely Istanbulite professional group, Venetian dragomans invested in forging affinal ties in situ more than through exogamous marriage. As a result, only a few of their members had the extended patronage networks in Rome, Paris, Leiden, or Vienna that would have allowed them to tap into the scholarly networks and Arabic-type printing presses operating there (or, for that matter, in Livorno, Lyon, or other metropoles with print shops that owned Arabic typeface in this period).[21] The clear shift in the center of gravity of a budding field of Orientalism away from its Italianate Renaissance roots northward by the mid-seventeenth century certainly did not help matters.[22]

A related factor was the Venetian program of dragoman apprenticeship, which, from its inception, sent youth to Istanbul rather than develop a formalized system for Ottoman language training in Venice. Indeed, there is little evidence that dragomans supported establishing a school for apprentice dragomans in Venice like the Parisian or Viennese models. Several decrees to that effect were passed by the Senate for almost a century, virtually to the end of the Venetian state. The school never opened. The first two initiatives came in 1692 from an Ottoman Muslim scholar turned Catholic convert, Abraham Albanese, and again in 1699 from the Damascene-born, Sorbonne-educated Salomon Negri. The former emphasized the need to study Arabic and Persian alongside Turkish. The latter, while focusing on Arabic and Turkish, similarly considered his a scholarly and philological, indeed a "scientific method" of instruction, based on reading in different genres. Negri openly bemoaned the lack of proper instruction in Arabic, which prevented dragomans, by his account, from understanding the higher registers of Ottoman.[23] The dragomans whom the Senate eyed as candidates for running such a school in its later incarnations, Giovanni Mascellini in 1746 and Giambattista Calavrò-Imberti in 1786, showed little interest in the job, and quickly returned to their families and careers in Istanbul when the plans fell through.[24]

Dragomans were likewise conspicuously absent from another Italian project to train Ottoman-language interpreters. The Neapolitan Collegio dei Cinesi was originally established by the Propaganda Fide in 1732 to prepare Chinese Christian youth for careers as missionary interpreters. In the 1740s, small quotas for Ottoman Christians were introduced among the college's students. However, as Marie Bossaert shows, even after Italian unification and the transformation of the papal college into a "Royal Asiatic College" in the 1860s, and eventually into an "Oriental Institute" in 1889, with the express intention to train a national corps to supplant Ottoman-born dragomans, hardly any of its graduates succeeded in securing a dragoman position in any major Italian consulates in the Ottoman Empire, let alone in the embassy in Istanbul, which remained the de facto sinecure of Ottoman "Levantine" families. Similarly, and unlike its Parisian and Viennese counterparts, the Neapolitan institution did not attract dragomans as teaching staff, nor dragomans' relatives as students.[25]

What might explain the repeated failure to open an Oriental academy in Venice, despite dozens of Senate decrees to that effect over the years? Quite possibly, Venice's dragomans sensed that a formalized program of instruction away from their home turf in Istanbul could break their hold on the profession, allowing Venetian competitors eventually to take their place. An explicit rationale for moving the apprentice dragomans' school to Venice was to increase the quotient of Venetian citizens' sons among students, and to minimize the well-noted distractions that the Ottoman capital offered to impressionable youth. Perhaps dragomans doubted the initiative's pedagogical merits, its assumption that the Ottoman language—and particularly the courtly register so essential to Porte diplomacy—could be taught as a set of grammatical rules abstracted from specific sites of inter-action and the experience of handling actual chancery documents. Finally, Venetian dragomans' training in formal chancery Italian as well as in Otto-man meant that they could communicate directly with members of the Ve-netian elite, unlike dragomans employed by other embassies—especially the British, Russian, Austrian, and Polish—in whose home countries Ital-ian was an intermediary language of limited purchase beyond diplomatic circles. It is yet to be documented whether dragomans actually acted be-hind the scenes to derail any plans to move the dragoman school to Venice. Be that as it may, without courses in Ottoman at the University of Padua, let alone a dedicated "Oriental academy" in Venice, few Venetians outside the dragomanate and missionary seminaries could obtain even minimal proficiency in the language. The absence of a potential readership reduced, in turn, the incentive for printing Ottoman textbooks, dictionaries, and grammars. Any short-term gains to be had from such publications would surely be offset in the long term by making dragomans' linguistic capital more widely available to outsiders.

Venetian dragomans' relative neglect of metalinguistic production in print thus evidently both relied on and further contributed to their un-derstanding of the Ottoman language as a specialized diplomatic register. Such a register could only be acquired in situ, through an extended sojourn in the Ottoman capital or in other Ottoman urban centers, under the tute-lage of a *hoca*. This system of face-to-face instruction by a local tutor was a long-standing practice in the Islamicate world, and was to remain in vogue among European diplomats (and later colonial administrators) through-out Ottoman, Safavid, and Mughal urban centers well into the nineteenth century.[26]

That the bailate adopted a pervasive Islamicate practice should come as little surprise. Beyond adaptability and prescient capacity to integrate into preexisting imperial structures, the Venetian institutionalization of this type of education at the heart of the Ottoman Empire also enabled, willy-nilly, particular pedagogies that proved much harder, if not entirely impossible, to implement elsewhere. Sojourning diplomatic representatives habitually lamented the lack of a mutual language between bailate *hocas* and young apprentice dragomans, which, in their telling, made the initial acquisition of Ottoman very difficult. Yet the teachers' ignorance of Italian and Greek also facilitated a de facto immersive model of language acqui-sition for their students.

These immersive features distinguish the Venetian dragoman apprenticeship program in both its contemporary diplomatic and pedagogical
contexts from the constant translation and commensuration that are a staple of the bilingual classroom, where teacher and students may share a
language different from the one being taught. Take, for example, the case
of Latin, early modern European scholars' paradigmatic second language.
Recent research has underscored that early modern Latin pedagogies were
far more diverse and sophisticated than once assumed. Yet few contemporary institutional settings sought, let alone achieved, even a modest
level of Latin immersion.[27] For most students, particularly at a younger
age, the grammar-translation method of the Jesuit schools was ascendant,
even as progressive educators continued to share earlier humanists' con-
viction "that oral proficiency was best acquired by using the language for
meaningful communication."[28] Not until the twentieth century would a
large-scale pedagogical alternative emerge to a prevailing model of second-language instruction that separated the teaching of language from the
teaching of content.[29] Venetian dragoman apprenticeship in Istanbul was
thus an outlier in an educational landscape that offered few immersive opportunities for second-language acquisition. That it developed at exactly
the same time that Jesuit pedagogy took hold of most Latin instruction in
seventeenth-century Catholic Europe further attests to the Venetian dragomanate's unique nature.

The immersive environment of the bailate's program of dragoman training contrasted not only with Latin instruction in contemporary academic
settings but with Ottoman instruction in the eighteenth-century Oriental
academies of Paris and Vienna, which increasingly emphasized a well-
rounded humanities curriculum and philologically grounded instruction
not only in Ottoman, but also, in parallel, in Arabic and in Persian.[30] And
yet the bailate's program held its own, notwithstanding its outlier nature and Venetian diplomats' lamentations. Indeed, over time, the Venetian dragomanate's durability confirmed the viability of its pedagogical
practice of embedding second-language learners in immersive contexts
of use. Despite its humble beginnings immersive language study eventually became a hallmark of a wider nascent field of Ottoman studies. It is
unsurprising, then, that seasoned diplomats, like English ambassador Sir
William Trumbull, left their copies of Meninski and De Paris at home in
London, realizing that "of more importance . . . than scholarly knowledge
about the Ottoman Turks was the ability to make sense of the political

vocabulary and practices of diplomacy of the Ottoman world: how to present an *'arz*, or petition, how to have a *hüccet* registered in the local court, or when to consult the Grand Mufti for a *fetva*."[31] In all these activities, dragomans' mastery, indeed de facto monopoly, remained virtually unchallenged across diplomatic chanceries.

Giovanni Battista Donà captured this duality between formal grammar and immersive language acquisition in his *Della Letteratura* of 1688, when he confirmed that Giovanni Agop's *Rudimento della Lingua Turchesca*, published in Venice three years prior,

> teaches the Turkish language with all the grammatical rules, as they do in the city of Constantinople. But those who are attached to the Ambassadors of Christian Princes in that city can attest that every day a Master of Turkish reading, writing, and grammar comes to instruct the young students of Turkish language of each Nation, as is practiced, especially with the Venetian language youth [i.e., apprentice dragomans], who resided with me.[32]

Grammars, in other words, were a poor substitute for properly learning Ottoman with a *hoca*.

One of the Venetian dragomanate's enduring legacies was precisely the proliferation into other institutional settings of its uniquely immersive training and keen metapragmatic awareness. When the famed Turkologist Jean Deny—himself a former apprentice dragoman and consular attaché in Beirut, Jerusalem, and Eastern Anatolia—published his monumental *Grammaire de la langue turque (dialecte osmanli)* in 1921, he noted: "This book does not pretend [. . .] to replace the oral teaching of a master, and the best master in this case is still the ferryman of the Golden Horn or the welcoming shopkeeper of the bazaar in Istanbul."[33] The social spaces where "real" linguistic knowledge was to be acquired, according to Deny, had shifted quite significantly from the courtly audience hall and diplomatic chancery of old. Yet his preferred spaces of encounter still represent the dragoman's decidedly Istanbulite perspective (here refracted through the unmistakable prism of fin-de-siècle flânerie) and emphasis on unmediated interaction, whether with a *hoca* or with a shopkeeper in the bazaar.

Immersion—facilitated through extended residential apprenticeship in embassy compounds and instruction by local tutors—was also at the heart of the US Department of State's training program for diplomatic and consular interpreters in Turkey, Japan, and China, established in the early twentieth century.[34] That this particular form of immersion bereft of prior language training at home was applied only to "Oriental" locales and languages speaks, once again, to the enduring entanglement of the dragomanate with orientalist knowledge production, and, eventually, with imperialist designs.

Other aspects of the Venetian dragomanate, too, were incorporated, albeit in different guise, into formal curricula, including in the Oriental academies of Vienna and Paris. The heavily endogamous and kin-based apprenticeship model of the seventeenth-century Venetian dragomanate morphed in both Vienna and, especially, Paris, into endogamous transmission of both knowledge and institutional authority, now mostly from master to student (though sometimes also from father to son or uncle to nephew). Reproduction, we might say, became sublimated in academic reproduction. Upon his death in 1713, François Pétis de la Croix's role as director of the Collège Louis-le-Grand was transferred—along with his Chair of Arabic at the Collège Royal and, eventually, the title of Royal Secretary-Interpreter—to his protégé Jean-Baptiste Hélin de Fiennes (1669–1744), himself a graduate of the Collège Louis-le-Grand. De Fiennes had accompanied Pétis de la Croix to Egypt in his youth and spent nearly two decades in Alexandria and Cairo as consular dragoman before returning to Paris in 1706. Following the Revolution, Pierre Amédée Jaubert (1779–1847), who had accompanied his own teacher, Jean-Michel Venture de Paradis, to Egypt with Napoleon's expedition the previous year, was appointed professor of Turkish at the École des Langues Orientales in 1799.[35] His diplomatic adventures in Istanbul, Persia, and as far as Tibet continued for decades to come, culminating in his mission to the Ottoman sultan in 1821 to represent the French position on the Greek Question.[36]

A career trajectory oscillating between diplomatic assignments in Istanbul, Salonica, Izmir, or Alexandria and lengthy incumbency as Chair of Turkish in the Parisian academy continued to typify several prominent French Ottomanists throughout the nineteenth and early-twentieth century. At least until the early decades of the Third Republic, virtually all holders of the Chair of Turkish at the Collège de France, and most professors of Turkish at the École des Langues Orientales (and, eventually, in their successor institution, INALCO) were former dragomans and apprentice dragomans turned royal secretary interpreters, who supervised the linguistic training of apprentice dragomans as a core academic duty.[37] This started with the first incumbent, Denis Dominique Cardonne (1721–1783), who sojourned as a dragoman in Istanbul for twenty years from age nine, later becoming Royal Secretary-Interpreter. It continued with Pierre Ruffin, Jean-Baptiste Perille, Jean-Daniel Kieffer (b. 1767, in Istanbul 1796–1803, Chair of Turkish 1805–1833),[38] and Alix Desgranges (1793–1854, Cardonne's grandson, who served as dragoman first in Salonica in 1815 and then in Istanbul in 1821, before being appointed Chair at the Collège in 1833). Desgranges's successor in the latter position in 1854, Abel Pavet de Courteille (1821–1889), was himself the grandson of the renowned professor of Arabic Antoine Isaac Silvestre de Sacy (1758-1838), and the first incumbent to forgo a diplomatic or consular career prior to appointment to the Collège. This exception notwithstanding, the same pattern emerges for professors of Turkish at the École: Charles Schefer (1820–1898), who served as its president from 1867 to his death, graduated from the Parisian school of apprentice dragomans and spent much of his twenties in Cairo, Beirut (where he served as dragoman), Jerusalem, Alexandria, and Istanbul.[39]

The self-starter Silvestre de Sacy proved a notable exception, pursuing a scholarly career largely detached from the Foreign Service. In this respect he diverged from his Arabic and Turkish teacher, Étienne Le Grand (ca. 1711–1784), himself a graduate of the École des Jeunes de langues. Le Grand spent over three decades as dragoman. He eventually directed apprentice dragomans' training in the French embassy in Pera before returning to Paris in 1764 to assume the title of Royal Secretary-Interpreter for Oriental languages and to offer Arabic and Turkish lessons to a new generation of student-apprentices.[40] Yet Sacy also differed from his heirs in the Parisian academy, many of whom reproduced the strong endogamy of their dragoman intellectual predecessors, whether through kinship (e.g., Sacy's grandson Abel Pavet de Courteille) or through intellectual filiation. In addition to Amédée Jaubert, mentioned above, another student of Sacy's, William McGuckin Baron de Slane (1801–1878), became chief interpreter for the French army in Africa. A third, Louis Dubeux (1798–1863), became Chair of Turkish at the École and authored a Turkish grammar.

A similar pattern of intellectual and institutional reproduction continued into the twentieth century. Charles Barbier de Meynard (1826–1908, the grandson of an Istanbulite physician) inherited the Chair of Persian from his teacher at the Collège de France, and eventually directed the École and presided over the Société asiatique. His student Jean Deny (1879–1963) directed the École from 1937 to 1948 and proceeded to a professorship of Turkology at the Sorbonne. Deny's student Louis Bazin (1920–2011)

inherited Deny's position at the École in 1949 and eventually held numerous other professorships of Turkish across Paris's top universities.[41]

It is here that Said's argument about Orientalism as the handmaiden of
colonial rule becomes most resonant. The same individuals who occupied
key positions in the French ministry of foreign affairs and whose career
paths embodied the peripatetic, Ottomancentric trajectories of the earlier
dragomanate, were to become the leading Ottomanists of the nineteenth
century, their political affiliation playing an important role in their promotion or demotion. The knowledge that they and other Orientalists produced
about "the Orient" (Ottoman or otherwise) was undoubtedly profoundly
shaped by their professional trajectories, political aspirations, deep identification with French foreign policy, and embedding in strict institutional
matrixes. But they were also the descendants of a dragomanate whose epistemological and methodological infrastructures predate and exceed Orientalists' own positionality.

Dragomans, to be sure, were never above the political fray either. But
during their formative era, the dragoman renaissance of the seventeenth
and early-eighteenth centuries, the imperial projects they were implicated
in were Ottoman and Venetian as much as French or Habsburg. In a memorable passage, Said writes:

> When around the turn of the eighteenth century the Orient defini-
> tively revealed the age of its languages—thus outdating Hebrew's di-
> vine pedigree—it was a group of Europeans who made the discovery,
> passed it on to other scholars, and preserved the discovery in the new
> science of Indo-European philology [. . .] At most, the "real" Orient
> provoked a writer to his vision; it very rarely guided it.[42]

It is no secret that the Ottoman Empire is largely absent from Said's *Orientalism*, figuring, very sporadically, as a literary trope, almost invariably
as a moribund polity. The Ottomans' glaring absence as active, agentive
historical actors from Said's account of Orientalism was shaped by his own
modernist biases. It also, as this book has suggested, skewed his analysis
of Orientalism's diverse genealogies and routes.

The porous boundary between scholarship and statecraft (whether in
authoring policy papers or serving in colonial government) marks modern
Orientalism (according to Said), and late-modern Middle East "experts"
eager to embrace the imperialist apologetics of neoconservative think
tanks.[43] These latest incarnations of scholars' ideological collaboration

with imperial states are essential to analyze. Yet as this book suggests, there was no prelapsarian moment of innocence when scholarly expertise about the Ottomans—linguistic, philological, historical—was somehow separate from statecraft. For centuries, the Ottomans were Venice's closest neighbors and its most powerful commercial allies and rivals, inherently tying dragomans' Ottomanist knowledge to their diplomatic work, patronage, and will to power. Both the strengths and the weaknesses of their body of knowledge and enduring methodological and epistemological legacies reflect dragomans' trans-imperial paths, but also attest to their deep embedding in Istanbulite courtly culture and capacity to reflect and refract Ottoman elites' own evolving understanding of their political project, history, and language.

Note on Names, Terms, and Transliteration

1. Gilbert 2018, 230–31.

Introduction

1. Said 1978, 15.

2. "Tergiman: ogn'Interprete, che frequenta il Divano, come và vestito; v'è il Divano del Gran Vesiro, dove quasi ogni giorno frequentano l'Interpreti dell'Imperatore de Romani, Interpreti della Porta, d'Inghilterra, Francia, Venezia, Polonia, Olanda, Ragusa & e vi stanno à sollecitare gl'interessi del loro Prencipe, altri de Mercanti, Consoli & e raramente si vedono al Divano, se non per qualche necessità, che gli preme di comparire' al Gran Divano, dove assistono appresso il Gran Vesiro li due Casiascheri, cioè dei due Gran Cancellieri per qualche cosa importante di Giustizia." ÖNB Cod. 8562 HAN MAG, vol. 1: 199r–v.

3. At least five exemplars of this album set survive. The two in the Bavarian State Archives in Munich, one of which was presented to Prince Elector Charles Albert, and the other previously kept in the Hanover court library in Mannheim, are identified as Mamuca della Torre's work. Three additional exemplars in the Austrian National Library in Vienna are improperly and only partially cataloged, and lack indication of Mamuca della Torre's authorship. They generally include the same series of miniatures (though each executed by a different artist[s]), and vary in size, number of volumes, binding, pagination, and orthography. BSB Cod. Icon. 349–351 and 352–354; ÖNB HAN Cod. 8562–8564; Cod. 8574; Cod. 8602–8604.

4. Stefani 1960, 31–41; Do Paço 2019a, 8–9.

5. The term Italianate is used throughout this book to call attention to a diffuse corpus of Italian-language texts and the highly diverse and trans-local reading public that engaged them. Both texts and their presumed readership defy simple categorization in terms of modern nation states ("Italians") and their bounded geographies ("the Italian peninsula"). This distinction is particularly apt here, given Italian's centrality to early modern diplomacy in general, and Mediterranean diplomacy in particular. The extensive corpus of Italian-language materials that the Mamuca della Torre dragomans generated for specifically Viennese (and other

Central European) readership well into the eighteenth century is a case in point. Tommasino 2015.

6. Cristoforo, like many of his relatives, proved successful in this quest. By the time of his death in 1760 he enjoyed the title of count conferred on his Vienna-based father, the Habsburg dragoman Marcantonio Mamuca della Torre, in 1701. After a youthful love affair in Istanbul with his teenage cousin Maria Tarsia resulted in an illegitimate daughter, Cristoforo evidently was able to parlay his noble title and Viennese connections into an advantageous marriage with Countess Maria Judith Khuen von Belasi und Lichtenberg of the Tyrolese nobility. The Mamuca della Torres's trans-imperial trajectories and social and spatial mobility are further discussed in the Epilogue.

7. Hitzel 1997; de Groot 2001; Hamilton and Richard 2004.

8. Bosworth 1999; Kaislaniemi 2009.

9. Wansbrough 1996.

10. Notable examples include Ali Ufki, né Wojciech Bobowski; Hürrem Bey; Zülfikar Ağa and Vincenzo Bratutti. Neudecker 2005; Krstić 2011b; Kármán 2018, and the additional references in Chapter 6.

11. Hermann 1956/2002; Mairs 2012.

12. Pym 2000; Hagen 2003; Paker 2011; Truschke 2016.

13. Zele 1990; Pedani 1994; Conley 2002; Williams 2002; Touzard 2005; Borromeo 2007; Lonni 2009; Grenet 2013; Ogborne 2013; Malcolm 2015; Gürkan 2017.

14. Veinstein 2000; Çiçek 2002; Ergene 2004; Janos 2006; Balcı 2013; Meral 2013.

15. Perocco 2010.

16. Eufe 2003; Papadia-Lala 2009; De Luca 2011; Rothman 2011a.

17. Dakhlia 2008; Peirce 2010.

18. Philliou 2001; Aydın 2007.

19. On Istanbulite polyglotism, see Dursteler 2012.

20. On Istanbul as a central node of early modern diplomacy, see Rudolph 2013; Berridge 2004; Goffman 2007; Ghobrial 2014a.

21. Höfert 2003; McJannet 2007.

22. Salzmann 2000; Bevilacqua and Pfeifer 2013.

23. Heywood 1972, 34.

24. Valensi 1993; Goffman 1998; Lindner 1998; Höfert 2003; MacLean 2004; Schülting et al. 2012.

25. For some recent exceptions, see Van Gelder and Krstić 2015; Talbot and McCluskey 2016.

26. Hitzel 1997; de Groot 2001; Hamilton and Richard 2004.

27. Valensi 1993, 14; Infelise 1997b, 2002; De Vivo 2007; Petitjean 2013.

28. "Ill[ustrissi]mo et Ecc[ellentissi]mo Sig[no]r mio Sig[no]r P[at]ron Col[entissi]mo Con tutta sommissione hò ricevuto li benissimi caratteri di V[ostra] E[ccellenza] rigati, sotto li 12–22 cadente, et con altretanta, consolatione ho intesa la di lei riverita sodisfatione, p[er] l'opera da me fatta nell' historia Turca.

Il libro comprato da V[ostra] E[ccellenza], et trasmesso à mè è proprio, al di lei insigne intento; Comincia dal tempo della Corronatione, di Sultan Mehmet, et finisce alla ressolutione presa la Porta d'incaminare, le sue Arme all'invasione dell'Vngaria, et poi segui l'Assedio di Viena, et a l'anno Mahomettano 1093, verso'l fine del Christiano 1682.

Jo in essecutione delli supremi Comandi di V[ostra] E[ccellenza], continuarò in questo, il filo dell'historia, et non ommettero tanto in q[ue]sto particolare q[ua]nto in ogn'altro, mi vedessi honorati delle sue preggiate prescrittioni di farmi in tutti li tempi, conoscer, che vivo

Di V[ostra] E[ccellenza]

Pera 20–30 Giugno 1695

Hum[ilissi]mo Dev[otissi]mo et Osseq[uietissi]mo Ser[vito]re

Giacomo Tarsia": Paget Papers, folder 7, 206, School of Oriental and African Studies, London (Giacomo Tarsia to William Lord Paget, 20–30 June, 1695).

29. Piterberg 2003; Tezcan 2007.

30. Schmidt 2002; Păun 2008; Dew 2009; Bevilacqua 2016. On the Spanish Crown's "Oriental Library," whose material objects were obtained through circuits spanning North Africa rather than the eastern Mediterranean, see García-Arenal and Rodríguez Mediano 2013; Hershenzon 2014.

31. As Eric Dursteler (2012, 61) notes, only one Venetian *bailo* after the 1550s actually learned Ottoman Turkish.

32. All of these tasks as performed by dragomans are amply documented in reports by scholars attached to French embassies in the Ottoman Empire in the seventeenth and early-eighteenth centuries. Omont 1902, 19, 179, 242, 385, 438, 510, 524–25, 528, 530–31, 556, 571, 573–74, 622, 629, 668–69, 693, 768; Hamilton 2018, 70, 110, 153, 183.

33. Hamilton et al. 2005 offers an important earlier contribution to this effort.

34. The term Islamicate, modeled after Italianate, was coined by Marshall Hodgson (1974, 59) to refer to "the social and cultural complex historically associated with Islam and the Muslims, both among Muslims themselves and even when found among non-Muslims."

35. Hanks 2010, 160.

36. Hanks 2015, 36.

37. Asad 1980, 649; Bardawil and Asad 2016, 161.

38. See, for example, Mills 2019 for an evocative example of missionary networks of Ottomanist knowledge production centered on Syria rather than Istanbul.

39. App 2010, xi.

40. Fleischer 1986; Turan 2007; Şahin 2013; Burak 2015.

41. Darling 2008; Kołodziejczyk 2012.

42. Barkey 2008, 8.

43. Aymes 2013, 32.

44. Sood 2011; Hagen 2003; Subrahmanyam 2006; El-Rouayheb 2015.

45. Necipoğlu 1989; Dale 2010.

46. Foundational groundwork for the study of early modern Ottoman-European connectivities was laid out by Kafadar 1995 and Goffman 2002. For recent case studies of specific knowledge domains, see Hagen 2000; Casale 2010; Krstić 2011a; Tezcan and Hagen 2012; Emiralioğlu 2014; Brummett 2015; Küçük 2019.

47. Rothman 2011, 11–15.

48. Subrahmanyam 2012; Raj 2016.

49. Pratt 1992; Rubiés 2007; Inglis 2011; Ramachandran 2015.

50. See, inter alia, Merle 2003; Andrea 2007; Meserve 2008; Harper 2011; Ingram 2015.

51. Wunder 2003; Boettcher 2004; Rubiés 2007; App 2010; Shalev 2012; Stolzenberg 2013; Davies et al. 2014; Miller 2015; Beasley 2018.

52. On Muslim scholars in early modern Europe in general, see Krstić 2015; for biographical case studies, see Hacker 1987; Hacker 1988; Wiegers 1988; Hamilton 1994; García-Arenal and Wiegers 2003; Davis 2006; Rietbergen 2006; Heyberger 2009; Coudert and Shoulson 2004; Hamilton 2006; Ghobrial 2014b; Girard 2019.

53. For cogent critiques of this assumption, though ones where trans-imperial mobility is not always fully thematized, see Schnapp 2014; Pollock et al. 2015; Grafton and Most 2016. Matthew Melvin-Koushki (2018, 226) has recently offered an even more profound critique of these assumptions, calling for a redefinition of "the [early modern] West" as encompassing the Arabic, Persian, and Latin philological cosmopolises. See also the discussion in Chapter 7.

54. For some examples of the thriving scholarship on early modern colonial officers-cum-scholars' endeavors in South Asia and their Indo-Persian interlocutors, see Flores and Saldanha 2003; Raj 2007; Trautmann 2009; Mantena 2012; Davies et al. 2014; Kinra 2016. Scholarship on the birth of Indology from engagements between European missionaries and South Asian elites is equally robust; see, e.g., Amaladas and Županov 2014; Lefèvre, Županov, and Flores 2015; Rubiés 2017.

55. For notable exceptions, see Brentjes 2010, Ghobrial 2014a, Bevilaqua 2018. Roberts 2015, Fraser 2017, and several of the contributors to Beaulieu and Roberts 2002 make similar arguments about Orientalist engagements with Ottoman and North African visual forms, though largely focused on the late-eighteenth and nineteenth centuries. On Said's own silence on Ottoman cultural production, and the modernist (and at times deeply Occidentalist) perspective informing some branches of the postcolonial project, see Bryce 2013. On Occidentalism, see Coronil 1996, Bracewell 2005, Mishkova 2008.

56. Goffman 2002.

57. Tavakoli-Targhi 2001, 18.

58. Burke 1980.

59. On the "dialogic emergence of culture," i.e., the processes through which "cultures are continuously produced, reproduced, and revised in dialogues among their members," see Tedlock and Mannheim 1995, 2.

60. See, e.g., Andrews and Kalpaklı 2004; Grehan 2006; Kafescioğlu 2009; Ghobrial 2014a; White 2017.

61. Cordier 1911; Paladino 1917; Babinger 1927; Neck 1950; Pippidi 1980; Lesure 1983; Zele 1990; Hering 1994; Infelise 1997a; Ács 2000; Conley 2002; Luca 2003a.

62. Tuncel 1973; Vranoussis 1973; de Groot 1994; Şeni 1997; De Testa and Gautier 2003.

63. Masson 1905; Testa and Gautier 1991; Bashan 1993; Hossain 1992; Hossain 1993; van den Boogert 1997; de Groot 2000; Berridge 2003; Miović-Perić 2013; Kármán 2014; Dörner 2015; Amelicheva 2016.

64. Matuz 1975; Marghetitch 1993; de Groot 1997; Veinstein 2000; Çiçek 2002.

65. For notable exceptions, see Römer 2008; Fraser 2010; Krstić 2011b; Zecevic 2014.

Chapter 1: Localizing Foreignness

1. "Figura della casa, ove habitano li Ecc[ellentissi]mi Baili, formata dalla parte dell'horto, et del corridor al di sop[r]a, p[er] il quale si passeggia[.] Sotto di esso sono le stanze, solite habitarsi da giovani di lingua": State Hermitage Museum, VAse 1782, 48r.

2. Fleischer 1986, 255–56, passim; Findley 1980; Goffman and Stroop 2004.

3. Imber 2002, 140–42; Ács 2000; Isom-Verhaaren 2004; Yılmaz 2009, 2017. Contemporary Ottoman commentators' repeated admonitions against unauthorized "outsiders" among the ranks of imperial household recruits only underscore their growing presence. Finkel 2005, 190.

4. Fleischer 1986, 256.

5. Minkov 2004, 67–68; Imber 2002. 134–37.

6. Imber 2002, 141; Minkov 2004, 74.

7. Kunt 1983; Necipoğlu 1991; Peirce 1993; Hathaway 1997; Pedani 2000; Hathaway 2008; Wilkins 2009.

8. On the consequences of elite endogamy for the Venetian patriciate's inability to reproduce itself as a class, see Sperling 1999. On the fraught relations between Venetian colonial nobilities on Crete and their metropolitan kin, see McKee 2000, 61–66 passim; and O'Connell 2004.

9. On the nexus of patrilineal consciousness, bilateral kinship orientation, and patronage strategies centered on the household in early modern Venice, see Grubb 1996; Romano 1996; Brown 2000; Chojnacki 2000; and Raines 2006. On the importance of personal and familial ties to the patriciate in consolidating citizens' hold on the lower echelons of the Venetian bureaucracy, see Pullan 1999, 162–63. On endogamy and patronage in the diplomatic corps, see Zannini 2000. On patrimonialism in early modern European familial states in general, see Adams 1994.

10. Spallanzani 1888, 192, quoted in Lucchetta 1985, 12.

11. On the Venetian term as a calque of the Turkish, see Sturdza 1983, 565.

12. "Non è dubio che il servizio de' suoi propri è più vantaggioso e con più dignità pubblica che quello de' sudditi turcheschi, perché quelli non temendo li rispetti parlano con ardire, mentre li turchi temono farlo": Quoted in Lucchetta 1989, 25.

13. Rycaut 1668, 90.

14. "Quelli di cotesta Città se sono di età tenera, ò non permettino li loro che se nè venghino, ò venendo non si può far tanto che non ristino sottoposti à mille strani accidenti; se sono in età matura, oltre che sono inhabili ad' apprender lingue, sono allevati non dirò con libertà, ma con licenza tale, che è impossibile si accommodino alli costumi di quà, et non perturbino le case de poveri Baili": Senato, Dispacci Costantinopoli (=SDispC), b. 104, 160v–161r (May 1, 1627).

15. The title of bailo, or *bajulus,* was first conferred on permanent Venetian representatives to Byzantine Constantinople in 1265. In 1575 the position was juridically equated to that of a regular ambassador, and the authority to appoint baili was transferred from the Venetian Great Council to the Senate. On the bailate as an institution, see Bertelè 1932; Coco and Manzonetto 1985; Dursteler 2006, 27–40.

16. According to Andre Pippidi (1980, 135), Serbians and Albanians of the seigniorial class were particularly prone to accept such employment. It should be noted, at the same time, that many families chose to "hedge their bets" by sending some sons to Venice and others to Istanbul. Wright 2006 offers a case in point; Arbel 2000 discusses the Cypriot nobility's relationship to Venice.

17. Belin 1894; Pistarino 1990.

18. On this relationship, see Boyar and Fleet 2010, 16–17. On the social geography and topography of early modern Ottoman Galata, see Mitler 1979. For a schematic map, see Dursteler 2006, 25.

19. Dalleggio d'Alessio 1969, 156–57; Belin 1894, 172.

20. Theunissen 1998; Van den Boogert 2005a, 64–70. On the transformation of foreigners into (protected) foreign residents, see also Goffman 2007, 64–65.

21. On Ottoman participation in early modern long-distance trade, see Trivellato 2009; Greene 2010; Aslanian 2011.

22. The French embassy in Istanbul, for example, was funded largely by the Marseille Chamber of Commerce, even after Colbert's massive reforms of 1669, intended to bring diplomacy more squarely under royal control. Takeda 2011.

23. Inalcık 1991; Dursteler 2004; Dursteler 2006.

24. This practice was not adopted in the recruitment of public dragomans in Venice proper until the 1660s, and even then was the result of repeated petitions by the then acting public pragoman Pietro Fortis, who himself was born in Pera and trained in the bailate. Rothman 2011a, 179–84.

25. SDispC, b. 118, 611r (17 October 1637); Senato, Deliberazioni Costantinopoli (= SDelC), filza 32, unfoliated (17 June 1641).

26. SDispC, filza 32, unfoliated (5 May 1641).

27. Trebbi 2001; Galtarossa 2003, and the bibliographies therein.

28. A seventh apprentice, Francesco Scaramelli, did achieve dragoman rank in 1635, but only served in Venice, where he was the first and only Venetian-born citizen to occupy the post of public dragoman in the seventeenth century. Rothman 2011b, 618.

29. These are aggregate numbers. Not all Ottoman apprentices secured a dragoman position, but at least one member of each Ottoman family in this pool did in the period under consideration.

30. Lodovico Marucini, a physician's son, began his apprenticeship in the bailate in 1553 and secured the title of grand dragoman in 1568. His younger brother Matteo apprenticed in the bailate from ca. 1569, achieving the title of dragoman in the late 1570s or early 1580s and leaving the bailate in 1584. Their nephew Giovanni Francesco began an apprenticeship ca. 1606, but left the service a few years later, without becoming a dragoman. Senato, Mar, reg. 37, 214 (28 December 1566), reg. 38, 13v–14 (24 March 1567).

31. The nature of the data does not allow us to distinguish conclusively between some apprentices and dragomans, nor to quantify the portion of each dragoman's time spent under Venetian employment as opposed to other embassies, hence the combined figures for the latter category.

32. In 1558 the bailo Marino Cavalli praised an apprentice's progress "in speaking, writing, and reading not only the Turkish language, but the Arabic one as well": SDispC, b. 2/b, fasc. 29, 73r–v (12 October 1558), quoted in Lucchetta 1989, 22; for reports on dragomans in baili's *relazioni*, see, inter alia, Albèri 1839, III.I., 103–5 (Bernardo Navagero in 1553), 181–82, (Domenico Trevisan in 1554), III.II. 50–56, (Daniele Barbarigo in 1564), 247–48, (Paolo Contarini in 1583), 318–20, (Gianfrancesco Morosini in 1585), 413–21 (Lorenzo Bernardo in 1592); Pedani-Fabris 1996, 391–92 (Lorenzo Bernardo in 1590), 467–72 (Girolamo Cappello in 1600); Barozzi and Berchet 1856, 251–53 (Simone Contarini in 1612), 426–31 (Alvise Contarini in 1641).

33. Lucchetta 1988, 1989. Among others, Bernard Lewis ventriloquizes diplomatic officials when he accepts dragomans' disloyalty as a fact rather than as a strategic claim deployed for specific ends by (some) participants in the power-laden interactions between dragomans and their patrician employers. Lewis 2004, 26.

34. Collegio, Risposte di dentro, b. 21, unfoliated (20 April 1630); SDispC, reg. 19, 23r–v (26 May 1629), 95v (24 January 1629 m.v.); Bailo a Costantinopoli (=BaC), b. 371, 25 (ca. 1630, includes a list in Turkish of Torre's creditors and an inventory of his possessions).

35. Dursteler 2018.

36. Dalleggio d'Alessio 1969, 157.

37. On Ottoman attempts to classify dragomans as subject non-Muslims, see Van den Boogert 1997.

38. Hitzel 1995, 53; De Groot 1978, 192.

39. SDispC, b. 133, 700r (10 April 1650), and b. 144, 118r–121r (15 July 1660); Inquisitori di Stato (=IS), b. 418, unfoliated (15 January 1658 m.v., and 6 October

1661). For Nicousios' biography, see Hering 1994; Janos 2006. For parallel cases in other embassies, see Cunningham 1961; De Groot 1978, 176; Bashan 1993; Amelicheva 2016.

40. On the Phanariots and the process of hellenization as spatio-social mobility among Ottoman Christians, see Philliou 2011, 15–16; Philliou 2009. On the Mavrocordatos' fierce anti-Catholic stance and Istanbul-centric identity, despite complex and far-flung marriage alliances and career paths, see Livanios 2013.

41. Among others, Marietta Mavrocordato, Alexander's cousin, married Stefano Ralli.

42. "[. . .] Ha questo Maurocordati [Alexander Mavrocordato] fatto sposo il di lui figlio primogenito [Nicholas Mavrocordato], in cui ha anco trasferita [formally from 1697] la sua carica di primo Interprete della Porta, in una figliola [Cassandra Cantacuzeno] di Demetrio Cantacuzeno fu prencipe di Moldavia, povera ma di buone e stimabili parentele et adherenze; mi sono valso della congiontura per coltivarlo,[ho] mandato alla sposa regalo di 4 vesti ripartite nelle seguentiqualità: velluto cremese, lastra bianca, samisquardo broccato a fiorid'oro e seta, damaschetto naranzino broccato a fiori d'argento agalloni, con altre galanterie": Archivio proprio Costantinopoli, b. 33, 133r–v, quoted in Luca 2008b, 667.

43. Philliou 2011, 8–11.

44. SDispC, filza 32, unfoliated (5 August 1641).

45. SDispC, b. 138, 546r, and 547r–548v (10 May 1655); IS, b. 418, unfoliated (15 January 1658 m.v., 20 July 1664, and 11 September 1664).

46. Veneri 2010, xiv.

47. Olivieri 2010 [1724], 10. Absent further details it is hard to determine which rendition of this popular legend was performed by bailate staff. It was clearly not Molière's 1665 version (in which the protagonist declares himself to be an atheist), which was printed only in 1672, but the libertine resonance of the work in other iterations as well would have been palpable to performers and audience alike.

48. Terzioğlu 1995; Hamadeh 2002; Ertug 2010; Fetvacı 2011; Şahin 2018.

49. Muir 2007; Henry 2009, though comedic theatrical spectacle could also be understood here as more broadly European, particularly given the choice of Don Giovanni, a story whose various Spanish, French, Italian, and German versions were performed by both *commedia dell'arte* and courtly troupes across Europe from the 1630s on. Pirrotta 1980.

50. Senato, Mar, reg. 31, 93r (21 February 1550 m.v.); Sturdza 1983, 565.

51. Hitzel 1995, 20, 41. On the significance of child labor to the French diplomatic enterprise in the Ottoman Empire (and elsewhere), see Gossard 2018.

52. Burkholder 1998, 86.

53. On the limited educational resources otherwise available to Catholic children and youth in contemporary Istanbul, see Dursteler 2004.

54. SDispC, filza 11, 135r–v (8 June 8 1577), cited in Lucchetta 1989, 24–25.

55. Capi del Consiglio dei Dieci (CCD), Lettere di Ambasciatori, Costantinopoli (LAC), b. 4, 159r (15 January 1574 m.v.).

56. "Perche stando in luogo dove non si parla, ne legge, et scrive, se non in Turco, si può crederre, che con presteza maggiore, si habbia da ricevere il frutto, che si deve giustamente spettare": SDispC, reg. 14, 145r–146r (21 February 1622 m.v.).

57. Senato, Mar, reg. 83, 185 (21 October, 1625).

58. BaC, b. 371, fasc. 3, unfoliated (3 July 1700).

59. Collegio, Risposte di dentro, b. 61, unfoliated (21 January 1663 m.v.).

60. "è cosa certo molto considerabile il vedere, che non solo gli adulti, & uomini fatti, ma etiamdio i fanciulli di pochi anni non sanno così presto balbetare, che snodano la lingua in trè, ò quattro idiomi differentissimi, e questi in perfezione. La lingua Greca è la loro originaria, essendo il parlar commune del paese, & in questa vengono educati dalle madri, che stilano tal linguaggio": Magni 1682, 65.

61. Quoted in Belin 1894, 180.

62. De Burgo 1686, 368.

63. Eldem 2016, 136.

64. Lesure 1983, 137.

65. SDispC, b. 11, fasc. 23, 135r–v (8 June 1577).

66. BaC, b. 263, fasc. 2.2, unfoliated (18 August 18, 1581).

67. SDispC, b. 50, 272r–276v (30 December 1599).

68. "Il loro maestro, che qui dicono il Coza, per opinione d'ogn'uno è huomo stimatiss[i]mo di doctrina, prattichiss[i]mo della legge turca, esguisitiss[i]mo nell' Idioma Arabo, Persiano, e Turco, ne intende punto l'Italiano, ò il Greco; Onde p[er] il p[ri]ncipianti non sarebbe atto ad ammaestrarli, perche non s'intenderiano l'uno con l'altro, ma p[er] quelli, che sanno qualche p[ri]ncipio vale molto p[er] ridurli à p[er]fett[io]ne quando in loro vi sia l'applicat[io]ne Q[ue]sto frequenta la casa. Non ha però stanza applicata p[er] tenervi la scola; ne q[ue]sta vi è, chi riccorre a lui, l'ammaestra, chi non vi và, non è da lui ne ripreso, ne ricercato; Non è però q[ue]sto senza li suoi contrarij ben grandi; egli è dedito al Vino in modo, che resta frequentiss[imamen]te da quello vinto, e con l'età, che si và avanzando, q[ue]sto è vitio, che sempre cresce. Veste l'habito di dervis, ch'è come di religioso, niente però egli è scropuloso della sua legge, et è concetto universale, che ne di quella, ne di altre molto si curi, il che causa, che in tanti anni, che lui serve la Casa non habbi mai detto parola ad alcuno de suoi scolari toccante le cose di religione, ò di p[er]suasione veruna al mahometismo, come potrebbe far facilmente chi ne fosse molto Zelante": SDispC, filza 32, unfoliated (7 June 1641).

69. "E perche hanno grand[emen]te bisogno li Giovani di lingua, massime quelli del Paese, d'apprender bene il parlar Italiano, co'l quale poi più facilmente si perfettionano nel turco, essendo, che il Coza, per altro valoroso nell'Idioma turco, Persiano, & Arabo, niente intende il Franco, e così non sapendo ne'l uno, ne'l altro la forza dei vocaboli, et il vero loro significato, vengono li giovani à perder li due ò tre primi anni dei loro studij, ò li passano con poco profitto: Raccordiamo con ogni riverenza, per com[mand]am[en]te necess[ari]o, il proveder essi Giovani di soggetto, che gl'instruisca nella lingua Italiana, et gl'insegni anco à scriver con buona frase, & carattere, che molto importa per le traduttioni di lettere, et

altre scritture, che si mandano da Ven[eti]a, et?oda gl'Ecc[ellentissi]mi Baili si scrivono: Questo soggetto potria essere ò il Capellano dell'attuale Ecc[ellentissi] mo Bailo, con qualche augumento di salario, ò alcuno dei Padri Franciscani, ò dominicani, che si mandano à Const[antinopo]li, che come sudditi godono anco certo annuo den[er]o, che gli paga il Cottimo di V[ost]ra Ser[enità]; Et potria in tal caso nell'esped[itio]ni ricercar li superiori, che à q[ue]sto effetto ne mandassero alcuo versato partic[olarmen]te in belle lettere, & nelle più proprie cond[itio]ni per tal ministerio": SDispC, filza 32, unfoliated (5 August 1641).

70. SDispC, b. 24, 82r (2 February 1642 m.v.).

71. SDispC, b. 139, 614v (23 September 1655), b. 140, 132v (23 November 1655), 133r (13 December 1655).

72. Collegio, Risposte di dentro, b. 43, unfoliated (18 September 1652).

73. Hitzel 2013, 28.

74. Lucchetta 1989, 21.

75. SDispC, b. 11, fasc. 23, 135r–v (8 June 1577).

76. SDispC, reg. 18, unfoliated (2 September 1627).

77. On the early French efforts to emulate the Venetian model of dragoman apprenticeship in Istanbul, see Hitzel 2013.

78. Baranowski 1949, 67–68.

79. Baranowski, 69–71.

80. Degros 1984; Hossain 1992; Hitzel 1995; Testa and Gautier 2003.

81. The Dutch, for example, sought to inculcate "loyalty" and channel the emotional attachments of the East Indies-born children of colonial officers to the metropole and away from Java, by forcing parents to send their sons to be educated in the Netherlands for many years before they were allowed to return to Java and assume a government position there. The French in Algeria, on the other hand, sought to establish local schools modeled on Islamic madrasas, where the sons of urban notables could be trained for careers in the colonial administration and promote a "Franco-Islamic alliance." On the East Indies, see Sutherland 2010; on Algeria, Christelow 1985.

82. Rathkolb 2004; Petritsch 2005; Wolf 2005; Do Paço 2019b. As Alastair Hamilton (2009, 241) notes, however, the Viennese Academy differed from its counterparts elsewhere in that it did not aim simply to train competent translators but to provide "the best education Austria had to offer. Besides mastering social accomplishments such as drawing, dancing, fencing and riding, they studied philosophy, logic, mathematics, physics, law, French, Italian, Latin, Greek, history and geography in addition to eastern languages (Turkish, Persian and Arabic). They could aspire to patents of nobility and to be ambassadors and statesmen."

83. Cáceres-Würsig 2012.

84. De Groot 1978; Hacker 1987; Bashan 1993; Berridge 2004.

85. As Yosef Hacker (1987, 41) notes, Jews (and, we should add, Armenians and Greeks) were better represented among consular dragomans in provincial settings

than among embassy dragomans in Istanbul, where Catholics tended to dominate the profession, with the exception of the Dutch legation.

86. "Pour ce qui concerne mes études en la langue turke, j'ai fait à Constantinople les mêmes choses que j'avois faites en Perse. J'ai eu des maîtres de langue, d'écriture, et de musique, j'ai fréquenté les savans, j'ai lu plusieurs bons livres en prose et en vers. Je me suis appliqué à entendre toutes sortes d'actes de justice, de finances et de chicane, même d'arithmétique, de philosophie et autres sciences, et j'ai étudié en dernier lieu le livre d'un savant homme, intitulé le parfait Secrétaire qui contient des lettres de tous Styles et de tous caractères pour rois, princes, vizyrs, amis, ennemis, et toutes autres sortes de conditions. Enfin j'ai tâché de savoir tout ce que l'on peut apprendre de cette langue et de ses différens caractères eu Qrmalı, Sulsy et Dyvany, et pour faire un plein exercice de ce que j'avois appris, j'ai traduit polir M. l'ambassadeur Nointel quantité de pièces Curieuses dont il m'a chargé, entre lesquelles étoient toutes les lettres écrites ci-devant de France à la Porte Othomane et de la Porte à la cour de France, qui composoient un gros volume, et plusieurs autres livres dans les langues que je savois, dont ce seigneur a rendu compte à la cour": Pétis de la Croix 1810 [1684?], 164–65.

87. Tuşalp Atiyas 2017.

88. Darakcıoğlu 2010, 51–57.

89. Likewise, dragomans of the Ottoman tributary states of Ragusa, Moldavia, Transylvania, and Wallachia often served as their states' top political functionaries in Istanbul. Miović 2001; Luca 2003b; Zecevic 2014; Kármán 2018.

90. SDispC, reg. 7, 27v and 38v (11 January 1585 m.v. and 10 May 1586); Gioveni's petition for a raise two years later, where he narrates his father's accomplishments, is in SDispC, b. 28, 67r–68v (24 September 1588, endorsed by the Senate on 11 March 1589).

91. BaC, b. 371, unfoliated (29 September 1619).

92. On Istanbulite dragomans' role in Venetian-Ottoman border negotiations in Dalmatia, see Poumarède 2020, 451–59 passim.

93. Rothman 2011a, 165–86. Although far less stringent in its citizenship requirements, the Habsburg monarchy also tended to appoint as dragomans in Vienna men who had long sojourned in Ottoman lands, either on private business or as formal apprentice dragomans in its legation in Istanbul. Wolf 2005.

94. De Luca 2011; Eufe 2003; Papadia-Lala 2009.

95. Krstić 2011b; Aydin 2007.

96. These included Tripoli, Jerusalem, Aleppo, Damascus, Cairo, Crete, Cyprus, the Peloponnese, Skyros, Timişoara, Budin, and Belgrade. Provincial dragoman titles included "Trablus Sancakbeyinin Tercümanı"; "Kudüs Subaşısı yanında tercüman"; "Kudüsi Şerif'te Rum Tercümanı"; "Arap Tercümanı"; "Girit Adası Tercümanlığı"; "Kıbrıs Divan Tercümanı"; "Mora Tercümanı"; "Sakız Tercümanı"; "Kandiye reaya tercümanı"; "Halep Tercümanı." Balcı 2006, 18. The lack of standardization of titles (some referring to territory, others to languages, other

still to specific communities) may indicate a rather haphazard system of dragoman recruitment and advancement, not unlike Venetian practice in its own maritime Greek-and Slavic-speaking colonies.

97. Balcı, 20–21.

98. Philliou 2011, 11; Balcı 2006, 26–7.

99. De Groot 1997; Heywood 2000; Van den Boogert 2005a; Castiglione 2014.

Chapter 2: Kinshipping

1. "L'havere i dragomani accasati a questa parte si deve considerare di non poco pregiuditio e impedimento a publici riguardi: come restano sgravati dall'abitacione del bailo cosi lo sono anche l'interesse, tutto lo studio e applicatione stando rivolta alle loro famiglie, quali, essendo stabilite in terra de Turchi, li obligano percio a circospettioni e risserve": quoted in Lucchetta 1984, 24.

2. The sixteenth-century Ottoman sequin coin was roughly equivalent to the Venetian gold ducat, with which it agreed in weight (3.5 grams).

3. "[I]n segno della satisfattione, che la Rep[ubbli]ca n[ost]ra hà delli servitij, che in diverse importanti occ[asi]oni, egli le hà prestati, et della p[ro]ntezza, che dimostra di voler continuar nel med[esi]mo p[er] l'avvenire . . . essendo à proposito del s[er]vicio publico il gratificarlo poiche è benissimo noto à cadauno, che essendo questo soggetto in grado principale à questa porta, puo fare molti importanti servitij, come ne hà fatti p[er] il passato, sicome si è inteso p[er] le l[ette]re del p[redet]to baylo n[ost]ro et di altri suoi p[re]cessori": SDelC, reg. 7, f. 71r. The vote was overwhelmingly in favor, with 140 ayes, six nays, and thirteen abstentions.

4. Not much is known about Hürrem Bey's personal life, but his enduring ties to the Venetian bailate and his multipronged diplomatic and spying maneuverings are fairly well attested. A manuscript of his Italian-language "Memoyre sur ung grand faict d'armes succedé à Servan combattant contre les Persans" is preserved in a compilation of diplomatic correspondence from the Porte dated to late 1578–1579 in BnF, Anc. 8078(3), Suppl. Fr. 503. That he spied for the French ambassador on other occasions is also suggested by a 1577 copy of an 'arz issued by the viceroy of Algiers in favor of a certain Süleyman Çavuş ("Soliman Chaoulx") and translated by Hürrem for the benefit of the French ambassador. Castries 1905, 356. Hürrem Bey was also on the Spanish king's payroll and played a significant role in the clandestine negotiations between the Habsburg representative Giovanni Margliani and the Ottoman grand vizier Sokollu Mehmed Paşa, described in some detail in Malcolm 2015, 227–74. For this and similar services King Philip II paid Hürrem 500 ducats annually beginning in 1573. Recently published account books of the Imperial Resident for 1581–1583 similarly attest to Hürrem Bey's annual payments of 100–400 taler: Graf 2016, 27, 59, 94–95. Gürkan (2015, 112–13) offers additional details of Hürrem's varied diplomatic exploits.

5. "Si è intesa dalle lettere del Baylo nostro in Cost.li de 30 Gennaro passato la humile supplicat.ne del fedel n'stro Pasqual Naon Dragom.o in constantin.li, che in questa occasione del maritar di una sua figliuola, gli sia usata dalla sig.a N'ra quella benignità, che è solita usare verso li Dragomani suoi, et che ha usato altre volte verso la sua propria persona in caso tale": Senato, Mar, Filza 104, unfoliated (24 June 24 1589).

6. An expenditure report attached to secretary Giovanni Battista Ballarino's dispatch to the Senate in 1655—and evidently loosely based on Ballarino's cash ledger studied below—lists, inter alia, gifts of twelve robes of *raso lattesin* (deep blue satin), crystals, and flowers from Bologna to "the sister of apprentice drago-man Michele Parada, who is marrying Peruca Silvestri, who had invited Ballarino to the wedding": SDispC, filza 139, 614v (19 September 1655). Another entry the following month mentions a gift to "the wife of dragoman Zuanne Olivieri, who had invited Ballarino to hold one of her daughters at baptism": SDispC, filza 139, 616r (17 October 1655). Tobias Graf (2016, 65, doc. 9, it. 14) notes a similar pattern of gifting on the occasion of marriage of an employee's offspring in the Imperial ambassador's account books.

7. Shryock, Trautmann, and Gamble 2011, 32.

8. On court physicians' roles in early modern Istanbulite diplomacy, see Arbel 1995b, 77–86; Lucchetta 1997; Luca 2015; Pugliano 2019.

9. A similar phenomenon can be seen in these families' incorporation into urban elites elsewhere in the region, as Malcolm (2015, 362–78) demonstrates in the case of the Bruttis' and Borisis' integration through marriage into the Capodistrian elite a generation earlier.

10. On Skovgaard's illustrious career and untimely death as both an Ottoman court physician and a Venetian spy, see Luca 2015.

11. Amelicheva 2016, 90, 127–28.

12. "Les choses estant en ce bon estat, Votre Excellence a envoyé Fornetty son drogman Grec de nation [1] dans une Eschelle où il y a un Consul françois qui n'a point de relation avec les Grecs, qui a postulé pendant 30 ans et qui a soutenu cette affaire avec facilité jusqu'alors a qui Fornetty se cacha dans son capot disant qu'il estoit un Arabe et me remit deux pacquets de Votre Excellence dans lesquels il n'est pas parlé de la commission de Fornetty pour Scio et de ma maison consulaire": Archives Nationales de France, Affaires Étrangères, B/I, vol. 382, ff. 182r–v (30 July 1696). Although the file is dated to 1696, Châteneuf's term in office ended in 1692, making the precise date of this correspondence difficult to determine. I thank Cesare Santus for bringing this case to my attention and for providing the transcription.

13. "[1] Qu'entend-il quand il dit que le sieur Fornetty est Grec de Nation? Veut-il dir qu'il est du rit Grec? Cela n'est pas vray, il fait profession de la Religion Catholique Apostolique et Romaine, dans laquelle tous ses ayeux ont esté elevez, ont vecu et son morts. Veut-il dire qu'il est né en Grèce? Il pourroit sans aucune ménagement dire qu'il est né en Turquie, mais cela ne concluroit pas qu'il fût Grec

ny Turc. Il est d'ancienne famille originaire des Gesnes, ses pères ont eu l'honneur de servir le Roy et sans interruption de père en fils en qualité de premier drogmans auprès des ambassadeurs de Sa Majesté a la Porte depuis environ 150 ans: son bisayeul avoit un brevet de cette charge du Roy Henry Trois. C'est par une suitte de cet attachement qui les a retenus et establis en ce Pays et que le sieur Fornetty y est né, et bien long que ce soit une chose a luy reprocher il croit au contraire qu'elle luy est honorable et le petits fils des drogmans françois qui sont aujourd'huy a la Porte seront dans le mesme cas où il se trouve quant a la naissance s'ils sont destinez au mesme employ": Quoted in Eldem 2016, 136.

14. BaC, 373, unfoliated (2 June 1682).

15. Testa and Gautier 2013, 131n1.

16. Archivio di Stato Vaticano, Segreteria di Stato, Venezia, 118, f. 649, quoted in Sangalli 2016, 109n31.

17. Collegio, Risposte di dentro, b. 35, unfoliated (20 December 1644); Faroqhi 1986, 367. On early-seventeenth-century Ottoman magistrates' and Venetian diplomats' differing conceptions regarding dragomans' intent to naturalize, see Goffman 2002, 175.

18. Collegio, Risposte di dentro, b. 40, unfoliated (18 June 1649). Significantly, Vecchia made no references to his wife or children in Pera either in his will of 1659 or in a 1655 petition from Istanbul requesting a monthly stipend for his sister in Venice. Notarile, Testamenti, b. 261, 131r–132r (21 November 1659); Senato, Mar, Filza 419, unfoliated (14 February 1654 m.v.).

19. Quoted in Coller 2010, 456. On eighteenth-century French efforts to prevent nationals from marrying or cohabiting with Ottoman Christian (especially Orthodox) women—a clear indication of the pervasiveness of this phenomenon—see also Celetti 2017.

20. Lucchetta 1984, 61.

21. Galland 1881, 59–64.

22. Galland 1881, 63, cited in Barbu 2015, 74n74. The family's Orthodox ties were consolidated further in the next generation, when their daughter Maria married Adam Kálnoky, then the Moldavian Boyard Constantin de Neniul.

23. Family History Library, microfilm roll 1037132, Santa Maria Draperis, Baptizatorum Liber Primus (=FHL, Bapt I), 56.

24. The church, overseen by Franciscans and closely associated with the Venetian community, had a tumultuous history, and was built and rebuilt numerous times from the late-sixteenth to the mid-eighteenth century. In fact, the origins of the parish record books in 1662 coincide with the relocation of the parish to Pera in the wake of the physical church's destruction in its previous location in Galata in the great fire of 1660. It remained a bastion of Pera's Catholic elites in the eighteenth century as well, when powerful local families regularly had their daughters marry sojourning apprentice dragomans from other metropoles. Baer 2004b. 171; Girardelli 2005; Do Paço 2018, 12.

25. FHL, Bapt I, 16.

26. FHL, Bapt I, 24.

27. The discussion that follows focuses on what domestic slavery can tell us about dragomans rather than about the institution of slavery itself, and inevitably provides only limited insights on the perspectives of the enslaved. The choice of nomenclature (e.g., "enslaved persons" rather than "slaves") cannot compensate for the historiographical weight of centuries of documentary practices and analytical lenses that have privileged the masters' perspective. It seeks, however, to call attention to the varied experiences of those who were trafficked and forced to labor and live as chattel but who also, in the words of Veruschka Wagner (2020, 232) "actively shaped the relationship to their masters, had an impact on the decisions they made, and influenced processes like manumissions and donations." For an illuminating discussion of the nomenclatural challenge, see Gac et al. 2010. I thank Tamara Walker for the reference and helpful suggestions.

28. Wilkins 2013; Sobers-Khan 2014; Wagner 2020.

29. Failure to record the status of an enslaved person may not have been pervasive in the parish records of Santa Maria Draperis, but does seem to have characterized the baptismal records of at least one other Galata church, the Dominican Church of SS Peter and Paul. This obviously makes it difficult to determine who among the baptized were enslaved, let alone which households they belonged to. I am grateful to Nur Sobers-Khan for sharing records from the archives of that church with me. For an inventory, see Palacios 2002, 2003.

30. FHL, Bapt I, 5–6.

31. FHL, Bapt I, 78, 81, 85.

32. FHL, Bapt I, 67.

33. FHL, Bapt I, 71 (1 March 1690). Antonio Piron and Smaragda Fortis married in 1680. Antonio's elder brother Giovanni died in 1687, and it is conceivable that Antonio's son was named after him, which would make him no older than three at the time of this baptism.

34. FHL, microfilm roll 1037132, Santa Maria Draperis, Mortuorum Liber Primus (=FHL, Mort I), 24.

35. FHL, Bapt I, 41 (21 October 1682), 44 (7 March 1683), 45 (14 March and 16 April 1683), 46 (25 April 1683), 47 (13 June 1683), 48 (26 September 1683), 49 (29 September 1683).

36. FHL, Mort I, 23 (23 April 1682).

37. FHL, microfilm roll 1037132, Santa Maria Draperis, Conjugatorium Liber Primus (=FHL, Conj I), 5 (26 November 1690).

38. FHL, Conj I, 5.

39. FHL, Conj I, 17 (1 February 1693), 18 (29 May 1695), 20–21 (12 April 1698), 21 (7 June 1699), 29 (5 May 1709).

40. Rothman 2012b; Wilkins 2013; McKee 2014.

41. Wilkins 2013.

42. For the wedding of "Giovanni Tedesco" (Johannes of Germany), formerly enslaved by Francesco Perone of Naples, and Elena Tedesca (Elena of Germany),

formerly enslaved by the grand dragoman to the Porte Alessandro Mavrocordato on February 2, 1698, see FHL, Conj I, 20.

43. Wilkins (2013, 349) notes a seventeenth-century surge in domestic slavery throughout Ottoman urban centers, encompassing the households of "both military and non-military social elites."

44. On master-slave sexual relations in the early modern Mediterranean and the methodological challenges of studying them, see McKee 2014.

45. FHL, Bapt I, 19, 22 (8 March 1676), 22 (17 December 1677), 23 (9 February 1678).

46. Peirce 1993, 6–7.

47. Başbakanlık Osmanlı Arşivleri, Ecnebi Defterleri (=BOA, ED) 13, 28, item 244 (undated, but ca. July 1608); 34, item 313 (14 [18] Cemaziyelahir 1018 AH [18 September 1609]).

48. On the Piron family's shipping prowess and close ties with both Venetian and Ottoman political elites, see Dursteler 2006, 147–49.

49. Van den Boogert 2009a.

50. BaC, b. 264, fasc. 2, 86r–87v (13 February 1585).

51. BaC, b. 287, fasc. 417, 20r–21v (18 July 1639–18 April 1641).

52. BaC, b. 317, fasc. "Atti Ballarino," 6v (18 November 1658), cited in Luca 2008a, 148–49.

53. BaC, b. 351, fasc. 3, 13r–v (12 August 1660), cited in Luca 2008a, 150–51.

54. BaC, B. 373 II, 35 (2 May 1675) cited in Luca 2008a, 158.

55. Luca 2013, 45 and 53–55 provides a full transcription of Tommaso Tarsia's will and related documents.

56. Gioia was the granddaughter of Mateca Salvago, niece of Giuliano, Gianesin, and Giovanni Battista Salvago, wife of Stefano Testa, and aunt of Pietro and Giacomo Fortis and of Antonio Coressi, all dragomans at one point or another. Eventually, in her effort to make the bailo pay for much-needed repairs to the house, in early 1666 she rented part of the compound to Mustafa Çelebi, a tutor of the daughter of the late Ottoman majordomo Bayram Ağa, much to the Venetians' embarrassment and discomfort. A translation of Mustafa Çelebi's rent contract was attached to the bailo Giacomo Querini's dispatch on 11 June 1672. Bertelè 1932, 232n18. Pedani (2013, 30–32) summarizes these negotiations.

57. BaC, b. 265, unfoliated (March 13–April 10, 1587).

58. BaC, b. 276, 237r–v (3 July 1610). On early modern Ottoman jurisdictional plurality, see Van den Boogert 2009b; on the broader questions this plurality raises for the study of trans-imperial dynamics, see Calafat 2019.

59. BaC, b. 369, it. 53 ("Casa Bailaggia"), "Raggioni pub[blich]e contro le pretese . . . della famiglia del Testa" (unfoliated, undated, ca. 1678). The context of these repairs was conveniently forgotten years later, when a new dispute erupted between the bailo and Caterina's heirs over ownership of the bailate. That the Venetian government rather than Salvago paid for the repairs served as key evidence in claiming that the property was owned by Venice, and that Salvago had

been only a pro forma owner to avoid the eventuality of confiscation in wartime. Pedani 2013, 31.

60. Olivieri 2010, 59–60.

61. BaC, b. 317, fasc. "Atti Ballarino 1658–1663," 6v (cited in Luca 2008a, 148–49).

62. BaC, b. 301, fasc. (I) 455, 1r (9 July 1681), 2r (2 August 1681), 3r (9 January 1681 m.v.). Gioggia's death on 9 February 1682 is mentioned on fol. 9l.

63. E.g., "Vesta una ormesin verde data ad una figliola del gia Dragoman Boris[i] p[er] li meriti di suo padre": BaC, b. 301, fasc. (II) 456, 32r (24 May 1625); "Al figliolo picolo del q. Boris[i] Dragomano vesta una": BaC, b. 301, fasc. (II) 456 31r (12 April 1625).

64. "Scovette" (*scopette*, or *scoette* in Venetian) were small dusters or brooms for sweeping, made of sorghum or dogwood.

65. BaC, b. 301, fasc. (II) 456, 38r, 39l, 40r, 41r, 42r, 43r, 44r. The last two items were only gifted to some recipients.

66. BaC, b. 301, fasc. (II) 456, 41r. The chief equestrian is described as "a man much loved by the Grand Signor."

67. According to Eric Dursteler, Orlandi was a prominent merchant from Bergamo based in Istanbul in the 1610s. His business dealings and commercial litigations appear regularly in the bailate chancery records, and he was also a member of the Council of Twelve—the bailo's "advisory board" that comprised prominent Istanbulite merchants claiming Venetian subjecthood. Orlandi appears to have petitioned the Venetian government for full citizenship, though the outcome of that application is unknown. (Dursteler, personal communication.) A Venetian ship belonging to an Orlandi—quite possibly Giambattista—was attacked by corsairs near Milos and taken to Izmir in early 1626; see Pedani 1994, 358–59 (#1334/cc. 48–50).

68. BaC, b. 301, fasc. (II) 456, 33r.

69. E.g., twice on fol. 40l in entries for gloves and perfumes, and once on fol. 40r for civet pelts.

70. That inviting the bailo to serve as the baptismal godparent for dragomans' children would become customary in the following decades is well attested by Antonio Olivieri, who describes a similar ritual for the child of Navon's grandson and namesake in 1701 ("com'il solito esser compare a un dragomano veneto, come a tenir una creatura al fonte"): Olivieri 2010, 56.

71. Pedani 1994, 135; Pedani and Bombaci 2010, 184 (773: VIII: 6).

72. On Nicolò, see Eufe 2003, 28. The Coressis' entanglements with bailate dragomans endured throughout the seventeenth century. Giovanni Battista Salvago's niece, Elisabetta, married another Coressi and, in 1675, petitioned for her son Antonio to be admitted as an apprentice dragoman, explicitly invoking the names of her four Salvago dragoman uncles as her inspiration. Documenti Turchi (=DT), b. 15, lt. 1604 (c. 1675). Another branch of the Coressi family wound up in Venice, where a certain Nicolò, son of Theodore of Crete, settled in 1642 and became the

president of the Greek confraternity in 1678. Koutmanis 2013, 194n86. A Nicolò Coressi, possibly the same one, served as the *ragionato* (accountant) under the Governor-General of Corfu, Girolamo Corner, in 1682–83, where he compiled a list of alms disbursed to several hundred Cretan refugee families. Mertzios 1951, 21, 31.

73. Members of the *famiglia alta* and of the ambassador's retinue appear as recipients of shirts throughout the cash ledgers. On 4 April 1624 four bailate drag-omans and three apprentice dragomans, along with the personal physicians and secretaries of the ambassador and the bailo, received one satin shirt each. Other shirts were given to all bailate staff, including dragomans and apprentices, two days later. The following December long breeches and shirts were prepared for two interpreters hired in Corfu upon the dragoman Brutti's death, Adamo da Corfu and Vassili dall Parga. BaC, b. 301, fasc. (II) 456, 34r–35r.

74. On semiotic fractal recursivity see Irvine and Gal 2000.

75. Quoted in Lucchetta 1997, 26.

76. Senato, Mar, reg. 37, 213 (27 December 1566); Compilazione Leggi, b. 146, unfoliated (21 October 1622); SDispC, reg. 19, fasc. 2, 57v (11 September 1630); reg. 23, fasc. 2, 51r (30 August 1636); filza 32, unfoliated (5 August 1641); SDispC, b. 124, 524v, 525r (8 October 1643), b. 139, 613r–v (1655); Cinque Savii, seconda serie, b. 61, fasc. 1, unfoliated (20 September 1695).

77. SDispC, reg. 19, fasc. 2, 8v (6 April 1630).

78. BaC 301 fasc II 456, 27r–34r at 34r; SDispC, filza 138, 374r–382v (1654).

79. SDispC, reg. 15 (29 March 1624), reg. 18, 78v (2 September 1627), filza 32, unfoliated (17 June 1641); Sacerdoti 1937, xi–xiii.

80. Ghobrial 2014a, 73; Salzmann 2000; Wasti 2005. On multidirectional cere-monial gifts, see Reindl-Kiel 2009.

81. This large northern falcon was especially prized by Ottoman elites as a hunting bird. Shehada forthcoming.

82. "Vestiti honorevolmente": CCD, LAC, b. 5, 73 (9 April 1579).

83. "Dovendo nel comparire nel Divano, et alle porte de Grandi à Const.li ve-stire con molta spese conforme all'uso del Paese, per publica riputatione, et per haver l'ingresso facile al trattare li negocij publici, rendersi grato segondo le oc-correnze": SDispC, reg. 14, 66r (26 July 1622).

84. "L'obligo di vestir degnam[en]te": Collegio, Risposte di dentro, b. 18, unfoli-ated (18 October 1627). "Le veste ordinarie p[er] comparir davanti ministri turchi": Collegio, Risposte di dentro, b. 26, unfoliated (22 November 1635). "Difficilmente posso durar in Costantinopoli con profession cospicua all' uso dispendioso di Corte": SDispC, b. 124, 539v (8 October 1643); BaC, b. 263, fasc. 2.1, 80v; SDispC, reg. 14, 65v (26 July 1622); SDispC, b. 104, 171r (12 May 1627), b. 118, 727v (9 Janu-ary 1637 m.v.), Collegio, Risposte di dentro, b. 18, unfoliated (25 January 1627 m.v.), b. 34, unfoliated (10 April 1643).

85. "Quattro vestiti, che pure vagliono à corrispondere al decoro della carica che sostento di pub[li]co Ser[vito]re e Ministro": Collegio, Risposte di dentro, b. 40, unfoliated (18 June 1643).

86. SDispC, b. 138, 374r–382v (21 October 1654). On Venetian textile terminology, see Newton 1988; Vitali 1992.

87. DT, b. 13, fasc. 1485 (1–10 April 1642). According to Pedani (2002, 92), the first permission for Venetian interpreters to dress as Ottoman subjects while on mission was granted during the War of Crete (1645–1669), further highlighting the unprecedented nature of Salvago's safe-conduct.

88. Tijana Krstić, personal communication.

89. Allerston 2000; Johnson 2005.

90. "Il n'est pas douteux que l'habillement oriental les confound avec les Rayas, et les fait regarder pour ce qu'ils ne sont pas. Les Puissances se méprennent tous les jours à cet extérieur, et très peu d'entre eux savent, très peu même veulent croire que nos Drogmans sont véritablement François. [. . .] On a vu souvent les Drogmans arrêtés pour le Carach et quand le Carachy s'est assuré qu'ils étoient François et exempts du tribute, il s'est contenté d'alléguer que ç'a été une méprise, et qu'après tout on ne peut lire sur le front d'un François habillé à la turque son nom ni son pais": Quoted in Testa and Gautier 1991, 20–21.

91. Van den Boogert 2005a, 65–66.

92. De Groot 2000, 246.

93. Keane 1997; Keane 2005.

94. "Li schiavi del nostro Imperatore non hanno bisogno d'esser vestiti da chi fà guerra seco": SDispC, 144, 18v–19r (15 July 1660).

95. "Con espressioni di stima del suo merito e brama di farle cimentar à tempo proprio con piu vivi effetti la sincera disposit.ne della Ser.ma Rep.ca verso di lui": SDispC, 144, 18v.

96. "Si è dimostrato oltrettanto pieno di affetto e di fede, che di valore": SDispC, reg. 23, fasc. 2, 58r (17 September 1636).

97. Albèri 1839 II, 185, quoted in Bertelè 1932, 122–23.

98. Mallett 1994, 235–36; Frigo 2008.

99. CCD, LAC, b. 4, 102r (20 July 1573). On garments as customary gifts in foreign diplomats' visits to Ottoman officials, see IS, b. 418, unfoliated (10 January 1663 m.v.). On the circulation of Italian silken cloth among Ottoman elite households, see Mackie 2001.

100. Albèri 1839, 104. Rüstem Paşa was a grand vizier and son-in-law of Sultan Süleyman the Lawgiver (1520–1566).

101. For Burke's description of his conversation with a tax collector in Alexandria, "a French gentleman who turned Turk" ("un Cauagliere Francese fatto Turco") who "listened to me while I spoke in French, but answered me through his dragoman, a Jew" ("egli mi ascoltaua mentre parlauo Francese, ma mi rispondeua per via d'vn Hebreo suo dragomano"), see De Burgo 1686, 192.

102. Arnauld and Nicole 1674, 649–50.

103. On the political and theological background of these publications, see Voulgaropoulou 2018. My deep thanks to Margarita Voulgaropoulou for alerting me to Tarsia's testimony and its context.

104. Arnauld and Nicole 1674, 645–47, at 647.
105. Gilbert 2020, 9.

Chapter 3: Inscribing the Self

1. *kuloğlu*, Turkish for "son of [the sultan's] slaves."
2. "Li turchi Asiatici, spacciati in Costantinopoli per rozi e rustici a paragon d'Europei, cimentati questi da gli Ottomani per valorosi e quelli per vili, non sono per ciò alla Porta ammessi, nè tra le militia nè tra li Ministri, in Barbaria, con tuttociò, avendo maggioranze e preminenze. Da tale differenza si può credere che nasca in Turchi Barbareschi un odio intestine colla Porta Ottomana loro ripudiatrice, e però, abbandonando i Turchi le natie capanne e l'aratro, corrono in fretta a nobilitarsi in Barbaria ove possono con More accasarsi et i suoi figli detti Culogli, cioè figli di soldati, subentrano al Padre ma, per la correlatione della madre Mora, come spurii in un certo modo e degeneri, non sono pregiati quanto i rinegati et i Turchi primitive. Questa mistione di rinegati e Turchi fa una tertia spetie di Turchi che parlano in Italiano e Castigliano. Li rinegati non capiscono la non vista grandezza Ottomana e li Turchi non aspettano da quella nè honori nè cariche, onde non è meraviglia se mancano di obedienza effettiva, in bocca sol professata": Salvago 1937 [1625], 78.
3. De Vivo 2011.
4. Motsch 2011, 212.
5. Galland 1881; Osman Ağa 1980; Tott 1784; Hammer-Purgstall 1940. On Rozsnyai, see Kármán 2016, 206 and its bibliography; on Zarini, see Miović-Perić 1995.
6. Benetti 1688.
7. Olivieri 2010. Olivieri, born and raised in Pera, was the son of the dragoman Giovanni Olivieri, nephew of the dragomans Giovanni Antonio Grillo and Marcantonio Borisi, and cousin of the dragoman Giovanni Battista Navon, all Venetian employees. His grandfather Olivier and brother Domenico served as French dragomans, while his brother-in-law, Francesco (Draco) Testa, served as a Dutch dragoman. Olivieri's nonlinear narrative offers fascinating glimpses into dragomans' daily lives in the second half of the seventeenth century.
8. The travelogue spans about thirty-four double-sided folios and survives in two manuscripts, a draft and a fair copy, both in Zadar State Archives, Mletački Dragoman, filza 109, items 1–2. These manuscripts are bundled with dozens of other writings by the dragoman Giambattista Calavrò-Imberti, all awaiting further study.
9. De Vivo 2011; Motsch 2011.
10. On entextualization, see Silverstein and Urban 1996.
11. De Vivo 2011, 32.
12. SDispC, b. 81, 18 (19 March 1616), 343r–345r (20 August 1616).

13. On early modern Islamicate travel genres, see, for example, Matar 2003; Alam and Subrahmanyam 2007.

14. Scholarship on Ottoman travel narratives in general, and diplomatic reports in particular, is only emerging. See Agai et al. 2013.

15. On polyphony as a compositional principle, see Bakhtin 1981.

16. On multiple mediations in the production of European perspectives on Ottoman lifeworlds, see also O'Quinn 2019, 18.

17. On the process of strategic suppression of difference see Woolard 1998; Woolard and Genovese 2007.

18. On this transition and its periodization, see Stagl 1995.

19. De Vivo 2007, 69.

20. As Paz further clarifies, "genre" is understood here as "a practice rather than the form of the text," but institutionalization can lead to the alterity becoming "typified and naturalized in ways that threaten to neutralize the boundary," making ongoing rearticulation necessary. Paz, personal communication.

21. To be sure, a trans-imperial perspective (combining distance and familiarity, self-awareness about written and oral modes of knowledge production) was inherent not only to dragomans' relazioni but to diplomatic writing from Istanbul more generally. This is evident from any casual reading of Venetian diplomatic *dispacci* (dispatches) from the Porte, where dragomans' daily interactions with Ottoman officials often are recorded in some detail and serve as the basis for much of the analysis of both current events and long-term political developments.

22. Berengo 1960.

23. For a partial list of surviving manuscripts in Italy, see Donazzolo 1928, 148–49. One of the manuscripts now in the Correr library in Venice seems to have been a copy prepared by Giacomo de Nores, who, while still enslaved, traveled to the Safavid frontier with his Ottoman master before being ransomed and arriving in Venice in 1587, where he eventually became a public dragoman. Donazzolo 1928, 148–49; Correr, Cod. Cicogna 1796; and, on de Nores, Chapter 6 below. Several of degli Alessandri's nine surviving Viennese copies seem to have arrived there shortly after the author read the text to the Venetian Senate—at least one bears the editorial marks of Sebastian Tengnagel, who served as Viennese court librarian from 1608. Hammer-Purgstall 1829, 616–17. At least a dozen copies of the text existed in French collections (mostly in the Royal Library in the Louvre) in the nineteenth century, as cataloged in Daru 1819, 691–92. At least nine copies survive in the British Library, mostly as part of early modern anthologies of Venetian diplomatic writings, i.e., Add MS 8290, 121v–145v; Add MS 8646, 41–51v; Add MS 16519, 125–152v; Add Ms 16543, 187–211v; Egerton MS 1087, 456–77; Harl. 3552, article 4, 214–40; Lansdowne 840.B, article 5, 75–85v; Royal 14.A.XIII, article 3, 95–120v; and Sloane 2908, the latter from among the papers of Engelbert Kaempfer. Kaempfer was a late-seventeenth-century German physicist and botanist, who collected, among other things, a series of contemporary travel accounts of Persia, likely in preparation for his own visit to and writings about Isfahan. A copy of

Alessandri's relazione also concludes the somewhat cryptically cataloged *Papeles varios políticos e históricos*, a compilation (mostly Italian, and occasionally Latin) of reports of foreign lands by Venetian state representatives originally kept in Philip V's library, and now in the Spanish National Library in Madrid, MSS 963, 261–86. Another late-sixteenth-century anthologized manuscript copy of the text, alongside Antonio Barbaro's, Giacomo Soranzo's, and Maffeo Venier's near contemporaneous relazioni from Istanbul, is kept in the University of Chicago Library's Special Collections Research Center, MS 1206. A French translation was anthologized in the *Recueil de relations venitiennes*, dating to the 1570s. BnF, Dupuy 769, 154–73. Both Italian and (abridged) English editions of the text—based on the manuscript in the Venetian State Archives—were printed in the nineteenth century as part of larger anthologies of travel narratives, e.g., Grey 1873. I have not been able to review these manuscripts, which await a detailed study.

24. Rota 2009a, 220.

25. Alessandri 1865 (1575), 160. This, and all subsequent citations of Alessandri refer to Berchet's print edition (1865), which reproduced the text previously printed in Alberì (Alessandri 1844) alongside other archival documents related to Alessandri's embassy to the Safavid court.

26. Sixteenth-and seventeenth-century Venetian relazioni from Istanbul averaged about double that, though they ranged widely, from under 1,000 words to over 48,000.

27. "io non dirò cosa che non abbia veduta, o che da relazione di diversi uomini degni di fede non mi sia stata detta con verità": Alessandri 1865. 168.

28. Alessandri 1865, 171.

29. Berchet 1865, 38.

30. On Ottoman petitioning, see Lafi 2011.

31. Babaie and Grigor 2015, 203.

32. Daniel 2001. On sacred kingship in Iranian history, see also Filipani-Ronconi 1978.

33. On Safavid political theology, see Babayan 1994.

34. Strathern 2014, 92.

35. On the extent to which sixteenth-century Venetian understandings of the Safavid Empire were beholden to official Ottoman accounts, see Cutillas Ferrer 2016.

36. "Vende esso re spesso gioje ed altre mercanzie, comprando e vendendo con quella sottilità che faria un mediocre mercante": Alessandri 1865, 174.

37. In a telling digression, Alessandri recounts the story of Kara Seraferin, an Ottoman merchant sojourning in Qazvin who is robbed by a group of Kurdish guards in the shah's employ. First he is thrown out in disbelief, and then, even once the truthfulness of his claims is proven in court, his money is expropriated to the shah's coffers, and justice is denied. Alessandri 1865, 171–72.

38. "Le donne sono per l'ordinario tutte brutte, ma di bellissimi lineamenti e nobili cere, sebbene i loro abiti non sono cosi attillati come quelli delle Turche": Alessandri 1865, 177–78.

39. Alessandri 1865, 181.

40. "le fabbriche sono bruttissime . . . ne' vi sono moschee ne' altro che possa render vaghe dette citta [. . .] Le strade sono brutte per la quantita' della polvere, e malamente vi si puo' andare, e conseguentemente l'inverno vi sono fanghi estremi": Alessandri 1865, 177.

41. Babaie and Grigor 2015. 185–88.

42. Gharipour 2017, 104.

43. See, for example, the descriptions of Isfahan in Ambrosio Bembo's journal, and the fifty-one line drawings by the French artist Guillaume Joseph Grélot that accompanied it, both based on direct eyewitnessing in the early 1570s. Interestingly, prior to traveling to Persia in the company of another merchant-diplomat, Jean Chardin, Grélot had spent the previous six years, from 1665 to 1671, in Istanbul, and his Ottoman sojourn clearly colored his representation of the Safavid world as well, as discussed in Welch 2007, 26–28.

44. Grey 1873, 167.

45. "è tutto giardini e mischite con volti biavi," "con marmari bell colorati," "una acqua molto bella," "quai meschita è tanto ben fabricata che né in terra del Turco né in tutta quanta la terra che ho visto, non ho ritrovato tal fabrica": Membré 1969, 58; English translation adapted from Membré 1993, 51.

46. Matthee 2011, 921. Bellingeri similarly notes how Venetian observations about the Safavids were often triangulated with those of the Ottomans, though in his interpretation the Safavids were generally read as "good Muslims" in contrast with the Ottoman "bad Muslims." As Alessandri's example shows, the dyadic relationship between Safavids and Ottomans, and the latter's understanding of the former, contributed to Venetian frameworks as well.

47. Veinstein 1992; Şahin 2013; Turan 2007; Tezcan 2010; Çipa and Fetvacı 2013.

48. E.g., "imperatori Ottomani" (168), "gli Ottomani" (169, 173, 181), "Ottomani" (181, 182), "imperatore Ottomano" (182).

49. E.g., "mercante Turco" (171), "[un] Turco" (173), "Il Turco" (179, 181, 182), "signorotti turchi" (182).

50. E.g., "Gisilbasci" in Ludovisi 1534, 24; "Chisil-bas" in Navagero 1553, 86; "Chizil-bas" in Trevisan 1554, 169; "Chisilpech" in Membré 1969 [1542], 35; "Chis-elbas" in Soranzo 1584, 290, and "chisillas" [sic] in Bernardo 1996 [1590], 350.

51. Among the Safavid offices that Alessandri silently glosses in Italian, without referring to a Persian or Turkish source term, are "consigliere del re" (169); "luogotenente del re" (174); "consiglio di stato" (175); "centurioni e capitani alla guardia del re" (176); "consiglio" (176); "sultani consiglieri" (176); "gran consiglieri" (176); and "capi di sestieri" (178).

52. "sultani, che non vuol dir altro che signori principali della milizia" (168); "sultanali che s'intendono essere governi delle provincie" (176); "sultani, uomini di esperienza e d'intelligenza nelle cose e governo di stato" (176). Other glossed terms include "caramè" (harem), "franchi" (Franks), "visiri" (viziers), and "*kurdi*" (Kurds). On the polysemy of "sultan" in Safavid usages see Güngörürler 2016, 53.

53. Sacerdoti 1937, xi.

54. DT, b. 13, fasc. 1485 (30 April 1642). Salvago acquired another similar safe-conduct in March 1645, although he apparently never used it.

55. He must have acquired some reputation for his studies, for in 1631 he was sent to the Ottoman kapudan paşa (lord admiral), who had expressed his interest in cosmography and who had asked the bailo for a person knowledgeable in cartography with whom he could discuss some maps he owned: SDispC, reg. III, 257b (4 February 1630 m.v.). I thank Giorgio Rota for the reference.

56. Donazzolo 1928, 207.

57. For Salvago's narrative of the deposition of Osman II and its possible sources, see Chapter 6.

58. On the corsairing episodes that led to the mission, and the broader diplomatic contest that framed—and ultimately doomed—it, see White 2017, 140–60.

59. The full text of Salvago's relazione, based on the extant copy preserved in the Archivio di Stato of Venice and supplemented by additional relevant archival documents, was published by Alberto Sacerdoti in 1937, at the height of the Italian colonial venture in Africa. All page numbers for Salvago's relazione refer to that edition.

60. Although the vast majority of Venetian ambassadors were patricians, Salvago was not the first non-noble to be entrusted with delicate diplomatic assignments by the Venetian Senate, but rather followed in the footsteps of Alessandri and Membré, and was followed, in turn, by another Pera-born Catholic subject, Ippolito Parada, who in 1633 was sent to Algiers to recover the possessions of Ambassador Cornaro in Spain. Upon his return to Istanbul, Parada became an apprentice dragoman, but died of the plague a few months later. Cinque Savii, Risposte, b. 149, 54r (10 May 1633); SDispC, b. 118, 611r (17 October 1637).

61. MCC, Cod. Morosini-Grimani, b. 547, fasc. 12 (51 pages, unnumbered), and BNM, MSS It. VII, 7610.

62. Valensi 1993, 15.

63. Salvago 1937, 7–9.

64. It is this numerical information about enslaved Venetians that has received most scholarly attention to date, as in Davis 2001.

65. On the perpetuation of a distinctly Ottoman ruling elite in North Africa through the restriction of marriage to local women from the late sixteenth century onward, see Shuval 2000b, 330.

66. On Ottoman metropolitan elites' Orientalist vision of the Arab provinces, albeit in a significantly later context, see Makdisi 2002.

67. On the Northern seaboard powers in the Mediterranean, see Fusaro 1996; Goffman 1998; Greene 2002. Salvago was, of course, not the only contemporary observer to note these alliances' significance; see, for example, the reports in early French periodicals in Turbet-Delof 1973, 15–16.

68. Salvago 1937, 75.

69. In Ottoman North Africa, this term usually referred to the male offspring of unions between local women and janissaries from the Ottoman heartland. Shuval 2000b, 331, Moalla 2004, 89.

70. Shuval 2000b, 327.

71. Pedani 2002, 95.

72. As discussed below, Tommaso Tarsia played a similar role a few decades later in elaborating the distinction between Turks and Ottomans.

73. "Chiamansi i corsari dalla provintia habitata Barbareschi, ma in effetto son una massa et una masnada di molte razze e generationi. Gli originarii furono Turchi e questi istituirono nuova militia di Gianiceri in Barbaria ordinando che, da Mori, Cingani et Ebrei in fuora, fossero ammesse tutte le Nationi": Salvago 1937, 77.

74. Here, as elsewhere, the issue is further complicated by the conflation of Turkish and Muslim, which was shared almost universally by Salvago's non-Ottoman contemporaries. Rothman 2011a, 198–247.

75. This perception is corroborated by the historiography. On the eclipsing of North Africa's indigenous Berber population by the occupying Ottomans, see Brett and Fentress 1996, 158–65. On the deep impact of the Ottomans on their North African provinces, see Shuval 2000a; Moalla 2004.

76. On the fraught relationship between the Ottoman janissary corps and the organization of the corsairs in Algiers, see Shuval 2000b, 328.

77. Salvago's erasure of North Africa's Roman past contrasts with later French colonial hyper-awareness of such legacies. Lorcin 2002; Davis 2007.

78. Salvago 1937, 75.

79. Salvago 1937, 76. Modern scholars do not agree on the introduction of gunpowder technologies to North Africa. Some support Salvago's observation by emphasizing the role played by Granadan refugees familiar with gunpowder technology in the Sa'dis' efforts to assert their power in Morocco in the 1470s. Others suggest it was actually the sultan in Istanbul—not Spanish or Portuguese monarchs—who supplied Granadan refugees turned corsairs with gunpowder technologies. Still others point out that gunpowder was already in use in Mamluk North Africa in the fourteenth century. Larguèche 2001; Buchanan 2016, 74. I thank Bert Hall for prodding me to explore further the historical veracity of Salvago's contentions about the provenance of Maghrebi gunpowder technology.

80. Salvago 1937, 77.

81. An early-sixteenth-century Muslim ambassador from Fez, Hassan Al-Wazzan, known later as Leo Africanus, was captured by corsairs and brought to Rome, where he converted to Catholicism and befriended a group of Christian and Jewish intellectuals. For Leo's intellectual biography, see Davis 2006; see also Hall 1995, 28–44 on Leo's own categories of African difference and Zhiri 2006 on Leo's representational strategies.

82. Davis 2006, 116–24. Leo was hardly alone. It is only recently that scholars have begun to study the dense commercial and intellectual ties that bound early

modern North Africa with the sub-Saharan societies "beyond the seas of sand." See, inter alia, Montana 2008, 132–50; Lydon 2009.

83. "L'Africa . . . ha ben nella rivolution de superni giri successivamente mutato e forma e signoria, ma non già mai essentia nè natura, poichè ne gli antichi et ne' moderni tempi sia o per influenza Celeste o per antipatia naturale, fu sempre in varie guise infesta e molesta all'opposta parte dell'Europa": Salvago 1937, 53.

84. As Francesc Relaño (2002) argues, a clear conception of "Africa" as a distinct continent, separate from the Mediterranean ecumene, emerged in European geographical and cartographic discourse only in the late Middle Ages.

85. "Gli abitatori della città, cioè i nobili, sono uomini veramente civili, e vestono il verno di panni di lana forestieri. . . .": Africano 1967 [1550], 183.

86. "Vestono i Corsari, e grandi e piccolo, positivissimamente di solo panno e non mai di seta, molto diversi dal superbo vestir Costantinopolitano": Salvago 1937, 69.

87. Salvago 1937, 69, 71. These pronouncements refer to Algiers and to Tunis, respectively. But see Moalla 2004, 12–18, who interprets the greater autonomy from Istanbul of the Tunisian dey post-1591 as predicated rather on a common Ottoman method of provincial governance.

88. On "classicizing" the Ottomans, see McJannet 2006; Burke 2007, 80. On the wider implications of spatiotemporal distancing, see Fabian 1983.

89. "Traci novelli, Tartari oriundi, popoli di Gog e Magog, nell'Apocalissi chiamati dall'Historico Divino San Giovanni, e così con occulto misterio intitolati; i quali, rinontiando a Monti Caspii la vita pastorale, con brama di signoreggiare, usciti già dalla Scithia, volgarmente Tartaria, et venuti ad occupar la Tracia, appò moderni Romania, posto che per processo di secoli, non che di lustri e d'anni, prattichino con tutte le sorti di gente civile, non havendo però ancor acquistato spetie d'urbanità, punto non tralignanti posteri del duro Scita e del feroce Trace, tuttavia conservano l'original durezza rustica e l'insita ferità non mai deposta nè dimenticata": Salvago 1937, 54.

90. On Gog and Magog in medieval thought and the significance of the "blurred" and unspecific nature of this category, see Westrem 1998, 56, 70. On medieval myths of the Scythian origins of the Turks, see Meserve 2008.

91. This was openly recognized by the Venetian Senate: in Salvago's letter of commission of 18 October 1624 the Senate lauded "la prattica che tieni con turchi" (the experience you have with Turks), urging him to make good use of it during the negotiations with the regents of North Africa; Salvago 1937, 14.

92. SDispC, b. 132, 756v and 757r (28 February 1648 m.v.).

93. IS, b. 418, unpaginated letters by Giovanni Battista Ballarino (16 and 22 August 1660).

94. Jones 1971, 398–99; Westrem 1998; Meserve 2008. On the connection between the Turks and Scythians in Aeneas Silvius Piccolomini's (later Pope Pius II) *Cosmographia* (1458–1460), see Bisaha 1999, 194.

95. Arbel 201, 254–55.

96. On Membré's proud ownership and annotations of a Mamluk Gospel Book in Arabic with Constantinopolitan Byzantine miniatures of ca. 1100 (now Cambridge, MS Gg. 5.27), acquired in Cairo in the 1560s, see Hunt 2007.

97. Rothman 2011a, 172–73.

98. Pedani 2020, 395–96.

99. Cited in Arbel 2002, 23.

100. Arbel 2002, 23

101. Morton 1993, xviii.

102. Membré 1969, 25.

103. "Rasonando con Seitler me disseno che io dovesse dirli perche causa li Veneziani hano per sua arma uno lion, perché si maravigliavano molto di questa cosa, digando loro che lo lion è cosa del chiach, perché Alì è uno lion invisibile. Alli omeni li pareva che fusse omo; ma lui era lion ordinato dal signor Dio per destruser li idolatri, siché, nelle istorie loro, si depingono le arme de Alì [come] uno lion, e per questo volevano saper. Per la qual cosa io li risposi che de qua si può veder per esperienza se la Signoria è amica del Chiach, over non; perché hano tanto amore in lo Alì che portano la sua arma e lo adorano, e sono più devoti de lui che altri; qual me disse che io dovesse dir a qual modo passa questa cosa; io li dissi: «in quel tempo che era vivo Alì, benché era in queste parti come figura de lione e appareva visibilmente, e parlava alle rechie delli omeni santi la teologia, li miracoli de Dio, le cose celeste, siché loro scrivevano tutto quanto, il qual ha fatto uno libro, che al presente lo chiamano evangelio e in turchesco ingil»; e lui me disse che confessano esser vero ditto evangelio, e credeno etiam loro in questo ingil, e con questo restò ben informato da me, e hano ditto che il dover era che me chiamasseno muvalì, cioè gente amata da Ali, e che seria più peccato amazzar uno Venezian che mille Ottomani": Membré 1969. 44–45. The English version is adapted from Membré 1993, 39–40.

104. On Safavid disputations, see Babayan 1994.

105. For his use of the honorific *seitler* to refer to the courtiers of Osku (*[H]uscup*) see Membré 1969, 22–24, 27, 32, 33, 35, 46.

106. Membré 1969, 10–13, 22.

107. Membré 1969, 58. Other examples include "lalà zoè governador" (10), "agosatti, zoè molettieri" (11), "ordu, zoè esercitto" (19), "musacap, cioè amati e amici del Re" (21) "meidan, cioè piazza" (22, 36), "mucurdar, cioè che bolla le cose del re" (23), "copech cran, cioè mazzacani" (23), "corchi, cioè li soldati a cavallo" (27, 34), "diassagoli, cioè officiali a questo deputati" (27), "califfa, cioè capo della villa e papasso" (28), "ichich agassi, cioè mastri di casa" (28), "tentur, cioè uno pitaro" (35), "Sofiani, cioè de li signori" (38), "ravavà, cioè tamburrini" (41), "Usbech, cioè de quelli delle berette verde" (42), "teperiach, cioè una cosa de stimulo" (47), "'chiachi pachichi,' cioè per la testa del chiach" (47), "chiach morati versi, cioè chiach li [li] dia il suo desiderio" (48), "carcanà, cioè li gambelli sui cargi" (49), "'allà, allà', che vol dire 'dio, dio'" (50), "nizille, cioè como ostarie" (54), "serafi, cioè quelli che cambiano le monede" (58), "palmera, cioè quello alboro che fa le nose grande de India" (63).

108. Morton 1993, xx.

109. "Corsa nella narata guisa la sfera dell'aversa mia sorte, et conoscendo esser statto per me, e per tutta la mia casa, il presente anno molto critico, per chiuder l'adito all'emuli di poter con qualch'impostura insidiar la mia vita, ho stimato conferente il ritirarmi in un villaggio pocco discosto, con pensiero di fermarmi in quello sin a tanto mi capiti qualche riverita prescrittione pubblica, per saper in virtù della medema con l'humiliatione dirigermi": Morton 1993, 755.

110. "Per esser la festa del santissimo Natale il giorno stesso che seguì la funesta funtione del fu primo vesir, con l'altre particolarità non mi portai per riverenza di quell venerabil giorno a corte, ma il secondo capitate lettere del Techieli fui con sollecitudine chiamato per tradurle. Mi portai immediate, e trovai che le preaccennate lettere erano portate dal cancellier grande all'agà de' giannizzari, già ello generalissimo, e perciò il capiggilar chiecaia col chiaus bassi, che si trovavan ivi, mi dissero che mi trattenessi con essi loro per qualch'hora non potendo tardar molto la comparsa del medesimo cancellier grande con lettere che dovevansi tradure, al qual effetto, fermatomi con essi, principiaron a discorrer meco di varie cose, et in conclusione, sotto siggilo di tutta confidente secrettezza, mi communicaron che infalibilmente il Maurogordato sarà deposto dal dragomanato della Porta, e che tenendo io qualche pocco di concetto buono appresso la medesima, havevan subodorato che fosse per appoggiar quella carica alla mia debolezza, per il che mi persuadevan da buoni amici di non far renitenza, ma anzi abbracciar volentier l'incontro che non disdice all'esser in servitio d'altro principe, essendo statti pure altre fiate dragomanni della Porta soggetti che servivan anco l'imperator cesareo, ed accellerar il mio viaggio vers' Andrianopoli per la consecutione. Sorpreso da tal stravagante proposta, non seppi per scansar l'impegno d'addur altro che la mia insufficienza per tal carica, con ch'essendosi fatta l'hora tarda, né comparendo le lettere, mi licentiai rimettendo al giorno seguente il tradurle. Presentita dal sudetto Maurogonato la mia chiamata dalli preaccennati ministry, insospetito fece subbito avanzar un suo biglietto al cancellier grande (con cui passava strettissima confidenza), supplicandolo, già che intendeva trovarsi esso in publico per tradur l'otrascritte lettere": Tarsia 1996 [1683], 738–39.

111. "ma bensi di viver e morir con quella incorrotta fede succhiata col latte sotto li auspicii faustissimi del mio natural invitissimo Principe": Tarsia 1996, 740.

112. A partial list includes: "L'estorsioni e violenze tiraniche and barbaramente" (687, the latter also on 693), "arrogante e cieca temerietà, pomposissima et comendabil ostentatione" (693), "cellerità" (694, 696), "laberinto di disgratie" (697), "oppressione de' Christiani, tiranicamente" (699), "questo barbaro decreto" (703), "cadaveri christiani stillanti sangue, con universal orrore" (704), "solita conatural loro barbaria, L'impeto furiosi de' Tartari et ottomani" (708), "patronanza despotica alli Christiani" (716), "lo fece inhumamente strozzare" (718), "fraude, solito stile di questa natione" (719), "barbara sua tiranide" (723), "l'ingorda conatural avaritia, sua tiranide" (729), "il terror dell'Europa" (730), "despotica auttorità,

Rigida et inhumana condana alla morte dell'inocente passà et officiali sì riguardevoli" (733), "rustiche spoglie" (735), "tiraniche procedure" (737).

113. Tarsia 1996, 709–14.

114. Tarsia 1996, 737.

115. On fourteen different occasions throughout the text he uses the phrase "supremo vesir(o)" or "supremo ministro" to calque the Ottoman title of "vezir-i Azam" or "sadrazam," rather than opt for the more conventional "primo vezir" or "gran vezir" (although he does use both systematically throughout, thirteen and seventeen times, respectively). The variation, it should be noted, does not seem to follow any discernible pattern, or conform to any rules of aesthetic variation. On dragomans' divergent approaches to glossing Ottoman nomenclature, see Chapter 6.

116. E.g., the explication of the Latin legal concept of *tantum frugi* (737) and the use of other Latin expressions such as *in scrittis* (735).

117. Examples include "campo ottomano" (689, 695, 704, 711, 716), "l'ottomano" (689), "Porta ottomana" (690), "insegna ottomana" (690), "essercito ottomano" (693, 699, 703, 713, 718), "statto ottomano" (689, 691, 694, 702, 705, 713, 716, 732), "Maestà Ottomana" (730, 732), and "arme ottomane" (734).

118. E.g., "schiavi turchi" (691, 704), "mercanti turchi" (743), and, more generically (and ambiguously), as "Turchi" (694, 695, 699, 705, 707, 711, 712, 713, 715, 716, 717, 720, 725, 752, 753) and "li Turchi" (692, 700, 702, 704, 705, 707, 708, 709, 711, 712, 715, 724, 725, 726). A few military usages blur these distinctions, as in "squadroni turcheschi" (714), "pressidio turco" (690, 691, 721), and "pressidio turchesco" (695).

119. For example, "Hassan passà della Grecia, nativo d'Albania" and "Ahmet agà crettense" (704), "il capiggilar chiecaia dell'interfetto, di nation francese" and "l'attual hasnadar Osman agà, di natione ciciliano" (737), and "Cara Ibrahim passa, nattivo d'Amassia, provincia dell'Asia" (740).

120. "Huomo di vilissimi natali, e che trahe origine da Marzuvan, terra situata nell'Asia": 737.

121. "il turco, per maggiormente vendicarsi corse alla fraude, solito stile di questa natione": 719.

122. Kunt 1974.

123. Taylor 2018, 298.

Chapter 4: Visualizing a Space of Encounter

1. According to Polona Vidmar (2010, 333) such caps marked the status of non-Muslim Ottoman subjects, while only dragomans and doctors enjoyed the right to wear kalpaks of astrakhan or sable fur.

2. As Vidmar (2010, 335) points out, however, the caption may have been added later, as the portrait itself dates to ca. 1700, and depicts Carli (b. 1646) as a middle-aged rather than an elderly man.

3. On the semiotics of bodily posture in early modern portraiture in general, and those of elite patriarchs in particular, see Bremmer and Roodenburg 1991. On protruding elbows, see the essay by Spicer therein.

4. I am thankful to an anonymous audience member at a public lecture I gave at the Bata Shoe Museum in 2010 for prompting me to explore further the potential meaning of the representation of an enslaved Black page in this portrait.

5. The iconography of Black pages was shared by Dutch, French, English, and Italian portrait artists throughout the early modern period. Bindman 2010.

6. On the "Turkish resonance" of Black pages in baroque art, see McGrath and Massing 2012, 17–19.

7. Necipoğlu 1992; Fleischer 1992; Kafadar 1995; Hagen 2003; Turan 2007; Kafescioğlu 2009.

8. For pioneering works in this vein, see McJannet 2007; Meserve 2008; Ghobrial 2016; Bevilacqua 2018.

9. Codex Cicogna 1971 was bequeathed to the City of Venice by the amateur Venetian historian Emmanuele Cicogna (1789–1868) as part of his enormous collection of 40,000 volumes and 5,000 manuscripts, all now housed in the Museo Civico Correr (=MCC) in Venice. Cicogna probably acquired the manuscript around 1828. Ms. VAse-1782 at the State Hermitage Museum Library in St. Petersburg was formerly in the possession of the renowned German Orientalist Franz Taeschner, who gave it the catalog number 114. Taeschner had acquired the codex from General von Bötticher, who had it displayed at the Exhibition of Islamic Art in Munich in 1910. In 1937, Taeschner lent the manuscript to the Berlin Staatsmuseum, from which it was removed by Soviet soldiers in 1945 and transferred to the State Hermitage Museum, alongside three other Taeschner manuscripts. On Taeschner and his collections, mostly at the Leiden University Library, see Schmidt 2010. On Cicogna and his collections, see Preto 1982; Romanelli 1994 and, especially, Istituto italiano di cultura di Istanbul 1995, which includes a reproduction of all the illustrations of the Cicogna Codex (albeit with skewed colors and with only a partial transcript of the gloss). The Taeschner Codex remains virtually unstudied except for a monochrome facsimile edition (with a few of the illustrations schematically recolored) published by Taeschner in 1925 and a preliminary study by Vasilyeva (2016). Even though Taeschner indicated in his brief introduction that the illustrations had been accompanied by an Italian text, he did not include a transcript, but only brief captions in German. I was fortunate enough to examine the manuscript in person in 2015, at the kind invitation of Dr. Daria Vasilyeva, head of the Byzantium and the Middle East Section of the Oriental Department of the State Hermitage Museum.

10. A portrait of Mustafa I (1617–1618) appears last (and out of chronological sequence) in Cicogna Codex, on folio 16.

11. Cicogna, 35–44 and 49 focus on the maltreatment of Venetian diplomatic representatives by Ottoman officials; folios 45–48 describe battle scenes; folios 55–59 depict Ottoman fortresses. Conversely, the three diplomatic scenes in Codex

Taeschner (fols. 51–53) all emphasize the positive aspects of diplomatic ceremonial. The other two illustrations in this category found in Codex Taeschner depict a siege of the island of Tenedos (fol. 14) and—in a scene ostensibly unrelated to Venetian-Ottoman diplomacy—janissaries attacking a tavern owner in the city in the wake of Sultan Murad IV's prohibition on wine and coffee consumption in 1633.

12. That Murad IV's portrait was included in the original manuscript is evident from a reference to Sultan Ibrahim at the opening sentence of folio 14r as "the brother of Murad."

13. The centrality of illustrations (sometimes problematically called "miniatures") to both courtly and urban literary production, and the politics of visual representation and narration in the early modern Ottoman capital are memorably captured by Orhan Pamuk in *My Name is Red* (2001). On the circulation of miniatures—both single-leaf and anthologized in albums—as aides to story-and fortune-tellers, part of seventeenth-century Istanbul's thriving coffeehouse culture, see Değirmenci 2011. On courtly miniature production, see Fetvacı 2013, and on the passion for album-making as a distinctly Ottoman imperial art form, Fetvacı 2020. Dozens of Ottoman albums, often with glosses and other customizations, also circulated outside the Ottoman Empire. Two such albums, Peter Mundy's 1618 *Brief Relation of the Turckes* (British Museum Add. 23880/1974-6-7-013) and the 1640s album in Warsaw's Biblioteka Narodowa (BOZ 165) are discussed in Collaço 2017. Claes Rålamb's album (ca. 1657), now in Stockholm (Royal Library, MS Rål. 8:o nr. 10), is discussed in Ådahl 2006. At least one other album of likely similar provenance is in Paris (*Recueil de costumes turcs et de fleurs*, BnF, Départment Estampes, OD. 26). For other seventeenth-century miniature albums of Istanbulite provenance, see Wilson 2003. At least thirty costume albums were produced before 1600, the earliest known exemplar being the 1570 Wolfenbüttel album (Blankenburg 206) discussed in Haase 1998 and Radway 2011. Lambert de Vos's 1574 album (Bremen SUB Ms. Or. 9), discussed in Koch 1991, was copied several times, with extant copies in Paris (the 1590 *Moeurs et costumes des Pays Orientaux*, BnF, Département Estampes, OD. 2), Athens (Gennadius Library, Arch.986), and Dresden (Kupferstickkabinett, Inv. Ca 114). Some of the striking stylistic and iconographic similarities between the De Vos and Wolfenbüttel albums and miniatures produced by the courtly miniaturist Nakkaş Osman under sultanic patronage for several mid-sixteenth-century official chronicles are analyzed by Paraldır 2007. For a comprehensive list of pre-1600 albums in this genre, see Radway 2012.

14. These include Claes Rålamb's album (ca. 1657), now in Stockholm (Royal Library, MS Rål. 8:o nr. 10), the *Gastallan Histori Tahtureks,* now in Istanbul (Deniz Müzesi Kitapliği, ms. 2380), Binney 1979 no. 62, a ca. 1660 album that was offered for sale by Sotheby's in 2012 (http://www.sothebys.com/en/auctions/ecatalogue/2012/an-eye-for-opulence-art-of-the-ottoman-empire/lot.186.html), and an unverifiable number of codices and single leaves in private collections. For a list of some albums' measurements and known locations, see Renda 1998, 171.

15. This resemblance was noted by Tadeusz Majda (Ådahl 2006, 213).

16. At the same time, the relative stylistic cohesion of both generic and custom miniatures (in terms of physiognomy, color schemes, and the representation of architectural space) precludes the possibility that they originated from widely different stocks. Rather, a Venetian patron may have either specified a list of miniatures to be painted in one commission, or purchased some generic preexisting miniatures and then commissioned from the same artist or workshop additional miniatures to fit a specific narrative. For details on late-sixteenth-century Ottoman miniature album production, which frequently involved more than one artist even for a single commission, see Renda 1976.

17. For a recent example of the older paradigm, see Kynan-Wilson 2017. On the multidirectional circulations that produced this genre, see Bevilacqua and Pfeifer 2013, 80–84; Fraser 2018; Fetvacı 2020.

18. On the Ottoman court atelier and the diffuse category of "court art," see Fisher and Garrett Fisher 1985; Fetvacı 2007. On the multiple interactions between courtly and so-called "bazaar" art, on the latter's audiences both within the court and around the city, and on the need to further explore the very category of "bazaar painters," see Değirmenci 2011.

19. On the careful education of Venetian diplomats destined for Istanbul, see Valensi 1993; Dursteler 2001; Frigo 2008.

20. On these multiple genres and their functioniong in the context of a Mediterranean space of encounter, see Rothman 2012a, 50–52.

21. Denny 1970, 51. On Ottoman representation of architectural space, see also Johnston 1971; Necipoğlu-Kafadar 1986; Rogers 1987.

22. "Forma di Cavarsera', ch[e] si fabrica in spatiose campagne, p[er] com'odo di viaggiansi, con dentro un gran cortile coperto, ove stan[n]o li cavalla, et d'ogni parte in qualch' magg[io]r eminenza, ma nel luogo stesso, s' accom[m]odano gl' huomini con lor ármi, et arnesi, essendoci quantità di camini, ordinatam.te, p[er] servitio d'ogn'uno il turco va con le chiavi ad' aprir la porta, et del Cavarsera' aperto si vede nella seguente carta la vera forma."

23. "Q[ue]sto è il Cavarsera aperto, con la porta, guardata da catena con li camini, et il foco p[er] com[m]odo di viaggianti, le cui armi pure si veggon' affise al muro, con li cavalli à basso, dentro il luogo med[esi]mo, ove capita ogni cond[itio]ne di turco, nel modo stesso che nella Christianità si usano le hosterie": Cicogna, 32r.

24. On the distinction between caravanserais and hans, see Ersoy 1999.

25. "Figura di un Can di Cost[antinopo]li, ove si riducono huomini, e cavalli da viaggio; la porta è attraversata da catene, guardata da custodi; al di fuori, attaccate all' istesso Can, vi sono botteghe di varie qualità di merci, p[er] com[m]odo delli stessi passaggieri, et viaggianti": Cicogna, 19r.

26. "Il Càn della Validè, cioè della Sultana madre di Sultan Amurat, è fabricato di marmi con gran maestria, et spesa; quantità di stanze al di dentro, p[er] custodir li capitali di mercanti; nel mezzo, una moschea, p[er] orare, et una fontana, p[er] lavarsi, et p[er] bere": Cicogna, 22r.

27. The Büyük Valide Han, the largest in Istanbul, was built by Kösem shortly before her death in 1650. Goodwin 1971, 359. On this and other architectural projects sponsored by the valide sultans, see Thys-Şenocak 2006.

28. Notably, these folios—15, 19, 22, 25, 26, 30, 35, 45, and 47, respectively—are all found in Taeschner. Cicogna only has one additional distinctly "Muslim" representation beyond the mosque in the courtyard of the Büyük Valide Han, i.e., the "Mosque of Santa Sofia" (34r), but the commentary on it remains remarkably sparse (no mention is made of the building's long and important history as a Byzantine church, for example).

29. On Süleymân's architectural projects, see the essays by Gülru Necipoğlu, Aptullah Kuran, and Nurhan Atasoy in Veinstein 1992.

30. On the appearance of scenes from everyday life in Ottoman albums during the reign of Ahmed I (1603–1617), see Atasoy and Çağman 1974, 65.

31. Wilson 2007.

32. "Varie sorti di papuzze, cioè scarpe, stivali, stivaletti, usati da huomini, e doñe turche": Cicogna, 21r.

33. "Varie qualità di turbanti, differenti fra loro usati da turchi secondo le cond[itio]ni et proffessioni, ch[e] han[n]o, come di sphai; d'huomo di legge, di scrittura, di religione, di arte, di nobiltà, di plebe, et simili": Taeschner, 33r.

34. On topographic drawings of Istanbul produced for Venetian military purposes, see Curatola 1999.

35. Babinger 1960; Mango 2000.

36. "La descrittione de gl' altri due forti, novam[en]te fabricati, è in altra carta, formata da mano assai dilig[en]te, et sarà nel fondo del p[rese]nte libro": Cicogna, 55r.

37. In the eighteenth century, Venetian need for expert visual-military knowledge of the Ottoman Empire led to Giovanni Francesco Rossini's sojourn in the bailate from 1723 to 1727 as military attaché. Rossini, who had extensive prior experience in creating topographic reliefs, produced several drawings of Istanbul, including "Hydrographic and Topographic Description of the Dardanelles completed in the year 1726," and "View of Constantinople from the garden of the Palace of Venice." Curatola 1999.

38. The appointment as Venetian Grand Chancellor often followed service as secretary to the bailo in Istanbul: of the five people elected Grand Chancellors from 1630 to 1660, four had served in Istanbul. Dursteler 2000, 177. On secretaries in the Venetian civil service in general, and on the importance of Grand Chancellors in particular, see Trebbi 1980; Neff 1985; Trebbi 1986; Zannini 1993; Grubb 2000; Galtarossa 2002.

39. Ballarino's extensive career in the Venetian civil service began at age nineteen, following his graduation in philosophy from the University of Padua, with an appointment as extraordinary secretary in the ducal chancellery. It subsequently included several lengthy sojourns outside the lagoon as secretary to the *provveditor generale* Francesco Molino on Crete (1627–1631) and to the *provveditor*

Francesco Zeno in Dalmatia (1632–1634), and as Resident in Vienna (1635–1638). In 1639 he was appointed secretary to the Council of Ten, and in 1643 he reached the delicate position of secretary to the *Inquisitori di Stato*. In Istanbul, Ballarino had first served as a secretary to Ambassador Simone Contarini and to the bailo Giorgio Giustinian (1624–1626), then to Ambassador Giovanni Soranzo while the latter was held captive by the Ottomans (1648–1650), and then, from 1653 on, as an aide and de facto replacement to the elderly Ambassador Giovanni Capello upon the latter's attempted suicide in 1654. Torcellan 1963 and the extensive biography by Ballarino's lifelong friend, the patrician Marco Trevisan (1671).

40. Dursteler 2000, 172.

41. Impalement in particular became a sign of Ottoman cruelty. Luigi Bassano (1545) devoted an entire section of his book to a very graphic description of Ottoman executions by impalement. Boerio's Venetian dictionary (1960, 326) even defines *impalar* as *infilare alla turchesca*. On Venetian understandings of impalement as part of a broader repertoire of Ottoman cruel execution techniques see Barzman 2017.

42. IS, reg. 148, 27 (6 June 1620). On the Borisis' involvement in Spanish espionage at the Porte, see also Malcolm 2015, 375–78.

43. The interrogation is described in some detail in Trevisan 1671, 92–95.

44. The apprentice in question could have been one of Christoforo's brothers, Marco and Giacomo, or sons, Leonardo, Tommaso, and Giacomo, who were all in Venetian service at some point during the war.

45. Romanelli's (1995, 229–30) suggestion that Marco Tarsia was involved in producing the album seems questionable, given Marco's premature death in 1650.

46. For example, Osman was "of vile birth, but sagacious and valorous, struck great terror and advanced violently (1r). Bayezid I "robbed" (*svaliggiare*) "Bosnia, Dalmatia, Albania, Croatia, and Wallachia" (4r). Mehmed I caused the "emptying out" (*insecutione*) of Christians, who were "forced to run away from his violence" and leave Serbia, Walachia, and parts of Dalmatia (5v). Bayezid II had the Venetian bailo dismissed and all the Venetian merchants imprisoned and robbed (8v). Selim I exercised "many cruelties" during his war against the Holy League (11v).

47. The complete list is as follows: The Serbian despot was "killed cruelly" by Murad I (3v); Murad II "harassed the Serbian despot," taking out the eyes and genitalia of his two sons (6r); Mehmed II "had his brother strangled and buried in his father's tomb, saying that this way, neither will have the displeasure of staying by himself" (7r); Mehmed II also had the Venetian bailo Girolamo Minio murdered, and two Venetian diplomats, Erizzo and Barbaro, impaled (7v); and, under pretence of peace, he had the prince of Misnia (Meissen) come visit him, and then had him skinned alive (*scorticare*) (7v); Selim I killed his brother as well as the captain of Cappadocia (9r), had one Mamluk sultan strangled and the other hanged (9r–9v); Selim II exercised "the cruelest acts of barbarity," skinning alive Marcantonio Bragadin (the Venetian commander of besieged Famagusta, Cyprus),

hanging another Venetian, Lorenzo Tiepolo, and decapitating or enslaving many other private masters and cavaliers (11v); Mehmed IV had the Venetian grand dragoman Grillo strangled by order of the grand vizier (15r, 38r); the ambassador of Prince George II Rákóczi of Transylvania was decapitated in the Divan (20r); the Venetian grand dragoman Grillo was strangled in 1649 (38r), while Grand Dragoman Borisi was hanged by the throat (39r) and two Venetian letter carriers were hooked and impaled (40r and 41r).

48. Rothman 2011a, 173–86.

49. Valensi 1993.

50. On "exotic" violence in early modern European prints, and their relationship to commodified travel literature, on the one hand, and the European Wars of Religion, on the other, see Schmidt 2015, 164–223.

51. As Gwendlyn Collaço recently noted in relation to two other contemporary costume albums from Istanbul, "compilers took an active role in the final product as both the selectors of images and those who controlled how and where these books were bound" (2017, 249). As I have shown here, however, Ballarino's role went far beyond mere selection and ordering of images, as his narrative gloss frames the visual program and deeply shapes its interpretation.

52. An interlinear comment provides information about territories conquered by the Ottomans from the Venetians in 1470 and about the impaling of two Venetian diplomats (7v); Bayezid's twenty-six year long reign is acknowledged above the line (8v); elsewhere, an interlinear date is added for a major Venetian loss during the War of Crete (14v). Other examples abound throughout.

53. Scholars agree that the portraits were not all created by the same artist. Over the years, several painters have been named as likely responsible for at least some of these portraits, including the Koper-based artist Natalis Bertolini, and the Udine-born, Venice-based Sebastiano Bombelli (1635–1719), the latter of whom created numerous portraits of Venetian nobility and specialized in full-length official portraiture. Bombelli became "the most sought after portraitist in the Venetian Republic in the second half of the seventeenth century," and his manner of ascribing "psychological introspection" to his sitters was deeply influential. Though settled in Venice, Bombelli is known to have traveled frequently to various European courts, as well as to his native Udine and nearby territories, where he often created portraits of local patricians. On Bombelli, see Bergamini 2016 and, on his style specifically, Rizzi 1969.

54. Gardina 2005.

55. On the pendant portraits of Stefano Carli and his wife, see Vidmar 2016. For Stefano's portrait, now presumed lost, see Cossàr 1950, 258.

56. Santangelo 1935, 137.

57. On other branches of the extended Tarsia family resident in Capodistria in the late seventeenth century, see Gardina 1993; Kokole 2012. On the Carlis, see Infelise 1997a.

58. Radossi 2003, 121, 384.

59. Cossàr 1950, 259. It was only around the turn of the nineteenth century that the Carli palace portraits were transferred to Parenzo/Poreč, some 60 kilometers south, in what is now Croatia. This was occasioned by the intestate death of Stefano Carli (b. 1726, Gian Rinaldo's great-nephew), who bequeathed the city all his possessions in 1813. In his will of February 11, 1813, the count asked that in return Poreč authorities establish a public library, endow four bursaries for students at the University of Padua, and provide dowries for four poor girls. An earlier will of March 7, 1810, mentions explicitly among his legacy "the seven portraits of dragomans which I have, and the family tree." Bralić and Burić 2005, 197–98. On Stefano Carli's endeavors to shape the future of the Istrian region under Habsburg rule in 1803, see Gottardi 1997.

60. Vidmar 2005, 276.

61. Vidmar 2010. On Ottoman dress, see Faroqhi and Neumann 2004.

62. Bevilacqua and Pfeifer 2013.

63. Waugh 2000.

64. On the portrayal of "Ottoman and Persian visitors to Europe holding a letter" as a common trope in European diplomatic portraiture see Matthiesson 2012.

65. Giustiniana's portrait lacks an inscription, but several stylistic and iconographic clues make it very likely that it served as a pendant with a previously unidentified/misidentified portrait of the dragoman Marcantonio Mamuca della Torre, Giustiniana's husband, as discussed below. On Bradamante's and Catterina's portraits generally, see Bralić and Burić 2005, 198–99.

66. Named after Louis XIV's mistress, the elaborate fontange headdress—replete with ribbon bows and wire frames to keep the hair up—became a Europe-wide de rigueur hairstyle starting in the 1680s.

67. On European sojourning artists' representations of Istanbulite elite headdress, see Vidmar 2010, 341–43.

68. On Pera's Genoese community, see Rohan 2015.

69. Vidmar 2005.

70. The three aigrettes and pearls in her headgear, the fur-trimmed outer garment, her confident posture with the outfacing elbow, and, of course, the drapery and landscape, all speak to her superior status.

71. Kokole 2012.

72. FHL, Bapt I, 34 (20 June 1680), 36 (6 June 1681), 69 (8 December 1688), 75 (August 1691).

73. School of Oriental Studies, Paget Papers, boxes 52–54.

74. Koper Regional Archives, KP 312 Tarsia.

75. I was not able to consult the Tarsia printed family tree, which dates to 1792. Kokole 2012.

76. Bralić and Burić 2005, 205.

77. On the conventionalized representation of Europeans in Safavid and early Qajar pictorial arts, see Langer 2013.

78. Dupont-Ferrier 1922, 117 quoted in Messaoudi 2015, 69n66.

79. Alexander Bevilacqua, personal communication; Eaton 2013; Riello 2018.

80. On the methodological significance of attending to family portraiture as strategic representations rather than reflective of social realities, see Hughes 1986. On the broad implications of shifting genealogical thinking in the human sciences, see Shryock and Smail 2011, 21–54.

81. The extent of the Istanbulite Tarsias' interactions with their relatives in Capodistria is hard to gauge at this point. However, ancedotal evidence suggests that family ties were enduring. For example, notarial records attest to interactions between Agostino Tarsia—the dragoman Ruggiero's son, and Tommaso and Giacomo's cousin—and Antonio Tarsia—a musician, notary public, and a distant cousin—who helped draw up the wedding contract for Agostino's daughter Appolonia in 1698. Earlier, in 1683, Tommaso Tarsia (presumably on his return from Vienna in the wake of the Ottoman armies) donated to the convent of Santa Chiara in Capodistria an expensive Gothic monstrance which Ottoman armies had looted in Austria and which Tarsia then purchased from "a Tatar" in the entourage of Kara Mustafa. Caprin 1907, vol. 1, 15n1; Kokole 2012.

82. Mamuca della Torre 1723; see Chapter 1 for details.

83. Bensheim, Institut für Personnengeschichte, Fondo Mamuca della Torre.

84. See, for example, Stefano Carli's five-act tragedy *La Erizia* (1765), which fictionalizes the capture and sexual enslavement of a Venetian governor's daughter in the Peloponnese in the wake of Ottoman conquest in 1470, and which, predictably, perpetuates every conceivable Orientalist trope about the Ottoman sultan as "barbarian, cruel, presumptuous, arrogant, fearful, terrible etc." Vidmar 2016, 67. The evident instrumentalization of Italian art history under Fascism to reclaim Istria (and, in particular, its early modern Italianate art forms) as integral part of a trans-historical "Italianità" remains to be written. On the Italian art establishment's cozy relationship with the Fascist state more broadly, see Stone 1998 and Lasansky 2004. On competing nineteenth-century appropriations of Dalmatian and Istrian antiquities, see Payne 2014; for the post-World War II contestations of affective belonging in the Istrian borderlands, see Ballinger 2003.

85. Jeffrey et al. 2011, 703.

86. The highly formalized interactional genre of audience at the divan should not obscure the fact that, in other contexts, Ottoman and foreign elites could engage in less prescribed forms of sociability. For suggestive comments in that vein, see Grehan 2006, 1363–65; Hamadeh 2007, 128–29 and 271n55; Ghobrial 2014a, 71. On the power of Ottoman officials' avoidance of direct communication with foreign representatives and insistence on linguistic mediation despite a shared idiom, see Perocco 2010, 65.

Chapter 5: Disciplining Language

1. "Quem usum habeat lingua Turcica?
Resp.Exiguum sanè in Theologia vel Philologia sacra: in Politicis non con-temnendum. Crebrò nobis cum porta Osmannica res est; Illic opus linguæ Turcicæ notitia": Pfeiffer 1672, 36.

2. "Es ist eine auffallende Erscheinung, dass urn jene Zeit die mannigfachen staatlichen V erbindungen mit dem Osmanischen Reiche, wie sie bereits im 15. Jahrhundert von verschiedenen westlichen Machten, vor all em den Venezianern unterhalten wurden, insbesondere aber die zahlreichen Unterhandlungen iiber Angelegenheiten des Krieges, und des Friedens sowie des Handels, in denen die Lagunenstadt, Frankreich und Oesterreich mit der Pforte standen, keine ein-dringlichere Beschaftigung mit der türkischen Sprache zu diesen rein praktischen Zwecken bewirken konnten": Babinger 1919, 106–7, quoted in Hamilton and Rich-ard 2004, 63. Translation mine.

3. Dursteler 2012, 61.

4. On this institution, see Rothman 2011a, 123–62.

5. Agop 1685; Drimba 1997.

6. On Agop, Donà, Agnellini, and their milieu, see Scarpa 2000 and below. On Agnellini's complex itineraries, see Heyberger 1995; Bevilacqua 2018, 60–61.

7. I am deliberately avoiding here the anachronistic nomenclature of "Turkol-ogy." Whereas by the nineteenth century a subdiscipline of Turkology coalesced around Ottoman Turkish philology and literature, the nomenclature was hardly prevalent earlier on. Moreover, as this chapter shows, the emergent seven-teenth-century field we might retroactively gloss as "Ottoman studies" encom-passed much historical and political knowledge, was more capacious in its themes and methods, and distinctly less interested in scriptural study than other Ori-entalist subspecializations, whether the religiously inflected study of "Oriental languages" such as Hebrew, Aramaic, and, to a lesser extent, Arabic, or what later morphed into comparative linguistics, e.g., in the study of Persian, Sanskrit, and Hindustani. On the latter, see Trautmann 2009; Kinra 2016. On Turkology, see Szurek 2014; Bossaert and Szurek 2015.

8. The classic monographic treatment of the subject remains Fück 1955, but see more recently Speer and Wegener 2006; Burman 2007; Tottoli 2015; Loop 2017; Tommasino 2018a. On Hebrew, see Coudert and Shoulson 2004; Vidro et al. 2014; Mandelbrote and Weinberg 2016.

9. Chan 2002; Xavier and Županov 2015.

10. Ben-Tov 2015, 105.

11. Ben-Tov 2015, 102. Belief that Turkish descended from Arabic was wide-spread enough among European scholars that in 1615 it was rehearsed by the Egyptian-born Copt Yusuf ibn Abu Dhaqn ("Josephus Barbatus"), an occasional university instructor of Arabic at both Leiden and Oxford (and a future Istanbu-lite dragoman). In the introduction to his Arabic grammar Abū Dhaqn wrote that

Turkish, Persian, Tatar, and Ethiopic all descended from Arabic "like daughters from a mother" (*quasi filiae a matre prodeunt*). Cited in Hamilton 1994, 135.

12. Malcolm 2007, 361.

13. The alt-academy, subaltern character of academic employment in the field of Turkology was to endure throughout the nineteenth century. On the employment of Ottoman Armenians as *répétiteurs* (lecturers) of Turkish language classes in Paris under the Third Republic, and on Turkish instruction as located mainly in commercial academies and vocational schools rather than universities, see Bossaert 2017.

14. As Stolzenberg (2015) himself concedes, his method has several limitations. The WorldCat union catalog, while ample, is incomplete, and the search term "linguae orientalis" in its various declensions only yields results in Latin, even though by the seventeenth century Orientalist scholarship in several vernacular languages (especially in Italian and French) was substantial. More fundamentally, his approach presupposes an already unified field of knowledge of "Oriental languages," whereas interest in specific languages, and especially in Ottoman Turkish, may have developed along parallel tracks that had little to do with the biblical, proselytizing, and antiquarian intent of Oriental studies as such. Finally, in a thriving manuscript culture such as that of the early Republic of Letters, an exclusive focus on print titles inevitably provides a very partial perspective, as Ghobrial (2016) notes.

15. On the contemporary duality of "Chaldean" as either (biblical) Aramaic or Syriac, itself sometimes understood as a variety of Aramaic, see Heyberger 2015, 496n4.

16. On the strong ties between English studies of Arabic and natural philosophy, see Russell 1995.

17. Stolzenberg 2015, 413.

18. An exception that proves the rule was the short-lived appointment of Giovanni Battista Podestà as professor of Oriental languages at the University of Vienna in 1674. Podestà had previously served as secretary of Oriental languages in the Imperial Council, and had studied Turkish in Vienna and Rome for a few years, which made him, at least by his own account, an expert on the language and authorized his long list of publications. Sprung and Mayr 1989; Fichtner 2008, 118–20.

19. On the case of the category "Levantine," see Rothman 2011a, 211–47.

20. On post-Reconquísta Arabic studies in Spain, see Rodríguez Mediano 2006; Hershenzon 2014; García-Arenal and Rodríguez Mediano 2017. On Jewish scholars and Christian Hebraists, see Burnett 2012. On Eastern Christians' roles in the study of Arabic in seventeenth-century Europe, see Ghobrial 2016; Heyberger 2009; Matar 2003, and the case studies in Hamilton 1994; Rietbergen 2006; Ghobrial 2017. On the Maronite College in Rome see Girard and Pizzorusso 2017.

21. Hamilton 2011, 300–1; Vrolijk and Van Leeuwen 2014.

22. Grafton and Weinberg 2011, 87, Hamilton 2011, 296–99.

23. Sebouh Aslanian suggests that the constitution of an Armenian diaspora that extended from Amsterdam and Venice to Goa can be traced, at least in part, to the massive dislocation of eastern Anatolian Armenian communities brought about by the Celali revolts and the Ottoman-Safavid wars of the early seventeenth century. While Armenians did play a certain role in the emergence of Ottoman studies, as discussed below, their involvement in teaching Ottoman and publishing Turkish-language books (mostly Turkish-Armenian, i.e., an Anatolian Turkish vernacular—rather than the high Ottoman register—written in the Armenian alphabet) dates mostly to the eighteenth century, and was fairly limited in scope. Shafir and Aslanian 2017. On the significantly larger role of Armenians—particularly graduates of the Armenian Mekhiterist college in Venice—as Ottoman language instructors throughout nineteenth-century Europe, see Bossaert 2017.

24. The philologist Joseph Justus Scaliger (1540–1609) complained that he "could not find a Turkish teacher to help him read the Arabic and Persian books he had"—this while residing in Leiden and enjoying access to a vast scholarly network. Palabiyik 2018, 119.

25. Quoted in Fleischer 1986, 22.

26. Fleischer 1986, 21.

27. Csató et al. 2010.

28. As Linda Darling (2012, 177) notes, "The ability to move between languages was an essential requirement of the [Ottoman] bureaucracy and played its part in diplomatic dealings from the foundation of the empire to the end."

29. On the development of the Ottoman courtly register, see Brendemoen 2012. On the sixteenth-century cultivation of Persian as integral to Ottoman's maturing as an imperial language, see Inan 2019.

30. My deep thanks to Atiqa Hachimi for encouraging me to explore this connection in the first place (personal communication) and for referring me to relevant works on Arabic historical linguistics. On histories of Arabic diglossia, see Zack and Schippers 2012.

31. On the extremely limited knowledge of Ottoman in late-seventeenth-century England see Heywood 2016, and Van den Boogert 2017 for the example of Johannes Heyman in Leiden.

32. On Meninski's printing woes, see Stachowski 2000, xxvi; Kent et al. 1978, 432.

33. See Heller and McElhinny 2017, 17, 117 passim.

34. Woolard 2002; Lee 2005; Durston 2007; Errington 2008; Hanks 2010.

35. On metalanguage, metapragmatic awareness, and their multiple interconnections, see Verschueren 2000.

36. Karttunen 1995.

37. On the relationship between translation, ideology, and "social context" as understood across disciplines, see Gilbert 2018.

38. Appendix 5.1 offers bibliographical details for the eighty-four works identified in this genre with the relevant scholarship on each, expanding on earlier

surveys, e.g., Yerasimos 1992; Berthier 1992; Rocchi 2013. Included are works in Latin, Italian, and French, as well as one in German and one in English. If works in Slavic languages were added, the corpus would grow only slightly, to include two Polish dictionaries. One, dated 1611, remains in manuscript, the other was published in Krakow in 1615. Stachowski 2013. I am unaware of contemporary works in this genre in other Romance languages, e.g., Spanish, Portuguese, or Romanian, and while a handful of works in other languages may still surface with future cataloging efforts, they will likely represent but a small fraction of the Romance-language corpus. The wide reach of Latin for linguistic studies of Ottoman is evident in this corpus, but Italian, too, played a decisive role, particularly in works intended for diplomatic rather than scholarly or missionary use. Traces of Italian's impact are evident in the ready availability of Italian-Ottoman materials in, e.g., Paris, London, and Madrid, as discussed below.

39. The anonymous manuscripts—all dating to the seventeenth century—include a small *Dictionnaire turquesque* that formed part of Colbert's library and that developed a unique system for abbreviating common Ottoman suffixes and verbs (BnF, MS Turc 233); a French-Ottoman bilingual dictionary (BnF, MS Turc 233); a partial Italian-Ottoman bilingual lexicon (BnF, Suppl. Turc 468); an Ottoman-Italian vocabulary with lexicographic notes (BnF, Suppl. Turc 469); the Illésházy manuscript now at the National Széchényi Library in Budapest (Oct. Lat. 13); and "an Italian-English-Turkish dictionary" now in the British Library (British Library, Add. Ms. 25872). The Illésházy compilation—evidently of divergent origins—includes a Turkish-Latin dictionary, a Latin-Turkish conversation guide, an abbreviated Turkish grammar in Italian (adapted from Molino 1641), and a Turkish dialogue, partially translated into Italian, all exhibiting strong Bosnian Turkish dialectal features. The trilingual dictionary in London remains virtually unstudied save for a brief mention in Lancashire 2012, 23 and a short catalog entry in Rieu 1888, 145. On the Paris manuscripts, see Berthier 1992. On the Budapest manuscript, see Németh 1970; Mollova 1997; Kappler 2001, 120–21.

40. Virtually all authors in this category were Catholics of various orders, including Capuchins, Jesuits, Theatines, Franciscans, Carmelites, French Oratorians, and Armenian-Catholics.

41. Hamilton and Richard 2004, 69.

42. On Du Ryer, see Kalus 1992, 84; Hamilton and Richard 2004; Hamilton 2017. On Meninski's enduring influence on eighteenth-century Ottoman grammars published in both Europe and the Ottoman Empire see Kappler 2014, 114–15 and below.

43. On Agop, see Drimba 1997; Scarpa 1998.

44. BnF, MS NAF 5405 and 5407, discussed in Gemayel 1984, 260, 297.

45. Toomer 1995, 30–31; Duverdier 1987; Girard and Pizzorusso 2017, 185–86.

46. For example, both Carradori and Mascis borrowed heavily from Molino, whereas Schieferdecker borrowed from Meninski. Some of these borrowings were of lexicographical matter, while others adopted the work's overall structure, ranging from outright plagiarism to subtle influence on structure. In all three

cases borrowings, in accordance with contemporary practice, were not explicitly acknowledged, and were often supplemented by additions and modifications, resulting in what may or may not have amounted to qualitative shifts in overall linguistic orientation. On Carradori, see Rocchi 2011; on Mascis, see Drimba 1992; on Schieferdecker, see Ben-Tov 2015.

47. Ekrem Caušević (2004, 249) notes the importance of training in Vienna's Oriental Academy for early-nineteenth-century Bosnian Franciscan friars' efforts to open similar schools in Fojnica and elsewhere. Unsurprisingly, the resulting teaching materials bore titles attesting to their great debt to Meninski.

48. This, of course, is true of the contributions of early modern secretaries and amanuenses more generally. Blair 2014.

49. Rocchi 2007, 2.

50. On Della Valle's manuscript grammar, see Rossi 1938.

51. Du Ryer 1630; Maggio 1643, 1670. As Kenessey (1974, 120) notes, no other evidence of Stephanus's grammar survives.

52. Kenessey 1974, 122. As Holdermann states in the preface to his own grammar of 1730, "Meninsky m'a paru le plus habile interprète et le meilleur maître des langues orientales. C'est lui que j'ay pris pour guide . . . Je me suis aussi exactement conformé à la methode des Grammairiens Latins et françois." Quoted in Berthier 1992, 78.

53. The *Vocabulario* was printed in Venice in five editions between 1574 and 1599 and again in Trento in 1684. The 1750 catalog of the French Bibliothèque du Roi lists copies of Molino's and de Paris's Ottoman-Italian dictionaries and of the Ottoman grammars of Megiser, Du Ryer, Seaman, and Meninski. *Catalogue* 1750: 19, 47–48, 72.

54. Rocchi 2011, 13.

55. Schmidt 2012, 273.

56. Rocchi 2007, 2; Kalus 1992, 86n13; Menz 2002; Schmidt 2012, 184, 273; Zwartjes 2014; Römer 2016.

57. Irvine and Gal 2000, 35; Gal and Irvine 1995; Woolard 1998.

58. "[L]a fatica dell'Argenti rappresenta il più ricco e importante lavoro sull'osmanlı redatto da un europeo nel corso dell'intero xvi secolo": Rocchi 2005, 39.

59. Adamović 2001, 14–15; Bombaci 1938; Merhan 2005; Rocchi 2007.

60. See the *Grammaire de la Langue Turque*, a French translation of Du Ryer, fair copied in Istanbul in 1688 and presented by a certain Philippe Desmartineaulx de Granvilliers (possibly a French apprentice dragoman) to Madame Girardin, wife of the French ambassador to the Porte. BL, Add. 27, 394, cited in Rieu 1888, 151. Du Ryer also authored a bilingual *Dictionarium turcico-latinum*, which remains in manuscript in at least two copies. BnF, MS Turc 464 and Suppl. Turc 465.

61. Kappler 1999; Święcicka 2020.

62. The copy currently at Uppsala University was purchased in Stockholm in 1758 by Carl Aurivillius (1717–1786), professor (and occasional government translator) of Oriental languages at the University of Uppsala. Another copy currently

at the Jagiellonian University Library in Krakow had previously belonged to Professor Tadeusz Kowalski (1889–1948). Święcicka 2020, 20. WorldCat and union catalog searches retrieved copies (sometimes multiple) in sixteen Italian libraries, as well as at least twenty-nine others throughout Europe. Additional copies are available at several libraries in Turkey and the US.

63. Couët's "Phrases Turques et Françoises composées par J. B. Couet, Enfant de Langue à Constantinople en 1712" is in BnF, Suppl. Turc 689. On Rizzi's work, see Kappler 2014.

64. Whereas Meninski proved the more scientifically sound of the two, it is the vitriolic and sarcastic nature of his rebuttals to Podestà's critiques that is most striking. For a sense of the intensity of their rivalry see Meninski's ascerbic notes on Podestà in an autographed manuscript of ca. 1669 now kept in the Royal Library of Belgium in Brussels, discussed in Geneja and Naster 1986.

65. Evans 1979, 428. On Meninski's enduring influence, see also De Groot 1994, 148n27. Even Sir James Redhouse—who worked as an Ottoman and later British dragoman for over twenty years—mentioned Meninski as one of his two chief sources for Turkish words in preparing his own "extensive Ottoman dictionary for Turkish use" in 1864. Quoted in Rieu 1888, 147.

66. Omont 1890, 3.

67. Dehérain 1930, 161.

68. Römer 2016. It is unclear whether the author argues that Meninski invented the first transliteration system for Ottoman or the first such system in Europe (and what transliteration actually meant in this context).

69. Hamilton and Richard 2004, 68.

70. Stachowski 2012 and its bibliography.

71. Baranowski 1949; Stachowski 2000, xxiv.

72. Geneja and Naster 1986. The authors note in passing (261–62) that Meninski's wife left him permanently in 1669 due to his "violent character" and that a legal process against him (likely for domestic abuse) was quietly resolved thanks to his prominent role in the imperial court.

73. The one outlier is Bernard de Paris's dictionary, which used the Ottoman Arabic script.

74. Csáto et al. 2010, 145.

75. Csáto et al. 2016. A notable exception in that volume is Richard Wittmann's study of the role of scribes in the preparation of petitions in early modern Istanbul, though it too falls short of addressing linguistic differentiation per se.

76. On routinized dispositions, "ways of seeing the world and oneself," as articulated in early modern linguistic encounter between missionaries and Maya in Yucatán, resulting in the (always imperfect) "reproduction of field positions in actors' dispositions" see Hanks 2010, 95 and passim.

77. On Roman—especially Franciscan, Jesuit, and Capuchin missionaries in the Ottoman Empire, see Van Droffelaar 1994; Tóth 2003, 2005; Causevic 2004; Borromeo 2005; Ruiu 2014, 2018.

78. Yağmur 2015; Rocchi 2016.

79. For a transcription of the pamphlet, now lost, see Lybyer 2013, 262–75. On its significance for introducing the Ottomans "on their own terms and in their own language" see Krstić 2011b, 133.

80. Rakova 2016, 29–31; Taylor 2018: 292–97.

81. Pedani Fabris 1994, 25, 141–48.

82. Hamilton and Richard 2004, 70. Curiously, the second manuscript of the dictionary does not include the ambassadorial address, but rather a selection of psalms in the Latin Vulgate with Arabic and Turkish translations and a literal, reverse translation of the Arabic into Latin.

83. Duverdier 1987, 329–30. French-Ottoman capitulation texts, in both languages, continued to be a staple of conversation guides well into the nineteenth century.

84. Du Vignau 1688, 30–36. On Du Vignau's identity, see Ghobrial 2014a, 5–6.

85. Mascis 1677, 281–90.

86. Hamilton 2017, 459.

87. Lupis 1527. This short work does not have a colophon and still awaits a detailed study to shed more light on its context of production and, especially, on its author—purportedly a Valencian Jew exiled from Spain who had settled in Ancona after a sojourn in Ottoman lands. For this identification, unfortunately without citations, see Rossebastiano 2000, 690. On the work's Ottoman linguistic contents, see Yağmur 2015.

88. Miselli 1682, 253-73 passim. Miselli, a pontifical courier and messenger, included in his vocabulary six languages: Italian, French, Spanish, German, Polish, and Turkish. The book enjoyed great popularity and went through seven editions between 1682 and 1699, including a German translation. On its Turkish linguistic materials, see Stackowski 1970; cf. Tinti 2014 on the work generally.

89. Palerne 1606, 522–54. Palerne's vocabulary includes headwords in French with their glosses in Italian, demotic Greek ("Grec vulgaire"), Turkish, Arabic ("Moresque"), and Slavic.

90. Palerne did, however, provide glosses for all four in other languages, namely "Hiasidich," "Hiasethi," "Mallem," (in colloquial Arabic) and "Draga" (in Slavic, though the gloss appears, curiously, under Arabic as well). Palerne 1606, 525.

91. Cited in Omont 1890, 7–9.

92. Megiser 1612.

93. Febure 1681, 525–28. The work was essentially an expanded edition of his earlier *Specchio overo Descritione della Turchia* (1674). Heyberger 2017.

94. Agnellini 1688, 13.

95. Agnellini 1688, 22–33.

96. While exceeding the scope of the current work, it would be interesting to compare Agnellini's chosen proverbs with the one hundred Persian proverbs with commentary produced in Levinus Warner's *Proverbiorum et sententiarum*

Persicarum centuria (Leiden, 1644), which were largely taken from Sa'dî's *Gulistân*. Vrolijk et al. 2012, 32.

97. Such an interpretation is supported by his biography. Agnellini (literally "lambkins," an Italian calque of his name, Karnûsh) was born as Humayli Ibn Da'fi in Mardin in the Ottoman eastern province of Diyarbakır ("Mesopotamia," as he called it), bordering on present-day Syria and Iraq. While serving as a Syriac Orthodox archbishop in his hometown (which was the patriarchate seat of the Syriac Orthodox Church) he converted to Catholicism and, ca. 1671, relocated to the Italian peninsula. He then traveled to France and Spain before accepting the Venetian cardinal Gregorio Barbarigo's invitation to come to his seminary in Padua. Agnellini was first entrusted with teaching Ottoman and, after the death of the previous holder of the chair of Arabic, with that language as well. He was also responsible for managing the Oriental section of the seminary's printing press, which published several of his other writings in Armenian and in Arabic. The second part of Agnellini's work, a pentalingual vocabulary alphabetized by Latin headwords, suggests its intended use for translating into rather than from Arabic, Turkish, and Persian. While it includes a few religious terms (Abbot, Resurrection), it covers mostly everyday lexemes (e.g., Tax, Provisions, Beer), including some fairly random ones (e.g., Rhinoceros, Western Breeze, Civet, Cockle). Jumping abruptly from the letter F to the letter R, it is hardly comprehensive or systematic, even for the letters it covers. Heyberger 1995; Scarpa 2000.

98. Rocchi 2015.

99. On Lupis, see Yağmur 2015; on the Bosnian Franciscans, see Adamović 1996; Causevic 2004; on the Illésházy manuscript, see Németh 1970, 15, 18–19, 24–25. Given the patterning of orthographic errors throughout the manuscript, it remains a distinct possibility that at least some sections—beyond the abbreviated grammar known to have been adapted from Molino—were also copied from a yet to be identified printed work. For another mid-eighteenth-century missionary Turkish dictionary reflecting "the south-eastern Turkish dialect, with strong Armenian overtones in its phonetics and, to some extent, also in its vocabulary," see Majda 2013, 7.

100. Schweickard 2014. On Montalbano's Ottoman sojourn and his long friendship with the Moldavian Voivode Graziani, whom he met in Istanbul as a young man, see Rocchi 2014.

101. El-Rouayheb 2015.

102. On the vital contributions of Central European religious refugees to the Ottoman court, not least in the field of diplomatic translation, see Krstić 2009.

103. Günergun 2007, 192–93; Peirce 2010; Petrovich 2013.

104. Balta and Kappler 2010.

105. Stein 2001, 165.

106. Zwartjes and Woidich 2012.

107. Rentzsch 2009, 370.

108. Strauss 1995, 190n2.

109. On the chronological arc of this development see Stein 2001.

110. Of further note is the greater incidence of combined works among missionaries, who perhaps intended their texts as practical, economical reference works in the field.

111. On Du Ryer's "attempt to find a Latin equivalent for Turkish grammatical concepts which could not in fact be translated," see Hamilton and Richard 2004, 66.

112. See Kappler 2014, Zwartjes 2014, 458–59. On Arabic paradigms in the study of Turkic grammar, see Ermers 1999.

113. Molino 1641, "Alli benigni lettori."

114. On vernacular Anatolian Turkish supplanting Armenian as a language of everyday communication, as well as literary production in Anatolian Armenian communities, see Aslanian 2016, 57–58.

115. Święcicka 2020, 41, 51.

116. "possede et parla bene la lingua turca, se bene non tanto culta, qualto quelli che sono allevati qui": SDispC, filza 102 (10 August 1626), quoted in Święcicka 2020, 44.

117. Molino was hardly unique in this regard. Johannes Heyman, in justifying an additional stint in Istanbul before returning to the Dutch Republic to assume his post as chair of Oriental languages at Leiden, explained that, while his sojourn in Izmir as a chaplain for the Dutch Consulate from 1700 to 1707 had provided him with a solid command of colloquial Turkish, "at the court of the Grand Signor and in all official writing the language of the scholars and courtiers is that which is mixed with Arabic and Persian words and phrases," for which he needed to immerse himself in the courtly environment of Istanbul. Quoted in Van den Boogert 2017, 301.

118. Stein 2001, 170.

119. Lewis 1999, 12.

120. As Römer 2016 notes, the Viennese tradition of teaching Ottoman has retained this principle, and still requires the study of Arabic in parallel with modern Turkish.

121. "ut qui has duas ignorarit, Turcicam rite callere nunquam dici possit . . . ": Meninski 1680a, 1.

122. Berthier 1992, 78–79.

123. Roper 2009, 84.

124. "Lingua Turcica magnam habet cum Persica & Tartarica cognationem; sed ab Arabica plane est diversa. In sacris tamen utplurimum hanc usurpant Turci: cum Alcoranus in ea sit conscriptus: Quinetjam, usdem omnino, quibus Arabes, in scribendo utuntur literarum characteribus: & iisdem quoque; punctis, seu vocalium potis": Megiser 1612, 2.

125. "[L]a Lingua Turca è come nell'Italia la Prouinciale, nella quale cadauno parla con le forme, e con la pronuncia, & accento del paese. Ma questa si rende

adornata dalla Persiana, si come noi facciamo con la Toscana. Tuttauia sarà di maggior proua di questa verità.

Che nello stesso modo pur anco si ritroua l'Arabo trà Turchi, si come il Latino trà noi; poiche sendo l'Alcorano scritto nella suddetta lingua, si rende l'Araba necessaria a loro, come alli nostri la lingua, in cui si ritroua la Sacra Scrittura. Vsando le maniere, le voci, e li periodi Arabi intieri per ornamento, per elocutione, e per decoro, massime nelli maneggi, nelli commandamenti, & altri ordini de' maggiori negotij, & arbitrij; lettere del Principe, Ministri, Bassà, e commando dell'Imperiale volontà. In somma presso loro l'eruditione maggiore si spiega, & vsa nelli huomini di Legge, che sono quelli, che s'impiegano nelli Tribunali di Giudicatura, nelli Parrochi, ò altri Sacerdoti loro, come si disse; come pure negli huomini più distinti nella Corte delle Nodarie, Segretarie, e Cancellarie, quali tutti per necessità di loro Ministero intendono, parlano, e scriuono l'Arabo": Donado 1688a, 6–8.

126. That he includes "parish pastors" (*parrochi*, clearly a commensuration of the office of *imam*) in this distinguished milieu may betray the extent to which Donà took his *ulema* interlocutors (and their at times inflated sense of self-importance) at their word: while the position of imam in a neighborhood mosque could provide a modest income to a *medrese* graduate, it was hardly the place to display one's erudition in Arabic. Beyond basic literacy and the recitation of Qur'anic prayers, neighborhood imams in early modern Istanbul seem to have served primarily as local scribes and property administrators. Literary flourish—in any language—was by no means a prerequisite for the job. On early modern Istanbulite imams and their duties, see Behar 2003, 67–71. On class and regional tensions within the seventeenth-century *ulema*, see Zilfi 2006.

127. "quali appariscono ritrosi, e di costume inciuili à quelli, che per non saper la loro lingua, con essi trattare non possono; mà quelli che la sanno li trouano domestici e affabili, e tanto più, quanto si parla con loro con maggior' eloquenza: per questo desiderando seruire all'vtilità publica, massimamente à quelli, che nell'Otomanno Impero pratticano, e facilitare l'acquisto della lingua Turchesca, ci siamo affaticati nell'imparare detta lingua, pratticando con li più dotti, leggendo li loro libri, considerando li commandamenti Regij, essaminando gl'Instromenti, e le scritture di giustitia con li più intelligenti Maestri si trouassero in Constantinopoli, li quali pagati dall'Eccellentissimo e Nobilissimo Signor Conte di Cesi di felice memoria, all'ora Ambasciatore per sua Maestà Christianissima, insegnauano il suo sempre lodato figliuolo Monsù di Conti, adesso per le sue rare virtù degnissimo Vescouo di Lodeues, al quale insegnauo ancora la lingua Latina, la quale possiede tanto puramente con la Turchesca, Italiana, e Greca, quanto la Francese à lui natural, al quale possiamo dire hauer l'obligo di questo Vocabolario; mentre con suo mezzo l'habbiamo compilato, raccogliendo, com l'Ape fà da diuersi fiori il suo liquore, non solamente li vocaboli volgari, mà ancora quelli, delli quali si seruono li Turchi nel parlar loro eloquente, nel comporre i libri, nel manifestare li ordini Regij, nel fare gl'Instromenti di giustitia, e nel scriuere le loro epistole: per questo è stato necessario di raccogliere molte parole

Arabe, e Persiane, per le quali forse che l'intelligenti sia nella lingua Araba, sia nella Persiana non esercitati nelle scritture Turchesche si marauigliaranno, che in questo Vocabolario si ritrouino tanti vocaboli, si d'vna lingua, come dell'altra, non sapendo la mescolanza, che fanno li Turchi di quelle lingue, mà al contrario crediamo che li pratichi delli libri Turcheschi restaranno attoniti, che con tanta fatica in vn libro si siano raccolte la maggior parte delle parole, delle quali si seruono li Turchi nelle scritture di giustitia, e nelle loro lettere, mentre in quelle si seruono delle Arabe, e in queste delle Persiane; nelli libri però adoprano tanto le Arabe, quanto le Persiane, & altre corrotte secondo la Prouincia dell'Autore": De Paris 1665, unpaginated.

128. "e saranno notati con le lettere T. A. P. e distinti con asterisci, ò stelluccie per leuar la confusion. E quando saranno doi, ò tre non notati, saranno da tutti intesi."

129. "Turcas non tantum ad supplendos defectus suae origine alias & usu barbarae linguae, sed etiam ad elegantiam sermonis, qui modo cultissimus dici potest, uti passim tam in loquendo, quam praecipue in scribendo vocibus, phrasibus sententiisque linguae Arabicae origine, ufu, majestate, & verborum copia nobilissimae ac antiquissimae, simul & Persicae nulli forte alii suavitate ac elegantia secundae, ita ut qui has duas ignorarit, Turcicam rite callere nunquam dici possit, ideoque singulis capitibus hujus Grammaticae Turcicae subjungi observationes ac praeceptiones utriusq; linguae Arabicae & Persicae": Meninski 1680b, 1. This and all following translations from Meninski's Latin are by Dylan Wilkerson, for whose expert help I am immensely grateful.

130. Meninski 1680b, prooemium.

131. Meninski 1680b.

132. On the steadily shrinking usage of (neo-)Latin outside scholarly communication from the mid-seventeenth century onward, see Helander 2012.

133. García-Arenal and Rodríguez Mediano 2017, 144; Gilbert 2020.

134. Hamilton and Richard 2004, 61.

135. It is quite telling that in the 1756 edition of Meninski's work, issued in conjunction with the opening of the Viennese Orientalische Akademie, the editor, Adam František Kollár, employee of the Imperial-Royal Library in Vienna, saw fit to add a reading excerpt for students from the *'ahdnâme* concluded under Sultan Ahmed I in 1669, at the end of the Ottoman-Venetian War of Crete. Meninski 1756, 2, 228–43.

136. The latter was probably the translation of Bellarmino's popular *Doctrina Christiana* undertaken by the Roman-educated Maronites Naṣrallāh Šalaq and Gabriel Sionita and printed by the Roman Typographia Savariana in 1615. The former was either Agostino Giustiniaini's 1516 multilingual edition, known as *Octaplum Psalterium* (Giustiniani 1516), or the Arabic Psalter printed by the Savariana in 1614, on which see Duverdier 1987, 323.

137. Kuru and Inan 2011.

138. Meninski 1680a, 196–216.

139. On the global permutations of this text, see Rajan 2006; Riedel 2010; van Ruymbeke 2016. On its complex Arabic, Anatolian Turkish, and Ottoman itineraries, see Paker and Toska 1997.

140. Bidpai 1654, 117–27.

141. Kuru 2016, 1201.

142. Kaya 2011.

143. Heller and McElhinny 2017, 43.

144. "les Turcs à Constantinople se voulant diverter font venire devant eux des Arabes, qu'ils font parler en cette langue; cependant c'est leur langue sainte, car leur Alcoran et toutes leurs priers sont en arabe, et ils dissent communément que la langue turque sert en ce monde et qu'en Paradis on parlera la langue arabe, et en Enger la Persienne, qui toutefois est belle, et fair la meilleure partie des poesies et chansons turques, mais comme ils haïssent extrêmement les Persiens, ils médisent de tout ce qui les regarde": Thévenot 1665, 297–98.

145. It remains a distinct possibility that Thévenot was actually revoicing here dragomans' unique perspective on the linguistic ecology of the Ottoman court. Not only was he hosted by the French embassy during his ten-month Istanbulite sojourn in 1656 but he was also a personal friend of d'Herbelot, who cited Thévenot in his *Bibliothèque Orientale*, and served as the godfather to the dragoman's son (and future dragoman himself) François Pétis de la Croix *fils*. Dew 2009, 85; Bevilacqua 2018, 270n65.

146. "Tota enim Lingua Persica et Tartara, immensumque arabicae linguae pelagus, esset uno volumine complectendum, nam Turcica Lingua inculta est et barbara, latrocinium omnium fere Linguarum orientalium, quibus Turcae promiscue ac indifferenter uti consueverunt": quoted in Hamilton and Richard 2004, 68.

147. "il parlar Turchesco vi è accompagnato dal Arabo, Persiano, Greco, e Tartaro, e per maggior sodisfattione delli curiosi, si ha' dichiarato in molti lochi le voci Arabe, Persiane, Greche, e Tartare": Molino 1641, "Letter to the reader."

148. "Turcismus Vulgaris & Literalis, idett: Arabismo & Persismo grammaticaliter & syntacticè mixtus."

149. "Pretendono i Turchi, e con ragione, esser lor fauella dell' Araba figliuola, ma dall'aiuto d'altre trè lingue arricchita, che sono Greca, Persiana, e Tartara, e questo ben puossi ragioneuolmente credere, auend'ella moltissimi vocaboli con quelle comuni, dal che nasce, che ouunque queste si parlano, altresì chi ha la lingua Turchesca con ogni facilità maggiore le già dette intende; ch'ella sia con le dette mescolata, che più ricca, e copiosa di voci la rendono, non è difficile dimostrarsi, mentre quelle parte d'Imperio Greco dell' Asia oue in Greco parlavasi, in oggi non altrimenti che in Turchesco si fauella, il che fanno ancora alter I Greci, I Persi, gli Armeni, Caldei, Tartari, e molte altre Nazioni, che il noro latte della falsa Dottrina Maomettana anno per lo somma disgrazia beuuto": Mascis 1677: "Letter to the reader" ("Al benigno lettore"). On Mascis's limited command of Ottoman and heavy reliance on Molino, see Drimba 1992, 112.

150. Errington 2008; Trautmann 1997. Meninski's influence on Jones's Persian (and pedagogy) has been amply documented, see, e.g., van Ruymbeke 2016, 314–15. We should add that Jones's theories, as Rajeev Kinra (2016) has shown so convincingly, were also deeply indebted to his Persian teachers in Calcutta, and to a long tradition of comparative philology in the Mughal court. The parallels with the case of Ottoman, though they remain to be explored in greater detail, seem unmistakable.

151. "[Q]uicunque in Aula hac Cæsarea aut alterius cujusvis Principis perfectus linguæ Turcicæ Interpres dici cupit, necessariò Arabicis Persicisque literis imbui debeat, non secus ac ipsi Turcæ statim atque legere incipiunt, utriusque linguæ studio singularem navant operatam, nec ullas deinceps scribunt sive ad suos sive ad extraneos literas, absque adscito ex vocibus phrasibusve Persicis ac Arabicis ornatu, elegantique intertexture: ita tamen, ut multi eorum minus docti non internoscant Arabicas à Persicis Turcicisve, ex usu tantùm cujusque vocis significationem intelligentes sermonique adaptantes": Meninski 1680b, prooemium.

152. Ferguson 2018.

153. Jones 1807 [1771], 610.

154. On Jones's encounter with Persian as a language of empire, and the importance of learning it from elite Mughal speakers, see Raj 2019.

Chapter 6: Translating the Ottomans

1. BaC, b. 252, fasc. 340, 87, undated.

2. For a general introduction to the *Carte Turche* and an inventory of the first dozen registers, albeit with little reference to translation practices, see Mumcu 2014.

3. The immediate context for Querini's request was an ongoing (and eventually successful) effort to turn the Franciscan complex into a mosque, in the wake of repeated fires that had destroyed the original structure. Girardelli 2010. For documents on the local congregation's efforts to renovate and preserve the complex, see also Matteucci 1967.

4. Tezcan 2011b, 269–70.

5. De Vivo 2007, 55; De Vivo 2010; Raines 2011; De Vivo 2013.

6. The currently known exemplars of this hybrid genre (of which others are likely to emerge) include British Archives, State Papers 105/216 ("Firmans, concerning the trade and diplomatic representation of English merchants"); 105/334 ("Book of Firmans, (Turkish) with Italian translations, concerning English merchants at Smyrna, 1678–1724"); 110/88 ("Letter book of Sir William Trumbull, resident ambassador to Turkey"); John Rylands Library, University of Manchester, MS Turkish 45 and 46 ("Ottoman documents with French translations, collected by French dragoman Jean-Baptiste Perille, 1732–1805/1806"); BnF, MS Turc 130; and several specimens in Leiden and Dubrovnik. Absent a synthetic study see the

specific case studies in Heywood 1993, 2000; Schmidt 1999, 2002, 2012; Kołodzie-jczyk 2011. On the compilation of such registers by dragoman-archivists in the Ragusan chancery, see Zecevic 2014, 391–92.

7. On European letterbooks, see Daybell 2012, 175–216. On equivalent Ottoman practices, see Faroqhi 1986; Goffman 1990; Riedlmayer 2008; Burak 2016.

8. At least one specimen, Rylands Turkish 46, was "collected by a family of dragomans of the French embassy in Pera," the Fornetti. Schmidt 1999, 376. Another, BnF, MS Turc 130, including "copies of two hundred sultanic decrees; the *'ahdnâme*s granted to France in 1569, 1581, and 1597; and a selection of twenty-two *fetva*s issued by several contemporary *şeyhülislam*s concerning trade, taxes, piracy, and captivity" was compiled by the former French ambassador to the Porte François Savary de Brèves upon his return to Paris in 1605 as a manual for his protégé, the future French consul in Egypt André Du Ryer. White 2015, 205; Panaite 2014. Mariusz Kaczka (2019, 204) describes the letterbooks of a dragoman in Polish employ in the eighteenth century, Francesco Giuliani, transferred along with Giuliani's entire personal archive and book collection to his successor (and based, at least partially, on that of his predecessor in that office, Giorgio Lomaca).

9. Liu 1995, 26.

10. On the nomenclature debates within Translation Studies, see Pym 2018; Pym and Torres-Símon 2014.

11. Sakai 2006; Gal 2015; Derrida 2001; Severi and Hanks 2015.

12. To my knowledge, the only corpus linguistic study of dragomans' writings to date is Muru 2016, which focuses exclusively on their Italian orthography and morphology.

13. On corsairing in the Adriatic and eastern Mediterranean and its diplomatic and commercial implications for Venetian-Ottoman relations, see Brummett 1994, 89–121; White 2017.

14. Both translations, along with the original Ottoman text, are in DT, b. 9, fasc. 1057–59. My deepest gratitude to Vera Costantini for taking photos of the Ottoman letter with the kind assistance of Dott.ssa Michela dal Borgo of the Venetian State Archives. For more information on the archival series of *Documenti Turchi* in general, and on the specific events that led to the diplomatic exchange between the sultan and the doge, see Pedani 1994, 271–72.

15. Established in 1446, the School of St. Mark admitted annually twelve students in their early teens "so that they might go to school to learn 'grammar, rhetoric and other subjects useful for the Chancery and how to write well.'" By the mid-sixteenth century, the School's state-funded lectureships in poetry, oratory, history, grammar, rhetoric, and especially Greek and Latin philology helped seal its humanist reputation. Ross 1976, 526, 532–35. On public schooling in sixteenth-century Venice more generally see Grendler 1989, 61–70.

16. BaC, b. 263, fasc. 2.1, 168r–v (10 March 1582). The idea of joining the bailate may have emerged from conversations with Matteo Marucini, another Venetian

citizen by birth who at the time served as a dragoman in Istanbul, and who in 1581 entrusted young Girolamo with the task of recovering monies owed him by Mehmed Çelebi, the bailate's Turkish-language instructor (*hoca*). BaC, b. 263, fasc. 2.2, 55r (18 August 1581).

17. SDispC, b. 28, 481r–482r (11 February 1588 m.v.). Examples of Alberti's translations of Ottoman texts in the course of his long career in Istanbul are in SDispC, b. 28, 397r, 445r–v (5 January 1588 m.v.); b. 50, 20r, 23r–25r (4 September 1599).

18. SDispC, b. 28, 481r (11 February 1588 m.v.); CCD, LAC, b. 6, 98r (22 August 1588).

19. SDispC, b. 50, 265r (10 January 1599 m.v.). A few years later, Alberti became secretary to the Venetian proveditor general in Crete. CCD, LAC, b. 6, 127r–v (17 November 1591); BaC, b. 275, fasc. 1, 41r–v, 147r–v (23 August 1605 and 25 January 1607 m.v.).

20. The de Nores were among the islands' Frankish feudatories, while the Podocataro were Greek-Cypriot Catholics. On the Cypriot nobility under Venetian rule, see Arbel 1995a.

21. Rudt de Collenberg 1983, 52, 60–61.

22. Notarile, Atti, b. 32, 41r–42v (17 February 1591 m.v.). Corazzol (1994, 776) discusses the deed for the ransom but does not identify de Nores as a future dragoman.

23. I thank the late Maria-Pia Pedani for emphasizing these issues in a personal communication.

24. The following analysis is informed by two separate transcriptions and translations of the original Ottoman document, one by Tijana Krstić and the other by Gülay Yılmaz. I am immensely grateful to both and remain solely responsible for the argument here.

25. Senato, Mar, filza 128, unpaginated (13 December 1594), my emphasis.

26. Hermans 1997.

27. De Nores too uses similar constructions, "l'eccelsa mia Corte Imperiale" (my sublime Imperial Court) and "sublime Corte Imperiale" (Sublime Imperial Court) later on.

28. As John Denton (1998, 70–71) suggests, use of explanatory glosses with textual markers such as "that is to say" to compensate for presumed gaps in readers' contextual knowledge was a common strategy among Renaissance vernacular translators of Latin antiquity. On early modern European translators' glosses of Ottoman terminology specifically, see McJannet 2006; Burke 2012, especially 146ff.

29. On Ottoman concepts of sovereignty, see Murphey 2008; Wigen 2013.

30. Rothman 2011a, 189–210.

31. MCC, Cod. Cicogna 2715, fasc. 38, fols. 315r–331v.

32. "Le rivolutioni Ottomane principate dalla Vita infortunata [etc.]": MCC, Cod. Morosini-Grimani 540, fasc. 24, unfoliated.

33. Cicogna's handwritten catalog gives the codex the title "Storia sacra e profana divisa per città e Provincie non Veneziane: Lettera C Costantinopoli = Turchi = Tartaria. MCC, Cod. Cicogna, Catalogo, 2, 448v.

34. MCC, Cod. Cicogna 2715, fasc. 31. The dragoman, identified by Salvago only by his last name, was likely Cristoforo Brutti, who translated numerous sultanic decrees in the *Carte Turche* in the early 1620s. See BaC, 251, fasc. 334.

35. MCC, Cod. Cicogna 2715, fasc. 32

36. MCC, Cod. Cicogna 2715, fasc. 33.

37. MCC, Cod. Cicogna 2715, fascs. 34–35.

38. MCC, Cod. Cicogna 2715, fasc. 36

39. On Minucci and his treatise, see Marani 1969.

40. MCC, Cod. Cicogna 2715, fascs. 22–27.

41. Krstić 2013. In the context of mounting military confrontations between the Ottomans and Safavids throughout the sixteenth and early seventeenth centuries, theological differences enabled both sultan and shah to recast themselves as universal leaders of the *ummah*, the community of believers. On the theological dimensions of Ottoman-Safavid rivalry, see Dressler 2005. On the multiplex processes of Ottoman Sunnitization that both predated and exceeded the parameters of Ottoman-Safavid rivalry, see Terzioğlu 2012; Erginbaş 2017; Krstić and Terzioğlu 2020.

42. DT, b.13, fasc. 1501, 1502; Pedani 1994, 407–9.

43. On the links between the historiography of the deposition of Osman II in 1622 and contemporary political and intellectual factions, see Tezcan 2002; Piterberg 2003; Hagen 2006.

44. Foscarini's mission never materialized, and Salvago was eventually sent to North Africa instead, as discussed in Chapter 3.

45. For Galland's unpublished account of the same events, see Abdel-Halim 1964, 219.

46. Tezcan 2002.

47. 320v, for governo: 317r, 318v.

48. Lybyer 2013 and Chapter 5.

49. Benetti uses the conjunction dozens of times in a fairly systematic way to gloss Ottoman nomenclature throughout his travelogue, for example "Asgì, cioè Cuoco, Carica di titolo fra questa Natione" (11), "Matarazì, e Tufeczì della sua Camera, cioè Bardacchiere, che gli somministra l'acqua, e Schioppettiere, che a piede appoggiauano la man sinistra sopra la groppa del cauallo" (12), "Chiaià, e Chiatip, cioè suo Vicario, e Notaio" (14), "Adil Chioschi, cioè Chiosco della Giustitia" (21), "Muteferachà, cioè Lancie spezzate" (36), and so forth.

50. Borovaya (2017, 148–49) notes the prevalence of "ke elyos lyaman" (Ladino for "which they call") in Moses Almosnino's *Crónica de los Reyes Otomanos* (ca. 1567), particularly in glossing Ottoman administrative and military terms, which the author, a Salonica-based scholar and rabbi, intended to teach his readership of elite Ottoman Sephardim in the hope of making them more serviceable to the empire.

51. Salvago, 320r, 326r.

52. 320v, 323v–324r, 326r–v.

53. "Arabi masnadieri, e maladrini": 320v.

54. "Che non vi andò mai niun Ottomano": 320v.

55. 322v–323v. In a further act of covert translation and commensuration, Salvago refers to the place as "Moschea di sultan Mehemmet," alluding to its eponymous patron, Sultan Mehmed the Conqueror (Fatih). He also mentions in passing that the neighborhood where the mosque is located was the residence of many *ulema*, thus providing a spatial rationale for the aggrieved party's route (and, in passim, underscoring his own nuanced familiarity with the social geography of the Ottoman capital).

56. *RELATIONE Delli Successi dell'Impero Ottomano, principiando dell'An'o di Mahometto 1047 sino li 1071 è DI CHRISTO N'RO SIGNORE 1638 sino li 1660 Composta in Lingua Turca DA HASSAN VEZHI è Tradotta all'Idioma Italiano DA GIACOMO TARSIA Dragomano Veneto In Pera di Costantinopoli li 20 Ottobre 1675*. BNM, MSS It. VI 84 (6053). The Marciana autograph came from the collections of the eighteenth-century antiquarian brothers Giacomo and Bernardo Nani, as attested by a bookplate. At least one other manuscript copy is known to have existed in the library of the book collector Richard Heber, Esq., and is recorded as It. 1604 in the library's auction catalog produced by the auctioneer R. H. Evans in the early 1830s. Evans 1836, 168. On the Nani brothers' collecting activities throughout Venice's maritime colonies, see Calvelli et al. 2017.

57. Atsiz 1977.

58. Tarsia, 82, 86.

59. Short excerpts in translation, including by Carli, appeared in Donà's *Della letteratura,* discussed above.

60. Donà 1688a, 1688b, Benetti 1688. Poletti was an established printer and publisher, responsible, among others, for several editions of Vincenzo Coronelli's geographical and cartographical works. Rhodes 1987, 78.

61. As Nabil al-Takriti (2017, 143–45) notes, extensions of the work continued well into the nineteenth century, attesting to its enduring popularity and utility among Ottoman literati. On Warner's efforts to acquire Katip Çelebi's library, as mediated by another Ottoman scholar, Muhammad al-'Urdi, see Witkam 2006.

62. Galland's *Chronologie mahométane* is in BnF, MS Fr. 5587 (1). Reiske's Latin translation remains uncataloged alongside his other papers in the Royal Library in Copenhagen. Haddad 2016, 21–22.

63. Hagen 2007.

64. Hagen 2007, 2.

65. Dew 2004; Bevilacqua 2016.

66. "vedere disingannato il Mondo della rea opinione, che non vi si conservi trà quei Barbari alcun seme d'erudizione": Carli 1697, dedication.

67. Marginal notes appear in dragomans' manuscript production as well. Giovanni Battista Salvago, for example, made abundant use of them in his narratives on Muslim rituals and theology discussed above.

68. Another term often used in Ottoman official records of the period is *mille-ti'l-Mesihiyye*, literally "the millet of the Messiah."

69. Carli 1697, 36, 49 (glossed), 8, 20, 37, 115, 165 (unglossed). The term "Christiani," referring to Christians as a collectivity of people, appears in the body of the text throughout (22, 120, 121, 128, 131, 137, 142, 154, 155, 162, 163, 186) and in the forms "Essercito Christiano" (Christian army, 155) and "Armata Christiana" (Christian Armada, 163). The "style sheet" seems to shift halfway through the book, around p. 120.

70. Carli 1697, 17.

71. Carli 1697, 82.

72. For representative critiques, see Boyden 2006, Milton 2008; Myskja 2013.

73. Botley 2004.

74. Tymoczko 2003 and Pym 1998 are exceptions that prove the rule, but still do not address translators' role in constituting the boundaries of the languages they purport to move across. On "translation" as a generative rubric for the host of mediation practices partaking in boundary-marking, see Gal 2015.

75. Wansbrough 1996, 77–78; Windler 2001, 85; Hermans 2012; Petitjean 2013; Tommasino 2015.

76. Abraham Hartwell's translation, *The Ottoman of Lazaro Soranzo* (1603), uses Italian orthography throughout (e.g., "gi" to render the Turkish postalveolar "c" sound, for example "Giaffer," "Sangiacches," "Giannizzaries") and pluralizes numerous Ottoman nouns with the Italianized suffix i (e.g. "Spahoglani," "Agiamoglani," "Timari"/"Timarioti," and "chiaussi"). The impact of Italian orthography is similarly apparent throughout Rycaut (1668), for example in the lexemes "hogia" (*hoca*), "Sanciack," "Ogiack" (*ocak*), "sarigia" (*sarıca*) and "Agiamoglans." Likewise, "sangiaccato," an Italian grammaticalization and orthographization of the Ottoman *sancak*, appears in numerous sixteenth-and seventeenth-century English, French, German, and Greek translations of assorted Italian chronicles (e.g., Robert Honywood's 1673 "Englishing" of Battista Nani's *The History of the Affairs of Europe in this Present Age*), throughout the *Calendar of State Papers*, and even as late as Charles Grey's translation of Angiolello (1873, 93). Finally, the imprint of Italian orthography and grammar is noticeable in other contemporary translations from Italian, e.g. "chiaussi" (plural form of the Ottoman *çavuş*) in Ogilby 1670, "sangiaco" and "Damasco" in Carr 1600, 61, 10–11,18, 22–23, and even in works by English authors, such as Fynes Moryson's *Itinerary* of 1617 ("Sangiaco," 222, "Chiauss," 269). On Ottoman (and Persian) lexemes in early modern English (albeit with little regard for morphological variation), see Cannon 2000. For the French case, see Stachowski 2015. On Italianisms in Ottoman "transcription texts," see Rocchi 2013.

77. Burke 2012, 151.

78. As Carter Findley (2019, 103) notes, the Swedish dragoman of Armenian and French descent Mouradgea d'Ohsson's *Tableau Général de l'empire othoman* includes various glosses, including lengthy "observations," which mimic the "digressions" (*istitrad*) found in Ottoman chronicles, even if "in spirit they may stray far from the way that subject is treated in Islamic law." For an emphasis rather on d'Ohsson's "contingency and entanglement" of Ottoman and French cultures, see Fraser 2010.

79. Tedlock and Mannheim 1995.

80. Carli 1697, n.p.

Chapter 7: Circulating "Turkish Literature"

1. Gilmore 1947, 722.

2. Colla 2015, 146.

3. Leibniz 1710, 1–16. On this essay's pivotal role in the development of historical linguistics, see de Buzon 2012; Baasten 2003. On the Royal Prussian Society, the *Miscellanea Berolinensia*, and the numerous challenges of bringing its first issue to print, see Kraft 2011. On the broader intellectual pursuits that led Leibniz to approach Podestà, see Carhart 2019, 98–100.

4. The exchange is summarized in Latin (sadly without dates or further details about the nature of the two scholars' exchange) in Leibniz 1718, 49–56 (reproduced in Leibniz 1768, vol. 6, part 2, 228–31). The same summary in French is in Pougens 1799, 70–73.

5. Erginbaş 2013, 136–37, 135.

6. Canatar 2005.

7. Cenābī 1680.

8. Roper 2014, 214. Especially ambitious in this regard was Podestà's three-volume *Cursus Grammaticalis* of Arabic, Persian, and Turkish, which totaled over 2,900 pages, and which Voigt printed in several editions from 1688 to 1703, using Arabic typeface throughout.

9. Podestà 1671, 1672a, 1672b. The German edition does not survive, but is alluded to by Podestà himself, and reported (with title and publication details) in Brunati 1837.

10. Gaudier 1567, on which see Höfert 2015 and below.

11. ". . . applicheremo con umlità, e daremo miglior perfettione a' nostri talenti, e con grand' utilità della Patria, alleuaremo, queste in Europa nuouamente nate lettere": Podestà 1672a, 190. He discusses the translation on pp. 3–4.

12. Similarly to Gian Rinaldo Carli's translation of Katip Çelebi some years later, Podestà's translation made ample use of marginal notes to provide analytical annotations. The vast majority of his notes consist of dates for events mentioned in the text, always in the format AC XXXX Heg. XXXX. Other notes gloss

culturally specific nomenclature, e.g., *oka*, which Podestà explains is a weight unit that equals two and a quarter Austrian pounds, "Except in Constantinople." Cenābī 1680, unpaginated.

13. Toomer 1995, 39. On Tengnagel's contributions to early Orientalism, see Römer 1996. On the central, and yet largely unacknowledged, role of Vienna's imperial librarians in the Republic of Letters, see Feola 2016; Molino 2016, 2017.

14. ÖNB, HAN, Cod. A. F. 12; Flügel 1865, 85–87.

15. According to WorldCat and Google Books, copies of the book are now available in Vienna, Prague, Munich, Göttingen, Weimar, Berlin, Wolfenbüttel, Budapest, Augsburg, Venice, Princeton, and Cleveland. Additional copies may also survive in a few private collections. It appears in several auction catalogs of private libraries from the late-eighteenth and nineteenth centuries, e.g., Panzer 1769, 343; Maison Silvestre 1838, 173; Martin 1850, 58; Grässe 1863, 638; Weigel 1865, 185.

16. Cody 2009.

17. De Zorzi 2017, 83.

18. Toderini 1787, vol. I, prefazione.

19. Toderini 1787, 212.

20. For a critique of the salvific properties of Ottoman print as ushering in a new civilizational phase for Islamicate societies, see Sajdi 2009; Schwartz 2017. On the complex circumstances that led Müteferrika to secure imperial permission to open his press in 1727, see Sabev 2018.

21. Toderini 1787, 213–22. It is noteworthy that Toderini describes Cala-vrò-Imberti's work not as a translation but rather as a "volgarizzamento," a vernacularization.

22. Fleischer 1986, 43.

23. Toderini 1787, vol. I, 63, 95. The only two known manuscript copies of Medun's translation are in the Marciana (BNM, MSS It. VI 272 [5686], likely an autograph), and in Bonn University Library (Manuscript Department, So 47, part of the bequest of the German Orientalist Johann Martin Augustin Scholz). On Kınalızade's moral philosophy, informed by Aristotle and al-Ghazali, among others, see Uysal 2007, 334; Götz and Sobieroj 1999, xvi. On the Marciana copy, see Zorzanello 1950, 99–100.

24. Infelise 1997a.

25. The translations in *Della letteratura* were undertaken for the most part by Gian Rinaldo Carli. The ones in the *Racolta curiosissima* were by Francesco Flangini, Stefano Fortis, and Antonio Benetti. On the collaborative nature of these publications, see Scarpa 2000; Preto 2013, 201–7. On Donà's ultimately failed Ottoman sojourn, see Gullino 1991.

26. De Zorzi 2017, 85.

27. On "invisible technicians," see Shapin 1989; Blair 2014.

28. Della Valle 2001, III (letter from Istanbul, 25 October 1614); Testa and Gautier 2003, 247.

29. On Gabai's wonderfully mercurial career as a printer and French dragoman between Istanbul and Izmir, see Hacker 1987.

30. Stoye 1994, 23.

31. Bologna, Biblioteca Universitaria, Fondo Marsigli (= BUB, FM), b. 51, 145v–148r (16 August 1680).

32. BUB, FM, b. 51, 127r, 136r, 137v (undated).

33. BUB, FM, b. 51, 141r (3 December 1685).

34. BUB, FM, b. 51, 154r–157r (undated).

35. BUB, FM, b. 52, unpaginated (ca. 1680). For further examples of Marsigli's double mediation of Ottoman courtly knowledge via (unnamed) dragomans' translation work, see D'Amora 2020.

36. On Busbecq, see Wunder 2003, and on his efforts to document systematically the linguistic variety of the Ottoman realm, see Considine 2008, 139–41.

37. Malcolm 2007, 329.

38. Ingram 2015; Darling 1994. *The Present State of the Ottoman Empire*, first printed in 1666, saw dozens of editions and translations both during Rycaut's lifetime (including French, Dutch, German, Italian, and Polish editions by 1678) and posthumously, "shap[ing] European perceptions of the Ottomans for a century." Anderson 2004. *The History of the Three Late Famous Impostors*, first published under the name of Rycaut's friend John Evelyn, was a highly influential and much-plagiarized account of Sabbatai Zevi, based in part on Rycaut's personal acquaintance with Zevi's father in Izmir. Popkin 1994. *The Present State of the Greek and Armenian Churches* went through several English and five French editions, in addition to a Dutch translation. A German edition of the *History* went through additional two reprints and "long remained an important source of knowledge to the Austrians about their mighty neighbor, with whom their own political and economic relations were far less extensive than those of the English": Anderson 1989, 230. Traces of Rycaut's lasting impact are evident throughout various eighteenth-century encyclopedic compendia.

39. Anderson 1989, 232–34, 237, 282.

40. Bevilacqua and Pfeifer 2013, 84.

41. On Vanmour, see Broos 2002; Gopin 2002; Sint Nicolaas 2003; O'Quinn 2019.

42. On Bellini, see Campbell and Chong 2005. On Rålamb, see Ådahl 2006. On the complex relations of transmission and re-appropriation between Ottoman and European portrait artists, see Majer 1991, 2000; Necipoğlu 2000. On embassy artists more generally, see Mansel 1988, 1996; Wilson 2003, 2007, 104–5. On the lasting artistic significance of embassy artists' representations of Ottoman lifeworlds see also Fraser 2017.

43. Hamilton 2004; Roper 2005; McJannet 2007; Malcolm 2007.

44. While never printed in his lifetime, multiple manuscripts of Busenello's *Lettere informative delle cose de Turchi*, dated 1744, circulated in Venice. Two different German translations were published in the 1770s, attesting to its reverberations in Enlightenment Ottomanist discourses beyond Venice. Preto 2013, 259–64.

45. The second volume seems to have enjoyed only limited circulation. Of the nine known surviving copies, seven are in Spain (including five in Madrid), one is in Gotha, and one in Zagreb. In other words, despite the relative accessibility of Italian, it remained confined to Habsburg territory. On Bratutti, see Gilbert 2020, 237–38.

46. On Wideman and his circle of elite clients, see Rózsa 2006; Etény 2014, 34.

47. Tellingly, in the 1654 volume, Bratutti included his portrait not as a frontispiece, but rather interleaved between the royal publication license and his letter to the reader.

48. Bratutti's insecurity about his position in Vienna and Madrid may have had strong psychological roots. In 1633, while still in Ragusan service in Istanbul, he was the subject of a poisoning attempt at a luncheon at the Viennese Resident's house, orchestrated by the Habsburg and Venetian authorities. Miović-Perić 2001, 88–89.

49. Bombaci 1969, 390–91. In an added irony, Sadeddin's chronicle was itself "essentially a translation," of a Persian text by Idris-i Bitlisi, a mid-fifteenth-century chancery official in Bayezid II's court. Stavrides 2001, 9.

50. Gelil 1678. The volume also included "sentencias filosóficas, compuestas por un doctor persa, llamado Seaid, y aora traducidas de lengua persiana en castellana por el mismo d. Vicente Bratuti." Rodríguez Mediano 2006, 261.

51. Babinger 1919, 110, who seems to have been aware only of the posthumous edition. I discuss Meninski's (uncredited) use of Bratutti's work in Chapter 5.

52. E.g., Adam Ebert's 1725 Latin translation of Bratutti, on which see Malcolm 2003, 90, n20 and bibliography.

53. Pétis de la Croix's compilation, like Galland's, appeared in multiple installments. The initial five volumes were printed before the translator's death in 1713, but at least ten more volumes were published posthumously in the course of the eighteenth century, followed by numerous other editions. They also spawned many "spoofs" over the next few decades, claiming to be translation-anthologies of Tatar, Peruvian, Mongol, ancient Gaul, and even French stories. Zakaria 2004.

54. Loop and van Leeuwen 2016.

55. Sebag 1978.

56. Galland 1724; Galland and Cardonne 1778.

57. Caylus 1743; Cardonne 1770 and the works cited in Loop and van Leeuwen 2016; see also Haddad 2016, 81–82, 89.

58. Boch 2005.

59. Aravamudan 2011.

60. On these translations, see Berthier 1997. On Müteferrika's intellectual enterprise, see Erginbaş 2014; Sabev 2018; van den Boogert 2005b.

61. Galland 1754, 1757.

62. Göçek 1987.

63. On Fonton, see Shiloah 1991; on Ali Ufki, see Haug 2016; on Cantemir, see O'Connell 2005.

64. Irving 2009, 385.

65. Theyls 1721, 1722. The work, which according to the author himself offered "the truth, directly gleaned from originals that I have in my possession," was translated into French the following year, and later served as a source for Voltaire's own history of Charles XII. Pierse 2003, 70–73; Baars 2014.

66. D'Ohsson 1787, 1788; Findley 2019, 39; Fraser 2010, 198–230.

67. This is the now lost *Essai sur la musique orientale ou explication du système des modes et des mesures de la musique turque.* Testa and Gautier 2003, 421–39.

68. Schmidt 2000.

69. Finkel 2015, 48–50.

70. Höfert 2015, 482; Molino 2016, 315–16.

71. Timonius 1714.

72. Pylarini 1714.

73. Testa and Gautier 2003, 238.

74. Bodleian Library, University of Oxford, Ms. Hyde 43. Neudecker 2005, 174, 182; Haug 2016.

75. Borromeo 2007, 855–58; Bayle 1820. An abridged English version of Ufki Bey's treatise on the palace also appeared in English print, and an unpublished French translation was found in the papers of Girardin, the French envoy to Istanbul, in 1686, who claimed to have authored it himself. Fisher and Garrett Fisher 1985, 118.

76. Neudecker 2005, 195.

77. Anderson 1989, 41.

78. SDispC, reg. III, 257b (February 4, 1630 m.v.). I thank Giorgio Rota for the reference.

79. Bombaci 1969, 401–2.

80. "J'avais entendu le jour précédent la lecture d'un discours italien écrit par le seigneur Maurocordato, touchant la force et la faiblesse de l'Empire ottoman": Galland 1881, vol. I, 236–37.

81. Pétis de la Croix 1696.

82. The work remains in manuscript: BnF, Suppl. Turc 694. Richard 2008, 5.

83. Bevilacqua 2016, 261, 215; as Bevilacqua argues, d'Herbelot strategically used several other Islamic compilations and anthologies, allowing him to cover immense ground, and also to refract their authors' perspective to some extent. Tommasino (2018b) introduces d'Herbelot's other possible interlocutor, the decidedly non-Ottoman Muslim scholar Ferdinando Medici/Muḥammad Bulghaith al-Darawi (b. 1624), a Moroccan formerly imprisoned in Livorno who became "reader of Arabic and Arabic letters" to Grand Prince Cosimo de' Medici and was eventually baptized in 1666, shortly before d'Herbelot first met and began corresponding with him.

84. Ansari and Schmidtke 2016, 108.

85. Bevilacqua 2016, 232. Galland also translated a section of the work in 1682, and sent it to Colbert in 1683, shortly before the latter's death, though it is unclear whether his translation was ever consulted by d'Herbelot. Richard 2008, 3.

86. Dew 2004, 239–41.

87. Two of Galland's main sources for these revisions were the poets Latifi and Kınalızade, luminaries of sixteenth-century Ottoman courtly literary culture. Bevilacqua 2016, 246–48.

88. Duverdier 1987, 326.

89. For examples of Istanbulite dragomans purchasing and inventorying Paris-bound early Arabic, Persian, and Ottoman manuscript collections (and the appointment of the future celebrity dragoman-scholar Antoine Galland as "royal antiquarian" in 1685), see Richard 1989, 5–11, 14–17; Richard 2008.

90. Melvin-Koushki 2018, 222n16 and 226.

91. Erginbaş 2013, 82.

92. Hagen 2003; Paker 2011. On the Islamicate cosmopolis more broadly, see Ricci 2011; El-Rouayheb 2015; Melvin-Koushki 2018.

93. Krstić 2011b. On Mehmed's Greek manuscript collection, which dates to the 1460s and 1470s, see Raby 1983. On printed books in sultanic libraries, see Roberts 2013, 154.

94. Mavroudi 2013. On the oral theological disputations at court that occasioned some of these translations see also Paker 2009, 555. On Mehmed's interest in Ptolemy's geography and the commissioning of its translation from his courtier George Amiroutzes of Trebizond in 1465, see also Pinto 2011, 157–58. As Mavroudi points out, the translation was likely carried out by Amiroutzes's elder son, Basileios/Mehmed Bey, who along with other youth from Trebizond formed a group of highly educated bilingual Greek/Arabic speakers in the sultan's court.

95. The first printed edition of the original (Vicenza, 1490) is now lost. It was reprinted by Ramusio in 1559 (66r–78r), with additional materials whose authorship is the subject of some scholarly debate. The author (or, by some accounts, translator) of the work, Giovanni Maria Angiolello, had taken part as an Ottoman captive in the campaign against the Ak Koyunlū Uzun Hasan with the Sultan's son Mustafa in 1474, and served as an Ottoman courtier for over a decade before returning to his native Vicenza. MacKay 2004, 219; Piemontese 2011.

96. Bombaci 1969, 324.

97. Günergun 2007, 197–98; Berardi 2017.

98. Tezcan 2011a, 199.

99. Günergun 2007, 202–3.

100. Stoye 1994, 25; Günergun 2007, 204–5; Erginbaş 2014, 71.

101. Günergun 2007, 206–10. On Ottoman courtly patronage of translations of scientific texts, see also Brentjes 2008, 428–29.

102. Osman Ağa 1998.

103. Du Halde 1732. According to Giambattista Toderini (1797, vol. 2, 146–47), who was shown the manuscript of the translation by Eremiani's son, himself a dragoman for the Danish embassy, the translators abbreviated any discussions of religion and other matters "disagreeable to the Turks." See also Van den Boogert 2005c, 247. On Lomaca, who in 1722–1723 traveled to France as Sultan Ahmed III's diplomatic envoy, see Calvi 2017, 24.

104. Krusinski 1730, Müteferrika 1732, discussed in Erginbaş 2014, 76–77, 81–82.

105. Findley 2019, 26.

106. Reychman and Zajączkowski 1968, 14–15.

107. Tezcan 2011a.

108. Özervarlı 2016.

109. Nuran Tezcan 2007, 1, 4. On the uniquely central position of poetry in Ottoman life in general, and courtly culture in particular, see Gamm 2011.

110. Aynur 2008, 497–99.

111. The Habsburg polymath and diplomatic envoy Count Karl Reviczky offers a case in point. Among Reviczky's most notable translations were a compilation of *ghazals* by the fourteenth-century Persian poet Hafez (based on collections in both Istanbul and Vienna), alongside eighteenth-century Ottoman treatises on government. O'Sullivan 2014, 80.

112. Sheikh 2016, esp. chapter 4.

113. Pfeifer 2015, 221. I thank Alexander Bevilacqua for raising this argument (personal communication).

114. Schellenberg 2016, 1.

115. As Strauss (2003) points out, even in the nineteenth century Europeans were confounded by an Ottoman reading public (and literary sphere) whose plurilingualism unsettled the expectations of a "national literature."

116. Wasti 2015.

117. Berthier 1997, 300; Blochet 1933, 75–76. On the long afterlife of these translations, disparaged as they may have been by later Orientalist readers, see the case of Istanbul-born Étienne Roboly, who in 1733 prepared a transcription and French translation of a sixty-four-folio chronicle attributed to the fifteenth-century Ottoman historian Uruç Bey, as discussed by Ménage 1971; Jasanoff 2005.

118. Casale 2017.

119. Indeed Al-Maqrizi became the focus of intense interest—through translations and critical editions—by French, Dutch, and German Orientalists from the late eighteenth century onward.

120. The early-twentieth-century Ottoman historian Ahmed Refik even used it as a source to quote (supposedly verbatim) a speech by Sultan Ahmed III. Erimtan 2008, 51.

121. Mignot 1787, i.

122. "je n'ai aucune connoissance des langues orientales": Mignot 1771, v.

123. Mignot 1787, v–vi. Not much is known about Bernard Bejault other than his position as royal librarian.

124. Mignot 1787, vi. Mignot's enthusiasm for this particular type of source ("These dispatches have discovered to me, more than any thing else, the genius, the force, the resources, the manners, of that nation I was desirous to describe") is especially noteworthy, as it suggests he was an "early adopter" of archival diplomatic reports as historical sources, well before Leopold von Ranke was to claim this as his methodological innovation. De Vivo 2011.

125. In Cardonne's case, his scholarly and bibliographic contributions continued in later years as royal secretary-interpreter, censor and inspector of the Royal Library, and, eventually, the holder of the chair for Turkish and Persian at the Collège Royal.

126. Naima's chronicle was the thirteenth book to be published by Müteferrika's press in 1741. It was printed in two volumes and sold especially well. The chronicles of Raşid and Asım were printed in a combined three-volume set in 1741. Woodhead 2012, 2017; Erginbaş 2014, 78–79; Kelecsényi n.d.

127. BnF, Supplément turc 917–19.

128. Tezcan 2007, 182.

129. See, for example, the 1844 illustrated edition of *Les mille et un jours* (Pajot 1844). Not only did the editor, "M. Sainte Croix Ajpot" (the orientalist Jules Pajot de Sainte Croix, who died in Yemen that year) expand Pétis de la Croix's original subhead of "contes persans" to read "contes persans, turcs, et chinois" and added to the list of translators "Cardonne, Caylus, etc.," but he also purported to have augmented their translations with additional new tales directly out of the Arabic, which he had acquired in Egypt some years earlier. It was, indeed, a truly Orientalist concoction, destined to have a long life of its own, with multiple editions and translations in the course of the nineteenth and twentieth centuries.

130. Makdisi and Nussbaum 2008, 1.

131. Ouyang and Gelder 2005; Yamanaka, Nishio, and Irwin 2006.

132. On Galland's various scribes and amanuenses in Istanbul and in Paris see Richard 2008. On his reliance on Diyab's orally mediated stories to supplement his collection and to give it its iconic stories, and for the European elements in Diyab's stories, see Bottigheimer 2014, Horta 2017. For Diyab's own account of these interactions, see Dyâb 2015. On the Anatolian mediation of Persian texts, and on the urban storytellers that Galland encountered during his sojourn in Istanbul, including Hoca Muzaffer, whose stories he recorded in his journal, see Marzolph 2015.

133. Tavakoli-Targhi 2001 and the Introduction.

134. Melvin-Koushki 2018, 221. Emphasis in the original.

Epilogue: Dragomans and the Routes of Orientalism

1. *Il Corriere Ordinario* 1712, 71.

2. Lodi 1701.

3. Fabris 2015.

4. Marcantonio's ancestors, the Mamuca and the Giustiniani, hailed from the Aegean island of Chios, but traced their roots to Messina and Genoa, respectively. Marcantonio's grandfather, Michele Mamuca, was a deputy in Chios, as was his uncle Giorgio, who was sent to Istanbul to negotiate on behalf of the community. Michele's wife, Marcantonio's paternal grandmother, was Girolama Giustiniani, descendant of the Giustiniani of Genoa. When the Genoese stronghold of Chios was captured by the Ottomans in 1566, both families—along with some of the island's remaining Catholic population—relocated to Istanbul, where their Italianate ancestry and Catholic bona fides proved highly fungible.

5. Through his aunt's marriage to the Greek Orthodox patrician Michalis Mavrocordato, Marcantonio became related to Alexander Mavrocordato, the illustrious Ottoman grand dragoman from 1673 to 1709, who himself established a dragoman dynasty in Ottoman service and secured for his descendants the title of Hospodars of Wallachia and Moldavia.

6. Stefani 1960, 31–41.

7. Ottoman historiography has resoundingly, and convincingly, rejected the paradigm of Ottoman decline. However, nineteenth-century Europeans undoubtedly understood the contemporary Ottoman Empire primarily through the lens of its shrinking territory and diminished political and military clout, magnified by assumptions about civilizational radical alterity. Neumann 1999; Çırakman 2002; Wigen 2018.

8. Szurek 2014, 351.

9. On the centrality of Arabic and Persian letters to the Palace School curriculum, see Miller (1941, 106), who suggests that the most popular texts in the seventeenth-century curriculum were in the genre of "Mulamma, narrative romances, or collections of short tales, characterized by a very ornate style with an unusually large admixture of Arabic and Persian words [. . .] As exercises in composition students wrote poetry and translated books, with commentaries appended, in both Arabic and Persian."

10. Pollock 2000; Melvin-Koushki 2018, 221 passim.

11. Messaoudi 2015, 25; Do Paço 2019b, 54.

12. Bevilacqua 2016. On the multiple provenances of the collection of "Turkish manuscripts" at the BnF, including the "Fonds des traductions," see Bibliothèque nationale de France 2007. The manuscript catalogue is in BnF, Suppl. turc 951 bis.

13. On the exercise books of Viennese *Sprachknaben* (apprentice dragomans) see, especially, Römer 2002. On the strong professional links between the Akademie, Vienna's Istanbulite diplomatic corps, and the office of Council Interpreter, see Reiter 2013. On the interplay between diplomacy and scholarship in Viennese-Istanbulite relations more broadly, see Do Paço 2015.

14. Kaczka 2019.

15. Richard 1989, 1.

16. Antoche 2015, 753–54.

17. On the De la Croix dragoman dynasty, see Sebag 1978; Ageron and Jaouhari 2014. On Galland, see Richard 2008; Marzolph 2015.

18. Chabert, who was born in Istanbul in 1766 to an Armenian mother and a Catholic father (himself a dragoman to the Polish and Sicilian legations), was sent at age thirteen to Vienna to attend the Oriental Academy, where he eventually became a professor of Oriental languages. Among others, he composed a simplified Turkish grammar and phrasebook based on Meninski's work, intended for use by military personnel on the Ottoman frontier. Römer 2018.

19. De Groot 2000, 244.

20. Beyond the bailate archives, manuscript exercise notebooks and other language-learning materials may well have been kept in dragomans' homes and lost over time, particularly with the political upheavals, professional mobilities, and physical dislocations that attended many Levantine families in the nineteenth and early-twentieth centuries.

21. On Venice's pioneering, if ultimately short-lived role in Arabic printing in the sixteenth century, see Vercellin 2001, 20–24. On the relative decline of Venetian printing houses after 1620, see Nuovo 2013, 421–23.

22. On this particular *translatio studii*, see Tommasino 2018a, 10–11 passim.

23. Quoted in Lucchetta 1983, 5.

24. Lucchetta 1983, 1984, 1985.

25. Bossaert 2020; Fatica 2006. For a list of Ottoman graduates of the Neapolitan college, see Elenchus Alumnorum 1917, 12–15.

26. Raj 2001; Kinra 2016.

27. Vittorino da Feltre's Casa Giocosa, an early immersion boarding school for the Duke of Gonzaga's children and select others, is a notable case in point. Musumeci 2009, 50.

28. Musumeci 2009, 49. As Musumeci notes, the celebrated educator John Amos Comenius (1592–1670) recommended sending boys between ten and twelve "to the place where the language that they wish to learn is spoken, and in the new language to make them read, write, and learn the class books of the Vernacular School" but his ideas were rarely implemented. Cited in Musumeci 2009, 56.

29. The insight that children's language acquisition is directly linked to psycho-cognitive processes that associate language with specific social contexts of use and their appropriate linguistic registers has guided the formation of modern language immersion education, most iconically and influentially the French immersion program established in Canada in 1965 to immerse Anglophone elementary school children in French. On the sociopolitical context in which French immersion programs first developed in Quebec, as well as their limitations, see Heller 1990.

30. Petritch 2005; Dupont-Ferrier 1922, 227–28.

31. Ghobrial 2014a, 41.

32. "s'insegna con tutte le regole grammaticali, come fanno nella suddetta Città di Costantinopoli, la Lingua Turca.

Ma quelli poi, che sono statti nella predetta Città presso gli Ambasciatori de' Principi Christiani, lo potarnno riferir loro, se in cadaun Palazzo vi vada ogni giorno Maestro di leggere, scriuere, e grammatica Turca, per insegnarla alli giouani studenti della Turca lingua di ciascuna Natione, si come si praticaua, massime con li giouani di lingua Veneti, che risedeuano presso di me": Dondado 1688, 10–11.

33. "Ce livre ne prétend nullement (. . .) remplacer l'enseignemt oral d'un maître, et le meilleur maître en occurrence c'est encore le passeur de la Corne d'Or ou l'accueillant boutiquier du bazar de Stamboul": Deny 1921, viii. On Deny's peripatetic life and enduring influence as the doyen of French Turkology, see also Szurek 2014.

34. Sawyer 2016.

35. The École des Languages Orientales was established in 1795. The first public school of Oriental languages in Europe and a Revolutionary institution par excellence, it replaced the dual training of French apprentice dragomans between the Collège Louis-le-Grand and the Collège Royal. Significantly, it retained the trifecta of Turkish, Persian, and Arabic language learning, which was a curricular staple of apprentice dragomans' training and which by that point was at the core of the Viennese Orientalische Akademie pedagogy as well. On shifts and continuities in the training of future dragomans under the Revolution, see Messaoudi 2015, 34–42.

36. De Groot 2000, 230–31.

37. Messaoudi 2015, 30.

38. Kieffer sojourned in Istanbul at a relatively older age than most dragomans. Indeed, his career in the Revolutionary Foreign Service was due at least in part to his detachment from old dragoman circles and their Levantine kin ties, as the latter were perceived to be irredeemably royalist in their political orientation. See Dehérain 1917; Bazin 1995, 985 on Revolutionary suspicion of royalist sympathies among dragoman faculty at the former Collège Louis-le-Grand.

39. Schefer's publication career highlights the role of dragomans in shaping the historiography of their field: he edited and published Galland's diaries, exhibiting, like Bazin a century later, a keen interest in his own professional ancestors.

40. Dehérain 1935.

41. Bazin 1995, 991–92.

42. Said 1978, 22.

43. Hudson 2005; Eyal 2006.

REFERENCES

Main Archival Series and Manuscript Libraries Consulted

Archivio di Stato di Venezia, Venice
  Bailo a Costantinopoli
  Capi del Consiglio dei Dieci, Lettere di Ambasciatori, Costantinopoli
  Cinque Savii alla Mercanzia
    Risposte
    Seconda serie
  Collegio
    Relazioni
    Risposte di dentro
  Documenti Turchi
  Inquisitori di Stato
  Notarile
    Atti
    Testamenti
  Senato
    Deliberazioni Costantinopoli
    Dispacci Costantinopoli
    Mar
Bibliothèque nationale de France, Paris
  MS Fr
  MS Naf
  MS Turc
  Suppl. Turc
Biblioteca Nationale Marciana, Venice
  MSS It. VI
  MSS It. VII
Başbakanlık Osmanlı Arşivleri, Istanbul
  Ecnebi Defteri
Biblioteca Universitaria, Bologna
  Fondo Marsigli

Family History Library, Salt Lake City
  Santa Maria Draperis (roll 1037132)
    Liber Baptizatorum
    Liber Conjugatorum
    Liber Mortuorum
Institut für Personnengeschichte, Bensheim (Germany)
  Fondo Mamuca della Torre
Koper Regional Archives (Slovenia)
  KP 290 (Borisi Family fonds)
  KP 312 (Tarsia Family fonds)
Museo Civico Correr, Venice
  Cod. Cicogna
  Cod. Morosini-Grimani
School of Oriental and African Studies, London
  Paget Papers
Zadar State Archives, Zadar (Croatia)
  Mletački Dragoman

Other Manuscript Sources

Mamuca della Torre, Cristoforo Conte. 1723. *Figure colorite che rappresentano gli abiti della corte ottomana, della città di Constantinopoli e di varie straniere nazioni barbare*. 3 vols. Bayerische Staatsbibliothek (Munich), Cod. icon. 349–51.

———. n.d. *Figure colorite che rappresentano gli abiti della corte ottomana, della città di Constantinopoli e di varie straniere nazioni barbare*. 3 vols. Bayerische Staatsbibliothek (Munich), Cod. icon. 352–54.

———. n.d. *Figurae 294 colorite che rappresentano le cariche, le professioni ecc. della città di Constantinopoli e di varie nazioni barbare colla descrizione*. 3 vols. Österreichische Nationalbibliothek (ÖNB), Cod. 8562–8564.

———. n.d. *Figurae 294 colorite che rappresentano le cariche, le professioni ecc. della città di Constantinopoli e di varie nazioni barbare colla descrizione*. 3 vols. Österreichische Nationalbibliothek (ÖNB), Cod. 8574–8576.

———. n.d. *Le duecento nouanta quattro figure colorite al uiuo, che rappresentano tutti quanti gl' abiti dell' un, e dell' altro sesso, tutte quante le cariche politiche, e militari; e tutti quanti gl' esercizij, e professioni della Corte Ottomana, della città di Constantinopoli, e di uarie straniere Nazioni barbare, colla distinta descrizione [. . .]*. 3 vols. Österreichische Nationalbibliothek (ÖNB), Cod. 8602–8604.

Salvago, Giovanni Battista. 1622. "Vita infortunata, e morte infelice di Sultan Osman, fig. lo di Sultan Acmed, et Nipote di Sultan Mustafà, al p'nte Rè de' Turchi." Biblioteca del Civico Museo Correr (Venice), Cod. Cicogna 2715, fasc. 38, fols. 315r–331v.

———. 1622. "Le Riuolutioni Ottomane principiate dalla Vita infortunata, e morte infelice di Sultan Osman, figliolo di Sultan Acmed, e nipote di Sultan Mustafà, al presente Rè de Turchi." Biblioteca del Civico Museo Correr (Venice), MSS Morosini-Grimani 540, fasc. 24, 32pp., unfoliated.

State Hermitage Museum, St. Petersburg, VAse-1782.

Vezhi, Hassan [Vecihi Hasan]. 1675. *RELATIONE Delli Successi dell'Impero Ottomano, principiando dell'An'o di Mahometto 1047 sino li 1071 è DI CHRISTO N'RO SIGNORE 1638 sino li 1660 [. . .]*. Translated by Giacomo Tarsia. Biblioteca Nazionale Marciana (Venice), MSS It. VI 84 (6053).

Printed Primary Sources

Adamović, Milan. 1996. *Die türkischen Texte in der Sammlung Palinić*. Göttingen: Pontus.

———. 2001. *Das Türkische des 16 Jahrhunderts: nach den Aufzeichnungen des Florentiners Filippo Argenti (1533)*. Göttingen: Pontus.

Africano, Giovanni Leone. 1967. "Della descrittione dell'Africa et delle cose notabli che ivi sono." In *Primo volume delle navigationi et viaggi*, edited by Giovanni Battista Ramusio. Venice: Giunti.

Agnellini, Timoteo. 1688. *Proverbi utili e virtuosi in lingua araba, persiana e turca gran parte in versi, con la loro ispiegatione in lingua latina et italiana et alcuni vocaboli di dette lingue*. Padua: Nella stamperia del Seminario.

Agop, Giovanni. 1685. *Rudimento della lingua turchesca*. Venice: Michel'Angelo Barboni.

Albèri, Eugenio, ed. 1839. *Relazioni degli ambasciatori veneti al Senato*. Florence: Società editrice fiorentina [. . .].

Alessandri, Vincenzo degli. 1844. "Relazione di Persia." In *Relazioni degli ambasciatori veneti al Senato*, edited by Eugenio Albèri, 3.2:103–27. Florence: Società editrice fiorentina.

———. 1865. "Relazione presentala al Consiglio dei Dieci il 24 settembre 1572 e letta l'11 ottobre da Vincenzo Alessandri, veneto legato a Thamasp re di Persia." In *La Repubblica di Venezia e la Persia*, edited by Guglielmo Berchet, 167–82. Turin: G. B. Paravia.

Angiolello, Giovan Maria, and Vincentio d'Alessandri. 1873. *A Narrative of Italian Travels in Persia, in the Fifteenth and Sixteenth Centuries*. Translated by Charles Grey. London: Hakluyt Society.

Arnauld, Antoine, and Pierre Nicole. 1674. *La perpetuité de la foy de l'Eglise catholique touchant l'Eucharistie [. . .]* vol. 3. A Paris: En la boutique de Charles Savreux. Chez Guillaume Desprez, au pied de la tour de Nostre Dame, du costé de l'Archevesché.

Bassano, Luigi. 1545. *Costumi et i modi particolari della vita de' Turchi*. Rome: n.p.

Bellarmino, Roberto Francesco Romolo. 1635. *Doctrina Christiana = Kitāb at-Taʿlīm al-masīḥī*. Translated by Gabriel Sionita and Naṣrallāh Šalaq. Paris: Antonius Vitray.

Benetti, Antonio. 1688. *Osseruazioni fatte dal fu dottor Antonio Benetti nel viaggio a Costantinopoli dell'illustriss & eccellent sig Gio Battista Donado spedito Bailo alla Porta Ottomana l'anno 1680 E nel tempo di sua permanenza, e ritorno seguito 1684 Dedicate all'alt sereniss del sig principe d Gio Gastone de Medici*. Venice: Poletti.

Bernardo, Lorenzo. 1996. "Relazione (1590)." In *Relazioni di Ambasciatori Veneti al Senato*, edited by Maria Pia Pedani, vol. 14: Costantinopoli relazioni inedite (1512–1789). Monumenta politica et philosophica rariora. Padua: Ausilio.

Bidpaï. 1654. *Espejo politico y moral para principes y ministros y todo genero de personas*. Translated by Vincenzo Bratutti. Madrid: Domingo García y Morràs.

Bobovius, Albertus [Ali Ufki Bey]. 1712. "A Treatise of Bobovius (Sometime First Interpreter to Mahomet IV) Concerning the Liturgy of the Turks, Their Pilgrimage to Mecca, Their Circumcision, Visitation of the Sick, &c [. . .]." In *Four Treatises Concerning the Doctrine, Discipline and Worship of the Mahometans*, edited by Adriaan Reelant, 104–50. London: Lintott and Sanger.

Burgo, Giovani Battista de. 1686. *Viaggio di cinque anni In Asia, Africa, & Europa del Turco*. In Milan: Agnelli.

Busbecq, Ogier Ghislain de. 2005. *The Turkish Letters of Ogier Ghiselin de Busbecq, Imperial Ambassador at Constantinople, 1554–1562 Newly Translated from the Latin of the Elzevir Ed of 1633 by Edward Seymour Forster*. Baton Rouge: Louisiana State University Press.

Carr, Ralph. 1600. *The Mahumetane or Turkish Historie [. . .]*. London: Thomas Este.

Catalogue des livres imprimés de la Bibliothèque du Roy. Belles lettres. Tome premier [-second]. 1750. Paris: Imprimerie Royale.

Caylus, Anne Claude Philippe. 1743. *Contes orientaux tirés des manuscrits de la Bibliothèque du Roy de France*. 2 vols. The Hague: n.p.

Cenabi, Muṣṭafā Ibn-Ḥasan al-. 1680. *D. Mustaphae Filii Hussein Algenabii De Gestis Timurlenkii, Seu Tamerlanis [. . .]*. Translated by Giovanni Battista Podestà. Vienna: Voigt.

Daru, Pierre-Antoine-Noël-Bruno. 1819. *Histoire de la Republique de Venise*. 6 vols. Paris: Didot.

De La Chappelle, George. 1648. *Recueil de divers portraits des principales dames de la Porte du Grand Turc, tirée au naturel sur les lieux*. Paris: Antoine Estienne.

Della Valle, Pietro. 2001. *La porta d'Oriente: lettere di Pietro della Valle, Istanbul 1614*. Edited by Chiara Cardini. Rome: Città nuova.

Dyâb, Hannā. 2015. *D'Alep à Paris: les pérégrinations d'un jeune Syrien au temps de Louis XIV.* Translated by Paule Fahmé-Thiery, Bernard Heyberger, and Jérôme Lentin. Arles: Actes Sud.

Donado, Giovanni Battista. 1688a. *Della letteratura de' Turchi.* Venice: per Andrea Poletti.

———, ed. 1688b. *Raccolta curiosissima d'adaggi turcheschi trasportati dal proprio idioma nell'italiano, e latino dalli giovani di lingua sotto il bailaggio in Costantinopoli dell'illustriss & eccell sig Gio Battista Donado.* Venice: Poletti.

Du Halde, Jean-Baptiste. 1732. *Description geographique, historique, chronologique, politique et physique de l'Empire de la Chine et de la Tartarie chinoise [. . .].* Paris: P. G. Le Mercier.

Du Ryer, André. 1630. *Rudimenta grammatices linguae Turcicae.* Paris: Antonius Vitray.

———. 1650. "Dictionarium Turcico-Latinum." BnF, MS Turc 464, 465.

Du Vignau, Sieur des Joannots. 1688. *Le Secretaire Turc: contenant l'art d'exprimer ses pensées sans se voir, sans se parler et sans s'écrire.* Paris: Guerout.

Elenchus alumnorum decreta et documenta quae spectant ad Collegium Sacrae Familiae Neapolis. 1917. Shanghai: Ex Tipographia Missionis Catholicae in Orphanotrophio T'ou-Sè-Wè. http://digituno.unior.it/document/811.

Evans, R. H. 1836. *Bibliotheca Heberiana. Catalogue of the Library of . . . Richard Heber [. . .].* London: W. Nicol.

Evelyn, John. 1669. *The History of the Three Late, Famous Impostors [. . .].* Savoy: Herringman.

Febure, Michele. 1681. *Teatro della Turchia [. . .].* Milan: Malatesta.

Fonton, Charles. 1751. "Essay sur la Musique Orientale Comparée à La Musique Européene." BnF, MS Fr. 4023.

Galland, Antoine. 1704. *Les mille et une nuits: Contes arabes.* Paris: Barbin.

———. 1724. *Les contes et fables indiennes de Bidpaï et de Lokman.* 2 vols. Paris: André Morin.

———. 1881. *Journal d'Antoine Galland pendant son séjour à Constantinople (1672–1673).* Edited by Charles Henri Auguste Schefer. Paris: E. Leroux.

Galland, Antoine, and Denis Dominique Cardonne, eds. 1778. *Contes et fables indiennes de Bidpaï et de Lokman.* 3 vols. Paris: P. G. Simon.

Galland, Julien-Claude. 1754. *Recueil des rits et des cérémonies du pèlerinage de La Mecque, auquel on a joint divers écrits relatifs à la religion, aux sciences et aux moeurs des Turcs. Par M. Galland.* Amsterdam et se vend à Paris: chez Desaint et Saillant.

———. 1757. *Sammlung von den Gebräuchen und Ceremonien der Wallfarth nach Mecca: nebst verschiedenen Schriften welche die Religion die Wissenschaften und die Sitten der Türken betreffen.* Translated by Johann Georg Angerer. Nuremberg: Monath.

Gaudier, Johannes, ed. 1567. *Chronica oder Acta von der Türckischen Tyrannen herkommen, vnd [und] gefürten Kriegen aus Türckischer Sprachen vordeutschet*. Frankfurt an der Oder: Johan Eichorn.

Gelil, Salih [Celālzāde Mustafa]. 1678. *Anales de Egipto: en que se trata de las cosas mas principales que han sucedido desde el principio del mundo hasta de cien años a esta parte*. Translated by Vincenzo Bratutti. Madrid: Melchor Alvarez.

Giustiniani, Agostino. 1516. *Psalterium, Hebraeum, Graecum, Arabicum, & Chaldaeum, cum tribus latinis interpretationibus & glossis*. Genoa: Pietro Porro.

Grässe, Johann Georg Theodor. 1863. *Trésor des livres rares et précieux ou Nouveau dictionnaire bibliographique*. 4 vols. Dresden: R. Kuntze.

Hammer-Purgstall, Joseph. 1827. *Geschichte des Osmanischen Reiches groszentheils aus bisher unbenützten Handschriften und Archiven*. Pest: Hartleben.

———. 1829. *Geschichte des Osmanischen Reiches groszentheils aus bisher unbenützten Handschriften und Archiven. Viertem Band. Vom Regierungsantritte Murad des dritten bis zur zweyten Entthronung Mustafa's I. 1574–1623*. 4 vols. Pest: Hartleben.

———. 1940. *"Erinnerungen aus meinem Leben" 1774–1852*. Edited by Reinhart Bachofen von Echt. Vienna: Hölder-Pichler-Tempsky.

Harsányi Nagy, Jakab. 1672. *Colloquia familiaria Turcico-Latina*. Cologne: Georg Schulz.

Herbelot, Barthélemy de. 1697. *Bibliothèque orientale, ou Dictionaire universel [. . .]*. Paris: Compagnie des Libraires.

Holdermann, Jean Baptiste Daniel. 1730. *Grammaire turque ou méthode courte et facile pour apprendre la langue turque*. Istanbul: Ibrahim Müteferrika.

Il corriere ordinario. 1712. "Vienna 16 Aprile." April 16, 1712.

Jones, Sir William. 1807. "Prefatory Discourse to an Essay on the History of the Turks." In *Memoirs of the Life, Writing, and Correspondence of Sir William Jones*, edited by John Shore Teignmouth, 594–621. London: J. Hatchard.

Katib Çelebi. 1697. *Cronologia historica scritta in lingua Turca, Persiana, & Araba, Da Hazi Halife' Mustafa', e tradotta nell'Idioma Italiano da Gio: Rinaldo Carli nobile justinopolitano, e Dragomano della Serenissima Republica di Venezia*. Translated by Gian Rinaldo Carli. Venice: Poletti.

Knolles, Richard. 1603. *The Generall Historie of the Turkes: From the First Beginning of That Nation to the Rising of the Othoman Familie: With All the Notable Expeditions of the Christian Princes Against Them*. London: Islip.

Krusinski, Judas Thaddaeus. 1142 AH [1729]. *Tarih-i Seyyah der Beyan-ı Ağnaviyan ve Sebab-i Inhidam-ı Bina Devlet-i Şahan-ı Safaviyan*. Edited and translated by Ibrahim Müteferrika. Istanbul: Dār-i Ṭibaʿa-yi ʿĀmira.

Kuçukçelebizade Ismail Asım. 1153 AH [1741]. *Tarih-i Çelebizade*. Istanbul: Dār-i Ṭibāʿa-yi ʿĀmira.

Leibniz, Gottfried Wilhelm. 1710. "Brevis designatio meditationum de Originibus Gentium, ductis potissimum ex indicio linguarum." *Miscellanea Berolinensia ad incrementum scientiarum* 1: 1–16.

———. 1718. *Otium Hanoveranum sive Miscellanea ex ore et schedis Godofr. Guilielmi Leibnitii quondam notata et descripta (etc.).* Leipzig: Martini.

———. 1768. *Opera omnia, Nunc primum collecta, in Classes distributa, praefationibus & indicibus exornata, studio Ludovici Dutens.* vol. 6. Geneva: De Tournes.

Leunclavius, Johannes. 1588. *Annales sultanorum Othmanidarum, a Turcis sua lingua scripti.* Frankfurt: Wechel.

———. 1591. *Historiae Musulmanae Turcorum, de monumentis ipsorum exscriptae, libri XVIII.* Frankfurt: Wechel.

Lodi, Vincenzo Giulio. 1701. *L'immortalita del cavalier Marc Antonio Mamuca della Torre, Conte del Sac Rom Imp consigliere attuale di guerra di Sua M Ces &c descritta.* Vienna: Heyinger.

Lupis, Pietro. 1527. *Opera nuova de M. Pietro Lupis Valentiano, la quale insegna a parlare Turchesco.* N.p.

Maggio, Francesco Maria. 1670. *Syntagmaton linguarum orientalium quae in Georgiae regionibus audiuntur libri duo.* Rome: Typographia Sacrae Congregationis de Propaganda Fide.

Magni, Cornelio. 1682. *Quanto di più curioso e vago ha potuto raccorre C M nel primo biennio da esso consumato in viaggi e dimore per la Turchia, parte I.* Venice: Abondio Menafoglio.

Maison Silvestre. 1838. *Catalogue de livres provenant de la librairie de M. Barrois l'aîné . . . Partie 2.* Paris: Silvestre.

Martin, Anton. 1850. *Katalog des K. K. polytechnischen Institutes in Wien.* Vienna: Polytechnisches Institut.

Mascis, Antonio. 1677. *Vocabolario toscano, e turchesco, arricchito di molte voci arabe, persiane, tartare, e greche necessarie alla cognizione della stessa lingua turchesca con l'aggiunta di alcuni rudimenti per impossessarsi del vero idioma turchesco.* Florence: Niccolo Nauesi.

Megiser, Hieronymus. 1612. *Institutionum linguae Turcicae libri quatuor [. . .].* Leipzig: printed by the author.

Membré, Michele. 1969. *Relazione di Persia (1542)*, Edited by Gianroberto Scarcia. Naples: Istituto universitario orientale.

———. 1993. *Mission to the Lord Sophy of Persia (1539–1542).* Translated with introduction and notes by A. H. Morton. London: School of Oriental and African Studies, University of London.

Meninski, Franciscus à Mesgnien. 1680a. *Linguarum Orientalium Turcicae, Arabicae, Persicae Institutiones Seu Grammatica Turcica [. . .].* Vienna: printed by the author.

———. 1680b. *Thesaurus Linguarum Orientalium Turcicae, Arabicae, Persicae [. . .] Nimirum lexicon [. . .].* 2 vols. Vienna: printed by the author.

———. 1687. *Complementum Thesauri linguarum orientalium, seu onomasticum latino-turcico-arabico-persici.* Vienna: printed by the author.

———. 1756. *Francisci à Mesgnien Meninski Institutiones linguæ Turcicæ, cum rudimentis parallelis linguarum Arabicæ & Persicæ.* Edited by Adamus Franciscus Kollar. 4 vols. Vienna: Ex Typographeo orientali Schilgiano.

———.1780. *Francisci a Mesgnien Meninski Lexicon arabico-persico-turcicvm adiecta ad singvlas voces et phrases significatione latina, ad vsitatiores etiam italica.* Edited by Bernhard Jenisch and Franz von Klezl. 4 vols. Vienna: Kurzböck.

Mignot, Vincent. 1771. *Histoire de l'empire Ottoman: depuis son origine jusqu'à la paix de Belgrade en 1740.* 4 vols. Paris: Le Clerc.

———. 1787. *The History of the Turkish, Or Ottoman Empire: From Its Foundation in 1300, to the Peace of Belgrade in 1740. To Which Is Prefixed An Historical Discourse on Mahomet and His Successors.* Translated by A. Hawkins. London: R. Thorn.

Miselli, Giuseppe. 1682. *Il burattino veridico, overo, Instrvzione generale per chi viaggia [. . .].* Rome: Michel'Ercole.

Molino, Giovanni. 1641. *Dittionario della lingua italiana turchesca.* Rome: Gioiosi.

Moryson, Fynes. 1617. *An Itinerary Vvritten by Fynes Moryson Gent, First in the Latine Tongue and Then Translated by Him into English [. . .].* London: Beale.

Mouradgea d'Ohsson, Ignatius. 1787. *Tableau général de l'empire othoman, divisé en deux parties, dont l'une comprend la législation mahométane; l'autre, l'histoire de l'empire othoman.* Paris: Imprimerie de monsieur.

———. 1788. *Oriental Antiquities, and General View of the Othoman Customs, Laws, and Ceremonies [. . .].* Philadelphia: Printed for the Select Committee and Grand Lodge of Enquiry.

Müteferrika, Ibrahim, ed. 1144 AH [1732]. *Füyuzat-ı Miknatisiye.* Istanbul: Dār-i Ṭibā'a-yi 'Āmira.

Naima, Mustafa. 1734. *Tarih-i Naima.* Istanbul: Dār-i Ṭibā'a-yi 'Āmira.

Nani, Battista. 1673. *The History of the Affairs of Europe in This Present Age, but More Particularly of the Republick of Venice.* Translated by Robert Honywood. London: Starkey.

Ogilby, John. 1670. *Africa, Being an Accurate Description of the Regions of Aegypt, Barbary, Lybia and Billedulgerid . . . Collected and Translated from Most Authentick Authors and Augmented with Later Observations . . . by John Ogilby.* London: T. Johnson.

Olivieri, Antonio. 2010. *Enciclopedia morale e civile della vita, costumi ed impegni di religione dell'abbate Antonio Olivieri, Cosmopoli, 1724.* Edited by Toni Veneri. Centro Interuniversitario Internazionale di Studi sul Viaggio Adriatico.

Osman Ağa. 1980. *Die Autobiographie des Dolmetschers Osman Aga aus Temeswar: der Text des londoner Autographen in normalisierter Rechtschreibung.* Edited by Richard F. Kreutel. Cambridge: EJW Gibb Memorial Trust.

———. 1998. *Prisonnier des infidèles: un soldat ottoman dans l'empire des Habsbourg.* Edited by Frédéric Hitzel. La bibliotheque turque. Arles: Sindbad.

Pajot, Jules, ed. 1844. *Les Mille et Un Jours, contes persans, turcs et chinois [. . .].* Paris: Pourrat Frères.

Palerne, Jean. 1606. *Pérégrinations du S. Jean Palerne [. . .] où est traicté de plusieurs singularités, & antiquités remarquées és provinces d'Egypte, Arabie deserte, & pierreuse, Terre Saincte Surie, Natolie, Grece, & plusiers isles tant la Mer Méditerranée, que archipelague.* Lyon: J. Pillehotte.

Panzer, Georg Wolfgang Franz. 1769. *Bibliotheca Thomasiana, sive thesaurus librorum quos olim possedit Gottofredus Thomasius de Troschenreut et Wiedersberg.* Nuremberg: Schwarzkopfius.

Paris, Bernard de. 1665. *Vocabolario italiano-turchesco, compilato dal M R P F Bernardo da Parigi tradotto dal francese nell' italiano dal P F Pietro d'Abbavilla.* Rome: Stamp. della soc. Congregationis de Propaganda Fide.

Pétis de la Croix, François. 1710. *Mille et un jour: contes persans.* Paris: Claude Barbin.

———. 1810. "Extrait des voyages de Pétis de la Croix." In *Relation de Dourry Efendy, ambassadeur de la Porte Ottomane auprès du roi de Perse [. . .],* edited by Louis Langlès. Paris: Ferra.

Pfeiffer, August. 1672. *Introductio in Orientem, sive synopsis quaestionum nobiliorum de origine, natura, usu et adminiculis linguarum orientalium et plerarumque extra Europam.* Wittenberg: Schmatz.

Podestà, Giovanni Battista. 1669. *Assertiones De principiis substantialibus, accidentalibus proximis & remotis, diversisque differentiis linguarum [. . .].* Vienna: Hacque.

———. 1671. *Verdolmetscher Türkischer Chronic.* Nuremberg: Endter.

———. 1672a. *Annali ottomanici.* Vienna: Voigt.

———. 1672b. *Translatae Turcicae Chronicae Pars Prima: Continens originem Ottomanicae stirpis, undecimq[ue] eiusdem stirpis Imperatorum gesta, iuxta traditionem Turcarum.* Nuremberg: Endter.

———. 1677. *Dissertatio academica, continens specimen triennalis profectûs in linguis orientalibus, Arabica nempè, Persica & Turcica, cui varia curiosa & scitu digna intermiscentur.* Vienna: Voigt.

———. 1678. *Elementa Calligraphiæ Arabico-Persico-Turcicæ: regulas scribendi et scripta vocalizata legendi, exhibentia (Tabella practica, pro elementis calligraphiæ Arabico-Persico-Turcicæ).* Vienna: Voigt.

———. 1688. *Cursus grammaticalis linguarum orientalium, Arabicae scilicet, Persicae et Turcicae*. Vienna: Voigt.

Pomis, David de. 1587. *Tsemah David / Dittionario novo hebraico, molto copioso, dechiarato in tre lingue Lexicon novum haebraicum*. Venice: Ioannem de Gara.

Pougens, Marie Charles J. de. 1799. *Essai sur les antiquités du Nord, et les anciennes langues septentrionales*. Paris: Charles Pougens.

Pylarini, Giacomo. 1714. "II. Nova & tuta vaiolas excitandi per transplantationem methodus, nuper inventa & in usum tracta." *Philosophical Transactions of the Royal Society of London* 29 (347): 393–99.

Ramberti, Benedetto. 1539. *Libri tre delle cose de Turchi [. . .]* Venice: Aldo Manuzio.

Ramusio, Giovanni Battista, ed. 1559. *Secondo volume delle navigationi et viaggi*. Venice: Giunti.

Raşid, Mehmed. 1153 AH [1741]. *Tarih-i Raşid*. Istanbul: Dār-i Ṭibāʿa-yi ʿĀmira.

Rycaut, Paul. 1668. *The Present State of the Ottoman Empire [. . .]*. London: John Starkey and Henry Brome.

———. 1679. *The Present State of the Greek and Armenian Churches, Anno Christi 1678*. London: Starkey.

———. 1680. *The History of the Turkish Empire from the Year 1623 to the Year 1677 [. . .]*. London: Starkey.

Saidino Turco [Hoca Sadeddin Efendi]. 1649. *Chronica dell'origine, e progressi della casa ottomana*. Translated by Vincenzo Bratutti. Vienna: Matteo Riccio.

———. 1652a. *Cronica dell' Origine e progressi della casa Ottomanna [. . .]* vol. 2. Translated by Vincenzo Bratutti. Madrid: Domingo García y Morràs.

———. 1652b. *The reign of Sultan Orchan, second king of the Turks*. Translated by William Seaman. London: Printed by T.R. and E.M. and are to be sold by John Sherley.

Salvago, Giovanni Battista. 1937. *"Africa overo Barbarìa" Relazione al doge di Venezia sulle reggenze di Algeri e di Tunisi*. Edited by Alberto Sacerdoti. Padua: Cedam.

Schieferdecker, Johannes David. 1695. *Nucleus institutionum arabicum . . . variis linguae ornamentls atque praeceptis dialecti turcicae illustratus [. . .]*. Leipzig: Hucho.

Seaman, William. 1670. *Grammatica linguæ turcicæ in quinque partes distributa*. Oxford: Millington.

Soranzo, Lazaro. 1603. *The Ottoman of Lazaro Soranzo [. . .]*. Translated by Abraham Hartwell. London: John Windet.

Spallanzani, Lazzaro. 1888. *Viaggio in Oriente*. Edited by Naborre Campanini. Turin: Fratelli Bocca.

Spey, Rutgherus. 1583. *Compendium Grammatices Arabicae*. Heidelberg: Jacob Mylius.

Tarsia, Tommaso. 1996. "Relazione dell'assedio di Vienna." In *Relazioni di Ambasciatori Veneti al Senato*, edited by Maria Pia Pedani. Vol. 14: Costantinopoli relazioni inedite (1512–1789): 684–755. Padua: Ausilio.

Theyls, Willem. 1721. *Gedenkschriften betreffende het leeven van Karel de XII, koning van Sweeden, gedurende sijn verblijf in het Ottomanische gebied [. . .]*. Leiden: Du Vivier.

———. 1722. *Mémoires pour servir à l'histoire de Charles XII roi de Suède: contenant ce qui s'est passé pendant le séjour de ce prince dans l'empire Ottoman [. . .]*. Leiden: Du Vivier.

Timonius, Emanuel. 1714. "V. An Account, or History, of the Procuring the Smallpox by Incision, or Inoculation; as It Has for Some Time Been Practised at Constantinople." Translated by John Woodward. *Philosophical Transactions of the Royal Society of London* 29 (339): 72–82.

Toderini, Giambattista. 1787. *Letteratura turchesca*. Venice: Giacomo Storti.

Tott, François. 1784. *Mémoires du baron de Tott, sur les Turcs et les Tartares*. A Amsterdam [Frankfurt]: n.p.

Trevisan, Marco. 1671. *L' immortalita di Gio Battista Ballarino caualiere [. . .]*. Venice: Pinelli.

Ufkî, Ali. 1690. *Tractatus Alberti Bobovii Turcarum Imp Mohammedis IVti olim interpretis primarii, De Turcarum liturgia: peregrinatione Meccana, circumcisione, aegrotorum visitatione &c*. Oxford: E Theatro Sheldoniano.

Vocabulario nuovo con il quale da se stessi, si puo benissimo imparare diversi linguaggi, cioe, italiano et greco, Turco, Todesco. Et di nuovo con somma diligentia, ricorretto. 1582. [Venice]: Bernardino de Franceschi.

Warner, Levinus. 1644. *Proverbiorum et Sententiarum Persicarum centuria*. Leiden: Ioannis Maire.

Weigel, Theodor Oswald. 1865. *Katalog des antiquarischen Lagers von T. O. Weigel*. Leipzig: Weigel. https://doi.org/10.1080/00263206.2015.1016505.

Yirmisekiz Çelebi Mehmed Efendi. 1757. *Relation de l'ambassade de Mehemet-Effendi à la cour de France en 1721*. Translated by Julien Galland. A Constantinople, et se trouve à Paris: Ganeau.

Secondary Sources

Abdel-Halim, Mohamed. 1964. *Antoine Galland, sa vie et son œuvre*. Paris: A.G. Nizet.

Ács, Pál. 2000. "Tarjumans Mahmud and Murad: Austrian and Hungarian Renegades as Sultan's Interpreters." In *Europa und die Türken in der Renaissance*, edited by Bodo Guthmüller, 307–16. Tübingen: Niemeyer. https://doi.org/10.1515/9783110933567.307.

Ådahl, Karin, ed. 2006. *The Sultan's Procession: The Swedish Embassy to Sultan Mehmed IV in 1657–1658 and the Rålamb Paintings*. Istanbul: Swedish Research Institute in Istanbul.

Adams, Julia. 1994. "The Familial State: Elite Family Practices and State-Making in the Early Modern Netherlands." *Theory and Society* 23 (4): 505–39. https://doi.org/10.1007/BF00992826.

Agai, Bekim, Olcay Akyıldız, and Caspar Hillebrand, eds. 2013. *Venturing Beyond Borders —Reflections on Genre, Function and Boundaries in Middle Eastern Travel Writing*. Istanbuler Texte und Studien 30. Würzburg: Ergon. https://doi.org/10.5771/9783956507076.

Ageron, Pierre, and Mustapha Jaouhari. 2014. "Le programme pédagogique d'un arabisant du Collège royal, François Pétis de La Croix (1653–1713)." *Arabica* 61 (3–4): 396–453. https://doi.org/10.1163/15700585-12341296.

Alam, Muzaffar, and Sanjay Subrahmanyam. 2007. *Indo-Persian Travels in the Age of Discoveries, 1400–1800*. New York: Cambridge University Press.

Allerston, Patricia. 2000. "Clothing and Early Modern Venetian Society." *Continuity and Change* 15 (3): 367–90. https://doi.org/10.1017/s0268416051003662.

Al-Tikriti, Nabil. 2017. "An Ottoman View of World History: Kātip Çelebi's Takvīmü't-Tevārīḫ." In *International Kātip Çelebi Research Symposium Proceedings / Uluslararası Kātip Çelebi Araştırmaları Sempozyumu Bildirileri*, edited by Turan Gökçe et al., 127–49. Izmir: İzmir Kātip Çelebi Üniversitesi Yayınları.

Amelicheva, Mariya Vladimirovna. 2016. "The Russian Residency in Constantinople, 1700–1774: Russian-Ottoman Diplomatic Encounters." PhD diss., Georgetown University.

Anderson, Sonia P. 1989. *An English Consul in Turkey: Paul Rycaut at Smyrna, 1667–1678*. New York: Clarendon Press.

———. 2004. "Rycaut, Sir Paul (1629–1700), Diplomat and Author." In *Oxford Dictionary of National Biography*. https://doi.org/10.1093/ref:odnb/24392.

Andrea, Bernadette Diane. 2007. *Women and Islam in Early Modern English Literature*. New York: Cambridge University Press. https://doi.org/10.1017/cbo9780511483424.

Andrews, Walter G., and Mehmet Kalpaklı. 2005. *The Age of Beloveds: Love and the Beloved in Early-Modern Ottoman and European Culture and Society*. Durham, NC: Duke University Press. https://doi.org/10.2307/j.ctv11sn3k7.

Ansari, Hassan, and Sabine Schmidtke. 2016. "Bibliographical Practices in Islamic Societies, with an Analysis of MS Berlin, Staatsbibliothek Zu Berlin, Hs. or. 13525." *Intellectual History of the Islamicate World* 4 (1–2): 102–51. https://doi.org/10.2307/j.ctv2dswqs.22.

Antoche, Emanuel Constantin. 2015. "Un ambassadeur français à la Porte Ottomane: Achille de Harlay, Baron de Sancy et de La Mole (1611–1619)." In *Istoria ca Datorie. Omagiu Academicianului Ion Aurel Pop*, edited by Bolovan Ghitta and Ov. Ghitta, 747–60. Cluj-Napoca: Académie Roumaine, Centrul de Studii Transilvane.

App, Urs. 2010. *The Birth of Orientalism*. Philadelphia: University of Pennsylvania Press. https://doi.org/10.9783/9780812200058.

Aravamudan, Srinivas. 2011. *Enlightenment Orientalism*. Chicago: University of Chicago Press. https://doi.org/10.7208/chicago/9780226024509.001.0001.

Arbel, Benjamin. 1995a. "Greek Magnates in Venetian Cyprus: The Case of the Synglitico Family." *Dumbarton Oaks Papers* 49: 327–37. https://doi.org/10.2307/1291717.

——. 1995b. *Trading Nations: Jews and Venetians in the Early-Modern Eastern Mediterranean*. Leiden: Brill.

——. 2000. *Cyprus, the Franks and Venice, 13th-16th Centuries*. Burlington, VT: Ashgate.

——. 2002. "Maps of the World for Ottoman Princes? Further Evidence and Questions Concerning 'the "Mappamondo" of Hajji Ahmed.'" *Imago Mundi* 54 (1): 19–29. https://doi.org/10.1080/03085690208592956.

——. 2013. "Translating the Orient for the Serenissima: Michiel Membrè in the Service of Sixteenth-Century Venice." In *La frontière méditeranéenne du XVᵉ au XVIIᵉ siècle*, edited by Albrech Fuess and Bernard Heyberger, 253–81. Turnhout: Brepols. https://doi.org/10.1484/m.er-eb.4.00190.

Asad, Talal. 1980. "Short Notices." *English Historical Review* 95 (376): 648–49. https://doi.org/10.1093/ehr/xcv.ccclxxvi.648.

Aslanian, Sebouh D. 2011. *From the Indian Ocean to the Mediterranean: The Global Trade Networks of Armenian Merchants from New Julfa*. Berkeley: University of California Press. https://doi.org/10.1525/california/9780520266872.001.0001.

——. 2016. "'Prepared in the Language of the Hagarites': Abbot Mkhitar's 1727 Armeno-Turkish Grammar of Modern Western Armenian." *Journal of the Society for Armenian Studies* 25: 54–86.

Atasoy, Nurhan and Filiz Çağman. 1974. *Turkish Miniature Painting*. Istanbul: R. C. D. Cultural Institute.

Atsız, Buğra. 1977. *Das osmanische Reich um die Mitte des 17 [ie siebzehnten] Jahrhunderts nach den Chroniken des Vecihi (1637–1660) und des Mehmed Halifa (1633–1660)*. Munich: Rudolf Trofenik.

Aydın, Bilgin. 2007. "Divan-ı Hümayun Tercümanları ve Osmanlı Kültür ve Diplomasisindeki Yerleri." *Osmanlı Araştırmaları* 29: 41–76.

Aymes, Marc. 2013. "Many a Standard at a Time: The Ottomans' Leverage with Imperial Studies." *Contributions to the History of Concepts* 8 (1): 26–43. https://doi.org/10.3167/choc.2013.080102.

Aynur, Hatice. 2008. "Ottoman Literature." In *The Cambridge History of Turkey. Vol. 3, The Late Ottoman Empire, 1603–1839*, edited by Suraiya Faroqhi, 3:481–520. New York: Cambridge University Press. https://doi.org/10.1017/chol9780521620956.021.

——. 2018. "Abdülmecid Firişteoğlu." In *Encyclopaedia of Islam, THREE*. https://doi.org/10.1163/1573-3912_ei3_com_35699.

Baars, Rosanne. 2014. "Constantinople Confidential. News and Information in the Diary of Jean-Louis Rigo (c. 1686–1756), Secretary of the Dutch Embassy in Istanbul." *LIAS: Journal of Early Modern Intellectual Culture and Its Sources* 41 (2): 143–71. https://doi.org/10.2143/LIAS.41.2.3064605.

Baasten, Martin. 2003. "A Note on the History of 'Semitic.'" In *Hamlet on a Hill*, edited by Martin F. J. Baasten and W. Th. Van Peursen, 57–72. Leuven: Peeters.

Babaie, Sussan, and Talinn Grigor. 2015. *Persian Kingship and Architecture: Strategies of Power in Iran from the Achaemenids to the Pahlavis*. London: Tauris. https://doi.org/10.5040/9780755611355.

Babayan, Kathryn. 1994. "The Safavid Synthesis: From Qizilbash Islam to Imamite Shi'ism." *Iranian Studies* 27 (1/4): 135–61. https://doi.org/10.1080/00210869408701824.

Babinger, Franz. 1919. "Die türkischen Studien in Europa bis zum Auftreten Josef von Hammer-Purgstalls." *Die Welt des Islams* 7 (3/4): 103–29.

———. 1927. "Der Pfortendolmetsch Murâd und seine Schriften." In *Literaturdenkmäler aus Ungarns Türkenzeit*, 33–54. Berlin: De Gruyter.

———. 1960. "Francesco Scarella e i suoi disegni di Costantinopoli (circa 1685)." *Rivista d'arte* 35: 153–67.

Baer, Marc David. 2004. "The Great Fire of 1660 and the Islamization of Christian and Jewish Space in Istanbul." *International Journal of Middle East Studies* 36 (2): 159–81. https://doi.org/10.1017/s002074380436201x.

Bakhtin, Mikhail M. 1981. "Discourse in the Novel." In *The Dialogic Imagination: Four Essays*, 259–422. University of Texas Press Slavic Series. Austin: University of Texas Press.

Balcı, Sezai. 2006. "Osmanlı devleti'nde tercümanlık ve bab-ı ali tercüme odası." Master's thesis, Ankara University.

———. 2013. *Babıâli tercüme odası*. Istanbul: Libra Kitapçılık ve Yayıncılık.

Ballinger, Pamela. 2003. *History in Exile: Memory and Identity at the Borders of the Balkans*. Princeton, NJ: Princeton University Press. https://doi.org/10.1515/9780691187273.

Balta, Evangelia, and Matthias Kappler, eds. 2010. *Cries and Whispers in Karamanlidika Books: Proceedings of the First International Conference on Karamanlidika Studies (Nicosia, 11th–13th September 2008)*. Turcologica, Bd. 83. Wiesbaden: Harrassowitz.

Baranowski, Bohdan. 1949. "F. Mesgnien-Meniński et l'enseignement des langues orientales en Pologne vers la moitié du XVIIᵉ siècle." *Rocznik Orientalistyczny* 15: 63–71.

Barbu, Violeta. 2015. "La Comtesse Maria Mamucca della Torre Kálnoky et sa famille aux carrefours des empires." *Études balkaniques* 2: 57–89.

Bardawil, Fadi A. and Talal Asad. 2016. "The Solitary Analyst of Doxas: An Interview with Talal Asad." *Comparative Studies of South Asia, Africa and the Middle East* 36 (1): 152–73. https://doi.org/10.1215/1089201x-3482183.

Barkey, Karen. 2008. *Empire of Difference: The Ottomans in Comparative Perspective*. New York: Cambridge University Press. https://doi.org/10.1017/cbo9780511790645.

Barzman, Karen-edis. 2017. *The Limits of Identity: Early Modern Venice, Dalmatia, and the Representation of Difference*. Leiden: Brill. https://doi. org/10.1163/9789004331518.

Bashan, Eliezer. 1993. "Jewish Interpreters in British Consular Service in the Middle East, 1581–1825 [in Hebrew]." *Sfunot* 6 (21): 41–69.

Bayle, Pierre. 1820. "Hali-Beigh." In *Dictionnaire historique et critique*, edited by Pierre Bayle, 7:479–80. Paris: Desoer, Libraire, rue Christine.

Bazin, Louis. 1995. "L'École des Langues orientales et l'Académie des Inscriptions et Belles-Lettres." *Comptes rendus des séances de l'Académie des Inscriptions et Belles-Lettres* 139 (4): 983–96. https://doi.org/10.3406/crai.1995.15544.

Beasley, Faith Evelyn. 2018. *Versailles Meets the Taj Mahal: François Bernier, Marguerite de La Sablière, and Enlightening Conversations in Seventeenth-Century France*. Toronto: University of Toronto Press. https://doi. org/10.3138/9781487516123.

Beaulieu, Jill, and Mary Roberts, eds. 2002. *Orientalism's Interlocutors: Painting, Architecture, Photography*. Durham, NC: Duke University Press. https:// doi.org/10.1215/9780822383857.

Behar, Cem. 2003. *A Neighborhood in Ottoman Istanbul: Fruit Vendors and Civil Servants in the Kasap İlyas Mahalle*. SUNY Series in the Social and Economic History of the Middle East. Albany: State University of New York Press.

Belin, François Alphonse. 1894. *Histoire de la latinité de Constantinople*. Paris: A. Picard et fils.

Bellingeri, Giampiero. 2015. "Turchi e Persiani fra visioni abnormi e normalizzazioni, a Venezia (secoli XV–XVIII)." *RILUNE — Revue des littératures européennes* 9. Visions de l'Orient: 14–89. http://www.rilune.org/images/mono9/BELLINGERI.pdf.

Ben-Tov, Asaph. 2015. "The Academic Study of Arabic in Seventeenth-and Early Eighteenth-Century Protestant Germany: A Preliminary Sketch." *History of Universities* 28 (2): 93–135. https://doi.org/10.1093/acprof: oso/9780198743651.003.0003.

Berardi, Luca. 2017. "The Sixteenth-Century Muhit Atlası: From a Venetian Globe to an Ottoman Atlas?" *Imago Mundi* 69 (1): 37–51. https://doi.org/10.108 0/03085694.2017.1242839.

Berchet, Guglielmo. 1865. *La Repubblica di Venezia e la Persia*. Turin: G. B. Paravia. https://www.gutenberg.org/files/34352/34352-h/34352-h.htm.

Berengo, Marino. 1960. "Alessandri, Vincenzo degli." In *Dizionario Biografico degli Italiani*, 2:174. Rome: Istituto dell'Enciclopedia Italiana. http://www. treccani.it/enciclopedia/vincenzo-degli-alessandri_(Dizionario-Biografico)/.

Bergamini, Giuseppe. 2016. "Bombelli, Sebastiano." In *Dizionario Biografico dei Friulani*. http://www.dizionariobiograficodeifriulani.it/bombelli-sebastiano/.

Berridge, G. R. 2003. "English Dragomans and Oriental Secretaries: The Early Nineteenth Century Origins of the Anglicization of the British Embassy Dragomanat in Constantinople." *Diplomacy & Statecraft* 14 (4): 137–52. https://doi.org/10.1080/0959229031233129574.

———. 2004. "Notes on the Origins of the Diplomatic Corps: Constantinople in the 1620s." *Clingendael Discussion Paper in Diplomacy* 92. https://www.clingendael.org/sites/default/files/2016-02/20040500_cli_paper_dip_issue92.pdf.

Bertelè, Tommaso. 1932. *Il palazzo degli ambasciatori di Venezia a Constantinopoli e le sue antiche memorie. Ricerche storiche con documenti inediti.* Bologna: Apollo.

Berthier, Annie. 1992. "À l'origine de l'étude de la langue turque en France. Liste des grammaires et dictionnaires manuscrits du fonds turc de la Bibliothèque nationale de Paris." *Varia Turcica* 19: 77–82.

———. 1997. "Turquerie ou Turcologie? L'effort de traduction des langues au XVIIᵉ siècle, d'après la collection des manuscrits conservée à la Bibliotheque nationale de France." In *Istanbul et les langues orientales*, edited by Frédéric Hitzel, 283–317. Istanbul: Isis.

Bevilacqua, Alexander. 2016. "How to Organise the Orient: D'Herbelot and the Bibliothèque Orientale." *Journal of the Warburg and Courtauld Institutes* 79 (1): 213–61. http://jstor.org/stable/26322524.

———. 2018. *The Republic of Arabic Letters: Islam and the European Enlightenment.* Cambridge, MA: Belknap Press of Harvard University Press. https://doi.org/10.4159/9780674985698.

Bevilacqua, Alexander and Helen Pfeifer. 2013. "Turquerie: Culture in Motion, 1650–1750." *Past & Present* 221 (1): 75–118.

Bibliothèque nationale de France. Département des manuscrits. 2007. "Présentation du fonds des manuscrits turcs." https://archivesetmanuscrits.bnf.fr/ark:/12148/cc4355v.

Bindman, David. 2010. "The Black Presence in British Art: Sixteenth and Seventeenth Centuries." In *The Image of the Black in Western Art*, edited by David Bindman and Henry Louis Gates. Cambridge, MA: Belknap Press of Harvard University Press. https://doi.org/10.37862/aaeportal.00140.007.

Binney, Edwin 3rd, ed. 1979. *Turkish Treasures from the Collection of Edwin Binney, 3rd.* Portland, OR: The Museum.

Bisaha, Nancy. 1999. "'New Barbarian' or Worthy Adversary? Humanist Constructs of the Ottoman Turks in Fifteenth-Century Italy." In *Western Views of Islam in Medieval and Early Modern Europe: Perception of Other*, edited by David R Blanks, 185–205. New York: St. Martin's Press. https://doi.org/10.1057/9780312299675_11.

Blair, Ann. 2014. "Hidden Hands: Amanuenses and Authorship in Early Modern Europe." A. S. W. Rosenbach Lectures in Bibliography, University of Pennsylvania Libraries, Philadelphia, March 17, 18, 20. https://repository.upenn.edu/rosenbach/8/.

Blochet, Edgar, ed. 1933. *Catalogue des manuscrits Turcs. Supplément, nos 573–1419*. Vol. 2. Paris: Bibliothèque nationale. https://doi. org/10.31826/9781463229740.

Boch, Julie. 2005. "De la traduction à l'invention: Aux sources des Contes orientaux de Caylus." *Féeries* 2: 47–59. https://journals.openedition.org/feeries/103.

Boerio, Giuseppe. 1960. *Dizionario del dialetto veneziano*. Turin: Bottega d'Erasmo.

Boettcher, Susan R. 2004. "German Orientalism in the Age of Confessional Consolidation: Jacob Andreae's Thirteen Sermons on the Turk, 1568." *Comparative Studies of South Asia, Africa and the Middle East* 24 (2): 101–15. https://doi.org/10.1215/1089201x-24-2-101.

Bombaci, Alessio. 1938. *La "Regola del parlare turcho" di Filippo Argenti: Materiale per la conoscenza del turco parlato nella prima metà del 16 secolo*. Naples: R. Istituto superiore orientale.

———. 1969. *La letteratura turca: Con un profilo della letteratura mongola*. Florence: Sansoni.

Borovaya, Olga. 2017. *The Beginnings of Ladino Literature: Moses Almosnino and His Readers*. Bloomington: Indiana University Press. https://doi.org/10.2307/j. ctt2005x2x.

Borromeo, Elisabetta. 2005. "Les Catholiques à Constantinople. Galata et les églises de rite latin au XVIIᵉ siècle." *Revue des mondes musulmans et de la Méditerranée* 107–10 (September): 227–43. https://doi.org/10.4000/remmm.2811.

———. 2007. *Voyageurs occidentaux dans l'empire Ottoman, 1600–1644*. Paris: Maisonneuve & Larose.

Bossaert, Marie. 2017. "La part arménienne des études turques. Enquête sur les subalternes de la turcologie en Europe." *European Journal of Turkish Studies. Social Sciences on Contemporary Turkey* 24 (November). https://doi. org/10.4000/ejts.5525.

———. 2000. "Poste in translation: Les drogmans des consulats italiens dans l'Empire Ottoman (1861–1911)." In *Consoli e consolati italiani dagli stati pre-unitari al fascismo*, edited by Marcella Aglietti, Mathieu Grenet, and Fabrice Jesné, 209–37. Rome: École française de Rome.

Bossaert, Marie and Emmanuel Szurek. 2015. "Toward a Transnational History of Turkish Studies (18th–20th Centuries)." *European Journal of Turkish Studies*, February. https://journals.openedition.org/ejts/5109.

Botley, Paul. 2004. *Latin Translation in the Renaissance: The Theory and Practice of Leonardo Bruni, Giannozzo Manetti and Desiderius Erasmus*. New York: Cambridge University Press.

Bottigheimer, Ruth B. 2014. "East Meets West: Hannā Diyāb and The Thousand and One Nights." *Marvels & Tales* 28 (2): 302–24. https://doi.org/10.13110/ marvelstales.28.2.0302.

Boyar, Ebru and Kate Fleet. 2010. *A Social History of Ottoman Istanbul*. Cambridge: Cambridge University Press. https://doi.org/10.1017/cbo9780511750427.

Boyden, Michael. 2006. "Language Politics, Translation, and American Literary History." *Target* 18 (1): 121–37. https://doi.org/10.1075/target.18.1.07boy.

Bracewell, Wendy. 2005. "Orientalism, Occidentalism and Cosmopolitanism: Balkan Travel Writings on Europe." International Interdisciplinary Conference Occidentalism. http://www.bulgc18.com/occidentalism/bracewell_en.htm.

Bralić, Višnja, and Nina Kudiš Burić, eds. 2006. *Slikarska baština Istre: djela štafelajnog slikarstva od 15. do 18. stoljeća na području Porečko-pulske biskupije*. Zagreb: Inst. za Povijest Umjetnosti.

Bremmer, Jan, and Herman Roodenburg. 1991. *A Cultural History of Gesture*. Ithaca, NY: Cornell University Press.

Brendemoen, Bernt. 2012. "Prestige Registers vs. Common Speech in Ottoman Turkish." In *High vs. Low and Mixed Varieties: Status, Norms and Functions across Time and Languages*, edited by Gunvor Mejdell and Lutz Edzard, 123–32. Wiesbaden: Harrassowitz.

Brentjes, Sonja. 2008. "Courtly Patronage of the Ancient Sciences in Post-Classical Islamic Societies." *Al-Qanṭara* 29 (2): 403–36. https://doi.org/10.3989/alqantara.2008.v29.i2.64.

——. 2010. *Travellers from Europe in the Ottoman and Safavid Empires, 16th–17th Centuries: Seeking, Transforming, Discarding Knowledge*. Burlington, VT: Ashgate, Variorum. https://doi.org/10.4324/9781003097778.

Brett, Michael and Elizabeth Fentress. 1996. *The Berbers*. Oxford: Blackwell.

Broos, Marianne. 2002. "Paintings of Receptions of the Ambassadors at the Sublime Porte by Jean Baptiste Vanmour (1671–1737) and Their Influence in Constantinople and Venice." In *I Guardi: Vedute, capricci, feste, disegni e quadri turcheschi*, edited by Alessandro Bettagno, 179–85. Venice: Marsilio, Fondazione Giorgio Cini.

Brown, Patricia Fortini. 2000. "Behind the Walls: The Material Culture of Venetian Elites." In *Venice Reconsidered: The History and Civilization of an Italian City-State, 1297–1797*, edited by John Martin, 295–338. Baltimore: Johns Hopkins University Press.

Brown, Rawdon. 1864. *Calendar of State Papers and Manuscripts, Relating to English Affairs Existing in the Archives and Collection of Venice, and in Other Libraries of Northern Italy*. London: Longman, Green.

Brummett, Palmira Johnson. 1994. *Ottoman Seapower and Levantine Diplomacy in the Age of Discovery*. Albany: State University of New York Press.

——. 2015. *Mapping the Ottomans: Sovereignty, Territory, and Identity in the Early Modern Mediterranean*. New York: Cambridge University Press. https://doi.org/10.1017/cbo9781316117316.

Bryce, Derek. 2013. "The Absence of Ottoman, Islamic Europe in Edward W. Said's Orientalism." *Theory, Culture & Society* 30 (1): 99–121. https://doi.org/10.1177/0263276412456562.

Buchanan, Brenda J. 2006. "Saltpetre: A Commodity of Empire." In *Gunpowder, Explosives and the State: A Technological History*, edited by Brenda J. Buchanan, 67–90. Burlington, VT: Ashgate. https://doi.org/10.4324/9781315253725-15.

Burak, Guy. 2015. *The Second Formation of Islamic Law: The Hanafi School in the Early Modern Ottoman Empire*. New York: Cambridge University Press. https://doi.org/10.1017/cbo9781316106341.

———. 2016. "Evidentiary Truth Claims, Imperial Registers, and the Ottoman Archive: Contending Legal Views of Archival and Record-Keeping Practices in Ottoman Greater Syria (17th–19th Centuries)." *Bulletin of the School of Oriental and African Studies. University of London* 79 (2): 233–54. https://doi.org/10.1017/s0041977x16000082.

Burke, Peter. 1980. "Did Europe Exist before 1700?" *History of European Ideas* 1 (1): 21–28. https://doi.org/10.1016/0191-6599(80)90004-2.

———. 2007. "Translations into Latin in Early Modern Europe." In *Cultural Translation in Early Modern Europe*, edited by Peter Burke and R. Po-chia Hsia, 65–80. Cambridge: Cambridge University Press. https://doi.org/10.1017/cbo9780511497193.005.

———. 2012. "Translating the Turks." In *Why Concepts Matter: Translating Social and Political Thought*, edited by Martin Burke and Melvin Richter, 141–52. Leiden: Brill. https://doi.org/10.1163/9789004194908_009.

Burkholder, Mark A. 1998. "Bureaucrats." In *Administrators of Empire*, edited by Mark A. Burkholder, 77–103. Expanding World. Aldershot: Ashgate. https://doi.org/10.4324/9780429457708-2.

Burman, Thomas E. 2007. *Reading the Qur'ān in Latin Christendom, 1140–1560*. Philadelphia: University of Pennsylvania Press. https://doi.org/10.9783/9780812200225.

Burnett, Stephen G. 2012. *Christian Hebraism in the Reformation Era (1500–1660): Authors, Books, and the Transmission of Jewish Learning*. Leiden: Brill. https://doi.org/10.1163/9789004222496.

Buzon, Frédéric de. 2012. "Leibniz étymologie et origine des nations." *Revue Française d'Histoire des Idées Politiques* 36 (2): 383–400. https://doi.org/10.3917/rfhip.036.0383.

Cáceres-Würsig, Ingrid. 2012. "The *Jeunes de Langues* in the Eighteenth Century: Spain's First Diplomatic Interpreters on the European Model." *Interpreting* 14 (2): 127–44. https://doi.org/10.1075/intp.14.2.01cac.

Calafat, Guillaume. 2019. "Jurisdictional Pluralism in a Litigious Sea (1590–1630): Hard Cases, Multi-Sited Trials and Legal Enforcement between North Africa and Italy." *Past & Present* 242 (14): 142–78. https://doi.org/10.1093/pastj/gtz041.

Calvelli, Lorenzo, Francesca Crema, and Franco Luciani. 2017. "The Nani Museum: Greek and Roman Inscriptions from Greece and Dalmatia." In *Illyrica*

Antiqua 2. In Honorem Duje Rendić-Miočević, edited by Dino Demicheli, 265–90. Zagreb: Department of Archaeology, Faculty of Humanities and Social Sciences, University of Zagreb.

Calvi, Giulia. 2017. "Translating Imperial Practices, Knowledge, and Taste across the Mediterranean: Giulio Ferrario and Ignatius Mouradgea d'Ohsson." In *Women, Consumption, and the Circulation of Ideas in South-Eastern Europe, 17th–19th Centuries*, edited by Constanţa Vintilă-Ghiţulescu, 12–46. Leiden: Brill. https://doi.org/10.1163/9789004355095_003.

Campbell, Caroline, and Alan Chong. 2005. *Bellini and the East*. New Haven, CT: Yale University Press.

Canatar, Mehmet. 2005. "Mustafa Cenabi." Historians of the Ottoman Empire. https://ottomanhistorians.uchicago.edu/tr/historian/mustafa-cenabi.

Cannon, Garland. 2000. "Turkish and Persian Loans in English Literature." *Neophilologus* 84 (2): 285–307. https://doi.org/10.1023/A:1004534102802.

Caprin, Giuseppe. 1907. *L'Istria nobilissima*. Trieste: Schimpff.

Carhart, Michael C. 2019. *Leibniz Discovers Asia: Social Networking in the Republic of Letters*. Baltimore: Johns Hopkins University Press. https://doi.org/10.1353/book.66175.

Casale, Giancarlo. 2010. *The Ottoman Age of Exploration*. New York: Oxford University Press. https://doi.org/10.1093/acprof:oso/9780195377828.001.0001.

———. 2017. "An Ottoman Humanist on the Long Road to Egypt: Salih Celalzade's *Tārīḫ-i Mıṣır Al-Cedid.*" *DYNTRAN Working Paper* 29. https://dyntran.hypotheses.org/2052,

Castiglione, Frank. 2014. "'Levantine' Dragomans in Nineteenth Century Istanbul: The Pisanis, the British, and Issues of Subjecthood." *Journal of Ottoman Studies* 44: 169–95. https://doi.org/10.18589/oa.562127.

Castries, Henry, ed. 1905. *Les sources inédites de l'histoire du Maroc de 1530 à 1845*. Paris: E. Leroux.

Causevic, Ekrem. 2004. "A Chronicle of Bosnian Turkology: The Franciscans and the Turkish Language." *International Journal of Turkish Studies* 10 (1): 241–53.

Celetti, David. 2017. "French Residents and Ottoman Women in 18th-Century Levant: Personal Relations, Social Control, and Cultural Interchange." In *Women, Consumption, and the Circulation of Ideas in South-Eastern Europe, 17th–19th Centuries*, edited by Constanţa Vintilă-Ghiţulescu, 47–64. Leiden: Brill. https://doi.org/:10.1163/9789004355095_004.

Chan, Albert. 2002. *Chinese Books and Documents in the Jesuit Archives in Rome, a Descriptive Catalogue Japonica-Sinica I-IV*. Armonk, NY: M.E. Sharpe.

Chojnacki, Stanley. 2000. *Women and Men in Renaissance Venice: Twelve Essays on Patrician Society*. Baltimore: Johns Hopkins University Press.

Christelow, Allan. 1985. "Algerian Interpreters and the French Colonial Adventure in Sub-Saharan Africa." *The Maghreb Review/Majallat Al-Maghrib* 10 (4–6): 101–6.

Çiçek, Kemal. 2002. "Interpreters of the Court in the Ottoman Empire as Seen from the Sharia Court Records of Cyprus." *Islamic Law and Society* 9 (1): 1–15. https://doi.org/10.1163/156851902753649252.

Çipa, H. Erdem, and Emine Fetvacı, eds. 2013. *Writing History at the Ottoman Court: Editing the Past, Fashioning the Future.* Bloomington: Indiana University Press.

Çırakman, Aslı. 2002. *From the "Terror of the World" to the "Sick Man of Europe": European Images of Ottoman Empire and Society from the Sixteenth Century to the Nineteenth.* New York: P. Lang.

Coco, Carla, and Flora Manzonetto. 1985. *Baili veneziani alla sublime porta: storia e caratteristiche dell'Ambasciata veneta a Costantinopoli.* Venice: Stamperia di Venezia.

Cody, Francis. 2009. "Daily Wires and Daily Blossoms: Cultivating Regimes of Circulation in Tamil India's Newspaper Revolution." *Journal of Linguistic Anthropology* 19 (2): 286–309. https://doi.org/10.1111/j.1548-1395.2009.01035.x.

Colla, Elliott. 2015. "Dragomen and Checkpoints." *The Translator* 21 (2): 132–53. https://doi.org/10.1080/13556509.2015.1071523.

Collaço, Gwendolyn. 2017. "Dressing a City's Demeanour: Ottoman Costume Albums and the Portrayal of Urban Identity in the Early Seventeenth Century." *Textile History* 48 (2): 248–67. https://doi.org/10.1080/00404969.2017.1369331.

Coller, Ian. 2010. "East of Enlightenment: Regulating Cosmopolitanism between Istanbul and Paris in the Eighteenth Century." *Journal of World History* 21 (3): 447–70. https://doi.org/10.1353/jwh.2010.0026.

Conley, Thomas. 2002. "The Speech of Ibrahim at the Coronation of Maximilian II." *Rhetorica* 20 (3): 263–73. https://doi.org/10.1525/rh.2002.20.3.263.

Considine, John. 2008. *Dictionaries in Early Modern Europe: Lexicography and the Making of Heritage.* New York: Cambridge University Press. https://doi.org/10.1017/cbo9780511485985.

Corazzol, Gigi. 1994. "Varietà notarile: scorci di vita economica e sociale." In *Storia di Venezia,* edited by Gaetano Cozzi, 6:775–91. Rome: Istituto della Enciclopedia Italiana.

Cordier, Henri. 1911. "Un interprète du général Brune et la fin de l'École des jeunes de langues." *Mémoires de l'institut national de France. Académie des inscriptions et belles-lettres,* 267–350. https://doi.org/10.3406/minf.1911.1594.

Coronil, Fernando. 1996. "Beyond Occidentalism: Toward Nonimperial Geohistorical Categories." *Cultural Anthropology* 11 (1): 51–87. https://doi.org/10.1525/can.1996.11.1.02a00030.

Cossàr, Ranieri Mario. 1950. "Epistolario inedito del conte Stefano Carli (1726–1813)." *Archeografo triestino* 16–17: 257–316.

Coudert, Allison P., and Jeffrey S. Shoulson. 2004. *Hebraica Veritas? Christian Hebraists and the Study of Judaism in Early Modern Europe.* Philadelphia: University of Pennsylvania Press.

Csató, Éva Ágnes, Lars Johanson, Heidi Stein, Claudia Römer, and Bernt Brendemoen. 2010. "The Linguistic Landscape of Istanbul in the Seventeenth Century." In *The Urban Mind: Cultural and Environmental Dynamics*, edited by Paul Sinclair et al., 415–39. Uppsala: African and Comparative Archaeology, Department of Archaeology and Ancient History, Uppsala University.

Csató, Éva Ágnes, Astrid Menz, and Fikret Turan, eds. 2016. *Spoken Ottoman in Mediator Texts*. Wiesbaden: Harrassowitz. https://doi.org/10.2307/j.ctvc7714z.

Cunningham, Allan. 1961. "'Dragomania': The Dragomans of the British Embassy in Turkey." *St. Antony's Papers (Middle Eastern Affairs No.2)* 11: 81–100.

Curatola, Giovanni. 1999. "Drawings by Colonel Giovanni Francesco Rossini, Military Attaché of the Venetian Embassy in Constantinople." In *Art Turc - Turkish Art: 10th International Congress of Turkish Art*, 225–31. Geneva: Fondation Max Van Berchem.

Cutillas Ferrer, José Francisco. 2016. "War and Diplomacy: A Letter Describing Shah Tahmasp I and His Ministers." In *The Spanish Monarchy and Safavid Persia in the Early Modern Period: Politics, War and Religion*, edited by Enrique García Hernán, Rudolph P. Matthee, and José Francisco Cutillas Ferrer, 29–40. Valencia: Albatros.

D'Amora, Rosita. 2020. "Luigi Ferdinando Marsili, Hezārfenn and the Coffee: Texts, Documents and Translations." *Oriente Moderno* 100 (1): 106–19. https://doi.org/10.1163/22138617-12340230.

Dakhlia, Jocelyne. 2008. *Lingua franca*. Arles: Actes Sud.

Dale, Stephen Frederic. 2010. *The Muslim Empires of the Ottomans, Safavids, and Mughals*. New York: Cambridge University Press. https://doi.org/10.1017/cbo9780511818646.005.

Dalleggio d'Alessio, Eugenio. 1969. "Listes des podestats de la colonie génoise de Péra (Galata), des prieurs et sous-prieurs de la Magnifica Comunita." *Revue des études byzantines* 27: 151–57. https://doi.org/10.3406/rebyz.1969.1418.

Daniel, Elton L. 2001. "Shah." In *The Oxford Encyclopedia of the Islamic World*. Oxford Islamic Studies Online. http://www.oxfordislamicstudies.com/article/opr/t236/e0724.

Darakcıoğlu, Mehmet. 2010. "Rebuilding the Tower of Babel: Language Divide, Employment of Translators, and the Translation Bureau in the Ottoman Empire." PhD diss., Princeton University.

Darling, Linda T. 2008. "Political Change and Political Discourse in the Early Modern Mediterranean World." *The Journal of Interdisciplinary History* 38 (4): 505–31. https://doi.org/10.1162/jinh.2008.38.4.505.

———. 2012. "Ottoman Turkish: Written Language and Scribal Practice, 13th to 20th Centuries." In *Literacy in the Persianatye World: Writing and the Social Order*, edited by Brian Spooner and William L. Hanaway,

171–95. Philadelphia: University of Pennsylvania Museum. https://doi. org/10.9783/9781934536568.171.

Davies, Simon, Gabriel Sánchez Espinosa, and Daniel Sanjiv Roberts. 2014. *India and Europe in the Global Eighteenth Century*. Oxford: Voltaire Foundation.

Davis, Diana K. 2007. *Resurrecting the Granary of Rome: Environmental History and French Colonial Expansion in North Africa*. Athens: Ohio University Press.

Davis, Natalie Zemon. 2006. *Trickster Travels: A Sixteenth-Century Muslim between Worlds*. New York: Hill and Wang.

Davis, Robert C. 2001. "Counting European Slaves on the Barbary Coast." *Past and Present* 172: 87–124. https://doi.org/10.1093/past/172.1.87.

Daybell, James. 2012. *The Material Letter in Early Modern England: Manuscript Letters and the Culture and Practices of Letter-Writing, 1512–1635*. New York: Palgrave Macmillan. https://doi.org/10.1057/9781137006066.0006.

De Groot, Alexander H. 1978. *The Ottoman Empire and the Dutch Republic: A History of the Earliest Diplomatic Relations, 1610–1630*. Leiden: Nederlands Historisch-Archaeologisch Instituut Leiden/Istanbul.

——. 1994. "The Dragomans of the Embassies in Istanbul 1785–1834." In *Eastward Bound. Dutch Ventures and Adventures in the Middle East*, edited by G. J. van Gelder, 130–58. Amsterdam: Rodopi.

——. 1997. "Protection and Nationality: The Decline of the Dragomans." In *Istanbul et les langues orientales*, edited by Frédéric Hitzel, 235–55. Istanbul: Isis.

——. 2000. "Dragomans' Careers: Change of Status in Some Families Connected with the British and Dutch Embassies in Istanbul 1785–1829." In *Friends and Rivals in the East: Studies in Anglo-Dutch Relations in the Levant from the Seventeenth to the Early Nineteenth Century*, edited by Alastair Hamilton, 223–46. Leiden: Brill.

——. 2001. "Die levantinischen Dragomanen: Einheimische und fremde im eigenen Land. Kultur-und Sprachgrenzen zwischen Ost und West (1453–1914)." In *Verstehen und Verständigung: Ethnologie, Xenologie, interkulturelle Philosophie*, edited by Wolfdietrich Schmied-Kowarzik, 110–27. Würzburg: Königshausen & Neumann.

De Luca, Lia. 2011. "L'interprete nella dimensione della testimonianza: il caso istriano." *Acta Histriae* 19 (1): 1–16.

De Vivo, Filippo. 2007. *Information and Communication in Venice: Rethinking Early Modern Politics*. New York: Oxford University Press. https://doi. org/10.1093/acprof:oso/9780199227068.001.0001.

——. 2010. "Ordering the Archive in Early Modern Venice (1400–1650)." *Archival Science* 10 (3): 231–48. https://doi.org/10.1007/s10502-010-9122-1.

——. 2011. "How to Read Venetian Relazioni." Things Not Easily Believed: Introducing the Early Modern Relation, special issue edited by Thomas Cohen and Germaine Warkentin of *Renaissance and Reformation / Renaissance et Réforme* 34: 25–59. https://doi.org/10.33137/rr.v34i1-2.16167.

———. 2013. "Heart of the State, Site of Tension: The Archival Turn Viewed from Venice, c. 1400–1700." *Annales. Histoire, Sciences Sociales* 68 (3): 459–85. https://doi.org/10.1017/s2398568200000030.

De Zorzi, Giovanni. 2017. "Giambattista Toderini and the 'Musica Turchesca.'" In *Theory and Practice in the Music of the Islamic World. Essays in Honour of Owen Wright*, edited by Rachel Harris and Martin Stokes, 83–105. London: Routledge. https://doi.org/10.4324/9781315191461-5.

Değirmenci, Tülün. 2011. "An Illustrated Mecmua: The Commoner's Voice and the Iconography of the Court in Seventeenth-Century Ottoman Painting." *Ars Orientalis* 41: 186–218.

Degros, Maurice. 1984. "Les Jeunes de langues sous la Revolution et l'Empire." *Revue d'histoire diplomatique* 98 (1–2): 77–107.

Dehérain, Henri. 1917. "Talleyrand et les chaires de langues turque et persane au collège de France en 1805." *Journal des savants* 15 (9): 415–28. https://doi.org/10.3406/jds.1917.4802.

———. 1930. *La vie de Pierre Ruffin, orientaliste et diplomate, 1742–1824*. 2. Paris: Paul Geuthner.

———. 1935. "Un maitre de Silvestre de Sacy l'orientaliste Étienne le Grand." *Journal des Savants* 1 (1): 17–31. https://doi.org/10.3406/jds.1935.6143.

Denny, Walter B. 1970. "A Sixteenth-Century Architectural Plan of Istanbul." *Ars Orientalis* 8: 49–63. http://www.jstor.org/stable/4629252.

Denton, John. 1998. "Renaissance Translation Strategies and the Manipulation of a Classical Text. Plutarch from Jacques Amyot to Thomas North." In *Europe et Traduction*, edited by Michel Ballard, 67–78. Ottawa: University of Ottawa Press. https://doi.org/10.4000/books.apu.6433.

Deny, Jean. 1921. *Grammaire de la langue turque (dialect osmanli)*. Paris: Éditions E. Leroux.

Derrida, Jacques. 2001. "What Is a 'Relevant' Translation?" Translated by Lawrence Venuti. *Critical Inquiry* 27 (2): 174–200. https://doi.org/10.1086/449005.

Dew, Nicholas. 2004. "The Order of Oriental Knowledge: The Making of d'Herbelot's Bibliothèque Orientale." In *Debating World Literature*, edited by Christopher Prendergast, 233–52. New York: Verso.

———. 2009. *Orientalism in Louis XIV's France*. New York: Oxford University Press. https://doi.org/10.1093/acprof:oso/9780199234844.001.0001.

———. 2014. "Islamic Manuscript Collecting and the Rise of the 'Oriental Library.'" Paper presented at the 128th Annual Meeting of the American Historical Association, Washington, DC.

Do Paço, David. 2015. *L'Orient à Vienne au dix-huitième siècle*. Oxford: Voltaire Foundation.

——. 2018. "A Social History of Trans-Imperial Diplomacy in a Crisis Context: Herbert von Rathkeal's Circles of Belonging in Pera, 1779–1802." *The International History Review*: 1–22. https://doi.org/10.1080/07075332.2 018.1482940.

——. 2019a. "Une collaboration économique et sociale: consuls et protecteurs des marchands ottomans à Vienne et à Trieste au XVIIIᵉ siècle." *Cahiers de la Méditerranée* 98: 57–74. https://doi.org/10.4000/cdlm.11291.

——. 2019b. "Patronage and Expertise: The Creation of Trans-Imperial Knowledge, 1719–1848." In *Transnational Cultures of Expertise*, edited by Lothar Schilling and Jakob Vogel, 48–62. Berlin: De Gruyter. https://doi. org/10.1515/9783110553734-004.

Donazzolo, Pietro. 1928. *I viaggiatori veneti minori: Studio bio-bibliografico.* Rome: Alla sede della Società. http://asa.archiviostudiadriatici.it/islandora/object/libria%3A316804

Dörner, Anton. 2015. "Literacy in the Service of Diplomacy: Transylvanian Emissaries, Translators and Scribes at the Ottoman Porte during the Reign of Michael Apafi I." *Anuarul Institutului de Istorie »George Barițiu« - Series HISTORICA - Supliment* LIV: 281–93.

Dressler, Markus. 2005. "Inventing Orthodoxy: Competing Claims for Authority and Legitimacy in the Ottoman-Safavid Conflict." In *Legitimizing the Order: The Ottoman Rhetoric of State Power*, edited by Hakan T. Karateke and Maurus Reinkowski, 151–73. Leiden: Brill.

Drimba, Vladimir. 1992. "La grammaire turque d'Antonio Mascis (1677)." *Wiener Zeitschrift für die Kunde des Morgenlandes* 82: 109–20.

——. 1997. "La grammaire turque de Giovanni Agop (1685)." In *Studia Ottomanica: Festgabe für György Hazai zum 65. Geburtstag*, edited by Barbara Kellner-Heinkele and Peter Zieme, 39–46. Wiesbaden: Harrassowitz.

Dupont-Ferrier, Gustave. 1922. "Les jeunes de langues ou 'arméniennes' à Louis-le-Grand." *Revue des études arméniennes* 3: 189–232.

Dursteler, Eric R. 2000. "Identity and Coexistence in the Early Modern Mediterranean: The Venetian Nation in Constantinople, 1573–1645." PhD diss., Brown University.

——. 2001. "The Bailo in Constantinople: Crisis and Career in Venice's Early Modern Diplomatic Corps." *Mediterranean Historical Review* 16 (2): 1–30. https://doi.org/10.1080/714004583.

——. 2006. *Venetians in Constantinople: Nation, Identity, and Coexistence in the Early Modern Mediterranean*. Baltimore: Johns Hopkins University Press. https://doi.org/10.1353/book.3253.

——. 2012. "Speaking in Tongues: Language and Communication in the Early Modern Mediterranean." *Past & Present* 217 (1): 47–77. https://doi.org/10.1093/pastj/gts023.

———. 2018. "Sex and Transcultural Connections in Early Modern Istanbul."
Studi e materiali di storia delle religioni 84 (2): 498–512.

Durston, Alan. 2007. *Pastoral Quechua: The History of Christian Translation in
Colonial Peru, 1550–1650*. Notre Dame, IN: University of Notre Dame Press.
https://doi.org/10.2307/j.ctvpg8689.

Duverdier, Gérald. 1987. "Savary de Brèves et İbrahim Müteferrika: deux drogmans culturels a l'origine de l'imprimerie turque." *Bulletin du Bibliophile*
3: 322–59.

Eaton, Natasha. 2013. *Mimesis across Empires: Artworks and Networks in India,
1765–1860*. Durham, NC: Duke University Press.

Eldem, Edhem. 2016. "The French Nation in Constantinople in the Eighteenth
Century as Reflected in the Saints Peter and Paul Parish Records, 1740–1800."
In *French Mediterraneans: Transnational and Imperial Histories*, edited by
Patricia M. E. Lorcin and Todd Shepard, 131–67. Lincoln: University of Ne-
braska Press. https://doi.org/10.2307/j.ctt1d8h8t4.10.

El-Rouayheb, Khaled. 2015. *Islamic Intellectual History in the Seventeenth Century: Scholarly Currents in the Ottoman Empire and the Maghreb*. New York:
Cambridge University Press. https://doi.org/10.1017/cbo9781107337657.

Emiralioğlu, M. Pinar. 2014. *Geographical Knowledge and Imperial Culture in
the Early Modern Ottoman Empire*. Transculturalisms, 1400–1700. Burlington, VT: Ashgate. https://doi.org/10.4324/9781315254494.

Ergene, Boğaç A. 2004. "Evidence in Ottoman Courts: Oral and Written Documentation in Early-Modern Courts of Islamic Law." *Journal of the American
Oriental Society* 124 (3): 471–91. https://doi.org/10.2307/4132276.

Erginbaş, Vefa. 2013. "The Appropriation of Islamic History and Ahl Al-Baytism in Ottoman Historical Writing, 1300–1650." PhD diss., Ohio State
University.

———. 2014. "Enlightenment in the Ottoman Context: İbrahim Müteferrika and
His Intellectual Landscape." In *Historical Aspects of Printing and Publishing
in Languages of the Middle East*, edited by Geoffrey Roper, 53–100. Leiden:
Brill. https://doi.org/10.1163/9789004255975_004.

———. 2017. "Problematizing Ottoman Sunnism: Appropriation of Islamic History and Ahl Al-Baytism in Ottoman Literary and Historical Writing in the
Sixteenth Century." *Journal of the Economic and Social History of the Orient*
60 (5): 614–46. https://doi.org/10.1163/15685209-12341435.

Erimtan, Can. 2008. *Ottomans Looking West? The Origins of the Tulip Age
and its Development in Modern Turkey*. London: I. B.Tauris. https://doi.
org/10.5040/9780755610013.

Ermers, Robert J. 1999. *Arabic Grammars of Turkic: The Arabic Linguistic Model Applied to Foreign Languages & Translation of ʾAbū Ḥayyān
Al-ʾAndalusī's Kitāb al-ʾIdrāk li-Lisān al-ʾAtrāk*. Leiden: Brill. https://doi.
org/10.1163/9789004348448_003.

Errington, James Joseph. 2008. *Linguistics in a Colonial World: A Story of Language, Meaning, and Power*. Malden, MA: Blackwell. https://doi. org/10.1002/9780470690765.

Ersoy, Bozkurt. 1999. "Façade Compositions of Ottoman City-Hans." In *Art Turc - Turkish Art: 10th International Congress of Turkish Art*, 297–303. Geneva: Fondation Max Van Berchem.

Ertuğ, Zeynep Tarim. 2010. "The Depiction of Ceremonies in Ottoman Miniatures: Historical Record or a Matter of Protocol?" *Muqarnas* 27: 251–75. https://doi.org/10.1163/ej.9789004185111.i-448.66.

Etényi, Nóra G. 2014. "The Genesis and Metamorphosis of Images in the Holy Roman Empire." In *A Divided Hungary in Europe: Exchanges, Networks and Representations, 1541–1699*, edited by Kees Teszelszky, 3:15–44. Cambridge: Cambridge Scholars Publishing.

Eufe, Rembert. 2003. "Politica linguistica della Serenissima: Luca Tron, Antonio Condulmer, Marin Sanudo e il volgare nell'amministrazione veneziana a Creta." *Philologie im Netz* 23: 15–43. http://web.fu-berlin.de/phin/phin23/p23t2.htm.

Evans, Robert John Weston. 1979. *The Making of the Habsburg Monarchy, 1550–1700: An Interpretation*. New York: Oxford University Press.

Eyal, Gil. 2006. *The Disenchantment of the Orient: Expertise in Arab Affairs and the Israeli State*. Stanford, CA: Stanford University Press.

Fabian, Johannes. 1983. *Time and the Other: How Anthropology Makes Its Object*. New York: Columbia University Press. https://doi.org/10.7312/fabi16926.

Fabris, Antonio. 2015. "A Description of the Ottoman Arsenal of Istanbul (1698)." *Mediterranea: Ricerche Storiche* 12: 435–44.

Faroqhi, Suraiya. 1986. "The Venetian Presence in the Ottoman Empire (1600–1630)." *Journal of European Economic History* 22: 345–84.

Faroqhi, Suraiya and Christoph K. Neumann, eds. 2004. *Ottoman Costumes: From Textile to Identity*. Istanbul: Eren.

Fatica, Michele, ed. 2006. *Matteo Ripa e il Collegio dei Cinesi di Napoli (1682–1869)*. Naples: Istituto universitario orientale.

Feola, Vittoria. 2016. "Paris, Rome, Venice, and Vienna in Peter Lambeck's Network." *Nuncius*, 107–28. https://doi.org/10.1163/18253911-03101005.

Ferguson, Heather L. 2018. *The Proper Order of Things: Language, Power, and Law in Ottoman Administrative Discourses*. Stanford, CA: Stanford University Press. https://doi.org/10.11126/stanford/9781503603561.001.0001.

Fetvacı, Emine. 2011. "Enriched Narratives and Empowered Images in Seventeenth-Century Ottoman Manuscripts." *Ars Orientalis* 40: 243–66. http://jstor.org/stable/23075937.

———. 2013. *Picturing History at the Ottoman Court*. Bloomington: Indiana University Press.

————. 2020. *The Album of the World Emperor: Cross-Cultural Collecting and the Art of Album-Making in Seventeenth-Century Istanbul.* Princeton, NJ: Princeton University Press. https://doi.org/10.2307/j.ctvsn3nrr.

Fichtner, Paula S. 2008. *Terror and Toleration: The Habsburg Empire Confronts Islam, 1526–1850.* London: Reaktion Books.

Filipani-Ronconi, Pio. 1978. "The Tradition of Sacred Kingship in Iran." In *Iran under the Pahlavis*, edited by George Lenczowski, 51–83. Stanford, CA: Hoover Institution Press.

Findley, Carter V. 1980. "Patrimonial Household Organization and Factional Activity in the Ottoman Ruling Class." In *Türkiye'nin Sosyal ve Ekonomik Tarihi (1071–1920). Social and Economic History of Turkey (1071–1920)*, edited by Osman Okyar, 227–35. Ankara: Meteksan Yayınları.

————. 2019. *Enlightening Europe on Islam and the Ottomans: Mouradgea d'Ohsson and His Masterpiece.* Leiden: Brill.

Finkel, Caroline. 2005. *Osman's Dream: The Story of the Ottoman Empire, 1300–1923.* London: John Murray.

————. 2015. "Joseph von Hammer-Purgstall's English Translation of the First Books of Evliya Çelebi's Seyahatnâme (Book of Travels) 1." *Journal of the Royal Asiatic Society* 25 (1): 41–55. https://doi.org/10.1017/S1356186314000108.

Fisher, Alan W, and Carol Garrett Fisher. 1985. "A Note on the Location of the Royal Ottoman Ateliers." *Muqarnas: An Annual on Islamic Art and Architecture* 3: 118–20. https://doi.org/10.2307/1523087.

Fleischer, Cornell H. 1986. *Bureaucrat and Intellectual in the Ottoman Empire: The Historian Mustafa Ali (1541–1600).* Princeton, NJ: Princeton University Press. https://doi.org/10.1515/9781400854219.

————. 1992. "The Lawgiver as Messiah: The Making of the Imperial Image in the Reign of Suleyman." In *Soliman le Magnifique et son temps*, edited by Gilles Veinstein, 159–78. Paris: Documentation française.

Flores, Jorge Manuel, and António Vasconcelos de Saldanha, eds. 2003. *The Firangis in the Mughal Chancellery: Portuguese Copies of Akbar's Documents (1572–1604).* New Delhi: Embassy of Portugal.

Flügel, Gustav, ed. 1865. *Die arabischen, persischen und türkischen Handschriften der Kaiserlich-Königlichen Hofbibliothek zu Wien.* Vienna: K. K. Hof-und Staatsdruckerei.

Fraser, Elisabeth. 2010. "'Dressing Turks in the French Manner': Mouradgea d'Ohsson's Panorama of the Ottoman Empire." *Ars Orientalis* 39: 198–230. http://jstor.org/stable/23075928.

————. 2017. *Mediterranean Encounters: Artists between Europe and the Ottoman Empire, 1774–1839.* University Park: The Pennsylvania State University Press.

Frigo, Daniela. 2008. "Prudence and Experience: Ambassadors and Political Culture in Early Modern Italy." *Journal of Medieval and Early Modern Studies* 38 (1): 15–34. https://doi.org/10.1215/10829636-2007-017.

Fück, Johann. 1955. *Die arabischen Studien in Europa bis in den Anfang des 20 Jahrhunderts*. Leipzig: Harrassowitz.

Fusaro, Maria. 1996. *Uva passa: una guerra commerciale tra Venezia e l'Inghilterra (1540–1640)*. Venice: Il Cardo.

Gac, Scott et al. 2010. "Re: use of 'enslaved'." H-Slavery Discussion Log. February 8, 2010. https://lists.h-net.org/cgi-bin/logbrowse. pl?trx=vx&list=H-Slavery&month=1002&msg=ipxCJim5wkqJnnd2syl8%2BQ.

Gal, Susan. 2015. "Politics of Translation." *Annual Review of Anthropology* 44 (1): 225–40. https://doi.org/10.1146/annurev-anthro-102214-013806.

Gal, Susan, and Judith T. Irvine. 1995. "The Boundaries of Languages and Disciplines: How Ideologies Construct Difference." *Social Research* 62 (4): 967–1001. http://jstor.org/stable/40971131.

Galtarossa, Massimo. 2002. "La formazione burocratica del segretario veneziano: il caso di Antonio Milledonne." *Archivio Veneto* CLVIII: 5–64.

———. 2003. "Cittadinanza e Cancelleria ducale a Venezia (XVI-XVIII sec)." *Storia di Venezia - Rivista* I: 147–52.

Gamm, Niki. 2011. "Ottoman Poetry - Ottoman Politics." *Journal of Turkish Studies* 35 (1): 1–14.

García-Arenal, Mercedes, and Fernando Rodríguez Mediano. 2013. *The Orient in Spain: Converted Muslims, the Forged Lead Books of Granada, and the Rise of Orientalism*. Leiden: Brill. https://doi.org/10.1163/9789004250291.

———. 2017. "Sacred History, Sacred Languages: The Question of Arabic in Early Modern Spain." In *The Teaching and Learning of Arabic in Early Modern Europe*, edited by Jan Loop, Alastair Hamilton, and Charles Burnett, 133–62. Leiden: Brill. https://doi.org/10.1163/9789004338623_007.

García-Arenal, Mercedes, and Gerard Albert Wiegers. 2003. *A Man of Three Worlds: Samuel Pallache, a Moroccan Jew in Catholic and Protestant Europe*. Baltimore: Johns Hopkins University Press. https://doi.org/10.1353/book.14092.

Gardina, Edvilijo. 1993. "La famiglia capodistriana dei Tarsia." In *Antonio Tarsia, 1643–1722, Koper-Capodistria, 350 let*, 11–24. Koper: Pokrajinski muzej Koper.

Gautier, Antoine, and Marie de Testa. 2013. *Drogmans, diplomates et ressortissants européens auprès de la porte ottomane*. Istanbul: Isis.

Gemayel, Nasser. 1984. *Les échanges culturels entre les Maronites et l'Europe: du Collège maronite de Rome (1584) au Collège de 'Ayn-Warqa (1789)*. Beirut: Imprimerie Gemayel.

Geneja, Czesława, and Paul Naster. 1986. "François à Mesgnien Meninski: A propos d'un manuscrit autographe à la Bibliothèque Royale de Belgique." *Orientalia Lovaniensia Periodica* XVII: 253–74.

Gharipour, Mohammad. 2017. "The Gardens of Safavid Isfahan and Renaissance Italy: A New Urban Landscape?" In *Gardens of Renaissance Europe and the Islamic Empires: Encounters and Confluences*, edited by Mohammad

Gharipour. University Park: Pennsylvania State University Press. https://doi.org/10.5325/j.ctv14gpbt3.11.

Ghobrial, John-Paul A. 2014a. *The Whispers of Cities: Information Flows in Istanbul, London, and Paris in the Age of William Trumbull*. New York: Oxford University Press. https://doi.org/10.1093/acprof:oso/9780199672417.001.0001.

——. 2014b. "The Secret Life of Elias of Babylon and the Uses of Global Microhistory." *Past & Present* 222 (1): 51–93. https://doi.org/10.1093/pastj/gtt024.

——. 2016. "The Archive of Orientalism and Its Keepers: Re-Imagining the Histories of Arabic Manuscripts in Early Modern Europe." *Past & Present* 230 (suppl. 11): 90–111. https://doi.org/10.1093/pastj/gtw023.

——. 2017. "The Life and Hard Times of Solomon Negri: An Arabic Teacher in Early Modern Europe." In *The Teaching and Learning of Arabic in Early Modern Europe*, edited by Jan Loop, Alastair Hamilton, and Charles Burnett, 310–31. Leiden: Brill. https://doi.org/10.1163/9789004338623_015.

Gilbert, Claire M. 2018. "Social Context, Ideology and Translation." In *The Routledge Handbook of Translation and Culture*, edited by Sue-Ann Harding and Ovidi Carbonell Cortés, 225–42. New York: Routledge. https://doi.org/10.4324/9781315670898-12.

——. 2020. *In Good Faith: Arabic Translation and Translators in Early Modern Spain*. Philadelphia: University of Pennsylvania Press.

Gilmore, Myron P. 1947. "The Turk in French History, Thought, and Literature (1520–1660). By Clarence Dana Rouillard." *American Historical Review* 52 (4): 722–24. https://doi.org/10.2307/1842319.

Girard, Aurélien. 2019. "Was an Eastern Scholar Necessarily a Cultural Broker in Early Modern Europe? Faustus Naironus (1628–1711), the Christian East, and Oriental Studies." In *Confessionalisation and Erudition in Early Modern Europe: An Episode in the History of the Humanities*, edited by Nicholas Hardy and Dmitri Levitin, 240–63. Oxford: Oxford University Press. https://doi.org/10.5871/bacad/9780197266601.003.0007.

Girard, Aurélien, and Giovanni Pizzorusso. 2017. "The Maronite College in Early Modern Rome: Between the Ottoman Empire and the Republic of Letters." In *College Communities Abroad. Education, Migration and Catholicism in Early Modern Europe,* edited by Liam Chambers and Thomas O'Connor, 174–97. Manchester: Manchester University Press. https://doi.org/10.7228/manchester/9781784995140.003.0007.

Girardelli, Paolo. 2005. "Architecture, Identity, and Liminality: On the Use and Meaning of Catholic Spaces in Late Ottoman Istanbul." *Muqarnas* 22: 233–64. https://doi.org/10.1163/22118993_02201011.

——. 2010. "Between Rome and Istanbul: Architecture and Material Culture of a Franciscan Convent in the Ottoman Capital." *Mediterranean Studies* 19 (1): 162–88. http://jstor.org/stable/41167033.

Göçek, Fatma Müge. 1987. *East Encounters West: France and the Ottoman Empire in the Eighteenth Century*. New York: Oxford University Press.

Goffman, Daniel. 1990. "Appendix 1: The Registers of Foreigners." In *Izmir and the Levantine World, 1550–1650*, 147–54. Seattle: University of Washington Press.

———. 1998. *Britons in the Ottoman Empire 1642–1660*. Seattle: University of Washington Press.

———. 2002. *The Ottoman Empire and Early Modern Europe*. New York: Cambridge University Press. https://doi.org/10.1017/CBO9780511818844.

———. 2007. "Negotiating with the Renaissance State: The Ottoman Empire and the New Diplomacy." In *The Early Modern Ottomans: Remapping the Empire*, edited by Virginia Aksan and Daniel Goffman, 61–74. New York: Cambridge University Press.

Goffman, Daniel, and Christopher Stroop. 2004. "Empire as Composite: The Ottoman Polity and the Typology of Dominion." In *Imperialisms: Historical and Literary Investigations, 1500–1900*, edited by Balachandra Rajan and Elizabeth Sauer, 129–45. New York: Palgrave Macmillan. https://doi.org/10.1057/9781403980465_8.

Gopin, Seth A. 2002. "The Influence of Jean-Baptiste Vanmour." In *I Guardi: Vedute, capricci, feste, disegni e quadri turcheschi*, edited by Alessandro Bettagno, 153–62. Venice: Marsilio, Fondazione Giorgio Cini.

Gossard, Julia M. 2018. "French Child Ambassadors in the East." *15 Minute History Podcast* 103 (blog). February 21, 2018. https://15minutehistory.org/podcast/episode-103-french-child-ambassadors-in-the-east/.

Gottardi, Michele. 1997. "Un progetto di governo di Gio. Stefano Carli (1803)." *Acta Histriae* 5 (5): 199–204. https://www.dlib.si/details/URN:NBN:SI:doc-SZIT9F31.

Götz, Manfred, and Florian Sobieroj. 1999. *Islamische Handschriften*. Stuttgart: F. Steiner.

Graf, Tobias P, ed. 2016. *Der Preis der Diplomatie: Die Abrechnungen der kaiserlichen Gesandten an der Hohen Pforte, 1580–1583*. Heidelberg: Universitäts-Bibliothek. https://doi.org/10.11588/heibooks.70.60.

Grafton, Anthony, and Glenn W. Most, eds. 2016. *Canonical Texts and Scholarly Practices: A Global Comparative Approach*. Cambridge: Cambridge University Press. https://doi.org/10.1017/cbo9781316226728.

Grafton, Anthony, and Joanna Weinberg. 2011. *I Have Always Loved the Holy Tongue: Isaac Casaubon, the Jews, and a Forgotten Chapter in Renaissance Scholarship*. Cambridge, MA: Harvard University Press.

Greene, Molly. 2002. "Beyond the Northern Invasion: The Mediterranean in the Seventeenth Century." *Past & Present* 174 (1): 42–71. https://doi.org/10.1093/past/174.1.42.

———. 2010. *Catholic Pirates and Greek Merchants: A Maritime History of the Mediterranean*. Princeton, NJ: Princeton University Press. https://doi.org/10.2307/j.ctv4w3sv3.

Grehan, James. 2006. "Smoking and 'Early Modern' Sociability: The Great Tobacco Debate in the Ottoman Middle East (Seventeenth to Eighteenth

Centuries)." *American Historical Review* 111 (5): 1352–77. https://doi. org/10.1086/ahr.111.5.1352.

Grendler, Paul F. 1989. *Schooling in Renaissance Italy: Literacy and Learning, 1300–1600*. Baltimore: Johns Hopkins University Press. https://doi.org/10.1093/obo/9780195399301-0005.

Grenet, Mathieu. 2013. "Alexis Gierra, 'interprète juré de langues orientales' à Marseille: une carrière entre marchands, frères et refugiés (fin XVIIIᵉ-premier tiers du XIXᵉ siècle." In *Langues et langages du commerce en Méditerranée et en Europe à l'époque moderne*, edited by Gilbert Buti, Michèle Janin-Thivos, and Olivier Raveux, 51–64. Aix-en-Provence: Presses universitaires de Provence.

Grey, Charles, ed. 1873. *A Narrative of Italian Travels in Persia, in the Fifteenth and Sixteen Centuries*. London: Printed for the Hakluyt Society. https://doi.org/10.4324/9781315564944.

Grubb, James S. 1996. *Provincial Families of the Renaissance: Private and Public Life in the Veneto*. Baltimore: Johns Hopkins University Press. https://doi.org/10.1353/book.67864.

———. 2000. "Elite Citizens." In *Venice Reconsidered: The History and Civilization of an Italian City-State, 1297–1797*, edited by John Martin and Dennis Romano, 339–64. Baltimore: Johns Hopkins University Press.

Gullino, Giuseppe. 1991. "DONÀ, Giovanni Battista." In *Dizionario Biografico degli Italiani* 40. http://www.treccani.it/enciclopedia/giovanni-battista-dona_(Dizionario-Biografico)/.

Günergun, Feza. 2007. "Ottoman Encounters with European Science: Sixteenth-and Seventeenth-Century Translations into Turkish." In *Cultural Translation in Early Modern Europe*, edited by Peter Burke, 192–211. Cambridge: Cambridge University Press. https://doi.org/10.1017/cbo9780511497193.012.

Güngörürler, Selim. 2016. "Diplomacy and Political Relations between the Ottoman Empire and Safavid Iran, 1639–1722." PhD diss., Georgetown University.

Gürkan, Emrah Safa. 2015. "Mediating Boundaries: Mediterranean Go-Betweens and Cross-Confessional Diplomacy in Constantinople, 1560–1600." *Journal of Early Modern History* 19 (2–3): 107–28. https://doi.org/10.1163/15700658-12342453.

———. 2017. *Sultanın Casusları: 16. yüzyılda istihbarat, sabotaj ve rüşvet ağları*. Istanbul: Kronik Yayıncılık.

Haase, Claus-Peter. 1998. "Das Kostümalbum von Lambert de Vos, sein osmanisches Pendant in Wolfenbüttel und die osmanische Textilkunst der Zeit Selims II." *EOTHEN: Jahreshefte der Gesellschaft der Freunde Islamischer Kunst und Kultur* 4–7: 39–44.

Hacker, Yosef. 1987. "An Emissary of Louis XIV in the Levant and the Culture of Ottoman Jewry [in Hebrew]." *Zion* 52 (1): 25–44. http://jstor.org/stable/23559517.

———. 1988. "Raphael Levi, Ahmed Bashi, Mehmet Bashi, Louis de Byzance—the Transformations of an Istanbulite Jew in the Seventeenth Century [in Hebrew]." In *Galut aḥar golah: meḥḳarim be-toldot 'Am Yiśra'el mugashim le-Profesor Ḥayim Bainarṭ li-melot lo shiv'im shanah*, edited by Aaron Mirsky, Avraham Grossman, and Yosef Kaplan, 497–516. Jerusalem: Ben-Zvi Institute.

Haddad, Jonathan. 2016. "Imagining Turkish Literature: Between the French Republic of Letters and the Ottoman Empire." PhD diss., University of California, Berkeley.

Hagen, Gottfried. 2000. "Some Considerations on the Study of Ottoman Geographical Writings." *Archivum Ottomanicum* 18: 183–93.

———. 2003. "Translations and Translators in a Multilingual Society: A Case Study of Persian-Ottoman Translations, Late 15th to Early 17th Century." *Eurasian Studies* 2 (1): 95–134.

———. 2006. Review of *An Ottoman Tragedy: History and Historiography at Play*, by Gabriel Piterberg. H-Net. https://networks.h-net.org/node/11419/reviews/11502/hagen-piterberg-ottoman-tragedy-history-and-historiography-play.

———. 2007. "Kātib Çelebī." In *Historians of the Ottoman Empire*, edited by Cemal Kafadar, Hakan T. Karateke, and Cornell H. Fleischer, 1–19. https://ottomanhistorians.uchicago.edu/en/historian/katib-celebi.

Hagen, Gottfried, and Baki Tezcan, eds. 2012. *Other Places: Ottomans Traveling, Seeing, Writing, Drawing the World: Essays in Honor of Thomas D. Goodrich*. A special double issue of the *Journal of Ottoman Studies / Osmanlı Araştırmaları* 39–40.

Hall, Kim F. 1995. *Things of Darkness: Economies of Race and Gender in Early Modern England*. Ithaca, NY: Cornell University Press. https://doi.org/10.7591/9781501725456.

Hamadeh, Shirine. 2002. "Splash and Spectacle: The Obsession with Fountains in Eighteenth-Century Istanbul." *Muqarnas* 19: 123–48. https://doi.org/10.1163/22118993-90000031.

———. 2007. *The City's Pleasures: Istanbul in the Eighteenth Century*. Seattle: University of Washington Press.

Hamilton, Alastair. 1994. "An Egyptian Traveller in the Republic of Letters: Josephus Barbatus or Abudacnus the Copt." *Journal of the Warburg and Courtauld Institutes* 57: 123–50. https://doi.org/10.2307/751466.

———. 2004. "Seaman, William (1606/7–1680)." In *Oxford Dictionary of National Biography*. https://doi.org/10.1093/odnb/9780192683120.013.24986.

———. 2006. *The Copts and the West, 1439–1822: The European Discovery of the Egyptian Church*. Oxford: Oxford University Press. http://hdl.handle.net/2027/heb.30658.

———. 2009. "Michel d'Asquier, Imperial Interpreter and Bibliophile." *Journal of the Warburg and Courtauld Institutes* 72: 237–41. http://jstor.org/stable/40593772.

———. 2011. "The Long Apprenticeship: Casaubon and Arabic." In *I Have Always Loved the Holy Tongue: Isaac Casaubon, the Jews, and a Forgotten Chapter in Renaissance Scholarship*, edited by Anthony Grafton and Joanna Weinberg, 293–306. Cambridge, MA: Harvard University Press.

———. 2017. "Du Ryer, André." In *Christian Muslim Relations: A Bibliographical History.* Vol. 9, *Western and Southern Europe (1600–1700)*, edited by David Thomas and John Chesworth, 453–65. Vol. 31, History of Christian-Muslim Relations. Leiden: Brill. https://doi.org/10.1163/2451-9537_cmrii_COM_27011.

Hamilton, Alastair, ed. 2018. *Johann Michael Wansleben's Travels in the Levant, 1671–1674: An Annotated Edition of His Italian Report.* Leiden: Brill. https://doi.org/10.1163/9789004362154.

Hamilton, Alastair, Maurits H. van den Boogert, and Bart Westerweel. 2005. *The Republic of Letters and the Levant.* Leiden: Brill.

Hamilton, Alastair, and Francis Richard. 2004. *André Du Ryer and Oriental Studies in Seventeenth-Century France.* London: Arcadian Library.

Hanks, William F. 2010. *Converting Words: Maya in the Age of the Cross.* Berkeley: University of California Press. https://doi.org/10.1525/california/9780520257702.001.0001.

———. 2015. "The Space of Translation." In *Translating Worlds: The Epistemological Space of Translation*, edited by Carlo Severi and William F. Hanks, 21–49. Chicago: HAU Books. https://doi.org/10.14318/hau4.2.002.

Harper, James G. 2011. *The Turk and Islam in the Western Eye, 1450–1750: Visual Imagery before Orientalism.* Burlington, VT: Ashgate. https://doi.org/10.4324/9781315085029.

Hathaway, Jane. 1997. *The Politics of Households in Ottoman Egypt: The Rise of the Qazdaglis.* New York: Cambridge University Press. https://doi.org/10.1017/cbo9780511470738.

———. 2008. *The Arab Lands under Ottoman Rule, 1516–1800.* Harlow: Longman. https://doi.org/10.4324/9781315838021.

Haug, Judith. 2016. "Being More than the Sum of One's Parts: Acculturation and Biculturality in the Life and Works of Ali Ufukî." *Archivum Ottomanicum* 33: 179–90.

Helander, Hans. 2012. "The Roles of Latin in Early Modern Europe." *L'annuaire du Collège de France. Cours et travaux* 111: 885–87. https://doi.org/10.4000/annuaire-cdf.1783.

Heller, Monica. 1990. "French Immersion in Canada: A Model for Switzerland?" *Multilingua - Journal of Cross-Cultural and Interlanguage Communication* 9 (1): 67–86. https://doi.org/10.1515/mult.1990.9.1.67.

Heller, Monica, and Bonnie S. McElhinny. 2017. *Language, Capitalism, Colonialism: Towards a Critical History.* Toronto: University of Toronto Press.

Henry, Chriscinda Claire. 2009. "Buffoons, Rustics, and Courtesans: Low Painting and Entertainment Culture in Renaissance Venice." PhD diss., University
of Chicago.

Hering, Gunnar. 1994. "Panagiotis Nikousios als Dragoman der Kaiserlichen
Gesandtschaft in Konstantinopel." In *Andrias. Herbert Hunger zum 80. Geb-
urtstag*, edited by W. Hörandner: 143–78. Vienna: Verlag der Österreichischen
Akademie der Wissenschaften.

Hermann, Alfred. 2002. "Interpreting in Antiquity." In *The Interpreting Studies
Reader*, edited by Franz Pöchhacker, 15–22. New York: Routledge.

Hermans, Theo. 1997. "The Task of the Translator in the European Renaissance:
Explorations in a Discursive Field." In *Translating Literature*, edited by Susan
Bassnett, 14–40. Cambridge: Brewer.

———. 2012. "De drooglieden van de Levantse handel: . . . de groote mobile van
de geheele machine . . ." *Filter, tijdschrift over vertalen* 19 (3): 23–31.

Hershenzon, Daniel. 2014. "Traveling Libraries: The Arabic Manuscripts of
Muley Zidan and the Escorial Library." *Journal of Early Modern History* 18
(6): 535–58. https://doi.org/10.1163/15700658-12342419.

Heyberger, Bernard. 1995. "La carrière manquée d'un écclésiastique oriental en
Italie: Timothée Karnush, archevêque syrien catholique de Mardin." *Bulletin
de la Faculté des Lettres de Mulhouse* XIX: 31–47.

———. 2009. "Chrétiens orientaux dans l'Europe catholique (XVIIᵉ–XVIIIᵉ
siècles)." In *Hommes de l'entre-deux. Parcours individuels et portraits de
groupes sur la frontière de la Méditerranée (XVIᵉ–XXᵉ siècle)*, edited by Bernard Heyberger and Chantal Verdeil, 61–93. Paris: Les Indes Savantes.

———. 2015. "L'Orient et l'islam dans l'érudition européenne du XVIIᵉ siècle."
Dix-septième siècle 268: 495–508. https://doi.org/:10.3917/dss.153.0495.

———. 2017. "Justinien de Neuvy, dit Michel Febvre." In *Christian Muslim
Relations: A Bibliographical History.* Vol. 9, *Western and Southern Europe
(1600–1700)*, edited by David Thomas and John Chesworth, 579–88. Vol. 3,
History of Christian-Muslim relations. Leiden: Brill.

Heywood, Colin J. 1972. "Sir Paul Rycaut, A Seventeenth-Century Observer of
the Ottoman State: Notes for a Study." In *English and Continental Views of
the Ottoman Empire, 1500–1800*, edited by Ezel Kural Shaw and Colin J. Heywood, 31–55. Los Angeles: William Andrews Clark Memorial Library.

———. 1993. "A Letter from Cerrāḥ Muṣṭafā Pasha, Vālī of Tunis, to Sir William
Trumbull (A.H. 1099/A.D. 1688)." *British Library Journal* 19: 218–29.

———. 2000. "A *Buyuruldu* of A.H. 1100 / A.D. 1689 for the Dragomans of the
English Embassy at Istanbul (Notes and Documents on the English Dragomanate, I)." In *The Balance of Truth. Essays in Honour of Professor Geoffrey
Lewis*, edited by Çigdem Balim-Harding, 125–44. Istanbul: Isis. https://doi.
org/10.31826/9781463231576-012.

———. 2016. "'More than Ordinary Labour': Thomas Hyde (1636–1703) and the Translation of Turkish Documents under the Later Stuarts." *Journal of the Royal Asiatic Society* 26 (1–2): 309–20. https://doi.org/10.1017/s1356186315000565.

Hitzel, Frédéric, ed. 1995. *Enfants de langue et drogmans*. Istanbul: Yapı Kredi Yayınları.

———, ed. 1997. *Istanbul et les langues orientales*. Paris: Éditions L'Harmattan.

———. 2013. "L'École des Jeunes de langue d'Istanbul, un modèle d'apprentissage des langues orientales." In *Langues et langues du commerce en Méditerranée (XVIᵉ–XIXᵉ siècle)*, edited by Gilbert Buti, Michèle Janin-Thivos, and Olivier Raveux, 23–31. Aix-en Provence: Presses universitaires de Provence.

Hodgson, Marshall G. S. 1974. *The Venture of Islam: Conscience and History in a World Civilization*. Chicago: University of Chicago Press. https://doi.org/10.7208/chicago/9780226346861.001.0001.

Höfert, Almut. 2003. *Den Feind beschreiben: "Türkengefahr" und europäisches Wissen über das Osmanische Reich 1450–1600*. Frankfurt: Campus.

———. 2015. "Hans Löwenklau." In *Christian Muslim Relations: A Bibliographical History*. Vol. *7, Central and Eastern Europe, Asia, Africa and South America (1500–1600)*, edited by David Thomas and John Chesworth, 481–88. Vo. 24, History of Christian-Muslim Relations. Leiden: Brill.

Hossain, Mary. 1992. "The Training of Interpreters in Arabic and Turkish under Louis XIV: France." *Seventeenth-Century French Studies* 14: 235–46. https://doi.org/10.1179/c17.1992.14.1.235.

———. 1993. "The Training of Interpreters in Arabic and Turkish under Louis XIV: The Ottoman Empire." *Seventeenth-Century French Studies* 15: 279–95. https://doi.org/10.1179/c17.1993.15.1.279.

Hudson, Leila. 2005. "The New Ivory Towers: Think Tanks, Strategic Studies and 'Counterrealism.'" *Middle East Policy* 12 (4): 118–32. https://doi.org/10.1111/j.1475-4967.2005.00229.x.

Hughes, Diane Owen. 1986. "Representing the Family: Portraits and Purposes in Early Modern Italy." *Journal of Interdisciplinary History* 17 (1): 7–38. https://doi.org/10.2307/204123.

Hunt, Lucy-Anne. 2007. "Illustrating the Gospels in Arabic: Byzantine and Arab Christian Miniatures in Two Manuscripts of the Early Mamluk Period in Cambridge." In *The Bible in Arab Christianity*, edited by David Thomas, 315–49. Leiden: Brill. https://doi.org/10.1163/ej.9789004155589.i-421.88.

Imber, Colin. 2002. *The Ottoman Empire, 1300–1650: The Structure of Power*. Houndmills: Palgrave Macmillan.

Inalcık, Halil. 1991. "Ottoman Galata, 1453-1553." In *Prèmiere rencontre internationale sur l'Empire Ottoman et la Turquie moderne*, edited by Edhem Eldem, 17–105. Istanbul: Isis.

Inan, Murat Umut. 2019. "Imperial Ambitions, Mystical Aspirations: Persian Learning in the Ottoman World." In *The Persianate World: The Frontiers of a*

Eurasian Lingua Franca, edited by Nile Green. Berkeley: University of California Press. https://doi.org/10.1525/9780520972100-005.

Infelise, Mario. 1997a. "Gian Rinaldo Carli senior, dragomanno della Repubblica." *Acta Histriae* 5: 189–98.

———. 1997b. "La guerra, le nuove, i curiosi: i giornali militari negli anni della Santa Lega contro il Turco (1683–1690)." In *I Farnese: corti, guerra e nobiltà in antico regime*, edited by Antonella Bilotto, 321–48. Rome: Bulzoni.

———. 2002. *Prima dei giornali: alle origini della pubblica informazione, secoli XVI e XVII*. Rome: Laterza.

Inglis, David. 2011. "Mapping Global Consciousness: Portuguese Imperialism and the Forging of Modern Global Sensibilities." *Globalizations* 8 (5): 687–702. https://doi.org/10.1080/14747731.2011.617570.

Ingram, Anders. 2015. *Writing the Ottomans: Turkish History in Early Modern England*. Houndsmills: Palgrave Macmillan. https://doi.org/10.1057/9781137401533.

Irvine, Judith T., and Susan Gal. 2000. "Language Ideology and Linguistic Differentiation." In *Regimes of Language: Ideologies, Polities, and Identities*, edited by Paul V. Kroskrity, 35–83. Santa Fe, NM: School of American Research Press.

Irving, David R. M. 2009. "Comparative Organography in Early Modern Empires." *Music and Letters* 90 (3): 372–98. https://doi.org/10.1093/ml/gcp010.

Isom-Verhaaren, Christine. 2004. "Shifting Identities: Foreign State Servants in France and the Ottoman Empire." *Journal of Early Modern History* 8 (1/2): 109–35. https://doi.org/10.1163/1570065041268915.

Istituto italiano di cultura di Istanbul, and Istanbul Topkapi Sarayi Muzesi ve Venedik Correr Muzesi koleksiyonlarindan. 1995. *Yuzyillar boyunca Venedik ve İstanbul görünümleri - Vedute di Venezia ed Istanbul attraverso i secoli dalle collezioni del Museo Correr-Venezia e Museo del Topkapi-Istanbul*. Istanbul: Güzel Sanatlar.

Janos, Damien. 2006. "Panaiotis Nicousios and Alexander Mavrocordatos: The Rise of the Phanariots and the Office of Grand Dragoman in the Ottoman Administration in the Second Half of the Seventeenth Century." *Archivum Ottomanicum* 23: 177–96.

Jasanoff, Maya. 2005. "Cosmopolitan: A Tale of Identity from Ottoman Alexandria." *Common Knowledge* 11 (3): 393–409. https://doi.org/10.1215/0961754x-11-3-393.

Jeffrey, Craig, Christine Philliou, Douglas Rogers, and Andrew Shryock. 2011. "Fixers in Motion. A Conversation." *Comparative Studies in Society and History* 53 (3): 692–707. https://doi.org/10.1017/s0010417511000302.

Johnson, James H. 2005. "Deceit and Sincerity in Early Modern Venice." *Eighteenth-Century Studies* 38 (3): 399–415. https://doi.org/:10.1353/ecs.2005.0027.

Johnston, Norman J. 1971. "The Urban World of the Matraki Manuscript." *Journal of Near Eastern Studies* 30 (3): 159–76. https://doi.org/10.1086/372116.

Jones, W. R. 1971. "The Image of the Barbarian in Medieval Europe." *Comparative Studies in Society and History* 13 (4): 376–408. https://doi. org/10.4324/9781315249292-13.

Kaczka, Mariusz. 2019. "Pashas and Nobles: Pawel Benoe and Ottoman-Polish Encounters in the Eighteenth Century." PhD diss., European University Institute.

Kafadar, Cemal. 1995. *Between Two Worlds: The Construction of the Ottoman State*. Berkeley: University of California Press. http://jstor.org/stable/10.1525/j. ctt4cgfms.

Kafescioğlu, Çiğdem. 2009. *Constantinopolis/Istanbul: Cultural Encounter, Imperial Vision, and the Construction of the Ottoman Capital*. University Park: Pennsylvania State University Press.

Kaislaniemi, Samuli. 2009. "Jurebassos and Linguists: The East India Company and Early Modern English Words for 'Interpreter'" In *Selected Proceedings of the 2008 Symposium on New Approaches in English Historical Lexis*, edited by R. W. McConchie, Alpo Honkapohja, and Jukka Tyrkkö, 60–83. Somerville, MA: Cascadilla Proceedings Project. http://www.lingref.com/cpp/hellex/2008/paper2167.pdf.

Kalus, Marielle. 1992. "Les premières grammaires turques en France et leur édition." In *Mélanges offerts à Louis Bazin par ses disciples, collègues et amis*, edited by Jean-Louis Bacqué-Grammont and Rémy Dor, 83–86. Paris: Éditions L'Harmattan.

Kappler, Matthias. 1999. "Eine griechische Übersetzung (1664) von Giovanni Molinos 'Brevi rudimenti del parlar turchesco.'" *Archivum Ottomanicum* 17: 271–95.

———. 2001. "Early European Grammars of Ottoman Turkish in Greek Translation: A Greek Version of Du Ryer's 'Rudimenta Grammatices Linguae Turcicae' (1630)." *Turkic Languages* 5 (1): 120–37.

———. 2014. "An Unedited Sketch of Turkish Grammar (1711) by the Venetian *giovane di lingua* Pietr' Antonio Rizzi." *Turkic Languages* 18 (1/2): 104–27. https://core.ac.uk/reader/41143469

Kármán, Gábor. 2014. "Translation at the Seventeenth-Century Transylvanian Embassy in Constantinople." In *Osmanischer Orient und Ostmitteleuropa: Perzeptionen und Interaktionen in den Grenzzonen zwischen dem 16. und 18. Jahrhundert*, edited by Robert Born and Andreas Puth, 253–77. Stuttgart: Steiner.

———. 2016. *A Seventeenth-Century Odyssey in East Central Europe: The Life of Jakab Harsányi Nagy*. Leiden: Brill. https://doi.org/10.1163/9789004306813.

———. 2018. "Grand Dragoman Zülfikar Aga." *Archivum Ottomanicum* 35: 5–30.

Karttunen, Frances E. 1995. "The Roots of Sixteenth-Century Mesoamerican Lexicography." In *Cultures, Ideologies, and the Dictionary*, edited by Braj B. Kachru and Henry Kahane, 75–88. Tübingen: Niemeyer. https://doi. org/10.1515/9783110957075.75.

Kaya, İbrahim. 2011. "Kemal Paşazâde'nin Dekâyıku'l-Hakâyık'ı üzerine bazı düşünceler." *Turkish Studies* 6: 671–704. https://arastirmax.com/tr/system/files/dergiler/79199/makaleler/6/4/arastirmax-kemal-pasazadenin-dekayikul-hakayiki-uzerine-bazi-dusunceler.pdf.

Keane, Webb. 1997. *Signs of Recognition: Powers and Hazards of Representation in an Indonesian Society.* Berkeley: University of California Press.

——. 2005. "The Hazards of New Clothes: What Signs Make Possible." In *The Art of Clothing: A Pacific Experience*, edited by Graeme Were, 1–16. London: University College London.

Kelecsényi, Ágnes. n.d. "The Mysterious Printer Ibrahim Müteferrika and the Beginning of Turkish Book Printing." http://muteferrika.mtak.hu/index-en.html.

Kenessey, Mary. 1974. "A Turkish Grammar from the 17th Century." *Acta Orientalia Academiae Scientiarum Hungaricae* 28 (1): 119–25.

Kent, Allen, Harold Lancour, and Jay E. Daily. 1978. *Encyclopedia of Library and Information Science.* Vol. 23: Poland. New York: M. Dekker.

Kinra, Rajeev. 2016. "Cultures of Comparative Philology in the Early Modern Indo-Persian World." *Philological Encounters* 1 (1–4): 225–87. https://doi.org/10.1163/24519197-00000010.

Koch, Hans-Albrecht. 1991. *Das Kostümbuch des Lambert de Vos.* Graz: Akademische Druck und Verlagsanstalt.

Kokole, Metoda. 2012. "Who Was Antonio Tarsia and from Whom Did He Learn How to Compose?" In *Barocco Padano 7. Atti del XV convegno internazionale sulla musica italiana nei secoli XVII–XVIII, Milano, 14–16 Luglio 2009.* Como: Antiquae Musicae Italicae Studiosi.

Kołodziejczyk, Dariusz. 2011. *The Crimean Khanate and Poland-Lithuania: International Diplomacy on the European Periphery (15th–18th Century). A Study of Peace Treaties Followed by Annotated Documents.* Leiden: Brill. https://doi.org/10.1163/ej.9789004191907.i-1098.

——. 2012. "Khan, Caliph, Tsar and Imperator: The Multiple Identities of the Ottoman Sultan." In *Universal Empire*, edited by Peter Fibiger Bang and Dariusz Kołodziejczyk, 175–93. Cambridge: Cambridge University Press. https://doi.org/10.1017/cbo9781139136952.009.

Koutmanis, Sotiris. 2013. "Greeks in Venice (1620–1710): Gender, Economy, Attitudes [in Greek]." PhD diss., University of Athens.

Kraft, Alexander. 2011. "'Notitia Cœrulei Berolinensis Nuper Inventi' on the 300th Anniversary of the First Publication on Prussian Blue." *Bulletin for the History of Chemistry* 3 (1): 3–9. http://acshist.scs.illinois.edu/bulletin_open_access/v36-1/v36-1%20p3-9.pdf.

Krstić, Tijana. 2009. "Illuminated by the Light of Islam and the Glory of the Ottoman Sultanate: Self-Narratives of Conversion to Islam in the Age of Confessionalization." *Comparative Studies in Society and History* 51 (1): 35–63. https://doi.org/10.1017/s0010417509000036.

———. 2011a. *Contested Conversions to Islam: Confessionalization and Community in the Early Modern Ottoman Empire*. Stanford, CA: Stanford University Press. https://doi.org/10.11126/stanford/9780804773171.001.0001.

———. 2011b. "Of Translation and Empire: Sixteenth-Century Ottoman Imperial Interpreters as Renaissance Go-Betweens." In *The Ottoman World*, edited by Christine Woodhead, 130–42. London: Routledge. https://doi.org/10.4324/9780203142851.ch9.

———. 2013. "Contesting Subjecthood and Sovereignty in Ottoman Galata in the Age of Confessionalization: The Carazo Affair, 1613–1617." *Oriente Moderno* 93 (2): 422–53. https://doi.org/10.1163/22138617-12340024.

———. 2015. "Islam and Muslims in Early Modern Europe." In *Oxford Handbook of Early Modern European History, 1350–1750*, edited by Hamish Scott, 1: 670–93. Oxford: Oxford Univeristy Press. https://doi.org/10.1093/oxfordhb/9780199597253.013.25.

Krstić, Tijana and Derin Terzioğlu, eds. 2020. *Historicizing Sunni Islam in the Ottoman Empire, c. 1450-c. 1750*. Ledien: Brill. https://doi.org/10.1163/9789004440296.

Küçük, Harun. 2019. *Science without Leisure: Practical Naturalism in Istanbul, 1660–1732*. Pittsburgh: University of Pittsburgh Press. https://doi.org/10.2307/j.ctvt1sgop.

Kunt, I. Metin. 1983. *The Sultan's Servants: The Transformation of Ottoman Provincial Government, 1550–1650*. New York: Columbia University Press.

Kuru, Selim S. 2016. "Turkish Literature." In *Encyclopedia of Islam and the Muslim World*, 2nd edition, edited by Richard C. Martin, 1199–1203. Farmington Hills, MI: Macmillan.

Kuru, Selim S. and Murat Umut Inan. 2011. "Reintroducing Hafez to Readers in Rum." Edited by Mehmet Kalpaklı. *Journal of Turkish Studies. Special Issue: Festschrift in Honor of Walter G. Andrews III* 35 (1): 11–34.

Kynan-Wilson, William. 2017. "Costume Albums." *Encyclopaedia of Islam, THREE*, edited by Kate Fleet et al., 1: 25–27. https://doi.org/10.1163/1573-3912_ei3_COM_26886.

Lafi, Nora. 2011. "Petitions and Accommodating Urban Change in the Ottoman Empire." In *Istanbul as Seen from a Distance: Centre and Provinces in the Ottoman Empire*, edited by M. Sait Özervarlı, Feryal Tansuğ, and Elisabeth Özdalga, 73–82. Istanbul: Swedish Research Institute in Istanbul.

Lancashire, Ian. 2004. "Lexicography in the Early Modern English Period: The Manuscript Record." In *Historical Dictionaries and Historical Dictionary Research*, edited by Julie Coleman and Anne McDermott, 19–30. Tübingen: Niemeyer. https://doi.org/10.1515/9783110912609.19.

Langer, Axel, ed. 2013. *The Fascination of Persia: The Persian-European Dialogue in Seventeenth-Century Art & Contemporary Art from Tehran*. Zurich: Scheidegger & Spiess.

Larguèche, Malenda. 2001. "The Mahalla: The Origins of Beylical Sovereignty in Ottoman Tunisia during the Early Modern Period." In *North Africa, Islam and the Mediterranean World from the Almoravids to the Algerian War*, edited by Julia Ann Clancy-Smith, 105–116. London: Frank Cass. https://doi.org/10.4324/9781315040011-6.

Lasansky, D. Medina. 2004. *The Renaissance Perfected: Architecture, Spectacle, and Tourism in Fascist Italy*. University Park: Pennsylvania State University Press.

Lee, M. Kittiya. 2005. "Conversing in Colony: The Brasílica and the Vulgar in Portuguese America, 1500–1759." PhD diss., Johns Hopkins University.

Lefèvre, Corinne, Ines G. Županov, and Jorge Manuel Flores, eds. 2015. *Cosmopolitismes en Asie du sud: Sources, itinéraires, langues (XVIe–XVIIIe siècle)*. Paris: Éditions de l'École des hautes études en sciences sociales. https://doi.org/10.4000/books.editionsehess.22987.

Lesure, Michele. 1983. "Michel Cernovic 'explorator secretus' à Constantenople (1556–1563)." *Turcica* 15: 127–54.

Lewis, Bernard. 2004. *From Babel to Dragomans: Interpreting the Middle East*. New York: Oxford University Press.

Lewis, Geoffrey L. 1999. *The Turkish Language Reform: A Catastrophic Success*. Oxford: Oxford University Press.

Lindner, Rudi Paul. 1998. "Icons among Iconoclasts in the Renaissance." In *The Iconic Page in Manuscript, Print, and Digital Culture*, edited by George Bornstein, 89–107. Ann Arbor: University of Michigan Press.

Liu, Lydia H. 1995. *Translingual Practice: Literature, National Culture and Translated Modernity—China, 1900–1937*. Stanford, CA: Stanford University Press.

Livanios, Dimitris. 2013. "Pride, Prudence, and the Fear of God: The Loyalties of Alexander and Nicholas Mavrocordatos (1664–1730)." Edited by David. Ricks and Michael B. Trapp. *Dialogos: Hellenic Studies Review* 7: 1–22.

Lonni, Ada. 2009. "Tradurre parole o tradurre culture? Identità nazionale e percezione di sé nella figura del dragomanno gerosolimitano del XIX secolo." In *Per le vie del mondo*, edited by Piero De Gennaro, 295–304. Turin: Università degli studi di Torino.

Loop, Jan, Alastair Hamilton, and Charles Burnett, eds. 2017. *The Teaching and Learning of Arabic in Early Modern Europe*. Leiden: Brill. https://doi.org/10.1163/9789004338623.

Loop, Jan, and Richard van Leeuwen. 2016. "The Arabian Nights in European Literature - An Anthology," Encounters with the Orient. https://www.kent.ac.uk/ewto/projects/anthology/index.html.

Lorcin, Patricia. 2002. "Rome and France in Africa: Recovering Colonial Algeria's Latin Past." *French Historical Studies* 25 (2): 295–329. https://doi.org/10.1215/00161071-25-2-295.

Luca, Cristian. 2003a. "Alcuni 'confidenti' del bailaggio veneto di Costantinopoli nel seicento." *Annuario dell' Istituto romeno di cultura e ricerca umanistica* 5: 299–310.

———. 2003b. "Veneziani, levantini e romeni fra prassi politiche e interessi mercantili nell'Europa sud-orientale tra cinque e seicento." In *Romania e Romània: Lingua e cultura romena di fronte all'occidente*, edited by Teresa Ferro, 243–60. Udine: Forum.

———. 2008a. *Dacoromano-Italica: Studi e ricerche sui rapporti italo-romeni nei secoli XVI–XVIII*. Cluj-Napoca: Accademia Romena Centro di Studi Transilvani.

———. 2008b. "Documentary Notes Relative to the Kinships of Levantines and Venetians with the Princely Families from Wallachia and Moldavia." In *Românii În Europa Medievală. Studii În Onoarea Profesorului Victor Spinei*, edited by Dumitru Țeicu and Ionel Cândea, 653–75. Brăila: Muzeul Brăilei, Editura Istros.

———. 2013. "Notes on the Family Wealth and Career Progression of Cristoforo Tarsia and His Sons, Dragomans of the Venetian Embassy in Constantinople (1618–1716)." *Acta Histriae* 21: 39–56. http://www.dlib.si/details/URN:NBN:SI:DOC-6ZIXXUUR.

———. 2015. "The Professional Elite in Mid-Seventeenth Century Constantinople: The Danish Physician Hans Andersen Skovgaard (1604–1656) in the Last Decade of His Life and Career." In *Social and Political Elites in Eastern and Central Europe (15th–18th Centuries)*, edited by Cristian Luca, Laurentiu Radvan, and Alexandru Simon, 147–56. London: School of Slavonic and East European Studies, University College London.

Lucchetta, Francesca. 1983. "Un progetto per una scuola di lingue orientali a Venezia nel settecento." *Quaderni di Studi Arabi* 1: 1–28. http://www.jstor.org/stable/25802545.

———. 1984. "Una scuola di lingue orientali a Venezia nel settecento: Il secondo tentativo." *Quaderni di Studi Arabi* 2: 21–61. http://www.jstor.org/stable/25802557.

———. 1985. "L'ultimo progetto di una scuola orientalistica a Venezia nel settecento." *Quaderni di Studi Arabi* 3: 1–43. http://www.jstor.org/stable/25802566.

———. 1988. "Lo studio delle lingue orientali nella scuola per dragomanni di Venezia alla fine del XVII secolo." *Quaderni di Studi Arabi* 5/6: 479–98. http://www.jstor.org/stable/25802624.

———. 1989. "La scuola dei 'giovani di lingua' veneti nei secoli XVI e XVII." *Quaderni di Studi Arabi* 7: 19–40. http://www.jstor.org/stable/25802654.

———. 1997. "Il medico del bailaggio di Costantinopoli: Fra terapie e politica (secc. xv–xvi)." *Quaderni di Studi Arabi* 15: 5–50. http://www.jstor.org/stable/23474023.

Lybyer, Albert Howe. 2013. *The Government of the Ottoman Empire in the Time of Suleiman the Magnificent*. Cambridge, MA: Harvard University Press. https://doi.org/10.4159/harvard.9780674337053.

Lydon, Ghislaine. 2009. *On Trans-Saharan Trails: Islamic Law, Trade Networks, and Cross-Cultural Exchange in Nineteenth-Century Western Africa*. New York: Cambridge University Press. https://doi.org/10.1017/cbo9780511575457.

MacKay, Pierre A. 2004. "The Content and Authorship of the *Historia Turchesca*." In *550th Anniversary of the Istanbul University, International Byzantine and Ottoman Symposium (XVth Century)*, edited by Sümer Atasoy, 213–23. Istanbul: İstanbul Üniversitesi.

Mackie, Louise. 2001. "Italian Silks for the Ottoman Sultans." *Electronic Journal of Oriental Studies. Proceedings of the 11th International Congress of Turkish Art* 4 (31): 1–21.

MacLean, Gerald M. 2004. *The Rise of Oriental Travel: English Visitors to the Ottoman Empire, 1580–1720*. New York: Palgrave Macmillan. https://doi.org/10.1057/9780230511767.

Mairs, Rachel. 2012. "Interpreters and Translators in Hellenistic and Roman Egypt." In *Actes du 26e Congrès International de Papyrologie Genève, 16–21 Août 2010*, edited by Paul Schubert, 30: 457–62. Geneva: Droz.

Majda, Tadeusz. 2013. *Turkish Religious Texts in Latin Script from 18th Century South-Eastern Anatolia: Transcriptions, Translations, and a Study of the Language*. Berlin: Klaus Schwarz.

Majer, Hans Georg. 1991. "Niğârî and the Sultans' Portraits of Paolo Giovio." In *9. Milletleraras Türk Sanatlar Kongresi. 9th International Congress of Turkish Art*, 2: 441–55. Ankara: Kültür Bakanligi.

———. 2000. "Giovio, Veronese und die Osmanen." In *Europa und die Türken in der Renaissance*, edited by Bodo Guthmüller, 345–59. Tübingen: Niemeyer. https://doi.org/10.1515/9783110933567.345.

Makdisi, Saree, and Felicity Nussbaum, eds. 2008. *The Arabian Nights in Historical Context: Between East and West*. New York: Oxford University Press. https://doi.org/10.1093/acprof:oso/9780199554157.001.0001.

Makdisi, Ussama. 2002. "Ottoman Orientalism." *American Historical Review* 107 (3): 768–96. https://doi.org/10.1086/532495.

Malcolm, Noel. 2003. "'Behemoth' Latinus: Adam Ebert, Tacitism, and Hobbes." *Filozofski Vestnik* 24 (2): 85–120. https://ojs.zrc-sazu.si/filozofski-vestnik/article/view/3388.

———. 2007. "Comenius, Boyle, Oldenburg, and the Translation of the Bible into Turkish." *Church History and Religious Culture* 87 (3): 327–62. https://doi.org/10.1163/187124107x232453.

———. 2015. *Agents of Empire: Knights, Corsairs, Jesuits and Spies in the Sixteenth-Century Mediterranean World*. London: Allen Lane.

Mallett, Michael. 1994. "Ambassadors and Their Audiences in Renaissance Italy." *Renaissance Studies* 8 (3): 229–43. https://doi.org/10.1111/1477-4658.00153.

Mandelbrote, Scott, and Joanna Weinberg, eds. 2016. *Jewish Books and Their Readers: Aspects of the Intellectual Life of Christians and Jews in Early Modern Europe*. Leiden: Brill. https://doi.org/10.1163/9789004318151.

Mango, Cyril. 2000. "The Triumphal Way of Constantinople and the Golden Gate." *Dumbarton Oaks Papers* 54: 173–88. https://doi.org/10.2307/1291838.

Mansel, Philip. 1988. "Between Two Empires: Hans Ludwig von Kuefstein, Ambassador from the Holy Roman Emperor to the Ottoman Sultan in 1628, and His Pictures." In *At the Sublime Porte: Ambassadors to the Ottoman Empire (1550–1800)*, 11–19. London: Hazlitt, Gooden & Fox.

———. 1996. "Art and Diplomacy in Ottoman Constantinople." *History Today* 46 (8): 43–49.

Mantena, Rama Sundari. 2012. *The Origins of Modern Historiography in India: Antiquarianism and Philology, 1780–1880*. New York: Palgrave Macmillan. https://doi.org/10.1057/9781137011923.

Marani, Alberto. 1969. "Relazione inedita sui Tartari Precopensi scritta nel 1585 da Minuccio Minucci, poi arcivescovo di Zara." *Il Mamiani* 4: 213–28.

Marghetitch, S. G. 1993 [1898]. *Étude sur les fonctions des drogmans des missions diplomatiques ou consulaire en Turquie*. Istanbul: Isis.

Marzolph, Ulrich. 2015. "A Scholar in the Making: Antoine Galland's Early Travel Diaries in the Light of Comparative Folk Narrative Research." *Middle Eastern Literatures* 18 (3): 283–300. https://doi.org/10.1080/14752 62x.2016.1199095.

Masson, Frédéric. 1905. "Les Jeunes de langues: Notes sur l'éducation dans un établissement de Jésuites au XVIIIᵉ siècle." In *Jadis*, 67–114. Paris: P. Ollendorff.

Matar, Nabil I. 2003. *In the Lands of the Christians: Arabic Travel Writing in the Seventeenth Century*. New York: Routledge. https://doi.org/10.4324/9780203615713.

Matteucci, Gualberto. 1967. *Un glorioso convento francescano sulle rive del Bosforo: il San Francesco di Galata in Costantinopoli, 1230–1697*. Florence: Studi francescani.

Matthee, Rudi. 2011. "Book Reviews." *Iranian Studies* 44 (6): 920–24. https://doi.org/10.1080/00210862.2011.586817.

Matthiesson, Sophie. 2012. "At the Edge of Empires: A Biedermeier Portrait from Trieste by Jožef Tominc." *Art Journal of the National Gallery of Victoria* 51. https://www.ngv.vic.gov.au/essay/at-the-edge-of-empires-a-biedermeier-portrait-from-trieste-by-jozef-tominc.

Matuz, Josef. 1975. "Die Pfortendolmetscher zur Herrschaftszeit Süleymân des Prächtigen." *Südost-Forschungen* 24: 26–60. https://freidok.uni-freiburg.de/dnb/download/4521.

Mavroudi, Maria. 2013. "Translators from Greek into Arabic at the Court of Mehmet the Conqueror." In *The Byzantine Court: Source of Power and Culture*, edited by Ayla Ödekan, Nevra Necipoğlu, and Engin Akyürek, 195–207. Istanbul: Koç University Press.

McGrath, Elizabeth, and Jean Michel Massing, eds. 2012. *The Slave in European Art: From Renaissance Trophy to Abolitionist Emblem*. London: Warburg Institute.

McJannet, Linda. 2006. "'History Written by the Enemy': Eastern Sources about the Ottomans on the Continent and in England." *English Literary Renaissance* 36 (3): 396–429. https://doi.org/10.1111/j.1475-6757.2006.00088.x.

———. 2007. *The Sultan Speaks: Dialogue in English Plays and Histories about the Ottoman Turks*. New York: Palgrave Macmillan. https://doi.org/10.1057/9780230601499.

McKee, Sally. 2000. *Uncommon Dominion: Venetian Crete and the Myth of Ethnic Purity*. Philadelphia: University of Pennsylvania Press. https://doi.org/10.9783/9780812203813.

———. 2014. "The Familiarity of Slaves in Medieval and Early Modern Households." In *Mediterranean Slavery Revisited (500–1800)*, edited by Stefan Hanss, Juliane Schiel, and Claudia Schmid, 501–14. Zurich: Chronos.

Melvin-Koushki, Matthew. 2018. "*Taḥqīq* vs. *Taqlīd* in the Renaissances of Western Early Modernity." *Philological Encounters* 3 (1–2): 193–249. https://doi.org/10.1163/24519197-12340041.

Ménage, V. L. 1971. "Another Text of Uruč's Ottoman Chronicle." *Islam* 47: 273–77.

Menz, Astrid. 2002. "'Pour apprendre une langue avec méthode, il faut commencer par étudier les termes de la grammaire': eine türkische Grammatik aus dem Jahre 1730." In *Scholarly Depth and Accuracy: a Festschrift to Lars Johanson*, edited by Nurettin Demir, 295–306. Ankara: Grafiker Yayıncılık.

Meral, Arzu. 2013. "A Survey of Translation Activity in the Ottoman Empire." *Osmanlı Araştırmaları / the Journal of Ottoman Studies* 42: 105–55.

Merhan, Aziz. 2005. "Filippo Argenti'nin 'Regola Del Parlare Turcho' Adlı Eserindeki Bazı Sözcükler Hakkında." *Türkiyat araştırmaları dergisi* 18: 115–29.

Merle, Alexandra. 2003. *Le miroir ottoman: une image politique des hommes dans la littérature géographique espagnole et française (XVIᵉ–XVIIᵉ siècles)*. Paris: Presses de l'Université de Paris-Sorbonne.

Mertzios, Konstantinos, ed. 1951. *Extracts from the Correspondence of the Venetian Ministers in Constantinople, Concerning the Patriarchate, 1556–1702* [in Greek]. Athens: Akadēmia Athēnōn.

Meserve, Margaret. 2008. *Empires of Islam in Renaissance Historical Thought*. Cambridge, MA: Harvard University Press. https://doi.org/10.4159/9780674040953.

Messaoudi, Alain. 2015. *Les arabisants et la France coloniale: savants, conseillers, médiateurs (1780–1930)*. Lyon: ENS Éditions. https://doi.org/10.4000/books.enseditions.3705.

Miller, Barnette. 1941. *The Palace School of Muhammad the Conqueror*. Cambridge, MA: Harvard University Press.

Miller, Peter N. 2015. *Peiresc's Mediterranean World.* Cambridge, MA: Harvard University Press. https://doi.org/10.4159/9780674425750.

Mills, Simon. 2019. *A Commerce of Knowledge: Trade, Religion, and Scholarship between England and the Ottoman Empire, 1600–1760.* New York: Oxford University Press. https://doi.org/9780198840336.001.0001.

Milton, John. 2008. "Foreignization: A Discussion of Theoretical and Practical Issues." *Yearbook of Comparative and General Literature* 54 (1): 103–13. http://muse.jhu.edu/article/402971.

Minkov, Anton. 2004. *Conversion to Islam in the Balkans: Kisve Bahasi Petitions and Ottoman Social Life, 1670–1730.* Leiden: Brill. http://hdl.handle.net/2027/heb.32169.

Miović-Perić, Vesna. 1995. "Dnevnik Dubrovačkog Dragomana Miha Zarinija." *Anali Zavoda za povijesne znanosti Hrvatske akademije znanosti i umjetnosti u Dubrovniku* 33: 93–135.

———. 2001. "Dragomans of the Dubrovnik Republic: Their Training and Career." *Dubrovnik Annals* 5: 81–94. https://hrcak.srce.hr/8300.

———. 2013. "Diplomatic Relations between the Ottoman Empire and the Republic of Dubrovnik." In *The European Tributary States of the Ottoman Empire in the Sixteenth and Seventeenth Centuries*, edited by Gábor Kármán and Lovro Kunčević, 187–208. Leiden: Brill. https://doi.org/10.1163/9789004254404_009.

Mishkova, Dianna. 2008. "Symbolic Geographies and Visions of Identity: A Balkan Perspective." *European Journal of Social Theory* 11 (2): 237–56. https://doi.org/10.1177/1368431007087476.

Mitler, Louis. 1979. "The Genoese in Galata: 1453–1682." *International Journal of Middle East Studies* 10 (1): 71–91. https://doi.org/10.1017/s0020743800053332.

Moalla, Asma. 2004. *The Regency of Tunis and the Ottoman Porte, 1777–1814: Army and Government of a North-African Ottoman Eyâlet at the End of the Eighteenth Century.* London: Routledge. https://doi.org/10.4324/9780203987223.

Molino, Paola. 2016. "World Bibliographies: Libraries and the Reorganization of Knowledge in Late Renaissance Europe." In *Canonical Texts and Scholarly Practices: A Global Comparative Approach*, edited by Anthony Grafton and Glenn W. Most, 299–322. Cambridge: Cambridge University Press. https://doi.org/10.1017/cbo9781316226728.015.

———. 2017. *L'impero di carta: storia di una biblioteca e di un bibliotecario (Vienna, 1575–1608).* Rome: Viella.

Mollova, Mefküre. 1997. "Le manuscrit turc d'Illésházy et ses problèmes textologico-linguistiques." *Zeitschrift für Balkanologie* 33: 39–75.

Montana, Ismael Musah. 2008. "The Trans-Saharan Slave Trade of Ottoman Tunisia, 1574 to 1782." *Maghreb Review: Majallat Al-Maghrib* 33 (2–3): 132–50. https://doi.org/10.1080/13629387.2014.983736.

Morton, A. H. 1993. Introduction to *Mission to the Lord Sophy of Persia (1539–1542)*, by Michele Membré, vii–xxviii. London: School of Oriental and African Studies, University of London.

Motsch, Andreas. 2011. "Relations of Travel: Itinerary of a Practice." *Renaissance and Reformation / Renaissance et Réforme* 34 (1/2): 207–36. https://doi.org/10.33137/rr.v34i1-2.16173.

Muir, Edward. 2007. *The Culture Wars of the Late Renaissance: Skeptics, Libertines, and Opera*. Cambridge, MA: Harvard University Press. https://doi.org/10.4159/9780674041264.

Mumcu, Serap. 2014. *Venedik Baylosu'nun Defterleri. The Venetian Baylo's Registers (1589–1684)*. Hilâl: Studi turchi e ottomani, 4. Venice: Edizioni Ca' Foscari. https://doi.org/10.14277/978-88-97735-57-1

Murphey, Rhoads. 2008. *Exploring Ottoman Sovereignty: Tradition, Image and Practice in the Ottoman Imperial Household, 1400–1800*. New York: Continuum. https://doi.org/10.5040/9781474210119.

Muru, Cristina. 2016. "La variazione linguistica nelle pratiche scrittorie dei Dragomanni." In *Dragomanni, Sovrani e Mercanti. Pratiche linguistiche nelle relazioni politiche e commerciali del Mediterraneo moderno*, edited by Margherita Di Salvo and Cristina Muru, 147–201. Pisa: Edizioni ETS.

Musumeci, Diane. 2009. "History of Language Teaching." In *The Handbook of Language Teaching*, edited by Michael H. Long and Catherine J. Doughty, 42–62. Chichester, West Sussex: Wiley-Blackwell. https://doi.org/10.1002/9781444315783.ch4.

Myskja, Kjetil. 2013. "Foreignisation and Resistance: Lawrence Venuti and His Critics." *Nordic Journal of English Studies* 12 (2): 1–23. https://doi.org/10.35360/njes.283.

Necipoğlu, Gülru. 1986. "Plans and Models in 15th-and 16th-Century Ottoman Architectural Practice." *Journal of the Society of Architectural Historians* 45 (3): 224–43. https://doi.org/10.2307/990160.

———. 1989. "Sultan Süleyman and the Representation of Power in a Context of Ottoman-Hapsburg-Papal Rivalry." *Art Bulletin* 71 (3): 401–27. https://doi.org/10.31826/9781463231774-013.

———. 1991. *Architecture, Ceremonial, and Power: The Topkapi Palace in the Fifteenth and Sixteenth Centuries*. Cambridge, MA: MIT Press.

———. 1992. "A Kânûn for the State, a Canon for the Arts: Conceptualizing the Classical Synthesis of Ottoman Art and Architecture." In *Soliman le Magnifique et son temps*, edited by Gilles Veinstein, 195–213. Paris: Documentation française.

———. 2000. "The Serial Portraits of Ottoman Sultans in Comparative Perspective." In *The Sultan's Portrait: Picturing the House of Osman*, edited by Ayse Orbay, 22–61. Istanbul: İşbank.

Neck, Rudolf. 1950. "Andrea Negroni: Ein Beitrag zur Geschichte der österreichisch-türkischen Beziehungen nach dem Frieden von Zsitvatorok." *Mitteilungen des österreichischen Staatsarchivs* 3: 166–95.

Neff, Mary Frances. 1985. "Chancellery Secretaries in Venetian Politics and Society, 1480–1533." PhD diss., University of California, Los Angeles.

Németh, Jenö U. 1970. *Die türkische Sprache in Ungarn im siebzehnten Jahrhundert*. Amsterdam: Grüner.

Neudecker, Hannah. 2005. "From Istanbul to London? Albertus Bobovius' Appeal to Isaac Basire." In *The Republic of Letters and the Levant*, edited by Alastair Hamilton, 173–96. Leiden: Brill. https://openaccess.leidenuniv.nl/handle/1887/16032.

Neumann, Iver B. 1999. *Uses of the Other: "The East" in European Identity Formation*. Minneapolis: University of Minnesota Press.

Newton, Stella Mary. 1988. *The Dress of the Venetians, 1495–1525*. Aldershot: Scolar Press.

Nuovo, Angela. 2013. *The Book Trade in the Italian Renaissance*. Translated by Lydia G. Cochrane. Leiden: Brill. https://doi.org/10.1163/9789004208490.

O'Connell, John Morgan. 2005. "The Edvâr of Demetrius Cantemir: Recent Publications." *Ethnomusicology Forum* 14 (2): 235–39. https://doi.org/10.1080/17411910500415887.

O'Connell, Monique. 2004. "The Venetian Patriciate in the Mediterranean: Legal Identity and Lineage in Fifteenth-Century Venetian Crete." *Renaissance Quarterly* 57 (2): 466–493. https://doi.org/10.2307/1261723.

Ogborn, Miles. 2013. "'It's Not What You Know . . .': Encounters, Go-Betweens, and the Geography of Knowledge." *Modern Intellectual History* 10 (1): 163–75. https://doi.org/10.1017/s147924431200039x.

Omont, Henri. 1890. *Documents sur les jeunes de langues et l'imprimerie orientale à Paris en 1719*. Nogent-le-Rotrou: Imprimerie de Daupeley-Gouverneur. ark:/12148/bpt6k6534667q.

———. 1902. *Missions archéologiques françaises en Orient aux XVIIe et XVIIIe siècles*. Paris: Imprimerie nationale. ark:/12148/bpt6k6348333x.

O'Quinn, Daniel. 2019. *Engaging the Ottoman Empire: Vexed Mediations, 1690–1815*. Philadelphia: University of Pennsylvania Press. https://doi.org/10.9783/9780812295535.

O'Sullivan, Michael. 2014. "A Hungarian Josephinist, Orientalist, and Bibliophile: Count Karl Reviczky, 1737–1793." *Austrian History Yearbook* 45: 61–88. https://doi.org/10.1017/s0067237813000611.

Ouyang, Wen-chin, and G. J. H. van Gelder, eds. 2005. *New Perspectives on Arabian Nights: Ideological Variations and Narrative Horizons*. London: Routledge. https://doi.org/10.4324/9781315874166.

Özervarlı, M. Sait. 2016. "Theology in the Ottoman Lands." In *The Oxford Handbook of Islamic Theology*, edited by Sabine Schmidtke,

567–86. Oxford: Oxford University Press. https://doi.org/10.1093/oxfordhb/9780199696703.013.027.

Paker, Saliha. 2009. "The Turkish Tradition." In *Routledge Encyclopedia of Translation Studies*, edited by Mona Baker and Gabriela Saldanha, 550–59. New York: Routledge. https://doi.org/10.4324/9780203359792.

———. 2011. "Translation, the Pursuit of Inventiveness and Ottoman Poetics: A Systemic Approach." In *Culture Contacts and the Making of Cultures*, edited by Rakefet Sela-Sheffy and Gideon Toury, 459–74. Tel Aviv: Tel Aviv University, Unit of Culture Research.

Paker, Saliha and Zehra Toska. 1997. "A Call for Descriptive Translation Studies on the Turkish Tradition of Rewrites." In *Translation as Intercultural Communication: Selected Papers from the EST Congress, Prague 1995*, edited by Mary Snell-Hornby, Zuzana Jettmarová, and Klaus Kaindl, 79–88. Amsterdam: J. Benjamins. https://doi.org/10.1075/btl.20.09pak.

Palabıyık, Nil. 2018. "The Last Letter from Étienne Hubert to Joseph Scaliger." *Lias* 45 (1): 113–143. https://doi.org/10.2143/LIAS.45.1.3285541.

Palacios, Arturo Bernal. 2002. "Fr. Benedetto Giovanni Palazzo OP (1892–1955) and His Catalogue of the Conventual Archives of Saint Peter in Galata (Istanbul)." *Dominican History Newsletter* 11: 215–50.

———. 2003. "Fr. Benedetto Giovanni Palazzo OP (1892–1955) and His Catalogue of the Conventual Archives of Saint Peter in Galata (Istanbul). II." *Dominican History Newsletter* 12: 157–86.

Paladino, G. 1917. "Due dragomanni veneti a Costantinopoli (Tommaso Tarsia e Gian Rinaldo Carli)." *Nuovo Archivio Veneto* 17 (33): 183–200.

Pamuk, Orhan. 2001. *My Name Is Red*. Translated by Erdağ Göknar. New York: Alfred A. Knopf.

Panaite, Viorel. 2014. "French Capitulations and Consular Jurisdiction in Egypt and Aleppo in the Late Sixteenth and Early Seventeenth Centuries." In *Well-Connected Domains: Towards an Entangled Ottoman History*, edited by Pascal Firges et al., 71–87. Leiden: Brill. https://doi.org/10.1163/9789004274686_006.

Papadia-Lala, Anastasia. 2009. "L'interprete nel mondo grecoveneziano (XIV–XVIII sec.). Lingua, comunicazione, politica." In *I Greci durante la venetocrazia: uomini, spazio, idee (XIII–XVIII sec.)*, edited by Chrysa A Maltezou, Angeliki Tzavara, and Despina Vlassi, 121–30. Venice: Istituto ellenico di studi bizantini e postbizantini di Venezia.

Parladır, Şebnem. 2007. "Sigetvar Seferi Tarihi ve Nakkaş Osman." *Sanat Tarihi Dergisi* 16 (1): 67–108. https://dergipark.org.tr/en/download/article-file/152365.

Păun, Radu G. 2008. "Réseaux de livres et réseaux de pouvoirs dans le sud-est de l'Europe: le monde des drogmans (XVIIᵉ–XVIIIᵉ siècles)." In *L'Europe en réseaux: Contribution à l'histoire intellectuelle de l'Europe: réseaux du livre, réseaux des lecteurs*, edited by Frédéric Barbier and István Monok, 63–107. Leipzig: Leipziger Universitätsverlag.

Payne, Alina Alexandra, ed. 2014. *Dalmatia and the Mediterranean: Portable Archeology and the Poetics of Influence*. Leiden: Brill.

Pedani, Maria Pia. 1994. *In nome del Gran Signore: Inviati ottomani a Venezia dalla caduta di Costantinopoli alla guerra di Candia*. Venice: Deputazione editrice.

———, ed. 1994. *I documenti turchi dell'Archivio di Stato di Venezia*. Rome: Ministero per i beni culturali e ambientali. http://www.archivi.beniculturali.it/dga/uploads/documents/Strumenti/5156eeece7a3c.pdf.

———, ed. 1996. *Relazioni di Ambasciatori Veneti al Senato*. Vol. XIV: Costantinopoli relazioni inedite (1512–1789). Padua: Ausilio.

———. 2000. "The Ottoman Venetian Frontier (15th–18th Centuries)." In *The Great Ottoman Turkish Civilization*, edited by Kemal Çiçek, 1:171–77. Ankara: Yeni Türkiye.

———. 2002. *Dalla frontiera al confine*. Venice: Herder Editrice.

———, ed. 2013. *Il Palazzo di Venezia a Istanbul e i suoi antichi abitanti*. Hilâl: Studi turchi e ottomani 3. Venice: Edizioni Ca' Foscari. https://doi.org/10.14277/978-88-97735-62-5.

———. 2020. "The Interpreter Michele Membrè's Life in Venice." In *Cultures of Empire: Rethinking Venetian Rule 1400–1700*, edited by Georg Christ and Franz-Julius Morche, 383–413. Leiden: Brill.

Pedani, Maria Pia and Alessio Bombaci, eds. 2010. *Inventory of the "Lettere e Scritture Turchesche" in the Venetian State Archives: Based on the Materials Compiled by Alessio Bombaci*. Leiden: Brill. https://doi.org/10.1163/ej.9789004179189.i-232.

Peirce, Leslie P. 1993. *The Imperial Harem: Women and Sovereignty in the Ottoman Empire*. New York: Oxford University Press.

———. 2010. "Polyglottism in the Ottoman Empire: A Reconsideration." In *Braudel Revisited: The Mediterranean World, 1600–1800*, edited by Gabriel Piterberg, Teofilo F. Ruiz, and Geoffrey Symcox, 76–98. Toronto: University of Toronto Press. https://doi.org/10.3138/9781442686854-006.

Perocco, Daria. 2010. "Tra Cinquecento e Seicento: incomprensione, ambiguità, reticenza davanti al sovrano straniero." In *Il potere della parola—La parola del potere*, edited by Antonella Ghersetti, 59–74. Venice: Filippi.

Petitjean, Johann. 2013. *L'intelligence des choses: une histoire de l'information entre Italie et Méditerranée (XVIᵉ–XVIIᵉ siècles)*. Rome: École Française de Rome. http://digital.casalini.it/9782728309641.

Petritsch, Ernst Dieter. 2005. "Erziehung in guten Sitten, Andacht und Gehorsam. Die 1754 gegründete Orientalische Akademie in Wien." In *Das osmanische Reich und die Habsburgermonarchie*, edited by Marlene Kurz,

491–501. Vienna: Oldenbourg Wissenschaftsverlag. https://doi.org/10.7767/boehlau.9783205160281.491.

Petrovich, Maya Xenia. 2013. "Between 'Serbian' and 'Chaghatay': The Janus-Faced Multilinguality of Ottoman Turks." Paper presented at the Conference Inter-Asian Connections IV: Istanbul—The Sounds and Scripts of Languages in Motion. Istanbul.

Pfeifer, Helen. 2015. "Encounter after the Conquest: Scholarly Gatherings in 16th-Century Ottoman Damascus." *International Journal of Middle East Studies* 47 (2): 219–39. https://doi.org/10.1017/s0020743815000021.

Philliou, Christine. 2001. "Mischief in the Old Regime: Provincial Dragomans and Social Change at the Turn of the Nineteenth Century." *New Perspectives on Turkey* 25: 103–21. https://doi.org/10.1017/s0896634600003629.

———. 2009. "Communities on the Verge: Unraveling the Phanariot Ascendancy in Ottoman Governance." *Comparative Studies in Society and History* 51 (1): 151–81. https://doi.org/10.1017/s0010417509000073.

———. 2011. *Biography of an Empire: Governing Ottomans in an Age of Revolution*. Berkeley: University of California Press. http://www.jstor.org/stable/10.1525/j.ctt1ppqj8.

Piemontese, A. M. 2011. "Angiolello, Giovanni Maria." In *Encyclopaedia Iranica*, 2.1: 31–32. http://www.iranicaonline.org/articles/angiolello-giovanni-maria-1451-ca-1525.

Pierse, Siofra. 2003. "A Sceptic Witness: Voltaire's Vision of Historiography." In *Cultural Memory: Essays on European Literature and History*, edited by C. E. J. Caldicott and Anne Fuchs, 69–84. Oxford: P. Lang.

Pinto, Karen. 2011. "The Maps Are the Message: Mehmet II's Patronage of an 'Ottoman Cluster.'" *Imago Mundi* 63 (2): 155–79. https://doi.org/10.1080/03085694.2011.568703.

Pippidi, Andrei. 1980. "Quelques drogmans de Constantinople au XVIIe siècle." In *Hommes et idées du Sud-Est européen à l'aube de l'âge moderne*, 133–59. Bucharest: Editura Academiei Republicii Socialiste România.

Pirrotta, Nino. 1980. "The Traditions of Don Juan Plays and Comic Operas." *Proceedings of the Royal Musical Association* 107 (1): 60–70. https://doi.org/10.1093/jrma/107.1.60.

Pistarino, Geo. 1990. "La caduta di Costantinopoli: da Pera genovese a Galata turca." In *Genovesi d'Oriente*, 281–382. Genoa: Civico Istituto Colombiano.

Piterberg, Gabriel. 2003. *An Ottoman Tragedy: History and Historiography at Play*. Berkeley: University of California Press.

Pollock, Sheldon I. 2000. "Cosmopolitan and Vernacular in History." *Public Culture* 12 (3): 591–625. https://doi.org/10.1215/08992363-12-3-591.

Pollock, Sheldon I., Benjamin A. Elman, and Ku-ming Kevin Chang, eds. 2015. *World Philology*. Cambridge, MA: Harvard University Press. https://doi.org/10.4159/harvard.9780674736122.

Popkin, Richard H. 1994. "Three English Tellings of the Sabbatai Zevi Story." *Jewish History* 8 (1/2): 43–54. https://doi.org/10.1007/bf01915907.Poumarède, Géraud. 2020. *L'Empire de Venise et les Turcs: XVIᵉ-XVIIᵉ siècle*. Paris: Classiques Garnier.

Pratt, Mary Louise. 1992. *Imperial Eyes: Travel Writing and Transculturation*. New York: Routledge. https://doi.org/10.4324/9780203106358.

Preto, Paolo. 1982. "Cicogna, Emmanuele Antonio." In *Dizionario Biografico degli Italiani*, 25: 394–97. Rome: Istituto dell'Enciclopedia Italiana. http://www.treccani.it/enciclopedia/emmanuele-antonio-cicogna_%28Dizionario-Biografico%29/.

———. 2013. *Venezia e i Turchi*. Rome: Viella.

Pugliano, Valentina. 2019. "Accountability, Autobiography and Belonging: The Working Journal of a Sixteenth-Century Diplomatic Physician between Venice and Damascus." In *Civic Medicine: Physician, Polity and Pen in Early Modern Europe*, edited by J. Andrew Mendelsohn, Annemarie Kinzelbach, and Ruth Schilling, 183–209. London: Routledge. https://doi.org/10.4324/9781315554693-8.

Pullan, Brian S. 1999. "'Three Orders of Inhabitants': Social Hierarchies in the Republic of Venice." In *Orders and Hierarchies in Late Medieval and Renaissance Europe*, edited by Jeffrey Howard Denton, 147–68. Toronto: University of Toronto Press. https://doi.org/10.1007/978-1-349-27580-9_10.

Pym, Anthony. 1998. *Method in Translation History*. Manchester: St. Jerome. https://doi.org/10.4324/9781315760049.

———. 2000. *Negotiating the Frontier: Translators and Intercultures in Hispanic History*. Manchester: St. Jerome. https://doi.org/10.4324/9781315760025.

———. 2018. "A Typology of Translation Solutions." *Journal of Specialised Translation* 30: 41–65. https://jostrans.org/issue30/art_pym.pdf.

Pym, Anthony and Esther Torres-Simón. 2014. "The Pedagogical Value of Translation Solution Types." *Perspectives*, July, 1–18. https://doi.org/10.1080/0907676x.2014.928334.

Raby, Julian. 1983. "Mehmed the Conqueror's Greek Scriptorium." *Dumbarton Oaks Papers* 37: 15–34. https://doi.org/10.2307/1291474.

Radossi, Giovanni. 2003. *Monumenta heraldica iustinopolitana: Stemmi di rettori, di famiglie notabili, di vescovi e della città di Capodistria*. Trieste: Unione italiana.

Radway, Robyn Dora. 2011. "Representing the Christians of Ottoman Europe: Self, Other, and the In-between in Sixteenth-Century Costume Books." *On the Art of Renaissance and Ottoman Hungary . . .* (blog). June 4, 2011. http://ottomanhungary.blogspot.com/2011_06_01_archive.html.

Raines, Dorit. 2006. *L'invention du mythe aristocratique: L'image de soi du patriciat vénitien au temps de la Sérénissime*. Venice: Istituto Veneto di Scienze, Lettere ed Arti.

———. 2011. "The Private Political Archives of the Venetian Patriciate—Storing, Retrieving and Recordkeeping in the Fifteenth-Eighteenth Centuries." *Journal of the Society of Archivists* 32 (1): 135–46. https://doi.org/10.1080/00379816.2011.564896.

Raj, Kapil. 2007. *Relocating Modern Science: Circulation and the Construction of Knowledge in South Asia and Europe, 1650–1900.* New York: Palgrave Macmillan. https://doi.org/10.1057/9780230625310.

———. 2016. "Go-Betweens, Travelers, and Cultural Translators." In *The Blackwell Companion to the History of Science*, edited by Bernard Lightman, 39–57. Malden, MA: Wiley-Blackwell. https://doi.org/10.1002/9781118620762.ch3.

———. 2019. "William Jones (1746–1794): Relating of the Original Inhabitants of India to the Other Families of Humanity." *History of Humanities* 4 (2): 243–46. https://doi.org/10.1086/704809.

Rajan, Chandra, ed. 2006. *The Pañcatantra*. London: Penguin.

Rakova, Snezhana. 2016. "Between the Sultan and the Doge: Diplomats and Spies in the Time of Suleiman the Magnificent." *CAS Sofia Working Paper Series*, no. 8: 1–35.

Ramachandran, Ayesha. 2015. *The Worldmakers: Global Imagining in Early Modern Europe.* Chicago: University of Chicago Press. https://doi.org/10.7208/chicago/9780226288826.001.0001.

Rathkolb, Oliver, ed. 2004. *250 Jahre: von der Orientalischen zur Diplomatischen Akademie in Wien.* Innsbruck: Studien.

Reindl-Kiel, Hedda. 2009. "Power and Submission: Gifting at Royal Circumcision Festivals (16th–18th Centuries)." *Turcica* 41: 37–88. https://doi.org/10.2143/turc.41.0.2049288.

Reiter, Clara. 2013. "'. . . wo der Dollmetsch allzeit interpretirt.' Das Hofdolmetscheramt am Wiener Hof: Vom Karrieresprungbrett zum Abstellgleis." *Lebende Sprachen* 58 (1): 197–220. https://doi.org/10.1515/les-2013-0009.

Relaño, Francesc. 2002. *The Shaping of Africa: Cosmographic Discourse and Cartographic Science in Late Medieval and Early Modern Europe.* Aldershot: Ashgate. https://doi.org/10.4324/9781315194554.

Renda, Günsel. 1976. "New Light on the Painters of the 'Zubdet Al-Tawarikh' in the Museum of Turkish and Islamic Arts in Istanbul." In *IVème Congrès International d'art Turc*, 183–200. Aix-en-Provence: Université de Provence.

———. 1998. "17 Yüzyıldan Bir Grup Kıyafet Albümü." In *17. Yüzyıl Osmanlı Kültür ve Sanat 19–20 Mart 1998: Sempozyum Bildirileri*, 153–78. Istanbul: Sanat Tarihi Derneği.

Rentzsch, Julian. 2009. "Deny, Jean." In *Lexicon Grammaticorum: A Bio-Bibliographical Companion to the History of Linguistics*, edited by Harro Stammerjohann, 370. Tübingen: Niemeyer.

Reychman, Jan, and Ananiasz Zajączkowski. 1968. *Handbook of Ottoman-Turkish Diplomatics*. The Hague: Mouton. https://doi.org/10.1515/9783110812695.

Rhodes, Dennis E. 1987. "Some Notes on Vincenzo Coronelli and His Publishers." *Imago Mundi* 39: 77–79. https://doi.org/10.1080/03085698708592618.

Ricci, Ronit. 2011. *Islam Translated: Literature, Conversion, and the Arabic Cosmopolis of South and Southeast Asia*. Chicago: University Of Chicago Press. https://doi.org/10.7208/chicago/9780226710907.001.0001.

Richard, Francis. 1986. "Aux origines de la connaissance de la langue persane en France." *Luqman. Annales des Presses Universitaires d'Iran* 3 (1): 23–42.

———. 1989. *Catalogue des manuscrits persans, Bibliothèque nationale de France, Département des Manuscrits. T. 1: Ancien fonds*. Paris: Bibliothèque nationale.

———. 2008. "Antoine Galland et sa quête inassable de manuscrits orientaux: de 'Alî Ufkî Bey à la liste de 1685." In *Actes du Colloque Antoine Galland et Ali Ufkî Bey interprètes de la civilisation ottomane* (Izmir, 2008).

Riedel, Dagmar. 2010. "KALILA WA DEMNA i. Redactions and Circulation." In *Encyclopaedia Iranica*, XV (4): 386–95. http://www.iranicaonline.org/articles/kalila-demna-i.

Riedlmayer, András J. 2008. "Ottoman Copybooks of Correspondence and Miscellanies as a Source for Political and Cultural History." *Acta Orientalia Academiae Scientiarum Hungaricae* 61 (1/2): 201–14. https://doi.org/10.1556/aorient.61.2008.1-2.17.

Riello, Giorgio, Anne Gerritsen, and Zoltán Biedermann, eds. 2018. *Global Gifts: The Material Culture of Diplomacy in Early Modern Eurasia*. New York: Cambridge University Press. https://doi.org/10.1017/9781108233880.

Rietbergen, Peter. 2006. "Ibrahim Al-Hakilani (1605–1664), or: The Power of Scholarship and Publishing." In *Power and Religion in Baroque Rome: Barberini Cultural Policies*, 296–335. Leiden: Brill. https://doi.org/10.1163/9789047417958_010.

Rieu, Charles. 1888. *Catalogue of the Turkish Manuscripts in the British Museum*. London: Gilbert and Rivington.

Rizzi, Aldo. 1969. "BOMBELLI, Sebastiano." In *Dizionario Biografico degli Italiani* 11. http://www.treccani.it//enciclopedia/sebastiano-bombelli_(Dizionario-Biografico).

Roberts, Mary. 2015. *Istanbul Exchanges: Ottomans, Orientalists, and Nineteenth-Century Visual Culture*. Berkeley: University of California Press. https://doi.org/10.3202/caa.reviews.2016.78.

Roberts, Sean. 2013. *Printing a Mediterranean World: Florence, Constantinople, and the Renaissance of Geography*. Cambridge, MA: Harvard University Press. https://doi.org/10.4159/harvard.9780674068070.

Rocchi, Luciano. 2005. "Appunti lessicali intorno al testo italiano della Regola del parlare turcho di Filippo Argenti." *Rivista italiana di linguistica e di dialettologia* 7: 39–46. https://doi.org/10.1400/90033.

———. 2007. *Ricerche sulla lingua osmanlı del XVI secolo: il corpus lessicale turco del manoscritto fiorentino di Filippo Argenti (1533).* Wiesbaden: Harrassowitz.

———. 2011. *Il dizionario turco-ottomano di Arcangelo Carradori (1650).* Trieste: Edizioni Università di Trieste.http://hdl.handle.net/10077/14761.

———. 2013. "Gli italianismi nei testi turchi in trascrizione." *Zeitschrift für Romanische Philologie* 129 (4): 888–931. https://doi.org/10.1515/zrp-2013-0088.

———. 2014. *I repertori lessicali turco-ottomani di Giovan Battista Montalbano (1630 ca.).* Trieste: Edizioni Università di Trieste.

———. 2015. "Bernardo da Parigi's Vocabolario Italiano-Turchesco (1665): An Ottoman-Turkish lexicographical monument still neglected." *Studia Linguistica Universitatis Iagellonicae Cracoviensis* 132 (4): 263–69. https://doi.org/10.4467/20834624sl.15.023.4430.

———. 2016. "Addenda from pre-Meninski transcription texts to Stanisław Stachowski's 'Osmanlı türkçesinde yeni farsça alıntılar sözlüğü'. Part IV." *Studia Linguistica Universitatis Iagellonicae Cracoviensis* 133 (4): 275–89. https://doi.org/10.4467/20834624SL.16.020.5689.

Rodríguez Mediano, Fernando. 2006. "Fragmentos de orientalism español del s xviii." *Hispania* 66 (222): 234–76. https://doi.org/10.3989/hispania.2006.v66.i222.8.

Rogers, J. M. 1987. "Itineraries and Town Views in Ottoman Histories." In *The History of Cartography*, edited by J. B Harley, 2.1: 228–55. Chicago: University of Chicago Press. https://press.uchicago.edu/books/HOC/HOC_V2_B1/HOC_VOLUME2_Book1_chapter12.pdf.

Rohan, Padraic. 2015. "The Genoese Levantine Colonies at the Birth of Ottoman Imperial Power: A Framework for Inquiry." Master's thesis, Istanbul Şehir University. https://core.ac.uk/download/pdf/38328689.pdf.

Romanelli, Giandomenico. 1994. *Il Museo Correr.* Milan: Electa.

Romano, Dennis. 1996. *Housecraft and Statecraft: Domestic Service in Renaissance Venice.* Baltimore: Johns Hopkins University Press.

Römer, Claudia. 1998. "An Ottoman Copyist Working for Sebastian Tengnagel, Librarian at the Vienna Hofbibliothek, 1608–1636." In *Essays on Ottoman Civilization: Proceedings of the XIIth Congress of the Comité International des Études Pré-Ottomanes et Ottomanes*, 331–50. Prague: Academy of Sciences of the Czech Republic, Oriental Institute.

———. 2002. "Die Übungsbücher der Zöglinge der K.K. Akademie orientalischer Sprachen." In *Auf den Spuren der Osmanen in der österreichischen Geschichte*, edited by Inanc Feigl, 155–60. Frankfurt: P. Lang.

———. 2008. "Contemporary European Translations of Ottoman Documents and Vice Versa (15th–17th Centuries)." *Acta Orientalia* 61 (1): 215–26. https://doi.org/10.1556/aorient.61.2008.1-2.18.

———. 2016. "Early Transcription Methods at the K. K. Akademie Orientalischer Sprachen in Vienna According to Students' Exercise Books." En Route to a Shared Identity (blog). September 20, 2016. https://dighist.hypotheses.org/1171.

——. 2018. *Meninski's Grammar Simplified: Thomas von Chabert's Manual Kurze Anleitung zur Erlernung der türkischen Sprache für Militär Personen, Vienna 1789.* Berlin: EB.

Roper, Geoffrey. 2005. "Turkish Printing and Publishing in England in the 17th Century." In *2nd International Symposium History of Printing and Publishing in the Languages and Countries of the Middle East*, edited by Philip Sadgrove, 77–87. Paris: Bibliothèque nationale de France.

——. 2009. "The Vienna Arabic Psalter of 1792 and the rôle of typography in European-Arab relations in the 18th century and earlier." In *Kommunikation und Information im 18. Jahrhundert: das Beispiel der Habsburgermonarchie*, edited by Johannes Frimmel and Michael Wögerbauer, 77–89. Wiesbaden: Harrassowitz.

——. 2014. "Music, Drama and Orientalism in Print: Joseph von Kurzböck (1736–1792), His Predecessors and Contemporaries." In *Ottoman Empire and European Theatre*. Vol. 2, *The Time of Joseph Haydn: From Sultan Mahmud I to Mahmud II (r.1730–1839)*, edited by Michael Hüttler and Hans Ernst Weidinger, 209–230. Vienna: Hollitzer. https://doi.org/10.2307/j.ctv6jmbqf.12.

Ross, James Bruce. 1976. "Venetian Schools and Teachers, Fourteenth to Early Sixteenth Century: A Survey and a Study of Giovanni Battista Egnazio." *Renaissance Quarterly* 29 (4): 521–66. https://doi.org/10.2307/2860032.

Rossebastiano, Alda. 2000. "La tradition des manuels polyglottes dans l'enseignement des langues." In *History of the language sciences*, edited by Sylvain Auroux, E. F. K. Koerner, Hans-Josef Niederehe, and Kees Versteegh, 688–98. Berlin: de Gruyter. https://doi.org/10.1515/9783110111033.1.17.688.

Rossi, Ettore. 1938. "Importanza dell'inedita Grammatica turca di Pietro Della Valle." In *Atti del XIX Congresso Internazionale degli Orientalisti (Rome, 23–29 settembre 1935)*, 202–9. Rome: Tipografia G. Bardi.

Rota, Giorgio. 2009a. "Safavid Envoys in Venice." In *Diplomatisches Zeremoniell in Europa und im Mittleren Osten in der frühen Neuzeit*, edited by Ralph Kauz, Giorgio Rota, and Jan Paul Niederkorn, 213–51. Vienna: Verlag der Oesterreichischen Akademie der Wissenschaften.

——. 2009b. *Under Two Lions: On the Knowledge of Persia in the Republic of Venice (ca. 1450-1797)*. Vienna: Verlag der Österreichischen Akademie der Wissenschaften.

Rothman, E. Natalie. 2010. "Genealogies of Mediation: 'Culture Broker' and Imperial Governmentality." In *Anthrohistory: Unsettling Knowledge and the Question of Discipline*, edited by Edward Murphy et al., 67–79. Ann Arbor: University of Michigan Press.

——. 2011a. *Brokering Empire: Trans-Imperial Subjects between Venice and Istanbul*. Ithaca, NY: Cornell University Press. https://doi.org/10.7591/9780801463112.

———. 2011b. "Conversion and Convergence in the Venetian-Ottoman Border-lands." *Journal of Medieval and Early Modern Studies* 41 (3): 601–33. https://doi.org/10.1215/10829636-1363963.

———. 2012a. "Visualizing a Space of Encounter: Intimacy, Alterity, and Trans-Imperial Perspective in an Ottoman-Venetian Miniature Album." *Osmanlı Araştırmaları / Journal of Ottoman Studies* 40: 39–80. https://dergipark.org.tr/en/pub/oa/issue/10938/130726.

———. 2012b. "Contested Subjecthood: Runaway Slaves in Early Modern Venice." *Quaderni Storici* 140 (2): 425–41. https://doi.org/10.1408/37888.

———. 2015. "Afterword: Intermediaries, Mediation, and Cross-Confessional Diplomacy in the Early Modern Mediterranean." *Journal of Early Modern History* 19 (2–3): 245–59. https://doi.org/10.1163/15700658-12342459.

Rózsa, György. 2006. "Elias Widemans druckgraphisches Porträtsammelwerk und der Westfälische Frieden." *Acta Historiae Artium* 47 (1–4): 103–17. https://doi.org/10.1556/ahista.47.2006.1-4.7.

Rubiés, Joan Pau. 2007. *Travellers and Cosmographers: Studies in the History of Early Modern Travel and Ethnology.* Aldershot, Burlington, VT: Ashgate.

———. 2017. "Ethnography and Cultural Translation in the Early Modern Missions." *Studies in Church History* 53 (June): 272–310. https://doi.org/10.1017/stc.2016.17.

Rudolph, Harriet. 2013. "The Ottoman Empire and the Institutionalization of European Diplomacy, 1500–1700." In *Islam and International Law*, edited by Andreas Th. Müller and Marie-Luisa Frick, 161–83. Leiden: Brill. https://doi.org/10.1163/9789004233362_010.

Rudt de Collenberg, Wipertus H. 1983. "Recherches sur quelques familles chypriotes apparentées au pape Clément VIII Aldobrandini (1592–1605): Flatro, Davila, Sozomenoi, Lusignan, Bustron et Nores." *Epeteris* 12: 5–68.

Ruiu, Adina. 2014. "Conflicting Visions of the Jesuit Missions to the Ottoman Empire, 1609–1628." *Journal of Jesuit Studies* 1 (2): 260–80. https://doi.org/10.1163/22141332-00102007.

———. 2018. "Missionaries and French Subjects: The Jesuits in the Ottoman Empire." In *A Companion to the Early Modern Catholic Global Missions*, 181–204. Leiden: Brill. https://doi.org/10.1163/9789004355286_009.

Russell, G. 1994. *The "Arabick" Interest of the Natural Philosophers in Seventeenth-Century England.* Leiden: Brill. https://doi.org/10.1163/9789004247062.

Ruymbeke, Christine van. 2016. *Kāshefi's Anvār-e Sohayli: Rewriting Kalila and Dimna in Timurid Herat.* Leiden: Brill. https://doi.org/10.1163/9789004314757.

Sabev, Orlin. 2018. *Waiting for Müteferrika: Glimpses on Ottoman Print Culture.* Boston: Academic Studies Press.

Sacerdoti, Alberto. 1937. Introduzione to *"Africa overo Barbarìa" Relazione al Doge di Venezia sulle reggenze di Algeri e di Tunisi*, by Giovanni Battista Salvago, i–xiv. Padua: Cedam.

Şahin, Kaya. 2013. *Empire and Power in the Reign of Süleyman: Narrating the Sixteenth-Century Ottoman World*. New York: Cambridge University Press. https://doi.org/10.1017/cbo9781139540643.

——. 2018. "Staging an Empire: An Ottoman Circumcision Ceremony as Cultural Performance." *American Historical Review* 123 (2): 463–92. https://doi.org/10.1093/ahr/123.2.463.

Said, Edward W. 1978. *Orientalism*. New York: Pantheon Books.

Sajdi, Dana. 2009. "Print and Its Discontents: A Case for Pre-Print Journalism and Other Sundry Print Matters." *The Translator* 15 (1): 105–38. https://doi.org/10.1080/13556509.2009.10799273.

Sakai, Naoki. 2006. "Translation." *Theory, Culture & Society* 23 (2–3): 71–78. https://doi.org/10.1177/0263276406063778.

Salzmann, Ariel. 2000. "The Age of Tulips: Confluence and Conflict in Early Modern Consumer Culture (1550–1730)." In *Consumption Studies and the History of the Ottoman Empire, 1550–1922: An Introduction*, edited by Donald Quataert, 83–106. Albany: State University of New York Press.

Sangalli, Maurizio. 2016. "La Piazza universale di tutte le religioni del mondo: Venezia e lo Stato da Mar tra Chiesa di Roma e chiese d'Oriente." In *Identidades cuestionadas: Coexistencia y conflictos interreligiosos en el Mediterráneo (ss. XIV–XVIII)*, edited by Borja Franco et al. Valencia: Universitat de València.

Santangelo, Antonino, ed. 1935. *Provincia di Pola*. Inventario degli oggetti d'arte d'Italia 5. Rome: Libreria dello Stato.

Sawyer, David B. 2016. "The U.S. Department of State's Corps of Student Interpreters: A Precursor to the Diplomatic Interpreting of Today?" In *New Insights in the History of Interpreting*, edited by Kayoko Takeda and Jesús Baigorri-Jalón, 99–134. Amsterdam: J. Benjamins. https://doi.org/10.1075/btl.122.05saw.

Scarcia, Gianroberto. 1969. "Presentazione." In *Relazione di Persia (1542)*, by Michele Membré, XI–LXX. Naples: Istituto universitario orientale.

Scarpa, Francesca. 1998. "Da Venezia a Costantinopoli, da Costantinopoli a Venezia: Giovanni Battista Donà." Master's thesis, Università degli studi di Venezia Ca' Foscari.

——. 2000. "Per la storia degli studi turchi e armeni a Venezia: il sacerdote armeno Giovanni Agop." *Annali di Ca' Foscari* 39 (3): 107–30. http://hdl.handle.net/11707/1847.

Schellenberg, Betty A. 2016. *Literary Coteries and the Making of Modern Print Culture: 1740–1790*. Cambridge: Cambridge University Press. https://doi.org/10.26530/oapen_611255.

Schmidt, Benjamin. 2015. *Inventing Exoticism: Geography, Globalism, and Europe's Early Modern World*. Philadelphia: University of Pennsylvania Press. https://doi.org/10.9783/9780812290349.

Schmidt, Jan. 1999. "French-Ottoman Relations in the Early Modern Period and the John Rylands Library MSS Turkish 45 & 46." *Turcica* 31: 375–436. https://doi.org/10.2143/turc.31.0.2004195.

———. 2000. "Franz von Dombay, Austrian Dragoman at the Bosnian Border 1792–1800." *Wiener Zeitschrift für die Kunde des Morgenlandes* 90: 75–168. http://www.jstor.org/stable/23864387.

———. 2002a. "An Ostrich Egg for Golius. The Heyman Papers Preserved in the Leiden and Manchester University Libraries and Early-Modern Contacts between the Netherlands and the Middle East." In *The Joys of Philology: Studies in Ottoman Literature, History and Orientalism, 1500–1923*, 2: 9–74. Istanbul: Isis.

———. 2010. "Franz Taeschner's Collection of Turkish Manuscripts in the Leiden University Library." In *The Joys of Philology: Studies in Ottoman Literature, History and Orientalism, 1500–1923*, 2: 237–66. Istanbul: Gorgias Press. https://doi.org/10.31826/9781463225636.

———, ed. 2012. *Catalogue of Turkish Manuscripts in the Library of Leiden University and Other Collections in the Netherlands: Minor Collections*. Leiden: Brill. https://doi.org/10.26530/oapen_421590.

Schnapp, Alain, ed. 2013. *World Antiquarianism: Comparative Perspectives*. Los Angeles: Getty Research Institute.

Schülting, Sabine, Ralf Hertel, and Sabine Lucia Müller, eds. 2012. *Early Modern Encounters with the Islamic East: Performing Cultures*. Transculturalisms, 1400–1700. Burlington, VT: Ashgate. https://doi.org/10.4324/9781315578422.

Schwartz, Kathryn A. 2017. "Book History, Print, and the Middle East." *History Compass* 15 (12): e12434. https://doi.org/10.1111/hic3.12434.

Schweickard, Wolfgang. 2014. "Türkische Wortgeschichte im Spiegel europäischer Quellen." *Zeitschrift für romanische Philologie* 130 (3): 815–32. https://doi.org/10.1515/zrp-2014-0063.

Sebag, Paul. 1978. "Sur deux orientalistes français du XVIIᵉ siècle F Pétis de la Croix et le Sieur de la Croix." *Revue de l'Occident Musulman et de la Méditerranée* 25: 89–118. https://doi.org/10.3406/remmm.1978.1805.

Şeni, Nora. 1997. "Dynasties de drogmans et levantinisme à Istanbul." In *Istanbul et les langues orientales*, edited by Frédéric Hitzel, 161–74. Istanbul: Isis.

Severi, Carlo, and William F. Hanks, eds. 2015. *Translating Worlds: The Epistemological Space of Translation*. Special Issues in Ethnographic Theory 1. Chicago: HAU Books. https://doi.org/10.14318/hau4.2.001.

Shafir, Nir. 2017. "Ports and Printers Across the Armenian Diaspora | Sebouh Aslanian." Ottoman History podcast 325. July 18, 2017. https://soundcloud.com/ottoman-history-podcast/sebouh-aslanian.

Shalev, Zur. 2012. *Sacred Words and Worlds: Geography, Religion, and Scholarship, 1550–1700.* Leiden: Brill. https://doi.org/10.1163/9789004209381.

Shehada, Housni Alkhateeb. 2020. "From the Far North to the Near East: Venice as an Intermediary in the Supply of Gyrfalcons to the Mamluks." In *Cultures of Empire: Rethinking Venetian Rule 1400–1700*, edited by Georg Christ and Franz-Julius Morche, 369–82. Leiden: Brill. https://doi.org/10.1163/9789004428874_015.

Sheikh, Mustapha. 2016. *Ottoman Puritanism and Its Discontents.* New York: Oxford University Press. https://doi.org/10.1093/acprof:oso/9780198790761.001.0001.

Shiloah, Amnon. 1991. "An Eighteenth-Century Critic of Taste and Good Taste." In *Ethnomusicology and Modern Music History*, edited by Stephen Blum, 181–89. Urbana: University of Illinois Press.

Shryock, Andrew and Daniel Lord Smail. 2011. *Deep History: The Architecture of Past and Present.* Berkeley: University of California Press.

Shryock, Andrew, Thomas R. Trautmann, and Clive Gamble. 2011. "Imagining the Human in Deep Time." In *Deep History: The Architecture of Past and Present*, edited by Andrew Shryock and Daniel Lord Smail, 21–54. Berkeley: University of California Press.

Shuval, Tal. 2000a. "Cezayir-i Garp: Bringing Algeria Back into Ottoman History." *New Perspectives on Turkey* 22: 85–116. https://doi.org/10.1017/s0896634600003289.

———. 2000b. "The Ottoman Algerian Elite and Its Ideology." *International Journal of Middle East Studies* 32 (3): 323–44. https://doi.org/10.1017/s0020743800021127.

Silverstein, Michael, and Greg Urban. 1996. *Natural Histories of Discourse.* Chicago: University of Chicago Press.

Sint Nicolaas, Eveline, ed. 2003. *Jean-Baptiste Vanmour: An Eyewitness of the Tulip Era.* Istanbul: Koçbank.

Sobers-Khan, Nur. 2014. *Building Our Collection: Mughal and Safavid Albums (Museum of Islamic Art, Doha).* Doha: Museum of Islamic Art.

Sood, Gagan D. S. 2011. "Circulation and Exchange in Islamicate Eurasia: A Regional Approach to the Early Modern World." *Past & Present* 212 (1): 113–62. https://doi.org/10.1093/pastj/gtr001.

Speer, Andreas, and Lydia Wegener, eds. 2006. *Wissen über Grenzen: Arabisches Wissen und lateinisches Mittelalter.* Berlin: De Gruyter. https://doi.org/10.1515/9783110194319.

Sperling, Jutta. 1999. "The Paradox of Perfection: Reproducing the Body Politic in Late Renaissance Venice." *Comparative Studies in Society and History* 41 (1): 3–32. https://doi.org/10.1017/s0010417599001851.

Sprung, Rainer, and Peter G. Mayr. 1989. "Franz Kleins Lehrtätigkeit an der k. und k. Orientalischen Akademie." *Mitteilungen des Instituts für Österreichische Geschichtsforschung* 97 (1–2): 83–103. https://doi.org/10.7767/miog.1989.97.jg.83.

Stachowski, Marek. 2012. "Remarks on the Phonetic Value of the Letters <Y> and <Ü> in Franciscus Meninski's Ottoman Turkish *Thesaurus* (1680)." *Studia Linguistica Universitatis Iagellonicae Cracoviensis* 129 (3): 189–97. http://info.filg.uj.edu.pl/zhjij/~stachowski.marek/store/pub/2012_Y_and_u_in_Meninskiss_Thesaurus.pdf.

———. 2013. "Marcin Paszkowski's Polish and Turkish dictionary (1615)." *Studies in Polish Linguistics* 8 (1): 45–56. https://doi.org/10.4467/23005920 SPL.13.003.1418.

———. 2015. "Louis Marcel Devic's Etymological Dictionary of Oriental Loanwords in French (1876) and a Few Turkological Comments." In *Oriental Studies and Arts*, edited by A Bareja-Starzyńska et al, 305–15. Warsaw: Dialog.

Stachowski, Stanisław. 1970. "Ein türkisches Wörterverzeichnis aus dem Jahr 1688." *Folia Orientalia* 11: 259–64.

———. 2000. "François à Mesgnien Meninski und sein *Thesaurus Linguarum Orientalium*." In *Thesaurus linguarum orientalium Turcicae-Arabicae-Persicae: Lexicon Turcico-Arabico-Persico*, edited by Mehmet Ölmez, Rerpint der Ausg. Wien 1680–1687, xxiii–xxxiv. Türk dilleri araştırmaları dizisi 27–32. Istanbul: Simurg.

Stagl, Justin. 1995. *A History of Curiosity: The Theory of Travel, 1550–1800.* Chur, Switzerland: Harwood.

Stavrides, Theoharis. 2001. *The Sultan of Vezirs: The Life and Times of the Ottoman Grand Vezir Mahmud Pasha Angelovic (1453–1474).* Leiden: Brill.

Stefani, Giuseppe. 1960. *I Greci a Trieste nel Settecento.* Trieste: Monciatti.

Stein, Heidi. 2001. "Some Notes on the Early History of Ottoman Turkish Lexicography in Europe (16th/17th c)." In *Uluslararası Sözlükbilim Sempozyumu bildirileri: 20–23 Mayıs 1999, Gazimağusa*, edited by Nurettin Demir and Emine Yılmaz, 165–77. Gazimağusa: Doğu Akdeniz Üniversitesi, Fen ve Edebiyat Fakültesi, Türk Dili ve Edebiyatı Bölümü.

Stolzenberg, Daniel. 2013. *Egyptian Oedipus: Athanasius Kircher and the Secrets of Antiquity.* Chicago: University of Chicago Press. https://doi.org/chicago/9780226924151.001.0001.

———. 2015. "Les 'langues orientales' et les racines de l'orientalisme académique: une enquête préliminaire." *Dix-septième siècle* 3 (268): 409–26. https://doi.org/10.3917/dss.153.0409.

Stone, Marla Susan. 1998. *The Patron State: Culture and Politics in Fascist Italy.* Princeton, NJ: Princeton University Press.

Stoye, John. 1994. *Marsigli's Europe, 1680–1730: The Life and Times of Luigi Ferdinando Marsigli, Soldier and Virtuoso.* New Haven, CT: Yale University Press.

Strathern, Alan. 2014. "Drawing the Veil of Sovereignty: Early Modern Islamic Empires and Understanding Sacred Kingship." *History and Theory* 53 (1): 79–93. https://doi.org/10.1111/hith.10696.

Strauss, Johann. 1995. "The Millets and the Ottoman Language: The Contribution of Ottoman Greeks to Ottoman Letters (19th–20th Centuries)." *Die Welt des Islams* 35 (2): 189–249. https://doi.org/10.1163/1570060952597860.

———. 2003. "Who Read What in the Ottoman Empire (19th–20th Centuries)?" *Middle Eastern Literatures* 6 (1): 39–76. https://doi.org/10.1080/14752620306881.

Sturdza, Mihail-Dimitri. 1983. *Dictionnaire historique et généalogique des grandes familles de Grèce, d'Albanie et de Constantinople.* Paris: M.-D. Sturdza.

Subrahmanyam, Sanjay. 2006. "A Tale of Three Empires: Mughals, Ottomans, and Habsburgs in a Comparative Context." *Common Knowledge* 12 (1): 66–92. https://doi.org/10.1215/0961754x-12-1-66.

———. 2012. *Courtly Encounters: Translating Courtliness and Violence in Early Modern Eurasia.* Cambridge, MA: Harvard University Press. https://doi.org/10.4159/harvard.9780674067363.

Sutherland, Heather. 2010. "Treacherous Translators and Improvident Paupers: Perception and Practice in Dutch Makassar, Eighteenth and Nineteenth Centuries." *Journal of the Economic and Social History of the Orient* 53 (1): 319–56. https://doi.org/10.1163/002249910x12573963244566.

Święcicka, Elżbieta. 2020. *Dictionary of Italian-Turkish Language (1641) by Giovanni Molino: Transcripted, Reversed, and Annotated.* Berlin: de Gruyter. https://doi.org/10.1515/9783110685039.

Szurek, Emmanuel. 2014. "Les Langues orientales, Jean Deny, les Turks et la Turquie nouvelle. Une histoire croisée de la turcologie française." In *Turcs et Français: une histoire culturelle, 1860–1960*, edited by Güneş Işıksel and Emmanuel Szurek, 327–52. Rennes: Presses Universitaires de Rennes. https://doi.org/10.4000/books.pur.51621.

Takeda, Junko Thérèse. 2011. *Between Crown and Commerce: Marseille and the Early Modern Mediterranean.* Baltimore: Johns Hopkins University Press. https://doi.org/10.1353/book.1852.

Talbot, Michael, and Phil McCluskey, eds. 2016. "Special Section: Contacts, Encounters, Practices: Ottoman-European Diplomacy, 1500–1800." *Osmanlı Araştırmaları / Journal of Ottoman Studies* 48: 269–416.

Tavakoli-Targhi, Mohamad. 2001. *Refashioning Iran: Orientalism, Occidentalism, and Historiography.* New York: Palgrave. https://doi.org/10.1057/9781403918413.

Taylor, Kathryn. 2018. "Making Statesmen, Writing Culture: Ethnography, Observation, and Diplomatic Travel in Early Modern Venice." *Journal of Early Modern History* 22 (4): 279–98. https://doi.org/10.1163/15700658-12342596.

Tedlock, Dennis, and Bruce Mannheim. 1995. Introduction to *The Dialogic Emergence of Culture*, edited by Dennis Tedlock, 1–32. Urbana: University of Illinois Press.

Terzioğlu, Derin. 1995. "The Imperial Circumcision Festival of 1582: An Interpretation." *Muqarnas* 12: 84–100. https://doi.org/10.2307/1523225.

———. 2012. "How to Conceptualize Ottoman Sunnitization: A Historiographical Discussion." *Turcica* 44: 301–38. https://doi.org/10.2143/TURC.44.0.2988854.

Testa, Marie de, and Antoine Gautier. 1991. "Les drogmans au service de la France au Levant." *Revue d'histoire diplomatique* 105 (1/2): 7–101.

———. 2003. *Drogmans et diplomates européens auprès de la porte ottomane*. Istanbul: Isis.

Tezcan, Baki. 2002. "The 1622 Military Rebellion in Istanbul: A Historiographical Journey." *International Journal of Turkish Studies* 8 (1–2): 25–43.

———. 2007. "The Politics of Early Modern Ottoman Historiography." In *The Early Modern Ottomans: Remapping the Empire*, edited by Virginia Aksan and Daniel Goffman, 167–198. Cambridge: Cambridge University Press.

———. 2010. *The Second Ottoman Empire: Political and Social Transformation in the Early Modern World*. New York: Cambridge University Press.

———. 2011a. "Ottoman Historical Writing." In *The Oxford History of Historical Writing*. Vol. 3: *1400–1800*, edited by José Rabasa, Masayuki Sato, Edoardo Tortarolo, and Daniel Woolf, 3:192–211. New York: Oxford University Press. https://doi.org/10.1093/acprof:osobl/9780199219179.003.0010.

———. 2011b. "The Frank in the Ottoman Eye of 1583." In *The Turk and Islam in the Western Eye, 1450–1750: Visual Imagery before Orientalism*, edited by James G Harper, 267–96. Burlington, VT: Ashgate. https://doi.org/10.4324/9781315085029.

Tezcan, Nuran. 2007. "Seventeenth-Century Ottoman Turkish Literature and the Seyahatnâme." *Eurasian Studies* VII (1–2): 1–8. http://hdl.handle.net/11693/49259.

Theunissen, Hans. 1998. "Ottoman-Venetian Diplomatics: The Ahd-Names. The Historical Background and the Development of a Category of Political-Commercial Instruments Together with an Annotated Edition of a Corpus of Relevant Documents." *Electronic Journal of Oriental Studies* 1 (2): 1–698.

Thys-Şenocak, Lucienne. 2006. *Ottoman Women Builders: The Architectural Patronage of Hadice Turhan Sultan*. Burlington, VT: Ashgate.

Tinti, Paolo. 2014. "Il paratesto del viaggiatore: il Burattino veridico di Giuseppe Miselli (1637–1695) e la sua fortuna editoriale." In *Il libro al centro: percorsi fra le discipline del libro in onore di Marco Santoro*, edited by Carmela Reale and Marco Santoro, 459–75. Naples: Liguori editore.

Tommasino, Pier Mattia. 2015. "Travelling East, Writing in Italian: Literature of European Travel to the Ottoman Empire Written in Italian

(16th and 17th Centuries)." *Philological Encounters* 2: 1–24. https://doi.org/10.1163/24519197-00000022.

———. 2018a. *The Venetian Qur'an: A Renaissance Companion to Islam.* Translated by Sylvia Notini. Philadelphia: University of Pennsylvania Press. https://doi.org/10.9783/9780812294972.

———. 2018b. "Bulghaith Al-Darawi and Barthélemy d'Herbelot: Readers of the Qur'an in Seventeenth-Century Tuscany." *Journal of Qur'anic Studies* 20 (3): 94–120. https://doi.org/10.3366/jqs.2018.0353.

Toomer, G. J. 1995. *Eastern Wisedome and Learning: The Study of Arabic in Seventeenth-Century England.* New York: Oxford University Press. https://doi.org/10.1093/acprof:oso/9780198202912.001.0001.

Torcellan, Gian Franco. 1963. "Ballarino, Giovanni Battista." *Dizionario Biografico Degli Italiani* 5: 570–71. Rome: Istituto dell'Enciclopedia Italiana. http://www.treccani.it/enciclopedia/giovanni-battista-ballarino_(Dizionario-Biografico)/.

Tóth, István György. 2003. "Between Islam and Catholicism: Bosnian Franciscan Missionaries in Turkish Hungary, 1584–1716." *Catholic Historical Review* 89 (3): 409–33. https://doi.org/10.1353/cat.2003.0179.

———. 2005. "Missions and Missionaries among the Csángó Hungarians in Moldova in the 17th Century." *Minorities Research: A Collection of Studies by Hungarian Authors* 7: 140–48.

Tottoli, Roberto. 2015. "The Latin Translation of the Qur'ān by Johann Zechendorff (1580–1662) Discovered in Cairo Dār Al-Kutub." *Oriente Moderno* 95 (1–2): 5–31. https://doi.org/10.1163/22138617-12340081.

Touzard, Anne-Marie. 2005. *Le drogman Padery: émissaire de France en Perse, 1719–1725.* Paris: Geuthner.

Trautmann, Thomas R. 1997. *Aryans and British India.* Berkeley: University of California Press. https://doi.org/10.1525/california/9780520205468.001.0001.

———, ed. 2009. *The Madras School of Orientalism: Producing Knowledge in Colonial South India.* New York: Oxford University Press.

Trebbi, Giuseppe. 1980. "La cancelleria veneta nei secoli XVI e XVII." *Annali della Fondazione Luigi Einaudi* 14: 65–125.

———. 1986. "Il segretario veneziano." *Archivio Storico Italiano* 144 (527): 35–73.

———. 2001. "I diritti di cittadinanza nelle repubbliche italiane della prima età moderna: gli esempi di Venezia e Firenze." In *Cittadinanza*, edited by Gilda Manganaro Favaretto, 135–82. Trieste: Edizioni Università di Trieste.

Trivellato, Francesca. 2009. *The Familiarity of Strangers: The Sephardic Diaspora, Livorno, and Cross-Cultural Trade in the Early Modern Period.* New Haven, CT: Yale University Press. http://www.jstor.org/stable/j.ctt1nq982.

Truschke, Audrey. 2016. *Culture of Encounters: Sanskrit at the Mughal Court.* New York: Columbia University Press. https://doi.org/10.7312/columbia/9780231173629.001.0001.

Tuncel, Bedrettin. 1973. "L'âge des drogmans." In *Istanbul à la jonction des cultures balkaniques, méditerranéennes, slaves et orientales aux XVIe–XIXe siècles*, 361–70. Bucharest: Association internationale d'études du Sud-Est européen.

Turan, Ebru. 2007. "The Sultan's Favorite: Ibrahim Pasha and the Making of the Ottoman Universal Sovereignty in the Reign of Sultan Süleyman (1516–1526)." PhD diss., University of Chicago.

Turbet-Delof, Guy. 1973. *La presse périodique française et l'Afrique barbaresque au 17e siècle (1611–1715)*. Geneva: Droz.

Tuşalp Atiyas, Ekin. 2017. "Eloquence in Context." *Turcica* 48: 113–55. https://doi.org/10.2143/TURC.48.0.3237137.

Tymoczko, Maria. 2003. "Ideology and the Position of the Translator: In What Sense Is a Translator 'in Between'?" In *Apropos of Ideology: Translation Studies on Ideology—Ideologies in Translation Studies*, edited by María Calzada-Pérez, 181–201. Manchester: St. Jerome. https://doi.org/10.4324/9781315759937.

Uysal, Enver. 2007. "Kınalızade's Views on the Moral Education of Children." *Journal of Moral Education* 36 (3): 333–41. https://doi.org/10.1080/03057240701552844.

Valensi, Lucette. 1993. *The Birth of the Despot: Venice and the Sublime Porte*. Ithaca, NY: Cornell University Press.

Van den Boogert, Maurits H. 1997. "Tussen consul en qâdî: De juridische positie van dragomans in theorie en praktijk." *Sharqiyyat* 9 (1): 37–53.

———. 2005a. *The Capitulations and the Ottoman Legal System: Qadis, Consuls, and Beratlıs in the 18th Century*. Leiden: Brill. https://doi.org/10.1163/9789047406129.

———. 2005b. "The Sultan's Answer to the Medici Press? Ibrahim Müteferrika's Printing House in Istanbul." In *The Republic of Letters and the Levant*, edited by Alastair Hamilton, 265–92. Leiden: Brill.

———. 2005c. "Patrick Russell and the Republic of Letters in Aleppo." In *The Republic of Letters and the Levant*, edited by Alastair Hamilton, 223–64. Leiden: Brill.

———. 2009a. "Intermediaries Par Excellence? Ottoman Dragomans in the Eighteenth Century." In *Hommes de l'entre-deux. Parcours individuels et portraits de groupes sur la frontière de la Méditerranée (XVIe–XXe siècle)*, edited by Bernard Heyberger, 95–115. Paris: Les Indes Savantes.

———. 2009b. "Legal Reflections on the 'Jurisprudential Shift Hypothesis.'" *Turcica* 41: 373–82.

———. 2017. "Learning Oriental Languages in the Ottoman Empire: Johannes Heyman (1667–1737) between Izmir and Damascus." In *The Teaching and Learning of Arabic in Early Modern Europe*, edited by Jan Loop, Alastair Hamilton, and Charles Burnett, 294–309. Leiden: Brill. https://doi.org/10.1163/9789004338623_014.

Van Droffelaar, Johan. 1994. "'Flemish Fathers' in the Levant: Dutch Protection of Three Franciscan Missions in the 17th and 18th Centuries." In *Eastward Bound. Dutch Ventures and Adventures in the Middle East*, edited by G. J. van Gelder, 81–113. Amsterdam: Rodopi.

Van Gelder, Maartje, and Tijana Krstić. 2015. "Introduction: Cross-Confessional Diplomacy and Diplomatic Intermediaries in the Early Modern Mediterranean." *Journal of Early Modern History* 19 (2–3): 93–105.

Vasilyeva, Daria. 2016. "An Alburn of Turkish Drawings of the Early 1660s from the Franz Taeschner Collection in the Hermitage [in Russian]." In *Belgrade Studies. Meeting of the 23th [sic] International Congress of Byzantine Studies*, 245–64. Saint Petersburg: State Hermitage Publishers.

Veinstein, Gilles, ed. 1992. *Soliman le Magnifique et son temps*. Paris: Documentation française.

———. 2000. "The Ottoman Administration and the Problem of Interpreters." In *The Great Ottoman Turkish Civilization 3: Philosophy, Science and Institutions*, edited by Kemal Çiçek, 3: 607–15. Ankara: Yeni Türkiye.

Vercellin, Giorgio. 2001. *Venezia e l'origine della stampa in caratteri arabi*. Padua: Il poligrafo.

Verschueren, Jef. 2000. "Notes on the Role of Metapragmatic Awareness in Language Use." *Pragmatics* 10 (4): 439–56. https://doi.org/10.1075/prag.10.4.02ver.

Vidmar, Polona, ed. 2005. *Image of the Turks in the 17th Century Europe*. Istanbul: Sakip Sabancı Museum.

———. 2010. "A Series of Portraits from the Bequest of the Counts of Carli at Poreč/Parenzo and Pictorial Representations of Central European Envoys to the Ottoman Court." *Annales. Series Historia et Sociologia* 20 (2): 331–48.

———. 2016. "Count Stefano Carli's *La Erizia* (1765): In the Harem of Sultan Mehmed II." In *Seraglios in Theatre, Music and Literature*, edited by Michael Hüttler and Hans Ernst Weidinger, 65–84. Vienna: Hollitzer. https://doi.org/10.2307/j.ctv6jmb85.7.

Vidro, Nadia, Irene E. Zwiep, and Judith Olszowy-Schlanger, eds. 2014. *A Universal Art: Hebrew Grammar across Disciplines and Faiths*. Leiden: Brill. https://doi.org/10.1163/9789004277052.

Vitali, Achille. 1992. *La moda a Venezia attraverso i secoli: lessico ragionato*. Venice: Filippi.

Voulgaropoulou, Margarita. 2018. "Orthodox Confession Building and the Greek Church between Protestantism and Catholicism: The Mission of the Marquis De Nointel to the Levant (1670–1673)." Paper presented at the Conference Entangled Confessionalizations? Dialogic Perspectives and Community-and Confession-Building Initiatives in the Ottoman Empire, 15th–18th Centuries, Central European University, Budapest.

Vranoussis, Leandre. 1973. "Les grecs de Constantinople et la vie intellectuelle à l'âge des drogmans." In *Istanbul à la jonction des cultures balkaniques, méditerranéennes, slaves et orientales aux XVIᵉ–XIXᵉ siècles*, 133–42. Bucharest: Association internationale d'études du Sud-Est européen.

Vrolijk, Arnoud, and Richard van Leeuwen. 2014. *Arabic Studies in the Netherlands: A Short History in Portraits, 1580–1950*. Leiden: Brill. https://doi.org/10.1163/9789004266339.

Vrolijk, Arnoud, Jan Schmidt, and Karin Scheper, eds. 2012. *Turcksche boucken: de oosterse verzameling van Levinus Warner, Nederlands diplomaat in zeventiende-eeuws Istanbul. The Oriental collection of Levinus Warner, Dutch diplomat in seventeenth-century Istanbul*. Translated by Beverley R. Jackson and David McKay. Eindhoven: Lecturis.

Wagner, Veruschka. 2020. "'Speaking Property' with the Capacity to Act: Slave Interagency in the 16th-and 17th-Century Istanbul Court Registers." In *Slaves and Slave Agency in the Ottoman Empire*, edited by Stephan Conermann and Gül Şen, 213–36. Göttingen: Vandenhoeck & Ruprecht. https://doi.org/10.14220/9783737010375.213.

Wansbrough, John E. 1996. *Lingua Franca in the Mediterranean*. Richmond: Curzon Press. https://doi.org/10.4324/9781315026206.

Wasti, Syed Tanvir. 2005. "The Ottoman Ceremony of the Royal Purse." *Middle Eastern Studies* 41 (2): 193–200. https://doi.org/10.1080/00263200500035116.

———. 2015. "On Charles Vernay and His 'DIVAN.'" *Middle Eastern Studies* 51 (5): 789–803.

Waugh, Daniel C. 2000. "The Development of Portraiture in Muscovy." http://faculty.washington.edu/dwaugh/rus/art/port.html.

Welch, Anthony, ed. 2007. *The Travels and Journal of Ambrosio Bembo*. Translated by Clara Bargellini. Berkeley: University of California Press. https://doi.org/10.1525/california/9780520249387.001.00.

Westrem, Scott. 1998. "Against Gog and Magog." In *Text and Territory: Geographical Imagination in the European Middle Ages*, edited by Sylvia Tomasch, 54–75. Philadelphia: University of Pennsylvania Press. https://doi.org/10.9783/9781512808018-006.

White, Joshua M. 2015. "Fetva Diplomacy: The Ottoman Şeyhülislam as Trans-Imperial Intermediary." *Journal of Early Modern History* 19 (2–3): 199–221. https://doi.org/10.1163/15700658-12342457.

———. 2017. *Piracy and Law in the Ottoman Mediterranean*. Stanford, CA: Stanford University Press. https://doi.org/10.11126/stanford/9781503602526.001.0001.

Wiegers, G. A. 1988. *A Learned Muslim Acquaintance of Erpenius and Golius: Aḥmad b. Kasim Al Andalusî and Arabic Studies in The Netherlands*. Leiden: Documentatiebureau Islam-Christendom, Faculteit der Godgeleerdheid, Rijksuniversiteit.

Wigen, Einar. 2013. "Ottoman Concepts of Empire." *Contributions to the History of Concepts* 8 (1): 44–66. https://doi.org/10.3167/choc.2013.080103.

———. 2018. *State of Translation: Turkey in Interlingual Relations*. Ann Arbor: University of Michigan Press. https://doi.org/10.3998/mpub.9910072.

Wilkins, Charles L. 2009. *Forging Urban Solidarities: Ottoman Aleppo 1640–1700*. Leiden: Brill, 2009. https://doi.org/10.1163/ej.9789004169074.i-328.

———. 2013. "Slavery and Household Formation in Ottoman Aleppo, 1640–1700." *Journal of the Economic and Social History of the Orient* 56 (3): 345–91. https://doi.org/10.1163/15685209-12341312.

Williams, Wes. 2002. "The Diplomat, the Trucheman and the Mystagogue: Forms of Belonging in Early Modern Jerusalem." In *Pilgrim Voices: Narrative and Authorship in Christian Pilgrimage*, edited by Simon Coleman, 17–39. New York: Berghahn Books. https://doi.org/10.3167/146526002782487882.

Wilson, Bronwen. 2003. "Reflecting on the Face of the Turk in Sixteenth-Century Venetian Portrait Books." *Word & Image* 19 (1/2): 38–58. https://doi.org/10.1080/02666286.2003.10406222.

———. 2007. "Foggie diverse di vestire de' Turchi: Turkish Costume Illustration and Cultural Translation." *Journal of Medieval and Early Modern Studies* 37 (1): 97–139. https://doi.org/10.1215/10829636-2006-012.

Windler, Christian. 2001. "Diplomatic History as a Field for Cultural Analysis: Muslim-Christian Relations in Tunis, 1700–1840." *The Historical Journal* 44 (1): 79–106. https://doi.org/10.1017/s0018246x01001674.

Witkam, Jan Just. 2006. "Precious Books and Moments of Friendship in 17th-Century Istanbul." In *Essays in Honour of Ekmeleddin İhsanoğlu*, vol. 1. *Societies, Cultures, Sciences: A Collection of Articles*, edited by Zeynep Durukal Abuhusayn and Mustafa Kaçar, 467–74. İstanbul: IRCICA.

Wolf, Michaela. 2005. "'Diplomatenlehrbuben' oder angehender 'Dragomane'? Zur Rekonstruktion des sozialen 'Dolmetschfeldes' in der Habsburgermonarchie." In *Das osmanische Reich und die Habsburgermonarchie*, edited by Marlene Kurz, 503–13. Vienna: Oldenbourg Wissenschaftsverlag. https://doi.org/10.7767/boehlau.9783205160281.503.

Woodhead, Christine. 2017. "Çelebizade İsmail Asım." *Encyclopaedia of Islam, THREE*, edited by Kate Fleet. https://doi.org/10.1163/1573-3912_ei3_COM_32043.

Woolard, Kathryn A. 1998. "Simultaneity and Bivalency as Strategies in Bilingualism." *Journal of Linguistic Anthropology* 8 (1): 3–29. https://doi.org/10.1525/jlin.1998.8.1.3.

———. 2002. "Bernardo de Aldrete and the Morisco Problem: A Study in Early Modern Spanish Language Ideology." *Comparative Studies in Society and History* 44 (3): 446–80. https://doi.org/10.1017/s0010417502000221.

Woolard, Kathryn A. and E. Nicholas Genovese. 2007. "Strategic Bivalency in Latin and Spanish in Early Modern Spain." *Language in Society* 36: 487–509. https://doi.org/10.1017/s0047404507070418.

Wright, Diana Gilliland. 2006. "The First Venetian Love Letter? The Testament of Zorzi Cernovich." *Electronic Journal of Oriental Studies* 9 (2): 1–20. https://www.medievalists.net/files/09090201.pdf.

Wunder, Amanda. 2003. "Western Travelers, Eastern Antiquities, and the Image of the Turk in Early Modern Europe." *Journal of Early Modern History* 7 (1–2): 89–119. https://doi.org/10.1163/157006503322487368.

Xavier, Ângela Barreto, and Ines G. Županov, eds. 2015. *Catholic Orientalism: Portuguese Empire, Indian Knowledge (16th–18th Centuries)*. New Delhi: Oxford University Press.

Yağmur, Ömer. 2015. "Pietro Lupis Valentiano'nun İtalyanca-Türkçe Çeviri Yazılı Sözlüğünde Ses Olayları (1520–1527)." *FSM İlmî Araştırmalar İnsan ve Toplum Bilimleri Dergisi* 0 (6): 243–78. https://doi.org/10.16947/fsmiad.97135.

Yamanaka, Yuriko, Tetsuo Nishio, and Kokuritsu Minzokugaku Hakubutsukan, eds. 2006. *The Arabian Nights and Orientalism: Perspectives from East & West*. London: Tauris. https://doi.org/10.5040/9780755612338.

Yerasimos, Stéphane. 1992. "Le Turc en Occident: La connaissance de la langue turque en Europe, XVᵉ–XVIIᵉ siècles." In *L'Inscription des langues dans les relations de voyage (XVIᵉ–XVIIIᵉ siècles)*, edited by Michèle Duchet. Special issue of *Les cahiers de Fontenay* 65–66: 181–210.

Yılmaz, Gülay. 2009. "Becoming a Devshirme: The Training of Conscripted Children in the Ottoman Empire." In *Children in Slavery through the Ages*, edited by Gwyn Campbell, Suzanne Miers, and Joseph Calder Miller, 119–34. Athens: Ohio University Press. https://doi.org/10.1353/chapter.258112.

———. 2017. "Change in Manpower in the Early Modern Janissary Army and Its Impact on the Devshirme System." *Rivista di studi militari* 6: 181–88.

Zack, Liesbeth, and Arie Schippers, eds. 2012. *Middle Arabic and Mixed Arabic: Diachrony and Synchrony*. Leiden: Brill. https://doi.org/10.1163/9789004228047.

Zakaria, Katia. 2004. "Pétis de la Croix, François, Les Mille et un jours, contes persans, texte établi, avec une introduction, des notices, une bibliographie, des jugements et une chronologie par Paul Sebbag, Phébus, Paris, 2003, 670 p." *Revue des mondes musulmans et de la Méditerranée* 103–104 (June): 282–86. https://journals.openedition.org/remmm/2393.

Zannini, Andrea. 1993. *Burocrazia e burocrati a Venezia in età moderna: i cittadini originari (sec XVI–XVIII)*. Venice: Istituto veneto di scienze, lettere ed arti.

———. 2000. "Economic and Social Aspects of the Crisis of Venetian Diplomacy in the Seventeenth and Eighteenth Centuries." In *Politics and Diplomacy in Early Modern Italy: The Structure of Diplomatic Practice, 1450–1800*, edited by Daniela Frigo, 109–46. New York: Cambridge University Press. https://doi.org/10.1017/cbo9780511523298.005.

Zecevic, Selma. 2014. "Translating Ottoman Justice: Ragusan Dragomans as Interpreters of Ottoman Law." *Islamic Law and Society* 21 (4): 388–418. https://doi.org/10.1163/15685195-00214p03.

Zele, Walter. 1990. "Alî bey, un interprete della Porta nella Venezia dell '500." *Studi Veneziani* 19: 187–224.

Zhiri, Oumelbanine. 2006. "Leo Africanus and the Limits of Translation." In *Travel and Translation in the Early Modern Period*, edited by Carmine Di Biase, 175–86. Amsterdam: Rodopi.

Zilfi, Madeline C. 2006. "The Ottoman Ulema." In *Cambridge History of Turkey*, edited by Suraiya Faroqhi, 3:209–25. New York: Cambridge University Press. https://doi.org/10.1017/CHOL9780521620956.011.

Zorzanello, Pietro. 1950. *Inventari dei manoscritti delle biblioteche d'Italia, vol. LXXVII: Venezia: Marciana: Mss. Italiani: classe VI*. Vol. 77. Florence: L. S. Olschki.

Zwartjes, Otto. 2014. "Una comparación entre la *Gramática turca* (1799) de Juan Antonio Romero y la *Grammaire turque* (1730) del jesuita Jean-Baptiste Holderman." In *Lenguas, estructuras y hablantes: estudios en homenaje a Thomas C. Smith Stark*, edited by Rebeca Barriga Villanueva and Esther Herrera, 1:451–82. Mexico City: El Colegio de México, Centro de Estudios Lingüísticos y Literarios. https://hdl.handle.net/11245/1.418218.

Zwartjes, Otto and Manfred Woidich. 2012. "Damascus Arabic According to the Compendio of Lucas Caballero (1709)." In *Middle Arabic and Mixed Arabic: Diachrony and Synchrony*, edited by Liesbeth Zack and Arie Schippers, 295–334. Leiden: Brill. https://doi.org/10.1163/9789004228047_018.

Page numbers followed by *t* refer to tables.